COPING WITH STRESS

IN A CHANGING WORLD

Richard Blonna Ed.D., C.H.E.S.

Associate Professor, Department of Community Health
William Patterson College

with 136 illustrations

Mosby

St. Louis   Baltimore   Boston   Carlsbad   Chicago   Naples   New York   Philadelphia   Portland
London   Madrid   Mexico City   Singapore   Sydney   Tokyo   Toronto   Wiesbaden

Mosby

Dedicated to Publishing Excellence

A Times Mirror
Company

Vice President and Publisher: James M. Smith
Senior Acquisitions Editor: Vicki Malinee
Developmental Editor: Catherine Schwent
Project Manager: Mark Spann
Production Editor: Holly Roseman
Electronic Production Coordinator: Terri Schwaegel
Manufacturing Supervisor: Tony McAllister
Designer: David Zielinski

Printed in the United States of America
Composition by Mosby Electronic Production, St. Louis
Printing and binding by RR Donnelley

Mosby–Year Book, Inc.
11830 Westline Industrial Drive
St. Louis, Missouri 63146

Library of Congress Cataloging-in-Publication Data

Blonna, Richard.
    Coping with stress in a changing world / Richard Blonna.
       p.   cm.
    Includes bibliographical references and index.
    ISBN 0-8151-0467-7 (pbk.)
    1. Stress (Psychology)   2. Stress management.   I. Title.
BF575.S75B57 1996
155.9′ 042—dc20   95-41489
                                        CIP

96 97 98 99 00 / 9 8 7 6 5 4 3 2 1

PREFACE

Stress is everywhere today. It seems that we cannot get away from this overwhelming player in our lives. As our world becomes more complicated, stress creeps in and affects our lives at all levels.

Coping With Stress in a Changing World approaches the topic of stress by presenting it uniquely in a wellness context. Stress is not an isolated phenomenon but rather a dynamic transaction influenced by one's overall level of well-being across the six dimensions of health. This book explains to students the interconnectedness of health and stress. It describes how all of the dimensions of health are involved in both the appraisal of potential stressors and the ability to cope with them. It explains how wellness (optimal health) can enhance our ability to manage stress.

The text is written in three parts and designed so that one part flows smoothly into the next. Part 1 is designed to introduce stress and explain how it is connected to health and wellness. Each of the dimensions of health are discussed with a focus on their connection to stress.

Part 2 presents an integrated approach to coping with stress. It describes four levels of coping with stress—rethink, reduce, relax, and release (the four *R*s)— and explains how to reorganize one's life in a more health-enhancing, stress-reducing way.

The final part presents a developmental look at stress and coping. Most stress management textbooks present a piecemeal approach to applying coping to typical stressors (school, work, relationships). *Coping With Stress in a Changing World* presents a systematic, developmental analysis of stress and coping. Stressors and coping strategies appropriate to each stage of life are examined in detail.

Audience

The text is written to appeal to both traditional college-age students as well as nontraditional students. It is the author's experience that a classroom mixture of numerous ages, backgrounds, and life experiences complement the teaching of stress management. The text is designed to provide examples, illustrations, and activities that are targeted toward and appeal to all groups of students.

Further, it is hoped that by presenting a developmental perspective on stress and coping, students will gain a deeper understanding and appreciation of the tasks and stressors faced by people at various points in their development. Traditional and nontraditional students will see how stressors and coping skills change in relation to life experience and development.

Features

Design

The text is designed to grab the student's attention. A single column text format was chosen to allow ample margins for presenting pedagogical aids. All key words and concepts are bold-faced to stand out easily. All key words are defined in the margins. The text also uses boxes to provide short examples or illustrations of supplementary material.

All artwork is designed to provide a crisp, clear visual picture to enhance the text. Many of the drawings employ cartoon-type figures that add humor wherever possible. This is consistent with our desire to lighten up the text.

Photographs have been chosen that portray a wide variety of people from varied races, ethnic groups, and genders. Many of the photographs portray active, healthy people enjoying life as they manage their stress.

Marginal Definitions

As previously mentioned, all important words are defined in the margins. These marginal definitions allow the students to quickly find the meaning of key words without having to flip pages.

Keys to Understanding

Important concepts, entitled *Keys to Understanding*, appear in the margin and provide simple explanations for important stress concepts.

Stress in Our World Boxes

This boxed feature provides a personal perspective concerning stress. The characters featured in Stress in Our World are used to give a human face to the discussion of stress. They also provide a cross-cultural perspective on stress.

Pedagogical Aids

The text incorporates a variety of pedagogical aids that assist instructors in conveying information as well as helping students explore the role of stress in their lives.

Chapter Objectives. Each chapter has a set of measurable objectives for students. This enables instructors and students to know what the goals are of each chapter.

Student Study Questions. Each chapter has a set of study questions that help students review and analyze the material covered in the chapter.

Chapter Summaries. Each chapter ends with a comprehensive summary that highlights key aspects of the chapter.

Assess Yourself. The Assess Yourself entries are self-surveys designed to provide personal information for students concerning their stress. The activities can serve as a springboard for group discussion or they can be used privately, as an aid for students to gain a broader understanding of stress in their personal lives. Because they are perforated for easy removal, they can be completed either in-class or as homework in preparation for classroom processing. They provide students an opportunity to share information about their personal stressors and coping strategies.

Documentation. All material referred to in the text is contained in the reference list. All references are current, with at least 75% from the past 5 years.

Ancillaries

A comprehensive ancillary package is available to qualified adopters of *Coping With Stress in a Changing World*. A unique feature of this package is that it was developed by the author, which ensures integration of the material.

Instructor's Manual and Test Bank. The instructor's manual features chapter overviews, learning objectives, suggested teaching outlines with recommended notes and activities for teaching each chapter, personal assessments, issues in the news, suggestions for guest lecturers, media resources, and 25 full-page transparency masters of helpful illustrations, charts, and tables. The test bank contains approximately 500 questions, including multiple choice, true/false, matching, and essay test questions.

Esatest III. This test bank software provides a combination of user-friendly aids that enable the instructor to select, edit, delete or add questions, as well as construct and print tests and answer keys. Available to qualified adopters of the text in IBM DOS and Macintosh formats.

Stress Management Audiotape. Packaged free with the textbook, this valuable cassette tape presents four relaxation techniques (diaphragmatic breathing, breath meditation, systemic muscle relaxation, and autogenic training) for the students to practice and incorporate into their everyday routine.

Mosby's Health Exchange. This newsletter provides instructors with the latest information concerning "hot topics" to supplement their Mosby stress, health, fitness, sexuality, drugs, and wellness texts. The newsletter is published twice a year and covers numerous health and wellness topics. In addition to being a useful resource for instructors, it features a pullout center section with information tailored to students.

Acknowledgements

The reviewers made excellent suggestions that were integrated whenever possible. Their contributions are present in every chapter. I would like to express my appreciation for their work.

John Janowiak
Appalachian State University

Patricia A. Tyra
University of Massachusetts - Lowell

Frank S. Lemmon
University of Utah

Marie Zannus
Nicholls State University

James L. Toman
University of Southern California

Special Acknowledgements

Coping With Stress in a Changing World is the culmination of 4 years worth of labor that started out as a dream. Since high school I have dreamed that someday I would be a college professor, serve as a consultant, and write books. Writing this book was the third, and final part of the dream. I guess it goes to show you that with enough hard work and discipline, a little luck, and belief in your dreams, fairy tales can come true.

I would like to acknowledge Dr. Jay Segal of Temple University, my professor of stress management in graduate school. Dr. Segal was the first person to stimulate my interest in stress management. Dr. Segal's help and encouragement helped me get my feet wet teaching my first classes in stress management as an adjunct faculty member finishing his dissertation.

Even though I have never met them, I would like to acknowledge Drs. Richard Lazarus, Susan Folkman, and Albert Ellis. Drs. Lazarus and Folkman, your work on the stress appraisal process is the cornerstone of this book. Your prolific scholarship has inspired me and helped shape my perspective on stress and coping. If this book seems a tome to the two of you it is because I believe strongly in your work.

Dr. Ellis, the principles and philosophy of Rational Emotive Therapy also serve as a major underlying foundation for this book as well as guidelines for my personal life. Your work has been a major influence on my thinking for the past 20 years.

Special thanks go to a bunch of hard-working people at Mosby for their help and support. First, I would like to thank Vicki Malinee and Jim Smith for the chance at writing this book. Thanks, Alyssa Naumann, for your help in solving a hundred nagging administrative issues and never ceasing to be calm, cool, and professional. Thanks, Holly Roseman, for your editorial expertise and precise attention to detail.

I also want to thank Catherine Schwent, who developed this project from the rough manuscript it started out as to the finished textbook before you. Catherine, like Yogi Berra, taught me that "it ain't over till it's over" (actually, it isn't over until you have a copy of the finished book in your hand). Thanks for your help, Catherine, this is your book as much as mine!

Finally, I would like to thank my family for their love and support throughout the entire project. Will and Mike, thanks for being patient with Dad and giving me the time and privacy I needed to complete this project. Your interest and support helped keep me motivated throughout the 3 summers and 4 years I worked on this book. Heidi, thanks for your support, encouragement and for listening to me when I needed someone to talk to. Thanks for being patient and helping me put things in their proper perspective when life and this project seemed to be getting out of control.

Richard Blonna

CONTENTS IN BRIEF

CONTENTS

7 REDUCE: THE SECOND LEVEL OF DEFENSE, 235

8 RELAX: PASSIVE RELAXATION STRATEGIES, 275

9 RELAX: ACTIVE RELAXATION STRATEGIES, 299

xviii

15 | STRESS IN ADULTHOOD, 517

16 | STRESS IN OLD AGE, 565

EPILOGUE, 607

Coping
With Stress

PART I

Stress and Wellness

Stress is everywhere. We are all familiar with the more exotic scenarios: air traffic controllers who know that their every move could result in the loss of a multimillion dollar aircraft and hundreds of lives; police in urban areas who face relentless danger and close public scrutiny; and the men and women who defend our allies in faraway places like Haiti, Kuwait, and Somalia. These situations represent the extremes. However, stress affects all of us regardless of our gender, age, race, or class.

Men and women are stressed. Some are stressed trying to balance the demands of husband/wife, mother/father, or homemaker/professional. Others are struggling to merely survive, doing the best they can in an economy that is recovering from the excesses of the 1980s. They are competing for jobs in a market flooded with the recently unemployed as companies downscale. Still others are caught in the cycle of unemployment, poverty, welfare, and despair.

Children are stressed. Some, like the typical 5 or 6 year old, are stressed adjusting to the new world of school. Others worry that their three-block walk to school may put them in the middle of cross fire between rival street gangs. Others are stressed from trying to cope with the pressures that accompany divorce, single-parent households, and blended families.

College students are stressed. Some are trying to cope with the demands of adapting to a new living environment, new peers, academic pressures, or sexual concerns. College can also put a financial stress on students and their families, and it seems as if there is never enough time to attend class, study, and work enough hours to pay the bills.

The elderly are stressed. Some are caught between the demands of forced retirement and the difficulty of meeting their financial needs. Others cope with the demands of frail health status and escalating health-care costs. Still others are stressed by the loss of their spouses or the dissolution of their families as their adult children leave home.

Such situations can leave us with trembling hands, tense muscles, migraine headaches, and multiple other symptoms of stress. They also can contribute to a host of chronic diseases, ranging from hypertension to peptic ulcers, and can predispose us to premature disability and death.

To understand and manage our stress, we need to view it in the context of our overall level of well-being across the six dimensions of health: physical, social, emotional, intellectual, spiritual, and environmental. Our overall well-being across these domains affects both our stress level and our ability to cope. Robust health with high levels of well-being is protective, helping to reduce our overall levels of stress and provide the energy and stamina necessary to cope with daily pressures. It can also facilitate coping as we draw upon resources ranging from social support to the inner strength that spiritual well-being provides.

Change is common in life, although it varies in intensity, frequency, and permanency. The only real constant in life is change; however, not everyone perceives change the same way. Some people view it positively, transforming change into challenge. For them these situations are catalysts for growth and action. Others view the change as a stressor and are mesmerized into inactivity.

In this book, we answer the many questions about stress and explore what stress is and what it does to us. Is it some physical symptom or problem, is it something within us, or is it an outside force? Is it some combination of events that pushes us over the brink? Isn't stress supposed to be good for us ? Don't we need it to succeed ? What does it really mean to be stressed out?

Stress is one of the most commonly referred to but least understood of all health problems. We examine the differences between stress and challenge, with an emphasis on the importance of the role of perception in distinguishing between the two. We examine the many common sources of stress for most people, understanding that not everyone perceives them the same way. We also examine strategies for managing stress. We show how to find the optimal levels of challenge and how to control stress instead of letting it control us.

CHAPTER 1

What is Stress?

CHAPTER OBJECTIVES

- Describe the four classical ways of defining stress.
- Compare the author's definition of stress with the classical definitions of stress.
- Explain the relationship between life events and the stress response.
- Describe the three phases of Selye's General Adaptation Syndrome (GAS).
- Describe the role of threat appraisal in the stress response.
- Define holistic health.
- Define wellness.
- Describe how the stress response is related to a person's level of functioning across the six dimensions of wellness.

What is Stress ?

Stress is different to everyone. Ten people would probably define stress ten different ways. However, there are four common perceptions of stress.

- Stress as a Stimulus
  People who view stress as stimulus define stress as an outside force that puts demands on them: "Stress is pressure." "Stress is having too much to do and too little time to do it." "My boss is stress."
- Stress as a Response
  Others define stress as a physical response going on within themselves: "Stress is a tension headache." "Stress is a knot in my stomach."
- Stress as a Transaction
  For others stress is a transaction, an exchange between a stimulus, our perception of it, and the response it causes: "Stress is the muscle tension I get when I think about giving a speech in front of the class."
- Stress as a Holistic Phenomenon
  Some describe stress as part of a larger whole. It is a part of an individual's physical, social, spiritual, emotional, intellectual, and environmental well-being: Stress is "being a student," or "feeling helpless in trying to control my life." It takes into account lifestyles and circumstances beyond single events that may trigger a stress response.

Each of these definitions is flawed to some extent. The *stress as a stimulus*, *stress as a response*, and *stress as a holistic phenomenon* definitions place too little emphasis on the role of perception in a stressful transaction. The *stress as a transaction* definition may examine the role of perception, but it does not take into account the individual's environment and overall level of well-being.

This book borrows from each of the four definitions of stress to create a more comprehensive definition of stress. For our purposes, we will define **stress** as a holistic transaction or an exchange between the individual and a stressor resulting in the body's mobilization of a **stress response**. A stressor is any stimulus appraised by the individual as threatening or capable of causing harm or loss.

This definition of stress recognizes the importance of perception in the appraisal of potential stressors. Perception of potential stressors is influenced by the individual's overall or holistic level of wellness (Fig. 1-1). This model emphasizes that stress does not occur in a vacuum. Similarly, coping with stress sometimes includes resources that extend beyond the individual.

stress
a holistic transaction between the individual, a stressor, and the environment resulting in a stress response

stress response
a set of physiological adaptations of the body to maintain homeostasis in the face of threat, harm, or loss

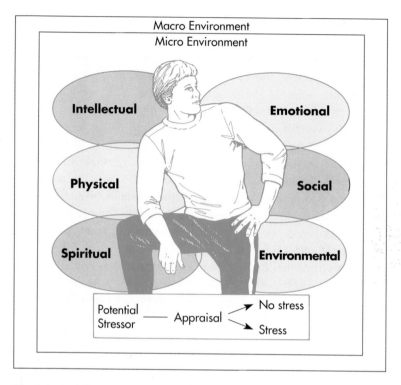

Macro Environment
Micro Environment

Intellectual

Emotional

Physical

Social

Spiritual

Environmental

Potential Stressor —— Appraisal < No stress / Stress

Fig. 1-1 A wellness model of stress places the stress appraisal process in the context of the individual's level of well-being across the physical, social, emotional, intellectual, spiritual, and environmental dimensions of health. Stress appraisal never occurs in a vaccuum. It is affected by our micro- and macro-environments.

This chapter examines the nature of stress, the theoretical issues and problems surrounding ways of viewing stress, and the evolution of the study of stress.

Early Pioneers
Bernard, Cannon, and Selye

The understanding of the physiological basis of stress grew largely out of the work of Claude Bernard, Walter Cannon, and Hans Selye. Bernard, a French physiologist, spent the last half of the nineteenth century refining the concept of the milieu interieur or, the body's internal environment. Long before the concept of stress was developed Bernard described how living organisms sought to maintain an internal constancy or balance and how this struggle went on despite changes in the outside environment.[10]

KEY
TO UNDERSTANDING

The stress response doesn't occur in a vacuum. It is influenced by what is going on in our immediate (micro) environment and the world at large (macro).

An example would be the body's attempt to maintain a balance in heart rate, temperature, and respiration when exposed to a change in weather conditions. As the temperature grows colder the body must stay in balance and not follow the environmental changes. Heart rate must continue in rhythm, internal temperature must be 98.6°, and breathing must be regular. If the body did not maintain its internal balance and fluctuated too greatly with the weather, it would begin to malfunction and breakdown.

Bernard's work was expanded on 50 years later by Walter Cannon,[2] a Harvard physiologist. In his original work, he refined Bernard's concept of the milieu interieur and renamed the process **homeostasis**, from the Greek words *homios* (meaning similar) and *stasis* (meaning position). This steady position or state of being was the normal pattern of internal functioning under which living things operated.

Cannon[2] theorized that living things seek to maintain homeostasis to prevent their various body systems from deviating too far from their normal limits of functioning. When body systems deviate from the norm too greatly they put the entire organism in danger. To prevent this from happening internal physiological processes are set into motion automatically, and in this way the body balances the effects of external environmental stressors.

Hans Selye[11], a Canadian endocrinologist (hormone specialist), continued Cannon's work. In 1926, as a second-year resident at the University of Montreal Medical School, Selye began his research in the area of homeostasis. In his physiological and pharmacological studies, he subjected laboratory animals to various extremes in harmful environmental stimuli (heat, cold, and chemicals) that placed demands on the body systems of these animals. He confirmed what Cannon had found: when an organism's normal operating systems (respiration, circulation, digestion, and temperature regulation) were thrown too far out of their normal range of functioning, the organism was in jeopardy of dying.[11] The demands created by the need to adapt to these external stimuli were far too great for their bodies to cope.

However, Selye went one step farther than Cannon. He found that not only did his laboratory animals adjust to these demands by initiating a complex pattern of physiological responses but that the responses were the same regardless of the source of the demand. Selye called this phenomenon the *nonspecific response to demand*. The nonspecificity of the response to any demand was the key factor in the development of Selye's stress theory,[11] and he later defined stress as the nonspecific response of the body to any demand.

homeostasis

the steady state of the body's internal processes

KEY
TO UNDERSTANDING

Nonspecificity refers to the theory that our bodies respond the same to different types of stressors.

General Adaptation Syndrome (GAS)

Selye developed a model for describing this nonspecific response and the adaptations it forces the body to make. He called it the **General Adaptation Syndrome (GAS)**, and it has three distinguishable phases: alarm, resistance, and exhaustion.[11] These three phases are sequential; that is, if the source of stress sounds the alarm and initiates the GAS and the stress is not removed or coped with, the body progresses to resistance and eventual exhaustion. However, recovery is an alternative outcome to exhaustion when the source of stress is either removed or coped with effectively (Fig. 1-2).

An underlying concept in Selye's GAS model is his belief that all living organisms are equipped with a vital force that he called *adaptation energy*. This adaptation energy is stored in the body and is drawn on whenever organisms have to adapt to demands from outside forces. When Selye's laboratory animals were exposed to outside stimuli, their internal alarms were triggered to initiate a complex set of physiological processes to mobilize energy for action.[11] **Fight or flight**, a phrase coined by

general adaptation syndrome (GAS)
the three-phase stress response identified by Selye

fight or flight
the state of physiological readiness for action created by the body during the alarm phase

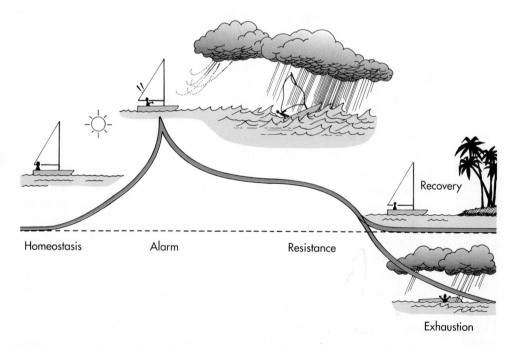

Recovery

Homeostasis   Alarm   Resistance

Exhaustion

Fig. 1-2 When we are not stressed, we are like a sailboat cutting a mild wake through our day. As stressors appear like clouds on the horizon, we get ready for turbulent seas and stormy weather. If we cope successfully, we resist the rough times and rechart a course through calmer seas. If we can't cope, like the sailboat, we crash and sink into exhaustion.

Canon,[2] is what Selye used to describe the state of the body at the alarm stage. The fight-or-flight response refers to the options available in coping with stressors at this point in the stress response. The body is primed to either confront the stressor or avoid it.

Selye found that when his laboratory animals could not fight or flee they had to adjust to the stimuli by shifting to a lower-level but more complex stress response. This response prompted various organs and glands of the animals to produce a variety of hormones, salts, and sugars needed to supply the energy necessary to *resist* the demands of the stimuli and keep the body in balance. Selye believed that the effects of the resistance phase of GAS result in the gradual wearing down of what he characterized as **weak links**, body parts or systems that bear the brunt of adaptive attempts during the resistance phase.[11] These weak links are the first body parts or systems to malfunction during the latter stages of resistance. When his animals were no longer able to resist the stimuli acting on them, they broke down, became *exhausted*, and died.

In studying this process of alarm, resistance, and exhaustion, Selye measured and quantified these physiological symptoms. His findings confirmed his earlier hypothesis about the nonspecificity of the response regardless of the type of stimuli.

Life Events Approach

Pressures associated with work, school, relationships, family life, and other environmental demands often cause people to describe themselves as "being under stress." In fact, such stressors have been found to affect physical health. Thomas Holmes and Richard Rahe,[7] pioneers in the study of life demands and their relationship to stress, noticed what seemed to be a relationship between stressful events and susceptibility to illness. In 1967, as researchers at the University of Washington School of Medicine, Holmes and Rahe examined the past medical records of their subjects and discovered that major life changes were often followed by the development of serious illnesses.

They wondered if this relationship was coincidental or if it could be used to predict the development of illness in people who might experience such changes in the future. They used the term **life events** to refer to life-changing experiences. Some of these events are joyous—marriage, the birth of a child, or a new job—and others are sad—the death of a loved one or the loss of a job. Holmes and Rahe[7] believed that these events, regardless of whether they were happy or sad, threw the body out of balance, forcing it to readjust. These readjustments use up energy and make demands on the body. Holmes and Rahe, like Selye, believed that the body has a finite amount of adaptation energy available to make these readjustments. If peo-

weak links
susceptible body part or systems that break down under the wear and tear of chronic stressors

life events
life-changing experiences that use energy and can cause stress

ple experience too many life events in too short a period of time, they will be at an increased risk for the development of disease.

To test this theory Holmes and Rahe[7], developed the Social Readjustment Rating Scale to measure these events. The scale consists of a variety of life events that are typically experienced by several people in any given year. They assigned a score for each event; serious events (death of a spouse, divorce) were awarded the highest score values. Subjects who took the test checked the events that they had experienced in the past year, and these events were tallied and the scores correlated with the presence or absence of disease. Holmes and Rahe's research findings supported their hypothesis that there is a relationship between life events and disease. In studies of naval officers, enlisted men, resident physicians, and medical students, they found that those subjects with the highest scores were most likely to develop a disease within the next year.

Assess Yourself 1-1 presents the Student Stress Scale, which is adapted from the original Holmes and Rahe test.[8] The events it contains are considered more relevant than the Social Readjustment Rating Scale for the typical college student. However, the original scale is also presented as Assess Yourself 1-2 so that students may choose for themselves the more appropriate test.

Critics of Holmes and Rahe's work argue that this type of stress theory ignores the role of perception in the stress response. They would argue that life events are only stressful if people perceive them to be. It is important to realize that these life events are normal occurrences and they are harmful only if too many of them occur in too short a time span. These arguments are examined in detail in Chapter 2.

Psychological Stress Researchers
Symbolic Threats

Simeons[12], a stress researcher in the early 1960s and a disciple of Hans Selye, believed that when modern people are confronted with stressors, such as an intolerable roommate or a dead-end relationship, their brains work in exactly the same way that their primitive ancestors did when confronted by a saber-toothed tiger. That is, they perceive the situation as threatening and mobilize energy for the body to fight or flee. Simeons calls these twentieth-century stressors *symbolic threats* because they are more of a threat to an individual's ego than to physical well-being.

According to Simeons[12] the human brain, particularly the part of the brain called the *diencephalon*, has not evolved to the point where it can discriminate between symbolic and physical threats and therefore cannot initiate different responses for these stressors. The brain still perceives all threats to our well-being as equally harmful. Simeons' work is the precursor for the

KEY
TO UNDERSTANDING

We all have demands on us. They become stressors when too many of them occur within too short a time.

third way of defining stress: stress as a transaction.[12] This transaction involves the perception of a stimulus as threatening and the subsequent triggering of an adaptive stress response.

Researchers studying psychological stress believe that very few stimuli are capable of causing stress responses without our perceiving them as potential stressors. They feel that with the exception of certain environmental stimuli (extremes in temperature, pollution, and noise), most of the things that cause us stress are people and situations that we determine as potential threats to our well-being. This perception involves the individual, the environment, and the potential stressor.

This way of viewing the stress response is entirely different from that of Selye, who never considered the role of perception in his nonspecific response. Unlike Holmes and Rahe, psychological stress researchers do not believe that there are life events that are universal stressors for everyone; people respond to these life events differently, depending on how they perceive them. An event such as a divorce may be perceived by one person as very stressful, whereas another might celebrate the occasion.

Researchers of psychological stress would take issue with the notion of **eustress** (good) versus **distress** (bad). They believe that people and things are stressors only if they are capable of initiating a stress response—that is, only if they are perceived as threatening or capable of causing harm or loss. In other words, eustress is not stress at all because it is associated with good feelings.

Perception of Threat

Richard Lazarus[5] is another psychological stress researcher. He is credited with developing a unique model of how our minds work when perceiving potential stressors. His theory of psychological stress revolves around the belief that people or things become stressors when they pose a threat to our well-being in some way. The threat may be physical harm but more often than not is psychosocial in nature. For instance, a comment someone makes about our clothing is not a direct threat to our well-being, yet it may be enough to initiate a stress response if we interpret it as a threat. Threat implies a state of anticipating a confrontation with a harmful condition. Whether the stressor is real or imagined is immaterial. It is the perception of the stimuli as threatening that determines whether or not they become stressors.

Lazarus[5,6] called the perception of potential stressors a *transaction* and called the actual evaluation of stimuli the *threat appraisal process*. Lazarus' model involves a three-part appraisal of the potential stressor: the first appraisal determines if the stressor is a threat; the second appraisal determines if the individual is capable of coping with the threat; and the third appraisal, the cognitive reappraisal, draws on the information from the first two appraisals. Fig. 1-3 illustrates Lazarus' perception of threat.

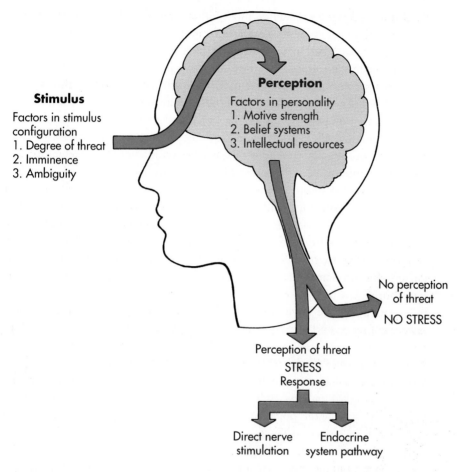

Stimulus

Factors in stimulus
configuration
1. Degree of threat
2. Imminence
3. Ambiguity

Perception

Factors in personality
1. Motive strength
2. Belief systems
3. Intellectual resources

No perception
of threat

NO STRESS

Perception of threat

STRESS

Response

Direct nerve
stimulation

Endocrine
system pathway

Fig. 1-3 Incoming stimuli are neutral until they are perceived as threatening or nonthreatening. This is determined by a combination of stimulus and personality factors.

Primary Appraisal: Is it a Threat?

The primary appraisal examines both stimulus and personality factors to determine if the potential stressor is a threat.

Stimulus Factors. The first stimulus factor, degree of threat, is the balance between the amount of danger perceived and our belief in our ability to cope with it. The second stimulus factor, imminence of confrontation, has to do with how near the threat is in space and time. The proximity of the stressor determines how much time we have to assess the threat and marshall whatever resources are necessary to cope with it. The last stimulus factor, ambiguity of a stimulus, will affect our perception of the stressor; stimuli that are not clear are often misinterpreted as threats because we cannot assess their true meanings.

Personality Factors. Lazarus' model also examines three personality factors related to the potential stressor: stimulus factors and individual personality factors. The first personality factor in Lazarus' model of threat appraisal is motive strength. If the stimulus is perceived as coming into conflict with our important goals or motives it will be considered threatening. However, if the stimulus does not conflict with these goals or only affects less important motives it may not be perceived as a threat. The second personality factor, belief systems, incorporates our fundamental values and ethics and our idealized picture of how the world should be. When people or events come into conflict with this picture, we feel threatened. The closer these threats come to our core values, the stronger we perceive them to be. For this reason our belief systems can be a major source of stress. The third personality factor, intellectual resources, has to do with our ability to use information. The more objective, accurate information we have at our disposal, the more resources we have to interpret and understand potential stressors. It is not only the sheer magnitude of information that is important; our ability to process it is also critical. We must be able to use the information that we have at our disposal. Being able to make connections, solve problems, and sort through lots of data is critical.

Secondary Threat Appraisal and Cognitive Reappraisal

Occurring simultaneously with the primary appraisal process is the secondary appraisal process, which attempts to answer the question "Can I cope with this threat?" Belief in one's ability to cope plays a big part in the stress appraisal process. The role of coping and the secondary appraisal are covered in detail in Chapter 2.

When both questions are answered ("Is it a threat?" and "Can I cope?"), the situation is reappraised and a determination is made by the brain concerning whether or not this potential stressor becomes a real stressor.

In the next section of this chapter we see how this transaction is influenced by our overall level of well-being across the six domains of health: physical, social, mental, intellectual, spiritual, and environmental.

health
a state of complete mental, physical, and social well-being; not merely the absence of disease

holistic health
process of moving toward optimal social, physical, emotional, spiritual, and intellectual functioning

Holistic Health Movement

The holistic health movement came into being in the 1960s as an attempt to expand the view of health that had been promulgated in 1947 by the World Health Organization (WHO).[13] At that time the leadership of WHO defined **health** as a state of complete mental, physical, and social well-being, not merely the absence of disease. This definition of health, although multifaceted, was flawed according to members of the new **holistic health** movement.

Halbert Dunn

Halbert Dunn (1962), one of the early pioneers in the field, believed that the WHO vision characterized health as a static state. Rather than call health a state of well-being, Dunn preferred to view it as a process of moving toward optimal functioning.[3] Dunn considered health to be a conscious and deliberate approach to life and being, rather than something to be abdicated to doctors and the health-care system.

Additionally, Dunn refined well-being to focus on functioning. How well does the organism function? He viewed functioning as evidence of well-being. Of course, people would suffer setbacks in their quest for optimal functioning, but the direction in which their lives were moving became an important criteria for evaluating their well-being. Daily habits and behaviors and overall lifestyle assumed primary importance in the holistic health movement.

Dunn's last criticism of the WHO definition of health revolved around its limiting the scope of well-being to only three dimensions: physical, social, and mental. Adherents of holism argued that the mental dimension alone had two separate components: the intellectual (rational thought processes) and emotional (feelings) that each dealt with different aspects of psychological well-being. Dunn added a last dimension, spiritual, because he felt that humans could not function optimally in a spiritual vacuum. Therefore a holistic definition of health has five dimensions: physical, social, emotional, intellectual, and spiritual.

KEY
TO UNDERSTANDING

Wellness affects the stress response because the way you appraise a potential stressor is influenced by both how you feel (health) and what is going on in your life (environment) on any particular day.

Wellness and Health

In the 1980s and 1990s the definition of health was expanded once again by the wellness movement.[1,9] Adherents to this discipline defined **wellness** as a state of optimal health. With wellness comes vigor, vitality, and the ability to live life to its fullest. Most recently adherents of wellness have added a sixth dimension of health, environmental, or planetary, health. This dimension involves both micro (immediate, personal) and macro (global/planetary) environments.[4]

wellness

a state of optimal health across the six dimensions (social, physical, emotional, intellectual, spiritual, and environmental)

Six Dimensions of Wellness

- *Physical:* How well the body performs its intended functions. Absence of disease, although an important influence on physical wellness, is not the sole criteria for health. The physical domain is influenced by factors such as genetic inheritance, nutritional status, fitness level, body composition, and immune status.

- *Social:* Being connected to others through various types of relationships. Individuals who function optimally in this domain are able to form friendships, have intimate relationships, and give and receive love and affection. They are able to give of themselves and share in the joys and sorrows of being part of a community.
- *Emotional:* Being in touch with feelings, having the ability to express them, and being able to control them when necessary. Optimal functioning involves understanding that emotions are the mirror to the soul and help us get in touch with what is important in our lives. Our emotions make us feel alive and provide us with a richness of experience that is uniquely human.
- *Intellectual:* The ability to process information effectively. Intellectual wellness involves the ability to use information in a rational way to problem solve and grow. It also includes factors such as creativity, spontaneity, and openness to new ways of viewing situations.
- *Spiritual:* Feeling connected to something beyond oneself. One way to express spirituality is through participation in organized religious activities. This usually involves the belief in a supreme being or higher supernatural force and a formalized code of conduct to live by. In a secular sense, spirituality can manifest itself through a connection to something greater than oneself. Whether it is being part of a community, working to save the environment, helping to feed the needy, or committing oneself to world peace, the underlying feeling is one of a perception of life as having meaning beyond the self.
- *Environmental:* The physical and societal surroundings that affect individuals' functioning on both the micro and macro levels. The well-being of our microenvironment includes the level of functioning of our school, home, work site, neighborhood, family, friends, and associates. Our social support system is also part of our microenvironment. This microenvironment greatly affects our health and affects our personal safety by influencing whether or not we are at risk for and fear such issues as theft, crime, and violence. Air and water quality, noise pollution, overcrowding, and other factors that influence our stress levels are also affected by our microenvironment.

The level of well-being of our macroenvironment (state, country, the world at large, and our planet) also affect our wellness. The effects of war, international disputes, famine, pollution, and ozone depletion all influence us to some extent. Decisions made by our political leaders also affect the way we think and live our lives. Our wellness and our ability to stay focused and whole is constantly challenged by media that bring the entire world and its problems into our living rooms each night.

Defining stress as a holistic transaction between the individual, a potential stressor, and the environment incorporates the individual's overall level of wellness across the six dimensions of health.

Stress and Wellness

Those who adhere to this wellness model of health also tend to feel that these six dimensions of health are as significant to stress as the combination of stimulus and response. Stress as a holistic phenomenon can be better understood when it is examined within the context of a person's level of functioning across the six dimensions of health. The amount of stress in peoples' lives and their ability to manage it is strongly influenced by the degree to which they function optimally in each dimension.

Because the stress response begins in the mind, people who have high levels of mental and emotional health are better able to discriminate true stressors from nonstressors. People with a high level of physical well-being can generally mobilize the energy necessary to cope with everyday stressors. Individuals with strong social support systems have a safety net for dealing with potential stressors. Spiritual people have a sense of inner calm that helps them stay focused and hopeful in troubled times. If living and work environments are safe and health-enhancing this will also support efforts at coping.

Adherents of a wellness view of stress would argue that people who function at high levels across the six dimensions of health are more resistant to stress and are able to get more out of each day. People on the dysfunctional end of the continuum are more susceptible to illness in general and potential stressors in particular. Assess Yourself 1-3 at the back of this chapter will help you assess your level of health across all six dimensions.

Over the next four chapters we will explore the multidimensional nature of stress and health. We will take a closer look at how each facet of our health is related to stress and the development of illness.

Summary

In this chapter, we examine the etiology of the author's definition of stress as a holistic transaction between the individual, a potential stressor, and the environment. We trace its roots in the four major ways of defining stress: stress as stimulus, stress as response, stress as a transaction, and stress as a holistic phenomenon. We clarify key definitions related to stress and briefly discuss the work of some of the pioneers in the field.

Claude Bernard, Walter Cannon, and Hans Selye were the pioneers in the research that qualified and quantified the effects of various stressful stimuli on the body. They showed us that the body attempts to maintain a balance, or homeostasis. When exposed to stimuli that put demands on it, the body mobilizes energy and attempts to maintain homeostasis through a complex physiological response involving many different body parts and systems. This response changes over time, and if the source of stress is not removed, resistance is lowered, and the body can become exhausted and break down.

Holmes and Rahe pioneered the investigation of the health effects of too many stressors. They coined the term, *life events*, to define everyday situations that place demands on people and force them to adapt. They quantified the effects of life events and their relationship to the stress response.

Psychological stress researchers examined the role of perception in the stress response. The stress response is viewed as a complex process involving factors concerning potential stressors, personality factors, and the resultant physiological changes that occur if stimuli are perceived as threats to our well-being. Richard Lazarus described various factors involving both the stimulus and the personality of the individual and examined their role in the assessment of potential stressors as threatening or not.

Halbert Dunn describes holistic health as the process of moving toward optimal functioning in the physical, mental, emotional, social, and spiritual dimensions. The stress response, according to adherents of holistic health, is viewed as a process mediated by a person's level of functioning across these five dimensions of health. People who are more whole, that is, functioning at high levels in each dimension, are better able to minimize their stressors and effectively cope with the stress in their lives.

A truly comprehensive view of health and stress, however, can never dismiss the effect of our environment on our attempts at achieving high levels of wellness and stress management. A wellness model of health adds an environmental dimension to the holistic definition. Our immediate microenvironment can contribute to either our stress or our ability to cope. It will affect our quality of life, safety, support systems, resources, and countless other factors related to stress. Our stress level is also affected by the "big picture." Events going on in our state, country, the world, and our planet (macroenvironment) filter through and affect our daily lives.

Defining stress as a holistic transaction between the individual, a potential stressor, and the environment draws from all of these classic definitions, weaving them together in an eclectic definition that incorporates all critical variables involved.

Study Questions

1. Describe the major differences in the four ways of defining stress.
2. Compare the author's definition of stress with the four classical definitions.
3. Explain a holistic transaction using a personal example.
4. What are life events, and how do they relate to stress ?
5. What is homeostasis, and how does it relate to the stress response?
6. What does Selye mean when he characterizes stress as "the non-specific response to any demand"?
7. Describe what happens during the fight-or-flight response.
8. What are a person's weak links?
9. What does Simeons mean by symbolic threats? Give an example of a symbolic threat to your well-being that is a source of stress.
10. What is the role of threat perception in the stress response?
11. Compare how high and low levels of wellness are related to stress.
12. What are the microenvironments and macroenvironments? How are they related to stress?

Reference list

1. Ardell, D.B. (1985). *The history & future of wellness.* Dubuque, IA: Kendall/Hunt.

2. Canon, W. (1932). *The wisdom of the body.* New York: WW Norton.

3. Dunn, H.L. (1962). High level wellness in the world of today. *Journal of the American Osteopathic Association*, 61, 9.

4. Insel, P.M. & Roth, W.T. (1993). *Core concepts in health.* Mountain View, CA: Mayfield Publishers.

5. Lazarus, R.S. (1966). *Psychological stress and the coping process.* New York: McGraw Hill.

6. Lazarus, R.S. (1977). *Stress and coping.* New York: Columbia University Press.

7. Holmes, H.T. & Rahe, H.R. (1967). The Social Readjustment Rating Scale. *Journal of Psychosomatic Research*, 11, 213.

8. Mullen, K. & Costello, G. (1986). *Health awareness through self-discovery.* Dubuque, IA: WC Brown.

9. Payne, W. & Hahn, D. (1992). *Understanding Your Health.* St. Louis: Mosby.

10. Selye, H. (1974). *Stress without distress.* New York: Signet Classics.

11. Selye, H. (1956). *The stress of life.* New York: McGraw Hill.

12. Simeons, A.T.W. (1961). *Man's presumptuous brain: An evolutionary inter-pretation of psychosomatic disease.* New York: EP Dutton.

13. World Health Organization. (1947). Constitution of the World Health Organization. *Chronicles of the World Health Organization*, 1, 29-43.

ASSESS YOURSELF 1-1

Student Stress Scale

The Student Stress Scale represents an adaptation of Holmes and Rahe's Life Event Scale. It has been modified to apply to college-age adults and should be considered a rough indication of stress levels and health consequences for teaching purposes.

In the Student Stress Scale, each event, such as beginning or ending school, is given a score that represents the amount of readjustment a person has to make in life as a result of the change. In some studies, people with serious illnesses have been found to have high scores on similar scales.

To determine your stress score ad up the number of points corresponding to the events you have experienced in the past 12 months.

1. Death of a close family member _____ 100
2. Death of a close friend _____ 73
3. Divorce between parents _____ 65
4. Jail term _____ 63
5. Major personal injury or illness _____ 63
6. Marriage _____ 58
7. Firing from a job _____ 50
8. Failure of an important course _____ 47
9. Change in health of a family member _____ 45
10. Pregnancy _____ 45
11. Sex problems _____ 44
12. Serious argument with close friend _____ 40
13. Change in financial status __✓__ 39
14. Change of major __✓__ 39
15. Trouble with parents _____ 39
16. New girlfriend or boyfriend __✓__ 37
17. Increase in work load at school __✓__ 37
18. Outstanding personal achievement _____ 36
19. First quarter/semester in college _____ 36
20. Change in living conditions _____ 31
21. Serious argument with an instructor _____ 30

Cont'd

Student Stress Scale (cont'd)

22.	Lower grades than expected	✓	29
23.	Change in sleeping habits	____	29
24.	Change in social activities	____	29
25.	Change in eating habits	____	28
26.	Chronic car trouble	____	26
27.	Change in the number of family get togethers	____	26
28.	Too many missed classes	____	25
29.	Change of college	____	24
30.	Dropping of more than one class	____	23
31.	Minor traffic violations	____	20

Total ____

Here's how to interpret your score. If your score is 300 or higher you are at high risk for developing a health problem. If your score is between 150 and 300 you have a 50-50 chance of experiencing a serious health change within 2 years. If your score is below 150 you have a 1-in-3 chance of serious health change.

The following can help you reduce your risk:

- Watch for early signs of stress, such as stomach aches or compulsive overeating.
- Avoid negative thinking.
- Arm your body against stress by eating nutritiously and exercising regularly.
- Practice a relaxation technique regularly.
- Turn to friends and relatives for support when you need it.

From: Mullen, K. & Costello, G. (1986). *Health Awareness Through Self-discovery*. Dubuque, IA: WC Brown.

ASSESS YOURSELF 1-2

Social Readjustment Rating Scale

The Social Readjustment Rating Scale was developed by Holmes and Rahe to assist people in quantifying their level of stress. In this scale, events such as marriage, divorce, retirement, etc., are given a score representing the amount of readjustment (and therefore stress) associated with the change. The score is measured in points called *life change units*. The events have been weighted so that more dramatic readjustments are worth more life change units.

To determine your score, check off the events that you have experienced in the past 12 months.

Rank	Life Event	Life Change Units
1	Death of spouse	100
2	Divorce	73
3	Marital separation	65
4	Jail term	63
5	Death of close family member	63
6	Personal injury or illness	53
7	Marriage	50
8	Fired at work	47
9	Marital reconciliation	45
10	Retirement	45
11	Change in health of family member	44
12	Pregnancy	40
13	Sex difficulties	39
14	Gain of new family member	39
15	Business readjustment	39
16	Change in financial state	38
17	Death of close friend	37
18	Change to different line of work	36
19	Change in number of arguments with spouse	35
20	Mortgage over $10,000	31
21	Foreclosure of mortgage or loan	30
22	Change in responsibilities at work	29

Cont'd

Social Readjustment Rating Scale (cont'd)

Rank	Life Event	Life Change Units
23	Son or daughter leaving home	29
24	Trouble with in-laws	29
25	Outstanding personal achievement	28
26	Spouse begins or stops work	26
27	Begin or end school	26
28	Change in living conditions	25
29	Revision of personal habits	24
30	Trouble with boss	23
31	Change in work hours or conditions	20
32	Change in residence	20
33	Change in school	20
34	Change in recreation	19
35	Change in church activities	19
36	Change in social activities	18
37	Mortgage or loan less than $10,000	17
38	Change in sleeping habits	16
39	Change in number of family get-togethers	15
40	Change in eating habits	15
41	Vacation	14
42	Christmas	13
43	Minor violations of the law	11

Total ____

Here's how to interpret your score. Life change units are points assigned to various experiences. If your score is 300 or higher you are at high risk for developing a health problem. If your score is between 150 and 300 you have a 50-50 chance of experiencing a serious health change within 2 years. If your score is below 150 you have a 1-in-3 chance of serious health change.

From Holmes T.H. & Rahe R.H. (1967). The social readjustment rating scale, *Journal of Psychosomatic Research*, 11, 213.

Name: _____ Date: _____

Wellness Test

Directions: Wellness involves a variety of components that work together to build the total concept. Below are some questions concerning the different aspects of wellness. Using the scale, respond to each question by circling the number that most closely corresponds with your feelings and lifestyle.

	Yes/always	Often	Once	Rarely	No/never
1. I exercise aerobically at least three times per week for 20 minutes or more.	(10)	7	5	3	1
2. When participating in physical activities, I include stretching and flexibility exercises.	10	(7)	5	3	1
3. I include warm-up and cool-down periods when participating in vigorous activities.	10	7	(5)	3	1
4. I engage in resistance-type exercises at least two times per week.	10	7	5	(3)	1
5. My physical fitness level is excellent for my age.	10	7	(5)	3	1
6. My body composition is appropriate for my gender (men, 10% to 18% body fat; women, 18% to 25%).	10	(7)	5	3	1
7. I have appropriate medical check-ups regularly and am able to talk to my doctor and ask questions that concern me.	10	7	5	(3)	1
8. I keep my immunizations up-to-date.	10	7	5	3	(1)
9. I keep up with the medical history of close relatives.	10	7	5	3	(1)
10. I keep records of the time, date, and results of medical tests.	10	7	5	3	(1)

Physical Wellness Assessment Score ___43___

	Yes/always	Often	Once	Rarely	No/never
1. I have at least one person in whom I can confide.	10	(7)	5	3	1
2. I have a good relationship with my family.	(10)	7	5	3	1

Cont'd

Wellness Test (cont'd)

	Yes/always	Often	Once	Rarely	No/never
3. I have friends at work or school with whom I gain support and talk with regularly.	10	(7)	5	3	1
4. I am involved in school activities.	(10)	7	5	3	1
5. I am involved in my community.	10	7	5	(3)	1
6. I do something for fun and just for myself at least once a week.	10	7	5	3	(1)
7. I am able to develop close, intimate relationships.	10	(7)	5	3	1
8. I engage in activities that contribute to the environment.	10	7	(5)	3	1
9. I am interested in the views, opinions, activities, and accomplishments of others.	10	7	(5)	3	1

Social Wellness Assessment Score __55__

	Yes/always	Often	Once	Rarely	No/never
1. I know what my values and beliefs are.	10	(7)	5	3	1
2. I live by my convictions.	10	7	(5)	3	1
3. My life has meaning and direction.	10	7	(5)	3	1
4. I derive strength from my spiritual life daily.	10	7	(5)	3	1
5. I have life goals that I strive to achieve every day.	10	(7)	5	3	1
6. I view life as a learning experience and look forward to the future.	10	(7)	5	3	1

Spiritual Wellness Assessment Score __36__

	Yes/always	Often	Once	Rarely	No/never
1. I feel positive about myself and my life.	10	(7)	5	3	1

Wellness Test (cont'd)

	Yes/always	Often	Once	Rarely	No/never
2. I am able to be the person I choose to be.	10	(7)	5	3	1
3. I am satisfied that I am performing to the best of my ability.	(10)	7	5	3	1
4. I can cope with life's ups and downs effectively and in a healthy manner.	10	7	(5)	3	1
5. I am nonjudgmental in my approach to others and take responsibility for my own decisions and actions.	10	(7)	5	3	1
6. I feel there is appropriate amount of excitement in my life.	10	(7)	5	3	1
7. When I make mistakes, I learn from them.	10	(7)	5	3	1
8. I can say "no" without feeling guilty	10	(7)	5	3	1
9. I find it easy to laugh.	10	(7)	5	3	1

Emotional Wellness Assessment Score 64

	Yes/always	Often	Once	Rarely	No/never
1. I believe my education is preparing me for what I would like to accomplish in life.	10	7	(5)	3	1
2. I am interested in learning just for the sake of learning.	10	(7)	5	3	1
3. I like to be aware of current social and political issues.	10	(7)	5	3	1
4. I have interests other than those directly related to my vocation.	10	(7)	5	3	1
5. I am able to apply what I know to real life situations.	10	7	5	(3)	1
6. I am interested in the viewpoint of others, even if it is very different from my own.	10	(7)	5	3	1
7. I seek advice when I am uncertain or uncomfortable with a recommended health or medical treatment.	10	(7)	5	3	1

Cont'd

Wellness (cont'd)

	Yes/always	Often	Once	Rarely	No/never
8. I ask about the risks and health benefits of a medical test before I use it.	10	7	(5)	3	1
9. When seeking medical care, I plan ahead how to describe my problem and what questions I should ask.	(10)	7	5	3	1
10. I keep abreast of the latest trends and information regarding health matters.	10	7	(5)	3	1

Intellectual Wellness Assessment Score ___63___

	Yes/always	Often	Once	Rarely	No/never
Micro Environment					
1. I use home safety devices (dead-bolt locks, window locks, etc.) to secure my personal environment.	10	7	5	3	(1)
2. I avoid areas in which my personal safety is compromised.	10	7	5	3	(1)
3. I have at least one person (neighbor, friend, etc.) close by whom I can call in an emergency.	10	(7)	5	3	1
4. I recycle and take other steps to reduce local environmental organization.	10	(7)	5	3	1
5. I am a member of at least one local safety or environmental organization.	10	7	5	3	(1)
Macro Environment					
6. I read a daily newspaper or weekly news magazine to keep abreast of world events.	10	(7)	5	3	1
7. I vote in national elections	10	(7)	5	3	1
8. I am a member of at least one national or global organization (UNICEF, Audubon Society, etc.)	10	7	5	3	(1)
9. I support (either financially or as a volunteer) national or global efforts aimed at preventing violence or global leaders.	10	7	5	3	(1)

Wellness (cont'd)

	Yes/always	Often	Once	Rarely	No/never
10. I express my views about environmental issues by writing to national or global leaders.	10	7	5	(3)	1

Environmental Wellness Assessment Score ___36___

Transfer the total score for each section to the spaces below. Add the scores and divide by eight to determine your average wellness score.

Physical Assessment Score................................... 43

Social Wellness Assessment 55

Spiritual Wellness Assessment 36

Emotional Wellness Assessment......................... 64

Intellectual Wellness Assessment........................ 63

Environmental Wellness Assessment.................. 36

Total 297

Average Wellness Score _____

(Divide total score by 6)

86-100—Excellent. You are engaging in behaviors and attitudes that can significantly contribute to a healthy lifestyle and a higher quality of life. If you scored in this range, you are an example to many.

70-85—Good. You engage in many health-promoting attitudes and behaviors that should contribute to good health and a more satisfying quality of life. However, there are some areas that could use some upgrading to provide optimal benefits. If you are at this level, you are showing how much you care about yourself and your life.

50-69—Average. You are typical of the average American who tends to act without really considering the consequences of your behaviors. Now is the time to consider your lifestyle and what ramifications it is having on you now and in the future. Maybe there are some positive actions that you can consider taking to improve your quality of life.

30-49—Below average. Perhaps you lack current information about behaviors and attitudes that can enhance your health and quality of life. Now is the time to begin to learn about positive changes that can improve your life.

Less than 30—Needs improvement. It is good that you are concerned enough about your health to take this test, but indications are that your behaviors and attitudes may be having detrimental effects on your health. You can easily begin to take action now to improve your prospects for the future.

Mental and Emotional Basis of Stress

CHAPTER OBJECTIVES

- Understand the influence of the mental and emotional dimensions of health on stress.
- Define personality and explain three different theories concerning its development.
- Explain how personality contributes to the stress response.
- Define the Type A personality and explain how it contributes to the stress response.
- Describe the role of anger and hostility in the development of stress.
- Explain the protective effects of the hardy personality.
- Compare Type A and B personalities.
- Describe rational emotive therapy.
- Describe the differences between primary and secondary stress appraisal.
- Describe the influence of perceived efficacy of coping in the stress appraisal process.

In this chapter we examine the mental and emotional basis of stress in great detail. We expand on the work of Lazarus and Ellis and explore the findings of a variety of other researchers in this area. We examine the notion of *stressful personalities* and *hardy* or *stress-resistant personalities*, as well as those specific personality attributes most related to stress. We also discuss an expanded version of Lazarus's threat appraisal model that integrates coping. This chapter examines the role of coping and one's perceived ability to cope. This perceived *efficacy* of coping is a vital part of the work of Lazarus and Folkman[20] and will tie the stress-related personality attributes together into a model of perception and coping.

Personality and Stress
Personality Development

Are some people better able to deal with life events and the daily hassles that confront all of us? Are there personality types that are more or less stress prone? In other words, are some people more easily stressed than others because of personality type? Many researchers believe that this is exactly the case. For these researchers, stressors, or potential stressors, are less important in the stress response than the personality of the individual experiencing these events.

personality

our unique collection of thoughts, attitudes, values, beliefs, perceptions, and behaviors that define who we are as people

Our **personality** is a collection of thoughts, attitudes, values, beliefs, perceptions, and behaviors that define how we see ourselves and our environment. Personality is constantly evolving and is the sum of everything we have experienced in our lives. Six different types of theories attempt to explain how personality develops, as shown in Table 2-1.

Behavioralists

Behavioralism, developed by John Watson[41], proposes that personality develops as a result of responses to generalized and specific stimuli. A stimulus-response model does not presuppose the existence of any innate, predetermined human personality attributes. Behavioralists believe our personalities are the result of a myriad of interactions between stimuli (people, places, events, situations, and images) and the responses they have evoked. Responses can be either positive or negative and can vary in their strength. The more powerful the response, the more likely we will either embrace (positive response) or reject (negative response) whatever stimuli prompted it.

Other theories use models that focus on developmental stages and tasks. These types of theories propose that personality develops in stages after certain tasks or needs are satisfied. Table 2-2 presents three such developmental personality theories.

TABLE 2.1

Traditional Models of Personality and Growth

View	Emphasis
Behavioralists	Responses to specific or generalized stimuli to explain human behavior
Freud	Growth as struggle between the unconscious-irrational forces and the conscious-rational resources of life
Erikson	Psychosocial aspects of growth
Maslow	Growth in terms of inner needs and motivation
Piaget	Intellectual-maturational aspects of growth
Kohlberg	Moral-ethical dimensions of growth

Freud

Freudian psychoanalytical theory promotes the notion that human personality develops as a result of a struggle between conscious and unconscious forces in our lives.[13] The conscious forces are directed by our ego and superego. Our ego (the rational, thinking mind) takes objective information into account, and our superego (our conscience) factors in our beliefs about right and wrong. These conscious forces struggle for control of our behavior with the id, the unconscious and irrational mind, which is driven by eros, a powerful life force striving for the pursuit of pleasure.

The fuel of this life force, libidinal energy, is channelled into various centers of our bodies during different stages of our development and creates a set of needs that must be satisfied. According to Freud our personality develops in response to our ability to satisfy these needs. If these needs are not satisfied, we become fixated, or stuck, at various stages of life and develop neurotic personality traits. These traits carry over into the successive stages of development unless resolved at some point in time. Freudian theory helps explain behaviors such as overeating or smoking, adult responses to our earliest needs for sucking and nurturing during the oral stage of development when libidinal energy was concentrated in the mouth.

Erickson

Eric Erickson[10] who studied with Freud also constructed a model that views personality development as a result of a struggle between opposing forces. These forces present themselves in a series of eight stages that occur throughout our lives (see Table 2-2). Erickson viewed development as a conflict between opposing psychosocial forces and qualities instead of the id and the ego/superego. Healthy personality development resulted

TABLE 2.2

The Developmental Theories of Freud, Erikson, and Piaget

Age	Freud	Erikson	Piaget
1	Oral	Trust vs. Mistrust	Sensorimotor
2	Anal	Autonomy vs. Shame/Doubt	
3	Phallic		Preoperational Thought
4		Initiative vs. Guilt	
5	Oedipal		
6			
7			
8			Concrete Operations
9	Latency	Industry vs. Inferiority	
10			
11			
12			
13			
14			
15	Adolescence	Identity vs. Role Confusion	Formal Operations
16			
17			
18			
Early Adulthood		Intimacy vs. Isolation	
Midlife		Generativity vs. Self-absorption	
Old Age		Integrity vs. Despair	

from accomplishing the developmental tasks required for each stage. Inadequate task resolution resulted in thwarted development in that particular area.

For example, infants who never successfully developed a sense of trust in themselves and others would grow up with a stronger sense of mistrust. This would stay with them throughout their lives and limit their ability to develop sustaining relationships and hope for a brighter future.

Piaget

Jean Piaget[31], a Swiss psychologist, was another personality theorist who focused on stages of cognitive development. Cognitive development is one facet of personality that influences who we are and how we view ourselves. Like Erickson, Piaget felt that our cognitive abilities progress as we move through a series of stages. These stages require increasingly more sophisticated types of thought processes and abilities that depend on neurological development and mastery of previous tasks. These tasks range from the simple ability of manipulating objects to using logical thought and abstract reasoning.

Kohlberg

Lawrence Kohlberg[17] proposed another developmental approach to understanding personality—a theory that emphasizes moral development. Kohlberg posits that there are stages of moral thinking and judging, and fully-functioning adult moral reasoning occurs as a result of successful progression through those various stages and levels. (See Table 2-3 for a presentation of Kohlberg's stages of moral development.)

Progression through Kohlberg's various stages and levels is shaped by various influences such as family, culture and subculture, and society. As in the other developmental theories, individuals are incapable of performing specific types of moral reasoning until they successfully master the tasks associated with that stage. For instance, young children will avoid breaking certain rules because they fear adult punishment and authority (Stage 1), not because they are acting in accordance with universal ethical principles (Stage 6). Kohlberg believed that not everyone progresses through all levels and stages and that only a minority of adults ever operate in Stage 6.

Maslow

The last developmental theory we examine is Abraham Maslow's[26] Hierarchy of Needs. Maslow, a humanist, believed that all humans are unique and capable of growing and reaching their utmost potential. He believed that humans are essentially good and have the ability to make choices about the direction in which they want their lives to move. Maslow believed that all people are capable of reaching their highest potential if they progress through a series of development stages that meet various basic human needs. Fig. 2-1 summarizes these needs.

Self-actualization, at the top of Maslow's pyramid, represents the pinnacle of human development. To reach that point one has to pass through all of the previous levels, successfully meeting the needs of those stages.

Maslow believed that as we work our way up this pyramid we often encounter *peak experiences*, moments that transcend mere existence and

TABLE 2.3

Kohlberg's Stages of Moral Development

Level and stage	What is right	Reasons for doing right
Level A: preconventional **Stage 1:** punishment and obedience	Avoiding breaking rules, obeying for obedience's sake, and avoiding doing physical damage to people and property	Avoiding punishment and the superior power of authorities
Stage 2: individual instrumental purpose and exchange	Following rules when it is in someone's immediate interest Using fairness, equal exchange, and agreement	Serving one's own needs or interests in a world where one must recognize that other people have interests as well
Level B: conventional **Stage 3:** mutual interpersonal expectations, relationships, and conformity	Living up to what is expected by relatives and friends or what is generally expected in one's role as son, sister, friend, and so on "Being good" is important	Needing to be good in one's own eyes and those of others Following the "golden rule"
Stage 4: social system and conscience maintenance	Fulfilling actual duties to which one has agreed Upholding laws that are to be upheld unless they conflict with other fixed social duties and rights Contributing to society, the group, or institution	Keeping institution going as a whole Using self-respect or conscience to meet one's defined obligations
Level C: transition		Basing reasons on emotions; conscience is arbitrary and relative
Level D: postconventional and principled **Stage 5:** prior rights and social contract or utility	Being aware that people hold a variety of values and opinions, most of which are relative to one's group Realizing that some nonrelative values and rights, such as life and liberty must be upheld in any society	Feeling obligated to obey the law because one has made a social contract to make and abide by laws for the good of all; the greatest good for the greatest number
Stage 6: universal ethical principle	Acting in accordance with principle when laws violate universal ethical principles Understanding the equality of human rights and respecting the dignity of human beings as individuals	As a rational person, seeing the validity of principles and becoming committed to them

crystalize for us what it means to be fully alive. Maslow believed that these peak experiences help us feel connected to the world around us and one with our universe (see the box on p. 36).

Dr. Daniel Girdano and others[12] describe self-worth, self-love, self-esteem, self-confidence, and self-respect as the critical components of a healthy personality. Development of these components relies on meeting specific needs that occur throughout our lives. Experiences in the first few years of life play a critical role in determining whether or not children will meet their needs for the development of these self components. Failure to meet these needs contributes to a personality and world view that can be a source of chronic stress throughout our lives.

Self-worth and self-love are described by Girdano[12] as inborn, something we do not have to earn or prove. Therefore we are born worthy and loving. Self-worth means feeling that we have value and are valued for who

Fig. 2-1 Maslow's hierarchy of needs.

Maslow's Self-actualized People

Abraham Maslow was interested in human potential. He felt that all people are born with unique qualities and the ability to maximize their genetically-determined potential. He was convinced that successful people, those who seemed to live life to its fullest, share certain unique qualities that allow them to live to their fullest potential. He compiled a list of 48 of the most influential historical and comtemporary figures of his time, people whom he considered to be fully self-actualized. Among those on his list were historical figures such as Abraham Lincoln, Henry David Thoreau, and Ludwig Von Beethoven. Contemporary figures of his time included Albert Einstein, Eleanor and Franklin D. Roosevelt, Eugene V. Debs, and Amelia Earhart.

In studying these and other fully self-actualized people, Maslow identified the following 16 common characteristics:

1. Do not distort reality
2. Have a high level of self-acceptance
3. Have loving and imtimate relationships with others
4. Are autonomous and independent
5. Are spontaneous in thought and emotion
6. Are task-oriented rather than self-oriented
7. Are open to newness and change
8. View and appreciate familiar things in new and different ways
9. Possess a sense of spirituality that connects them to all living things and the universe
10. Have empathy toward those from cultures other than their own
11. Relate to others as individuals
12. Have their own unique ethical sense of right and wrong
13. Resist acculturation
14. Are able to tolerate and enjoy silence and solitude
15. Are creative and inventive
16. Have a sense of humor and an appreciation of their own and other human failings

These characteristics set self-actualizers apart from others and enable them to continue to grow and fully develop their potential. These characteristics create and maintain a personality that enables self-actualizers to take advantage of situations that can contribute to their growth and to learn from negative experiences that could be detrimental to their well-being.

we are, and self-love is the sense of caring for, forgiving, and nurturing ourselves. However, for various reasons many people feel unworthy and do not love themselves. They feel they have to earn self-worth and self-love and spend much of their lives punishing themselves.

Self-esteem, self-confidence, and self-respect, on the other hand, are not innate.[12] These components evolve and develop in response to our successes and failures as we grow and interact with the world around us.

Of the five components of the self characterized by Girdano[12], self-esteem seems to be the most critical component of a healthy personality. Self-esteem literally means feeling good about oneself and is essential to happiness and well-being. Self-esteem slowly evolves as our sense of trust in ourselves and others grows. We test our abilities and learn from our successes and failures. We are rewarded, both intrinsically and by others, as our successes build and as we grow.

Our successes breed self-confidence and we feel increasingly more capable and confident. With greater self-confidence we rely less on the approval of others and trust our intuition to help us anticipate the future. In time, our confidence breeds self-respect, the ability to honor what we value in life. Self-respect is our anchor and helps keep us steady in times of emotional upheaval. It allows us to appreciate who we are and what we are feeling. Our self-confidence and self-esteem enable us to own those feelings and trust in their appropriateness.

These aspects of the self are central to our personality. They build upon each other and work together to define who we are and how we view our world. The next section examines the significance of personality types and how they are related to stress.

Personality Types

It seems reasonable to assume that our personality will influence, if not determine, how we react to potentially stressful events and people. Most arguments about the effects of personality on stress do not challenge this belief. Rather, theorists argue about the relative significance of personality or how much effect it has on stress in our lives.

There is a substantial amount of literature on *stress-resistant* versus *stress-prone* personality types. Research shows that some of us are more prone or resistant to potential stressors because of our personalities. Furthermore, personalities can be grouped into categories that are more or less prone to stress.

Type A Personality

One of the most widely documented relationships between personality, behavior, and stress is the link between the **Type A personality** and stress, pioneered by Friedman and Rosenman,[11] cardiologists working in San Francisco. They first described the Type A behavior pattern in their patients.

Type A personality

a stress-prone personality characterized by aggressive, competitive, and hostile attitudes and behavior

They described the typical Type A individual as someone who was always trying to achieve or acquire more and more things in less and less time. The Type A person is a chronic overachiever usually in competition with others. Even though Type As put themselves under enormous pressure on a regular basis, they do not react to this by getting anxious. Rather, they confidently grapple with these self-imposed challenges.[33]

The typical Type A personality has the following characteristics:

Competitive—Type As want to win at everything; even a child's board game can turn into a battleground. Type As often bring their competitive nature to their play and recreational pursuits become competitive athletic events.

Verbally aggressive—Often the speech of Type As, besides being rushed, is peppered with explosive accentuation of key words.

Hard-driving—Type As push themselves to limits that most people resist. They routinely perform two or more tasks simultaneously and overbook their schedules. They jump from one task to another with little or no downtime. Because of this Type As are often rewarded for their efforts. They work long hours and still take work home.

Unable to relax—Even while on vacation Type As tend to feel guilty about not doing something productive.

Very time conscious—A Type A personality would have a very hard time getting through the day without a watch. They maintain strict schedules with little flexibility and they hate to "waste" time.

Easily angered—Type As are easily angered. They have very short fuses. This anger or strong feeling of displeasure cuts across all barriers.

Hostile—Although anger is general and can be directed at events or objects, hostility is focused on people. Type As are hostile and other people are the target of their anger.

In addition to the aforementioned traits, Type As also exhibit body language and speech patterns that are noticeably different from non-Type As.[33,34]

The following body language and speech patterns typify Type As when responding to potentially stressful situations:

Tightening of facial muscles—noticeably tense muscles of the face, neck, and forehead.

Gesturing with a clenched fist—clench their fists and punch home their points.

Grimacing—contort their facial muscles to express displeasure.

Using explosive speech—change their vocal intonation and use loud bursts of key words to make their points.

Interrupting the interviewer—cut off the interviewer to make their points.

Hurrying the pace—try to speed along the pace of the interview by finishing the interviewer's sentences and by other means.

This chronic combination of both substance (beliefs/behaviors) and style (the manner in which they are expressed) characterizes the Type A behavior pattern. Assess Yourself 2-1 identifies tendencies toward Type A behavior.

Type A personalities usually are highly successful people. Their hard work, fanatical drive, and competitiveness are rewarded with financial success and the admiration of their peers who often wonder how they sustain their high level of activity (Fig. 2-2). Unfortunately, there is a price to pay for this.

Friedman and Rosenman[11] wondered whether the presence of these personality attributes was merely a coincidence or whether there was some relationship between them and an increased risk for coronary heart disease. In looking back at the medical records of their patients, they examined whether or not those exhibiting Type A traits developed coronary heart disease (CHD) at a greater rate than those with a calmer, more relaxed personality. CHD, also known as coronary artery disease, involves damage to the vessels that supply blood to the heart muscle.

Friedman and Rosenman found that Type As did in fact experience a greater rate of CHD than patients not displaying the Type A behavior patterns. Their research controlled the other factors associated with CHD, such

KEY
TO UNDERSTANDING

The Type A personality is a construct involving both behavior and beliefs.

Fig. 2-2 Type A personalities are always trying to do more and more in less and less time.

as diet, lack of exercise, smoking, and high blood pressure. Their work has become so well-known that the phrase *Type A* has become synonymous with people who are aggressive, competitive, and hard driving. Their research and the countless studies that have followed it have uncovered a strong relationship between the Type A behavior pattern and an increased risk for heart disease and premature death from all causes.

Other subsequent long-term studies have noted similar associations between Type A behavior and increased risk for CHD in groups of healthy subjects.[14,33] The Type A personality is relatively stable; 61% of subjects rated as Type A between 1960 and 1961 retained that classification in a 27-year follow-up study,[4] perpetuating their risk for over 2 decades.

The increased risks associated with the Type A behavior pattern are not gender specific. Although the majority of Type A studies are of men, research shows that both Type A men and women are at increased risk for CHD.[1,18,30] One large research project, the Framingham Study, showed that Type A women are more than three times more likely than Type B women to develop heart disease.[14]

Type B Personality

Friedman and Rosenman[11] went one step further and identified a second type of personality pattern, **Type B**, that is the opposite of Type A. In a sense the Type B personality could almost be classified as non-A because of its absence of Type A traits. Type B personalities are relaxed and easy-going, not as competitive as Type As, and do not exhibit the same tendencies of time urgency and anger. Friedman and Rosenman found that in subjects who are free from other risk factors for coronary heart disease (diabetes, hypertension, and elevated cholesterol), a Type B personality is protected against heart disease.

Similar findings concerning the protective effects of Type B characteristics were also found in another study.[23] For example, Type B individuals have a lower incidence of daily hassles than Type A personalities because they are not as easily frustrated.[24]

Because of inconsistencies in results and problems in research associated with Type As, some researchers have attempted to isolate which Type A factors are more significantly related to risk for CHD. The studies point to two factors as the most predictive of all Type A variables: anger and hostility. **Anger**, in general, is directed at anything, and **hostility** is a type of anger that is directed specifically at people. Anger seems to be more of a reaction to a situation, whereas hostility is an enduring trait; it is difficult to isolate and measure either trait independently. Evidence supports that a significant relationship exists between hostility and anger and negative health outcomes.[2,25]

Type B
a stress-resistant personality characterized by a relaxed, easygoing, friendly manner

KEY
TO UNDERSTANDING

The Type B personality is the opposite of Type A.

anger
a strong feeling of displeasure targeted at anything

hostility
anger that is directed at someone

A significant relationship between the degree of hostility and the severity of the disease was found in the Williams et al[42] study of subjects who already had coronary atherosclerosis.[42] In healthy subjects, hostility level was significantly related to both heart attack and death from CHD.[29,38] Additionally death rates from all causes were significantly related to high levels of hostility.[3,29,38] Two recent studies[9,27] discovered that men and boys have higher hostility scores than their female counterparts, possibly explaining the heightened risk of CHD in males.

Hardy Personality

As a University of Chicago doctoral student, Suzanne Kobassa[16] identified another personality type, the **hardy personality**. Like Type B, the hardy personality may also help fight stress and disease. Kobassa studied two groups of middle- and upper-level managers of a large public utility. All managers took an initial battery of tests designed to measure their stress levels and illness levels; each subject was given a total stress score and a total illness score based on their test results. Two groups were formed based on these scores—a high stress/high illness group and a high stress/low illness group. All low-stress subjects were removed from the study.[16]

> **hardy personality**
> a stress-resistant personality characterized by commitment, control, and challenge

To categorize the personality attributes of high-stress subjects, Kobassa administered a variety of psychological tests. When analyzing the results she found that some subjects had certain personality traits that protected against the ravages of stress. These managers she entitled *hardy*. These hardy managers do more than survive the daily pressures of corporate life; they thrive on pressure. Hardy subjects have the following characteristics: low blood pressure, few sick days, happy personalities, and little psychological distress.[16] Additionally, three personality attributes are associated with hardiness: commitment, control, and change.

Commitment refers to having a sense of purpose and meaning to life and relationships. Kobassa describes this as being "committed to, rather than alienated from, oneself."[16] Committed individuals are actively involved in life. Kobassa characterizes this as "vigorousness vs. a vegetativeness"[16] with their environment.

Closely related to commitment is control, a feeling of being in charge of your life. People in control feel they are actors in life, not objects being acted on. This internal *locus of control* has been studied for several years. Rotter,[36] a pioneer in this area of research, found that people with a high internal locus of control feel in charge of their lives. These people also believe they are responsible for their actions and therefore are more likely to take steps to ensure their well-being.

STRESS IN OUR WORLD

Shakir

Shakir is a perfect example of the hardy personality in action.

Shakir is a mid-level bureaucrat in a large state agency that monitors federally funded family planning services for low-income populations. Shakir has seen it all in his 15 years of state service. He has survived the policy changes of four United States presidents, two governors, three health commissioners, and three division directors. These policy makers have come and gone, each changing the face of Shakir's agency according to their political philosophies. Each has created new procedures, forms, and protocols that were scrapped as they moved on to other positions. Shakir has outlasted them all.

Shakir knows he could earn twice the salary he makes in his present job if he left for work in the private sector. His MBA from a premiere graduate school, years of managerial experience, and polished communication skills would qualify him for a variety of high-paying, less politically volatile private-sector jobs. However, despite the constant change, lower salary, and lack of prestige Shakir stays.

Shakir stays because he is committed and he feels his work has some meaning. He realizes that by staying he provides the continuity needed to deliver important services to people in need. Besides doing a good job at work, Shakir also volunteers his time to work with professional organizations and grassroots committees that are related to his profession.

Shakir also feels in control. He is the quintessential bureaucrat and he is proud of that title. He operates smoothly within the slowly moving bureaucratic machinery and has learned how to get things done despite the bureaucracy. People respect him and help him overcome obstacles that others feel are beyond their control. Shakir is a valued and respected member of his division and is given a lot of authority to work within the parameters of the organization.

Lastly, after 15 years Shakir still feels challenged by his work. Rather than fearing change he looks forward to it. He views the policy changes that often accompany the political maneuvers in his state as healthy and challenging. Confident in his ability to adapt to change, Shakir views change as essential and actively solicits ideas from others concerning his work. He is more than a survivor, he has flourished.

Even in situations where decisions are made above their level, managers with high control scores believe they have the final word on events that affect their lives. Individuals who feel in control of their lives are better able to withstand the pressures of the business world, a place where few individuals have complete control of 100% of their work. Assess Yourself 2-2 helps you discover how much control you have over your life.

The third personality attribute associated with hardiness is challenge, which relates to how people perceive change. Hardy individuals welcome change and view it as a normal part of life. They understand that no one is ever free from change. Instead they view change as the only constant in life. Hardy people are flexible and can adapt to life's changes.

As an example, hardiness is a buffer against stress and burnout among nurses.[43] Nurses who score higher than their peers on hardiness tests are more capable of combating the effects of job stress and burnout.

However, Kobassa's work has been criticized by Hull et al.[15] who contend that all of Kobassa's three components of hardiness (control, commitment, and challenge) may not operate together in all stressful situations. Hull et al. feel that hardiness may be more related to either a combination of control and commitment or any of the three variables working independently. As discussed later in this chapter, Lazarus and Folkman[20] build on Kobassa's concept of challenge and operationally define it so that its role in personality and the stress response is clearer.

Irrational, Illogical Personality

Albert Ellis,[6-8] the founder of a type of therapy called *rational emotive psychotherapy (RET)*, discusses a group of personality attributes that he has labeled as *illogical beliefs,* and that underlie his theory on stress and neurotic behavior. RET is based on the philosophy that people and things do not make us feel bad and behave neurotically. Instead our negative thoughts and illogical beliefs about these people and things are the basis for our stress and neuroses. Ellis believes our perception of situations determines whether or not these situations become stressors.

The underlying theory of RET is based on Ellis' ABC model. In this model the presence of an activating event, *A*, triggers a series of illogical beliefs. These illogical beliefs, *B*, cause a variety of negative mental, emotional, physical, behavioral, and social consequences, *C*.[7] In essence, A + B = C.

In their clinical work with neurotic patients, Ellis and Harper[6] identified 10 commonly held illogical beliefs about life (see the box on p. 44). Such beliefs form the basis of an irrational **belief system** that gives a distorted perspective for assessing potentially stressful situations. In other words, chronically irrational or illogical people think unclearly and interpret potential stressors incorrectly; therefore they are in a state of stress when it is not warranted.

These illogical/irrational thinkers are more predisposed to stress or neuroses than others because their distorted view of the world creates more potentially stressful situations. Relatively mild stimuli and situations are more likely to develop into stressors for people with an illogical belief system.

KEY
TO UNDERSTANDING

An internal locus of control means that, regardless of the situation, we ultimately have the final word on our thoughts, feelings, and behavior.

KEY
TO UNDERSTANDING

Nothing in life is constant except change.

belief system
a collection of values, attitudes, and beliefs about the world and interactions between people

Ten Irrational Beliefs

1. You must have love or approval from all the people you find significant.

2. You must prove thoroughly adequate, competent, or achieving.

3. When people act obnoxiously or unfairly, you should blame and damn them and see them as bad, wicked, or rotten individuals.

4. You have to view things as awful, terrible, horrible, and catastrophic when you get seriously frustrated, treated unfairly, or rejected.

5. Emotional misery comes from external pressures, and you have little ability to control or change your feelings.

6. If something seems dangerous or fearsome, you must preoccupy yourself with it and make yourself anxious about it.

7. You can more easily avoid facing many life difficulties and self-responsibilities than undertake more rewarding forms of self-discipline.

8. Your past remains all-important and, because something once strongly influenced your life, it has to keep determining your feelings and behavior today.

9. People and things should turn out better than they do, and you must view it as awful and horrible if you do not find good solutions to life's grim realities.

10. You can achieve maximum human happiness by inertia and inaction or by passively and uncommittedly enjoying yourself.

These people are unable to see the bright side or view the situation in a more rational way.[5]

Ellis[7] noticed his clients engaged in subvocal speech patterns (talking to oneself) that reinforced any irrational beliefs. His clients would repeat negative messages about a stressful event to themselves. In addition, they would direct much of the negative subvocal speech patterns inward, making themselves the target of the negative self-talk.

John is a perfect example (Fig. 2-3). He was walking down the hall to class when a friend from an earlier class walked past him, oblivious of his presence. John immediately perceived this illogically by thinking to himself, "I can't believe she did that to me—how terrible." He backed this up by asking himself subvocally; "What did I do wrong ? I must be a total jerk."

This interaction between the irrational/illogical thought pattern and the negative subvocal speech transformed a relatively benign event into a stressor that stayed with John all morning.

In a revision of his original ABC model, Ellis[8] discusses the importance of goals, values, and desires in perceiving activating events. His

Fig. 2-3 John was just passed by one of his classmates who didn't even acknowledge his presence. John then engages in subvocal speech.

revised theory explains how healthy people can use reason and intellect to logically evaluate the threat posed by activating events. Irrational people, on the other hand, are unable to do this and use disordered thinking based on illogical beliefs when confronted by activating events. Ellis carries this theory further by explaining that the irrational beliefs themselves can be activating events. When this happens, even the thought of the activating event can trigger a stress response or another negative consequence.

In trying to understand Ellis's illogical beliefs theory, it is important to realize that all of us hold some of these views at one time or another. People who hold several of these beliefs and regularly view the world in this irrational and illogical way are more stress-prone. Assess Yourself 2-3 evaluates your tendency to think irrationally.

The negative self-talk also keeps the stress response alive longer. Negative self-talk, particularly if it persists beyond the stressful situation, transforms thoughts about the **primary stressor** into a **secondary stressor**.

To make Ellis and Harper's theory easier to use and understand Walen and others[40] grouped the 10 illogical/irrational beliefs into four categories:

1. "Awfulizing" statements—exaggerate the negative effects of a situation
2. Shoulds/musts/oughts—set illogical demands on oneself and others
3. Evaluation of worth statements—imply that some people or things are worthless or a complete waste of time
4. Need statements—set unrealistic, unattainable requirements for happiness

Awfulizing statements are often used by people who blow every little misfortune out of proportion; for them everything is a catastrophe. They are like the boy who cried wolf in that after a while we tune out their complaints because we have become desensitized to them.

These people prolong their stress responses by continually reminding themselves how horrible or terrible their situation is. Tom is a perfect example (Fig. 2-4). He woke up late for school because his alarm did not go off. He had forgotten to take his slacks out of the dryer the night before and had no time to iron them, so he ran to class with wrinkled pants. Totally annoyed at the situation, Tom told himself, "How horrible! I can't go to class looking like this. This is awful." As he scurried across campus to get to class Tom constantly reminded himself how terrible this all was and wondered, "Why does this always happen to me?" All day Tom stoked the fires of his stress by telling everybody about his misfortune. At three o'clock Tom was in the snack bar still recounting the morning's events. What could have been a minor annoyance or inconvenience (alarm not going off, being late for one class) turned into an all-day stressor that wasted a tremendous amount of energy.

Shoulds, oughts, and *musts* are often spouted by people who believe things must be a certain way (usually their own) or else it is wrong. These people often complain about how others should act or how they must behave. They tend to see things as either black or white and have little patience for different views.

People who illogically evaluate the worth of things commonly refer to other people or situations as "worthless" or "a complete waste of time." These people have a very low frustration tolerance and tend to overreact to shortcomings of people or situations. For example, some people with this thinking go crazy waiting in line at the supermarket (Fig. 2-5) when the person in front of them has to fumble with money or write a check. They con-

Fig. 2-4 Tom is late for school. His alarm did not go off. His pants are wrinkled. He has no time to iron them. The whole day is horrible for him.

Fig. 2-5 People who illogically evaluate the worth of things usually have a low frustration tolerance and tend to overreact.

sider this time spent in line to be a complete waste of time. A waiter who is slow or who makes a mistake on the bill might be viewed as totally incompetent. A school course that does not meet expectations might be a complete waste of money. Instead of judging a particular aspect of a person or situation as having low value, these irrational thinkers rate the entire person or situation.

Irrationally needy people set unrealistic standards for happiness. Whether it is for a spouse, boyfriend or girlfriend, teacher, or employer, these people set their expectations too high to ever be met. They are constantly finding faults and are rarely satisfied, regardless of the situation or outcome.

Anxious-Reactive Personality

The anxious-reactive personality characterized by Girdano and others[12] is similar to the irrational personality described by Ellis. The anxious-reactive personality creates a self-perpetuating anxiety reaction that keeps the stress response alive long after the stressor disappears. People with this personality type are similar to Ellis's catastrophizers or Walen's awfulizers. They are hypersensitive to stressors and initiate stress by anticipating that the worst will happen.

Similiar to Ellis's irrational beliefs, the catastrophic, illogical thoughts about the activating stressful event can not only trigger the stress response but can also serve as activating events without the presence of the original stressor. This is an anxiety feedback loop in which cognitive anxiety keeps the stress response alive.[12] Fig. 2-6 provides an example.

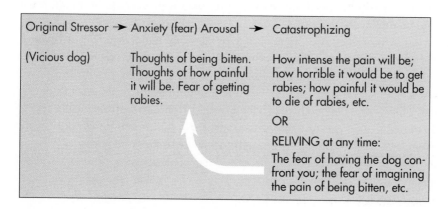

Fig. 2-6 Cognitive activity in the anxiety feedback loop.

Perception and Stress

Ellis, Kobassa, Friedman and Rosenman, and the other researchers discussed so far have proven that certain personality types and personality behavior patterns are associated with increased stress and illness levels. Although no one is exactly sure how personality develops and the extent to which biological and psychosocial factors influence our personalities, it is safe to say that our perception of the world around us is intricately linked to our personalities.

With the exception of certain unpleasant environmental stimuli, most stressors are people or situations that we have learned to consider stressful. The people and things that are our stressors are learned over the course of a lifetime and are very individualistic—what we perceive as stressful someone else may not.

Lazarus and Threat Appraisal

In Chapter 1 the work of Richard Lazarus is introduced, which provides a rich theoretical framework that ties together the works of this chapter's researchers. Lazarus's[19] initial book revolved around the concept of threat appraisal. He believed things stress us because they threaten our well-being in some way. Threat is a state of anticipated confrontation with a harmful condition and includes physical harm, psychological pain, or social discomfort. For instance, some people may perceive exercise as stressful because of the physical discomfort. Others may avoid becoming intimate with a partner because getting too close makes them vulnerable. Still others may avoid certain social gatherings because the environment makes them feel out of control. If the event provokes a perception of threat, it will lead to the stress response.

Examine the case of Hiroko, a psychology major who has a midterm in her abnormal psychology course. Hiroko has an *A* average in her major and has gotten excellent grades on all of her midterms during the past 2 years. She is well prepared for her upcoming midterm and knows the material. However, even with this background, if Hiroko perceives this test as threatening then the test will cause her stress. The mere perception of the event, however irrational, is enough to initiate a stress response.

As briefly discussed in Chapter 1, the presence of a potential stressor initiates the stress appraisal process (Fig. 2-7). In his later work with colleague Susan Folkman, Lazarus[19] expanded on threat appraisal. Primary and secondary appraisal are actually misnomers because they imply something that Lazarus never intended: the notion that primary appraisal is more impor-

KEY
TO UNDERSTANDING

It does not matter whether or not something is truly threatening. If one perceives something as threatening, it is.

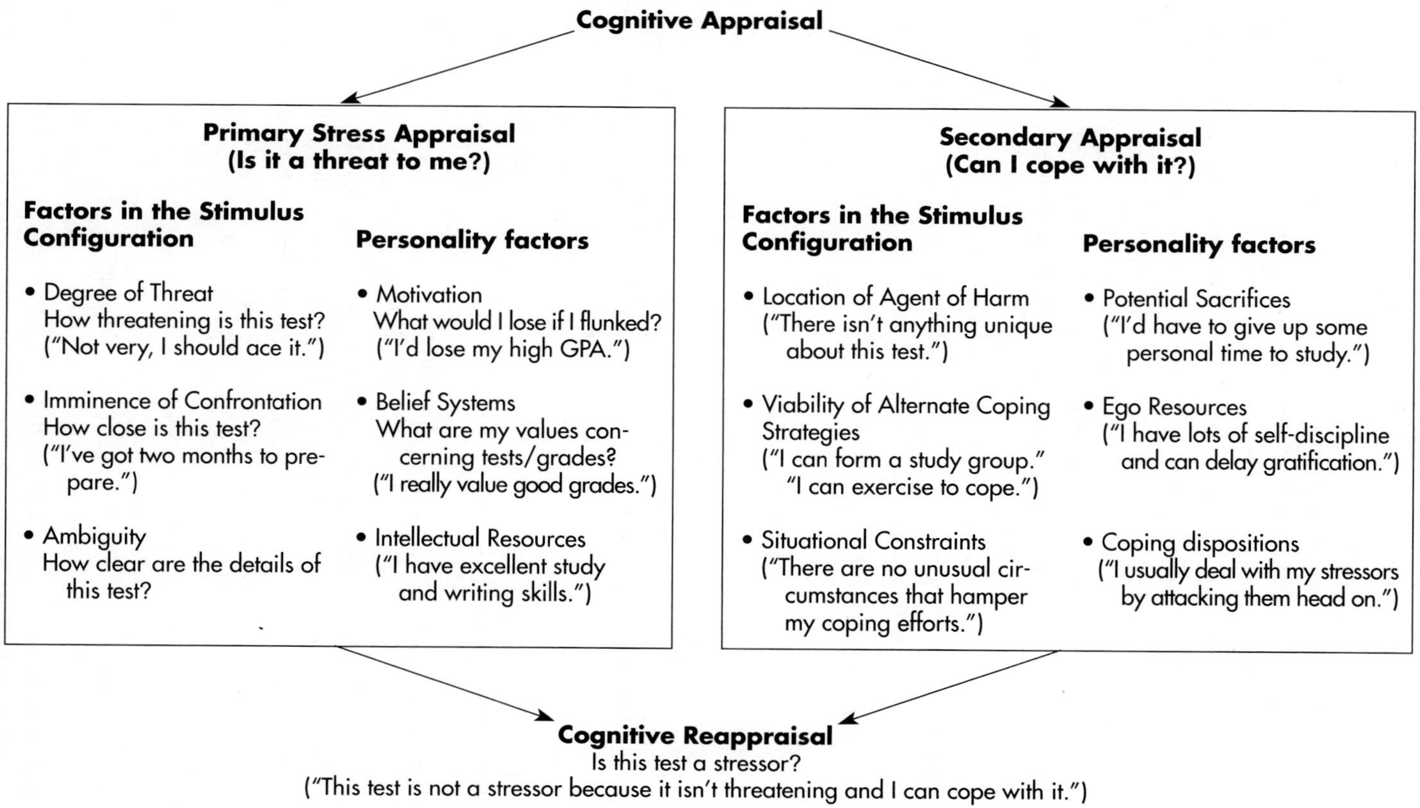

Cognitive Appraisal

Primary Stress Appraisal
(Is it a threat to me?)

Factors in the Stimulus Configuration

- Degree of Threat
  How threatening is this test?
  ("Not very, I should ace it.")

- Imminence of Confrontation
  How close is this test?
  ("I've got two months to prepare.")

- Ambiguity
  How clear are the details of this test?

Personality factors

- Motivation
  What would I lose if I flunked?
  ("I'd lose my high GPA.")

- Belief Systems
  What are my values concerning tests/grades?
  ("I really value good grades.")

- Intellectual Resources
  ("I have excellent study and writing skills.")

Secondary Appraisal
(Can I cope with it?)

Factors in the Stimulus Configuration

- Location of Agent of Harm
  ("There isn't anything unique about this test.")

- Viability of Alternate Coping Strategies
  ("I can form a study group."
  "I can exercise to cope.")

- Situational Constraints
  ("There are no unusual circumstances that hamper my coping efforts.")

Personality factors

- Potential Sacrifices
  ("I'd have to give up some personal time to study.")

- Ego Resources
  ("I have lots of self-discipline and can delay gratification.")

- Coping dispositions
  ("I usually deal with my stressors by attacking them head on.")

Cognitive Reappraisal
Is this test a stressor?

("This test is not a stressor because it isn't threatening and I can cope with it.")

Fig. 2-7 Primary and secondary stress appraisals.

tant and comes before secondary appraisal.[20] Actually each step is equally important in the appraisal process and occur simultaneously. Both are followed by reappraisal, which involves looking at the potential stressor with the new information from the primary and secondary appraisals (Fig. 2-8).

Another important distinction in the newer Lazarus theory is the description of the appraisal process as a stress transaction (a concept also introduced in Chapter 1). The appraisal process is a transaction between primary and secondary appraisal in a specific context. Each time the same potential stressor presents itself, it is appraised differently because the context in which it occurs is different than the first time it was experienced.[20] We bring new insights and experience to each potentially stressful encounter, and sometimes as the transaction unfolds the situation changes and things work out differently.

In his recent works, Lazarus[21,22] explains how space and time affect our ability to cope. Past experience and successful coping strengthen us and add new strategies to our coping skills. This feeds into the appraisal process and changes the way we view the same potential stressor. In essence, Lazarus believes our past successes help reduce present and future stressors.

KEY
TO UNDERSTANDING

The stress transaction does not take place in a vacuum.

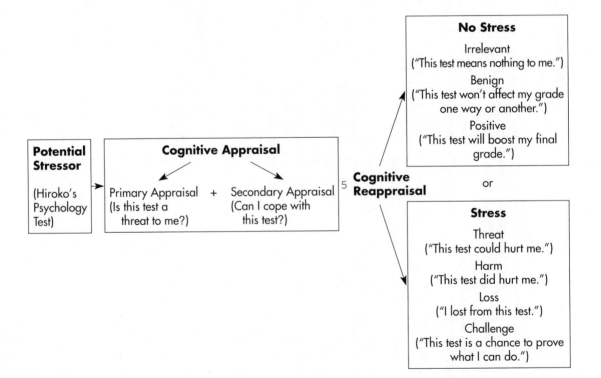

Fig. 2-8 Lazarus and Folkman's stress appraisal model.

Primary Stress Appraisal

In the revised model, Lazarus and Folkman distinguish between three different types of **primary appraisal**: irrelevant appraisal, benign/positive appraisal, and stressful appraisal.[20] This distinction makes it easier to understand how we differentiate between stressful and nonstressful situations.

1. Irrelevant appraisal is the assessment of encounters with potential stressors that have no relevance to us—there is no personal investment of time, energy, or emotions. Consequently we have nothing to gain or lose from a particular experience, which is why we often have a hard time understanding how someone can get stressed about something that to us is not a big deal.

2. **Benign/positive appraisal** is the assessment of encounters with people or situations that are either benign or positive (gaining something pleasurable or enhancing our well-being). This stressor category is similar to Selye's eustress. These appraisals are usually characterized by pleasurable emotions such as happiness, love, joy, euphoria, peacefulness, or exhilaration (Fig. 2-9).
   Lazarus and Folkman[20] disagree with the physiological stress researchers' description of benign/positive appraisal's effects on the body. Although they agree with Selye that eustress throws the body out of balance and necessitates initiation of a stress response to achieve homeostasis, they believe the physiological response is different from the response caused by distress. The physiological response is short-term, and the accompanying positive emotions enhance our overall well-being and use energy at the same time.

3. **Stress appraisal**, the third type of appraisal, is similar to but more expanded than Lazarus's[19] initial threat appraisal. Stress appraisal has three subtypes: threat appraisal, harm/loss appraisal, and challenge appraisal.

   - Threat appraisal is anticipatory because it is the assessment of harm or loss that has not yet occurred. Based on the threat appraisal, personality resources, and ability to cope with the situation, a person anticipates if something bad will happen.
   - Harm/loss appraisal is similar to threat appraisal but involves the appraisal of situations that have already occurred and the assessment of the consequences.
   - Challenge appraisal is the assessment of a situation focusing on positive things that can result from it. Challenge appraisal involves looking at a situation for its growth potential or for what might be gained from the challenge. Like threat appraisal

primary appraisal
the initial part of the stress transaction when an individual questions whether a potential stressor is a threat

benign/positive appraisal
a type of primary appraisal that determines whether the situation in question has the potential for either a neutral or positive outcome

stress appraisal
a type of primary appraisal that determines whether the situation involves threat, harm/loss, or challenge for the person

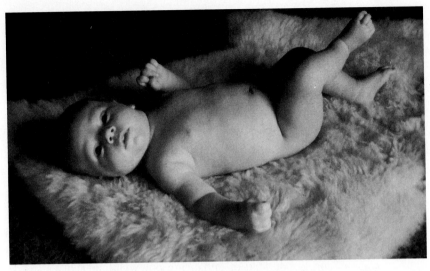

Fig. 2-9 Positive events like birth, although stressors, can energize us.

KEY
TO UNDERSTANDING

Though both threat and challenge trigger the same mobilization of energy, the latter is accompanied by positive rather than negative emotions.

it involves total mobilization of energy for fight or flight. However, the intention is not to protect against harm but to gain strength by overcoming a challenge. When we are challenged, we feel eagerness, excitement, and exhilaration rather than the negative feelings that are part of threat appraisal, such as sadness, fear, anxiety, anger, and hostility. Even though this energy mobilization is as intense as the energy resulting from threat appraisal, it is short term, goal directed, and enables us to accomplish positive results. These positive results can include our psychological, physical, or financial well-being.

In our example (Fig. 2-10) Hiroko's midterm in abnormal psychology is the potential stressor. Hiroko may perceive the examination as a threat and therefore a stressor. On the other hand, Hiroko may not perceive the exam as a threat, based on a combination of factors about the test and her own personality.

Stimulus Factors

According to the Lazarus and Folkman[20] model, the first stimulus factor in Hiroko's situation involves her appraisal of the degree of threat posed by the test. Hiroko evaluates how important this test is to her grade in the class, her overall grade point average, and her academic success in general.

In Hiroko's situation, success or failure on this test should not pose too much of a threat because she is an excellent student. However, even with her academic background if Hiroko's personality were a certain type, past

Fig. 2-10 A test could be appraised as an opportunity to showcase our talents or an opportunity to fail. Our perception of the test determines this.

academic performance would not matter much in judging the degree of threat of this test.

The second stimulus factor, imminence of confrontation, measures how close the threat is; the closer the threat, the greater the stress. Again, using Hiroko's test as an example, it would be more threatening if the test were tomorrow rather than next month. An unannounced quiz would be even more of a threat (Fig. 2-11).

The third factor associated with the potential stressor is the ambiguity of the stimulus. Much of the stress associated with this examination is how much is known about it. Did the instructor clearly state what will be covered on the test? Will it be an essay or multiple-choice test? Do the students have a pool of study questions or examples of the instructor's test questions? Anything that makes the examination less ambiguous reduces the stress surrounding it.

Personality Factors

The first personality factor related to threat appraisal is motivation. If a stimulus is perceived as a conflict with an important goal or motive it will be considered threatening. Consider Hiroko's test, if the test results are perceived as conflicting with something that is very important to Hiroko, such as having a perfect *A* average or graduating *summa cum laude*, she will perceive the test as a threat. Even given her history of success, if she believes that this one test could negatively affect all of her previous hard work, she will perceive it as a threat. At this point Hiroko may not be thinking rationally; if she allows irrational thoughts to dominate her appraisal of the test it will be perceived as a threat.

Fig. 2-11 If we have time to plan and study, examinations need not be too stressful.

On the other hand, if Hiroko perceives the examination as an opportunity to improve herself and to demonstrate her superior abilities, she may view it as a challenge rather than a threat. This part of Lazarus and Folkman's[20] theory ties together with Kobassa's[16] work on challenge. If Hiroko has a hardy personality (to use Kobassa's terminology), feels in control of her own destiny, and is committed to excellence, she probably will view the examination as a challenge. Whereas Kobassa viewed her three components of a hardy personality as standing alone, Lazarus and Folkman integrate them into their comprehensive model of stress appraisal.

A second personality factor associated with threat appraisal is one's belief system. If Hiroko's beliefs about herself, school, tests, and life in general are logical, she can put this test in its proper perspective. She can use her intellectual abilities and thinking skills to logically assess this potential stressor. However, if Hiroko is illogical and has a distorted picture of her abilities, the school, or the test, she will be more likely to perceive the test as a threat rather than a challenge (Fig. 2-12). If she is a catastrophizer or an awfulizer, she probably will be more likely to have self-doubt and view the test as a

Fig. 2-12 Illogical, irrational thoughts often turn into negative self-talk, a factor involved in keeping the stress response alive.

threat. She will overexaggerate the significance of the test or criticize her own abilities and distort the reality of the situation. The role of irrational and/or illogical thought processes in perception fits perfectly within the broader theoretical framework of stress appraisal presented by Lazarus and Folkman.[20]

The third personality factor, intellectual resources, also affects whether Hiroko perceives the test as a threat or as a challenge. If Hiroko thinks clearly and processes information accurately she will have a good chance of viewing the test as a challenge. Objective evidence from her past successes, overall success in school, and her ability to achieve good grades are all pieces of information she can use to problem solve and realize that she has the ability to succeed. However, she might view this test as a threat if she does not accurately analyze the information.

Hiroko's creativity also plays a part in her ability to process information. Hiroko's creativity is an intellectual resource that should enable her to find several different ways to view and solve problems related to the test. The more creative she is, the easier it is for her to seek alternate solutions to problems when encountering any obstacles related to the test. Creativity is a valuable commodity that can help us cope with stress. Assess Yourself 2-4 is designed to help you assess your creative tendencies.

As Lazarus and Folkman[20] point out, primary and secondary appraisals occur simultaneously. During secondary appraisal, Hiroko analyzes her ability to cope with the perceived threat/challenge posed by the examination. At the same time, she is appraising her ability to cope with this threat/challenge.

Secondary Appraisal

As in primary appraisal, the process of secondary appraisal involves both stimulus and personality factors. The stimulus factors include the potential stressor and the specific environmental context in which the potential stressor occurs. The personality factors occur in the mind of the individual.

Stimulus Factors

Location of harm is a stimulus factor that specifies exactly what about the situation is potentially threatening or challenging. If an exact determination can be made then an individual appraising a potential can try to match the situation with an appropriate coping strategy. If the situation is similar to one from the past, the person will feel more sure of his or her ability to cope with the present potential stressor. A different situation, however, does not allow the same coping strategy; the person has to seek an alternate route for coping. This situational constraint might hinder the person's perceived ability to handle the new stressor.

Again using Hiroko's test example, as she examines the test as a potential stressor, she tries to pinpoint exactly what is stressful about it. Is it the effect of a negative grade on her overall GPA? Is it a threat to her ego? Is it fear that her parents will get angry? Whatever the true reason is, identifying the exact threat/challenge is important in assessing her coping ability with the situation.

Once Hiroko knows exactly what is threatening or challenging about this test, she can decide what will work in dealing with the situation. She can assess, for example, whether a short run would alleviate the stress (Fig. 2-13) or whether a long talk with a trusted friend would work better. Using the coping options available to her, Hiroko tries to match them to this unique stressor.

Hiroko remembers that the last time she had test anxiety, she went home and had a long talk with her brother who helped her put the situation in perspective. Eventually, after talking with him she was able to refocus and did very well on her test.

However, in this situation Hiroko realizes that she will not be able to use this coping strategy. Situational constraints (her brother is overseas in the military) prevent her from using what worked in the past. She will have to use another coping strategy for this present situation. Hiroko instantly reassesses the other coping strategies at her disposal.

Personality Factors

Hiroko's own personality also has a significant effect on all of the situational factors. As Hiroko weighs the pros and cons of the various situational factors, she assesses what personal sacrifices she must make to cope with this threat/challenge and whether those sacrifices are worth it. Even if she perceives that she can cope with this situation, she may not feel it is worth it. She may feel that the sacrifices (time spent studying, lost hours at work) are not worth the price of success.

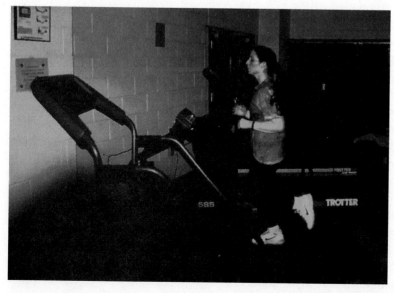

Fig. 2-13 Often a brisk run or other aerobic exercise will clear out the stress from our minds and bodies.

Hiroko's ego and previous coping dispositions also come into play. The way in which Hiroko copes with her problems has a lot to do with the type of person she is. Hiroko is usually very self-confident and tends to meet her problems head on. Occasionally, when she faces situations that are very threatening, she backs off and lets things settle before she attacks them. Usually, however, she prefers to deal with her problems in a straight-forward, objective way, even if it means exposing some of her own personal weaknesses.

Other people may cope in less direct ways. People who are shy or nonassertive, for example, might use avoidance as a coping strategy. In Chapter 11 we will talk in detail about the variety of ways to cope with stressors. However, for the purpose of describing Lazarus and Folkmans' model, Hiroko is now ready to reappraise the potentially stressful situation to determine if it is a stressor.

Reappraisal

In his recent work, Lazarus[21] describes the importance of what he calls the core relational themes in stress appraisal. As stress transactions unfold, they arouse complex emotions that are juxtaposed with people's thoughts, motives, and beliefs about the meaning of the situation. A core relational theme refers to this underlying meaning. Primary and secondary appraisals therefore are affected by both the emotions that are aroused and the underlying core relational theme. A core relational theme in Hiroko's case might be the importance of academic success and the dishonor her family would feel if she did poorly.

After weighing the potentially stressful situation and all of the situational factors, using her personality attributes, and assessing her ability to cope, Hiroko reassesses the potential threat to determine whether or not her situation is a stressor or not. Initially, Hiroko does perceive the test as a stressor. After a couple of days, however, as the situation unfolds, she talks to her mother and begins to review her class notes; she modifies her initial assessment and the test loses its status as a stressor. Both the environment and the situation have changed, as well as Hiroko's perceptions of both. A stress transaction has occurred in Hiroko's life.

Hiroko's example demonstrates how Lazarus and Folkman's[20] stress transaction model ties together the key aspects of the psychological basis of stress. The example demonstrates how factors related to the stimulus (the test), Hiroko's personality, and her environment (family and school situations) influence the stress transaction. The next chapter examines the physiological basis of stress that begins with the appraisal of a potential stressor as threatening.

Summary

We begin this chapter with a critical examination of the influence of psychosocial factors on stress. We pose the question of whether or not some people, by virtue of their personalities, were more susceptible to stress than others.

Rosenman and Friedman and others present compelling evidence that the hard-driving, hurried, competitive, time-conscious man or woman is at an increased risk for cardiovascular disease. Their conceptualization of the Type A individual and the risks inherent in a Type A behavior pattern have become common knowledge and have helped us understand the role our personalities play in determining our stress and health.

In applying their findings to help people correct their Type A ways, Friedman and Rosenman describe a Type B personality that is more stress-resistant. Type Bs are more relaxed and easygoing and have a lessened risk of heart disease.

Matthews, Barefoot, and others, in clarifying Friedman and Rosenman's work, isolated the two most destructive Type A attributes: hostility and anger. Their work illustrates that even a hard-driven, competitive person need not be at an increased risk for stress or health problems if they are not hostile or angry. Hostility and anger seem to be the two attributes that account for most of the health risks associated with the Type A behavior pattern.

Kobassa's work illustrates how people are more stress-resistant if they are hardy. Hardiness refers to people who feel in control of their lives, are committed rather than aimless, and who view situations as challenges rather than stressors. Kobassa's work ties research on Type As with accepted knowledge of the virtues of possessing an internal locus of control and the power of positive thinking.

Ellis shows us how our belief system affects how we view things and whether or not these beliefs transform neutral situations into stressors. Ellis's work introduces the notion of our thoughts as the mediators between potential stressors and the stress response. He reaffirms the psychological stress researchers' beliefs that stress does not exist in situations and things but instead it is our perception of these that determines whether or not we make them into stressors.

In expanding his initial theory, Lazarus joined with Folkman to present a unified psychological theory of stress.[20] Integrating the disparate research of Friedman and Rosenman, Matthews, Kobassa, and Ellis into a unified framework supports the notion that our perceptions coupled with our perceived abilities determine whether or not we allow ourselves to be stressed or challenged.

The work of Lazarus and Folkman enables us to understand how some people are able to thrive on leading a busy, challenging, and demanding life. They describe how individual differences allow some of us to be able to handle much more than others.

Study Questions

1. What is personality and how is it related to stress?
2. Compare three different theories of personality development.
3. Describe the Type A personality behavior pattern.
4. List and describe the two key attributes of the Type A personality that are most related to stress.
5. Describe the Type B personality.
6. Hardy personalities are characterized by what three attributes?
7. What is the underlying assumption of rational emotive psychotherapy concerning the role of perception in the stress response?
8. Describe Lazarus and Folkman's stress transaction concept.
9. What is the difference between primary and secondary appraisal?
10. Describe the three types of primary appraisal.
11. What is the role of coping in stress appraisal?
12. What turns a potential stressor into a challenge?

References

1. Anderson, J.R. & Waldron I. (1983). Behavioral and content components of the structured interview assessment of Type A behavior pattern in women. *Journal of Behavioral Medicine, 6,* 123-134.

2. Barefoot, J.C. (1993). Keeping conflicting findings in perspective: the case of hostility and health. *Mayo Clinic Proceedings, 68,* 192-193.

3. Barefoot, J.C., Dahlstrom W.G., and Williams, R.B. (1983). Hostility, CHD Incidence, and Total Mortality: a 25 year Follow-Up study of 255 physicians. *Psychosomatic Medicine, 45*(1), 59-63.

4. Carmelli, D., Dame, A., Swan, G., & Rosenman, R. (1991). Long-term changes in Type A behavior: a 27 year follow-up of the western collaborative group study. *Journal of Behavioral Medicine, 14*(6), 593-606.

5. De Moor, W. (1988). A rational-emotive ABC model of emotional disturbances: a stress model. *Psychotherapy in Private Practice, 6*(2), 21-33.

6. Ellis, A. & Harper, R. (1975). *A guide to rational living.* Englewood Cliffs: Prentice Hall.

7. Ellis, A. (1991a). The philosophical basis of rational emotive therapy. *Psychotherapy in Private Practice 8*(4), 97-106.

8. Ellis, A. (1991b). The revised ABC's of rational-emotive therapy (RET). *Journal of Rational-Emotive Therapy, 9*(3), 139-167.

9. Engebretson, T. & Matthews, K. (1992). Dimensions of hostility in men, women, and boys; relationships to personality and cardiovascular responses to stress. *Psychosomatic Medicine,* 54(3), 311-23.

10. Erickson, E. (1986). *Childhood and society.* New York: WW Norton

11. Friedman, M. & Rosenman, R. (1974). *Type A behavior and your heart.* Greenwich Conn: Fawcett.

12. Girdano, D., Everly, G., & Dusek, D. (1993). *Controlling stress and tension: a holistic approach.* Englewood Cliffs: Prentice Hall.

13. Hall, C. (1954). *A primer of freudian psychology.* London: World.

14. Haynes, S.G., Feinleib, M., & Kannel, W.B. (1980). The relationship of psychosocial factors to coronary heart disease in the Framingham Study 111: eight year incidence of coronary heart disease. *American Journal of Epidemiology, 111,* 37-58.

15. Hull, J.G., Van Treuren, R., & Virnelli, S. (1987). Hardiness and health: a critique and alternate approach. *Journal of Personality and Social Psychology, 53*(3): 518-530.

16. Kobassa, S. (1979). Stressful life events, personality, and health: an inquiry into hardiness. *Journal of Personality and Social Psychology, 37*(1). 1-11.

17. Kohlberg, L. (1981). *The philosophy of moral development* (Vol. 1). San Francisco: Harper and Row.

18. Lawler, K. & Schmied, L. (1992). A prospective study of women's health: the effects of stress, hardiness, locus of control, Type A behavior, and psychosocial reactivity. *Women and Health, 19*(1), 27-41.

19. Lazarus, R.S. (1966). *Psychological stress and the coping process.* New York: McGraw-Hill.

20. Lazarus, R.S. & Folkman, S. (1985). *Stress appraisal and coping.* New York: Springer.

21. Lazarus, R. (1993a). From psychological stress to the emotions: a history of changing outlooks. *Annual Reviews in Psychology, 44,* 1-21.

22. Lazarus, R. (1993b). Coping theory and research: past, present, and future. *Psychosomatic Medicine, 55,* 234-247.

23. Lyness, S. (1993). Predictors of difference between Type A and Type B individuals in heart rate and blood pressure reactivity. *Psychological Bulletin, 114*(2), 266-295.

24. Margiotta, E., Davilla, D., & Hicks R. (1990). Type A-B behavior and the self-report of daily hassles and uplifts. *Perceptual and Motor Skills, 70*(3), 777-778.

25. Maruta. (1993). *Mayo Clinic Proceedings, 68,* 109-114.

26. Maslow, A. (1968). *Toward a psychology of being.* Princeton: Van Nostrand.

27. Manuck, S. & Saab, P. (1992). The influence of age , sex, and family on Type A and hostile attitudes and behavior. *Health Psychology, 11,*(5), 317-323.

28. Matthews, K.A. & Haynes, S.G. (1986). Type A behavior pattern and coronary disease risk: update and critical evaluation. *American Journal of Epidemiology, 123,* (6), 923-960.

29. Matthews, K.A. et al. (1977). Competitive drive, pattern A and coronary heart disease; a further analysis of the Western collaborative group study. *Journal of Chronic Disease, 30,* 489-498.

30. Meninger, J. (1983). The validity of Type A behavior scales for employed women. *American Journal of Epidemiology, 118,* 424.

31. Piaget, J. *The psychology of intelligence.* London: Routledge and Kegan Paul.

32. Ragland, D.R. & Brand R.J. (1988). Type A behavior and mortality from coronary heart disease. *The New England Journal of Medicine, 318*(2), 65-69.

33. Rosenman, R. & Chesney, M.A. (1985). Type A behavior and coronary disease. In Spielberger, C.D. & Sarason, I.G. (Eds.), *Stress and anxiety* (Vol. 9). (pp. 207-229). Washington DC: Hemisphere.

34. Rosenman, R. (1978). The interview method of assessment of coronary-prone behavior pattern. In T.M. Dembroski, Weis, S.M., Shields, J.L., Haynes, S.G. & Feinleb, M. (Eds.), *Coronary prone behavior.* New York: Springer.

35. Rosemnan, R., Brand, R.J., Jenkins, C.D., Friedman, M., Straus, R., & Wurm, M. (1975). *Journal of the American Medical Association, 233*(8), 872-877.

36. Rotter, J.B. (1975). Some problems and misconceptions related to the construct of internal vs. external control of reinforcement. *Journal of Consulting and Clinical Psychology, 43,* 56-67.

37. Deleted in page proofs.

38. Shekelle, R.B., Gayle, M., Ostfield, A.M., & Oglesby, P. (1983). *Psychosomatic Medicine, 45*(2), 109-114.

39. Thoresen, C. & Powell, L. (1992). Type A behavior: new perspectives on theory, assessment and intervention. *Consulting and Clinical Psychology, 60*(4), 595-604.

40. Walen, S., DiGuiseppi, R., & Wessler, R. (1980). *A practitioner's guide to RET.* New York: Oxford University Press.

41. Watson, J. (1928). *Psychological care of infant and child.* Salem, NH: Ayer.

42. Williams, R.B. Jr., Haney, T.L., Lee, K.L., Kong, Y., Blumenthal, J.A., & Whalen, R.E. (1980). Type A behavior, hostility, and coronary atherosclerosis. *Psychosomatic Medicine, 42,* 539-549.

43. Wright, T., Blache, C., Ralph, J., & Luterman, A. (1993). Hardiness, stress and burnout among intensive care nurses. *Journal of Burn Care Rehabilitation, 14*(3), 376-81.

Name: _____ Date: _____

Type A Behavior

This scale, based on the one developed by Friedman and Rosenman,[11] will give you an estimate of your type A tendencies.

Directions: Answer the following questions by indicating the response that most often applies to you.

Yes	No	Statement
____	____	1. I always feel rushed.
____	____	2. I find it hard to relax.
____	____	3. I attempt to do more and more in less and less time.
____	____	4. I often find myself doing more than one thing at a time.
____	____	5. When someone takes too long to make their point, I finish the sentence for them.
____	____	6. Waiting in line for anything drives me crazy.
____	____	7. I am always on time or early.
____	____	8. In a conversation, I often clench my fist and pound home important points.
____	____	9. I often use explosive outbursts to accentuate key points.
____	____	10. I am competitive at everything.
____	____	11. I tend to evaluate my success by translating things into numbers.
____	____	12. Friends tell me I have more energy than most people.
____	____	13. I always move, walk, and eat quickly.
____	____	14. I bring work home often.
____	____	15. I tend to get bored on vacation.
____	____	16. I feel guilty when I am not being "productive."
____	____	17. I tend to refocus other people's conversations around things that interest me.
____	____	18. I hurry others along in their conversations.
____	____	19. It is agonizing to be stuck behind someone driving too slowly.
____	____	20. I find it intolerable to let others do something I can do faster.

Scoring: Add up the number of items for which you checked yes. The greater the number of yes items, the more likely it is that you are a Type A personality.

ASSESS YOURSELF 2-2

Internal vs. External Control

Directions: Circle the statement that best describes how you feel.

1. a. Children get into trouble because their parents punish them too much.
   b. Children get into trouble because their parents are too easy with them.

2. a. Many of the unhappy things in people's lives are partly due to bad luck.
   b. People's misfortunes result from the mistakes they make.

3. a. One of the major reasons we have wars is because people do not take enough interest in politics.
   b. There will always be wars no matter how hard people try to prevent them.

4. a. In the long run people get the respect they deserve in this world.
   b. Unfortunately, an individual's worth often passes unrecognized no matter how hard he tries.

5. a. The idea that teachers are unfair to students is nonsense.
   b. Most students don't realize the extent to which their grades are influenced by accidental happenings.

6. a. Without the right breaks one cannot be an effective leader.
   b. Capable people who fail to become leaders have not taken advantage of their opportunities.

7. a. No matter how hard you try some people just do not like you.
   b. People who cannot get others to like them do not understand how to get along with others.

8. a. Heredity plays the major role in determining one's personality.
   b. It is one's experiences in life that determine personality.

9. a. I have often found that what is going to happen will happen.
   b. Trusting to fate has never turned out as well for me as making a decision to take a definite course of action.

10. a. In the case of the well-prepared student there is rarely if ever such a thing as an unfair test.
    b. Many times examination questions tend to be so unrelated to course work that studying is really useless.

11. a. Becoming a success is a matter of hard work—luck has little or nothing to do with it.
    b. Getting a good job depends mainly on being in the right place at the right time.

12. a. The average citizen can have an influence in government decisions.
    b. This world is run by the few people in power and there is not much the little guy can do about it.

13. a. When I make plans, I am almost certain that I can make them work.
    b. It is not always wise to plan too far ahead because many things turn out to be a matter of good or bad fortune anyway.

cont'd

Internal vs. External Control (cont'd)

14. a There are certain people who are just no good.
 b. There is some good in everybody.

15. a. In my case getting what I want has little or nothing to do with luck.
 b. Many times we might just as well decide what to do by flipping a coin.

16. a. Who gets to be the boss often depends on who was lucky enough to be in the right place first.
 b. Getting people to do the right thing depends on ability—luck has little or nothing to do with it.

17 a. As far as world affairs are concerned, most of us are the victims of forces we can neither understand nor control.
 b. By taking an active part in political and social affairs, the people can control world events.

18. a. Most people do not realize the extent to which their lives are controlled by accidental happenings.
 b. There really is no such thing as "luck."

19. a. One should always be willing to admit mistakes.
 b. It is usually best to cover up one's mistakes.

20. a. It is hard to know whether or not a person really likes you.
 b. How many friends you have depends on how nice a person you are.

21. a. In the long run the bad things that happen to us are balanced by the good ones.
 b. Most misfortunes are the result of lack of ability, ignorance, laziness, or all three.

22. a. With enough effort we can wipe out political corruption.
 b. It is difficult for people to have much control over the things politicians do in office.

23. a. Sometimes I cannot understand how teachers arrive at the grades they give.
 b. There is a direct connection between how hard I study and the grades I get.

24. a. A good leader expects people to decide for themselves what they should do.
 b. A good leader makes it clear to everybody what their jobs are.

25. a. Many times I feel that I have little influence over the things that happen to me.
 b. It is impossible for me to believe that chance or luck plays an important role in my life.

26. a. People will like you more the harder you try to please them.
 b. There's not much use in trying too hard to please people—if they like you, they like you.

27. a. There is too much emphasis on athletics in high school.
 b. Team sports are an excellent way to build character.

28. a. What happens to me is my own doing.
 b. Sometimes I feel that I do not have enough control over the direction my life is taking.

Internal vs. External Control (cont'd)

29. a. Most of the time I cannot understand why politicians behave the way they do.
    b. In the long run the people are responsible for bad government on a national and on a local level.

Scoring: Give yourself 1 point for each of these circled choices: 1b, 2a, 3b, 4b, 5b, 6a, 7a, 8a, 10b, 11b, 12b, 13b, 15b, 16a, 17a, 18a, 20a, 21a, 22b, 23a, 25a, 26b, 28b, 29a.

Scores range from 0 (most internal) to 23 (most external).

ASSESS YOURSELF 2-3

Rational Beliefs Inventory

Directions: For each of the following 20 statements select either 1 (most like me), 2 (somewhat like me), 0 (not sure), or 3 (not like me) to describe your feelings.

—— 1. I need approval from family, friends, and acquaintances.

—— 2. Things that happened to me in the past control who I am.

—— 3. I must be good at everything I try.

—— 4. I have little control over my emotions.

—— 5. Other people and things tend to make me feel bad.

—— 6. I deal with tough problems by avoiding them.

—— 7. Things should really turn out better than they do.

—— 8. My motto is, "Never Volunteer."

—— 9. I cannot seem to get fearful things off my mind.

——10. Unfair people are rotten and should be blamed for their misdeeds.

——11. It is terrible when things do not go my way.

——12. I really need love and approval from everyone.

——13. Worrying about fearful things helps me cope with them.

——14. Because the past strongly influences who we are, it determines our present emotions and behavior.

——15. It is really easier to avoid problems and responsibilities than to face them.

——16. I am happiest when I do not commit myself to things.

——17. There are some people who are just plain rotten and deserve all the misery they get.

——18. People really should do their best at everything.

——19. There really is a perfect solution to every problem—that is why it is so terrible when it is not found.

——20. It is horrible when things in my life are not the way I want them to be.

Scoring: Add all of the numbers you placed in the left-hand column. The lower the score the more illogical/irrational you tend to be.

 0 - 20 If you scored in this range you tend to believe in many of the 10 illogical beliefs.

20 - 40 You have a moderately illogical belief system.

40 - 60 You tend to be logical and rational.

Remember, this is an estimate of how your beliefs about life match up to the 10 illogical beliefs of Rational Emotive Therapy. All of us share some of these beliefs at times.

ASSESS YOURSELF 2-4

Creative Brainstorming

Brainstorming is a well-known, time-tested activity for breaking down mental barriers to problems and enhancing creativity. It allows us to free our minds from self-imposed restrictions on our creative tendencies by encouraging us to use our imaginations in coming up with numerous solutions to any given problem.

Brainstorming can be done alone but is best performed in a group.

Groundrules:

1. No evaluation of any kind is permitted in the initial session. Participants will spend more time thinking about defending their suggestions rather than generating new ideas if criticism is allowed.

2. All participants are encouraged to think of any ideas possible. It is easier to tone down ideas than tune up conventional ones.

3. Quantity is important. Do not stop until all ideas are exhausted. Rapid-fire generation of many ideas helps keep evaluation of ideas in check and quantity usually leads to quality.

4. Participants are encouraged to build on or modify the ideas of others. This often leads to new ideas that are superior to the original ones that sparked them.

Instructions for Brainstorming

1. Pick a common problem that seems to be a stressor for most of the sutdents in the class (e.g., long lines for registration, lack of adequate parking, lack of income, income burden).

2. Ask students to think up as many options as possible for solving the problem.

3. Encourage them to come up with the craziest solutions possible. Have fun!

4. Encourage them to be as specific as possible. For instance, when dealing with long lines for registration, "The registrar could set up a phone-in registration policy," is more specific than "They should shorten the lines."

5. Write all solutions down without evaluation. You are allowed to ask for clarification but be careful about evaluative comments and vocal intonation.

_____

_____

_____

_____

_____

_____

cont'd

Creative Brainstorming (cont'd)

_____

_____

_____

_____

_____

_____

Process the activity by explaining that there are several different ways of viewing and solving any problem. Not all solutions are equally acceptable to everyone but many different solutions exist. If an acceptable solution for eliminating a problem (stressor) cannot be found, we then have to find an acceptable way of coping with it until it can be worked out.

The Physical Basis of Stress

CHAPTER OBJECTIVES

- List and describe functions of the
  four parts of the brain most directly
  related to the stress response.
- Give an example of how sensory and
  motor brain areas work in initiating
  the fight-or-flight stress response.
- Trace the course of neural impulses
  through the central and peripheral
  nervous systems as they respond to
  a stressor.
- Compare and contrast the role of
  neural impulses and circulating
  hormones during the alarm and
  resistance phases of the GAS.
- Define homeostasis and its
  relationship to the stress response.
- Describe how the sympathetic and
  parasympathetic nervous systems
  are involved in the stress response.
- Analyze the interplay between the
  cerebral cortex and the limbic
  system in the resistance phase of
  the stress response.

cont'd

CHAPTER OBJECTIVES (cont'd)

- Compare and contrast the role of the endocrine system in acute and chronic stress responses.
- Describe Selye's general adaptation syndrome.
- Critically analyze Selye's concepts of nonspecificity and eustress/distress.

psychological
pertaining to functions of the human mind

physiological
pertaining to functions of the human body

KEY
TO UNDERSTANDING

Our thoughts and feelings are influenced by our physiological well-being. Conversely our physical health is influenced by our thoughts and feelings about it.

This chapter explores the physiological aspects of both acute and chronic stress responses. We begin our journey with an examination of the brain and what happens once it perceives a potential stressor as threatening. The stress messages sent by the brain to the nervous and endocrine systems will be studied, and we examine in detail the direct effects of activation of these two systems on the body. We will see how the stress response changes in relation to whether the type of stressor is acute and life threatening or chronic and less intense.

Although this chapter is devoted to physiology, in actuality we cannot separate the **psychological** from the **physiological**; all of our thoughts, feelings, and beliefs have physiological components. A key to understanding this is to remember that the interpretation of our thoughts and feelings is influenced by our overall physical health and the condition of our body parts and systems. Conversely, all bodily sensations we experience are interpreted by our brain and are subject to our mental health and the thoughts and feelings we have about those sensations.

The brain and spinal cord are like the central switchboard of a telephone system that interconnects and directs a dizzying number of incoming and outgoing calls. Many of these "calls" are stress-related messages that can literally short-circuit our switchboards. Have you ever felt so stressed out that it seemed as though you could not think clearly?

Fight or Flight: An Alarm Reaction

A prehistoric man was crouching behind some brush at the edge of the savanna. Hunting a small deer-like creature, he was quietly stalking his prey. As he peered out from his hiding place, a large sabre-toothed tiger was staring directly into his face (Fig. 3-1).

Instantly the alarm was sounded. His eyes, picking up the image, sent to his brain a picture that was instantly deciphered as a clear and imminent threat. Instantaneously, messages were sent to various parts of his body to mobilize the energy needed to either stand and fight or run.

Fig. 3-1 The fight-or-flight response has been with us since the dawn of civilization.

STRESS IN OUR WORLD

Maya

About 2 million years after our prehistoric man came face to face with his sabre-toothed tiger, Maya puts on her left blinker and pulls onto the entrance ramp to the Los Angeles freeway. Not very far from the spot where her long-lost ancestor defeated the sabre-toothed tiger, Maya, late for work, will have sabre-toothed tigers of a different kind to deal with today on the job. As she slowly enters the traffic flow, mulling over how she will explain her lateness, out of the corner of her eye she catches an 18-wheel tractor-trailer bearing down on her. All at once the truck blasts its horn and jams on its brakes, causing the sickening combination of the smell of burning rubber and the screeching of brakes and skidding tires.

In a flash, Maya's eyes, ears, and nose send images to her brain that are instantly deciphered as a clear and imminent threat. Her brain sounds the same alarm that saved her ancestor 2 million years ago. Nerves begin to fire furiously, triggering muscles, glands, and organs into action. The mobilization is enhanced by hormones stimulated by nerve transmissions and by chemicals secreted from her brain.

Maya grips the steering wheel tightly, hits the gas, downshifts, and spins the wheel, throwing her small car off the road and careening down an embankment. Wild-eyed, nostrils flared, heart pumping, lungs and muscles aching, she holds the car on line until she comes crashing to a halt at the bottom. She slumps over the wheel of her car, exhausted but alive (Fig. 3-2).

Fig. 3-2 (1) Maya's brain senses danger and she sounds the alarm. (2) Her body quickly responds by producing energy. (3) Fueled by the stress response, she flees the onrushing truck and seeks safety. (4) Safe at the bottom of the embankment, the threat removed, Maya's body begins to return to normal.

KEY
TO UNDERSTANDING

The stress response can be viewed as a series of stages that continues to exact a toll on our bodies until we either remove or cope with the source of our stress.

Nerves began to fire furiously; their targets were the muscles, organs, and glands involved in supplying the energy and force needed to combat this threat. Some of these nerve transmissions stimulated glands that dumped hormones into his blood, intensifying this state of readiness.

In a split second he was on his feet. Wild-eyed, nostrils flared, and muscles coiled like springs, he summoned all of his courage and thrust the sharpened stick he used as a spear into the belly of the beast. With his heart pounding in his chest, his lungs gasping, and his muscles burning, he thrust his spear again and again until the tiger lay dying. Stopping only when he was sure he was out of harm's way, the man fell back onto the ground, exhausted but alive.

As a species for more than 1 million years, we have relied on this fight-or-flight stress response to help us get out of harm's way. Indeed, many of us would not be here were it not for our ability to mobilize such an intense, life-saving response to acute, short-term threats to our well-being. As we discuss in Chapter 1, the fight-or-flight response is a result of the alarm phase of Selye's general adaptation syndrome (GAS) (Fig. 3-3). It is our first response to acute, life-threatening stressors such as Maya's (see box on p. 77). The fight-or-flight response shuts down after either the stressor is removed or is dealt with effectively.

When confronted with chronic, non–life-threatening stressors, fight or flight changes into a less intense response that makes up the resistance phase of GAS. If the stressor is not removed or coped with successfully,

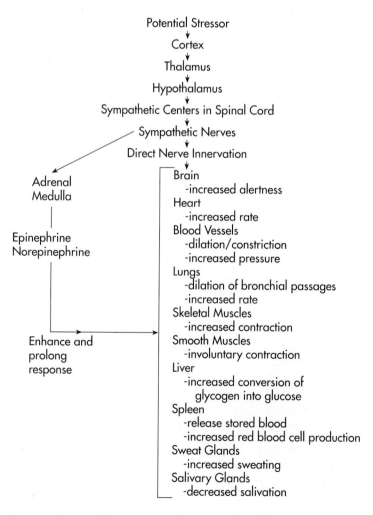

Fig. 3-3 Selye's fight or flight response (alarm phase). Fight or flight quickly mobilizes energy through neural and hormonal stimulation of various organs, glands, and tissue.

resistance eventually ends in the final phase of GAS, exhaustion. A key to understanding the stress response is to view it as a series of stages that continue to exact a toll on our bodies until we either remove or cope with the stressor that initiates it.

The Brain and Fight or Flight

The fight-or-flight response originates with the brain's perception of threat. The average human brain weighs about 3.5 lb (1.58 kg), is pinkish grey, wrinkled like a walnut, and about the size of two fists. Although there are several ways to divide the brain, for our purposes we focus on the parts of the brain most directly related to the stress response: (1) the cerebral cortex (2) the diencephalon (3) the limbic system, and (4) the brain stem (Fig. 3-4). We will discuss how each part is involved in the fight-or-flight response.

Cerebral Cortex

The entire surface of the brain is very irregular, with ridges (gyri), shallow grooves (sulci), and deep grooves (fissures) dividing it into sections. The deepest of the grooves, the longitudinal fissure, divides the cerebrum into

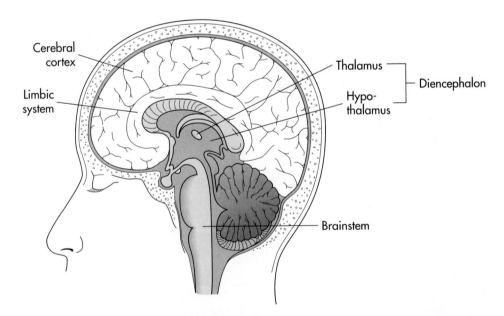

Fig. 3-4 For the purpose of illustrating the stress response, we can divide the brain into four components: the cortex, the diencephalon, the limbic system, and the brain stem.

its two halves (hemispheres). The cerebral hemispheres form the outermost part of the brain. Each hemisphere is concerned with the **motor**, **sensory**, and **associational** functions of the opposite side of the body. The left hemisphere controls the right side of the body and the right hemisphere is responsible for the left side of the body.

When Maya sensed imminent danger from the approaching tractor-trailer, motor activity on the right side of her body (e.g., removing her right hand from the steering wheel, downshifting, removing her right foot from the gas and applying it to the brake pedal) was directed by messages from the left hemisphere of her brain.

In addition to separating the brain in half, the fissures, grooves, and ridges divide the cerebrum into four sections called *lobes*. The frontal, parietal, occipital, and temporal lobes of each hemisphere are responsible for controlling a variety of motor, sensory, and associational brain functions, which are directly involved in the stress response.

The entire cerebrum is covered by the cerebral cortex, a thin ($1/8$ inch [0.3 cm]) convoluted mass of neural cell bodies that makes up about 40% of our total brain mass. This "executive suite" of the nervous system, enables us to perceive, communicate, remember, understand, appreciate, and control voluntary movement. The cerebral cortex is the seat of consciousness and conscious behavior.[9]

Motor Control

The primary motor area, located in the posterior part of the frontal lobe of the cerebral cortex, controls the gross motor activity of our skeletal muscles (Fig. 3-5). This is the part of the brain that allowed Maya to control her car and get out of harm's way. Messages from this part of her brain triggered the muscular activity she needed to focus her eyes, steer, brake, downshift, decelerate, and get to safety.

Sensory Areas

The conscious awareness of sensations (sight, sound, smell, taste, and touch) is controlled by the parietal, occipital, and temporal lobes of the cerebral cortex identified in Fig. 3-5.

These are the parts of Maya's brain that transmitted the messages indicating the danger posed by the rapidly approaching tractor-trailer. Although it's hard to distinguish which messages arrived first, several sensations signaled imminent harm.

In one split-second glance into her left rear-view mirror, Maya's visual cortex and association areas picked up the rapidly approaching image of the skidding, smoking truck; the visual cortex actually saw the image of the truck and the association area determined what it was.

motor
relating to nerve impulses going out to muscles

sensory
relating to nerve messages coming into the brain

associational
connecting together individual sensory inputs

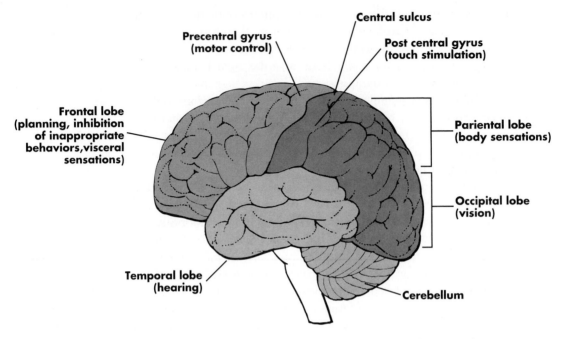

Fig. 3-5 The brain is divided into four lobes by its folds (gyri) and grooves (sulci). Each lobe controls specific sensory functions.

Simultaneously, as Maya saw the truck skidding, she also heard the blast of its horn and the screech of its skidding tires. These incoming sounds were received and interpreted as dangerous by the primary auditory cortex and auditory associational areas, respectively.

She is not sure when she first became aware of it, but Maya recalls almost becoming nauseated by the sickening smell of the burning rubber caused by the truck's tires trying to grip the pavement and stop. The olfactory cortex located in the middle of the temporal lobes analyzed and interpreted the incoming smells as burning rubber.

Although the visual, auditory, and olfactory sensations involved in Maya's stressful interlude with the tractor-trailer entered as distinct, separate entities, they were quickly assimilated, sorted out, deciphered, and refitted together as a danger signal. This interplay relied on Maya's stored memories of past experiences, which influenced her assessment of the present incoming stimuli. The combination of interpretation of new information and review of similar past experiences formed a new construct—I am in danger.

The Diencephalon

The diencephalon, which forms the central core of the brain, contains the thalamus and hypothalamus. This area plays a critical role in the continuation of the stress response that begins with the interpretation of an incoming stimulus as potentially threatening.

The thalamus is a hidden region of the brain might best be described as the relay center for all inputs to the cerebral cortex. The sensations that informed Maya of impending danger all converged in her thalamus. The thalamus also plays a key role in mediating all sensations, motor activities, cortical arousal, and memory. The thalamus is truly the gateway to the cerebral cortex.[11]

If the thalamus is the gateway to the cerebral cortex, the hypothalamus located directly underneath it and at the end of the brain stem, is the actual gate. Despite its small size, the hypothalamus exerts a tremendous amount of control over body functioning. It works in consort with the nervous and endocrine systems, sending its messages via direct nerve transmissions and chemicals called **hormonal-releasing factors**. These nervous and endocrine systems provide two of the main pathways of the fight-or-flight response.

You may remember from Chapter 1 that Canon hypothesized that our bodies continually adjust to demands from the environment to maintain a steady, homeostatic state in which metabolic processes function smoothly. Goldstein,[4] in a description of neurotransmitters and stress, explains that there actually are several homeostatic mechanisms that function similarly to thermostats. He refers to these as **homeostats** and explains how they employ feedback from different body systems to regulate homeostasis throughout the body.

Normal, everyday occurrences, such as standing up or digesting a meal, throw the body out of equilibrium and force adjustments in a variety of systems that control homeostasis. Extreme threats to our well-being, such as Maya's impending crash, throw our bodies out of this steady state and force us to rapidly readjust. A key to understanding the stress response is to view it as a very energy-intensive adjustment to demands placed on the body. To meet the demands of stressors, the body must rapidly mobilize and use a tremendous amount of energy. These adjustments are mediated by the electrical and chemical messages sent by the hypothalamus.

When Maya perceived the tractor-trailer bearing down on her, her hypothalamus instantaneously sent direct nerve transmissions and hormonal releasing factors to the following targets involved in her fight-or-flight response: her heart, blood vessels, lungs, skeletal muscles, liver, spleen, salivary glands, sweat glands, and smooth muscles. Once stimulated, these target muscles, glands, and organs were responsible for saving Maya's life.

Her heart, responding to electrical and chemical stimulation, increased the volume of blood being pumped throughout her body by increasing its rate and pressure. This increased pumping of blood was necessary for supplying the extra oxygen and other fuels she needed to act.

hormonal-releasing factors
chemicals secreted by the hypothalamus that trigger the pituitary to release specific hormones

homeostats
thermostat-like mechanisms that regulate a variety of autonomic functions

Her blood vessels helped in this process. The blood vessels supplying her brain and skeletal muscles dilated, allowing increased blood flow to the areas that would be called on to save her life. Blood vessels to noncritical areas, such as her digestive system, constricted, facilitating the rerouting of the blood to where it was needed most.

Her lungs responded instantly by increasing her rate and depth of breathing. Her airways expanded, allowing maximum intake of air so vital oxygen could mix with her blood.

Her skeletal muscles, fueled by her oxygen-rich blood and her stored blood sugars, contracted to exert maximum force.

Her digestion shut down, and the blood used for that process was diverted. Smooth muscle contractions and salivation, necessary components of digestion, stopped, which is why Maya had a dry, cotton-mouth sensation after her ordeal was over.

Her liver started metabolizing additional sugar for energy. It also began liberating fats and converting these and proteins into useable energy sources to supply the tremendous amount of fuel needed to cope with the stressor.

Her sweat glands, preparing for the tremendous energy expenditure to come, initiated a cooling response by activating increased perspiration.

Maya's kidneys were stimulated to increase water volume and retention. This served to increase blood volume, raise blood pressure, and get more blood to where it was needed. Later this reaction triggered thirst receptors in her brain, causing her to drink to replace her lost fluids.

Finally, Maya's adrenal glands were activated and began to pump out adrenaline and noradrenaline providing the chemical basis to enhance and sustain her stress response (Fig 3-6).

The Limbic System

The limbic system, a complex arrangement of nervous tissue, is also referred to as our "emotional brain." It links physical reactions to sensory and emotional stimuli. It encircles the upper part of the brain stem including the following structures: the diencephalon, cingulate gyrus, hippocampus, fornix, septal nucleus, and amygdaloid nucleus.

The limbic system, or emotional brain, interacts with the thinking, rational brain (cerebral cortex), establishing a relationship between our thoughts and our feelings. Sometimes this relationship is clear cut and appropriate as our emotions accurately reflect our knowledge about something. It was quite clear to Maya that the fear she was feeling as a result of the close call with the tractor trailer was accurate and justified. At other times our intellect may inhibit us from expressing our emotions, or our emotions may keep us from thinking clearly. Either of these situations can result in triggering and perpetuating a stress response.

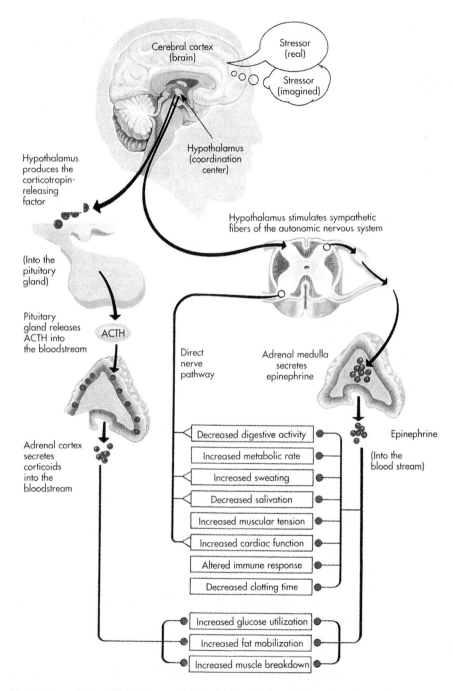

Fig. 3-6 In an instant Maya's senses pick up the tractor-trailer. Her cortex perceives the message as threatening and stimulates the hypothalamus to sound the alarm. Energy is mobiled to fight or flee through a series of chemical and nerve transmissions.

The Brain Stem

The brain stem, consisting of three regions—the midbrain, pons, and medulla oblongata—produces the autonomic functions necessary for our survival and also serves as the pathway for connections between the higher and lower brain functions.

The reticular formation, also known as the reticular activating system (RAS), is a collection of neurons running through the three regions of the brain stem. It is responsible for sending messages between the higher parts of the brain that control thoughts and awareness to the lower parts that are responsible for the activities of organs, muscles, and glands. As is described later in this chapter, these organs, muscles, and glands are capable of activating the stress response as the body mobilizes tremendous amounts of energy to cope with threats to its well-being. The messages can travel in either direction; they can emanate from conscious thoughts and travel to organs, muscles, and glands influencing their functions, or they can originate in the organs, muscles, and glands and send messages back to the brain where this information is interpreted.

The RAS is responsible for both general and specific arousal of the brain. During general arousal the RAS is responsible for maintaining the alertness of the cerebral cortex. Both RAS and cortical activity change during various states of wakefulness. When we are fully awake, RAS activity levels are at their highest. They decrease during the varied stages of sleep and during meditation, which is best characterized as a wakeful, resting state.

During specific arousal the RAS is responsible for magnifying and increasing our awareness of specific stimuli. It allows us to hone in or focus on details of a stimulus as messages are passed back and forth from various parts of the brain. With the help of associations, memories, feelings, and thoughts we are able to decode and decipher the stimuli.

Most of the time we are unaware of the role of the RAS. We do not realize that the RAS is filtering out a tremendous amount of stimuli, allowing us to attend only to the important information.

Because this complex set of neurons is capable of sending such an enormous amount of messages back and forth, the brain needs a filter to screen out unimportant messages. The RAS acts as that screen and disregards more than 90% of all familiar, repetitive, or weak sensory stimulation as unimportant while allowing new, unusual, or strong stimuli to penetrate. This helps us to focus our attention on important stimuli. This also explains why Maya was oblivious to everything else going on around her as the truck was bearing down. She was no longer aware of the music on the radio, the other cars on the road, or the sun reflecting off her windshield. All of her attention was riveted on the truck.

Think about a time when your attention was riveted on something as your brain tried to make it out. Have you ever been camping in the middle of the woods where, in the darkness of night, each new rustle of leaves or snapping twig is frightening until you figure out what they are? How about the creaks and pops that emanate from your basement, attic, or garage and always seems to occur late at night when everyone else is fast asleep? It seems as if every fiber of your being is focused on the sounds as your brain furiously works to decipher what they represent.

If the RAS did not screen out the majority of insignificant stimuli, we would be overwhelmed by overstimulation and in a state of chronic stress activation. The sensory stimulation of the average mall would be sheer madness. Driving in traffic would be impossible. Walking down a crowded city street would be mystifying as we examined each face, car, and passing building. Even sitting in a classroom would be difficult as we scanned the walls, ceilings, and desks.

Close your eyes for a minute and try to recount the composition of the classroom in which this course is being taught. What is on the walls? How many desks are there? How many windows? What color is the paint? What is the type, color, and pattern of the floor covering? Is the ceiling made of tiles, cement, or sheetrock? Most of us do not pay attention to these and many other such details because they are unimportant or distracting.

As we will discuss in Chapter 7, we are stressed because there are too many things going on in our lives. We run from one thing to the next. We are overbooked, overcommited, and pulled in several directions at the same time. When this happens, we are in a chronic state of RAS activation; our minds and bodies are continually aroused and need to slow down and rest.

The Nervous System and Fight or Flight

Because we have already covered the role of the brain in Maya's stress response, we will turn our attention to the rest of her nervous system. As we introduced in Chapter 1, the human nervous system is composed of two parts: the central nervous system and the peripheral nervous system. The **central nervous system** is made up of the brain and spinal cord, whereas the **peripheral nervous system** comprises all other nerves and connects the spinal cord to various target organs, glands, and tissues.

central nervous system
that part of the nervous system comprising the brain and the spinal cord

The Spinal Cord

The 17-inch (43 cm) inch long, 3/4-inch (1.90 cm) thick, glistening white, ropelike spinal cord can be compared with a fiber optic telephone cable. Both are made of a multitude of threadlike fibers that are capable of sending

peripheral nervous system
all other nerves emanating from the spinal cord

somatic nervous system
the part of the peripheral nervous system under our voluntary control

autonomic nervous system
the part of the peripheral nervous system that is automatic and involuntary

sympathetic
the part of the autonomic nervous system that is responsible for activating the organs that maintain homeostasis

parasympathetic
the part of the autonomic nervous system responsible for turning off the autonomic system

KEY
TO UNDERSTANDING

Sympathetic nervous system responses can be called *stress responses,* whereas parasympathetic responses can be labeled *relaxation responses.*

and receiving a tremendous amount of electrical messages in a split second. The spinal cord is the lifeline between the brain and the rest of the body.

The initial information concerning the oncoming tractor trailer was passed along as electrical impulses from Maya's brain, through her spinal cord, to her peripheral nervous system, and ultimately to the specific glands, organs, and tissues involved in the stress response.

The Peripheral Nervous System

The peripheral nervous system is made up of two divisions, the **somatic nervous system** and the **autonomic nervous system**.

Somatic Nervous System. The somatic nervous system transmits messages that are under our conscious control. The somatic nervous system comes into play during a stress response when we are aware that we are being stressed and we consciously initiate some action as a result. We will discuss its role in the stress response later in this chapter when we meet Mario, a man with a different kind of stressor than Maya.

Autonomic Nervous System. The autonomic nervous system controls functions that are unconscious and go on without us thinking about them. Unlike the somatic nervous system, the autonomic nervous system operates at a subconscious level. Body processes, such as breathing, digestion, and heart beat, are operated by this system and go on without our conscious control.

The autonomic nervous system is the part of the peripheral nervous system that deserves the most attention as far as the stress response is concerned. The autonomic nervous system serves as the pathway for all of the electrical messages sent by the hypothalamus to the myriad organs, glands, and tissues involved in maintaining homeostasis or adjusting to the demands of a stressor. These body parts are activated in response to the perception of threat and are deactivated once the stressor is dealt with or removed. This activation and deactivation is controlled respectively by the two branches of the autonomic nervous system, the **sympathetic** and **parasympathetic** branches of the autonomic nervous system (Table 3-1). A key to understanding these branches is to refer to sympathetic responses as *stress responses,* whereas parasympathetic responses are referred to as *relaxation responses.* These are the most sensitive, rapidly acting, and powerful of the body's stress systems.[4]

In Maya's case, her sympathetic nervous system was responsible for passing along nerve transmissions sent from her hypothalamus in response to the presence of the tractor trailer bearing down on her. These messages

TABLE 3.1

Effects of the Sympathetic and Parasympathetic Divisions of the Autonomic Nervous System

Target organ/system	Sympathetic effects	Parasympathetic effects
Digestive system	Decreases activity of digestive system and constricts digestive system sphincters (e.g., anal sphincter)	Increases smooth muscle mobility (peristalsis) and amount of secretion by digestive system glands; relaxes sphincters
Liver	Causes glucose to be released to blood	No effect
Lungs	Dilates bronchioles	Constricts bronchioles
Urinary bladder/urethra	Constricts sphincters (prevents voiding)	Relaxes sphincters (allows voiding)
Kidneys	Decreases urine output	No effect
Heart	Increases rate and force of heartbeat	Decreases rate; slows and steadies
Blood vessels	Constricts blood vessels in viscera and skin (dilates those in skeletal muscle and heart); increases blood pressure	No effect on most blood vessels
Glands–salivary, lacrimal	Inhibits; result is dry mouth and dry eyes	Stimulates; increases production of saliva and tears
Eye (iris)	Stimulates dilator muscles; dilates pupils	Stimulates constrictor muscles; constricts pupils
Eye (ciliary muscle)	Inhibits; decreases bulging of lens; prepares for distant vision	Stimulates to increase bulging of lens for close vision
Adrenal medulla	Stimulates medulla cells to secrete epinephrine and norepinephrine	No effect
Sweat glands of skin	Stimulates to produce perspiration	No effect
Arrector pili muscles attached to hair follicles	Stimulates; produces "goosebumps"	No effect
Penis	Causes ejaculation (emission of semen)	Causes erection because of vasodilation
Cellular metabolism	Increases metabolic rate; increases blood sugar levels; stimulates fat breakdown	No effect

triggered the initiation of her stress response, leading to her swerve her car off the road and down the embankment.

Once her car came to a halt and the threat of the accident was gone, her parasympathetic nervous system took over, initiating responses that began to reverse those set into motion sympathetically. Her heart rate, respiration, and muscle tension began to return to normal; hormone and blood sugar levels began to drop off and get back to their normal ranges.

The Endocrine System and Fight or Flight

The endocrine system is responsible for the production and secretion of the potent hormones, which initiate and perpetuate the stress response, in addition to a variety of other functions ranging from sexual response to growth. The endocrine system is made up of the pituitary, thyroid, parathyroid, adrenal, pancreas, thymus, and pineal glands, as well as the ovaries and the testes. These glands produce and secrete various hormones that provide much of the fuel for the stress response (Fig. 3-7).

As already mentioned, the endocrine system works on the principle of feedback, with the hypothalamus acting as a thermostat that senses the level of a particular hormone circulating in the bloodstream. Just as the thermostat in your home senses the level of heat in your house and turns on your heating or cooling system, your hypothalamus regulates the functioning of various organs, glands, and systems by sensing their levels of activity and turning them on and off as needed.

If the level of a particular hormone is too low, the hypothalamus secretes specific releasing factors into the bloodstream. The pituitary gland,

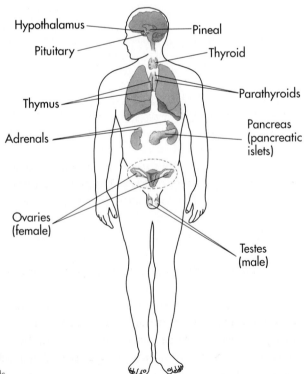

Fig. 3-7 The locations of the major endocrine glands.

sensing the presence of those releasing factors, secretes one of its own hormones that travels through the bloodstream to the target endocrine gland, prompting it to begin producing hormones. The pituitary gland has earned the nickname "the master gland" because of its role in orchestrating this complex regulatory process.

The Role of the Adrenal Glands

The adrenal glands play the most significant role in the stress response. They are the primary endocrine glands involved in fight-or-flight acute stress responses like Maya's. They also are the key endocrine glands involved in the resistance phase of the general adaptation syndrome where stressors are low level and chronic.

For the purpose of understanding their role in the stress response, the adrenal glands can be divided into two primary parts—the medulla and the cortex. The medulla, or inner part, comes into play during the initial mobilization of energy needed to fuel the fight or flight response, and the cortex, or outer shell, plays the key role in sustaining stress responses of longer duration. Hormones secreted during such long-term stress responses are associated with Selye's resistance and exhaustion phases of GAS.

A key to understanding the endocrine system's role in the stress response is to realize that it gets involved because nerves cannot continue to fire indefinitely without malfunction. In a sense, nerves will short circuit without adequate downtime.

The hypothalamus gets the adrenal glands involved in the stress response in two ways. The first way is by sending direct nerve transmissions to the **adrenal medulla** during fight or flight. This can be referred to as the *adrenomedullary stress system* because it revolves around the actions of epinephrine and norepinephrine (also known as *adrenaline* and *noradrenaline*), the hormones secreted by the medulla.[4]

Adrenaline and noradrenaline are powerful hormones that stimulate almost all body systems. Their role in the fight or flight response is to enhance and prolong the activation of the various muscles, glands, and organs that are triggered by direct nerve stimulation from the hypothalamus.

The second way the hypothalamus gets the adrenal glands involved in a stress response is through the secretion of releasing factors that trigger the pituitary gland to activate the production of adrenal cortical hormones necessary for longer-lasting stress responses. One of these adrenal cortical hormones, cortisol, does this by inhibiting the breakdown of epinephrine and norepinephrine and enhancing the body's sensitivity to those chemicals. Cortisol also provides additional fuel for the stress response by helping the body convert stored fats and proteins to useable glucose energy.

KEY
TO UNDERSTANDING

Just as your thermostat regulates the temperature in your house by responding to feedback from its thermometer, your hypothalamus regulates bodily functions by responding to the electrical and chemical feedback from your nervous and endocrine system.

adrenal medulla
the inner core of the adrenal gland

STRESS IN OUR WORLD

Mario

Mario hasn't been feeling very well lately. He has had nagging muscle tension in his neck, he thinks he is developing an ulcer, and he hasn't been feeling rested, even after 10 hours of sleep. He has been thinking about going to the doctor to see what's wrong.

Mario has been in a very unhappy relationship for more than a year now. There have been times when he's felt like he was going to blow his top. He gets so angry at his wife that he screams and calls her names that even surprise himself. He feels his heart pounding in his chest, his muscles tightening, and his breath coming out in gasps. Unable to vent this rage, he turns it inward, bites his lip and goes into another room to simmer down. In time his symptoms disappear and he falls asleep, exhausted by his ordeal.

After a few of these confrontations without any resolution, Mario has realized that he isn't ready or able to rectify the problems in his marriage. He also feels that he has no options and has to stay in it. He has resolved that he isn't going anywhere, and sadly, will have to endure things.

Over the past few months since he made this decision to maintain his status quo, Mario has begun to feel ill because his body has been experiencing a different kind of stress response—one that is less intense but every bit as complex and energy-intensive as the life-saving alarm response that Maya experienced. His body simply cannot maintain the high levels of activation during his confrontations with his wife. Since he has neither fought not fled, and because the source of his stress (his wife) still exists, his body has shifted into a lower intensity response.

Daily, Mario's senses and brain sound the alarm signaling threat, but his body's response is less intense. His heart and lungs are still working overtime but he doesn't realize it until the end of the day when he is exhausted and wonders why. If he checked it, he would see that his heart rate, blood pressure, and respiration are all elevated. It is his body's way of mobilizing the energy needed to meet the threat that his brain and senses are perceiving. Every time he sees his wife, smells her scent on his clothing, or thinks

about her, his brain receives these messages, mixes them with memories and past associations, and interprets this as a threat, keeping the stress response alive.

This routine requires a tremendous amount of energy. To keep this stress response alive, his body uses energy from all available sources. It takes the calories from the food Mario eats and it also draws extra energy from reserves in his skeletal muscles. This, however, isn't enough, so his liver is triggered to synthesize energy from other sources such as protein and fats. Hormones also help out; various glands secrete a variety of hormones into his bloodstream to provide energy, raise blood pressure, and increase his metabolic rate.

Mario does not even realize all of this is going on. It is only after he begins to feel tired all of the time, starts developing an ulcer, and cannot get his muscle cramps to stop that he realizes that something is going wrong. Mario is in the resistance stage of a long-term stress response and is on the verge of exhaustion.

Resistance: A Long-Term Stress Response

The alarm response is acute, intense, and necessary for survival. It does not cause harm to the body; rather, it is designed to save our lives. Without it we would not have an immediate response to life-threatening situations. If, however, the stressor is not dealt with by fighting or fleeing, or if it is chronic and persists for long periods (see the box opposite), our bodies must shift into a lower-level type of stress response. We simply cannot keep the intense, energy-demanding alarm response alive indefinitely. To cope with chronic stressors that are not life threatening, we move into the resistance phase of Selye's stress response.

The resistance phase of the general adaptation syndrome is similar to the fight or flight response or alarm phase in that it requires the body to mobilize energy to meet the demands imposed by stressors. However, it differs in several key ways. The same body parts and systems mobilized during alarm are still working but at a less intense level. The body is not at rest, nor is it in the throes of the alarm response, it is somewhere in between. The result is similar to an automobile that idles faster than it should. The engine works harder to simply keep its operating parts in balance. It uses more gas, performs less efficiently, and will break down sooner than a car idling at the proper rate (Fig. 3-8).

Mario's body in resistance works the same way. He feels chronically fatigued, is more susceptible to illness, and is less efficient and happy. He suffers from a decreased quality of life; all of the energy he uses in maintaining the stress response is lost. Rather than use all of this energy to try to maintain homeostasis in the face of his constant stressor, he could be putting it to much better use. He could be using that energy to enjoy and get the most out of his life rather than having to use it to cope with the stress of his relationship.

A key to understanding our body's response in resistance is to envision it as not being energy efficient. When we are chronically stressed, we waste a tremendous amount of energy, our body's most precious resource.

KEY
TO UNDERSTANDING

Chronic stress responses reduce our day-to-day quality of life by wasting energy we could be using more productively.

The Brain and Resistance

One big difference between Maya's and Mario's stress responses is the role of conscious thought and emotions. In Maya's case, her alarm response was triggered by a direct, immediate, life-threatening stressor (the tractor trailer). It was mediated primarily by sensations (visual images, sounds, smells) that were clear-cut warning signs of imminent harm. In Mario's stress response his stressor (his relationship) is less direct, more diffuse, and not immediately life threatening.

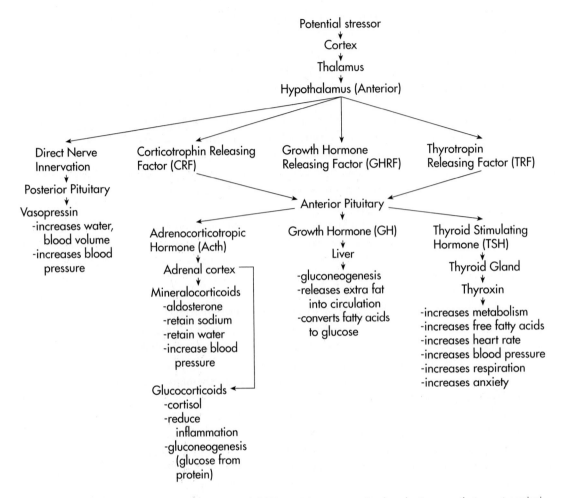

Fig. 3-8 The resistance and exhaustion phases of GAS occur in response to chronic stressors that exert gradual wear and tear on the body.

At times Mario isn't completely sure that his relationship is as bad as it often appears. He has doubts about his wife's words and actions and isn't always clear about their intentions and meaning. His feelings often cloud his ability to think rationally, making it hard to sort things out. The past and the present seem to merge, confusing things even more.

Unfortunately, our brains have not evolved to the point where we can differentiate between direct, life-threatening events and symbolic, less-threatening stressors. Mario's brain responds to his less-threatening stressor in the same way as Maya's brain does to hers. The difference is the role played by the thinking, analyzing, and emotional parts of Mario's brain.

The Cerebral Cortex

Mario spends a good part of his waking day sorting through the myriad of thoughts and emotions associated with his deteriorating relationship. He sifts through the hundreds of bits of information about his life, his wife, and their relationship, trying to figure out where, why, and how things began to turn the way they did.

This rational, analytical assessment is carried out by the cerebral cortex, the part of the brain responsible for rational thought processes, such as judgement, reasoning, planning, and producing abstract ideas. It is also plays a role in mood and is linked to the limbic system, the emotional brain. This is why his feelings keep creeping into what he wishes could be an entirely rational assessment of his situation.

The cerebral cortex is the part of the brain that decides whether or not Mario has the resources to cope with his relationship. If you remember from Chapter 1, Lazarus and Folkman referred to this decision-making process as the stress transaction. Mario uses his brain to assess factors concerning his potential stressor and his personality. If he had decided that the potential stressor could be improved and he had the personality resources to do it, the situation would pass and he would not be stressed. However, he is stressed because he feels that the problems in his relationship are too large and deep-seated, and he simply cannot cope with them.

The importance of cortical functions in initiating and sustaining the stress response cannot be understated. The greatest distinction between the work of the stress pioneers such as Selye and Cannon and those who have followed, like Mason, and Lazarus and Folkman, is the understanding and documentation of the role of perception in the stress response. A stress response can be triggered merely by our thoughts and feelings. We do not need to be confronted with immediate threats to our well-being, such as Maya's tractor trailer. If we feel something is a threat, regardless of the accuracy of this assessment, we will trigger a stress response. A key to understanding this is to realize that our perception of people and situations determines whether or not they are stressors. They are only potential stressors until we perceive them as otherwise.

KEY
TO UNDERSTANDING

Our perception of situations determines whether or not they will become stressors.

The Diencephalon, Limbic System, and Brain Stem

Mario's stressor is much more complex than Maya's. In fact, at times things seem to be going fine between Mario and his wife. Sometimes he is not really sure what their problems are or whether his wife's comments and behavior are intentionally hurtful.

For example, last night as they were getting ready to go out to dinner with friends, Mario's wife made a comment about his suit. "Nice suit, it makes you look 20 years younger," she said. It's not so much what she said, but the way she said it. Mario's limbic system was working overtime as thoughts and emotions intermingled and were relayed through his thalamus, back and forth between his cortex and limbic system. Mario's mind was racing as his wife made her comment. Twenty years worth of feelings for this woman, their relationship, himself, and his life blended with each other and with Mario's attempts to rationally think through the moment.

The tension built up inside him as his hypothalamus set a variety of physiological responses into motion. Mario did everything he could to resist the temptation to strike back or break down and scream, thus totally sabotaging a potentially enjoyable evening out with friends.

Mario tried to relax but seemed supersensitive to everything going on around him; he was acutely aware of every detail of the rest of the evening. Getting dressed seemed to take forever because he felt his wife was evaluating everything about him. Their silence in the drive to their friends' house seemed deafening to him because his RAS had his brain aroused and focused on every sensation. He tried to shut down his brain a little by having a few drinks, but he drank too much and wound up getting his wife even more aggravated with him. Unfortunately for Mario, his body would soon suffer the toll for turning his rage inward. His developing ulcer and muscle spasms were the price he was paying.

The Endocrine System and Resistance

cortex
the outer shell of the adrenal gland

corticoids
adrenal cortical hormones

glucocorticoids
adrenal cortical hormones that control the sugar balance in the body

mineralocorticoids
adrenal cortical hormones that control the salt balance in the body

Although less intense, the resistance phase is more complex than the alarm phase because it involves various hormones maintaining increased levels of activation of body parts and systems. While in resistance the anterior part of Mario's hypothalamus produces releasing factors that stimulate his pituitary gland to activate the manufacturing and secretion of hormones in the adrenal cortex and thyroid glands. Additionally, the pituitary gland directly releases its own hormones, vasopressin and oxytocin, into circulation. These hormones are responsible for maintaining the stress response during long periods of chronic stimulation.

Adrenal Function

During resistance the outer shell of Mario's adrenal glands, the **cortex**, plays a major role in perpetuating his stress response. This can be referred to as the pituitary-adrenocortical system because of the primary role played by adrenal cortical hormones.[4] Mario's adrenal cortex produces hormones called **corticoids**. Two major types of corticoids, **glucocorticoids** and **mineralocorticoids**, are involved in perpetuating his stress response (Fig. 3-9).

Glucocorticoids work with other hormones by maintaining Mario's increased metabolism; they make sure enough energy is available. Cortisol is

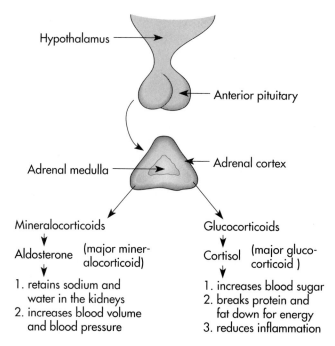

Hypothalamus

Anterior pituitary

Adrenal medulla — Adrenal cortex

Mineralocorticoids

Aldosterone (major miner-
            alocorticoid)

1. retains sodium and
   water in the kidneys
2. increases blood volume
   and blood pressure

Glucocorticoids

Cortisol (major gluco-
          corticoid)

1. increases blood sugar
2. breaks protein and
   fat down for energy
3. reduces inflammation

Fig. 3-9 The role of adrenal hormones in the stress response.

the glucocorticoid responsible for providing the gas needed to fuel the stress response. Cortisol provides fuel by working with Mario's liver to create new sources of **glucose**, the body's main source of fuel.

The liver plays a major role during the resistance phase of Mario's stress response. The liver is responsible for producing energy by absorbing nutrients from recently eaten food and converting them into glucose. In addition, the liver can change excess simple sugars called *monosaccharides* into glycogen and fat and store them for later use. When Mario's glucose is exhausted, he taps into the glucose stored in his skeletal muscles and liver. This stored glucose provides additional fuel to keep his stress response alive and maintain homeostasis.

Eventually, Mario uses all of his glycogen reserves. Once they are depleted, cortisol helps his liver synthesize **amino acids** into glucose. Additionally, cortisol increases the level of fats in his bloodstream by releasing free fatty acids from stored fat tissue to be used as a source of fuel. This process of converting amino acids and fats into energy for the body is called gluconeogenesis.

Mineralocorticoids, the second group of adrenocortical hormones, help control the volume of water and electrolytes in Mario's body by maintaining his levels of sodium and potassium. Working on a feedback system with the hypothalamus, kidneys, and adrenal glands, mineralocorticoids

glucose

a simple sugar; the main energy source for the body

amino acids

the building blocks of protein

keep his body's essential fluids in balance. Aldosterone, a key mineralocorticoid, helps prevent the rapid loss of sodium from Mario's body by conserving sodium ions and eliminating potassium. This increases Mario's blood volume, thereby raising his blood pressure.

Thyroid Function

The thyroid gland helps keep Mario's stress response alive during the resistance phase by increasing his metabolic rate and assisting in gluconeogenesis. Thyroxine, the major thyroid hormone, affects virtually every cell in Mario's body and is a key component in regulating his basal metabolic rate. The role of the thyroid is well documented in Selye's[10] work.

Hyperthyroidism, caused by excessive thyroid stimulation, was part of the key triad Selye documented as indicative of exhaustion.[10] During prolonged exposure to stressors the thyroid is overstimulated and increases the body's metabolic rate to meet the demands for fuel for the stress response.

Pituitary

Besides secreting releasing factors that trigger the adrenal and thyroid glands, the pituitary gland itself is stimulated by the hypothalamus during the stress response and secretes vasopressin. Vasopressin, also known as antidiuretic hormone (ADH), works with the kidneys in retaining water to elevate the total body water content. This in turn increases blood volume and pressure.

The Physiology of Exhaustion

After a period of time Mario's body simply will not continue to run at this increased level of energy demand. The stress response, fueled by the hormonal influences of his adrenal, thyroid, and pituitary glands, will begin to exact a toll. Something has to give, and what goes first is what we referred to in Chapter 1 as Selye's[10] "weak links." Selye believed that we have a finite amount of energy available to adapt to the demands of stress. After we use it all, we suffer from exhaustion. This adaptation energy, or stored reserve, systematically gets depleted during the resistance phase if we do not remove the source of our stress or do things to relax and offset the demands of the stressor.

Selye believed the weak link to be a body part or system that is predisposed to breakdown because of some inherent weakness. According to Selye, this inherent weak point, whether resulting from heredity or environment, is the most likely part to falter when faced with the ravages of stress. It seems clear now, years after Selye introduced this concept, that exhaustion occurs as a result of three physiological causes: (1) the loss of potassium ions, (2) the loss of adrenal glucocorticoids, and (3) the weakening of vital organs.

The long-term effect of mineralocorticoids keeping sodium levels high through the suppression of potassium and hydrogen ions is that cells begin to die. Potassium, the chief positive ion in cells, plays a vital role in the effective functioning of cells. When potassium levels fall, cells function less effectively and eventually die. Exposure to chronic, low-level stress can contribute to this process.[10]

The long-term result of excessive adrenal gland stimulation is the depletion of adrenal glucocorticoids. When this happens, blood glucose levels fall dramatically and result in the loss of nutrients to the cells.

As these physical responses indicate, chronic stress resulting from long-term resistance puts a heavy demand on strategic body parts. The heart, blood vessels, and adrenal and thyroid glands are particularly susceptible to sudden breakdown from the strain of this continual stress response.[12] We examine in detail the effects of stress on the development of disease in Chapter 4.

A Critical Look at GAS

Selye's[10] three-phase general adaptation syndrome has remained among the most accepted and well-known explanations of stress in the field (Fig. 3-10). In recent years, however, the two key elements of Selye's theory—nonspecificity and the comparability of eustress and distress—have been challenged.

If you remember from Chapter 1, nonspecificity refers to Selye's belief that all stressors trigger the same kind of response in the body. Selye believed that there are no specific stress responses matched to specific stressors. In other words, you do not have one stress response for relationship problems, one for traffic, and one for flunking a test. According to Selye, your body responds the same to each of these. Additionally, he believed that the body responds the same to positive (eustress) and negative (distress) stressors; all stressors throw the body out of equilibrium, forcing adaptation. This adaptation puts increased demands on your body, and in Selye's eyes, positive events exact the same toll as negative events.

These two issues represent the core of Selye's definition of stress. Doubts about their validity challenge the very notion of stress held by many people in the field.

Much of Selye's initial work on the general adaptation syndrome occurred before 1950 and was hampered by the lack of a sophisticated instruments and measurement techniques now available for the study of bio-

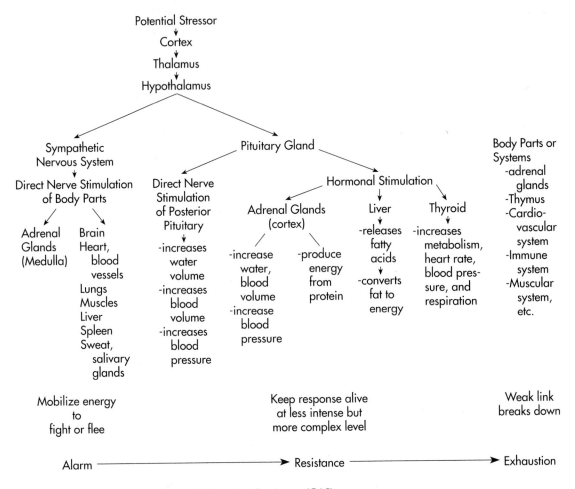

Fig. 3-10 Summary of Selye's General Adaptation Syndrome (GAS).

morphological
concerned with the
structure and function
of an organism

chemical activity within the human body. As a result, many of his findings and interpretations of the effects of stress were attributed to **morphological** changes in the adrenal and thyroid glands rather than actual measurement of the hormonal activity of these glands while his subjects were under stress. In the 1960s and 1970s, however, advances in instrumentation, scientific technology, and the emergence of the field of neuroendocrinology, which studies the relationship between the brain and the endocrine system, began to cast serious doubts about Selye's findings concerning nonspecificity.

David Goldstein,[3] a researcher at the National Institute of Health in Maryland, poses a fundamental challenge of Selye's nonspecificity concept based on acceptance of evolutionary theory. Citing evidence stemming from Darwin's work, Goldstein claims that a nonspecific response to any demand conceptualization is contrary to accepted beliefs about the evolutionary process. In fact Goldstein asserted, stress responses have a "primitive specificity" that makes sense in terms of processes that go on during evolutionary adaptations to situations. Stress responses evolve like all processes and depend on cognitive aspects such as the perceived meaning of the stressor, one's perceived ability to cope with it, genetic factors, and the effects of learning (conditioning).

Additionally, Goldstein[3] has identified different responses to seven specific stressors: water deprivation, salt deprivation, changes in posture, eating a large meal, exercise, hemorrhage, and alterations in temperature. During exposure to each of these stressors, different homeostats regulate different systematic responses. This seems to indicate that there are at least seven specific stress responses to environmental stimuli alone.

If, in fact, there are seven specific responses to simple environmental stressors, it is logical to assume that there also might be different responses to specific psychosocial stressors. Most of us are much more likely to be stressed by emotional arousal stemming from psychosocial stressors than by the extremes in environmental conditions created by Selye in the laboratory. In fact, as Mason[7] reported, emotional stimuli are among the most potent in stimulating pituitary-adrenocortical activity.

Because emotional stimuli can trigger the same stress response as the noxious environmental stimuli used by Selye in his laboratory studies, was he actually measuring a response to these stimuli or to the emotional arousal created by them? It is hard to assess because there seems to be a high degree of intercommunication between psychosocial/emotional inputs and physiological outputs.[1]

Citing research that minimizes psychological reactions to physical stimuli, Mason[7] provides evidence that contradicts Selye's nonspecific response concept. In certain studies where psychological reactions to increased physical stimuli were minimized, human and monkey subjects did not react with a nonspecific triggering of adrenal hormones.[8] This information lends credibility to the idea that the psychological perception of threat posed by Selye's noxious environmental stimuli was the key variable—not the actual noxious stimuli themselves. This distinction fundamentally changes the view of the stress response from that of a nonspecific response being elicited by a diversity of stimuli to that of a hormonal response being elicited largely by a single stimulus or stimulus class.[7]

In other words, stress is not the nonspecific response to *any* demand—just those demands capable of triggering emotional arousal. *Emotional arousal* is another term for feeling threatened or harmed, which supports Lazarus and Folkman's[5] view of the stress response as being mediated by the perception of threat/harm or challenge.

Cortisol seems to be the main hormone whose presence indicates stress rather than challenge. Frankenhaeuser[3] has shown that cortisol secretion is linked to the perception of threat. He studied subjects exposed to threatening and nonthreatening tasks. Both types of tasks were considered potential stressors; each threw the body out of equilibrium, required energy to accomplish the task and elevated the levels of norepinephrine, the hormone related to sympathetic nervous system arousal. When the tasks were accomplished, the levels of norepinephrine returned to normal.

In addition to heightened norepinephrine levels, the threatened group also had elevated blood levels of cortisol. This seems to lend credibility to the specificity of a stress response in relation to one's perception of the stressor. Also, it seems that the perception of threat is necessary for continued activation of the stress response. Other studies have also reported presence of cortisol in subjects exposed to threatening and challenging tasks.[6]

These findings seem to indicate that there is not just one, nonspecific stress response to all demands; there are in fact different responses that occur depending on whether one perceives stimuli as a threat, harm/loss, or challenge. Therefore eustress may be an outdated concept and at the very least, a misnomer.

Although positive, challenging stimuli throw us out of equilibrium and force our bodies to adapt through increased energy utilization, our perception of these stimuli surely determines the extent and the duration of our bodily involvement. Getting psyched up for an athletic competition, for instance, gets our "juices flowing" in a positive way (Fig. 3-11).

We perceive such a stimulus as a challenge and our bodies respond by producing extra energy through glycogenesis and gluconeogenesis. However, this mobilization ceases once the stimulus is removed and the challenge is over. This is different from the kind of energy mobilization that occurs during the resistance phase in response to a chronic stressor such as a relationship gone bad. Lazarus and Folkman[5] would say that our perception (and therefore our body's involvement) of the latter is different from the former. Although the types of physiological processes triggered for energy mobilization are similar, the perception of the stimuli and the duration and intensity of exposure are entirely different. Activation of adaptive mechanisms that enable the body to adjust to the demands of challenge are not the same as those involved in adjusting to harm, loss, or threat.

Further, our sense of being clear about and in control of the athletic competition is likely to be very different than the relationship stressor. We can consciously focus on the challenge and, through our cerebral cortex, trigger the mobilizing of the energy needed to get us through our ordeal.

In the short term, the hormones that mobilize blood sugars and fats enable extra effort and higher performance levels. In the long term, sus-

Fig. 3-11 Being challenged can bring you to the edge of peak performance.

tained release of these same chemicals in response to situations involving perceived harm, loss, or threat lead to fatigue and the depletion of reserves.

There is evidence to support the theory that chronic stressors can leave the body in a state of excessive sympathetic arousal. It has been found that individuals suffering from post-traumatic stress disorders (PTSD) have abnormally high levels of adrenal hormones and elevated blood pressure and heart rate.[8] Reactivation of memories, thoughts, and feelings about traumatic events are presumed to be the cause of the continual stimulation of the adrenal glands in PTSD sufferers.

Though short-term eustress demands energy, there is little evidence that long-term eustress leads to the same negative health effects associated with distress. It may well be that the cognitive stress appraisal of situations that could be labeled eustress would eventually reduce these to what Lazarus and Folkman[5] would refer to as benign/positive events that are no longer capable of triggering a stress response.

Summary

We started this chapter with a re-creation of the fight-or-flight response and traced this response from its origins in the various sensory and motor centers of the brain. The anatomy and physiology of the brain was discussed in detail, with particular attention to the way the various components of brain functioning come into play during the stress response. The reader should understand more fully how potentially stressful stimuli is received, interpreted, and reacted to by an individual.

The brain's relationship to the central and peripheral nervous systems was compared to a switchboard and telephone system, with the brain receiving and routing incoming messages. These messages travel along different circuits, ultimately reaching their destinations and transmitting their messages. The transmissions fired off by the nervous system can be considered electrical message units carried along the various branches of the nervous system. They stimulate the various organs and tissues involved in initiating the stress response and in mobilizing the energy needed to maintain homeostasis in the face of a stressor.

We discussed the endocrine system and focused on its role in keeping the stress response alive once nerve transmissions have been stretched to their limit. A detailed discussion of the various endocrine glands and hormones was presented to give the reader an appreciation of the complexity of this system and its role in the stress response. Selye's general adaptation syndrome (GAS), the classic model used to describe the physiological changes associated with the stress response, was presented in detail and tied all of the information from the first part of the chapter. We also discussed the three phases of GAS, (alarm, resistance, and exhaustion), citing the involvement of the various body parts and systems involved.

The chapter ends with a critical analysis of Selye's work, citing where it diverges from more recent insights gleaned from the fields of psychoneuroendocrinology and stress appraisal.

Study Questions

1. What are the four parts of the brain most directly related to the stress response? Describe their components and functions.
2. What are the differences between the motor and sensory areas of the brain? How do they react during the fight or flight response?
3. Trace the course of a nerve impulse as it travels along the central and peripheral nervous systems in response to a potential stressor.
4. Describe the actions of nerve impulses and hormones during the alarm and resistance phases of the general adaptation syndrome? What are their similarities and differences?
5. What is the relationship between homeostasis and stress?
6. What are the effects of sympathetic nervous system activation and parasympathetic deactivation?
7. How do higher (cortical) and lower (limbic) brain functions interact during a chronic stress response?

8. What is the primary function of the endocrine system during resistance?
9. What are the three phases of the general adaptation syndrome? Discuss how these phases are affected by the passage of time.
10. What are the major challenges to Selye's concepts of nonspecificity and eustress/distress?

References

1. Daruna, J.H., and Morgan, J.E. (1990). Psychosocial effects on immune function. *Psychosomatics, 31*(1), 4-11.

2. Dembroski, T.M. & Blumchen, D. (Eds.). (1983). *Behavioral bases of coronary heart disease*. Basel, Switzerland: Karger.

3. Frankenhauser, M. (1983). The sympathetic-adrenal and pituitary-adrenal responses to challenge; Comparison between the sexes. In T.M. Dembroski and D. Blumchen (Eds.) *Biobehavioral bases of coronary heart disease*. Basel, Switzerland: Karger.

4. Goldstein, D.S. (1990). Neurotransmitters and stress. *Biofeedback and Self-Regulation, 15*(3), 243-271.

5. Lazarus, R.S., and Folkman, S. (1985). *Stress appraisal and coping*. New York: Springer.

6. Lovallo, W.R., Pincomb, G.A., Brackett, D.J., and Wilson, M.F. (1990). Heart rate reactivity as a predictor of neuroendocrine responses to aversive stimuli and appetite changes. *Psychosomatic Medicine, 52*, 17-26.

7. Mason, J.W. (1975). A historical view of the stress field. *Journal of Human Stress, 1*, 22-36.

8. McFall, M.E., Murburg, M.M., Roszell, D.K., and Veith, R.C. (1989). Psychophysiologic and neuroendocrine findings in post traumatic stress disorder: a review of theory and research. *Journal of Anxiety Disorders, 3*, 243-257.

9. Seely, R.R., Stephens, T.D., & Tate, P. (1995). *Anatomy and physiology*. St. Louis: Mosby.

10. Selye, H. (1956). *The Stress of Life*. New York: McGraw Hill.

11. Thibodeau, G.A. & Patton, K.T. (1993). *Anatomy and physiology*. St. Louis: Mosby.

12. Tortora, G.J. and Anagnostakos, N.P. (1987). *Principles of anatomy and physiology* (5th ed.) New York: Harper and Row.

Name: _____ Date: _____

Physiological Symptom Checklist

Circle the number which indicates the frequency of occurrence of each symptom.

	Never	> 1X in past 3-6 months	> 1 X/month	> 1 X/week
1. Tension headache	0	1	2	3
2. Migraine (vascular) headache	0	1	2	3
3. Stomachache	0	1	2	3
4. Cold hands	0	1	2	3
5. Acid stomach	0	1	2	3
6. Shallow, rapid breathing	0	1	2	3
7. Diarrhea	0	1	2	3
8. Muscle cramps	0	1	2	3
9. Burping	0	1	2	3
10. Gasiness	0	1	2	3
11. Increased urge to urinate	0	1	2	3
12. Sweaty hands/feet	0	1	2	3
13. Oily skin	0	1	2	3
14. Fatigue/exhausted feelings	0	1	2	3
15. Dry mouth	0	1	2	3
16. Hand tremor	0	1	2	3
17. Backache	0	1	2	3
18. Neck stiffness	0	1	2	3
19. Gum chewing	0	1	2	3
20. Grinding teeth	0	1	2	3
21. Constipation	0	1	2	3
22. Tightness in chest or heart	0	1	2	3
23. Dizziness	0	1	2	3
24. Nausea/vomiting	0	1	2	3
25. Butterflies in stomach	0	1	2	3
26. Skin blemishes	0	1	2	3

Cont'd

Physiological Symptom Checklist (cont'd)

	Never	> 1X in past 3-6 months	> 1 X/month	> 1 X/week
27. Heart pounding	0	1	2	3
28. Blushing	0	1	2	3
29. Palpitations	0	1	2	3
30. Indigestion	0	1	2	3
31. Hyperventilation	0	1	2	3
32. Skin rashes	0	1	2	3
33. Jaw pain	0	1	2	3

Interpretation:

Add up your total score.

< 38 = low physiological symptoms score

38-50 = moderate physiological symptoms score

51-75 = high physiological symptoms score

76-99 = excessive physiological symptoms score

The Social and Spiritual Basis of Stress

- Describe the social dimension of health and how it relates to stress.
- Describe the relationship between social relationships and stress.
- Explain three types of resources one can get from social support systems.
- Understand the relationship between life events and stress.
- Understand the relationship between PTSD, life events, and stress.
- Describe the moderating effects of uplifts on daily hassles and stress.
- Describe the effect of chronic, negative social problems on stress.
- Explain the relationship between economic insecurity and stress.
- Explain how stereotypes, prejudice, and discrimination contribute to stress.
- Describe the differences between spirituality, religiosity, and faith.
- Explain how spirituality is related to stress.

interpersonal

events that go on between two or more people

intrapersonal

events that go on within an individual

This chapter examines the social and spiritual basis of stress. Although it is impossible to discuss these dimensions of health without there being some overlap with Chapter 2, Mental and Emotional Basis of Stress, there are aspects of stress that are more related to **interpersonal** issues than **intrapersonal** ones. We examine the relationship between our connectedness with others and our susceptibility to stress. We also look at how our spirituality is related to both our social health and our stress.

The Social Dimension: Social Support and Stress

What exactly do we mean by the social dimension? Aren't all people social creatures who come into contact with other humans regularly? It is true that by virtue of being human we are social creatures. We need human contact to be fully alive. However, is there a way to qualify and quantify the social dimension? Are there resources that we can examine that give breadth and depth to our social relationships?

The Social Dimension Defined

Lazarus and Folkman[31] categorize two facets of our social resources: (1) social networks—the existence, types, number, and interconnectedness of our social relationships; and (2) social support—the perceived resources we get from our relationships, both in terms of the extent and quality of support (e.g., financial, emotional, child care).

The people who make up our social support network are our family, friends, associates, co-workers, church members, teammates, and so on; these are the people we turn to in troubled times.

Our social support system changes as we age. When we are young, we turn mainly to our family; as we grow, our friends supplement whatever family support we have; and when we reach adulthood, our main source of support is our primary partner—our husband, wife, or lover. These primary support people are augmented by others who share our work, play, worship, and community involvement. The depth and richness of our involvement with these other people can make all the difference when we lose our primary support system (see Assess Yourself 4-1).

Our social dimension can either be a rich source of human interaction that nourishes and sustains us through troubled times, thereby reducing stress, or it can be a void that only magnifies our sense of aloneness and isolation.

Social Relationships and Stress

There has been a great deal of research to support the notion that people with supportive social relationships are better able to cope with problems, manage stress, and prevent premature death and disability (both physical and psychological). The exact mechanism of these protective effects, however, is unknown. There are two theories used to explain the effects of social support on stress: the direct effect theory and the stress buffering theory.[35]

The direct effect theory asserts that an extensive social network exerts a protective effect against stress, regardless of the degree of stress one is experiencing.[35] In other words, if you have an extensive social network, it will insulate or protect you from life's stresses. Its effects are preventive in nature; aloneness and isolation are two risk factors for many physical and psychological illnesses, and having many social ties protects against those two factors.[31] The direct effect theory equates an extensive social network with a high level of social support (Fig. 4-1).

The stress buffering theory, on the other hand, states that a well-functioning social-support network helps offset or disperse the negative effects of stressors when you are exposed to them. In other words the benefits of

Fig. 4-1 Our social networks can be a rich
source of support in troubled times.

social support come into play when you need them. People with strong
social support derive benefits from this only when needed.[35]

No one is sure which theory is correct; however, there seems to be
good evidence to support each. The direct effect theory assumes that people need to be embedded in a social network to feel good about themselves
and their lives.[31] This seems to fit with what we know about the need for
humans to have nurturing social interactions to develop and thrive. The
early work of Harlow, a psychologist interested in the effects of human
bonding,[23] demonstrated that monkeys deprived of social contact, physical
touch, and nurturing do not develop normally and are significantly more
likely to suffer premature disability and death than monkeys who do receive
social contact. Indeed, Harlow demonstrated that even monkeys "cared for"
by an artificial wire and cloth mother fare better than the monkeys devoid
of any mother figure to cling to.

As Lazarus and Folkman[31] put it, "without ongoing social relationships, much of the meaningfulness of human existence is lacking or impaired. Viable social relationships make possible identification and involvement which can be viewed as the polar opposite of alienation and anomie." Social interaction helps reduce our overall stress level by making us feel connected and not separate and alone.

However, social networks also have the potential to create stress. To use the stress-reducing properties of social networks, you first have to invest a lot of time and energy to cultivate these relationships. Additionally, social relationships require nurturing, which also takes time. There is a certain amount of sacrifice involved in forming relationships and belonging to groups. A person must continually evaluate whether or not the stress-reducing benefits of extensive social networks compensate for the stress created by the demands of social networks.

The stress buffering theory rests on the assumption that social support is a commodity that we have to draw on when it is needed. A key to understanding this is to view social resources as very tangible things whose presence can help us through troubled times, thereby reducing the associated stress. Just knowing these resources exist can affect our perceived ability to cope, a key element in the stress transaction.

There are many kinds of social support, and the benefits derived from them can make the difference between being able to cope or being overwhelmed with stress. Having a supportive social network could mean having someone there to listen when you need a friend. It could mean there is someone to loan you money during a tough financial time. It could translate into someone being there to watch your child in an emergency or take care of your pet while you are away. It could also mean having someone there to nurse you back to health after an illness or help you find preventive care to protect your health.

Although these are concrete examples of where one's social supports can meet specific needs, many times just knowing someone is there in case you need them can make all the difference in the world between feeling safe and secure or alone and vulnerable. This faith in friends and neighbors may account for the differences in health status between those with strong social networks and those without them. In a sense this is a spiritual bond— a sense of connectedness that is based on faith and the belief that someone will be there for us when we are in need.

Social Support, Stress, and Illness

Regardless of which theory you believe, there is ample evidence to suggest that a lack of social support is a contributing factor to the development of

KEY
TO UNDERSTANDING

Social relationships make us feel connected to others—not separate and alone.

KEY
TO UNDERSTANDING

We must continually evaluate our social relationships to see if their benefits outweigh the stress created by the time and energy we must use to maintain them.

morbidity

the number of cases
of a disease/condition

psychological and physical illness. Conversely, an extensive network of supportive social relationships is related to reduced **morbidity** and mortality associated with a variety of physical illnesses.[21]

Among the literature associated with social resources and psychological stress, there is a growing body of literature suggesting the link between social support and depression. Several studies point to the level of social support in an individual's life as the key moderator between life stressors and the development of depression. Higher levels of pessimism, depressive symptoms, and suicidal tendencies are found in subjects who report a lack of social supports.[35,48]

Physical illness is also related to social support. A study by Kiecolt-Glaser et al.[27] showed that social isolation is related to reduced immunity. In the study, subjects with the lowest levels of social support also had lower levels of killer cells, the immune system components responsible for destroying invading substances responsible for the development of disease.

Several studies have found a relationship between social isolation and premature death. People who have rich social networks tend to live longer than those who do not. A 9-year prospective study[5] of 7000 Californians showed that those with close social ties lived longer than those who were more isolated. Those classified as having the fewest social relationships had the highest death rate and those classified as most lonely died at a rate three times that of those with good social supports.

Other studies, both in this country and in foreign countries, have found similar results. In Michigan and South Carolina, subjects with the greatest social support systems had the lowest death rates, regardless of age. Among Japanese and Swedish men similar findings were obtained; those with the worst social supports (lived alone, few friends, limited activities and group affiliations) had the highest death rates.[21]

Although studies seem to indicate that extensive social networks seem to be protective against disease, no one is exactly sure why this is so. It may be that people who are able to cultivate extensive social networks are also better able to take advantage of resources than others. They may have better social skills that enable them to more effectively use the resources available to them. In other words the protective effect may not come from the relationships per se but from the individuals' ability to get what they need from these relationships.

Life Events and Stress

In Chapter 1, we introduced the concept of defining stress in terms of the number of major life events a person experiences over a short period of time. We examined the work of Holmes and Rahe[25] and presented evidence to support the notion that a person's physical and psychological well-being is related to the amount of major life stress they experience in a given time. Since Holmes and Rahe pioneered the development of the first scale, several studies have been conducted using various types of life events instruments. Measuring stress using life events scales has become the dominant way of determining whether or not a person is stressed. However, there are many troubling facts associated with this approach.

The most troubling aspect of a life events approach to measuring stress and its effects on the body is the poor correlation found in the majority of research studies. Most statistical analyses of the relationship of life events to illness have been only weakly significant.[39] A tremendous amount of effort has gone into improving the Social Readjustment Rating Scale. Attempts have been made to weigh certain items more heavily than others, omit undesirable items, expand the breadth of the events and make it less subjective.[26] However, those who have developed broader instruments including various life events categories have found these changes to be problematic. Considerable variability was found within the categories—a fact attributed to the dependence of such instruments on subjects' personal biographical data.[15]

Another downfall of using life events to measure stress is that it does not take into account, a person's perception of the event or the specific context in which it occurs. Life events scales assume that all persons will respond the same to each occurrence of any event. However, each life event is part of a specific transaction involving the individual's perception of the stressor and his or her perceived ability to cope with it.[16] It makes sense for people to minimize making too many major life changes in a short period of time and to be sure they give themselves a break to rest and rejuvenate after experiencing a particularly stressful period. However, not everyone perceives these changes in the same way and care must be taken in generalizing about the effects of life events.

The benefit of using life events to help us understand our stress is that it is a simple way to quantify assessment technique. Life events scales are good tools for helping us assess the level of change in our lives. Coupled with an assessment of our physical, emotional, social, spiritual, and environmental well-being, they can help us know when we need to slow down.[12]

Daily Hassles and Uplifts

A better way to look at the influence of psychosocial forces that affect our lives and cause us stress is to examine the role of daily hassles and uplifts. "Hassles are the irritating, frustrating, distressing demands that to some degree characterize everyday transactions with the environment."[26] These include everything from traffic jams to financial concerns, from arguments to bad weather. Uplifts are happy, satisfying experiences ranging from hearing your favorite song on the radio to taking a day off work. Daily hassles and uplifts are much more individualistic than life events.

Hassles Defined

The centrality of hassles also plays a key role in their relationship to stress.[20,30] In studies, central hassles have been defined as those that reflect ongoing themes or problems in a person's life (Fig. 4-2). Even though the presence and quantity of central hassles were relatively constant for all studied subjects over time, types of hassles differed among the groups studied (elderly people, mothers with young children, older students, and a random sample from the community).[10] What was central differed from group to group, reflecting different interpersonal and social contexts.

In addition to their link with stress, the frequency and intensity of daily hassles is also significantly related to overall health. In fact, researchers have found that daily hassles are much more strongly related to health outcomes than life events. The frequency and intensity of hassles has an especially strong association psychological illness,[26] and similar results have been found with physical health problems.[14,50] Additionally, the association of hassles to the development of illness has been found to exist independent of major life events. That is, people who experience a lot of daily hassles are more likely to

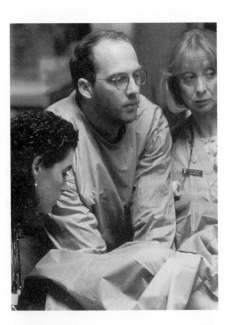

Fig. 4-2 Watching shows like NBC's *ER* gives a person a good idea of the amount of daily stress medical personnel can have on the job.

become ill than people with fewer hassles, regardless of the overall number of life events they experience.[14] Stress-related illnesses, ranging from cardiovascular problems like hypertension to disorders of the muscular system, such as low back pain and tension headaches, are covered in detail in Chapter 5.

Uplifts Defined

The effects of uplifts on stress are less convincing than those of hassles. Uplifts by themselves seem to have little protective effect against stress. When examined in conjunction with hassles, however, they seem to play a mediating role. Uplifts seem to defuse the effects of daily hassles in people who have a lot of both.[14] In many instances, people who are very productive and are involved in a variety of work, community, family, and social responsibilities experience more daily hassles than those who are less involved. However, these people also seem to get many uplifts from their involvement in these activities. A key to understanding this is to view uplifts as having the ability to cancel out the negative effects of daily hassles.

KEY
TO UNDERSTANDING

Uplifts can cancel out the stress created by too many daily hassles.

If one's activities are hassle-intensive but do not also produce many uplifts, they will be perceived as stressors. One's cognitive perception of the uplifts seems to imply that the work was worth it because the benefits outweighed the hassles.[14]

Although many major life events can and do appear suddenly and are beyond our immediate control, daily hassles usually are a result of forces within our ability to change. Because daily hassles are controllable and are more significantly related to the development of health problems than life events, we can minimize our risks for stress-related illness by paying more attention to them. However, an integrated approach to studying both is needed. There is a need for longitudinal studies that will track individuals in their natural surroundings to examine the combined effects of life events and daily hassles over time.[49] Such studies would examine not only life events and daily hassles, but the person-environment interactions in which they occur.

Post-Traumatic Stress Disorder

As we have discussed, one of the criticisms of using life events tests as measures of stress is that they can be perceived differently by individuals. However, there are events that are so traumatic and personally devastating that they come as close as possible to being characterized as universal stressors. These traumata are so outside the realm of the usual human experience that they are capable of causing enough intense fear, terror, and helplessness to literally leave their victims numb.

Such traumata can be characterized as either personal (rape, incest, robbery, torture) or community (earthquake, flood, war, terrorism). The event does not have to happen to the individual for it to be traumatic. It could affect a child, spouse, family member, stranger, or the community as a whole.

The most common traumata involve a threat to one's life, serious personal physical harm, a threat to one's family or individual family members, catastrophic destruction of one's home or community, viewing another person being seriously harmed or killed, or learning about these events though not actually experiencing them first-hand.[1]

The nation's response to the bombing of the Alfred P. Murrah Federal Building in Oklahoma City on April 19, 1995 is an example of such traumata (Fig. 4-3). The bombing was not only personally devastating to those who lost family members and friends, but it shocked the entire nation. President

Fig. 4-3 The Alfred P. Murrah federal building in Oklahoma City after the bomb on April 19, 1995.

Clinton declared a national day of mourning, and teams of social workers, psychologists, and clergy were mobilized to help people deal with the grief and numbness they felt in response to the senseless murders.[41]

Ultimately, when all efforts to find any remaining victims were exhausted, Oklahoma City and federal officials had the remains of the building razed in the hope of helping the community heal its wounds and cope with its grief. As the building imploded, hundreds of spectators held hands and hugged one another. Many openly wept, hoping their tears would help wash away their pain.[20]

PTSD Defined

Experiencing such traumata can lead to post-traumatic stress disorder (PTSD), which has four characteristic symptoms. These symptoms must persist for at least 1 month to be characterized as PTSD.[1]

1. *Reexperiencing the traumatic event*

    Traumata are reexperienced in many ways. They can be relived through dreams that recreate the event or parts of it. Occasionally sufferers dissociate from reality and slip into trancelike states for seconds, minutes, hours, and even days as they relive the traumatic event. In other cases, daily activities that contain aspects of the traumatic experience can symbolize the event and trigger intense psychological stress.[1]

2. *Avoiding any stimuli associated with the event*

    Avoidance of stimuli associated with the trauma can mean avoiding thoughts or feelings about the event. PTSD sufferers make deliberate attempts to avoid these stimuli in hopes of suppressing the psychological distress associated with them. Recounting these thoughts and feelings, as well as experiencing physical or visual stimuli associated with the trauma, can arouse recollections of the event.

3. *An overall numbing of responsiveness*

    Associated with the avoidance of trauma-related stimuli is a more generalized "psychic numbing" or "emotional anesthesia" that begins soon after the experience. The person has an overall inability to feel emotions of any type. It is as if the pain associated with the trauma is so deep that it deadens any feelings at all. PTSD sufferers often feel detached from others and generally disinterested in life and the things that used to bring them happiness and joy.[1]

4. *Increased emotional and physiological arousal*

    The fourth characteristic PTSD symptom, increased emotional and physiological arousal, can take many forms. Sleep disorders are common; PTSD sufferers have difficulty falling asleep, as well as staying asleep. Recurrent nightmares involving the reliving of the event can disturb the duration and depth of sleep. Increased emotional arousal can also make concentrating on tasks difficult.

Many sufferers with milder cases report an increase in aggression manifested as increased irritability and tension. In more severe forms, particularly among war veterans who have committed acts of violence, the sufferer might experience unpredictable outbursts of aggressive behavior and expressions of anger.[1]

In its relationship to PTSD, the Vietnam War seems to be unique among all wars fought by Americans. Not just the jungles, booby traps, and guerilla tactics but having women and children as combatants challenged western notions of what you can do to defend yourself against an armed enemy.[38] Not only was the war unique but so was the homecoming. Never before did veterans return to face such ridicule, shame, or a "collusion of silence"[38] that made it politically incorrect to discuss the war.

An article about PTSD recounts the story of Joe (a nondrinker and Vietnam veteran), whose PTSD-driven rage lead him to go into bars, pretending to be drunk, and start fights with the biggest guys in the place in the hope of getting shot or stabbed and ending his misery. Like Joe, many veterans suffering from PTSD turn their anger and rage inward, secretly hoping someone will put them out of their misery. Many take their own lives or take risks that increase their likelihood of dying from such causes as motor vehicle accidents.[38]

An impressive review of the theory and research surrounding PTSD and neuroendocrine activation found strong evidence of chronic autonomic nervous system activation among PTSD sufferers.[33] This activation seems to be triggered by memory-evoking stimuli associated with the original traumatic event and results in chronic overstimulation of the adrenal glands. PTSD sufferers were found to have significantly higher resting heart rates, blood pressure, and levels of circulating adrenal hormones than nonsufferers.

Chronic, Negative Social Conditions

Somewhere on the spectrum between tragic life events and minor daily hassles lie chronic, negative social situations such as poverty, unemployment, and discrimination. These are neither acute, tragic events, nor are they minor annoyances. Rather they are ongoing sources of tension that often leave people caught up in a cycle of despair and hopelessness.

Poverty

A key to understanding the effects of poverty on stress is to view it as a two-edged sword—it serves as both a source of stress and as a barrier to effective coping. Poverty exposes people to a greater amount of traumatic situations, negative life events, and daily hassles. However, at the same time it attacks and limits many potential sources of social support.

Poor women especially experience more frequent, more threatening, and more uncontrollable life events than the general population. They are exposed to higher levels of violence, crime, and murder than the general population and suffer from a higher rate of illness and death among their children and a higher rate of imprisonment of their husbands. These traumatic situations and negative life events expose poor women to considerably more potential stressors than more affluent women.

Poverty also imposes chronic conditions that tax the coping abilities of the poor. Conditions that are endured daily include overcrowding, inadequate housing, dangerous neighborhoods, and financial uncertainty.[4] Also, role conflicts between poor women and their male partners often occur because of such issues as the high rate of unemployment and underemployment among poor men. Poor women are forced to work unskilled jobs that provide limited salaries and inadequate benefits. Additionally, many poor women are forced to put their children in child-care arrangements that are less than adequate.[4]

Although studies show that women with adequate social support systems are better able to cope with the stresses associated with being poor, poverty itself can erode these very support systems. A reliable spouse or partner, the cornerstone of support systems for most women, is not present for most poor women. Poverty also takes its toll on friends and neighbors. With more affluent women, it is usually these friends and neighbors who come to the rescue in times of need; they provide the child care, emotional support, and financial resources to fall back on in times of need. With poor women, however, these friends, family, and neighbors are often in the same dire straights. In fact, there is almost a contagion effect in such social networks where involvement in the social network exacted a higher cost than the benefits derived through participation.[4] Because everyone is in need, continually experiencing catastrophes and crises, involvement in these social networks is often more stressful than helpful.

Poverty takes many forms, and for most Americans it is a temporary condition lasting only 1 or 2 years. For certain groups, however, such as single parent mothers, poverty often is a chronic condition lasting several years.[4] As such, poverty can be viewed as a chronic, long-term stressor, capable of creating the same negative physiological responses as any other stimuli. Although being poor itself is not a stressor and only becomes one

KEY
TO UNDERSTANDING
Poverty is a two-edged sword that is both a source of stress and a barrier to effective coping.

epidemiology

the study of the distribution and determinants of diseases/conditions in populations

when appraised as such, few people trapped by this condition are able to view it as a challenge rather than a threat. As a result, the association between poverty and mental health problems is one of the most well established in all of psychiatric **epidemiology**.[4] Low income and low socioeconomic status are associated with high rates of mental disease.

Unemployment

A consequence of tough economic times, such as the recession of the late 1980s and early 1990s, is that millions of Americans are out of work. A variety of potential stressors arise for someone who becomes unemployed: the challenge of meeting basic economic needs for survival, difficulty finding future work, loss of health/medical benefits, decline in lifestyle, and loss of self-esteem are just a few. Catalano[9] reviewed a variety of individual and ecological (community-based) studies concerning the health effects of economic insecurity. He defines economic insecurity as either the rate of unemployment in an area or losing a job and being unable to meet financial needs.

In Catalano's[9] study, economic insecurity tended to result in psychological distress and nonspecific physiological illness.[9] There was also a relationship, although weak, between economic insecurity and suicide,[16] child abuse, adverse birth outcomes, and heart disease.[9]

Among his findings, the least controversial was the strong association between psychological distress and economic insecurity. Several studies he reviewed point to the increased psychological distress associated with involuntary job loss.

Expectations about finding a new job, and the length of job loss are significant mediators of unemployment.[2] The longer one is without a job, the greater the perception that he or she will be unable to find one. This combination has proved to be very stressful (Fig. 4-4).

Sometimes this pessimism can extend beyond individual persons and communities. Yankelovich[53] a leading national pollster claims that the mood of the entire nation in response to the recession of the late 1980s to early 1990s was one of gloom; people did not believe things were going to get better. This type of climate, coupled with the reality of jobs lost through corporate restructuring, downsizing, and plant closures, left people wondering if they would be next.[40]

Not only did unemployed individuals have increased psychological distress, but the effects of economic insecurity extended to their spouses.[4] In fact, in one study of stress and unemployment in rural, nonfarm families, the wives of recently unemployed men suffered greater stress than their laid-off husbands.[51] It was the wives, in most cases who were responsible for the household budget. They were faced with the task of figuring out how to take care of the family's needs now that their husbands were unemployed.

Fig. 4-4 Losing our jobs can be a source of economic insecurity and a major source of stress.

The number of people seeking mental health services increases in times of high unemployment.[9] This phenomenon even extends to professionals in the upper socioeconomic brackets. Tetzeli[46] cites a 50% increase in visits to a major New York City hospital for stress testing among bankers, stockbrokers, and managers. Many of these people were still employed but anticipated being let go from their positions.

Catalano's[9] last finding was the strong association between economic insecurity and the level of physical illness among individuals and communities—what he refers to as nonspecific illness. The strong association between economic insecurity and nonspecific physical illness is consistent with the stress-illness model discussed in Chapter 2 (see p. 43). The chronic, low-level effects of unemployment and economic insecurity create an ongoing stress response that manifests itself in a variety of ways. In Catalano's research there were higher levels of illness even when other variables (age, gender, socioeconomic status, and other stressors) were controlled.

However, we must be careful in generalizing about the health effects of job loss. Many factors are involved in understanding how job loss results in a feeling of economic insecurity. Findings are mixed, concerning the consistency of the effects of job loss across socioeconomic and demographic groups. For instance the effects of job loss among auto workers (a heavily unionized industry) were most pathogenic (disease producing) for minorities.[9] However, in some studies of representative samples across job categories the effects of job loss were found to be equally pathogenic for middle- and upper-income workers as for those with lower incomes.[9] Although it seems implausible, not everyone responds to losing their jobs in the same way.

In a study of Latinas (women of Latino origin), Romero et al[41] found that few studies existed concerning the health effects of unemployment on women. They speculate that this was due to a large extent to the prevalence of sexist attitudes among researchers who assumed that participation of most women in the workforce was an option, not a necessity. These researchers held very traditional viewpoints concerning the male partner's preeminence as the "breadwinner" in a family.[41] Consequently, these traditionalists viewed a woman's job loss as not being very stressful because it was just supplementary in nature. However, Romero et al[41] proposed that most women are in the workforce not just to supplement their partner's income, but because their salaries are needed to survive or sustain a standard of living higher than mere subsistence.

In their study, Romero et al[41] found that Latinas who lost their jobs because of the closing of a local manufacturing plant suffered from a variety of psychological stressors. They grouped these stressors into three categories: family events, occupational events, and economic events.

More than half of the women reported stress because of the effect their job loss had on family events. Losing their jobs meant that they could not provide the things to which their families were accustomed, and they had a hard time explaining this reduced quality of living to their children. Additionally, they reported that relationships with their children had deteriorated since their job loss.

Almost all of the women reported feelings of sadness for the loss of their jobs and for the loss of contact with former co-workers. A large majority also felt insecure about their ability to find another job, and almost all reported difficulties in making ends meet. They reported difficulties meeting both basic daily economic needs (food and other commodities) and special needs (presents for their children).

A job meant more than just a paycheck to these women, and their job losses presented stressors that went beyond the loss of income.[41] The extent of their stress depended on the length of unemployment and the age of the women. Those unemployed the longest reported the greatest stress levels. Higher stress levels were also reported among the older women. The older the woman, the longer she needed to adjust to her job loss and cope with her stress.

Another study of employed and unemployed, male, blue-collar workers found mixed results concerning the effects of job loss.[19] The results challenged the notion that most people react to unemployment with loss of self-esteem, increase in stressful life events, and an external locus of control. The findings of the study showed no significant relationship between being unemployed and the three expected outcomes.

The lack of self-esteem loss among the unemployed men is attributed to general levels of unemployment in the community.[19] There seems to be greater acceptance of one's lack of work if many in the community are experiencing the same thing.

In cases where financial needs could be met with unemployment compensation benefits, job loss was actually perceived as a way to reduce stressful life events. Some of the men who were laid off viewed this as time to rest, spend time with family, pursue other interests, and investigate other jobs. Blue-collar workers seem to develop a tolerance and expectation for periods of unemployment. This "it comes with the territory" attitude seems to have a buffering effect for the blue-collar worker when he actually loses a job.

Other studies have also identified variables that seem to mediate how one perceives the loss of a job. All of these studies lend credibility to the perception of stress as a holistic transaction involving the perceived ability to cope with a potential stressor. In cases where job loss was perceived as an event that could be coped with, there was minimal stress. In other cases, such as with the Latina women, where job loss interfered with their ability to cope with economic needs, they felt stressed by the closing of their plant.

Job Loss and Violence

One very troubling aspect of stress related to job loss is the increasing number of violent crimes associated with it. At least 750 people have been killed at work each year between 1980 and 1993.[41] A government report from the National Institute of Occupational Safety and Health shows that from 1980-1988 there were 6965 cases of work-related homicides.[43] Although many are quick to place the blame on the easy availability of firearms, particularly handguns, one researcher asserts that it is people's attitudes, not weapons, that are to blame.[28] Weapons have always been available in this country and these increases in violent behavior are recent—within the past decade. In a sense one can view this work-related stress as stress associated with irrational beliefs about how work and the economy should be.

Stress and Stereotypes, Prejudice, and Discrimination

Although discrimination based on race, ethnicity, gender, age, or sexual orientation can be a tremendous source of stress, it is much more difficult to study empirically than poverty and unemployment. There are few studies that examine the specific effects of discrimination on stress. Instead, most studies describe the effects of such issues as poverty, crime, violence, and unemployment, and then analyze the demographics of those who are poor, involved in violent crimes, or are unemployed. As we have previously discussed, nonwhites and women make up the largest segment of those affected by these conditions.

Many people will make the argument that by virtue of the objective numbers alone, nonwhites and women are disproportionately represented in the statistics on poverty, crime, and unemployment and the fact that such disparity is allowed to exist is cited as discrimination perpetuated by the dominant culture. Whether one agrees with this conceptualization or not, a case can be made for a relationship between stress and stereotypes, prejudice, and discrimination. One can even carry the discussion further and argue that the net effect of this ongoing, chronic stress is a collective outburst at the community level. It was just such a combination that precipitated the rioting in south-central Los Angeles in 1992.[42] Shoemaker et al[42] assert that unequal distribution of civic and state resources in health care, education, and economic opportunities coupled with the paramilitary "law and order" posture of the police department created an incendiary community environment just waiting to explode.

Stereotypes

A stereotype is a set of assumptions and beliefs about the physical, behavioral, and psychological characteristics assigned to a particular group of people. Stereotypes abound for almost every class of people imaginable. People are stereotyped according to age, education, occupation, profession, national origin, religion, family role, interests, and disability status just to name a few. Stereotypes related to gender, race, ethnicity, and sexual orientation seem to be the deepest seated and most disturbing in our culture.[13]

Although we hate to admit it, all of us use stereotypes at times. A key to understanding stereotypes is that they make it easy for us to categorize and make sense out of people and experiences. Stereotypes are based in part on reality and personal experience. We tend to generalize to all members of a particular group, attributes that we have observed as belonging to particular members of that group.

An example could be the stereotype that some people have about football players being insensitive brutes, pumped up on steroids, and wanting to knock someone's head off. There have been enough reports about steroid abuse among football players to provide evidence that this exists and is a problem. In addition to this, most football fans have read books or interviews about hard-hitting linebackers and defensive backs who have had fantasies about tackling an opponent so hard that they literally take his head off. These kinds of reports create a stereotype about football players that is somewhere between fact and fiction.

Stereotypes make us lazy; they can become substitutes for observation and for finding out what people and the world are really like. In this sense, they can impoverish us[24] and can be a source of stress for us.

Most of us resist being personally stereotyped. We want others to acknowledge our uniqueness and to understand those characteristics that set us apart from others. We resent when others categorize us in a stereotypical fashion, yet most of us use stereotypes at times to pigeonhole others. In particular, we apply stereotypes to others who are different than us. We do this because those who are different represent the unknown; they have unknown qualities and they make us uneasy. We stereotype them because it then makes it easier for us to categorize them. We can create a picture of who they are without having to take the time to get to know them.[24]

In the book *Missing People and Others,*[32] the author, Arturo Madrid, refers to those who are different as "others." Being other means that you are dissimilar, on the outside, or excluded (see Stress In Our World box below).

Unfortunately, besides impoverishing us, stereotyping and seeing people as "other" sows the seeds of prejudice and discrimination. By stereotyping, we prejudge. Usually when one stereotypes, the type of prejudging that accompanies this is adverse, not positive. Prejudice, or adverse prejudging, is easy to foster when one does not take the time to get to know or understand those who are different. When prejudice leads to unequal treatment, it results in discrimination.

KEY
TO UNDERSTANDING

Stereotypes make it easy to categorize people.

STRESS IN OUR WORLD

Missing People and Others

Being the other means feeling different. It is awareness of being distinct or consciousness of being dissimilar. It means being outside the game, outside the circle, outside the set. It means being on the edges, on the margins, on the periphery. Otherness means feeling excluded, closed out, precluded, even disdained or scorned. It produces a sense of isolation, of apartness, of disconnectedness, of alienation.

Being the other involves a contradictory phenomenon. On the one hand, being the other frequently means being invisible. Ralph Ellison wrote eloquently about that experience in his magisterial novel The Invisible Man. *On the other hand, being other sometimes involves sticking out like a sore thumb.*

If one is the other, one will inevitably be perceived unidimensionally; will be seen stereotypically; will be defined and delimited by mental sets that may not bear much relation to existing realities. There is a darker side to otherness as well. The other disturbs, disquiets, discomforts. It provokes distrust and suspicion. The other makes people feel anxious, nervous, apprehensive, even fearful. The other frightens.

KEY
TO UNDERSTANDING

You can understand
the effects of stereo-
types, prejudice, and
discrimination on
stress by plugging
each variable into
Lazarus and
Folkman's stress-
appraisal model.

A key to understanding the variables stereotypes, prejudice, and discrimination is to plug them into Lazarus and Folkman's[32] transactional model to understand how they relate to stress. All three of these variables can either fit into stimulus configuration factors or personality factors.

Being treated in a stereotypical fashion, or not being allowed access to something for instance, could be a stressor in itself (stimulus factors). On the other hand, stereotypes, prejudice, and discrimination can negatively affect one's personality, reducing their perceived ability to cope. We examine a few examples of this using different types of discrimination.

The Male Role Stereotype and Stress

In his book *The Male Role Stereotype,*[47] Doug Cooper Thompson describes the role men are expected to play in American society and how this can be a source of stress. The following is his male stereotypical "code of conduct."

1. Act tough—Most boys and men are brought up to believe that they have to show that they are strong and tough; they have to be able to "take it" and "dish it out."
2. Hide emotions—"Big boys don't cry" is an epithet that most men learn early and adhere to rigidly throughout their lives.
3. Earn "big bucks"—Most men are dissuaded from choosing careers that do not have great earning potential. Men are trained to believe that they have to be the family breadwinner.
4. Get the "right" kind of job—Boys learn early on that men who pursue the wrong kinds of jobs (e.g., kindergarten teacher, nurse, secretary, librarian) are perceived as strange.
5. Compete intensely—Boys learn early on that to be a man is to be an intense competitor, whether on the playing field, in the classroom, or in the bedroom.
6. Win - Men are taught to do almost anything to win. Getting ahead and winning, whether it is at Little League or in the boardroom is crucial, regardless of the personal or family sacrifice it may entail.

Thompson[47] discusses what the cost of this code is for men. Playing this game and living up to this stereotype can be intensely stressful.

1. Acting tough has its price. Men are far more likely than women to use violence to settle their differences. Fighting is an accepted part of men's sports. Men commit a disproportionate share of violent crimes. Homicide is the leading cause of death for young black males.
2. Hiding emotions can be a risk factor for mental and physical illness. Men who keep their emotions bottled up run the risk of a variety of illnesses ranging from hypertension to depression. Hiding emo-

tions or not clearly expressing them can also put a strain on most relationships in which clear, open communication is vital.

3. The emphasis on having to be the breadwinner can put a tremendous amount of pressure on men. Some men choose careers that they really do not like but that pay well. Others put in an inordinate amount of time (overtime, nights, weekends) striving to get to the top. They have less time for themselves, their families, and their community.

4. In striving for the big salary, many men forgo careers that would be more personally rewarding. Many men would be happier in less competitive jobs or jobs that are more nurturing and involve helping others.

5. With its overemphasis on competition, the traditional male role carries over from work to play. There is no "down time." Many men have not learned how to relax—to let down their guard and be playful. A casual jog with a friend often becomes a competitive race to the finish line.

6. A "win-at-all-costs" attitude can be damaging both on the job and when it extends to home life and friendships. Much more in life is accomplished through compromise and accommodation than through winning and intimidation. Men who grow up learning to win at all costs have a harder time negotiating and compromising.

Race and Gender Stereotypes

Sometimes stereotypes converge and create a special kind of stress. In the Stress In Our World box on p. 130, Brent Staples[42] describes what it is like to grow up both black and male in urban America in the 1980s.

Staples' depiction of what it is like being a black male in urban America is a vivid example of the chronic, daily exposure to a stressful situation and the adjustments he has had to make in his life as a result of this.

Sometimes stereotyping and stress are associated with anger that boils over in rage, a hatred so deep that it sometimes makes logical, rational behavior difficult to maintain. Such a rage was used in the defense of Colin Ferguson, a black man accused of killing 6 and wounding 19 people on the Long Island Railroad. Ferguson's lawyers claimed that when he lost control and committed his crime, their client was overcome with "black rage," a hatred of whites based on years of oppression and discrimination against blacks.[38] Police also believed Ferguson was motivated by racial hatred because they found a note in his pocket at the time of his arrest that contained writings attacking whites.[3]

The jury found that, although Ferguson may have felt such rage at the time of the killings, it was no excuse for such a heinous crime, and they convicted him for the murder of six innocent people. At a presentencing hear-

STRESS IN OUR WORLD

Just Walk on By

My first victim was a woman—white, well dressed, probably in her late twenties. I came upon her late one evening on a deserted street in Hyde Park, a relatively affluent neighborhood in an otherwise mean, impoverished section of Chicago. As I swung onto the avenue behind her, there seemed to be a discreet, uninflammatory distance between us. Not so. She cast back a worried glance. To her, the youngish black man—a broad 6 feet 2 inches with a beard and billowing hair, both hands

shoved into the pockets of a military jacket-seemed menacingly close. After a few more quick glimpses, she picked up the pace and was soon running in earnest. Within seconds she disappeared into a cross street.

That was more than a decade ago. I was 22 years old, a graduate student newly arrived at the University of Chicago. It was in the echo of that terrified woman's footfalls that I first began to know the unwilling inheritance I had come into—the ability to alter public space in ugly ways. It was

clear she thought herself the quarry of a mugger, a rapist, or worse. Suffering a bout of insomnia, however, I was stalking sleep, not defenseless wayfarers... I was surprised, embarrassed, and dismayed all at once. Her flight made me feel like an accomplice in tyranny. It also made it clear that I was indistinguishable from the muggers who occasionally seeped into the area from the surrounding ghetto... I soon gathered that being perceived as dangerous is a hazard in itself.

ing, survivors of the shooting and family members of the slain victims confronted Ferguson and pleaded with the court for the death penalty. One of those who testified was a woman, Mi Won Kim, whose sister, Mi Kyung, was herself a victim of prejudice and racism. She recounted how her sister suffered because of discrimination but, unlike Ferguson, had the courage to face up to her hardships.[42]

Sexual Orientation Stereotypes

KEY
TO UNDERSTANDING

Homophobia is based in part on a stereotypical assumption about what it means to be a gay man or lesbian.

Homophobia is the irrational fear and hatred of homosexuality in ourselves and others. A key to understanding homophobia is to realize that it is based in part on prejudice founded on stereotypical assumptions about what it means to be gay or lesbian. The Stress In Our World box on p. 132 contains a short excerpt from Burg et al.[7] to illustrate how prejudice based on sexual orientation can be an ongoing source of stress (Fig. 4-5).

Although this excerpt focuses on lesbians, gay men and bisexuals share in the same kind of daily tension associated with the need to be on guard concerning their sexual orientation. One serious issue that underscores the necessity of being on guard and hiding one's gayness is the continuing high level of gay bashing and work-related discrimination that still exists in this country.

In 1990 the Federal Bureau of Investigation (FBI) began collecting data on hate crimes against gays and lesbians. As part of the national movement to identify and effectively deal with hate crimes, several states and municipalities have included sexual orientation in laws dealing with hate crimes. In the first year of data collection, hate crimes against gays and lesbians increased 15%. Although a 15% increase represents a dramatic increase, the real increase is probably much higher than that.[11] Many gays and lesbians fail to report hate crimes for fear of abuse at the hands of police, disclosure of their sexual identity to employers and the community, and fear that doctors will treat them badly. Even when gays and lesbians report hate crimes and win their cases in court, prosecutions often result in either acquittal or light sentences for those convicted.[34] This might reflect the homophobic attitudes of juries and judges and the pervasive belief that somehow gays provoke these bashings through sexual advances.

Fig. 4-5 Being gay often means having to hide these public displays of love and affection.

STRESS IN OUR WORLD

On Being a Lesbian

Heterosexuals can hold hands in public, go anywhere together, be welcomed as a couple by their families and friends, celebrate their relationships openly, make decisions for each other in times of sickness and provide for each other's material well-being in case of death. Gays and lesbians can take none of these commonplace things for granted.

In the faculty room where I work, I hear the other teachers talking about their relationships...nothing real heavy, but they do give each other a lot of support. Since being out to them (informing them of my lesbianism) would mean losing my job, I can't let off steam all day; if Ann's sick and I'm worried about her, I can't get any comfort at work. If we have a big decision to make, I can't ask for help from my co-workers in sorting it out. All this makes our lesbian friends terribly important, especially the ones who talk with us about our relationship.

The first half of this chapter examined the nature of social influences on stress. For many people, their spirituality is powerful enough to sustain their faith and help mediate even the most oppressive social conditions. The next half of the chapter examines the nature of spirituality and how it relates to stress.

Spirituality and Stress
Differences Between Faith, Religion, and Spirituality

Spirituality, religion, and faith are separate entities yet they are often used interchangeably.[29] Part of the confusion lies in the fact that, although all three are different, they are related. Faith is a part of both spirituality and religion, and our spiritual beliefs underlie our religiosity. Let's examine each in greater detail and assess how they relate to stress.

Faith

Faith is a generic and dynamic human experience.[18] It is generic because faith cuts across all religions, races, ethnic groups, and cultures. It is dynamic because it is ever changing and adaptive. Faith evolves and develops as it passes through stages in our lives.

There are three dimensions to faith:

1. Faith involves a pattern of personal trust in and loyalty to a set of core values. These core values are referred to as our *centers of*

value[18] and are made up of the people, institutions, ideals, and causes that give our lives meaning and direction.

2. Faith involves trust in and loyalty to images and realities of power. The biblical passage, "the Lord is my shepherd, I shall not want" reflects a Christian's ultimate trust in the image of an all-powerful God who will watch over his flock. Others faith may be in their government, spouse, father, or mother.

3. Faith involves trust in and loyalty to a master script or story for our lives. This master script is our internalized picture of our lives. It evolves from our first day of life and provides a picture of who we are, where we are going, and what we shall do along the way. This vision, whether completely accurate or not, provides us with direction and meaning in our lives.

All three dimensions of faith rely on the underlying premise—trust and loyalty to that which cannot be proven empirically. Whether or not our beliefs have been explicitly nurtured through religious participation, we base our faith on forming relations of trust and loyalty to others with no guarantee of anything. Faith in this sense is a covenant.[18] We are not alone in our faith. Faith involves loyalty to others through a shared trust that involves our centers of value, images of power, and a master script. Beyond this, however, faith involves a trust in and loyalty to God, something, someone, or some reality that transcends us.

It is this transcendent nature of faith that distinguishes it from mere beliefs that are usually rooted in some empirical evidence. Faith is the belief in something that cannot be proven. One can have faith in a variety of things. One can be faithful without being spiritual or religious. However, faith is a key component of spirituality and religiosity (see Assess Yourself 4-3).

Religion

Religion is a cumulative historical tradition linking expressions of faith from people of the past with those of the present and future.[18] Religion includes but is not limited to scriptures, theology, ethical teachings, prayers, architecture, art, music, and patterns of teaching and presenting. Religion is an organized system of worship. Religion includes spirituality but goes beyond it by institutionalizing specific spiritual tenets and codes. At the core of most religions is faith in God or a higher power. Religious faith is the personal appropriation of a relationship to a god through one's religious tradition. Religions, by their very nature are exclusionary because the faithful differ from the nonfaithful by their adherence to their religious dogma.

Organized religions provide an explanation for such questions as, What is the meaning of life? Where did we come from? What happens to us after death? Additionally, they provide a code of living that revolves around ethical principles and laws governing human behavior despite the legal statutes of countries.

Spirituality

Spirituality is a belief in or relationship with some higher power, creative force, divine being, or infinite source of energy.[29] Spirituality is a very misunderstood subject. When asked about their spirituality most people automatically associate it with God and formal, organized religion. However, as we mentioned in Chapter 1, spirituality can be defined in either a religious or secular way.

Our spirituality is a two-dimensional concept.[18] The vertical dimension is the relationship with the transcendent/God or set of supreme values that guide a person's life. The horizontal is the person's relationship with self, others, and the environment. There is a continual interrelationship between the two dimensions (see Fig. 4-6).

Spiritual faith may or may not involve a religious dimension. All formal religious scripture refers to the spiritual domain. However, people can be spiritual without being religious. Spirituality can revolve around a faith

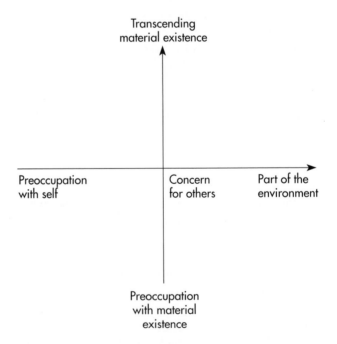

Fig. 4-6 Spirituality involves movement along two dimensions. On the vertical dimension one transcends being overly concerned with the material world and earthly possessions. The horizontal dimension involves a lack of preoccupation with the self and a growing interest in others and the environment as a whole.

and trust and forming a covenant with a higher order other than God. Those who are spiritual but not religious may form their covenant with nature and the natural world. Rather than look to God for their faith, these people might look to science, history, or nature. Faith for them might not come from a belief in God but rather from a belief in the inherent goodness of humans or all living things. Their rules for living may not originate in religious law but from ethical standards that are based on a respect and love for all living things and the universe in general.

M. Scott Peck, the author of *The Road Less Traveled*, was heavily influenced by Fowler's[17] earlier writings concerning the seven stages of faith and the evolution of spiritual development. In Peck's[38] book, *The Different Drum: Community Making and Peace*, the author describes spiritual development as a four stage process:

- Stage 1: chaotic and antisocial
- Stage 2: formal institutional
- Stage 3: skeptic and individual
- Stage 4: mystic and communal

Stage 1 is made up of young children and perhaps one in five adults. It is a stage of undeveloped spirituality characterized as chaotic and antisocial. People in this stage are chaotic in the sense that their lives are basically unprincipled. There is nothing that governs them but their own will. They lack integrity and their movement is guided by whim, not principle. Individuals in this stage are antisocial in that they are generally incapable of loving others. Their actions are self-serving and manipulative, even if they say otherwise. Many spend their entire lives at this level. Others move to the next stage.

Stage 2 is inhabited by the majority of churchgoers and believers as well as emotionally healthy children. In this stage of spiritual development the person is strongly attached to the formal, institutional religious experience versus the essence of that religion. There is strict adherence to the traditions and dogma of the religion. Change and nontraditional interpretations of the religious experience are viewed with disfavor by persons in this stage.

Stage 3 of spiritual development is characterized by an increasing skepticism about the formal interpretations and expressions of the religion. There is a focus on an individual interpretation of the teachings and practices that may include rejection of some things. However, this is not to be confused with the antisocial aspect of Stage 1. Stage three individuals are often more socially committed and community oriented than Stage 2 people. Their individuality often manifests itself in examining issues and seeking the truth– -going beyond mere adherence to dogma.

Stage 4, the mystic, communal part of spiritual development, is made up of people who have moved beyond narrowly defining their faith; the communal aspect of this stage is one of inclusiveness rather than exclusion. It is made up of people whose spirituality does not exclude others of a different faith or who pray to a different god or who do not believe in a god. It is made up of people who believe that all spiritual persons belong to the same group and that what connects them is a mystery. The interconnectedness of humans, and other life forms and environments cannot always be explained rationally or objectively. They believe that some things are beyond rational explanation and remain a mystery. Stage 4 individuals take comfort in the interconnectedness of life and revel in the mystery that surrounds their faith.

Religiosity, Spirituality, Faith, and Stress Management

Regardless of the source of their faith, those with a rich spiritual dimension seek solace in the belief that life matters and that we belong here. We are all in this struggle to be human and make sense of this life together. No living thing is an island—we are all interconnected. We are all together on this planet called Earth careening through space from who knows where to who knows where.

In addition to this sense of interconnectedness, we also possess a sense of awe and wonder at experiences that somehow transcend us. These experiences speak to us with an inner voice that defies logic and rational explanation. It is a primal voice that is based on faith and needs no rational, empirical justification. It echoes a common thread that runs through our being and ties us to all of humankind and every living thing. The box on page 137 lists 10 of these life experiences that evoke a sense of spirituality that defies explanation. How many more can you add to the list?

A key to understanding spirituality is to view it as a moderator of life events, daily hassles, and chronic pressures. It is one of the factors that gets taken into consideration when evaluating our ability to cope with a potential stressor. Spirituality can be a valuable resource from which we draw strength. It can also serve as an uplift, not necessarily connected to a stressor.

Several studies point to the relationship between spirituality, religiosity, and an increased ability to cope with crises. A study[21] of very successful professional men and women who had suffered severe psychological or physical trauma found that the key variable that they all shared was a strong sense of spirituality. The study showed that those with a deep sense of spirituality reported fewer minor illnesses, less use of medical care, and more complete recovery from minor illnesses than the national average.

KEY
TO UNDERSTANDING

Spirituality can serve as a moderator of life events, daily hassles, and chronic problems.

10 Spiritual Events

1. The emergence of a child from the birth canal

2. The death of a loved one

3. The power of a natural disaster, such as a hurricane, tornado, or flood

4. An orgasm

5. A brilliant sunset

6. A moonlit night in the desert

7. The endless pounding of the surf

8. A walk through the woods on a crisp autumn day (Fig. 4-7)

9. The pain and suffering of a starving child—belly swollen, eyes bulging

10. A picture of earth sent back from a spacecraft

In a study[6] of 1473 Americans of similar age, income, and education, religious participation was almost as significant an influence on health as age and social class. Those who were not regular participators in religious activities were more than twice as likely to report health problems as practicers. The study found that formal religious activity affected health in several ways:

- Some churches require healthful behavior—from avoiding cigarettes and alcohol to having only one sexual partner.

Fig. 4-7 For many of us spirituality includes peaceful, reflective moments outdoors.

- Most churches advocate using their Sabbath as a day of rest, and reflection (a buffer against stress).

- Sharing a religion fosters networks of social support that you can turn to in times of need.

The study[6] also found that among the religious, people who were members of more liberal denominations were in better health than those from more conservative sects.

Spiritual Distress and Illness

So established is the relationship between spirituality, religiosity, and healing, that in certain hospitals nurses take spiritual assessments of hospitalized patients. A spirituality scale has even been developed to assist nurses in this evaluation.[36] Spirituality affects patients' perceptions of their illnesses, their faith in their ability to get well, their will to live, their sick role behavior, and their preparation for death, just to name a few.

Spiritual distress has been associated with the following diagnoses: sleep pattern disturbance, hopelessness, powerlessness, self-esteem disturbance, impaired adjustment, and ineffective coping.[29] All of these problems can affect the prognosis of the sick person.

spiritual distress

the state in which an individual experiences or is at risk of experiencing a disturbance in the belief or value system that provides strength, hope, and meaning to life

Spiritual distress a term used to describe stress associated with a lack of spirituality, is defined as "the state in which the individual experiences or is at risk of experiencing a disturbance in the belief or value system which provides strength, hope, and meaning to life."[8] Some of the defining characteristics of spiritual distress include questioning the credibility of one's belief system, feeling a sense of spiritual emptiness, expressing the feeling that there is no reason to go on living, feeling emotionally detached from oneself and others, and demonstrating discouragement and despair. Patients who are spiritually distressed are at greater risk for undesirable outcomes concerning their treatment and recovery.

Spiritual distress can be grouped into three categories:

1. Inability to practice spiritual rituals
2. A conflict between religious or spiritual beliefs and the prescribed health regimen
3. The crisis of illness, suffering, or death

The inability to practice spiritual rituals can arise out of the constraints placed on patients by hospitalization or being in a nursing home. These constraints revolve around issues such as the inability to physically assume normal position for prayer or meditation, the inability to maintain a religious diet or fast, or separation from spiritual articles, clothing, and texts.

Sometimes spiritual distress arises over a conflict between religious or spiritual beliefs and the prescribed health regimen. The person may object to prescribed or legally required medical procedures such as autopsy, blood transfusions, or immunization. Sometimes a prescribed diet or medication will conflict with spiritual dietary restrictions.

Lastly, spiritual distress may be specifically related to the nature of the crisis, illness/suffering or specter of death. In this case the distress is associated with a breach of faith rather than an inability to practice or conform to one's beliefs. The person asks questions such as, What did I do to deserve this? Is this God's will? Why is this happening to me? Is my faith too weak?

Because spiritual and religious practices cut across all cultures and groups, it is important to use a multicultural approach in understanding these needs. Table 4-1 summarizes some of the major spiritual and religious considerations for a variety of groups that affect spiritual distress.

Summary

We began this chapter with an examination of the social dimension. We described the two facets of social resources—social networks and social support—and examined how these are related to stress. Although no one knows for sure exactly how social networks affect stress, two theories, the direct effects theory and the stress buffering theory, were presented.

Keeping with our adherence to a transaction model of stress, we examined the role of perception, cautioning the reader about weighing the costs associated with developing and nurturing extensive social networks against the benefits derived from these.

The chapter examined the relationship between life events and stress, citing research criticizing a life-events approach. Post-traumatic stress disorder was presented as a type of extreme example of a negative life event.

The use of daily hassles and uplifts was described as a more accurate method of analyzing social and spiritual stress. Research was presented that supports the notion that daily hassles are a more accurate indicator of a person's social stress than life events. The role of uplifts was found to be relatively benign except in cases where they coexisted with high levels of hassles, in which case, they had a moderating effect.

Chronic, negative social problems such as poverty, unemployment, and discrimination were examined as a sort of middle-ground social stressor, falling somewhere between life events and daily hassles. Examples were given concerning how these ongoing problems are related to chronic, low-level stress.

Text continued on p. 144

TABLE 4.1

Overview of Religious Beliefs

Baptist

Illness
Laying on of hands, divine healing through prayer
May request communion
Some prohibit medical therapy
May consider illness divine punishment or intrusion of
Satan

Diet
No alcohol
No coffee, tea, tobacco, pork, or strangled animals
Some fasting

Birth
Opposes infant baptism

Text
Bible

Beliefs
Some practice speaking in tongues

Buddhism

Illness
Considered trial that develops the soul
May wish counseling by priest
May refuse treatment on holy days

Diet
Strict vegetarianism
Discourages use of alcohol, tobacco, and drugs

Death
Last-rite chanting by priest
Death leads to rebirth.

Text
Buddha's sermon on the "eightfold path"
The Tripitaka, or "three baskets" of wisdom

Beliefs
Cleanliness is of great importance
Suffering is universal

Christian Science

Illness
Caused by errors in thought and mind
May oppose drugs and other medical interventions
Accepts only legally required immunizations
May desire support from a Christian Science reader
or treatment by a Christian Science nurse or
practitioner
Healing is a spiritual renewal

Death
Autopsy permitted only in cases of sudden death

Text
Bible
Science and Health with Key to the Scriptures by Mary
Baker Eddy

Eastern Orthodox (Greek Orthodox, Russian Orthodox, Armenian)

Illness
May desire Holy Communion, laying on of hands,
anointing, or sacrament of Holy Unction
Most oppose euthanasia and favor every effort to
preserve life

Russian Orthodox males should be shaved only if
necessary for surgery

TABLE 4.1 (CONT'D)

Overview of Religious Beliefs (cont'd)

Eastern Orthodox (Greek Orthodox, Russian Orthodox, Armenian) (cont'd)

Diet
May fast Wednesdays, Fridays, during Lent, before
    Christmas, or before communion
May avoid meat, dairy products, and olive oil during fast

Birth
Baptism 8 to 40 days after birth, usually by immersion
May be followed immediately by confirmation

Death
Last rites and administration of Holy Communion
May oppose autopsy, embalming, and cremation

Texts
Bible
Prayer book

Religious articles
Icons (pictures of Jesus, Mary, saints)
Holy water and lighted candles
Russion Orthodox wears cross necklace that should
    be removed only if necessary

Other
Greek Orthodox opposes abortion
Confession at least yearly
Holy Communion four times yearly

Episcopal

Illness
May believe in spiritual healing
May desire confession and Communion

Diet
May abstain from meat on Fridays
May fast during Lent or before communion

Birth
Infant baptism is mandatory

Death
Last rites optional

Texts
Bible
Prayer book

Hinduism

Illness
May minimize illness and emphasize its temporary
    nature
Considered important only as it affects spiritual quest
Illness or injury may represent sins committed in
    previous life

Diet
Many are vegetarian
Beef and pork are forbidden
Many abstain from alcohol

Death
Seen as rebirth
Priest may tie thread around neck or wrist
Water is poured into mouth, and family washes body
Cremation preferred

Beliefs
Self-control, self-discipline, and cleanliness emphasized
Opposes artificial insemination

Cont'd

TABLE 4.1 (CONT'D)

Overview of Religious Beliefs (cont'd)

Hinduism (cont'd)

Texts
Vedas
Upanishads
Bhagavad-Gita

Worship
Usually in home
May involve various images, statues, and symbols of gods
May include use of water, fire, lights, sounds, natural
    objects, special postures, and gestures

Jehovah's Witness

Illness
Opposes blood transfusions and organ transplantation
May oppose other medical treatment and all modern
    science
Opposes faith healing
Opposes abortion

Diet
May eat meats that have been drained

Texts
Bible

Judaism

Illness
Medical care emphasized
Rabbinical consultation necessary for donation and
    transplantation of organs
May oppose surgical procedures on the Sabbath
May prefer burial of removed organs or body tissues
May oppose shaving
May wear skull cap and socks continuously, believing
    head and feet should be covered

Diet
Fasting for 24 hours on certain holy days
Matzo replaces leavened bread during passover week
May observe strict Kosher dietary laws

Birth
Ritual circumcision 8 days after birth
Fetuses are buried

Death
Ritual burial; society members wash body
Oppose cremation
Many oppose autopsy and donation of body to science
Most do not believe in afterlife
Generally oppose prolongation of life after irreversible
    brain damage

Texts
Torah
Talmud
Prayer book

Religious articles
Menorah
Yarmulke
Tallith
Tefillin, or phylacteries
Star of David

Lutheran, Methodist, Presbyterian

Illness
May request communion, anointing and blessing, or
    visitation by minister or elder
Generally encourages use of medical science

Birth
Baptism by sprinkling or immersion of infants, children,
    or adults

TABLE 4.1 (CONT'D)

Overview of Religious Beliefs (cont'd)

Lutheran, Methodist, Presbyterian (cont'd)

Death
Optional last rites or scripture reading

Texts
Bible
Prayer book

Mormon (Church of Jesus Christ of Latter-Day Saints)

Illness
May come through partaking of harmful substances
    such as alcohol, tobacco, drugs, etc.
May be seen as a necessary part of the plan of
    salvation
May desire sacrament of the Lord's Supper to be
    administered by a Church Priesthood holder
Divine healing through laying on of hands
Church may provide financial support during illness

Diet
Prohibits alcohol, tobacco, and hot drinks
Sparing use of meats

Birth
No infant baptism
Infants are born innocent

Death
Cremation is opposed

Texts
Bible
Book of Mormon

Religious articles
Special undergarment may be worn by both men and
    women and should not be removed except during
    serious illness, childbirth, emergencies, etc.

Beliefs
Oppose abortion
Vicarious baptism for deceased who were not
    baptized in life

Muslim (Islamic, Moslem) and Black Muslim

Illness
Oppose faith healing
Illness is God's will
Group prayer may be helpful
Favors every effort to prolong life

Diet
Pork prohibited
May oppose alcohol and traditional Black American
    foods
Fasts sunrise to sunset during Ramadan

Birth
Circumcision practiced with accompanying ceremony
Aborted 30-day fetus is treated as human being

Death
Confession of sins before death

Family follows specific procedure for washing and
    preparing body, which is then turned to face Mecca
May oppose autopsy

Texts
Koran
Hadith

Prayer
Five times daily—facing Mecca and kneeling on prayer
    rug
Ritual washing after prayer

Beliefs
All activities restricted to what is necessary for health
Personal cleanliness very important
Gambling and idol worship prohibited

Cont'd

TABLE 4.1 (CONT'D)

Overview of Religious Beliefs (cont'd)

Roman Catholic

Illness

Allowed by God because of man's sins but not
    considered personal punishment
May desire confession and communion
Anointing of sick for all seriously ill patients
Donation and transplantation of organs permitted
Burial of amputated limbs

Diet

Fasting or abstaining from meat mandatory on Ash
    Wednesday and Good Friday
Fast from solid food for 1 hour and abstain from
    alcohol for 3 hours before receiving Communion

Birth

Baptism of infants and aborted fetuses mandatory

Death

Anointing of sick
Extraordinary artificial means of sustaining life are
    unnecessary

Texts

Bible
Prayer book

Religious articles

Rosary, crucifix, saints' medals, statues, holy water,
    lighted candles

Other

Attendance at mass required on Sundays or late
    Saturday and on holy days
Sacrament of Penance at least yearly
Oppose abortion

The chapter ended with an examination of how spirituality, religiosity, and faith are related to the stress response. Although used interchangeably, each represents a different phenomenon with its own relationship to stress. In essence, those who are spiritual and/or religious have greater faith in life and tend to experience greater physical and psychological health.

Student Study Questions

1. List and describe the components of the social dimension of health.
2. Explain how social relationships affect personal stress.
3. List and describe three different types of resources that people can get from social support systems.
4. Describe how social relationships can be a source of stress in some instances.
5. Explain the theory behind life events and stress.
6. Explain two weaknesses in using life events scales to assess personal stress.
7. Describe PTSD, and explain how it is related to stress.
8. How do uplifts work in moderating daily hassles?
9. Describe economic insecurity and explain how it is related to stress.

10. Explain how stereotypes, prejudice, and discrimination fit together.

11. Explain how stereotypes can create stress.

12. Describe the differences between spirituality and religiosity.

13. What is spiritual distress, and how is it related to stress?

References

1. American Psychiatric Association. (1991). *Diagnostic and statistical manual of mental disorders.* Washington, DC: American Psychiatric Press.

2. Baik, K., Hosseini, M., & Priesmeyer, H.R. (1989). Correlates of psychological distress in involuntary job loss. *Psychological Reports 65*(3), 1227-1233.

3. Beck, M. (December 20, 1993). Rage, resentment, and a ruger; motives of mass-murderer Colin Ferguson. *Newsweek 122*(25), 3.

4. Belle, D. (1990). Poverty and women's mental health. *American Psychologist,* March, 45(3), 385-388.

5. Berkman, L.R., & Syme, S.L. (1979). Social networks, host resistance, and mortality: a nine year follow-up of Almeada County residents. *American Journal of Epidemiology, 109,* 186-204.

6. Brown, L. (1993). A prayer a day. *American Health,* March, 27.

7. Burg, B. et al. (1992). Loving women: lesbian life and relationships. In *Boston women's health collective. The new our bodies ourselves* (pp. 177-182) New York: Touchstone.

8. Carpentino, L.J. (1992). *Nursing diagnosis: Application to clinical practice* (3rd ed.). Philadelphia: J.B. Lippincott.

9. Catalano, R. (1991). The health effects of economic insecurity. *The American Journal of Public Health 81*(9), 1148-1152.

10. Chamberlain, K. & Zika, S. (1990). The minor events approach to stress: support for the use of daily hassles. *British Journal of Psychology,* 81, 469-81.

11. Cotton, P. (1992). Attacks on homosexual persons may be increasing but many "bashings" are still not reported to police. *Journal of American Medical Association* 267(22), 2999-2931.

12. Creed, F. (1993). Life events and stress. *Current Opinion in Psychiatry 6* (2), 269-273.

13. Cyrus, V. (1993). *Experiencing race, class, and gender in the United States.* Mountain View, CA: Mayfield.

14. Delongis, A.D., Coyne, J.C., Dakof, G., Folkman, S., & Lazarus, R.S. (1982). Relationship of daily hassles, uplifts, and major life events to health status. *Health Psychology, 1*(2), 119-136.

15. Dohrenwend, B.P., et al. (1990). Measuring life events: the problem of variability within event categories. *Stress Medicine 6*(3), 179-187.

16. Dooley, D., Catalano, R., Rook, K., & Serxner, S. (1989). Economic stress and suicide: multilevel analyses. *Suicide and Life Threatening Behavior, 19*(4), 337-351.

17. Fowler, J.F. (1986). *Stages of faith: the psychology of human development and the quest for meaning.* New York: Harper & Row.

18. Fowler, J.F. (1991). Stages in faith consciousness. In Oser, F.K., & Scarlett, W.G. (Eds.), *Religious development in childhood and adolescence.* San Franscisco: Jossey-Bass.

19. Frost, T.F., & Clayson, D.E. (1991). The measurement of self-esteem, stress-related life events, and locus of control among unemployed blue-collar workers. *Journal of Applied Social Psychology, 21*(14), 1402-1417.

20. Goode, E. (1995, June 5). Eight seconds to a new beginning. *U.S. News & World Report,* 8-9.

21. Gruen, R., Folkman, S., & Lazarus, R. (1989). Centrality and individual differences in the meaning of daily hassles. *Journal of Personality, 56,* 743-762.

22. Hafen, B.Q., Frandsen, K.J., Karren, K.J., & Hooker, K.R. (1992). *The health effects of attitudes, emotions, and relationships.* Provo, UT: EMS Associates.

23. Harlow, H.F. (1953). Mice, monkeys, men and motives. *Psychological Review, 60,* 23-32.

24. Heilbroner, R. (1993). Stereotypes, prejudice and discrimination. In Cyrus, V. (Ed.) *Experiencing race, class, and gender in the United States* (pp. 144-145). Mountain View, CA: Mayfield.

25. Holmes, T.H., & Rahe, R.H. (1967). Social readjustment rating scale. *Journal of Psychosomatic Medicine, 11,* 213-218.

26. Kanner, A.D., Coyne, J.C., Schaefer, C., & Lazarus, R.S. (1981). Comparison of two modes of stress measurement: daily hassles and uplifts versus major life events. *Journal of Behavioral Medicine. 4*(1), 1-37.

27. Kiecolt-Glaser, J.K., et al. (1988). Marital discord and immunity in males. *Psychosomatic Medicine, 50,* 213-229.

28. Klinghoffer, D. (1993). Fired, ready, aim: the evolution of violent behavior from disgruntled employees and others who do not get what they want. *National Review, 45*(8), 56-58.

29. Kozier, B., Erb, G., & Olivieri, R. (1991) *Fundamentals of Nursing.* Redwood City, CA: Addison Wesley.

30. Lazarus, R.S. (1990). Theory-based stress measurement. *Psychological Inquiry, 1*(1), 3-13.

31. Lazarus, R., & Folkman, S. (1985) *Stress appraisal & coping.* New York: Springer.

32. Madrid, A. (1993). Missing people and others. In Anderson, M.L. (Ed.), *Race, class, and gender: an anthology* (pp. 6-11). Belmont, CA: Wadsworth Pub.

33. McFall, M., et al. (1989). Psychophysiologic and neuroendocrine findings in posttraumatic stress disorder: a review of theory and research. *Journal of Anxiety Disorders, 3,* 243-257.

34. Minkowitz, D. (1992). It's still open season on gays. *The Nation, 254*(11), 368-381.

35. Overholser, J.C., Norman, W.H., & Miller, I.W. (1990). Life stress and social support in depressed patients. *Behavioral Medicine, Fall,* 125-131.

36. Paloutzian, R.T., & Ellison, C.W. (1982). Loneliness, spiritual well-being, and the quality of life. In Peplau L.A., & Perlman, D. (Eds.). *Loneliness: a sourcebook of current theory research, and therapy.* New York: J Wiley and Sons.

37. Peck, M.S. (1987). The different drum: community making and peace. New York: Simon and Schuster.

38. Pooley, E. (April 18, 1994). Capitalizing on a killer: a spurious "black rage" defense. *New York Magazine,* 16(27), 38-40.

39. Poppy, J. (1993, Jan/Feb). War without end. *Men's Health,* 8, (1), 70-92.

40. Rabkin, J.G., & Streuning E.L. (1976). Life events, stress, and illness. *Science, 194,* 1013-1020.

41. Richmond, S. (1991). Depression in a recession. *Kiplinger's Personal Financial Magazine, 45*(3), 78.

42. Roberts, S.V. (1995, April 3). Staring back into the eyes of evil. *U.S. News & World Report,* 118, (3).

43. Roberts, S.V., Gest, T., Walsh, K.T., & Popkin, J. (1995, May 8). After the heartbreak. *U.S. News & World Report,* 118, (18), 27-29.

44. Romero, G.J., Castro, F., & Cervantes, R.C. (1988). Latinas without work. *Psychology of Women Quarterly, 12,* 281-297.

45. Shoemaker, W.G., et al. (1993). Urban violence in Los Angeles in the aftermath of the riots: a perspective from health care professionals with implications for social reconstruction. *Journal of the American Medical Association, 270*(23), 2833-2838.

46. Smith, S.L. (1993). Violence in the workplace: a call for help. *Occupational Hazards, 55*(10) 39-34.

47. Solomon J., & King, P. (July 19, 1993). Waging war in the workplace: violence on the job. *Newsweek, 122*(3), 30-33.

48. Staples, B. (1993). Just walk on by. In *Experiencing race, class, and gender in the United States* (pp. 180-182). Mountain View, CA: Mayfield.

49. Tetzeli, R. (October 5, 1991). Economy creates more stress. *Fortune,* Oct, 11-13.

50. Thompson, D.C. (1993). The male role stereotype. In *Experiencing race, class, and gender in the United States* (pp. 146-148). Mountain View, CA: Mayfield.

51. Turner, R.J. (1983). Direct, indirect, and moderating effects of social support on psychological distress and associated conditions. In Kaplan, H. (Ed.), *Psychosocial stress: trends in theory and research.* New York: Academic Press.

52. Wagner, B.M. (1990). Major and daily stress and psychopathology: On the adequacy of the definitions and methods. *Stress-Medicine, 6*(3), 217-226.

53. Weinberger, M., Hiner, S.L., & Tierney, W.M. (1987). In support of hassles as a measure of stress in predicting health outcomes. *Journal of Behavioral Medicine, 10*, 19-31.

54. Wilhelm, M.S., & Ridley, C.A. (January, 1988). Stress and unemployment in rural non-farm couples: a study of hardships and coping resources. *Family Relations, 37*, 50-54.

55. Wolf, T.M., et al. (1989). Relationships of hassles, uplifts and life events to psychological well-being in 55 medical students. *Behavioral Medicine, 15*(1), 37-45.

56. Yankelovich, D. (February 20, 1992). What economists don't understand. *Fortune, 125*(3).

Name: _____ Date: _____

Social Support Table

1. Draw a picture of a large conference table.

2. Place any number of chairs at the table.

3. Decide who sits at the head of the table and why.

4. Fill the other seats at the table with members of your personal social network.

5. For each person, answer the following questions:

    - What type of support do I need from this person?

    - What type of support do I get from this person?

    - What type of support would I never ask for from this person?

    - What do I give up in return for this support?

    - Is it worth it? (If yes, why?).

6. If you could add one more chair, what type of support would you like to receive from the person who would occupy it?

Hassles/Uplifts Inventory

Directions: On the following pages, circle the events that have affected you in the past month. (This is not a complete listing.) Then look at the numbers to the right of the items you circled. Indicate by circling a 1, 2, or 3 how often each of the circled events has occurred in the last month. If an event did not occur in the last month, do not circle it.

UPLIFTS	HOW OFTEN		
	Somewhat Often	Moderately Often	Extremely Often
Getting enough sleep	1	2	3
Practicing your hobby	1	2	3
Being lucky	1	2	3
Saving money	1	2	3
Nature	1	2	3
Liking fellow workers	1	2	3
Not working (on vacation, laid-off, etc.)	1	2	3
Gossiping; "shooting the bull"	1	2	3
Successful financial dealings	1	2	3
Being rested	1	2	3
Feeling healthy	1	2	3
Finding something presumed lost	1	2	3
Recovering from illness	1	2	3
Staying or getting in good physical shape	1	2	3
Being with children	1	2	3
"Pulling something off"; getting away with something	1	2	3
Visiting, phoning, or writing someone	1	2	3
Relating well with your spouse or lover	1	2	3
Completing a task	1	2	3
Giving a compliment	1	2	3

Cont'd

Hassles/Uplifts Inventory (cont'd)

HASSLES	SEVERITY		
	Somewhat Severe	Moderately Severe	Extremely Severe
Not enough money for food	1	2	3
Too many interruptions	1	2	3
Unexpected company	1	2	3
Too much time on hands	1	2	3
Having to wait	1	2	3
Concerns about accidents	1	2	3
Being lonely	1	2	3
Not enough money for health care	1	2	3
Fear of confrontation	1	2	3
Financial security	1	2	3
Silly practical mistakes	1	2	3
Inability to express yourself	1	2	3
Physical illness	1	2	3
Side effects of medication	1	2	3
Concerns about medical treatment	1	2	3
Physical appearance	1	2	3
Fear of rejection	1	2	3
Difficulties with getting pregnant	1	2	3
Sexual problems that result from physical problems	1	2	3
Sexual problems other than those resulting from physical problems	1	2	3
Concerns about health in general	1	2	3

Scoring:

Tally your scores for both the Hassles and Uplifts scales. There is no absolute cut-off score for either hassles or uplifts that you can use in evaluating your risk for stress-related illness. In general, the higher your hassles score, the greater your risk for stress-related disorders. The higher your uplift score, the greater your ability to cancel out the negative effects of hassles. Both scales should be taken and evaluated together.

Name: _____ Date: _____

Faith Assessment

1. List three things in which you have faith.

   _____

   _____

   _____

2. Describe the feelings you have about these three things.

   _____

   _____

   _____

3. Describe one incident when your faith in any/all of these things helped you either prevent or cope with a physical or mental illness.

   _____

   _____

   _____

CHAPTER 5

The Effects of Stress on the Body and Mind

CHAPTER OBJECTIVES

- Define psychosomatic illness.
- Differentiate between psychogenic and somatogenic disease.
- Describe the effects of chronic stress on the following body systems:
    - Endocrine system
    - Muscular system
    - Cardiovascular system
    - Immune system
    - Digestive system
- Describe the role of chronic stress in the development of a variety of diseases/illnesses.
- Describe the role of stress in the development of a variety of psychological problems.

In this chapter, we examine the relationship between stress and disease, paying particular attention to psychosomatic illness. We differentiate between the effects of short-term, acute stress and long-term, chronic stress. The positive effects of challenges are compared with the negative consequences of too much stress. An in-depth look at the effects of long-term stress on the quality of our lives is provided. Explaining how chronic stress affects the physiological functioning of key body systems and examining how breakdowns in those systems lead to specific types of illnesses and disease is also discussed.

Psychosomatic Disease and Stress

psychosomatic

the interaction of the mind and body in the disease process

The term **psychosomatic** was coined by Philip Deutsch[16] to illustrate the interaction between the mind and body in the disease process. Diseases associated with stress have often been trivialized as being "all in one's head," or *psychosomatic*. In our culture, there seems to be a bias against diseases that are not linked to a clear, causative organism or a germ that is responsible for the problem.

In actuality, susceptibility to infectious diseases and the development of any type of illness, whether caused by an infectious or communicable organism, never occurs without mental processes. As we have seen in chapters 2 and 3, our brains are intimately linked with physiological functioning at the cellular level. Our perception of the events going on around us affect nerve impulses, chemical reactions, and other physiological processes. Why one person develops a disease and another similarly receptive person does not, often has to do with a variety of factors beyond the disease-producing germ itself.

KEY
TO UNDERSTANDING

In actuality, susceptibility to infectious diseases and the development of any illness, whether caused by an infectious or comunicable organism, never occurs without mental processes.

Psychogenic Disease

psychogenic

psychosomatic illnesses without a causative germ

Psychogenic and **somatogenic** are two categories of psychosomatic disease.[20] Psychogenic disease refers to psychosomatic illnesses that are without a causative organism, or germ. These diseases, such as bronchial asthma, chronic backache, migraine headaches, peptic ulcers, and colitis, are conditions that arise when the structure and function of body parts and tissues are altered by a chronic stress response.

somatogenic

psychosomatic illness that involves a causative germ

Chronic stress is a risk factor that contributes to the development of some diseases, such as cardiovascular disease. The degenerative process of atherosclerosis is worsened by the physiological changes in the body caused by the ongoing stress response. There is, however, no causative germ involved.

Somatogenic Disease

With somatogenic disease, a causative organism exists. The long-term effects of the stress response weaken the body's defenses, making a person more susceptible to infection and the development of disease. A person in college may be susceptibe to mononucleosis, for instance, due in part to the effects of chronic stressors on his or her immune system. The link between somatogenic disease and stress is less direct and more difficult to prove because many other factors, ranging from a person's behavior to the **virulence** of the invading germ, must be taken into consideration.

virulence

the strength of an organism; related to its ability to infect a susceptible person

The Effects of Acute, High-Level Stress on Disease

In acute, alarm phase stress we are in a state of complete mental and physical readiness. We have an abundance of energy at our disposal because our digestive system shuts down and our liver works overtime to convert all available energy sources, such as sugars, fats, and proteins, into a usable state.

Our endocrine system contributes to this energy mobilization by secreting the powerful adrenal hormones, epinephrine and norepinephrine. Our cardiovascular system pumps oxygen- and energy-rich blood through our arteries at a greater rate and force, supplying every critical area in our body, from our brains, so we can think clearly, to our skeletal muscles, so we can act quickly. Our nervous system quickly responds to all incoming stimuli and fires off nerve impulses at an astounding rate. Our muscles are contracted, energized, and ready to move. Our pupils are dilated, with our eyes scanning the scene clearly. In this alarm state, we are at the brink, ready to fight or flee. Whether the stimulus is a perceived harm, loss, or challenge, and whatever the stressful situation may be, we are energized and primed for action. Fig. 5-1 illustrates the steps in this reaction.

The effects of acute, or alarm phase, stress responses are not harmful as long as we act and use this energy. The rapid mobilization of energy created to assist us in confronting a threat, a harm, or a challenge is a positive, life-saving adaptive mechanism. Although the effects are intense, they are short-lived and begin to reverse once the source of stress is removed or coped with effectively.

The result of this type of stress response on the body is fatigue. With a lifestyle that is balanced and includes proper nutrition, exercise, and adequate rest, the body can rejuvenate itself and not suffer any harm. The greater the frequency of events that provoke alarm reactions, the greater the

2. Hypothalamus sends
message via pituitary
to rest of body through
nerves and adrenals.

3. Direct nerve stimulation and
chemicals released by adrenals
cause the physiological
fight or flight response.
- Brain shifts into
full alert
- Breathing and
heart rates increase
- Increased sweat
production
cools the body
- Blood coagulability
increases
- Glucose fuel stored
in liver and muscles
becomes available
for action
- Blood supply to
kidneys and intestines
decreases
- Blood and fuel are
sent to muscles in
preparation for
movement

1. Nervous system
perceives
stressors.

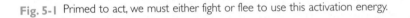

Fig. 5-1 Primed to act, we must either fight or flee to use this activation energy.

need for rest to help the body restore the energy that was used up in coping with the stressor. The effects of a moderate amount of short-term stress on psychogenic and somatogenic disease is negligible.

Unfortunately, we are often stressed by situations and people that we cannot fight or run away from—stressors that are going to be around for some time. When we do not act and use the energy that has been mobilized to either eliminate or cope with the source of stress, the body cannot remain in this state of activation for long periods. Our bodies then shift into a low-level, resistance phase response, and we begin to suffer the effects of coping with a long-term, chronic stressor.

The Effects of Chronic, Low-level Stress on the Body

The effects of chronic low-level stress on disease are most clear with psychogenic diseases. Over time the stress response exerts a generalized wear and tear on the body. When body parts and systems are forced to work overtime for long periods without rest and rejuvenation, they begin to malfunction and eventually break down. The relationship between stress and psychogenic disease is most direct with five body systems: the endocrine, muscular, digestive, cardiovascular, and immune systems. Excess strain on these systems results in inefficiency and a gradual breakdown in their performance, followed by an increased susceptibility to a host of illnesses. In the next section, we examine this phenomenon, first by explaining the relationship between stress and the body system under study and then by looking at individual diseases and conditions that are associated with malfunction of this system.

Stress and the Endocrine System

The stress response is intimately linked to endocrine system functioning. Besides being the key component in perpetuating the chronic, low-level stress response, the endocrine system is responsible for a variety of other functions, ranging from reproduction to growth. Chronic stress has the potential to interfere with and shut down these other endocrine functions.

The endocrine system, as discussed in Chapter 3, relies on a feedback mechanism involving the hypothalamus, the pituitary, other endocrine glands, the bloodstream, and hormones. The whole system must work together; if one component breaks down, the whole system can go down.

Research in the area was hampered for years by a lack of sophisticated instruments and methodology. Selye[41] and others, working with laboratory animals, observed structural changes in their subjects caused by exposure to acute and chronic stressors. Because they lacked the sophisticated instruments and methods needed to pinpoint and quantify specific hormones, they used **morphological** changes, such as enlarged adrenal glands and heavier pituitary glands, to indicate the response to stressors. Adrenal gland weight, before and after exposure to stressors, was used as an indicator of adrenal functioning while under stress.[30] Selye[41] characterized the following syndrome associated with chronic stress: increased activity followed by enlargement of the adrenal cortex, swollen lymph glands, atrophy of the thymus, and stomach ulcers.

Early findings in animal research have been replicated with human subjects. The same physiological changes been noted in humans and the link between these responses and the brain has been clarified, establishing the relationship between our thoughts and the stress response.[30]

There are many varied effects of the disruption in normal endocrine functioning. Chronic hormonal imbalance is related to a host of illnesses, ranging from sexual dysfunction to lowered immune system functioning.

KEY
TO UNDERSTANDING

When body parts or systems ar forced to work overtime for long periods without rest and rejuvenation, they begin to malfunction and eventually breakdown.

morphological
having to do with the form and structure of organisms

Chronic Endocrine System Stress and Disease

A discussion of how hormones are associated with the stress response takes place in Chapter 3. In this section, we examine how the three hormones, epinephrine (adrenaline), norepinephrine (noradrenaline), and cortisol are implicated in a variety of medical problems.

Heart Disease. Epinephrine and norepinephrine work together to speed up circulation, helping to mobilize the energy needed to fight or flee. Epinephrine causes blood vessels, especially the smaller ones in our extremities, to constrict, thereby forcing the heart to pump under greater pressure. Chronically increased blood pressure results in a condition called *hypertension*, which is a primary risk factor for stroke and heart attack.

Norepinephrine also causes blood vessels to constrict and it interferes with blood platelets and the red blood cells. Platelets are cell fragments found in blood and are involved in clotting. Red blood cells are primarily involved in transporting oxygen throughout the body. Excess norepinephrine has been shown to disturb platelets and red blood cells, causing damage to the endothelium, which is the lining of the heart and blood vessels.[23] Damage to the endothelium is considered to be a precursor to the development of atherosclerosis, or hardening of the arteries. Norepinephrine also converts another stress hormone, testosterone, into estradiol, a little-understood chemical that is significantly elevated in men who have heart attacks.[23] Although not completely understood, estradiol and other estrogens play a role in controlling fluid and electrolyte balance, which contribute to the regulation of blood pressure.

Cortisol, a very potent hormone, inhibits the breakdown of epinephrine and norepinephrine and increases the body's sensitivity to these substances. In doing this, it interferes with the body's ability to relax and to reverse the process of stress activation. Cortisol increases blood cholesterol and fat levels by releasing these substances from fatty tissue so they can be converted to energy through gluconeogenesis. A chronic stress response can result in continual activation of this process, unnecessarily elevating serum cholesterol and fat, which are recognized risk factors for heart disease. Excess cortisol levels have also been connected to damage to the endothelium.[23]

Sexual disorders. Another result of chronic stress and endocrine system functioning is diminished sexual response (Fig. 5-2). Stress is implicated in the development of problems associated with the sexual desire and sexual response among men. Profound physiological and endocrine changes that accompany depression, fatigue, and stress states contribute to a loss of sexual motivation; the central nervous system and neurotransmitters are affected and the available supply of androgen, a sex hormone that controls

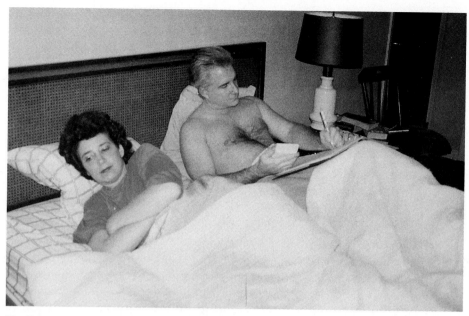

Fig. 5-2 Stress can diminish your interest in sex.

testosterone production is lowered. Men under chronic stress show a significant and consistent depression in levels of testosterone, a gonadal hormone linked to sexual desire. When the source of stress is removed or coped with and testosterone levels return to normal, sexual desire begins to return.[28]

The mechanism of this action, although not completely understood, centers around messages passed from the hypothalamus to the pituitary in response to perceived stress. The hypothalamus triggers a decrease in the secretion of the pituitary hormones, follicle-stimulating hormone (FSH), and luteinizing hormone (LH). These hormones are responsible for stimulating the testes to produce testosterone. This decreased level of FSH and LH results in decreased levels of testosterone, which affect the sex centers in the brain and result in a loss of sexual desire and decreased sexual response.[28]

Another endocrine link to sexual disorders is related to a byproduct of excess corticosteroid production. Increased blood cortisone levels are related to the suppression of male sex hormones.

Kaplan[28] speculates that the effects of chronic stress on male sexual response are somewhat varied, with not all men responding equally. She states that some men may be more susceptible than others to impaired sexual response because of a hereditary predisposition, or "a weak link," to use

Selye's terminology. Kaplan[28] also describes the role of emotions and comfort level in sexual response and discusses how stress interferes with one's ability to relax and let the sexual response unfold.

Premenstrual syndrome. Another endocrine disorder affected by stress is premenstrual syndrome (PMS). PMS is characterized by myriad physical and psychological symptoms that appear anywhere from 2 to 6 days before the onset of menstruation. Psychosocial symptoms include negative emotions, such as anxiety, irritability, depression, anger, insomnia, confusion, and social withdrawal. Physical symptoms include fluid retention, breast tenderness, weight gain, headaches, dizziness, nausea, increased appetite, and a craving for sweets.[12]

Most discussions of PMS emphasize its negative physiological and psychological aspects. PMS has also been used as a legal defense for women who have committed violent acts, implying that the overwhelming power of their emotional distress rendered them incapable of controlling their behaviors. The politicizing of PMS and its use as a legal defense may work against women as this feeds into continuing negative gender role stereotypes of female emotions, menstruation, and the inability of women to hold positions of responsibility.[38] This emphasis on the negative aspects of the syndrome ignores the fact that for many women, menstruation is also a time of peak creativity and productivity.[38]

Research about the causes, nature, and treatment of PMS lack consistency. Although most PMS researchers believe that shifting hormonal balances play a key role in the etiology of the condition, the specific hormones and exact mechanisms of action are unclear. A change in the ratio of estrogen to progesterone has been implicated as has a change in the level of mineralocorticoids that control fluid retention. Still other theorists propose that the key hormones involved in menstruation are those of the brain that influence mood.[32]

Although estimates of the number of PMS sufferers vary from to 20% to 75% of women,[32] most researchers agree that between 3% to 5% of women have serious enough symptoms to interfere with normal daily functioning.[38] One of the many problems in studying the extent and nature of PMS is the fact that symptoms are often transient, do not always occur, and are often unobservable.[32]

An interesting aspect of PMS is the relationship between womens' moods, attitudes and emotions, and the physiological symptoms that characterize the syndrome. Researchers are still trying to ascertain whether it is the negative emotions about menstruation and PMS that trigger the hormonal and other physiological changes or whether it is the physical discomfort that precipitates the psychological and social distress. As we have seen in this chapter, the two are intimately related through cortical, hypothalamic, pituitary, and adrenal functioning. There is evidence that dissatisfaction with one's gender role and marriage can increase the severity of PMS symptoms.[13] Marital distress, as discussed in Chapter 2, can be the cause of chronic, resistance-level stress capable of causing imbalances in circulating hormones.

For years, stress management has been advocated as part of a comprehensive PMS treatment program.[25] Stress-management techniques can help control the negative emotional and negative physical symptoms of PMS. Carefully controlled studies examining the role of stress management in the treatment of PMS are needed.

Stress and the Muscular System

Each muscle is actually a mass of millions of muscle cells, capable of being stimulated by nerve innervation during a stress response. When muscle contraction occurs and muscles are stimulated fully, they shorten, and movement, or work, is accomplished. When stimulated partially, **tension** occurs but no work is accomplished.[30] Muscles that are chronically tense, or partially contracted, result in a state of **bracing**. The three types of muscles are skeletal, smooth, and cardiac (Fig. 5-3).

tension

partial shortening of a muscle

bracing

a state of chronic muscle tension

Skeletal muscles. Skeletal muscles are also known as *striated muscles* because they have long bands of fibers, called *striations*, and can be controlled voluntarily. Skeletal muscles attach to and cover the skeleton. They are remarkably adaptable and allow us to perform a variety of tasks ranging from playing a violin to power-lifting massive weights (Fig. 5-4).

Smooth muscles. Unlike skeletal muscles, smooth muscles are neither striated nor capable of voluntary action. Smooth muscle tissue is found in the walls of vital internal organs, such as the stomach, bladder, and lungs. These muscles contract in response to involuntary chemical and nerve messages. We do not have to voluntarily contract our intestines, for instance, to move food along as it is digested.

Cardiac muscles. Cardiac muscle tissue, like skeletal muscle tissue, is striated. However, unlike skeletal muscle tissue, the movement of cardiac muscle is involuntary. The steady rates of a heart beat are set by a natural pacemaker that electrically stimulates the heart, causing it to beat.

Chronic Muscle Tension and Disease

Chronic, low-level stress results in constant muscle tension in all three types of muscle tissue. Acute, strenuous muscle contractions are not as harmful as chron-

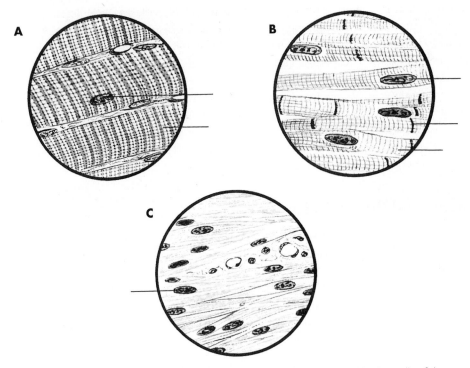

Fig. 5-3 **A**, Skeletal muscle is attached to bones. **B**, Cardiac muscle is found in the walls of the heart. **C**, Smooth muscle is most often found in visceral (hollow) organs, such as the stomach.

ic, mild tensing contractions. Chronic muscle tension is a continual byproduct of resistance-phase stress, which is the mild, low-level state of activation that our bodies are put in when we are continually stressed. Often the effects of chronic muscle tension go unnoticed until symptoms present themselves.

The usual symptom of chronic muscle tension in striated, skeletal muscles is pain in a muscle or muscle group. This pain is not attributed to acute overexertion, such as the muscle pain you feel after vigorous physical work. Pain symptoms can range from mild tension headaches to very painful spasms requiring rest and treatment. A symptom of chronic smooth muscle tension is disrupted functioning, such as a case of chronic constipation when tensing of the smooth muscles of the digestive system result in changes in digestion and elimination.

Furthermore, chronic muscle tension contributes to the perception of stress in the mind by conveying messages that are perceived by the brain as stressful.[20] In other words, when our muscles are tense, we feel "stressed" and this perception reinforces the tension. It is a vicious cycle that is only broken when we can get our muscles to relax (Fig. 5-5).

Fig. 5-4 Skeletal muscles are remarkably adaptable to a wide range of tasks, from playing the piano to working out with large amounts of weight.

Chronically tense muscles have been associated with negative health conditions related to skeletal muscles including headache, backache, temporomandibular joint (TMJ) disorder, eye disorders, and muscle spasms, pulls, and tears.[20]

Headache. Headache associated with chronic muscle tension is caused by involuntary contractions of the muscles of the eyes, forehead, neck, and jaw, which are usually unnoticable. Chronic tension in this region results in tension headaches. Tension headaches have a close relationship to emotional conflict; like migraines, they can be quite painful and debilitating.[40]

Backache. Backache, especially in the lower back region, is often the result of chronic muscle tension. As with tension headaches, backaches are the result of chronic, involuntary contractions of skeletal muscles. People who have lower back problems because of other conditions, such as obesity, poor posture, or disc injury, can compound their illness if they are also chronically stressed.

TMJ Syndrome. Temporomandibular joint (TMJ) syndrome, a disorder of the jaw, is often a result of a chronic grinding and clenching of the teeth called *bruxism*. This behavior occurs most often at night. In TMJ syndrome,

Fig. 5-5 When our muscles are tense, our brains tell us we are stressed.

a combination of facial pain, sensitive teeth, headaches, ringing in the ears, and clicking or popping sounds when a person opens and closes the mouth often occurs.[47]

Muscle pain. Chronically tense muscles are muscles that are constantly overworked; therefore these muscles are more susceptible to pulls, spasms, and tears. Muscle spasms, which are unrelenting, extreme contractions of a muscle or muscle group, are often the end-product of ignoring the early-warning signs of muscle tension, such as mild pain or tension.[20]

Stress and the Cardiovascular System

The relationship between stress and cardiovascular disease is perhaps the most studied and documented of all the stress-related disorders. When the cardiovascular system is stressed, it does not work entirely independently of other body systems, especially the endocrine system. Because of this, there is a considerable connection between the two systems in relation to the effects of the stress response.

The cardiovascular system can best be described as a closed system consisting of a pump, tubes, and fluid. The pump (heart) operates automatically at a predetermined rate, providing vital nutrients and removing waste products in the fluid (blood) as it moves under pressure through an interconnected network of flexible tubes (blood vessels) of varying diameters (Figs. 5-6 and 5-7). As we will see, stress affects all three components of this system.

The role of the cardiovascular system is to supply the body with oxygen-rich blood and nutrients and to remove waste products from the tissues and the cells. It does this in conjunction with the lungs, which provide fresh oxygen to the blood and remove carbon dioxide waste. These functions are critical, not only for the long-term health of the entire body but also for a zestful day-to-day quality of life.

People with impaired cardiovascular functioning simply do not have the amount of energy and ability necessary to perform at high levels for long periods of time; their bodies are being robbed of the vital nutrients and oxygen supplied by efficient heart and lung operation. Because all living tissue requires an ongoing, fresh supply of blood to perform effectively, cardiovascular problems affect all body systems. Long-term problems of the cardiovascular system can lead to malfunctioning, premature aging, and death of the body parts, systems, or the individual.

The health of the cardiovascular system is based on three factors. The first factor is the heart's ability to receive nourishment through its own coronary arteries. For the heart to pump efficiently, it must receive nourishment

KEY
TO UNDERSTANDING

The cardiovascular system is a closed system consisting of a pump (the heart), tubes (blood vessels), and fluid (the blood).

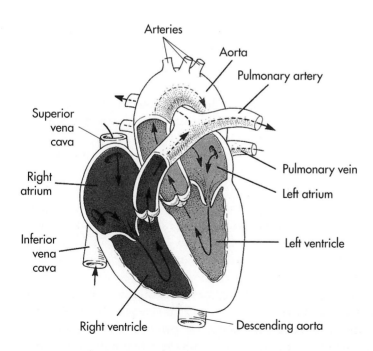

Fig. 5-6 The cardiovascular system.

arrhythmias

irregular heart
rhythms

spasms

sudden, involuntary
muscle twitches that
range in severity from
mild to very painful

veins

large blood vessels
that carry blood to
the heart

venules

small blood vessels
that carry blood to
the heart

arteries

large blood vessels
that carry blood away
from the heart

arterioles

the smallest vascular
branch of arterial
circulation

from the blood through its own network of coronary blood vessels. Although the heart's job is to pump blood to all body parts, it does not draw its own nutrients from this process. It is served by its own blood vessels, which must remain open and flexible, delivering an adequate supply of blood regardless of the demands on the heart muscle.

The second factor critical for a healthy heart is the heart's ability to maintain a steady, rhythmic beat despite varying demands made on it. For the heart to supply blood to critical parts of the body (the brain and heart muscle in particular) on a continuous basis, it must pump rhythmically under all situations. **Arrhythmias**, **spasms**, and irregular beating patterns are potentially life threatening because they could possibly lead to a failure to maintain an adequate supply of blood to critical tissue, especially in the brain.

Lastly, for a person to have a healthy heart, the blood vessels must be able to facilitate the passage of nutrient-rich blood by remaining open and flexible and maintaining normal pressure. The **veins**, **venules**, **arteries**, and **arterioles** facilitate the movement of blood by expanding and contracting in response to the heart's beating action. The beating of the heart and the pumping of blood exert pressure against the walls of blood vessels. This pressure is mediated by the blood vessels' ability to stretch during the work, or systolic, phase and bounce back during the rest, or diastolic, phase of a heartbeat. Blood vessels that are clear and pliable allow maximum blood flow under minimum pressure, a state that provides the optimal supply of nutrients and removal of waste without exerting undue wear and tear on the system.

Effects of Stress on the Cardiovascular System

Chronic, low-level stress can affect all three components of the cardiovascular system and jeopardize the health of the entire body. It is impossible to isolate these effects from endocrine system functioning in many cases because hormones are directly involved in stimulating cardiovascular functioning on several levels.

Chronic, low-level stress can accelerate the heart rate, making it pump faster and under greater pressure than necessary. It can also change the chemistry of the blood itself, flooding it with excess, life-threatening cholesterol, fats, and other substances. Lastly, low-level stress can change the makeup of the blood vessels, speeding up the process of atherosclerosis, or hardening of the arteries.

Chronic stress can also speed up the development of cardiovascular disease in persons with other risk factors, such as sedentary lifestyles, smoking, and diets high in fats and cholesterol. The combination of chronic stress and other risk factors can often be synergistic, resulting in negative consequences beyond the individual risks attributed to each separately.

Specific Effects of Stress on the Heart

As we have already examined in great detail, chronic, low-level stress results in accelerated heart rate and elevated blood pressure. What makes this combination a potentially deadly result of a chronic stress response is its insidious nature. Often, because these effects in resistance are less dramatic than during an alarm reaction, we do not notice them. Unless we check our resting pulse routinely, and monitor our blood pressure with a **sphygmomanometer**, we are usually unaware of elevations in either.

Additionally, it is long-term elevation of these functions that can cause severe health problems. Our heart rate and blood pressure normally respond to increased demands by elevating, thereby supplying extra blood to meet energy needs. When these needs are met, heart rate and blood pressure should return to their normal ranges.

Problems arise when they remain elevated for long periods. Chronic hypertension damages the **endothelium** of the blood vessels, making them more susceptible to the development of atherosclerosis. Chronic hypertension is also a major risk factor for stroke and heart attack. The increased blood pressure can dislodge **plaques** and send them coursing through the blood vessels. If they lodge in a blood vessel servicing the brain, a stroke occurs. If one lodges in a blood vessel servicing the heart, a heart attack results. Both conditions can be fatal.

sphygmo-manometer
instrument for measuring blood pressure

endothelium
squamous tissue that lines the walls of the heart, blood vessels, and lymphatic vessels

plaques
accumulations of fat and cholesterol on the endothelium

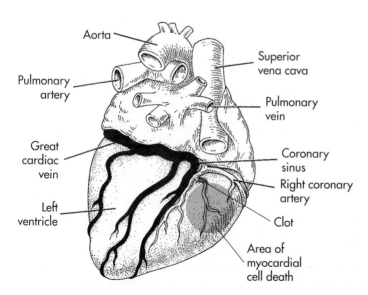

Fig. 5-7 A heart attack (myocardial infarction) occurs when a clot in one of the arteries that feeds the myocardium cuts off the blood supply, causing the cells in that area to die.

Specific Effects of Stress on Blood Chemistry

Chronic stress also affects blood chemistry, which contributes to changes in the structure of the blood vessels themselves. As we have already discussed in Chapter 3, under normal conditions the liver is responsible for producing more than 75% of all the cholesterol needed by the body. Any excess cholesterol that is not needed by the body is removed by the liver. The liver works overtime when under chronic stress, producing extra cholesterol to fuel the stress response while at the same time trying to get rid of any cholesterol that is not needed by the body.

The liver simply cannot keep up with these demands, and a certain amount of the cholesterol in circulation is deposited in the interior walls of the blood vessels. Eventually, these deposits accumulate, which results in a condition called *atherosclerosis.* Besides increased levels of cholesterol, hormonal changes disrupt the normal chemistry of the blood, making it a contributing factor to the hardening process in atherosclerosis.[23,35,49]

Specific Effects of Stress on the Blood Vessels

Arteriosclerosis is the general term used to describe any of a number of degenerative changes in the arteries leading to their decreased elasticity and reduced blood flow. *Atherosclerosis* is a specific term used to describe changes in the walls of large arteries caused by deposits of fatty plaque, fibrin (a clotting factor), cholesterol, and calcium (Fig. 5-8). These changes decrease the diameter of the artery's interior and make the arterial walls brittle. Once the blood vessels lose their elasticity, they become less efficient in transporting and processing nutrients and waste products.

Atherosclerosis is directly linked to increases in blood pressure. When the diameter of the blood vessels gets smaller and the body still requires the same volume of blood, the heart must pump more frequently and under greater pressure to meet this need. The loss of elasticity also contributes to the demands for increased pressure. This deadly combination contributes to both stroke and heart attack.

Chronic Stress and Migraine Headaches

Migraine headaches are another major problem associated with stress and the cardiovascular system. Migraine headaches are also referred to as vascular headaches because they involve the carotid artery. The common carotid artery that carries blood from the heart up each side of the head splits into two branches: the external carotid, which terminates in front of the ear; and the internal carotid, which disappears under the bones of the skull.

Migraine headaches typically affect only one side of the head. At some point before the migraine attack, the carotid arteries on the affected side of the head narrow, which may result in a flushing, or pallor, of the skin. This

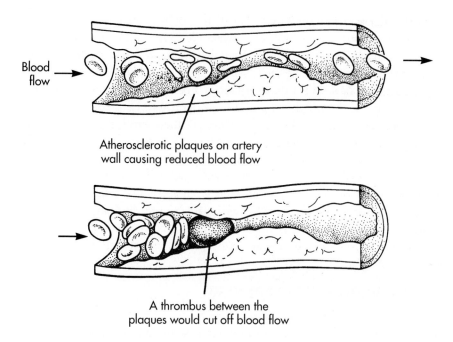

Atherosclerotic plaques on artery
wall causing reduced blood flow

A thrombus between the
plaques would cut off blood flow

Fig. 5-8 Atherosclerotic plaque in an artery.

narrowing of the arteries before the actual onset of a migraine produces a collection of symptoms called the **prodrome**. These prodromal symptoms include increased irritability, nausea, sensitivity to noise and light, and a sensation of seeing flashing lights. The prodrome starts 1 to 2 hours before the actual headache itself.[21]

After the prodrome and a period of constriction, the carotid arteries begin to swell. This dramatic constriction, followed by expansion, is responsible for the onset of the headache. Migraine headaches produce painful throbbing and intense pain that can last for several hours or days. Other accompanying symptoms can include nausea, vomiting, chills, sweating, edema, irritability, and extreme fatigue. An attack is often followed by dull neck and head pains and a great need for sleep. The constriction and dilation are believed to be associated with the release of the potent chemicals serotonin, which is a vasoconstrictor, and bradykinin, which is a vasodilator. Together they mediate the respective narrowing and widening of the carotid arteries.

Both physiological and psychological factors seem to be involved in migraine headaches. Migraines often run in families; an inherited migraine trait, carried through a recessive gene, is thought to be the cause.[40] Low serotonin levels, or deficiencies in the enzyme that metabolizes it, are believed to be related to the onset of migraines.[20]

prodrome

a group of symptoms occurring before the onset of illness

Migraine headache sufferers also share a personality type characterized as ambitious, perfectionistic, rigid, tense, or resentful, yet efficient and poised. In many cases, these individuals have experienced emotional crises before the onset of the headaches.[40] They often harbor resentment and hostility and are unable to vent these emotions. Feelings of anger and repressed rage are often present. These emotions are often well concealed and sometimes not even realized by migraine sufferers themselves. Psychotherapists treating patients with migraines find that symptoms are sometimes short-circuited when patients are able to vent their underlying hostility.[36]

As we discuss in Chapter 2, there is considerable evidence to support the relationship between illness and stress, anger, and hostility. Emotions, especially powerful emotions, such as hostility, rage, and anger, are quite capable of triggering an alarm response, which can evolve into chronic, resistance-level stress if the source is not alleviated or coped with effectively.

Stress and the Immune System

Another area in which the risks associated with chronic, low-level stress are clear and well documented is our immune system. Our immune system is a part of our body's defense network against illness and disease originating from factors and conditions both outside (exogenous) or inside (endogenous) ourselves. Our bodies are equipped, through mechanical and chemical defenses, with the ability to protect ourselves from exogenous invaders such as microorganisms, allergens, and other substances, or endogenous factors such as mutating cells or improperly functioning tissue.

Mechanical barriers are our first line of defense against invaders. Intact skin and mucous membranes set up a formidable barrier against invaders. However, germs, chemicals, and carcinogens, sometimes do break through, and when they do our immune system takes over.

The immune system is really a functional system rather than an organ system. Various organs that have other functions produce a variety of immune system components. Immune system organs are generally referred to as lymphoid organs because they are involved with the growth and utilization of lymphocytes, white blood cells that play a major role in immune system functioning. The lymph system is a major component of the immune system, with trillions of individual immune cells produced in bone marrow, the thymus, lymph nodes, spleen, tonsils, appendix, and other lymphatic tissue in the small intestine, called Peyer's patches[23] (Fig. 5-9).

Lymphocyte cells originate in the soft tissue within the long bones of the body. From the bone marrow, some of these cells migrate to the thymus. Lymphocytes that grow and mature in the thymus are called *T* **cells**. Other lymphocytes are called *B* **cells**.

T cells

a small, circulating lymphocyte that matures in the thymus and mediates cellular immune response

B cells

lymphocytes that grow and mature in bone marrow and places other than the thymus

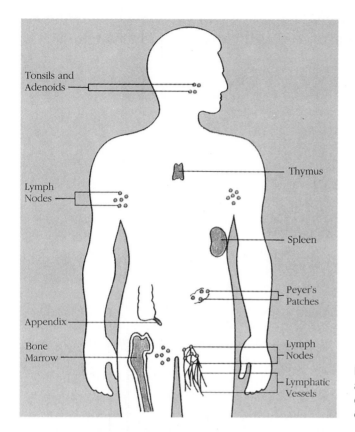

Tonsils and Adenoids

Lymph Nodes

Appendix

Bone Marrow

Thymus

Spleen

Peyer's Patches

Lymph Nodes

Lymphatic Vessels

Fig. 5-9 The organs of the immune system, also known as lymphoid organs. They are concerned with the growth, development, and deployment of lymphocites.

Lymphocytes are most responsible for orchestrating the functions of the immune system. The immune system has about 1 trillion lymphocytes. *B* cells secrete **antibodies**, chemicals that match with specific invaders called **antigens**. These antibodies are responsible for inactivating antigens, thereby making them incapable of causing disease.

T cells do not secrete antibodies but act as messengers and killers, locating and destroying invading antigens. Some *T* cells, called *helpers*, help activate the production of other *T* and *B* cells (see box on p. 174). Other *T* cells, called *suppressors*, stop the production of antigens, calling off the attack (Fig. 5-10).

The number of *T* and *B* cells must be balanced for them to perform effectively. When the ratio of *T* to *B* cells is out of balance, the immune response is compromised and does not work effectively.

Other key chemicals that are produced by the immune system are macrophages, monocytes, and granulocytes. These chemicals envelop, destroy, and digest invading microorganisms and other antigens. Known generally as phagocytes, they team up with more than 20 types of proteins

antibodies

chemicals of the immune system that are protective and are produced in response to specific invaders

antigens

foreign substances perceived by the body as invaders

Functions of Cells and Molecules Involved in Immunity

Element	Function in the immune response
B cell	Lymphocyte that resides in the lymph nodes, spleen, or other lymphoid tissues where it is induced to replicate by antigen-binding and helper *T* cell interactions.
Plasma cell	Produces huge numbers of the same antibody (immunoglobulin); represents further specialization of *B* cell clone descendants.
Helper *T* cell	A regulatory *T* cell that binds with a specific antigen presented by a macrophage; on circulating into the spleen and lymph nodes, it stimulates the production of other cells (killer *T* cells and *B* cells) to help fight the invader.
Killer *T* cell	Recruited by antigen presented by a macrophage; activity enhanced by helper *T* cells; its specialty is killing virus-invaded body cells, as well as body cells that have become cancerous.
Suppressor *T* cell	Slows or stops the activity of *B* and *T* cells once the infection (or attack by foreign cells) has been conquered.
Macrophage	Engulfs and digests antigens that it encounters and presents parts of them on its plasma membrane for recognition by *T* cells bearing receptors for the same antigen; this function, antigen presentation, is essential for normal, cell-mediated responses; also releases chemicals that activate *T* cells.

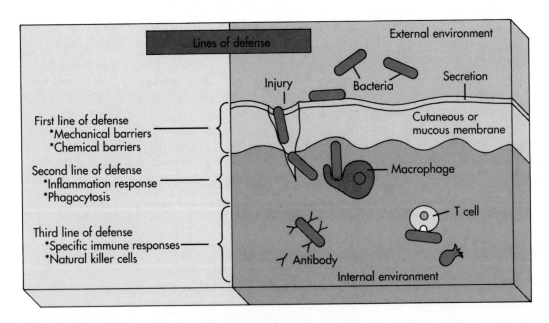

Fig. 5-10 The cell wars that occur in our bodies everyday.

that make up the immune system's complement system. This system is triggered by antibodies that lock onto antigens and cause redness, warmth, swelling, and inflammation, all components of the war against invaders.[23]

The lymphatic system, much like the cardiovascular system, is a network of vessels, each smaller than the next. The vessels connect all of the body's tissues, bathing them in a clear lymph fluid (Fig. 5-11). Lymph nodes are like dams, where foreign particles and other cellular debris are trapped and filtered out of the fluid by webbed tissue. The system of small tributaries merges with the larger branches at the base of the neck where **lymphatic ducts** merge their fluid with the bloodstream. There, lymphocytes and other chemicals of the immune system are carried through the blood to tissues throughout the body where they might be needed. Gradually, they filter through the tissues back into lymphatic fluid and the process starts over again.[23]

The immune system has five primary responsibilities:[48]

1. recognizing foreign substances that do not belong in your body, such as germs, allergens, and irritants
2. defending you by attacking these invaders
3. protecting you from reinfection from these same invaders in the future

lymphatic ducts
portals where the lymph system empties into the bloodstream

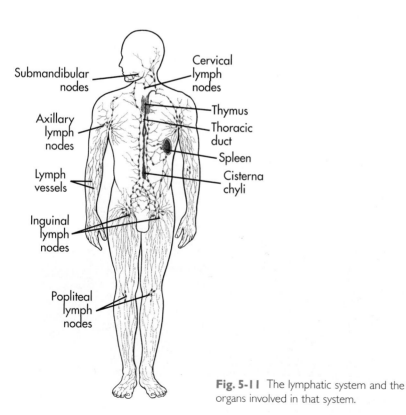

Fig. 5-11 The lymphatic system and the organs involved in that system.

4. performing surveillance for and destroying mutant cells before they can become cancerous

5. resisting recurrences of chronic infections because of untreatable conditions such as viral infections

A breakdown in any part of the immune system can compromise its ability to perform any of these five functions and can lead to a variety of health problems including immunosuppression or hyperimmunity. Immunosuppression results in a diminished ability of one or more of the components of the system. Hyperimmunity has the opposite effect, resulting in uncontrolled activation of one or more parts of the system. In either case, there is an imbalance in the finely tuned precision required for the system to work at peak efficiency.

There are two types of immunity—natural and acquired (Fig. 5-12). Natural immunity is nonspecific, offering general protection against all types of illness and invaders. The chemicals, proteins, and white blood cells that make up this line of defense are not produced in response to specific types of invading organisms; they are produced routinely by the organs and tissues that contribute to immune system functioning. As long as our bodies are healthy and well nourished, these substances will be available to help us.

Acquired immunity is distinguished from natural immunity by three characteristics: specificity, diversity, and memory. Acquired immunity is specific to individual antigens. It is estimated that there are more than 1 million antigens and our bodies are capable of mounting a few specific immune response against each one.[44]

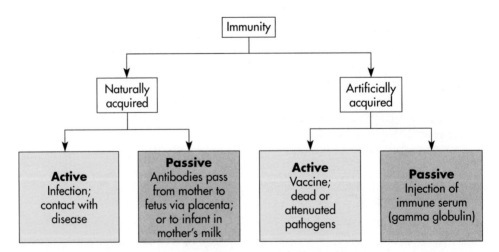

Fig. 5-12 The blue boxes signify active types of immunity in which the immune system has built up defenses. The gray boxes signify short-lived, passive types of immunity in which the immune system has no memory established.

The immune system is also able to remember its actions. Each antigen triggers the production of individual memory cells that circulate constantly through our bodies to ensure lifelong protection. If we are ever invaded by the same organism in the future, these memory cells ensure that future immune responses will be both potent and immediate.[44]

We obtain acquired immunity in three ways: by a temporary supply of antibodies from our mothers at birth, which lasts for 3 months; by becoming infected with and surviving certain diseases; and by vaccination.

Psychoneuroimmunology, Stress, and Immune Disorders

Much of what we know about the relationship between the brain, the nervous system, and the immune response has come out of the field of psychoneuroimmunology (PNI). PNI was developed in 1964 by Robert Ader, the Director of the Division of Behavioral and Psychosocial Medicine at the University of Rochester.

Psychoneuroimmunology is the study of the intricate interaction of consciousness (psycho), brain and central nervous system (neuro), and the body's defense against external infection and aberrant cell division (immunology).[36] Although a relatively new medical discipline, the philosophical roots of the connection between physical health, the brain, and emotions can be traced to Aristotle.[22] Much of what we know about the effects of stress on the body has come from this science. Three major reviews of psychoneuroimmunology literature, by Pelletier and Herzing in 1988, O'Leary in 1990, and Vollhardt in 1991, chronicle this emerging field and discuss some of its major findings.

Psychoneuroimmunology and immunosuppression. Vollhardt[50] found that, according to most major PNI theorists, stress and psychiatric disorders such as depression and anxiety are the most common neurological links to immune system dysfunction. Vollhardt chronicled some of the major studies implicating such negative emotional states and immune suppression. Pelletier and Herzing[36] also described the role of stress, loneliness, hopelessness, and depression in immunosuppression. O'Leary[34] described the effects of chronic stress on immunosuppression, paying particular attention to the variables of social disruption, psychological depression, and negative personality attributes.

Several studies have shown that chronic stress exerts a general **immunosuppressive effect** that suppresses or withholds the body's ability to initiate a prompt, efficient immune reaction.[2,19,23] This has been attributed to the abundance of corticosteroids produced during chronic stress, which produces an imbalance in corticosteroid levels and weakens immunocompetence.[37] This weakening of immune function is also attributed to gen-

immunosuppressive effect
anything that slows down or interferes with correct immune response

eral strain on the various body parts associated with the production and maintenance of the immune system.

For example, atrophy of the thymus, a key component of the immune system, has been documented by Selye.[41] Shrinking of the thymus results in its inability to produce *T* cells or the hormones needed to stimulate them. This can lead to an imbalance and inefficiency of the entire immune response.

Furthermore, chronic stress can deplete nutritional factors associated with immune system functioning. Key nutrients, particularly the water-soluble vitamins C and B complex, are depleted as a result of chronic stress.[37]

Stress has also been implicated in weakening the part of the immune system responsible for surveillance of the body's own mutating cells. During stress these mutant cells are not routed out and destroyed because they are not identified by the weakened immune system. Left unchecked, they proliferate and spread, causing cancer.[37]

Psychoneuroimmunology and Hyperactive Immunity. The effects of stress and other psychological attributes on hyperactive immunity have also been examined.[50] Although most PNI research focuses on immune suppression and its effects on disease, there is literature linking stress and psychological disorders with hyperimmunity. Hyperimmunity is characterized as an exaggerated autoimmune response, meaning that the body literally turns on itself, perceiving self as an antigen. Autoimmune disorders linked to stress include, but are not limited to, rheumatoid arthritis, ulcerative colitis, psoriasis, and systemic lupus erythematosus.

There are both behavioral and immunological adaptations that occur during stressful situations. Because of a central nervous system link mediated by the production of corticotropin-releasing hormone, the stress response can affect certain inflammatory diseases such as rheumatoid arthritis.[46] The perception of threat activates not only the stress response but also an autoimmune inflammatory response. Because of the link, ongoing stress and affective psychological disorders, such as depression, may be related to the chronicity of the inflammatory response.

Hyperactive immunity also plays a big part in allergies. Common allergens ranging from pollen and household dust to foods such as chocolate are responsible for triggering an immune response in susceptible individuals. The presence of these allergens, which are perceived by the body as invaders (antigens), triggers the production of a potent immune system chemical called *histamine*. In a normal immune response, histamine deactivates the invading antigens, rendering them harmless to the body. However, in hyperactive immunity excess histamine is responsible for triggering an inflammatory response that can include swollen tissues, mucus secretion, and constricted air passageways. These result in a runny or stuffy nose, watery eyes, itching, and difficult breathing characteristic of allergic reactions.

In someone with irritable lung syndrome who is susceptible to asthma, exogenous allergens can trigger an asthma attack. During an asthma attack, the large air passageways (bronchi) of the lungs swell, become clogged with mucus, and constrict, making breathing extremely difficult and often frightening.

Stress and negative emotions can serve as endogenous factors capable of triggering an asthma attack in an asthmatic, further demonstrating the mind-body connection in the absence of exogenous antigens. Stress can also exacerbate existing attacks when the attack is perceived negatively thus creating a feedback loop of attack, causing physical symptoms that the body perceives as stressful, thus perpetuating the attack.

Stress and the Digestive System

As discussed in Chapter 3, our digestive system is responsible for processing food from ingestion to elimination. It is directly related to the muscular system because much of the work associated with digestion is controlled by autonomic, smooth muscle contractions and the release of digestive juices. Fig. 5-13 illustrates the organs involved in digestion.

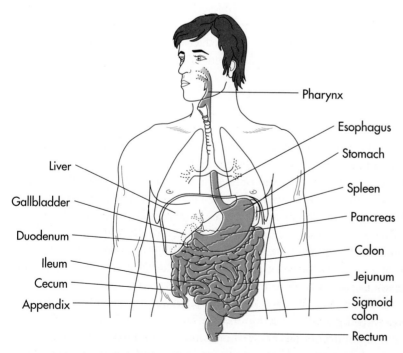

Fig. 5-13 The gastrointestinal system digests food through the use of mechanical and chemical digestions. Once excess chemicals, particularly hydrochloric acid, are secreted, this mucus can break down, allowing ulcers to form.

Chronic stress upsets the digestive process; chronic smooth muscle tension, combined with excessive levels of stomach acids and decreased levels of saliva, leads to a variety of digestive difficulties. These are even worse in people who are both chronically stressed and have genetic predispositions to digestive disorders.

Chronically tense smooth muscles can result in diarrhea, constipation, spasms of the esophagus and colon,[20] and ulcers.[41] Chronic smooth muscle tension also affects the **peristaltic action** of the digestive system, slowing it down and sometimes causing spasms associated with colitis or irritable bowel syndrome. Partially digested food is not moved smoothly through the digestive system, resulting in constipation or diarrhea.[23] Mucus production in the stomach lining is also diminished during chronic stress, resulting in a greater susceptibility to the effects of digestive juices, particularly hydrochloric acid, which has been implicated in the development of ulcers, which are erosions in the lining of the stomach.[23]

peristaltic action
contracting and relaxing of the smooth muscles of the digestive system that pushes partially digested food along

Chronic Stress and Psychological Illness

Acute and chronic, low-level, unresolved stress may be viewed as a contributing factor in a variety of psychological problems and in some cases, may be considered the first stage in the development of certain forms of these illnesses. Chronic stress is a risk factor for psychological problems, such as burnout, anxiety disorders (general anxiety, panic, phobias, posttraumatic stress disorder), depression, and suicide.[51]

Burnout

Burnout, although not an officially classified psychological illness, is a condition in which people lose their concern and feelings for others. Burnout can be defined as a way "to deplete oneself, to exhaust one's physical and mental resources. In effect, to wear out oneself by excessively striving to meet unrealistic expectations imposed by oneself or by the values of society."[8] In most cases, burnout is a response to self-induced psychological stress caused by illogical and irrational beliefs about work and job performance.

Risk factors for burnout include extreme dedication to work, putting in long hours, taking work home on a regular basis, taking personal responsibility for all uncompleted work (even if amounts are unrealistic), and feeling anxiety and guilt about work undone.[11]

Although burnout has been studied mostly among social workers, psychologists, child-care workers, prison personnel, and other service-oriented professionals whose jobs revolve around helping others, burnout can affect

KEY
TO UNDERSTANDING

Chronic stress is both a risk factor for psychological illness and a symptom of a broader problem.

anyone.[9,10,17,26] People who are burned out lose their concern and empathy for the clients they serve and they begin to treat them in a detached, mechanical way. Cherniss[10] noted the following symptoms of burnout in human service workers he studied:

- Loss of concern for clients
- Tendency to treat clients in a detached, mechanical fashion
- Increasing discouragement, pessimism, and fatalism about work
- Decline in motivation, effort, and involvement in work
- Apathy, negativism, irritation, and anger with coworkers and clients
- Preoccupation with one's own comfort and welfare on the job
- Tendency to rationalize failure by blaming clients and "the system"
- Resistant to change, growing rigidity, loss of creativity

Burnout is a response to the intense, unrelenting stress of caring for others' interpersonal needs. Chance,[8] cites four stages of burnout:

- **Stage 1.** enthusiasm–positive feelings about self, work, and ability to help
- **Stage 2.** stagnation–feelings of a lack of personal or organizational growth and/or progress; sense of sameness; not moving forward
- **Stage 3.** frustration–feeling that nothing can be done or no one is willing to try
- **Stage 4.** apathy–no longer caring; more concern for personal comfort

Workers experiencing personal stress from non–job-related sources tend to carry this over to their work.[10] This contributes to their overall stress levels and enhances the opportunity for burnout.

Anxiety

Anxiety is a vague uneasy feeling, the source of which is often nonspecific or unknown to the individual.[4] Anxiety can be caused by threats to both biological integrity (unmet needs for food, water, or sex) or security of the self (unmet needs for self-respect, approval, or status). Mild anxiety is frequently coupled with fears, doubts, guilt, and obsessions. Higher levels of anxiety are characterized as the most uncomfortable feelings an individual can have—a terror so strong that individuals try to get rid of it as soon as possible.[51]

Anxiety can be focused or general. A **phobia** is an anxiety disorder that is characterized by an obsessive, irrational, and intense fear of a specific thing (dog, spider, dirt), activity (leaving the house), or situation (exposure to heights). These phobic reactions can leave a sufferer with feelings of

General

phobia
a type of anxiety that is focused on a particular object, activity, or situation

faintness, fatigue, nausea, tremors, palpitations, and panic.[4] The causes of phobias are not entirely clear, although a very stressful, traumatic life event or generalized fear about life is commonly reported.[51]

Generalized anxiety disorder is characterized as an unrealistic, excessive anxiety about two or more life circumstances for a period of 6 months or longer. The focus of the anxiety does not revolve around another classifiable disorder, such as a phobia, panic attack, or excessive-compulsive disorder. The disturbance is not due to the effects of substances, such as drugs or a general medical problem, and it does not occur exclusively during other types of disorders, such as mood disorders or psychosis. Instead, an individual suffering from general anxiety is bothered by circumstances almost continually.

General anxiety sufferers feel irritable and tense and have difficulty concentrating. These mental signs are coupled with physical symptoms, such as shortness of breath, increased heart rate, cold, clammy hands, dry mouth, nausea, diarrhea, chills or hot flashes, muscle tension, aches, and soreness.[3]

Anxiety can be measured on a continuum and is related to the ability to focus and concentrate (Fig. 5-14). Mild anxiety (+) can help people focus on the task at hand; it can serve as a motivator or catalyst for action and heightens our sensory awareness and ability to perceive stimuli. As the level of anxiety increases to moderate anxiety (++) it narrows our perceptual field, distorting our ability to focus on a situation. When we reach the level of severe anxiety (+++), it results in selective inattention, and we are

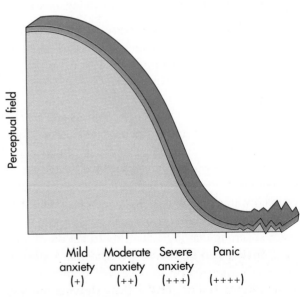

Fig. 5-14 The effect of anxiety on the perceptual field.

unable to focus on certain parts of the environment. When the level of anxiety reaches panic, (++++) we are unable to focus on anything and are overcome with dread.[51]

Panic attacks are discrete periods of intense fear and discomfort that come on unexpectedly and reach their peak within 10 minutes. The DSM-IV diagnoses a person as having a panic disorder when they have experienced four or more attacks in a 4-week period, or one or more attacks followed by a period of at least a month of persistent fear or worry of having another attack. Additionally, sufferers experience at least four of the following symptoms:

- Shortness of breath
- Racing heartbeat
- Chest pain
- Smothering, choking sensation
- Dizziness, vertigo, or unsteady feelings
- Tingling in the hands or wobbly legs
- Hot and cold flashes
- Sweating
- Feelings of unreality
- Faintness, trembling, or shaking
- Nausea, vomiting, or diarrhea
- Fear of going crazy or dying[3]

In community-based epidemiological studies, it is estimated that 3% of the adult population suffers from recurrent panic attacks,[29] approximately 10% of the adult population suffers from isolated or infrequent attacks, and about a third of all young adults have had at least one panic attack.

Although the causes of generalized anxiety, phobias, and panic attacks are many and varied, stress is implicated in all three. Perceived threats are a major cause of anxiety and panic.[51] These threats, whether real or imagined, focus on two areas: biological integrity and security of the self. People who feel in danger of impending physical or psychosocial threats become anxious, and if the threats are not removed or coped with effectively, a generalized state or anxiety could result in or lead to a breakdown or panic attack.

Mood Disorders

Mood disorders are divided into two categories: bipolar disorders and depressive disorders. Bipolar disorders are characterized by opposite reac-

manic episodes

a distinct period when a person's predominant mood is either elevated, expansive, or irritable and is accompanied by other manic symptoms

major depressive episodes

at least 2-week periods of depressed mood or loss of pleasure

grd

chronic / reactive

tions. People with bipolar disorders alternate from **manic episodes** to **major depressive episodes**; they feel elated and then sink to the depths of despair. In depressive disorders a person can have excessive feelings of sadness, melancholy, dejection, worthlessness, emptiness, and hopelessness that do not match up to the reality of a person's life.[51]

Bipolar disorders are characterized as either bipolar 1 or bipolar 2. The essential feature of bipolar 1 disorders is the presentation of some type of manic episode followed by a depressive episode. The essential feature of bipolar 2 disorders is the presentation of some form of depressive episode followed by at least one manic episode.

People with manic or bipolar depression alternate between manic episodes and major depressive episodes. The manic state is characterized by high levels of energy, psychomotor activity, goal-directed behavior, productivity, and a decreased need for sleep. An increase in self-esteem (bordering on self-aggrandizement), rapid flights of ideas, easy distractibility, and irritability are also characteristic of the manic state.

The depressive state, on the other hand, is characterized by a depressed mood or loss of interest or pleasure in almost all activities for a period of at least 2 weeks.[3] Depression is a normal reaction when we suffer a loss or tragedy or when things do not work out the way we would like. However, when depression lasts more than 2 to 3 weeks, it is time to seek help.

Two of the major types of depressive disorders are major depression (single or recurrent episodes) and chronic depression (dysthymia). Major depression is defined as having suffered from one (single episode) or more (recurrent episodes) depressive episodes without an intervening manic episode. Over 50% of all people having one major depressive episode will have another before returning to normal functioning. Estimates of major cases of depression range between 4.5% to 9.3% of the U.S. adult female population and 2.3% to 3.2% of adult males.[3]

Some of those who suffer from major depression are affected with a seasonal pattern specifier. Formerly called seasonal affective disorder (SAD), it occurs during the short, gray days of winter, the lack of exposure to sunlight is a stressor. From October to March people with this disorder are depressed and lose interest in work, sex, and other pursuits, while craving sweets and rich foods.[3] Fig. 5-15 shows the prevalence of SAD across the United States. It varies with latitude, being more prevalent in northern states, which experience longer, harsher winters.

Chronic depression (dysthymic disorder) is characterized by a mild, low-level depressed mood that lasts for more than 2 years (1 year for children and adolescents). The diagnosis is based on a person never being without symptoms for more than 2 months during a 2-year period. Although

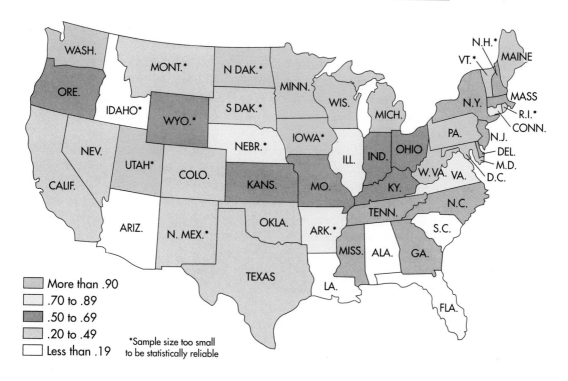

Fig. 5-15 The prevalance of SAD in the United States varies with latitude, making those living in the northernmost states more susceptible.

individuals with chronic depression are able to function, they do so at a less than optimal level. They may suffer constant fatigue, feel hopeless, have difficulty making decisions, have low self-esteem, and have difficulty concentrating. They may either have a poor appetite or overeat and may either have difficulty sleeping or may oversleep regularly.[3]

Although there are many causes of depression, acute and chronic stress are considered major risk factors. Many people become depressed after suffering a traumatic life event. In some cases, events that occur early in a person's life, such as the loss of a parent through death or divorce at a critical stage of development, undermine the development of self-esteem. Later in life, psychological stress that evokes the earlier loss can trigger the onset of depression.[14,39]

It is not uncommon for people experiencing events such as divorce, death of a loved one, abuse, or neglect to become depressed. For others, a chronically stressful environment, whether at work or at home, is a trigger for depression. These traumatic life events make some people vulnerable to depression.[6]

Suicide

Suicide can be characterized as a permanent solution to a temporary problem. However, people who take their own lives are desperate; they do not see the options that may be open to them for solving or reducing some of their problems. They cannot cope with their lives and feel lonely, ashamed, and hopeless.

Suicide rates for adolescents and college-age people are rising. Suicide is now the second-leading cause of death for young adults between the ages of 15 and 24 (automobile accidents are the first).[43] Brought on by the unrelenting pressures of modern life and the inability of many young people to cope, depressed young people see suicide as a reasonable way of dealing with their insurmountable problems.

demographic factors
nonmedical background data, such as factors about a person's age, sex, race, occupation, and residence

Although there are many risk factors for suicide among the adolescent and college-age population, three of them are stress-related: depression, major loss, and stressful life events. Other risk factors include **demographic factors**, psychiatric disorder, and biological problems, such as decreased levels of serotonin, growth hormones, and corticotropin-releasing factors. However, depression is linked to more than two thirds of all suicides.[7]

Summary

In this chapter we examined the relationship of acute and chronic stress responses in the development of health problems. We began the chapter with a discussion of the concept of psychosomatic illnesses. We differentiated between the two types of psychosomatic illnesses, psychogenic and somatogenic, and discussed the interplay between the mind and the body in the development, onset, and progression of disease.

Acute stress responses, or alarm reactions, help us mobilize the intense amount of energy needed by the fight-or-flight response to save our lives. We discussed how this energy mobilization is crucial to our well-being and can be used positively when meeting challenges as well as threats.

We discovered that chronic stress responses, those low-level physiological reactions to persistent unrelieved stressors, although milder in nature, are the ones that ultimately cause us more harm. We explored this in detail, examining the effect of chronic stress on those body parts and systems most directly affected by it. We detailed how stress upon these body parts and systems leads to their decreased efficiency, breakdown, and sometimes death.

We also explored the relationship of chronic stress to the development of psychological illnesses. Several categories of psychological problems, ranging from burnout to suicide, were also examined, with a focus on the role of stress in their development.

Study questions

1. What is psychosomatic illness?
2. List and describe the two different types of psychosomatic disease.
3. Discuss the similarities and differences between acute and chronic stress responses.
4. Describe the role of chronic stress in the weakening and eventual breakdown of various body parts and systems.
5. How does chronic stress affect the muscular system?
6. Describe the effects of chronic stress on the endocrine system.
7. How does chronic stress affect the digestive system?
8. Discuss how chronic stress affects the three components of the cardiovascular system.
9. Describe how chronic stress upsets the functioning of the immune system.
10. How is chronic stress implicated in depression?
11. Describe the role of stress in suicide.

References

1. Ader, R. (1981). *Psychoneuroimmunology*. New York: Academic Press.

2. Amkraut, A. & Solomon, G. (1974). From symbolic stimulus to the pathophysiologic response: Immune Mechanisms. *International Journal of Psychiatry in Medicine, 5*, 541-563.

3. American Psychiatric Association (1994). *Diagnostic and Statistical Manual of Mental Disorders (4th ed.)*. (4th ed.). Washington DC: American Psychiatric Association.

4. Anderson, K.N., & Anderson, L.E., & Glanze, W.D. (1994). *Mosby's Medical, Nursing, and Allied Health Dictionary (4th ed.)*. (4th ed.). (Rev. ed.). St Louis: Mosby.

5. Blumenthal, S.J. (1990). Youth Suicide: The Physician's Role in Suicide Prevention. *JAMA, 264*(24), 3194-3196.

6. Brown, G.W., Bifulco, A. & Harris, T.O. (1987). Life Events, Vulnerability, and the Onset of Depression. *British Journal of Psychiatry, 150*, 30-42.

7. Buros, O.K. (1978). The Eighth Mental Measurements Yearbook (Vol. 1). Highland Park, N.J.: Gryphon Press.

8. Chance, P. (1981, January). That Burned Out, Used Up Feeling. *Psychology Today*, 88-92.

9. Cherniss, G. (1992). Long-term consequences of burnout; an exploratory study. *Journal of Organic Behavior, 13*(1) 1-11.

10. Chernis, G. (1980). *Burnout in Human Service Professionals*. NY: Praeger Press.

11. Clark, C.C. (1980). Burnout, Assessment, & Intervention. *Journal of Nursing Administration, 10*(9), 39-43.

12. Crooks, R., & Baur, K. (1993). *Our Sexuality* (5th ed.). Redwood City: Benjamin Cummings.

13. Coughlin, P. (1990). Premenstrual syndrome; how marital satisfaction and role choice affect symptom severity. *Social Work, 35,* 351-55.

14. Cummins, R. (1990). Social Insecurity, Anxiety, and Stressful Events as Antecedents of Depressive Symptoms. *Behavioral Medicine, 16*(4), 161-164.

15. De Longis, A., Coyne, J.C., Dalcob, G., Folkman,S., & Lazarus, R. (1982). Reliability of Daily Hassles, Uplifts, and Major Life Events To Health Status. *Health Psychology, 1*(2), 119-136.

16. Deutsch,F. (1959). *On the Mysterious Leap From Mind to Body.* NY: International Universities Press.

17. Evans, B.K., & Fischer, D.G. (1993). The nature of burnout; a study of the three factor model of burnout in human service and non-human service samples. *Journal of Occupational and Organizational Psychology, 66,* 29-38.

18. Everly, G.S. & Rosenfeld, R. (1981). *The Nature and Treatment of the Stress Response.* NY: Plenum Press.

19. Glaser, R., Rice, J, Sheridan, J., and others. (1987). Stress-Related Immune Suppression; Health Implications. *Brain Behavior-Immunity, 1*(1), 7-20.

20. Girdano, D.A., Everly, G.S., & Dusek, D. (1990). *Controlling Stress and Tension; A Holistic Approach.* Englewood Cliffs, N.J.: Prentice Hall.

21. Goodell H. (1967). Thirty Years of Headache Research in the Lab of the Late Dr. Howard G. Wolf. *Headache, 6,* 158-171.

22. Hall, S.S. (1989, June). A molecular code links emotions, mind, and health. *Smithsonian,* 67-71.

23. Hafen, B.Q., Frandsen, K.J. Karren, K. & Hooker, K.R. (1991). *The Health Effects of Attitudes, Emotions, and Relationships.* Provo: EMS Associates.

24. Hales, D. (1992). *An Invitation to Health.* Redwood City: Benjamin Cummings.

25. Harrison M. (1982). *Self-Help for Premenstrual Syndrome.* Cambridge: Matrix Press.

26. Huebner, H.S. (1992). Burnout among school psychologists; an exploratory investigation into its nature, extent, and correlates. *School Psychology Quarterly, 7*(2), 129-36.

27. Kanner, A.D., Coyne, J.C., Schaefer, C. & Lazarus, R.S. (1981) Comparison of Two Modes of Stress Measurement: Daily Hassles and Uplifts vs. Major Life Events. *Journal of Behav. Med, 4*(1), 1-36.

28. Kaplan, H.S. (1974). *The New Sex Therapy.* NY: Brunner Mazel.

29. Klerman, G.L., Weissman, M.M., Ovellette, R., Johnson, J, & Greenwald, S. (1991). Panic Attacks in The Community: Social Morbidity and Health Care Utilization. *JAMA, 265*(6), 742-746.

30. Mason, J. (1968) A Review of Psychoendocrine Research on the Pituitary-Adrenal Cortical System. *Psychosomatic Medicine, 30*(5), 576-580.

31. Mason, J. (1968). The Scope of Psychoendocrine Research. *Psychosomatic Medicine, 30*(5), 565-576.

32. Masters, W.H., Johnson, V.E., & Kolodny, R.C. (1992) *Human Sexuality* (4th ed.). New York: Harper Collins.

33. Monroe, S. (1983). Major and Minor Life Events as Predictors of Psychological Distress: Future Issues and Findings. *Journal of Behav. Med,* 6, 189-205.

34. O'Leary, A. (1990) Stress, emotion, and human immune function. *Psychological Bulletin, 108*(3), 363-382.

35. Oliver, M.F. (1981). Diet and Coronary Heart Disease. *BR Med Journal,37,* 49-58.

36. Pelletier, K.R., Herzing, D.L. (1988). Psychoneuroimmunology; Toward a mind-body model: a critical review. *Advances, 5*(1), 27-56.

37. Pellitier, K.R. (1977). *Mind as Healer, Mind as Slayer.* NY: Dell.

38. Reid, R.L. (1991). Premenstrual syndrome. *New England Journal of Medicine, 324,* 1208-1211.

39. Rosenfield, A.H. (1985, June). Depression: Dispelling the Despair. *Psychology Today,* 29-34.

40. Sargent, J.D., Green, E.E., & Walters, E.D. (1973). Use of Autogenic Feedback Techniques in the Treatment of Migraine and Tension Headaches. *Psychosomatic Medicine, 35,* 129-133.

41. Selye, H. (1976). *The Stress of Life.* NY: McGraw Hill.

42. Seward, B.L. (1994). *Managing Stress.* Boston: Jones & Bartlett.

43. Shafer, D., Vreeland, V., Garland, A., Rajos, M., Underwood, M., & Busner, C. (1990). Adolescent Suicide Attempters: Response to a Suicide Prevention Program. *JAMA, 264*(24), 3151-3155.

44. Staines, N., Brostoff, J, & James, K. (1993). *Introducing Immunology* (2nd ed.). St Louis: Mosby.

45. Stein, M., Miller, A.H., & Trestman, R.L. (1991). Depression, the immune system, and health and illness. *Archives of General Psychiatry, 48,* 171-77.

46. Sternberg,E.M., Chrousos, G.P., & Gold,P.W. (1992). The stress response and the regulation of inflammatory diseases. *Annals of Internal Medicine 117*(10), 854-66.

47. Tasner, M. (1986, November/December). Medical Self Care TMJ., 47-50.

48. Thibodeau, G.A., & Patton, K.T. (1993). *Anatomy and physiology* (2nd ed.). St. Louis: Mosby.

49. Van Dorner, C.J.P., & Orlebeke, K.F. (1982, December) Stress, Personality & Serum Cholesterol Level. *Journal Human Stress,* 24-28.

50. Vollhardt, L.T. (1991). Psychoneuroimmunology; a literature review. *American Journal of Orthopsychiatry, 61*(1), 35-47.

51. Wilson, H.K., & Kneisl, C.R. (1992). Psychiatric Nursing (4th ed.) Redwood City: Benjamin Cummings & Addison Weseley.

52. Wolf, T.M., Elston, R.C., & Kissling, G.E. (1989). Relationship of Hassles, Uplifts, and Life Events to Psychological Well-Being of Freshman Medical Students. *Behavioral Medicine, 15*(1), 37-45.

PART II

A Wellness Model of Stress and Coping

As we defined it in Chapter 1, stress is a holistic transaction between an individual and a stressor, resulting in the body's mobilization of a stress response. Because the stress transaction is a holistic phenomenon, so to should be our coping. A wellness model of coping takes this into account. As you set general goals for improving your overall level of health and wellness you can also set specific goals for reducing stress.

A key to effective stress management is developing a more stress-resistant lifestyle, as well as having a repertoire of specific coping strategies. In other words, if we pay attention to our lifestyles and develop a higher level of wellness, we will have more energy, a clearer head, better social supports, and greater spiritual peacefulness. All of this will make us hardier and more stress-resistant.

We can view this holistic lifestyle as our core level of defense against stress. We call this core level *reorganize* because it is based on changing our lifestyles and priorities to reflect a greater concern for our health and stress management. Surrounding this core are four levels of defense that focus on different types of coping strategies.

The first of these levels is called *rethink* because it focuses on changing our illogical views about the world around us. The next level is named *reduce* because it concerns reducing the overall quantity of stressors in our lives. The third level is entitled *relax* because it focuses on helping us learn how to put our bodies into a relaxed state on a regular basis. Finally, the fourth level is *release*, which focuses on active ways to purge the byproducts of stress and tension from our lives.

Each level by itself is a different and useful line of defense against stress, but combined with the others becomes much stronger. A **synergistic effect** occurs when all the levels are working together simultaneously. The combined result is greater than the sum of its parts.

synergistic effect
the total effect is greater than the sum of 2 or more effects taken independently

For maximum effectiveness we can incorporate all four levels of coping into our daily lives so that we are constantly striving to rethink, reduce, relax, and release. A key to effective stress management is to become more proactive than reactive about stress. We need to be on the offensive against stress rather than always reacting to its presence.

Each of us is different in terms of what stress management techniques work for us. Our personalities guide us in determining which coping strate-

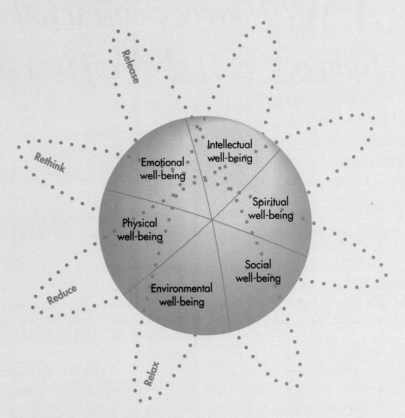

A wellness model of coping integrates all six dimensions of health with specific levels of coping strategies.

gies and lifestyle choices we will make in our stress-management efforts. Additionally, what works against one stressor or on one particular day may not work for a different stressor or on another occasion. The greater your repertoire of choices from each level, the better your ability to manage stress. The likelihood of situational constraints inhibiting your coping will be small if you have a wide variety of strategies to choose from.

In the next five chapters, we examine a number of strategies of defense against stress. Try them all out. Play with them. Find out what works best for you and your types of stressors. Mold them into a personal stress management plan that fits your lifestyle.

CHAPTER **6**

Rethink: Changing Your Thoughts About Potential Stressors

CHAPTER OBJECTIVES

- Explain the concept of a wellness model of coping.
- Describe the five levels of coping.
- Describe how to develop a multi-level coping plan.
- Clarify values concerning a number of issues.
- Describe how perspective about life relates to stress.
- Explain and give examples of the three humor skills.
- Apply Ellis's ABCDE model of Rational Emotive Therapy.
- Explain how Morita psychotherapy ideas relate to coping.
- Explain the role of humor in stress management
- Demonstrate competence with humor skills

The only constant in life is change! Perhaps if we all grew up believing in this, we would be less stressed when life throws us a curve. Instead, we grow up believing in the fallacy that someday we will be "home free." We believe that if we control as many variables as we can, everything will work out as planned. Furthermore, if it does not work out we get stressed, angry, or depressed. "How can life be so unfair?" we lament when things don't go our way.

It would be nice if life did always work out according to plan. Unfortunately, however, the best intentions sometimes go awry. Just when everything is going the way we want it to, something happens to set us back or force us to shift into "plan B."

To thrive, not merely survive, we must adapt to change or be left behind. We must always be ready with a plan B, even if that plan is simply to be open enough to allow ourselves to view something differently than we have in the past. Rethinking starts with the acceptance of change and ends with the creative application of new ways to manage it.

Believing that change is the only constant in life does not mean letting go of all control over our lives. Rather it means developing a mind-set that allows us to be fluid and to adapt to the inevitable change that being truly human entails. Such an attitude enables us to see stressful situations in the proper light. We are at least in control of the way we view our lives. We should also develop an understanding of the kinds of people, places, and situations that are stressors for us and use this knowledge to anticipate stressful situations before they happen. In this way, we can plan around potential stressors, short-circuiting them before they become overwhelming.

KEY
TO UNDERSTANDING

To cope with change is to recognize that it is inevitable and to welcome it.

Knowing What You Value

KEY
TO UNDERSTANDING

To be clear about the things you value.

When we use rethinking as a coping strategy, we really are taking another look at potential stressors. We are reviewing them in terms of whether or not they truly are a threat to us and the things we hold dear. Therefore a key to understanding what stresses us and then coping with it effectively is being clear about the things that we value. Our values are the mirror of our personality and are most central to defining who we are as people. Although our knowledge, attitudes, and beliefs strongly influence who we are and paint a picture of us for others, it is our values that are the foundation on which these other facets are built.

Because of this, values clarification must be part of any efforts to change health behavior, such as beginning an exercise program, stopping smoking, or managing stress. How can a person truly commit to these changes if they do not really value their health? Although it is relatively easy to teach someone new information, it is much harder to change his or her values. In many cases, the first necessary step in changing our values is acknowledging what they are.

Values clarification, also known as values education, is an often misunderstood process. It has been attacked as a way to brainwash or inculcate students with a teacher's values. However, values clarification as envisioned by its creators is exactly the opposite. It is a process of helping individuals clarify and stand up for what they truly value.[22]

The three-part process for values clarification involves prizing, choosing, and acting on one's values.[18]

- Prizing beliefs and behaviors—During the first step of values clarification individuals explore their values and are given opportunities for publicly affirming and prizing them. This process allows individuals to stand up for those things they hold sacred.
- Choosing beliefs and behaviors—The next value clarification step involves examining values against other options. After consideration of consequences, students are allowed to freely choose either their values or other values from the alternatives examined in clarification activities.
- Acting on beliefs—This third and final step in the value clarification process involves taking action that is consistent with your beliefs. Students are supported in their attempts to use their values to shape a lifestyle that helps them act with consistency.

Values clarification is a process for helping students understand, affirm, and be true to those things in their lives that are truly important. Sometimes we need to take the time to stop and examine our values—to check and see whether our lives are still on course with what we perceive to be important and meaningful. Assess Yourself 6-1 helps you identify your values.

Not surprisingly, when we are put into situations where we perceive that our values are being threatened, we often become stressed. We might refer to this type of stressor as an **intrapersonal conflict**. Understanding our values helps us view potential stressors with the proper perspective. We judge situations and people in relation to what we value. That is why stress is so individualistic; what is important and worth defending to one person may be totally insignificant to another.

Values clarification as a stress-management technique is useful because it allows us to clarify those things that are truly worth getting stressed about. The things that do not matter much to us are not really worth added stress. Gradually we can learn to control our thoughts and the emotions that are aroused in relation to these insignificant things. With the help of some cognitive coping techniques we can learn to analyze potential stressors more rationally and objectively—to judge whether or not they pose a real threat to the things we value.

intrapersonal conflict

problems arising because of conflicts within a person, such as an assault on their values

STRESS IN OUR WORLD

Maria

Maria is feeling stressed. She is in the middle of her first examination for her philosophy class and notices that the woman next to her, Dawn, is cheating. Dawn has a small piece of paper with tiny notes written on it taped to her arm and covered by her sweatshirt. Every time the professor turns his head or walks away, Dawn rolls her sleeve up and glances at her notes. Other students seem aware of this but go about their business and ignore Dawn.

Maria is not used to this. As a Roman Catholic of Italian-American descent, Maria grew up in a strict Catholic family and attended parochial schools throughout her primary and secondary grades. She was taught that cheating was a sin against God. To view another person cheating and not do something was considered almost as bad.

As a result of this Maria is feeling very confused. Although she has heard other students talk about cheating, she has never observed such a blatant attempt herself. Should she say something to Dawn, the professor, her classmates? Why doesn't somebody else say something to Dawn? Why doesn't the professor see what is going on? Why is Dawn cheating? Isn't it immoral to cheat? Why should I care so much? These and a hundred other questions go through Maria's mind as she becomes increasingly more distracted by Dawn's cheating.

She finds herself thinking more about Dawn than her own performance on the test. Maria then gets angry. She realizes that she is becoming stressed by this inner values conflict brought on by Dawn's cheating. Maria is in the throes of an intrapersonal stress episode.

Goal Setting

The goals we set for ourselves usually revolve around the things we value in life. For instance, we plan to go to college because it is a necessary prerequisite for acquiring the type of career and lifestyle we value. We choose a partner because he or she shares our values and sense of what is important and meaningful in life.

Often, when we are without focus or direction in our lives, we are like ships adrift at sea without anchors. We move in and out of relationships, schools, jobs, seemingly at the whim of fate.

Our goals, like our values, help define who we are. We define ourselves not only by who we are in the present, but what we might become in the future. Setting short- and long-term goals is an excellent way of moving toward greater direction in life. When we have no goals, we tend to be aimless and take each day as it comes, unconnected to a more meaningful whole. Without goals we can be overwhelmed by the limitless choices available to us each day. We also can be overwhelmed by the demands of others whose requests often conflict with what we need to do. Goals help us focus on what is important in our lives and give us some structure and purpose.

Measurable Objectives

Our goals can be as lofty as we want; however, the best goals are those that are realistically within reach. By setting realistic goals we can guarantee ourselves a better chance of success. When we successfully reach our goals it enhances our self-esteem and motivates us to set bigger and more difficult goals. Setting unrealistic goals sets us up for failure. Continual failure to reach our goals can lead to disappointment and can reinforce doubts and negative beliefs we may harbor about our abilities. In actuality, all of us have had our share of success. We just tend to forget these. Take time to remember your successes by doing Assess Yourself 6-2.

One way to ensure that your goals are met is to set concrete, measurable objectives for each goal. Because our goals are often lofty, and immeasurable, establishing measurable objectives helps us keep our focus. Measurable objectives answer the following question: Who will do how much of what by when? John's case is a perfect example. His overall goal is to get better grades in college. He could refine that goal by restating that he would like to raise his grade point average by 0.5 points. To accomplish this he could set the following objective: "By the end of next year (by when) I (who) will earn at least a *B* (how much) in all five of my classes (of what) each semester."

It is also important to remain flexible when we set our goals and evaluate our results. Sometimes things happen that change the course of events midway through the process of working toward our goal. We need to be fluid and adapt to these new demands. Sometimes we will need to reformulate our goals, but other times just stretching the time frame for completion will suffice (Assess Yourself 6-3).

KEY
TO UNDERSTANDING

Effective goal setting requires thinking small.

Putting Things in Proper Perspective

Sometimes we become stressed as a result of blowing things out of proportion. We may make a big deal out of little events that when viewed in a broader perspective really are not that important. Somehow we lose our perspective and overemphasize our plight, making us "the center of the universe."[13] In other words, we become so important in our own minds, it is as if everything revolves around us. Therefore the things that involve us take on added significance. If anything goes wrong with our lives it is very stressful. We sim-

Tips for Effective Goal Setting

1. Complete Assess Yourself 6-1—Values Self-Survey.

2. Decide on which aspects of your life you want to work, improve, or explore (e.g., improve your level of fitness, save some money, learn a new hobby).
   * Remember, you cannot meet all of your goals at the same time.

3. Prioritize your goals. Rank them on a scale of 1 to 10 (1 being the most important) and start working on the most important ones.

4. Break large goals down into smaller segments. If you eventually want to be able to run marathons, start by getting into shape for a 10,000-meter run.

5. Set goals you can reach. You can ensure success by setting goals that are within your reach. Success in reaching these smaller goals will eventually get you to your overall goal.

6. Make your goals measurable. Be as specific as possible. "I would like to lose 10 lbs in the next 3 months" is an example of a specific, measurable goal.

7. Set a reasonable time frame for each goal. Without linking your goal to a time frame your commitment may wane. Make sure you give yourself enough time to reach your goal.

8. Reward yourself for success. Put some money aside or get someone you love to commit to doing something nice for you. Your reward could be as simple as putting aside the time to take a bubble bath and relax.

ply must do something to regain control. Metcalf and Felible[13] describe the top three indicators that you may view yourself as the center of the universe:

1. *Nothing is ever your fault.*
   When at the center of the universe, some think that nothing is ever their fault; someone else always screws up. By blaming others, they have an illusion of control.

2. *Everything is always your fault.*
   Others feel that they are so important that they control everything in their lives. When something goes wrong they always blame themselves. They feel as if they should be able to plan for and control even the most minute details of their lives and relationships.

3. *Any combination of 1 and 2.*

Why do people develop this center of the universe position and take on such an attitude of importance (Fig. 6-1)? Probably because they have a hard time accepting the absurdity of life.[13] They may have grown up with the belief that they could control all of the variables in life. However, just when they think everything is under control, life throws them a curve. According to Metcalf and Felible,[13] one must develop the first humor skill, accepting absur-

Fig. 6-1 When you look objectively at the universe and your place in it, it can sometimes make your problems and stress seem pretty insignificant.

dity, to escape from the center of the universe. You cannot control everything in life so you might as well laugh over the absurdity of it all. To do this, however, takes training. In many cases, we have to relearn just how absurdly humorous life can be. Metcalf believes that to do this we need to go back and look at our lives to see where we lost the ability to laugh at the absurd.

Assess Yourself 6-4, the humor inventory, evolved out of the idea of using inventories in the treatment of people with addictive disorders. This activity helps individuals bring to the surface all of the fears, resentment, and anger masked by their addiction. In many cases, it is the turning point in recovery. Metcalf and Felible[13] were so taken with this activity that they developed a humor inventory to help free people from the things that block their ability to lighten up.

Rethinking the Pace of Your Life

It is not too hard to lose sight of the perspective of your life and what is really important considering the pace at which most of us live. We rush our way through the day, often at such an intense pace that we miss many of the details that give our lives texture, depth, color, and richness. We

STRESS IN OUR WORLD

Norman Cousins

In 1979, Norman Cousins, an editor for the magazine Saturday Review, *wrote a book entitled* Anatomy of an Illness as Perceived by the Patient. *The book chronicled Cousin's successful and unorthodox battle in 1964 with the potentially devastating degenerative connective tissue disease, ankylosing spondylitis.*

The disease developed mysteriously after Cousins returned from a trip to Russia in a state of complete mental and physical exhaustion. It started with a feeling of listlessness throughout his body and fatigue extending to his arms, legs, neck, and back. Within a week, Cousins was nearly immobilized with intense pain and stiffness because of inflammation in all of his joints. Additionally, he proved to be hypersensitive to the medications being given to him to reduce the pain and swelling, and consequently he developed a severe case of hives and nodules under his skin, which made him feel itchy and as though things were crawling all over him.

After failing to respond to traditional chemotherapeutic and pain-killing agents and discovering that he was hypersensitive to some of them, Cousins, with the consent of his physicians, decided to stop the drugs. In their place, he substituted homeopathic treatments for the chemotherapeutic agents, and laughter for the painkillers. Cousins had studied the brain's ability to produce its own endorphins through laughter. He devised a regular schedule of humor and laughter, watching endless comedy movies and reading funny books and magazines. To his delight, Cousins found that 10 minutes of genuine laughter produced 2 hours of pain-free sleep without taking drugs. When the effects of his laughter wore off, he repeated the regimen and added another dose of comedy.

Cousins also felt that the noisy, impersonal atmosphere of a hospital was not conducive to rest and to maintaining an optimistic outlook on his prognosis. The hospital was having a hard time with his comedy festivals, self-directed treatment, and overall need to be in control, so Cousins checked out of the hospital and into a hotel. There, with some essential medical equipment, his physician, and his family and friends, he was able to proceed with his unorthodox treatment.

Within days, Cousins began to respond to his new treatment regimen. His allergic symptoms disappeared, he was able to rest, and his immune function improved. Over the next few months he recovered from his illness and was eventually able to return to work. Although he cannot prove it, Cousins feels that his laughter routine, positive outlook, and will to live were key elements in his recovery from his near fatal illness.

put things off until one day we simply run out of time. Harry Chapin's famous song, "The Cats in the Cradle" spins the tale of an old man literally dying to spend time with his grown son only to find out that "the boy was just like me"—too busy, too preoccupied, and too hardened to respond to the pleas of his own father. It is a sad tale, but one that chides us to remember to take time to stop from time to time and pay attention to the little things that give our lives meaning. Assess Yourself 6-5 rates your pace of life.

The Power of Positive Thinking

Norman Vincent Peale[15] wrote a book more than 40 years ago that is as timely today as the day it was written. His message is about the incredible power in thinking positively about things. We have already seen in Chapter 2 how our brains translate neutral stimuli into either stress or no stress according to our perception of harm, challenge, or ambivalence. Peale explains not only how we can use positive thinking to reduce stress but also how to use it to maximize psychological well-being.

Although Peale's message is delivered in religious terms, and his ultimate source of strength is belief in God, secular people can learn a great lesson from it as well. In a sense, what Peale is saying is that it is up to the individual. You can focus on the negative, debilitating aspects of your life and be stressed, or you can cut those loose and focus on the positive.

F. Scott Peck[16] in *The Road Less Traveled* in a way shares this sentiment with Peale. Peck believes that we need to acknowledge the fact that life is difficult and sometimes we will find it very hard to keep going. However, we need not fixate on this. Wallowing in self-pity we can miss out on all of the beauty and fun in life. Peck[16] believes that we need to acknowledge that life is tough before we can get move on.

Focusing on the bright side does not mean denying the existence of pain. It simply means making the most of a bad situation without denying its existence. It also means cutting loose from the experience once you have grieved long enough (see Stress In Our World box on p. 202). Assess Yourself 6-6 helps you focus on the bright side.

Whose Life is it Anyway?

In *How I Found Freedom in an Unfree World*, Harry Browne[1] suggests that most of us are caught up in living someone else's life. Often, we live by an agenda that is set by someone else. One of the primary tasks involved in

STRESS IN OUR WORLD

The Fisherman

There is an old fable about a fisherman who went out to sea one day with his two sons. The day started off like any normal day in their Mediterranean fishing village. The men in the village spent time getting their hand-held nets ready as their sons got the 20-foot wooden rowboats ready for the day's fishing. The three men took turns rowing out to the fishing grounds a couple miles offshore. It was a beautiful day and the fishing was good.

Around noon, however, their luck changed. The skies began to darken quickly as the wind picked up. Before they knew it a storm roared in and they were being tossed around in 25-foot waves, their sense of direction lost. Not knowing which way to row, they let the tide take them and prayed for the best. Conditions worsened and the father feared for the lives of his sons. All seemed lost when suddenly a beacon appeared in the darkness, pointing the way to shore. Summoning all of their strength, they rowed toward the beacon, crashing through the waves as they steadily approached the shoreline.

As the boat neared the safety of the shore, the old fisherman realized what the beacon was. Apparently, his house had been struck by lightning during the storm and the resulting fire was lighting the way home. As they approached the smoking, charred remains, the fisherman's wife came running up and threw her arms around her men, thanking God for their safe return.

Have you ever experienced anything like this in your life? Could you turn a tragedy around and see the bright side? Has it proved true in your life that there is a silver lining to every dark cloud?

becoming an adult is to become more self-directed and break away from the control and excessive influence of parents and others. This separation and movement toward greater self-direction is a fundamental rite of passage of traditional American culture.

Older adults entering another phase of their lives also go through rites of passage: the widower, alone after a lifetime of being part of a couple; the mother, returning to college after taking 20 years off to raise her children; the worker, starting all over after his or her employer of 25 years shuts down. Each of these older adults face the same questions as the 18-year-old freshman, away from home for the first time. Who am I? What do I want out of life? What's right for me? These people are struggling with the same issues of striving for independence but trying to stay connected to the significant others in their lives.

This is a hard balance to achieve in our society. Although American culture encourages independence, at the same time it romanticizes the idea of being out of control. Soap operas and romantic novels are full of characters who are passionately overwhelmed and out of control of their emotions and behavior. Song lyrics also romanticize the loss of control. "Born to Run" or "Born to be Wild" connote a romantic and free-spirited image that is appealing to much of America's youth.

Carol Cassell[2] in her book *Swept Away* describes how women in our culture grow up believing that losing control of their emotions and sexual behavior while in the throes of passion is acceptable and even desirable. A byproduct of this attitude, however, is the abdication of any responsibility for their behavior. Being "out of control" becomes an excuse for not assuming responsibility for behavior. Some distressing results of this lack of control are the alarmingly high rates of adolescent pregnancy and sexually transmitted diseases (STDs). HIV and AIDS rates, which have dropped off significantly for some groups at risk, have continued to rise among the youth, with teenagers now representing the largest group of new cases each year.[9]

Unfortunately, our cultural fostering of this lack of control is coupled with what has been labeled as the retarded sexual development of American youth.[12] In a large multinational study of teenage sexuality and adolescent pregnancy, American teens scored the lowest of five similarly developed industrialized countries (Canada, Sweden, France, England, and the Netherlands) on tests of knowledge and attitudes concerning sexuality and contraception.[4] Lack of basic information concerning sexual anatomy and physiology, contraception, and pregnancy were cited among other findings as indicators of what international experts would consider arrested sexual development. Sexuality and sexual behavior were regarded by the other five countries as normal aspects of life that were openly discussed and dealt with responsibly. School curricula and societal attitudes focused on being in control through a combination of education and greater access to information and health services. As a result, all of the other five countries have much lower adolescent pregnancy and STD rates than the United States.

Our culture makes it seem as though we have no control over our emotions or behavior once life throws us a curve. People who can adjust, pick themselves up, and get on with their lives if things do not go their way are viewed as emotionless automatons. People love to share in our grief and wallow in our self-pity. They feel cheated if we handle things and do not get swept away.

Some people are more self-directed than others. They know who they are, where they are going, and have a sense of control in trying to chart it. They rely more on their own judgments and are less concerned about pleasing others, even if it means they sometimes have to disappoint the ones they love.

In Chapter 2, we discuss the work of Susan Kobassa[10] who found that people with more stress-resistant personalities, which she termed *hardy*, feel more in control of their lives. They have an internal focus of control and are able to "pull their own strings,"[5] which involves understanding and being true to personal values. People who pull their own strings resist being swayed by others. They make their own plans and decisions based on a rational assessment of the issues and how they relate to their lives.[6] They sometimes go against conventional wisdom because it is not right for them, and they do not buy into many of the illogical assumptions that were outlined in Chapter 2.

Rational Emotive Therapy

Rational emotive therapy (RET) uses logical thinking and positive self-talk as an aid in reducing stress and neuroses. In fact, the underlying premise of RET is that people or things do not cause us stress—it is our illogical beliefs and irrational self-talk that are the culprits. Logically, RET techniques revolve around understanding our illogical beliefs and substituting more rational thoughts in their place.[7]

Ellis and Harper's[6] ABCDE technique (see Fig. 6-2) for reducing distress embraces this concept. The acronym stands for the following:

A   (activating event)-the primary stimulus that activated the stress response

B   (belief system)-our illogical beliefs about the primary stimulus (accompanied by specific negative self-talk)

C   (consequences)-the negative physical, mental, and behavioral effects of our illogical beliefs

D   (dispute)-a process of substituting more rational, logical beliefs and self-talk for each illogical belief

E   (effects)-an assessment of the effects of the dispute process on the consequences

We can illustrate this by discussing Rich, a first-semester college senior who wants to change his major from international marketing to education. Rich has decided after an intern experience during the summer that the high-powered world of international marketing is not for him. He thinks that he really wants to work with young people and teach high school business. After making the decision to switch, he informs his girlfriend who is very upset by the news. She is disappointed that he wants to teach, and she claims that he will never be able to support a family on a teacher's salary. She is annoyed that he did not know what he wanted sooner. His parents are also worried about him changing focus so late in his college career.

(activating event) — The primary stimulus that activated the stress response.

 (belief system) — our illogical beliefs about A (accompanied by the specific negative self-talk).

 (consequence) — the negative physical, mental, and behavioral effects of B.

 (dispute) — a process of substituting more rational, logical beliefs and self-talk for each B.

 (effects) — an assessment of the effects of the dispute process on C. Did D result in diminished consequences?

Fig. 6-2 The ABCDE technique for reducing stress.

In Rich's situation, the ABCDE technique would work like this:

A - Rich's girlfriend and parents react negatively to Rich deciding to change his major.

B - As a result of all the flack he is getting, Rich subvocalizes the following illogical beliefs:

- "I shouldn't make this change so late in my college career."
- "I should really enter a career in which I can earn more money than teaching."
- "I should have known what I wanted sooner."
- "I shouldn't disappoint my girlfriend and my parents."
- "I'll never amount to anything."
- "I'll never be able to support a family as a teacher."
- "I never do anything right."
- "I'm a total jerk."

C - As a result of all of this negative self-talk and illogical thinking, Rich is experiencing the following symptoms:

Physical
- Muscle tension in his neck and upper back
- Tension headaches
- Difficulty sleeping
- Fatigue

Mental
- Loss of self confidence
- Anxiety
- Difficulty concentrating

Behavioral

- Rich hasn't wanted to go out much on the weekend.
- He hasn't seen his girlfriend in a week.
- He's been arguing with his parents almost every day over little things.
- He's been out late a few nights a week, drinking at the local bar by himself.

D - Rich decides to tackle his problem by analyzing each of these illogical beliefs and substituting more rational thoughts in their place.

- "I know it's not going to be easy, but I need to make this change now. I know I will not be happy and productive if I stay in international marketing."
- "Money is important, but I'll never be good at something I don't want to be doing."
- "It certainly would have been easier if I knew at 19 that I wanted to teach. The truth is I didn't find out until this summer when I did some work with a neighborhood youth group. Besides, most of my marketing courses will fit with my new major, business education."
- "Although I don't like to cause my family and girlfriend pain, I've got to be true to myself if we are to have honest relationships."
- "I've already accomplished a lot. There is no reason to believe I can't be an excellent teacher."
- "It may be difficult on a teacher's salary, but there are a lot of men that teach who support their families. If I ever marry, I need to have a wife who also wants to earn part of the family income."
- "I've made tons of correct decisions in the past. This is the right decision for me."

E - As a result of working through the dispute and coming up with a more rational belief system concerning his decision, Rich experiences the following changes:

Physical

- Muscle tension relaxes
- Tension headaches lessen
- Able to sleep soundly

Mental

- Regains confidence in decisions
- Still anxious, but able to discuss it
- Regains concentration

Behavioral

- Spending more time with his girlfriend
- Stopped arguing with those closest to him

- More social
- Seeking support of his friends

Work through your own ABCDE scenario in Assess Yourself 6-7.

Morita Psychotherapy

What about those of us who have tried to change our illogical thoughts about events but find ourselves unable to do so? What happens when our thoughts and feelings mesmerize us into inactivity? What does it mean if we cannot be as rational as Ellis[7] and we feel controlled by our illogical thoughts and the emotions they evoke?

David Reynolds[18], in his classic work on **Morita psychotherapy** *Playing Ball on Running Water*, talks about how we can learn to accept our negative thoughts and feelings without letting them control our behavior. He clarifies the key Moritist viewpoint related to stress management: we cannot always understand and control our negative thoughts and feelings, but we can control our behavior.[18]

Moritists believe that neurotic individuals are caught in a vicious cycle that is characterized by a hypersensitivity to any physical and mental condition that they perceive as threatening, which results in paying increased attention to the thoughts or feelings that aroused the threat. The increased attention to the negative thoughts and feelings results in making the perception of threat even sharper, immobilizing the individual.[14]

Moritists would say that the best way to deal with negative thoughts and feelings is to acknowledge their existence, accept them for what they are, and get on with the things you need to do for the rest of that day. In time, all feelings will pass and be replaced by others. This acceptance of mental symptoms for what they are is an important Moritist concept that is borrowed from Zen Buddhism.[14] A key to understanding this is to realize that feelings do not need to control your behavior. Being sad, for instance, does not have to stop you from getting out of bed, washing your face, getting dressed, and getting on with your day. You may not be as happy as you would like to be, but you will not feel any better by staying in bed and feeling sorry for yourself.

In his book *Even in Summer the Ice Doesn't Melt*, Reynolds[19] explains that we will never truly understand the reasons behind our feelings. Trying to gain insight into our feelings is useful if we apply that information to problem solve and give ourselves ideas about how to reduce the likelihood of certain feelings. However, we will never be certain about why we are feeling what we are feeling at any given time. We cannot control our feelings anymore than we can control the weather. As a consequence of this

Morita psychotherapy
a type of psychotherapy developed in Japan that contends that, although we cannot always understand or control our emotions, we do not have to let them control our behavior

KEY
TO UNDERSTANDING

To cope with our emotions, we must realize that we may never be able to understand and control them. We can, however, be in control of how we behave in relation to them.

type of thinking, we begin to accept, rather than try to control, create, or dissolve our feelings. Our feelings are part of who we are, and we do not need to solve or resolve them to get on with our lives.

Productivity: The Key to Morita Psychotherapy

Morita therapy helps people acknowledge their feelings and then get beyond them by engaging in productive work; it recognizes action as the key to successful living. Morita therapists teach people to accept the curative effects of nature, manual labor, and channelling disruptive feelings into productive behavior.[8,14,20]

For instance, let's suppose you wake up at 3:00 AM and are unable to get back to sleep because of troubling thoughts and negative emotions. A Moritist would say that it is your choice—you can stay in bed, tossing and turning for hours trying to figure out what the problem is, or you can acknowledge your discomfort and do something productive. If you choose the latter, in time the feelings will pass and be replaced with a new set of emotions.

Morita training would teach you to get out of bed (respect this natural reaction to wakefulness), accept the troubling thoughts and feelings for what they are, and do something productive like clean the bathroom tiles. Not only should you clean them, but it is preferable to fully immerse yourself in the task at hand, using a toothbrush to scrub each tile and taking your time to do the best job you can do. After completing the bathroom you may or may not have the same feelings. What has changed, however, is that you now have a sparkling clean bathroom. You have proven to yourself that you can engage in productive living despite having distressing thoughts and feelings.

Enjoying Life More

How much do you enjoy your life? Are you having as much fun now as you would like to be having? Are you doing the things that you enjoy, or have you lost sight of the notion that life is supposed to be enjoyed and that you deserve to have fun? Assess Yourself 6-8 is a quick activity designed to help you assess your fun level.

If there is not much fun in your life at this time, lighten up—you are not alone. Many of us have lost sight of the fact that we need and deserve to have fun. As a culture we have become so self-conscious of having to be good at everything we do that we have lost our ability to try something that looks like fun, even if we cannot be good at it. That childlike innocence that we are born with—the ability to spontaneously let loose, free from concern about what other people might think—has been replaced with a concern for how well we can do things. Our fun has become so organized that we feel we cannot even play unless we have taken lessons first.

In some cases we simply have forgotten how to laugh. We have been surrounded by so much sadness that we forget what it means to be happy. Our home life, instead of contributing to our happiness, has robbed us of the joy we should be experiencing. Sometimes we surround ourselves with people who are joyless. Like the mythical Scrooge, they scowl their way through life, bah humbugging everything that is happy. They overanalyze and approach life through a pseudosophisticated cynical haze that finds most simple and fun things boring.

In other cases, we may just work too hard. We have bought into the Puritan work ethic to such an extent that we have forgotten that the purpose of work is to enable us to live the kind of life we truly enjoy. Instead of trying to work smart, we are obsessed with working hard. Instead of working to live, we live to work; our work becomes our life.

Most Americans define themselves by their jobs rather than how they live their lives off the job. As a culture we are obsessed with work. We have bought into the belief that we should feel guilty if we do not strive our hardest to work our way to the top. Today simply working is no longer good enough; we now must have careers. Instead of viewing work as a way to provide for our needs, most people view work itself as a need. It is no wonder that people have a hard time leaving their work at the office. Taking work home or on vacation or feeling that one is too valuable to even take a vacation are other examples that our work has become central in our lives. This partially explains why many of us have a hard time relaxing on our days off (see box on p. 210).

Other cultures perceive work in an entirely different light. Southern European and Latin American cultures build midday breaks or siestas into the middle of the day. These extended "lunch hours" are not spent hunched over a desk, furtively munching a sandwich while trying to get in extra work. Rather, they are spent in the company of family or friends, sharing a meal, and often include a restful nap or break. Work is resumed after this break. Additionally, in most European countries people go "on holiday" for at least 4 weeks in the summer. The pace of work slows down and operations revolve around human needs. However, productivity in these countries remains high and in some cases higher than in the United States. West Germany, for instance, before its merger with East Germany, enjoyed a standard of living second to none though its workers toiled for fewer hours on the job than Americans.[11] Even Japanese workers, famous for their intensity, long hours, and level of commitment, try to infuse into the work envi-

Do You Really Know How To Play?

What did you do with your extra day off last Memorial Day weekend? Did you spend it picnicking with friends? Taking the first swim of the season? Enjoying the latest box-office hit?

Or did you feel compelled to spend the long holiday weekend involved in much less pleasurable pursuits, such as painting the house, cleaning the yard, or worst of all, catching up on work that you brought home from school or the office? If you did any of these, or were plagued with guilt because you did not do anything "productive" with your weekend, you are not alone.

Many people feel that they must always be doing something productive. This is fine when it concerns our work. However, when we carry this attitude over into our leisure time, it can become a source of stress.

The problem for most of us is that we have so much to do during our free time, that it is becoming less and less "free." It is estimated that Americans spend almost half of their weekend time doing chores or working at their jobs. Our lives are so committed to careers, family responsibilities, and social activities that we are not leaving any time for our brains and bodies to recuperate. The result is that we feel no more energetic by Sunday than we felt on Friday night.

The following are some tips to make your leisure time more fun:

- Keep work and play separate. - Although the weekend golf outing with the boss is inevitable, keep this and other forms of mixing work with leisure to a minimum.

- Do not turn play into work. - Do not turn each game of tennis into the finals at Wimbledon. Leisure time sports and hobbies are played for fun--not to win at all costs.

- Find new playmates. - If you spend most of your free time with the same circle of friends, you are probably doing the same things. Meet new people and create new playful opportunities by changing your socializing patterns.

- Expand your leisure horizons. - Devote one day a month or every other month to trying a different play activity.

- Do what you really enjoy, not what you think you should do. - Rollerblading may be all the rage, but if it is not for you, participating will be a source of stress.

- Don't rule something out because you think you will not excel. - Skiing the novice trails can be just as exhilarating as the expert slopes. You do not have to be an expert at an activity to enjoy it.

- Do not put off until tomorrow, the fun you can have today. - Too many of us promise that someday when we have the time we will try this or that. Make the time today! Pencil into your schedule a certain amount of "fun" time each day.

A final word about play. Do not feel guilty about being idle or wanting your play time. You work hard. You deserve your play! Go out and have some fun (and don't worry about it)!

ronment activities that reduce stress and increase productivity. Exercise sessions, singing, and team-building efforts all work to build the body and the spirit and help diffuse the pressures of the job.

Putting Humor into Life

We need to recapture our childlike innocence about play and relearn how to put some humor back into our lives. Humor has as its root the Latin word _umor,_ which means fluid, like water. Humor helps us be more fluid and go with the flow of our lives. Fluid is also the opposite of rigid and tense. It is not coincidental that when we laugh, we cannot be stressed. It is physiologically impossible to be laughing (a relaxation response) and stressed at the same time. Humor can be "a set of survival skills that relieve tension, keeping us fluid and flexible instead of allowing us to become rigid and breakable in the face of relentless change."[13] Viewing humor this way is empowering because it implies that we can learn these humor skills. Like any new skills, They must be practiced for them to eventually become conditioned responses to the absurdity of life and the reality of change.

There are three humor skills, according to Metcalf:[13] (1) the ability to see the absurdity in difficult situations, (2) the ability to take yourself lightly while taking your work seriously, and (3) having a disciplined sense of joy in being alive.

Seeing the Absurdity in Difficult Situations

Life and people can be very absurd when you think about it. In a recent nationally televised, professional football playoff game, the favored team was getting blown out. Everything they tried backfired. On-target passes were dropped, tackles were missed, and balls were fumbled and then recovered by the opposing team. By the end of the first half the team was down 35-3—a truly absurd situation for the quarterback of this team. It would have been easy for him to give into the temptation to just quit.

Instead, however, he gathered his team and said, "Listen, we've got nothing more to lose, let's go out there, open it up, and have some fun. Let's take it one down at a time." In doing this, he took the pressure off. Sometimes it takes getting to a point where we feel we have nothing more to lose before we can lighten up and see the absurdity of it all.

That quarterback was able to march his team back, play by play, to eventually tie the game at 38 and throw it into overtime, then they won it on a field goal. Assess Yourself 6-9 allows you to create your own Absurdity Library.

Taking Yourself Lightly while Taking your Work Seriously

This second humor skill is one that exemplifies grace and modesty. It is characterized by a humble attitude and a proper perspective. As we have already discussed in this chapter, it is hard to take yourself lightly when you view yourself as the center of the universe.

Metcalf[13] uses the example of a young boy with cancer to explain what he means by this second humor skill. This young cancer patient would imitate the sounds of various animals when undergoing chemotherapy. He would squeal like a pig, bark like a dog, or cluck like a chicken. The medical staff would go along with him and his treatment sessions would be light-hearted exchanges of animal sounds. For most people, chemotherapy is a painful, serious situation. Metcalf could not understand how this boy could be so playful under such circumstances. The boy explained it by saying that he was not the cancer. Cancer was only part of his life. He took the disease seriously and attended treatment faithfully, believing that the discipline involved in seeing it through just might save his life. However, he did not dwell on it. He was doing all that he could do. He did not take himself so seriously that he had to stop being a kid and having fun. In fact, the silliness helped; it made him and everyone else feel better.

Having a Sense of Joy in Being Alive

The third humor skill is having a sense of joy in being alive. How many of us stop long enough to just reflect on how great it feels to be alive? Sometimes we take it for granted. Do you know someone who has been very close to death—someone who has suffered a life-threatening illness or accident? They often seem like changed people. Suddenly they are able to see the absurdity of life and all the time they wasted on meaningless things. They sense the preciousness of each day and live each as if it were their last. These people have a renewed zest for living and joy in the simple things in life. Assess Yourself 6-10 encourages you to create your own joy list.

Summary

This chapter introduces the first level of coping with stress—rethink. It starts with a discussion of values clarification. By clarifying our values we examine the things in life that are most central to who we are. This is a critical step in stress management because it gives us a frame of reference and helps us understand why we get stressed when we are in situations where things that are important to us are in jeopardy.

Our values guide us in setting goals for life and stress management. Goals help shape our lives and give them meaning. Goals put us on a course and give our lives direction and purpose.

The chapter moves on to look at how we sometimes lose sight of what is important to us. It describes the whole issue of perspective. Are we able to view daily events in a rational, sensible perspective, or do we blow everything out of proportion? Do we, as Metcalf[13] says, view ourselves as the center of the universe? We also need to reevaluate the pace of life. Are we constantly rushing about from one commitment to the next? This chapter looks at how the pace of our lives is related to our stress.

The chapter continues by reexamining the work of Albert Ellis[7], the father of rational emotive psychotherapy. Ellis believes that it is not people or things that cause us stress but rather our illogical beliefs and negative self-talk. The chapter describes Ellis's ABCDE technique for handling potential stressors rationally.

Morita therapy goes one step beyond RET by saying that even though our illogical beliefs and the negative emotions created by them are a source of stress, we can still live productive lives. Moritists believe that although we may not be able to control our distressing emotions, we can control our behavior. In time, our negative emotions will pass and will be replaced by new ones. Moritists teach us how to accept and live with negative emotions and still lead productive lives.

The chapter ends with a discussion of the importance of fun and humor in our lives and in stress management. The chapter explores the definition of humor and explains how humor involves both attitudinal and skill building components. That is, humor is both an outlook and a set of useful skills. The chapter ends by describing how we can develop both.

Student Study Questions

1. Describe what the author means by a wellness model of stress.
2. List and describe the five levels of coping.
3. What is meant by the synergistic effect created by the combination of the five levels of wellness and the five levels of coping?
4. Using a personal example, what is the true purpose of values clarification?
5. What is the perspective "Lighten Up" all about?
6. List and describe Metcalf's three humor skills.
7. How does the ABCDE model of Rational Emotive Therapy work to reduce stress?
8. Define humor.
9. How does humor cancel out stress?

References

1. Browne, H. (1973). *How I found freedom in an unfree world.* New York: Macmillan.

2. Cassell, C. (1984). *Swept away: why women fear their own sexuality.* New York: Simon & Schuster.

3. Cousins, N. (1979). *Anatomy of an illness as perceived by the patient.* New York: WW Norton.

4. Dryfoos, J. (1985). What the United States can learn about prevention of teenage pregnancy from other countries. *SIECUS Report, 14*(2), 1-7.

5. Dyer, W. (1978). *Pulling your own strings.* New York: Crowne.

6. Ellis, A., & Harper, R. (1975). *A new guide to rational living.* North Hollywood: Wilshire Books.

7. Ellis, A. (1993). Reflections on rational emotive therapy. *Journal of Consulting and Clinical Psychology, 61*(2), 199-201.

8. Goddard, K. (1991). Morita therapy: a literature review. *Transcultural Psychiatric Research Review, 28*(2), 93-115.

9. Jemmott, J.B., Jemmott, L., & Fong, G.T. (1992). Reductions in HIV risk-associated behaviors among black male adolescents: effects of an AIDS prevention intervention. *American Journal of Public Health, 82*(3), 372-77.

10. Kobassa, S. (1979). Stressful life events, personality & health: an inquiry into hardiness. *Journal of Personality & Social Psychology, 37*(1), 1-11.

11. Lawday, D. (1991). Letter from a productive lover of leisure. *US News & World Report, 111*(6), 6-8.

12. Martinson, F.M. (1982). Against sexual retardation. *SIECUS Report, 10*(3), 3.

13. Metcalf, C.W., & Felible, R. (1992). *Lighten up: survival skills for people under pressure.* Reading, MA: Addison Wesley.

14. Nathan, J. (1990). Sitting, laboring, and changing; a critical examination of the indigenous Japanese psychotherapies. *Psychologia, 33,* 163-170.

15. Peale, N.V. (1952). *The power of positive thinking.* Greenwich, CN: Fawcett Crest.

16. Peck, F.S. (1978). *The road less traveled.* New York: Simon & Schuster.

17. Raths, L., Harmin, M., & Simon, S. (1966). *Values and teaching.* Columbus: Charles E. Merrill.

18. Reynolds, D. (1984). *Playing ball on running water.* New York: William Morrow.

19. Reynolds, D. (1986). *Even in summer the ice doesn't melt.* New York: William Morrow.

20. Reynolds, D. (1992). The teacher-student relationship in Japanese culture and Morita Therapy. *International Bulletin of Morita Therapy, 5*(1), 18-21.

21. Simon, S.B., Howe, L.W., & Kirschenbaum, H. (1978). *Values clarification: a handbook of strategies for teachers and students.* New York: A&W Visual Library.

Name: _____ Date: _____

Strength of Values

Purpose

This strategy provides students with an opportunity to assess the strength of their feelings on the issues they themselves identify.

Procedure

This worksheet contains several unfinished sentences. (See below.) Students use the stems to write complete sentences or paragraphs if they wish.

The worksheet may then be filed for later reference, or an optional class discussion or small group discussion might follow.

Worksheet

Complete the statements below. You may write one sentence or a whole paragraph. Write "nothing" for any sentence for which you have no answer, or "pass" if you would prefer not to say.

1. I would be willing to die for . . .

    _____

    _____

2. I would be willing to physically fight for . . .

    _____

    _____

3. I would argue strongly in favor of . . .

    _____

    _____

4. I would quietly take a position in favor of . . .

    _____

    _____

5. I will share only with my friends my belief that . . .

    _____

    _____

6. I prefer to keep to myself my belief that . . . (This is for the student's private record.)

    _____

    _____

From Simon, S.B., Howe, L.W., & Kirschenbaum, H. (1978). *Values clarification: a handbook of strategies for teachers and students.* New York: A&W Visual Library.

Name: _____ Date: _____

Success Analysis

Everybody has been good at something in life. We have all had our successes. Unfortunately, however, most of us tend to dwell on our failures instead. This activity is designed to help us recall successful events from our pasts so that we can use these as a stimulus for future success.

Instructions:

1. Divide your life into the following time segments:
   - Childhood (elementary school years)
   - Early adolescence (middle school years)
   - Adolescence (high school)
   - Young adulthood (late teens, early twenties)
   - Early adulthood (mid-twenties to late thirties)
   - Middle adulthood (40s to 50s)
   - Older adulthood (60 +)

2. Describe one personal success for each time segment. A success could be as simple as something you did well during that time of life or it could be a formal honor you received.

   _____

   _____

   _____

   _____

   _____

   _____

   _____

3. Try to capture the feelings you felt at this time.

4. Where will your next success come from? Why?

5. Take turns sharing your successes with others in small groups.

Name: _____ Date: _____

Goals and Objectives Worksheet

Accomplishing your goals takes planning, hard work, discipline, determination, organization, and faith. This worksheet will help you organize your goals and set objectives to keep you on course.

Life Goals

A. Personal Goals

    1st Goal

    _____

    _____

        Objectives

        a. _____

        b. _____

        c. _____

    2nd Goal

    _____

    _____

        Objectives

        a. _____

        b. _____

        c. _____

    3rd Goal

    _____

    _____

        Objectives

        a. _____

        b. _____

        c. _____

B. Professional Goals

    1st Goal

    _____

    _____

Goals and Objectives Worksheet (cont'd)

Objectives

a. _____

b. _____

c. _____

2nd Goal

_____

_____

Objectives

a. _____

b. _____

c. _____

3rd Goal

_____

_____

Objectives

a. _____

b. _____

c. _____

ASSESS YOURSELF 6-4

Humor Inventory

The Humor Inventory is really a simple tool. It consists of four parts:

1. What happened?

2. How did it make you feel?

3. What were you left with?

4. What can you do about it?

Instructions:

- What Happened?

  Describe the event that contributed to distorting or blocking your sense of humor.

- How did it make you feel?

  List the specific feelings you can remember about this incident.

- What were you left with?

  Discuss the belief(s) about humor you took away from this.

- What can you do about it?

  Consider how you can take this information and change your views about humor and the way you use it.

Example:

1. What Happened?

   When I was about 5 years old, I remember waiting with my father and brother outside a hospital as my mother visited a sick friend. The hospital had a fringed awning covering the walkway into the front door. To amuse ourselves, we had a contest to see who could jump up and touch the fringe. My father easily reached it. My older brother got very close. I, chubby and sickly, could barely get off the ground. This was hilarious to my father and brother who laughed heartily, rolled on the ground and made remarks such as, "what a load," and "fat boy."

2. How did it make me feel?

   I was embarrassed. I wanted to run away and hide from them and all the people on the street who I imagined were staring at me.

3. What was I left with?

   I realized that humor could be a powerful weapon. Teasing and bringing attention to someone's shortcomings could bring someone to their knees.

4. What can I do about it?

   I am trying to stop using this kind of humor against my own sons. I slip up occasionally but always apologize and try not to repeat my mistakes.

Humor Inventory (cont'd)

Divide your life up into the following segments:

- Grade school (ages 5 to 11)
- Junior high (ages 12 to 15)
- High school (ages 15 to 18)
- College and career (ages 18 to 29)
- Parenthood
- Middle years (ages 36 to 65)
- Elder years (70+)

Take a humor inventory for each of the stages that are appropriate for you. Share them with your classmates in small groups.

From Metcalf, C. W., & Felible, R. (1992). *Lighten up: survival skills for people under pressure*. Reading, MA: Addison Wesley.

ASSESS YOURSELF 6-5

Slow the Pace: When Was the Last Time You . . .

Check off whether you performed this activity in the past month.

	Yes	No	Activity
1.			Walked instead of driving or taking the bus
2.			Intentionally took the back roads or streets so you could take your time
3.			Took the train or bus so you could sit back and gaze out of the window
4.			Took a walk in the woods or a park
5.			Took a bicycle ride off the beaten path
6.			Went on a nature walk
7.			Stopped to smell or observe the flowers or scenery along the side of a road
8.			Watched a sunset
9.			Sat quietly and listened to the birds in the trees
10.			Listened to the wind blowing through the trees
11.			Sat on the beach and just watched and listened to the waves
12.			Rocked a baby to sleep
13.			Explored a tidepool, pond, or frozen shoreline
14.			Examined a handful of beach sand or snow
15.			Planted a garden
16.			Watched the clouds roll by
17.			Looked at the stars and the moon on a clear night
18.			Brushed your pet's fur or someone else's hair
19.			Gave someone else a shampoo

Scoring: Yes _____   No _____

Add up the total number of responses for the past month. The greater the number of yes responses, the better. If you did not have at least 4 yes responses, you need to slow down and rethink the pace of your life before it slips away or you forget how to slow down.

These are just a few activities that require you to slow down and pay attention to the small things that give our lives the richness that makes us fully human. These things will also help you reduce your stress by helping you rethink your priorities and the relative unimportance of all the rushing around you do.

ASSESS YOURSELF 6-6

Bright-side Scenarios

There are at least two ways to view every situation. Often we choose to focus on the negative side of a situation. Try to focus on the bright side of the following scenarios. Describe as many bright-side interpretations as possible for each scenario.

1. You lose your job.

   _____

   _____

2. You do your best but are beaten by an opponent in the championship (individual or team sport).

   _____

   _____

3. Your company relocates to another part of the country and offers to take you with them.

   _____

   _____

4. Your boyfriend/girlfriend wants to date other people.

   _____

   _____

5. Your parents get divorced.

   _____

   _____

6. Your parents get remarried to someone else.

   _____

   _____

7. Your old clunker car dies in the driveway.

   _____

   _____

8. You flunk the CPA exam the first time around.

   _____

   _____

9. You must do your term paper over because it is unacceptable.

   _____

   _____

10. It rains for the first 2 days of your vacation.

   _____

   _____

ASSESS YOURSELF 6-7

ABCDE Scenarios

Think of a situation in which you became stressed because of your illogical beliefs about that situation. Make sure the beliefs you had really were illogical and inappropriate for the situation. For instance, it is reasonable to be upset if a good friend lets you down, but it is illogical or for you to blame yourself and use negative self-talk.

Work through your scenario using Ellis and Harper's[6] ABCDE technique. Refer to the list of illogical beliefs from Chapter 2 for help in identifying your illogical beliefs about the situation. Make sure you list each belief separately. Share these scenarios with your classmates in small groups.

A - Activating event (the stressor that activated your response)

B - Illogical beliefs (the specific illogical beliefs and negative subvocal self-talk related to the activating event)

C - Consequences (the negative effects of your beliefs—could be mental, physical, social, behavioral, etc.)

D - Dispute (rephrasing each belief into a more logical/rational statement)

E - Evaluate effects (the effects of the dispute on the consequences)

Name: _____ Date: _____

Am I Having Fun Yet?

List your top 10 favorite activities and the number of times you have done them this week:

Activity	Times Done
1. _____	_____
2. _____	_____
3. _____	_____
4. _____	_____
5. _____	_____
6. _____	_____
7. _____	_____
8. _____	_____
9. _____	_____
10. _____	_____

What is the total number of times you have has fun this week?

If your weekly fun count was less than 10, you're not doing pleasurable things as often as you should. Make time for at least one of these activities every day.

Name: _____ Date: _____

Absurdity Library

This activity is designed to help us remember just how absurd and humorous the world can be. When we get caught up in taking things too seriously, we sometimes need to be reminded of the absurdity of it all.

Instructions:

1. Starting today, begin to put together your own personal absurdity library. Compile cartoons, song lyrics, stories, letters from friends, advertisements, and photographs. You can even add records, tapes, and videos to your collection. In no time, your collection will be overflowing with goodies to dig into when the need arises.

2. Look for things that have personal meaning for you, even if others do not view them as special.

3. Add to your collection daily!

4. Whenever you feel the need, stop what you're doing and go to your absurdity library.

Adapted from Metcalf, C.W., & Felible, R. (1992). *Lighten up: survival skills for people under pressure.* Reading, MA: Addison-Wesley.

Name: _____ Date: _____

Joy List

Here is the perfect companion when you begin to question what life is all about. It is called the joy list and it takes off where Assess Yourself 6-8 leaves off. It is amazing how many people cannot come up with 10 things they really enjoy. This activity, the joy list, will help you keep track of the things that bring your life joy.

Instructions:

1. Dedicate a small spiral pad for this activity.

2. Carry the pad with you daily.

3. Every time you do something that you enjoy write it down.

4. Look back over your list frequently.

5. Try to build these things into your schedule.

6. Share your list with someone you love.

Start now by writing down 10 things that bring you joy.

1. _____
2. _____
3. _____
4. _____
5. _____
6. _____
7. _____
8. _____
9. _____
10. _____

From Metcalf, C.W., & Felible, R. (1992). *Lighten up: survival skills for people under pressure.* Reading, MA: Addison Wesley.

Reduce: The Second Level of Defense

CHAPTER OBJECTIVES

- Define reduce, the second level of coping with stress.

- Compare and contrast rethink and reduce.

- Analyze the relationship between level of stimulation and efficiency.

- Describe the three *As* of coping using a personal stressor as an example.

- Assess and evaluate your time management.

- Using personal examples, describe the ACT method of time management.

- Explain the relationship between stress management and assertiveness, nonassertiveness, and aggressiveness.

- Describe the three-part communication model used in the text.

Cont'd

CHAPTER OBJECTIVES (cont'd)

- **Describe the relationship between communication and stress.**
- **Identify aspects of your life that may be areas for downscaling.**

In Chapter 6, we explored the first line of defense against stress, rethink. We learned that many of us are stressed because of the way we view the world and the events that happen to us. Our beliefs about time, our activity level, and the pace of our lives play major roles in our stress level. We need to think about these issues and ask ourselves some tough questions about them.

Do we schedule every minute of every passing day? Do we build downtime or playtime into our schedules? Do we say yes to every request? Do we feel that we are unproductive if we are not always busy? Do we feel that there is enough time in our lives to meet our needs and do the things we truly enjoy? These are just a few of the many questions we answer and issues we explore in this chapter as we seek to understand ways to reduce stress in our lives.

How Much Stress Is Too Much?

As we discussed in Chapter 2, stress is a very individualistic phenomenon. What stresses some people does not even affect others. Some events that may drive you crazy roll right off your friend's back. Just as the nature of stimuli are individually perceived as either stressful or not, so is the amount of stimuli. The amount of stimuli that challenges you to dig down and work harder might mesmerize your friend into inactivity. Trying to keep up with the pace that challenges you may render them useless; they simply cannot keep up because they are stressed to the limit. How much stress is enough or too much? What amount of stimulation will get us to perform at our peak efficiency without burning out? The following inverted U-shaped curve (Fig. 7-1) helps us answer these questions.

This curve clearly illustrates the effects of excess stress on our level of functioning. The horizontal axis plots the level of stimulation or demand and runs from low to high. The vertical axis plots the level of performance, ranging from inefficient to optimal efficiency. The curve shows that too low a level of stimulation results in inefficient functioning. In other words, when we are not challenged, we fail to live up to our potential. As we take on more responsibilities and demand more of ourselves, we begin to perform

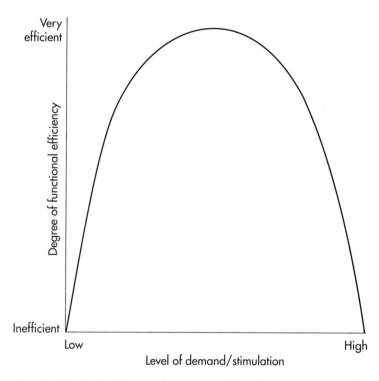

Fig. 7-1 This drawing illustrates how our level of performance is negatively affected by too many demands. The key is finding our optimal level.

at a higher level of efficiency. This is what was referred to in Chapter 2 as being challenged. It is not stress because we perceive it positively—we sense the exhilaration and energy it mobilizes. As we near our optimal level of stimulation or challenge, we approach peak efficiency.

Without this illustration, one would logically think that if a person is performing at peak efficiency at this peak level of demand there is no reason to think that they cannot do even better with a little more stimulation. In fact, however, the opposite is true. A little more demand results in a decrease in our performance. We begin to miss deadlines, hand in sloppy work, forget meetings, etc. With a lot more demand, challenge is replaced by stress and we sink to the same level of inefficiency as when we were not challenged enough. Good coaches realize this and strive to challenge each player and the team just enough to reach that point of peak efficiency. In addition, they try to have this peak coincide with the end of the season drive for the playoffs (see the box about Coach Brown on p. 238).

What do you do if you do not have a personal coach? How do we determine how much stimulation is enough? How do we know what the effects of a certain level of demand will be? Trial and error is the key to find-

STRESS IN OUR WORLD

Coach Brown

Coach Brown is a good example of someone who knows just how far to push his players to get them to perform at optimal efficiency. When he accepted the coaching position, he inherited a team that many people felt had failed to live up to their potential by not making the NCAA playoffs the year before. However, in his first year Brown took that same team to the playoffs and within a game of beating the NCAA champions.

He was able to achieve this in part because he is a master of determining how hard to push his players. Brown pushed when he needed to and laid back when his team needed to regroup. Rather than treat each player the same, Brown worked with the individual men, using the appropriate type and amount of stimulation to push each to his highest level of efficiency.

Have you ever had a similar experience with a coach, parent, or other leader? Have you ever had an experience with a person who was not very skillful in motivating you and either pushed you too hard or not hard enough? What kinds and how much pressure motivates you toward peak efficiency?

KEY
TO UNDERSTANDING

Understanding your optimal level of demand requires trial and error.

ing out how much stimulation is appropriate. We take on a certain amount of work and commitment and assess how well we are performing. We examine not only the end result of our labor but also how we feel during the labor. Do we feel challenged or stressed? Are our emotions positive or negative?

An example might be the amount of credit hours you choose to register for in a semester. How do you know where to start? Your school advisor may give you some rough parameters for how many credits you need to graduate in 4 years. Beyond that you are on your own. One of your friends might do well with 16 credit hours per semester; however, that might be far too many for you. You may find that at 16 credit hours your grades are mostly *C*s and *D*s and you feel terrible because you stay up late every night to study. Unlike your friend, you simply cannot cut it. You are constantly tired, feel pushed to the limit, and do not have any time to socialize and have fun.

You need to decide whether the amount of pressure is enough or too much. Part of your decision will be based on how well you are functioning across the six dimensions of health. If you have high levels of physical, mental, emotional, spiritual, social, and environmental well-being, you will have more energy and a zest for life. You will feel more able to cope with the demands of extra work.

Regardless of what you ultimately decide, it is your decision. No one else can tell you how much is right for you. Trust your intuition and stand by your decision. Keep in mind, however, the only constant in life is change, and you might be better positioned next year to push yourself harder. At any given point in your life, your six dimensions of wellness will influence your perceived ability to cope.

Categories of Stressors

The first step in reducing your overall stress level is taking an inventory of the amount and types of stressors in your life. Assess Yourself 7-1 describes a personal stressor diary that will help you understand what stresses you, the intensity of those stressors and how you respond to them.

If you have determined that there are too many stressors in your life, then you need to take action. You need a plan to control as many of those stressors as possible. Unfortunately, you never will be able to control all of your stressors. Some of the things that cause us stress come without warning. It is important to realize this so you do not set up unrealistic expectations about being able to control all of your stress. Psychologist David Elkind[5] describes three categories of stressors: stressors that are foreseeable and can be controlled, stressors that are foreseeable and cannot be controlled, and stressors that are neither foreseeable nor controllable.

Because we cannot do much in advance to prepare for the third category of stressor, do not worry about it. When things happen unexpectedly, you need to adapt to the change and go with the flow. A key to stress management is not getting overly upset about things that are beyond your control.

We can, however, work with categories 1 and 2. Once you have kept your personal stressor diary for a few weeks, you will begin to get a handle on the kinds of things that cause you stress. Look for patterns: types of people, kinds of situations, and combinations of events. After you know the kinds of things that are stressors for you, examine whether or not you can anticipate these things in advance and whether or not you can exert any control over their occurrence. If you do have some control over their occurrence (category 1), you can formulate a plan for reducing their likelihood. If you cannot control the occurrence of this stressor (category 2), you have to use a different type of strategy to cope with it.

Three *As* of Coping

There are three ways of coping with some category 1 stressors: 1) *abolish* means completely eliminating stressors; 2) *avoid* refers to minimizing your exposure to stressors; and 3) *alter* means somehow changing the way you are exposed to the stressor.

Fig. 7-2 If there really is such a thing as a universal stressor, it is traffic. Traffic is the bane of commuters everywhere.

Take traffic as an example (Fig. 7-2). Suppose, after keeping your stressor diary for a few weeks, you find that your commute to school is a major source of stress for you. You have 9:00 AM classes four days a week and getting to school at this time puts you right in the middle of rush hour traffic.

Abolish

Using the three ways of coping, you begin with abolish—you consider dropping out of school. This way you have no school and therefore no commute. Realistically, however, you still want to attend school, so you shift to plan B—abolish your 9:00 AM classes. By taking either 8:00 AM or 11:00 AM classes you change your commute, leaving either before or after the rush hour. Using your problem solving skills and knowledge of the area and assessing your time needs for the rest of the day and week, you decide which classes will fit your schedule better.

Avoid

If the first *A* is impractical, you can shift into the second *A*, avoid. Using this strategy, you do not completely eliminate the stressor—you simply minimize your exposure to it. Again using the rush hour traffic as an example, you can simply choose to expose yourself to it less frequently. Instead of taking 9:00 AM classes four days a week, you may choose to take them only twice a week. In a sense, you cut your stress in half by cutting your exposure in half.

Alter

If neither of these solutions are acceptable, you can use the third *A*, alter, to somehow change the stressor or your exposure to it. You can alter this stressor to defuse it. You may decide to carpool. By being a passenger, you can sit back, read the paper, or take a nap during the ride to school. Some people, however, might find being a passenger more stressful than driving themselves. You also could try a different route; a back road may take a little longer but might provide a break from the traffic. Simply the change of scenery might be enough to defuse the commute as a stressor. You could also install a cassette deck or compact disk player in your vehicle and listen to comedy or peaceful music while stuck in traffic. You might even choose to listen to notes from class, using the commute as a time to study. Assess Yourself 7-2 shows how to cope with stressors using abolish, avoid, and alter as ways of coping.

A word of caution about the triple *As*—they do not work for all types of stressors. They work well for situational stressors, like traffic, that are not interpersonal in nature. However, they may not be appropriate for stressors between individuals. It may not be practical or possible, for instance, to use them with a roommate whom you do not like being around or with your boss who works in the same office as you. You may try them and find that they are inappropriate. If that is the case, move on to another reduce strategy or another level of coping.

Managing Your Time

Do you feel that there is not enough time in the day to do what needs to be done? Do you feel that you could use a couple more hours to finish up things at night? Are you the kind of person who would be lost if you forgot to wear your watch one day? Most people feel that they could use a little more time. Unfortunately, we cannot add more hours to our day or more days to our lives. What we can do is examine how we choose to spend our time and realize that it is truly our choice. We can determine whether or not we use our time efficiently.

Goal Setting and Time Management

The first step in time management is setting goals for our lives. As we discussed in Chapter 6, having a set of clear goals for your life helps reduce stress because it provides structure and purpose. It also serves as a basis for the planning and use of time.

All of this emphasis on efficiency and use of time does not mean that we should not have time to relax. Indeed, people who manage their time effectively realize that building free time into their schedules is just as important as building in time to study and work. One of the things time management teaches us is that there is enough time for both work and play if we plan wisely.

Assessing Your Time Use

Once you have clarified your goals and decided they are worthy of serious time considerations, you are ready to examine exactly how you use your time. You need to take a look at a few weeks worth of time logs to get a sense of how you use your time (Assess Yourself 7-3). Once you have completed your assessment, you can begin to look for patterns and trends in your use of time. Can you identify blocks of time that are not being used efficiently? Is your log so cluttered with commitments that there is very little time left for personal use? Remember, the most important thing to assess is how your use of time either compliments or inhibits your values and goals.

If your use of time inhibits your values and goals, you need to specify exactly how and where this is occurring. It may be that your schedule is not whole or balanced. You may spend too much time engaged in things such as watching TV or talking with friends. Or you may find that too much of your time is spent in work-related activities and that you do not allow yourself to indulge in a little "vegging out" now and then. When making these kinds of global assessments of your time use, keep the following types of time in mind:

1. School time—time spent attending classes, studying, researching at the library
2. Work time—time spent in actual work (your job, housework, community service, or child care)
3. Commuting time—time spent getting to and from work, school, and other commitments
4. Before and after time—this is your "cushion" from one commitment to the next
5. Playtime—time spent doing things that are fun
6. Sleep time—actual hours spent sleeping

Each segment of your time can be analyzed for quantity and quality. You need to ask yourself not only how much time you are spending, but whether it is quality time. Once again, remember that you are the ultimate judge of what works for you.

School time. School time involves the hours spent in all of the activities related to completing assignments. This includes the time spent in class, studying, going to the library, writing papers, and attending performances. Students often underestimate the amount of out-of-class time that is required to be successful in college.

Work time. Work time is that period of the day when you are engaged in tasks that are required of you according to your role. Obviously, the job you are paid for is the type of work most people include in this category. Other types of labor, ranging from child care to community service, can also fall into this category and must be assessed.

For instance, a person engaged in full-time child care who is also active in community service might actually put in more work hours than a person with a traditional 9-to-5 office job. The former does not share the same schedule of mandatory coffee breaks, free lunch hours, and personal time afforded by the for-pay work world of many people. Students engaged in classwork, homework, part-time jobs, childcare of siblings, housework, and community service can be stretched to the limit. Theses types of activities need to be evaluated as work when assessing time use. People engaged in this type of labor can easily find themselves as overextended and stressed out as the typical harried executive.

Commuting time. In today's society, we are dependent on automobiles and we spend much of our time in transit. Commuting time needs to be taken into account when examining our schedules. How many hours do we spend getting to and from school and work? How is this commuting time spent? Are their ways to alter it to make it less stressful?

Before and after time. Often we get into trouble with our use of time by not scheduling enough before and after time. We cut things so close that the slightest deviation from normal can throw our schedule off for the rest of the day. Students are notorious for scheduling three or more classes back-to-back in an effort to use time more efficiently. In actuality, what this does is set them up for stress because invariably things happen between classes that throw off these precise schedules. A class running overtime or a long line in the school cafeteria can wreak havoc on tight schedules.

Playtime. Playtime is important for total wellness and it needs to be built into each day as a stress-preventive strategy (Fig. 7-3). Playtime needs to be scheduled in just like work time. Playtime also needs to be given the same priority as work time. Remember the efficiency curve—more is not necessarily better when dealing with stress and time demands.[13]

Playtime is usually the first to be sacrificed when we overbook our commitments. Rather than accept this practice as standard operating procedure, we need to view this loss of playtime as a warning of our lack of balance. We also need to constantly assess our playtime to ensure that it stays play and not work. All too often our competitive instincts take over, and a relaxing game can become a struggle for dominance. Instead of using the game to relieve stress and tension, the game becomes a stressor itself. There is nothing wrong with competitive play as long as it is not the sole source of play.

Fig. 7-3 Playtime is critical for combatting stress. Make sure you build some into every day.

Sleep time. Sleep time is another highly variable phenomenon. Although some of us get by on 5 hours of sleep and feel refreshed, others need 8 to 9 hours to recharge their energy. Sleep needs vary from day to day and are influenced by a host of variables, ranging from overall level of health to energy expended during the day. Sleep needs also vary throughout the life cycle. Your body will let you know if you are not getting enough sleep. Pay attention to your fatigue warning signs.[8]

Time Management: A Matter of Priority

In addition to thinking globally about our use of time, we also need to look at how we spend time in a given day and week when we have specific tasks and deadlines that must be met. There are several ways to approach this type of time management.

The ACT Technique

The ACT technique is an approach to time management that revolves around making priority lists of things that you need and would like to accomplish during any given day. Each activity is assigned a different priority status and is approached based on its priority.

> A—activities that *absolutely* must be done today or you will suffer immediate, severe consequences. These are things you cannot put off until tomorrow. Only you can determine what these activities are but for the most part these are things such as paying bills,

Factors Related to Fatigue

1. Stress—Excess stress can sap your energy by wasting it to maintain the stress response. Make stress-management activities a part of each day.

2. Lack of sleep—Sleep needs vary greatly from person to person. While most people need between 5 to 10 hours a night, others get by on just 5 hours. If you are groggy after what you consider a good night's sleep, you may need a couple more hours.

3. Lack of exercise—If you are out of shape, your body is not performing up to its capabilities. Regular exercise will help your heart and lungs get more energy-producing oxygen into your bloodstream. Additionally, you will not have to work as hard to maintain your current level of activity.

4. Poor diet—A balanced diet with selections from all five food groups will provide all the essential nutrients to your body, ensuring it has the energy it needs to carry on.

5. Illness—Medical problems can rob you of energy and interfere with your body's normal functioning. Many energy-robbing illness such as anemia can go undetected without diagnostic tests.

6. Substance use—Both legal and illegal drugs often have fatigue and drowsiness as a side effect. Make sure you understand the possible side effects of all medication you are taking. If the symptoms persist, see your doctor.

handing in school and work assignments, and meeting personal obligations. Remember, playtime is essential. Do not neglect to schedule some in as an *A* list activity.

C—activities that *could* get done when the *A* list tasks are finished. Working on an assignment that is due next month is an example of this kind of task. Although you would like to begin the project, failure to do so will not result in any negative consequences today. *C* list activities will become *A* list activities in time as their deadlines approach.

T—activities you could *try* to do if all of your *A*s and *C*s get finished. Things like shopping for a new car or writing a letter you have been meaning to get to would be *T* list activities.

The best time to make up these priority lists is at the end of the day. You begin by assessing which *C* and *T* list activities remain from during the day. Taking these and tomorrow's *A* list activities, you plan your schedule for the next day. If you have fewer *A*s, today's unfinished *C*s may move up and become *A* list activities as their deadlines approach. You may even be able to get to some *T* list entries.

Some people simply tape these lists to their desk and check things off as they are finished. Others spend lots of money on color-coded schedule books or notebook computers. Others keep a daily calendar datebook that comes in handy when scheduling future commitments.

A word about working through your *A* list: some people like attacking the more difficult items first. In this way, they attack the most difficult problems when they are the freshest and have the most energy. Others like to knock off several smaller tasks first to get a sense of accomplishment right off the bat. There is no correct formula; whatever works for you is the best approach.

The key aspect of a priority system such as this is to finish your *A* list before moving on to your *C* or *T* lists. It is tempting to stop doing what has to be done to pursue something else that is more fun or less important. This invariably leads to stress, however, as *A* list deadlines get closer and you have not made the necessary progress in meeting them. This is when you find yourself taking unfinished work home or staying up late to accomplish things that could have been finished on time.

One way of achieving true **hedonism** is becoming more organized and using time effectively. This way, when you are off, you do not worry about unfinished business because there is none. You can be concerned about one thing—the pleasure that you can get out of this free time.

KEY
TO UNDERSTANDING

Finish your A list activities first.

hedonism

the pursuit of pleasure or happiness as the chief goal in life

Downscaling Your Life

Sometimes the reason we feel that there is too much to do and not enough time to do it is that our lives have gotten away from us. When you examine your personal stressor diary and time-management log, you might find that you need to cut back or downscale your life.

As has been the recurring theme of this chapter, only you know whether or not this needs to be done. It is so easy to get caught up in other people's expectations of how much you should be doing that it can be a challenge to finally take charge and say, "enough is enough." Sometimes this means letting other people down or failing to live up to others expectations. However, for you to be productive and whole, you need to live and work within your limits. Pushing too hard can be counterproductive.

KEY
TO UNDERSTANDING

Being productive requires working within your limits.

Downscaling can be achieved in several ways. It may simply involve cutting back your number of commitments. You may be happy with the lifestyle you have and the direction your life is going but you simply are too busy. In this case, downscaling does not mean changing the direction and focus of your life. All that is required is cutting back your activities and responsibilities.

In other cases, downscaling may involve changing the present focus and future direction of your life. You may decide that you are in a rut and your life is moving in a direction that is more stressful than enjoyable. In this

STRESS IN OUR WORLD

Karen

Karen is a second semester junior in college. She is very popular and everyone wants to be her friend. She is on the dean's list, takes 18 credit hours a semester, works 20 hours a week, and is a member of three clubs on campus. She is also the President of her sorority and an officer in each of the other clubs.

Karen's life is a whirlwind. She is forever dashing from one responsibility to the next. She gets up and rushes out of her dorm room to class, grabbing a cup of coffee and a doughnut from the student center on the way. Having three courses back-to-back, she rushes from one class to another, pausing only to grab a quick snack from a vending machine. She jumps in her car after her 12:30 class and races across town to get to her job as a part-time bank teller. At 4:00 PM she races back to campus, grabbing a quick burger at a drive-through so she can make a sorority meeting. When the meeting is over she heads back to her room to study for an hour before heading off to hang-out with friends at the student center. Back in her room by 11:00 PM, she collapses and is asleep instantly.

Karen has been having some problems recently. It seems that her grades are off and she will not make the dean's list this semester. She has been feeling tired lately and has been sick three times this year so far. She has been on edge lately with a very short fuse. Her boyfriend just broke up with her because he never got to spend any time with her. Her life is beginning to break at the seams.

Do you know any Karens? How long can she keep up this pace? What would you recommend to help her get her life in order?

case you will not only have to cut back but also change course. You will need a new direction and new plan to get you where you want to be.

The blueprint for downscaling is very similar to everything else we have been discussing in this chapter in that it begins with a look at your values and goals. From this assessment we decide in which areas we would be happier with less.

Asserting Yourself

Reducing activities, whether they involve the three As of coping, time management, or downscaling, often require that we assert ourselves in our desire to cut back on life demands. In many cases these demands on our time and energy revolve around the needs of other people, and the decision to downscale will affect others who will try to pressure us to get their needs met. Therefore if our attempts at reducing stress are to succeed, then assertiveness is key.

Assertiveness is often confused with aggressiveness, and many people fail to develop assertiveness skills because of this confusion. In their attempts to control what they perceive as aggressiveness, they act nonassertively and fail to get their needs met, allowing hostility and frustration to build up inside

In actuality, assertiveness is not a negative attribute. It is based on mutual respect and democracy in relationships. Assertiveness is understanding your wants and needs and pursuing them without infringing on others. Aggressiveness, on the other hand, is pursuing your needs and wants without any regard to how this affects the rights of others; often, aggressive people get their needs met at the expense of others. Nonassertiveness is failing to pursue your needs and wants while allowing others to meet theirs. Nonassertive people often fail to stick up for their rights and allow others to take advantage of them, often denying that this is going on.[15] Lack of assertiveness is a key factor in becoming overburdened with commitments that demand time and interfere with doing what you want or need to do.

Nonassertive people are also often filled with resentment and hostility toward others. Originally, in an attempt to avoid conflict, the nonassertive will say yes when they really mean no. This temporarily relieves them from feeling guilty. Unfortunately, however, when they do this they get trapped

KEY
TO UNDERSTANDING

Lack of assertiveness is a key factor in becoming overburdened.

Assertiveness Bill of Rights

The following "Assertiveness Bill of Rights" may help strengthen your resolve to speak up for yourself:

- You have the right to judge your own behavior, thoughts, and emotions and to take responsibility for their initiation and consequences upon yourself.

- You have the right to offer no reason or excuses for justifying your behavior.

- You have the right to judge if you are responsible for finding solutions for other people's problems.

- You have the right to change your mind.

- You have the right to make mistakes and be responsible for them.

- You have the right to say, "I don't know."

- You have the right to be independent of the good will of others before coping with them.

- You have the right to be illogical in making decisions.

- You have the right to say, "I don't understand."

- You have the right to say, "I don't care."

From Hales, D. (1992). *An invitation to health.* Menlo Park, CA: Benjamin Cummings.

into doing things they do not want to do or do not have the time to do. When this happens they begin to feel miserable because they have lost control of their lives and time. They are constantly fighting back anger and hostility directed at other people. They also realize that the only way this will stop is if they begin to say no, which brings them full circle to the same situation as the initial one—having to say no. If they were assertive to begin with, they could have avoided all of that aggravation and stress.

Assertiveness begins, as do all of the reduce strategies, with an assessment of our use of time, level of commitment, goals, and values. Once we have evaluated these areas, we can decide whether to allow new demands on our time. Saying no and meaning it are the hard parts. The box below helps you learn to say no.

How to Say No

Saying no is not always easy but it is essential if you are to be assertive and reduce your stress. Remember, you have the right to say no. The following are clear guidelines for saying no.

1. Face the other person from a normal distance.
    - If you are too far away, you may appear timid.
    - If you crowd the person, you border on aggressiveness.
2. Look the other person directly in the eyes.
    - Averting eye contact is a sure give-away that you will cave in.
3. Keep your head up and your body relaxed.
    - Don't be a shrinking violet.
4. Speak clearly, firmly, and at a volume that can be heard.
5. Just say no.
    - You do not need to clarify why.
6. Be prepared to repeat it.
    - Sometimes people are persistent.
7. Stick to your guns.
    - Do not give in—it gets easier with practice.

If you feel a need to explain why you are declining, here are a few tips for setting the stage:

1. Thank the person for the offer.
2. Express appreciation.
3. Affirm your friendship.
4. Reject the offer, not the person.

Often, lack of assertiveness is a cultural issue that transcends stress management. Some cultures demand subjugating personal desires for the good of a larger whole. Children are expected to put their needs behind those of others and respect the wishes of parents, grandparents, and elders.

The conflict between these traditional ways of behaving and American cultural values that focus on the individual and self-actualization can be a source of stress for traditional students.

STRESS IN OUR WORLD

Susie Chen

Susie Chen was a senior marketing major and she was the youngest daughter of a first generation Chinese-American family. Susie's two sisters were married and worked with their husbands in the family business comprised of three laundries. Susie, the first of the family to attend college, managed one of the three laundries.

Susie enrolled in a stress-management class because she needed help managing her time more efficiently. She attended college during the day and worked at the family business more than 40 hours a week and on weekends. She also lived at home with her mom, dad, and grandparents.

After a few weeks of class it became apparent that time management was not Susie's problem; she had excellent time-management skills.

Susie's real problem was that she was feeling extremely anxious and stressed anticipating her impending graduation. Upon graduation, her family expected her to become more involved in the family business, perhaps opening a fourth outlet, and to continue to live at home. The issue was never discussed—they just assumed that Susie would obey their wishes.

However, Susie had no desire to either remain in the family business or continue to live at home. She longed to join a multinational company and see the world as an international marketing representative. She also wanted her own apartment.

When she was asked by her professor whether or not she had explained these desires to her family, she exclaimed, "Oh no! I couldn't do that. They would never

understand or accept it. Plus it would be considered impolite." When her professor probed further concerning how she was going to pursue her plans, she explained that they would have to wait until either her parents died or she would do something shameful like run away and leave them a letter, praying for their future forgiveness.

The professor was dumbfounded. He really did not know what to do. It was obvious that cultural reasons were keeping Susie, an excellent student with great communication skills, from using the assertiveness techniques that her professor recommended. They decided that she was better off learning how to live with this stressor and cope with it using other techniques rather than to try to eliminate it through the use of assertiveness.

Communicating Effectively to Reduce Stress

Communicating effectively is the best prevention against stress that arises from interpersonal relationships. Conversely, ineffective communication or miscommunication can often become a source of stress. Usually, as Lazarus and Folkman[11] pointed out, people feel stressed when things are ambiguous. When people are unsure of what situations or messages mean, they feel threatened by them and therefore become stressed. Clearing up misunderstandings before they are left to fester is a good preventive strategy for reducing stress. Rarely, do unresolved issues clear up without any attempts to clarify and fix them.

Metacommunication

Communication is defined as the process by which information is exchanged between individuals through a common system of symbols, signs, or behaviors. It involves all the modes of behavior that an individual uses to affect another person, including spoken and written words as well as nonverbal messages such as gestures, facial expressions, bodily posture, and artistic symbols.[4] Communication also includes the interpersonal relationship between communicators. When we are in the presence of others, according to Watzlawick, Beavin, and Jackson[16] it is impossible to not communicate; both activity and inactivity, speech and silence, communicate messages.

Communication occurs at two levels: the content level (what is actually being said) and the relationship level (what is going on between the communicants). This second relationship level is referred to as metacommunication, or communication about communication. Watzlawick, Beavin, and Jackson[16] use the term *pragmatics* to refer to the relationship between communicators and they identify two types of relationships: symmetrical and complementary. Symmetrical relationships are based on equality, with each communicator treating the other in a like fashion, minimizing differences and conflict. Complementary relationships, on the other hand, are based on differences. Communicators maximize their differences causing inequality and disharmony. Complementary relationships therefore often result in stress.

Transactional Analysis

Erich Berne's[1] transactional analysis is a communication model that examines relationships that are either symmetrical or complementary. Berne proposes that all people have three sources of behavior, or ego states: the parent, adult, and child. Each ego state manifests itself in a different communication style. Fig. 7-4 illustrates the three ego states of transactional analysis.

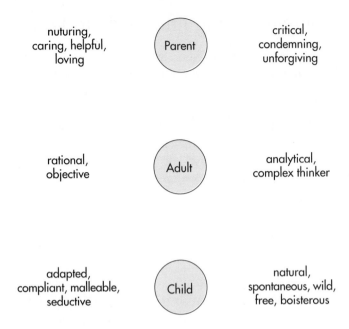

Fig. 7-4 The three transactional analysis ego states.

The Child. The child manifests itself through childish use of verbal and non-verbal communication. The child uses coyness, naivete, charm, boisterousness, giggling, and whining and is spontaneous, irresponsible, and manipulative.

The Adult. The adult is rational and objective, uses logic and analysis, and exhibits sound decision making based on accurate perception and analysis. The adult is fair, responsible, and sociable.

The Parent. The parent incorporates the feelings and behaviors learned from authority figures. The parent communicates the conscience of the person through words, actions, postures, behaviors, expectations, and the use of guilt or reward. The parent can be nurturing or critical.[1]

According to Berne,[1] when we communicate, our message is sent from one of our three ego states and is received by a specific ego state of another. Ideally, the ego state from which we send messages matches that of the person to whom we are talking. In other words, if we are speaking from our adult state to another person, they should be receiving our message in their adult state. If they are not, a mismatch occurs. A mismatch is similar to a complementary message in Watzlawick, Beavin, and Jackson's[16] metacommunication model. Mismatches between messages sent from one state and received by another can be a source of stress.

Fig. 7-5 illustrates a mismatch that occurs when we are talking to a peer and we use our parent ego state instead of our adult state. Our friend,

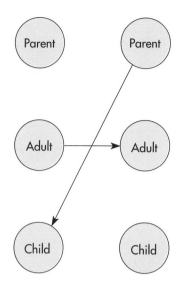

Fig. 7-5 Crossed TA transactions. One adult addresses another adult. However, the second adult receives the message in an adult ego state and responds as if to a child ego state.

receiving in an adult ego state, expects us to send an adult message. Instead, we send a parent message to a child ego state, which creates a mismatch and is a source of stress.

A Circular Model of Communication

Effective communication is a circular process that involves sending and receiving coded messages. Fig. 7-6 illustrates what happens when a message is sent, received, and responded to.

A sender wishing to communicate puts the idea and feeling of the message into a form that can be transmitted. This process of formulating a message and choosing appropriate words, symbols, tone, and expressions to represent it is called **encoding**.

The encoded message is transmitted and received by the receiver and then translated by the receiver's personal storehouse of knowledge and experience. This perceiving and translating process is called **decoding**.

As you can see in Fig. 7-6, both encoding and decoding take place within the context of the interpersonal and physical relationship of the communicants. What is being said involves not only the actual message but also the physical environment and the relationship between sender and receiver. A sender might alter the message depending on whether the environment is friendly or unfriendly, familiar or unfamiliar, safe or unsafe, formal or informal. Additionally, a sender might send a different message in the same environment depending on the nature of the relationship with the receiver. The

encoding

the selection of signs, symbols, emotions, and words to transmit a message

decoding

the use of knowledge, memory, language, context, and personal history and experience to interpret a message.

Sender   Receiver

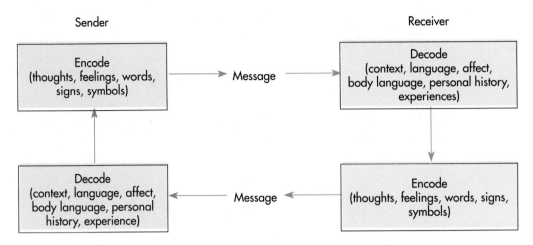

Fig. 7-6 A model of communication.

message might be affected by whether the sender and receiver are friends or enemies, strangers or acquaintances, peers or of unequal status.

As seen in Fig. 7-6, communication involves sending and receiving both verbal and nonverbal messages. Each type of message is capable of transmitting information and is part of the encoding and decoding process.

Verbal Communication

Verbal communication is two dimensional in that it involves transmitting both thoughts and feelings by putting them into words. The cognitive dimension is concerned with communicating thoughts about things, while the affective dimension involves putting feelings into words. Most people find communicating cognitive information easier than expressing feelings.

Specificity is crucial in effective verbal communication; the more specific the message, the more likely it is to be transmitted clearly. Vocabulary plays a big part in the specificity of our verbal communication. Having a large working vocabulary allows us to specify exactly what we want to say.

The level of language we use also affects the forcefulness of verbal communication. There are four levels of language: childhood, street, everyday discourse, and scientific.

Childhood language. Childhood language is simple, cute, fun, and often used to disguise embarrassment. Lovers have their own brand of childhood language. They may use it to describe their sexual anatomy and physiology, sexual desire, or needs for pleasure. Pet names and phrases are part of this language. People also often use childhood language when they make mistakes and seek forgiveness. "Oops, sowwy (sic) about that," they may say in mock childhood tones.

Street language. Street language is tough, expressive, and emotional. Street language can be disarming and is often used to level the playing field when communicants are not equal. Tough talk can bestow power and superiority. Street language also serves to create bonds between members of subcultures through the sharing of a language that is often not understood by members of mainstream society.

Everyday discourse. Common discourse is the language level in which most people communicate. Its words, expressions, and speech patterns are used by people in communicating information that is neither intimate nor scientific. It is the language taught in schools and used in most communications.

Scientific language. Scientific, or professional, language is the discourse of the work world. It is the language shared by professional peers as they communicate about the subtleties of their chosen professions. Like street language, it is usually understood only by those who share its culture. Computer professionals are famous for having a unique vocabulary, as are doctors and other medical professionals.

Nonverbal Communication

How we say things is as important as what we say. Body language is a term used to describe the nonverbal messages we send through our posture, gestures, movement, physical appearance, and even silence. Our body language intentionally or unintentionally sends messages to receivers.

Positive body language. Positive, or open, body language involves a relaxed posture, steady eye contact, nods of the head, and an occasional smile or happy expression. All are cues that you are an approachable sender or receptive receiver.

Negative body language. Negative, or closed, body language includes visible signs of tension, such as clenched fists, tight jaw muscles, a "closed" posture (e.g., arms folded, body shifted sideways), and facial expressions ranging from anger to disbelief. Negative body language can indicate that you are either apathetic or disturbed about something.

Physical appearance. Physical appearance can convey a variety of messages. A messy or ungroomed appearance may represent a variety of encoded messages ranging from positive (comfortable and relaxed) to negative (apathy and disrespect). Clothing and adornment might be intentionally or unintentionally erotic and seductive. This can affect both the encoding and decoding process; the sender might be trying to convey one message ("I'm trying to look my best"), while the receiver may perceive another ("This person is trying to manipulate or come on to me").

Silence. Silence is a form of nonverbal communication that can be both a source of stress and a sign of comfort. Silence is a stressor when wordless pauses are perceived as signs of a breakdown in the communication process. At other times, silence communicates comfort and acceptance between friends and lovers who understand that a loving bond exists despite a lack of conversation. Silence is a necessary part of effective communication that is often overlooked. People need time to listen, digest, and understand messages. It allows us time to reflect as we formulate our thoughts and words.

Touch and space. Touch is another way to nonverbally communicate a wide range of messages. A firm handshake, a pat on the head, a gentle squeeze of the shoulder, or a reassuring touch on the arm all convey messages without speaking a single word. Appropriately used, they add another dimension of communication that sometimes reaches deeper than mere words. When used inappropriately, however, the effects of touch can be devastating. A simple pat on the head can be a sign of endearment to your child but can embarrass or infuriate another adult. A squeeze on your friend's shoulder can show him you understand his problems, but the same squeeze on your secretary's shoulder can be a form of sexual harassment.

The space between sender and receiver also affects communication. Hall[9] has identified four space zones common to communication in North America:

1. Intimate pace (less than 18 in [.45 m])—space reserved for communication between intimate partners
2. Personal space (18 in to 4 ft [.45 to 1.22 m])—space appropriate for close relationships that may involve touching
3. Social/Consultive space (4 to 12ft [1.22 to 3.66 m])—space for non-touching, less intimate relationships that may involve louder verbal communication
4. Public space (greater than 12 ft [3.66 m])—space used for formal gatherings, such as addressing a large group

Stress can arise when senders and receivers violate these commonly accepted space parameters. For instance, we are stressed by situations where nonintimate persons get within the boundaries of intimate space. We find ourselves backing up to reclaim our violated space. Sometimes we place objects as barriers between us and others to define our space and set allowable communication zones.

Cultural Considerations in Communication

Communicating effectively requires awareness of and sensitivity to various cultural influences related to verbal and nonverbal communication. The following are a few examples of common cultural considerations to keep in mind.

Verbal Communication

Not all cultural groups and subcultures share a common language. Although English is the first language spoken by most Americans, and common discourse is the level most frequently used to communicate, this is not the case for many individuals and groups. For many Americans, English is a second language and common discourse is not always completely understood.

Some subjects and forms of communication may be unacceptable to certain cultures. Such forbidden topics of discussion may include emotions, feelings, or intimate sexual and other personal matters. The use of humor as a form of communication may also be disagreeable in some cultures.

Nonverbal Communication

Just as there are cultural differences related to the spoken word, there are also a variety of nonverbal factors that vary according to culture. For example, there are differences in territoriality and personal space. In general, people of Arabic, southern European, and African origins frequently sit or stand relatively close to each other when talking. People of Asian, northern European, or North American countries are more comfortable talking farther apart.[10]

Perception of time and the relationship of the past, present, and future also vary by culture. Americans and Canadians are very time and future oriented; in daily life these people are triggered to action at specific times of the day and schedules are strictly adhered to. However, in other cultures people are much less concerned with the future and do not follow such rigid schedules. Many Native American homes do not even have clocks because people are more concerned about the present and live one day at a time.[10]

Body language also varies significantly according to culture. Anglo-Americans like to maintain and place a high value on direct eye contact when speaking to one another. Native Americans, however, view continuous direct eye contact as insulting and disrespectful. Rules about eye contact also vary by gender in certain cultures. In Islamic cultures, for example, women are taught to divert eye contact, although it is acceptable for men. The meaning and acceptability of other nonverbal behaviors such as pointing fingers, shaking hands, and other forms of touch also vary by culture.

Cont'd

Cultural Considerations in Communication (cont'd)

The following can be helpful in managing cultural considerations with verbal and nonverbal communication.

1. Slow down—People for whom English is a second language can have a hard time keeping up with and understanding the speech of someone whose first language is English.

2. Minimize nonverbal distractions—Be conservative rather than flamboyant in your use of gestures, personal space, etc.

3. Look for feedback—People who do not understand, cannot keep up, or are uncomfortable with something you do or say will often send nonverbal or verbal cues. They can be as blatant as asking for clarification or as subtle as a turned head or lack of eye contact. It is your responsibility to seek clarification of these cues.

4. Use an interpreter—Get someone to translate your message into the other person's language of choice.

5. Avoid talking louder—When we are not sure we are being understood, we sometimes raise our voices assuming the person cannot hear us. Talking loudly can be perceived as threatening or condescending and is rarely helpful.

6. Show respect—Even if you make a mistake, being humble and respectful of cultural differences will convey the message that you care and want to understand and improve communication.

Communication Skills

Communication involves three specific sets of skills: initiating, listening, and responding skills[12] (Fig. 7-7).

Initiating Skills

KEY
TO UNDERSTANDING

Effective communication requires assuming responsibility for clearing up misunderstandings.

Initiating skills are those encoding techniques you can employ to begin to express yourself. The key in communicating to reduce stress is understanding that it is your responsibility. If you have a problem with something someone says or does, it is your responsibility to bring it to their attention. They may or may not even be aware of the way their words or actions affect you. Furthermore, the fact that they said it is evidence that either they do not realize the power of their words or that they do and did it intentionally. In either case it is illogical for you to wait for them to apologize or bring it up. It is not their problem but yours.

　　If possible, the best time to clear up problems associated with communication is when they first occur. Taking time to clear things up before

Fig. 7-7 This model illustrates the circular nature of a dialogue. Each person is actively involved in either giving messages, listening, or responding.

they are allowed to progress can prevent the problem from escalating. Often, however, it is impossible to do this because of situational constraints. In these cases, tell the other person that you need some time alone with them to discuss something important. Try to get them in a neutral territory where you feel safe and emotionally strong. Make time to talk.

Important in initiating communication is the use of *I* language. When you use *I* language, you take responsibility for your feelings. *I* language does not blame your feelings on other people. For example, let us say that your friend made fun of you in front of three other common friends. Rather than blame your friend by saying, "*You* really made me feel terrible." you could say, "*I* really feel terrible when you...". Rather than blame your friend for what you are feeling, you own up to your feelings and state them in *I* language.

It is important to describe both the situation and your feelings about what happened in clear, simple terms. Try to avoid general statements like, "I hate it when you treat me bad," or "I hate it when you do things like that." It is better to specify exactly what the other person did that you dislike. It is better to say things like, "I hate it when you make fun of me in front of our friends," or "I really feel like a fool when you make fun of me in front of our friends." The phrase *in front of our friends* clarifies the situation by making it more specific.

It is also important to criticize the behavior, not the person. You must be sure that the person understands that you still like them but that you do not like it when they behave a certain way. Remember, the person probably is totally unaware of the nature of their language and behavior and its effects on you. The more precise you are in describing exactly what is bothering you, the better the chance you have for clearing up the problem without hurting the person's feelings. Assess Yourself 7-5 will help you assess your communication ability.

Initiating also includes nonverbal messages. As we have discussed, our posture, position, and expression all factor into the verbal message that is being sent. Sometimes we initiate using only nonverbal communication. A simple stare can send a message that is infinitely more powerful than a hundred words.

Listening Skills

Once you have expressed yourself clearly, the second phase of the communication cycle, listening, comes into play. Effective listening is a critical decoding skill.

passive listening
one-way listening that
provides no feedback

There are two types of listening, passive and active. **Passive listening** is one-way listening; the listener merely soaks in what is being sent by the initiator. Passive listening is what we all do when watching television or a movie or listening to the radio. Passive listening, however, is not the most effective form of listening to another person when trying to reduce stress.

active listening
listening with under-
standing and feedback

Active listening is much better for dealing with interpersonal communication because it requires feedback. Active listeners show that they are listening by providing both nonverbal and verbal feedback. For this reason, active listening is very demanding. It takes a lot of energy and concentration, and it is very easy to get distracted and lose interest. The box below illustrates some common bad habits that inhibit active listening.

BAD LISTENING HABITS

Dismissing the subject as uninteresting
Careful listening always presents us with new questions to be considered and new decisions to be made. Being a good listener requires a bit of courage and an inquisitive mind. One can always learn something—even from a bad speaker.

Faking attention
All of us have the "skill" of fixing glassy eyes on a speaker while our thoughts are miles away. However, efficient listening is dynamic and energy consuming. It is active, not passive. To listen well, we must do some of the work ourselves.

Avoiding difficult material
As listeners we often indulge ourselves in entertaining programs that demand very little attention. However, a certain amount of expository material is necessary for learning in life. We should consider it a challenge and give our receptive brains a little workout.

Creating or tolerating distractions
Do you clip your nails during a speech? Do you drum your fingers on the table? Do you allow the persons near you to carry on a private chit-chat? We should do our best to keep such distractions to a minimum.

Listening only for facts
Some listeners have a psychological set for listening only for what they think to be facts. These are usually sums of money, dates, or influential names. A good speaker will signal you by some device when he is about to impart to you some never-to-be-forgotten fact. Listen to all that he says. You can weed out the trivia after the conversation has ended.

Simple verbal and nonverbal cues such as a nod followed by an "uh huh" are enough to let the speaker know that you are listening. Once the initiator is finished you then move into the third phase of the cycle, responding.

Responding Skills

Responding skills involve reacting to the initiator's message and encoding some type of feedback using verbal and nonverbal communication. If the message is clear and no further clarification is necessary, a simple declarative statement can be used to acknowledge that you hear them and agree, disagree, or have new information to provide. If you disagree or have problems, remember to use *I* language to express your opinions.

BAD LISTENING HABITS (cont'd)

Judging the person instead of the delivery

Do you let the fact that a speaker's clothes do not match detract from what he or she is saying? Or perhaps you simply don't like the person and tune him or her out. However, that person might have something worthwhile to say and it is important to withhold judgment until evaluation is complete.

Getting overstimulated

A familiar fact presented from an unusual point of view or a chance word or phrase is often stimulus enough to trigger our imagination. We may go off on a mental tangent and often return only to hear the end of a question directed at us. Avoid this pitfall with the power of concentration.

Letting emotion-laden words and personal prejudice interfere

Emotional bias is one of the most formidable barriers to clear comprehension. When emotion enters the picture, we cease to think with our heads. It is important to respond rationally rather than emotionally, because some shrewd speakers deliberately use emotion to throw you off track.

Wasting the differential between through speed and speech speed

The average speech speed is approximately 125 words per minute, but it is not difficult to think 1000 words per minute. However, it is good to think at the comfortable rate of 500 words per minute. This means that we can let the speaker use 125 words a minute and still keep 375 for ourselves. This 375 is called the differential, and we can use it to our distinct advantage if we mentally recapitulate the speaker's words or ideas about every 4 minutes. Therefore resist the temptation to let your mind wonder, and use the differential time to recapitulate the speaker's message for maximum comprehension.

From Cicatelli Associates. (1985). *Ten bad listening habits: and what to do about them.* New York: Cicatelli Associates.

open-ended statements
statements that cannot be answered with a simple yes/no answer

paraphrasing
repeating back your version of the initiator's message

mirroring
repeating the initiator's exact words while mimicking their exact body posturing

Often responding skills are used to get additional information needed to understand an issue or solve a problem. Keeping the conversation going or requesting more information relies on being able to draw more information out of the initiator. Four techniques for doing this are: **open-ended statements**, **paraphrasing**, **mirroring**, and simple yes/no questions.

Open-ended statements. Using open-ended statements, such as "tell me more" or "what else do you know about that," are easy ways to get information and keep a conversation going. They require the initiator to provide additional information beyond a simple yes/no answer. The box on p. 263 provides more open-ended statements.

Paraphrasing. Paraphrasing, putting the person's message into your own words and interpreting what they mean, is another way to provide feedback and get more information. You can start off a paraphrase by stating "So, what you're saying is..." or "I sense that you...". When you paraphrase, you interpret the person's message, and he or she will usually let you know if you are on target or off base concerning your interpretation of what they said.

Mirroring. A more powerful technique for keeping a person talking is mirroring. Mirroring is restating the person's exact words while mimicking their body posturing. This is done intentionally for impact. Mirroring is very useful when someone says something that has strong emotional connotations attached to it. Their message was so powerful that you want to hear more before risking weakening or misinterpreting it. For example, if a friend told you she was so angry at her boyfriend she could kill him, you would mirror it by saying in a surprised and questioning tone of voice, "You're so angry at him you could kill him!" This usually will provoke the person to continue and go into the greater detail you desire.

Yes-and-no questions. The weakest type of response in a dialogue, and the way most of us seek additional information is to ask direct yes/no questions. Yes/no questions do not require explanation like paraphrasing and mirroring do because they can be answered by a simple yes or no. Although they are very useful for verifying facts, they are easy to overuse and they can shut down a dialogue.

Once the receiver encodes a response using one or more of the four techniques, the communication process shifts back to the sender. We have now come full circle with sender encoding, receiver decoding, receiver encoding and providing feedback that now becomes information to be decoded by the sender as the cycle begins all over again.

10 Open-Ended Statements for Keeping People Talking

Open-ended statements tend to begin with different words than closed-ended questions which for the most part can be answered with one- or two-word replies. Open-ended statements require the person to elaborate.

Close-Ended	**Open-Ended**
Are?	How?
Do?	Why?
Who?	In what way?
When, where, which?	

From: Garner, A. (1980). *Conversationally Speaking.* New York: McGraw Hill.

The following are examples of open-ended statements.

1. "No kidding, tell me more."
2. "Tell me how you feel about..."
3. "What are your thoughts about...?"
4. "I'm not sure I understand, please explain that..."
5. "In what way did...?"
6. "Why do you think that?"
7. "How did you come to that...?"

Verbal Assertiveness: The DESC Model

One useful technique that combines both assertiveness and effective verbal communication is the DESC model.[2,7] It is a powerful tool that will help you become more precise in asserting yourself, and it is an excellent technique to use when the source of your stress is interpersonal, such as another's behavior, remark, or a social situation.

The DESC model has four parts:

1. **D**escribe—paint a verbal picture of the situation or other person's behavior that is a source of stress. Be as precise as possible.
2. **E**xpress—express your feelings about the incident using *I* language.
3. **S**pecify—be specific in identifying alternative ways you would prefer the person to speak or behave.
4. **C**onsequences—identify the consequences that will follow if the person does or does not comply with your wishes.

Example: Mary has just walked out of a meeting with her sorority sisters when the president of the sorority walks up and announces in a loud voice, "Mary, you did such a good job chairing last year's homecoming float committee, I'd like you to do it again this year." Mary really does not want the job again. It took a lot of time and was a tremendous amount of work. Feeling trapped, however, Mary says, "Sure Erica, I'd be glad to do it." As she walks away, Mary's stomach is churning and she is angry with both Erica, for putting her on the spot, and herself, for agreeing to something she does not want to do.

Instead, Mary could have used the DESC model to respond to Erica's request.

1. **D** - "Erica, when you come up to me in front of several sisters and ask me to do something..."
2. **E** - "I feel trapped, angry, and taken advantage of."
3. **S** - "I'd prefer that you either bring this up at our meeting or speak to me about it personally."
4. **C** - "In the future, if you do this again I won't volunteer and it will hurt our friendship. Furthermore, I'll be less likely to do anything for the sorority if you continue to behave this way. If you do change, I still may not volunteer for everything, but at least I'll think about it and we'll remain friends.

When using this model be as precise as possible in describing the other person's offending behavior or actions. Remember, do not criticize the person, just their offensive behavior. It is also very important to take responsibility for your feelings and use *I* language when describing them. Rather than blaming Erica, Mary was very clear in saying "I feel trapped, angry, and taken advantage of." Assess Yourself 7-6 has additional scenarios you can use to practice the DESC model.

Summary

This chapter introduces reduce, the second level of defense against stress. Aimed at cutting back on the sheer volume of potential stressors in our lives, reduce begins with an assessment of the things that cause us stress, and how our bodies respond. It also examines our use of time and our daily stressors against the context of our values and goals to see where they come into conflict.

We discuss the variable nature of stress and how the amount of tolerable stress varies from person to person and day to day. We discuss the fine line between challenge and threat and how we only learn that dividing point through experience and attention to our early warning signs of stress.

This chapter presents many strategies for reducing stressors when they come into conflict with our goals and values. We talk about the three ways of coping, abolish, avoid, and alter, that allow us to eliminate, minimize, or change our exposure to stressors.

We then learn about time management. We look at ways of evaluating whether our use of time is consistent with our values and goals, and discuss prioritizing the activities that make up our days.

We examine the idea of downscaling, emphasizing how only you can determine if the direction of your life is healthful or stressful.

Assertiveness is covered next, with an emphasis on how nonassertiveness is often a major contributing factor toward feeling too stretched or overextended. We discuss strategies for saying no and assuming control for the level of commitments in our lives.

Finally, we examine the notion of using effective communication as a way to prevent stress caused by ambiguity and miscommunication. We discuss a four-part communication model that emphasizes personal responsibility for clearing up communication breakdowns before they became sources of stress. We also learn how to use the DESC model, which combines assertiveness and verbal communication skills. This chapter builds upon the assessment and management skills introduced in Chapter 6. The next chapter deals with channeling energy and tension once the stress response kicks in.

References

1. Berne, E. (1960). *Transactional analysis in psychotherapy.* New York: Grove Press.

2. Bower, S.A., & Bower, G. (1976). *Asserting Yourself: A practical guide for positive change.* Reading Mass: Addison-Wesley.

3. Cicatelli Associates. (1985). *Ten bad listening habits: and what to do about them.* New York: Cicatelli Associates.

4. Edelman, C.L., & Mandel, C.L. (1994). *Health promotion throughout the life-span.* St Louis: Mosby.

5. Elkind, D. (1984). *All grown up and no where to go: teenagers in crisis.* Reading, MA: Addison Wesley.

6. Garner, A. (1980). *Conversationally speaking.* New York: McGraw Hill.

7. Greenberg, G. (1993). *Comprehensive stress management.* Dubuque, IA: Brown/Benchmark.

8. Hales, D. (1992). *An invitation to health.* Menlo Park, CA: Benjamin Cummings.

9. Hall, E. (1973). *The silent language.* Garden City, NY: Doubleday/Anchor Press.

10. Kozier, B., Erb, G., & Olivieri, R. (1991). *Fundamentals of nursing.* Redwood City, CA; Addison-Wesley/Benjamin Cummings.

11. Lazarus, R., & Folkman, S. (1984). *Stress appraisal and coping.* New York: Springer.

12. Mandel, B. (1980). Communication: a four-part process. *Hotliner, 1* (4), 6.

13. Parade (1992). Do you really know how to play?

14. Payne, W. & Hahn, D. (1994). *Understanding your health.* St. Louis: Mosby.

15. Smith, J.C. (1993). *Creative stress management.* Englewood Cliffs, NJ: Prentice Hall.

16. Watzlawick, P. Beavin, J.H., & Jackson, D.D. (1967). *Pragmatics of human communication.* New York: WW Norton.

Name: _____ Date: _____

Stressor Diary

For the remainder of the semester keep a personal stressor diary. Keep track of your stressors, how your body/mind responds to them, their level of intensity, and how you cope. This will help you identify trends or patterns in your stressors and assist you in your stress-management plan.

Day/date	Stressor	Response	Intensity	Coping	Specific details that bothered you
Example:					
Monday Sept. 1	stuck in traffic	muscle tension in neck; anger	8	yelled at other drivers	felt trapped, like there was nothing I could do
Tuesday Sept. 2	fight with girlfriend	anger; stomach churning	9	stormed out the room; avoided her	fought over silly comment made by a TV talk-show host

Stressor Diary (cont'd)

Day/date	Stressor	Response	Intensity	Coping	Specific details that bothered you

ASSESS YOURSELF 7-2

Triple *A*s Scenarios

The following scenarios represent common stressors that respond very well to a three *A*s approach. Work through each of the *A*s, abolish, avoid, and alter, for each scenario. Do all three apply to each scenario? If not, why?

1. You love your mother, but she can drive you nuts. She insists on having you come over two nights a week for dinner. You do not mind seeing her, but her apartment is cramped, and parking is very difficult. Besides that, you really do not want to commit to such a rigid schedule.

    _____

    _____

    _____

    _____

    _____

2. Your roommates seem to think that college is one nonstop party. They are up late five nights a week and out the other two. They never study and are on academic probation.

    _____

    _____

    _____

    _____

    _____

3. Although your apartment is small, the housework seems never-ending. You do not get much help from your roommate who abuses your generosity in preparing food, shopping, and cleaning up.

    _____

    _____

    _____

    _____

    _____

Name: _____ Date: _____

Time-Management Log

Day/Time	Activity
5:00 am	
5:30 am	
6:00 am	
6:30 am	
7:00 am	
7:30 am	
8:00 am	
8:30 am	
9:00 am	
9:30 am	
10:00 am	
10:30 am	
11:00 am	
11:30 am	
12:00 pm	
12:30 pm	
1:00 pm	
1:30 pm	
2:00 pm	
2:30 pm	
3:00 pm	
3:30 pm	
4:00 pm	
4:30 pm	
5:00 pm	

Time-Management Log (cont'd)

Day/Time	Activity
5:30 pm	
6:00 pm	
6:30 pm	
7:00 pm	
7:30 pm	
8:00 pm	
8:30 pm	
9:00 pm	

Name: _____ Date: _____

How Well Do I Communicate?

Answer by circling 0 (rarely), 1 (sometimes), or 2 (often).

	Rarely	Sometimes	Often
In conversation, how frequently do you interrupt?	0	1	2
How often do you joke, saying in a funny way something that is really important to you?	0	1	2
Do you think that if your partner or friend really cared about you, she or he would understand your needs without your having to explain everything?	0	1	2
When you do not understand something, do you dislike having to ask questions?	0	1	2
How often do you hint about things you want rather than asking directly?	0	1	2
How frequently do you say yes when you really want to say no?	0	1	2

Total _____

Interpretation

If your score is around three, you are an above-average listener and communicator. You understand and get your message across. If you score around six, you are like most people. Sometimes you do not understand what another person wants or you are not able to get your own meaning across. Scores of eight to ten suggest that you frequently do not communicate well. A careful reading of this chapter should help you listen and speak much more effectively greatly increasing your ability to communicate and to enjoy good relationships.

To carry this further...

Having completed this personal assessment, did you find that you are a more or less effective communicator than you would have anticipated? Do you better understand why a high score in a particular area might be perceived as unsupportive of effective verbal communication?

From: Payne W. & Hahn D. (1994). *Understanding Your Health*. St. Louis: Mosby.

Relax: Passive Relaxation Strategies

In the past two chapters we have explored stress-management techniques that focus on changing your environment or the way you perceive it. However, sometimes this is impossible. When this is the case, you need to find other ways to cope with your situation. This chapter introduces techniques designed to help you relax in just such situations.

This chapter focuses on passive relaxation techniques, which are distinguished from the active relaxation techniques described in Chapters 9 and 10. The main difference between the two is that passive techniques do not employ vigorous, physical exertion.

Relaxation Defined

KEY
TO UNDERSTANDING

To be truly relaxed requires having a passive mental state.
Proper breathing is the key to all relaxation.

The passivity referred to in the context of this chapter has as much to do with your mental state as it does with the level of physical activity employed by these techniques. A key to being truly relaxed is having a passive mental state. Essentially, this means allowing your mind to slow down and, as thoughts and emotions arise, allowing them to pass. In a sense, relaxation means letting things go in one ear and out the other. We cannot totally eliminate the intrusion of thoughts and emotions, but we can minimize their occurrence and significance by acknowledging them and letting them pass. It takes discipline and practice; do not think you are failing at any of the techniques if intrusive thoughts and emotions crop up. In time they will decrease in frequency and consequence.

When most people think of stress management, they think of the types of activities covered in this chapter. Strategies such as deep breathing, systematic muscle relaxation, meditation, and biofeedback readily come to mind. These and the other less known relaxation techniques that we discuss in this chapter share the ability to put the body into a state that is incompatible with stress. When a person is relaxed, he or she simply cannot be stressed. Through systematic relaxation training we can learn to automatically shift into a relaxation response whenever we feel stressed.

The Physiology of Relaxation

To get a sense of what it means to be truly relaxed, watch your dog or cat seek out a warm spot in the sun. It finds a quiet spot, away from the main traffic of the house, circles it a few times, stretches its legs, rolls its head and neck, lays down and fully arches its back, takes a deep breath and exhales deeply, and then curls up or sprawls in the warm rays (Fig. 8-1).

Fig. 8-1 To understand what relaxation is about, watch a dog have a good stretch and lie down in front of a warm window.

When we are relaxed, our minds are clear, our muscles are without tension, and our breathing is free, easy, and deep. The box on p. 278 illustrates the physiological processes that are related to relaxation.

When we are relaxed, there is a decrease in both skeletal and smooth muscle tension. Our muscles are not in the chronic state of mild contraction that characterizes the stress response. This protects them from the cumulative negative effects of being constantly tensed.

Our breathing rate decreases and the depth of breathing increases. We breathe more evenly and fully, allowing efficient oxygen utilization and carbon dioxide removal.

The number of times our hearts beat per minute decreases, and our blood pressure also decreases; both of these reduce the wear and tear on our cardiovascular system. In addition, we have more efficient circulation. Blood is allowed to move freely throughout the body, no longer pooling in the internal organs. Our extremities warm up as circulation is restored.

Our blood volume decreases and normal water balance is restored because we no longer are producing extra mineralocorticoids that retain sodium and increase blood volume and pressure.

Our metabolic rate returns to normal and our parasympathetic nervous system exerts control over the many processes set into motion by sympathetic activation.

In a sense, we slow down and return to normal, cancelling out the effects of stress. This is what relaxation training is all about—putting our bodies in this relaxed state on a regular basis to cancel out the effects of stress. Through regular practice our bodies will begin to relax more fully. We will be able to slow down and relax more easily, sensing when we are stressed more quickly.

Relaxation versus Stress

Stress	Relaxation
Increased body metabolism	Decreased body metabolism
Increased heart rate	Decreased heart rate
Increased blood pressure	Decreased blood pressure
Increased breathing rate	Decreased breathing rate
Increased oxygen consumption	Decreased oxygen consumption
Increased cardiac output	Decreased cardiac output
Increased muscular tension	Decreased muscular tension
Decreased blood clotting time	Increased blood clotting time
Increased blood flow to the major muscle groups involved in fight-or-flight (including the arms and legs)	

From: Curtis, J. & Detert, R. (1985). *Learn to relax: a 14-day program*, LaCrosse, WI: Coulee Press.

Breathing and Relaxation

Breathing is the basis of both life and relaxation. By breathing correctly, we can strengthen and train lung functioning, increase cardiovascular response, increase oxygenation of the blood, calm the nerves, and increase restfulness.[4]

The parts of the brain that control breathing also are related to those that control stress arousal. Controlled, deep, even breathing facilitates relaxation. Rapid, shallow, irregular breathing disrupts relaxation.[4] Therefore learning to control our breathing will provide immediate benefits in learning to control our stress responses.

All relaxation techniques begin with getting in touch with the pace and depth of your breathing. One of the main bases for understanding whether or not you are stressed is the pace and depth of your breathing. If it is rapid and shallow, chances are you are stressed. Deep breathing activities reduce stress. They also form the basis of most other relaxation techniques.

KEY
TO UNDERSTANDING

Proper breathing is the
key to all relaxation.

Breathing to Reduce Stress

Most of us use only a portion of our lungs when we breathe. We tend to breathe with only the top third of our lungs. To receive the stress-reducing benefits of breathing, we must learn how to get our entire lungs involved. We need to learn how to fill our lungs from the bottom up. You do this by pushing your stomach out as you inhale, making room for the air to fill the lower portion of your lungs. Fig. 8-2 clarifies this procedure by illustrating the shape of your lungs.

As you slowly take air in, your lungs begin to fill from the bottom up. Sometimes it helps to let the shoulders rise and fall with inhalation and exhalation, respectively.

Most of us breathe too quickly. Breathing slowly means that it should take several seconds to fill your lungs with air. It is not unusual to take 10

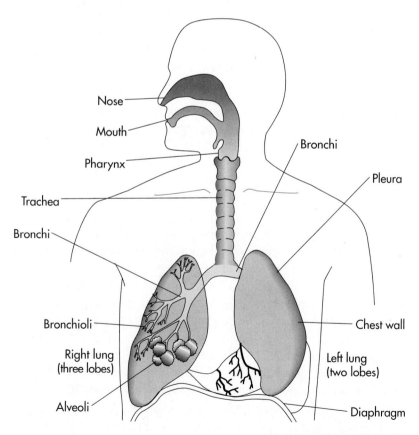

Fig. 8-2 Sometimes it is helpful to visualize your lungs while performing deep breathing exercises or when meditating.

seconds or longer to either inhale or exhale in breathing exercises. The following instructions will help you begin to breathe deeply.

1. Find a quiet place away from others to practice.
2. Minimize distractions by closing doors and turning off the radio, television, and phone.
3. Sit on a chair with your back straight, head up.
4. Visualize a picture of your lungs.
5. Slowly breathe in through your nose.
6. As you breathe in, push your stomach forward.
7. Let your ribs expand and your shoulders rise as the air fills your lungs completely from the bottom up.
8. When your lungs feel full, slowly begin to exhale through your mouth.
9. Let your shoulders fall and your ribs shrink back as the air slowly passes through your mouth.
10. Gently pull your stomach back in with your stomach muscles, fully draining all of the air from the lower portion of your lungs.
11. Repeat this activity for 5 minutes.
12. Practice this activity a few times a day.

In time, with regular practice, you will automatically shift into a deeper, more even breathing pattern whenever you feel stressed. Deep breathing is an excellent first choice for reducing stress. It is also the starting point for the remaining techniques described in this chapter.

Meditation

When most people think of meditation, they visualize an old man in diaphanous robes, with a long white beard and dark, leathery skin. This imaginary man sits alone, in a full lotus position, on top of a mountain in Tibet or some other exotic location. He is in a deep trance, engaged in a mystical communication with a higher being. Seated at his feet is a disciple, who after making the long, arduous climb to the mountaintop, seeks the true meaning of life.

In truth, most meditators are average people like you and me. Some are young; others are old. Most do not have long, flowing beards, and very few are interested in sitting on top of high mountains for extended periods (Fig. 8-3).

Origins of Meditation

People have been meditating for thousands of years. Meditation originated in India and Tibet, as part of the practice of Zen Buddhism and raja yoga.

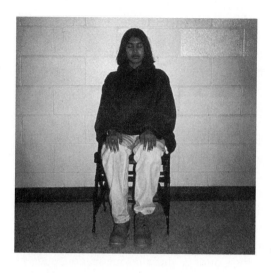

Fig. 8-3 Although the full lotus position is most often associated with meditation, sitting comfortably with your back straight will do fine.

Meditation in its religious or spiritual context is intended to train disciples in achieving the fullest control over their minds as possible. Yogis claim that in achieving this control and heightened awareness, disciples can transcend normal stages of consciousness and reach the highest levels of connectedness and spirituality. One form of meditation, **transcendental meditation (TM)**, derives its name from this belief in transcendence to another plane.[1]

Meditation in general, and transcendental meditation in particular, received a lot of attention in the 1960s and 1970s when the English rock group, the Beatles, studied TM with the Maharishi Mahesh Yogi. Millions of Americans became acquainted with this previously unknown practice. The Maharishi's face was on the cover of almost every major magazine, and TM training courses and schools popped up all over the country.

Benefits of Meditation

Besides the spiritual dimension of meditation, disciples of TM alluded to its distinct physiological benefits, ranging from reduced muscle tension to increases in brain wave patterns that were more conducive to relaxation. These claims were studied and well documented in the 1970s when the Harvard Medical School undertook a group of research studies to examine the physiological benefits of TM. Through a series of carefully controlled studies, Harvard researchers were able to reach the following conclusions concerning the benefits of TM:[1]

1. Decreased metabolic rate and oxygen consumption, called **hypometabolism**, occurs only during two other states: sleep and hibernation. Mediators were able to achieve hypometabolism

transcendental meditation
a type of focused meditation popularized by Maharishi Mahesh Yogi from India

hypometabolic state
a restful waking state characterized by decreased metabolic rate and respiration

alpha waves

slow, low-amplitude brain waves associated with a wakeful, resting state

without being asleep or hibernating. The meditative state is a restful but awake state. During meditation the body needs and burns less energy. It slows down and, as with sleep, provides a period of rest. The meditative state, however, uses even less oxygen than the sleeping state.

2. Brain wave activity also changes during meditation (Fig. 8-4). **Alpha waves** increase in intensity and frequency. These low-amplitude, slow, synchronous brain waves are the type associated with the restful awake state.

3. Heart rate decreases during meditation. In the Harvard study the researchers found that heart rate decreased by an average of three beats per minute during meditation.

4. Blood pressure remains unchanged during meditation, but the researchers found that regular mediators had lower blood pressure than nonmeditators, before, during, and after meditation, suggesting the long-term effects of the practice.

5. Respiration also decreases during meditation. The rate and depth of breathing slow down. There is a decreased need for oxygen because of the lessening of the metabolic rate.[1]

Other studies have documented findings that go beyond those found in the Harvard research. Two studies[7,12] found that mediators experience a carryover of the trophotropic effects of meditation. Although many studies document that mediators experience various short-term stress-reducing effects, these characteristics become a more stable trait for regular media-

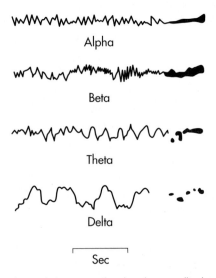

Fig. 8-4 Alpha waves, pictured above, are the slow, low-amplitude waves associated with a restful waking state.

tors. The benefits, particularly a calmer, more peaceful view of the world, become a part of the meditator's day-to-day existence.

In general, the meditative state is relaxed and restful, ideal for cancelling out the effects of stress. Being in a meditative state is incompatible with stress. You cannot be stressed and relaxed at the same time. For this reason, and for practice, teachers of meditation urge their students to meditate for 20 minutes, twice a day. This successfully cancels out the effects of the stress response while training the mind to sink into the meditative state more easily.

In a sense, what meditation does is help us unclutter our minds. It slows our minds and limits our thoughts, giving us a temporary break from the countless thoughts and feelings that our brains encounter each day.

Types of Meditation

Focused Meditation

There are many forms of meditation. The main difference between them concerns the use of some form of a focal point. In focused meditation the focal point can be anything. Mediators concentrate all of their energy on their established focal point and when distractions occur, their attention is refixed on the focal point.

Object Meditation. The focal point can be an object such as a candle, or the point in a room where the ceiling meets the wall. A candle is a traditional meditative object; mediators can lose themselves in the flickering flame of the candle as it hypnotically waves back and forth.

Word, Phrase, Mantra Meditation. The focal point could also be a word, phrase, or personally meaningful word, or a **mantra**. In transcendental meditation the bestowing of a mantra by the teacher is a sacred ritual. Your personal mantra in TM is not to be shared with others. It has personal value to you alone.

Some people meditate to simple words such as *one* when inhaling, and *two* while exhaling. These words themselves are meaningless except to serve as a focal point. Still others use a word that helps create a relaxing visual image. Words such as *beach* or *sun* can help create this effect.

Sound Meditation. Some people like to meditate to music. Music has been shown to affect the following physiological processes: metabolic rate, muscular activity, respiration, heart rate, and blood pressure.[2] Music also has the ability to profoundly affect our emotions.

KEY
TO UNDERSTANDING

During meditation you must get back to your deep breathing if you are distracted.

mantra
a personally meaningful word used as the focal point in TM

Music can act in positive, stress-reducing ways by slowing physiological processes and producing positive emotions. Unfortunately, like noise, it can also act as a stimulus that increases these responses and creates negative emotions.[2] One person's music, however, is often another person's noise, and therefore the subject of which music will relax versus which will stress continues to be controversial. Common sense will tell you which types of music and artists help relax you.

Other people find it relaxing and helpful to meditate to natural sounds ranging from the sound of waves (Fig. 8-5) to the wind whistling through the trees. To do this, meditate outdoors or listen to commercially prepared audio tapes and compact disks.[5]

A third type of sound that people use to meditate is the sound associated with a repetitive, physical activity. Some people even combine physical activity with meditation. (See Chapter 10 for a detailed discussion of the benefits of exercise.) To achieve a meditative state, these people often focus on the rhythmic sounds of their own breathing and footsteps as they walk or run; hands knifing through the water as they swim; or "swoosh" of skis moving through the snow as they cross-country ski. The repetitive nature of the activities is perfect for meditation because people can tune into their breathing while tuning out external stimuli.

Breath Meditation. Visualizing your breathing instead of listening to it is another focusing method. Watching the air travel in, around, and out of the nose, throat, and lungs helps mediators maintain concentration on their focal point while forgetting about everything else going on in their lives. You can learn to watch the air go in and out by first looking at a picture of the respiratory system to visualize the structure of the body parts involved in breathing. After you can visualize the body parts used in breathing, you can close your eyes when you breathe and follow the flow of the air using your imagination. This will help minimize distractions.

Fig. 8-5 Some people would find a secluded beach on a warm day an ideal place to meditate. The combination of warm sun, gentle wind, and hypnotic pounding of the waves is hard to match.

Nonfocused Meditation

Nonfocused, or open focus, meditation does not involve paying attention to a focal point. Rather the meditator allows all incoming visual stimuli to enter and exit consciousness without paying them any special attention. These stimuli are simply acknowledged and released. Nonfocused meditation is difficult for many beginners because there is a greater tendency for the mind to wander and for the person to be unsure of his or her role in the process.

Moving Meditation. Moving meditation is a type of open-focus meditation that is done during exercises such as walking, cross-country skiing, or swimming. Although it is done while moving, it is not the same as sound meditation, where one concentrates and focuses on rhythmic breathing or foot pounding. Instead, during moving meditation, one is open to the sights and sounds of the immediate environment. The idea is to be immersed in the immediate environment, to be fully open to it while shutting off distracting outside thoughts and ideas that drift in. A walk in the woods is a sensory delight as we allow ourselves to fully experience all of its sights, sounds, and smells (see Assess Yourself 8-1).

Benson's Relaxation Response

One type of meditation that is easy to learn is the **relaxation response**, developed by Benson[1] after the Harvard studies of TM. It borrows all of the key elements of meditation from eastern teaching and demystifies the practice by deemphasizing parts such as personal mantras.

There are four things you need for learning the relaxation response: a quiet environment, a mental device, a passive attitude, and a comfortable position.

A Quiet Environment.

Meditating, for most people, requires a quiet environment with minimal distractions. The choices are endless. Some people prefer to meditate outdoors, where they can experience the warmth of the sun, the sounds of birds, or a running brook. Others prefer the peace and solitude of a carpeted room with the shades drawn and the windows closed. It is not a good idea to meditate in an area with people entering and leaving or other distractions. Turn off the television, radio, or stereo. Temporarily disconnect the phone or turn down the volume.

A Mental Device.

Benson[1] and his colleagues referred to a focal point as a mental device. The relaxation response is a type of focused meditation. As we just described,

relaxation response
an Americanized form of focused meditation

KEY
TO UNDERSTANDING

Minimal distractions are important for successful meditation.

your focal point can be a visual object, your breathing, or a repetitive sound, word, or phrase.

If you choose to focus on your breathing, a sound, a word or a phrase, closing your eyes while you meditate will help you stay focused. Match the repeated sound, word, or phrase to the inhalation and exhalation of your breathing. Some people use two different words: one to repeat while inhaling and one for exhaling.

A Passive Attitude

KEY
TO UNDERSTANDING

Do not worry about
your performance
during meditation.

Do not worry about distractions; they will occur. The phone will ring, other noises will occur, and your focus will be disrupted by competing thoughts. When this happens, simply acknowledge the distractions and refocus. Do not worry about your performance.

A Comfortable Position

You do not have to be a yoga master and sit in a full lotus position to meditate. You need only to be comfortable and relaxed. Stretch beforehand, loosen or remove any tight clothing, and make sure you are not chilled.

Sitting in a chair with a straight back or sitting on the floor with your legs crossed are good positions for meditation. Do not meditate while lying down. You will have a tendency to fall asleep.

Instructions for the Relaxation Response

1. Sit quietly in a comfortable position.
2. Close your eyes or focus on your visual focal point.
3. Completely relax all of your muscles from your feet to your head.
4. Breathe easily and naturally, repeating your word, phrase, or sound with every inhalation and exhalation.
5. Continue for 10 to 20 minutes. You can check your watch, but do not use an alarm to signal the end.
6. Maintain a passive attitude. Get back to your focal point when you are distracted.

Initially, 10 minutes will seem like an eternity. Be patient. With time and practice you will come to enjoy the time and be surprised that it passes so quickly.

Visual Imagery

Visualization goes hand-in-hand with several relaxation techniques. Visualization, or the mental creation of relaxing visual images and scenes, can be used with other techniques such as deep breathing, yoga, stretching, meditation.

Visual imagery, by itself or in conjunction with the aforementioned techniques, works by using relaxing images to facilitate a relaxation response. It does this in two ways: by offsetting the effects of stress-arousing scenarios and by creating relaxing scenes.

Think for a moment about a scary scene from a horror movie. Think about all of the ways you might use to describe your reaction. "It made my flesh crawl," "It was hair raising," "It made me shiver," "I got a lump in my throat." All of these statements reflect the physiological processes set into motion by the stress response. In fact, the visual images we have can be as arousing as the actual events. Although viewing a horror film can set these physiological processes in motion, just recalling the scene in our mind can have the same effect.

Conversely, if we visualize a relaxing scene, our bodies can facilitate a relaxed state. Such stress-reducing visual imagery can be focused on our own bodies or on outside scenarios. For instance, if we envision warm sensations in our arms and legs, we actually feel them getting heavy and warm. If we focus on the sun's warming rays, we feel them radiating over us, making us warm and relaxed.

In deep breathing, we visualize air entering the deepest passageways and spaces of our lungs, filling them with oxygen. In meditation we might focus on a warming word, such as *sun*, or a warming scene, such as the image of floating on a raft in a pool with the warm sun beating down. All of these positive images can help us relax, warm up, and cancel out the negative effects of stress. Because these warming words and scenes are so personal and subjective, what works for one person might be ineffective for another.

The Quieting Reflex and the Calming Response

Charles Stroebel[10] developed a quick, 6-second relaxation technique called the *quieting reflex*. He named it this because with practice it can be triggered almost reflexively. The quieting reflex incorporates deep breathing, muscle relaxation, and visual imagery and can be used with any type of stressor.

Instructions for the quieting reflex

1. Think about whatever it is that is making you stressed.
2. Smile to relax facial muscle tension.

3. Repeat to yourself, "I can keep a calm body and an alert mind."
4. Take a quiet, easy breath.
5. Exhale through parted teeth, allowing your jaw to go slack.
6. Visualize heaviness and warmth flowing throughout your body.

Jay Segal[9] from Temple University developed a slightly modified version of the quieting reflex called the *calming response*. This technique also is quick and utilizes deep breathing, muscle relaxation, and visual imagery.

Segal's technique, like Stroebel's, can be used anywhere and anytime you are stressed or are anticipating stress. It is designed to quickly help you relax and stop the stress response from progressing.

Six steps of the calming response

1. Take a personal inventory of stressors.
2. Whenever you are stressed or are about to be confronted with any of your stressors, stop what you are focusing on and get in touch with the depth and pace of your breathing. Is your breathing shallow, irregular, and uneven?
3. Think of a relaxing, warming word and a visual image.
4. Take three deep abdominal breaths. On the first breath, repeat to yourself, "I will not let my body get involved," or "My body will stay uninvolved."
5. On the second breath, identify any muscle or muscle group that is tense and:

   ■ on inhalation contract and hold it for 3 seconds.
   ■ on exhalation release the contraction.

6. On the third deep, slow breath, close your eyes and think of your calming word and relaxing image.

You can repeat this sequence again if you are still tense and use it as often as you want during the day.

Autogenic Training

Autogenic training is a form of hypnosis that incorporates visual images of our bodies becoming warm and relaxed. Two normal by-products of hypnosis, warmth and a feeling of heaviness in the limbs, are associated with increased peripheral blood flow and reduced muscle tension. These are also associated with other techniques designed to facilitate a relaxation response similar to what you would experience through meditation. Autogenics just gets you there in a different way. Meditation relaxes your mind first, which leads to your body relaxing and getting warm. Autogenics begins with your body, and your mind in turn slows down and relaxes.

Autogenic means self-generating. Essentially, autogenic training is a type of self-hypnosis that uses imagery to systematically relax and warm up our bodies. Instead of focusing on external scenarios, the images conjured up through autogenics are of the arms and legs, stomach, and forehead. These body parts are imagined to be warm, heavy, and relaxed.

Autogenics was developed by a Johannes Schultz, a German psychiatrist, and his student, Wolfgang Luthe, for use in the practice of psychotherapy.[8] They used hypnosis as a tool to help relax their patients by reducing muscle tension, increasing blood flow to the peripheries, and slowing heart rate and respiration. They were able to teach their patients to induce this state themselves, thereby facilitating their psychotherapy and helping them gain some self-control over their lives.

It became apparent to Luthe[8] and others that the use of autogenics could be expanded to include nonpsychotherapeutic settings, where clinically well people could use the technique for stress reduction.

Instructions for Performing Autogenics

You can perform autogenic training either sitting or lying down. Begin by getting in touch with your breathing.

Breathing. Take a few deep abdominal breaths and contract and relax any muscles that are tense. Repeat the following sentences to yourself: "My breathing is slow an even." "My breathing is smooth and rhythmic." "My breathing is effortless and calm."

As you continue to breathe, visualize you are on a warm, sunny beach. As the waves move in, they cover your body with warmth and relaxation. Feel the waves of warmth and relaxation wash over your shoulders and chest and through your arms and hands. Feel the waves of warmth rush over your stomach and hips, down your back and legs, and over your feet. Feel the warmth and continue to breathe.

Heart. As you continue to breathe slowly and deeply, visualize your heart and say to yourself, "My heartbeat is calm and regular."

As you continue to repeat this message to yourself, visualize your heart beating calmly and regularly, sending warm blood throughout your body. See the blood flow out of your heart, through your internal organs and your brain, and out through your arms and legs, all the way out to your fingers and toes. Continue for a few seconds to breathe slowly and deeply, watching your blood course slowly throughout your body.

KEY
TO UNDERSTANDING

During autogenic training, visualize that your body is heavy and warm.

Visualize the center of your body, your solar plexus, that part of your body right behind your navel. Imagine it is warm and relaxed and repeat, "My solar plexus is warm and relaxed."

Repeat to yourself, "I am relaxed. I am calm. I am quiet. My breathing is smooth and rhythmic. My heartbeat is calm and regular. My solar plexus is relaxed."

Arms and Hands. Starting with your right arm, repeat the following statement as you continue to breathe slowly and deeply and visualize the warm blood flowing throughout your arm all the way to your fingers: "My right arm and hand are heavy and warm." Switch your focus to the left arm and hand and, following the same instructions, repeat: "My left arm and hand are heavy and warm." Now focus on both arms and hands and repeat, "Both of my arms and hands are heavy and warm." "It would take a great effort to raise my arms." Continue to breathe slowly and deeply, watching the blood flow into your arms and hands, making them feel heavy and warm.

Legs and feet. As you continue to breathe slowly and deeply, visualize the blood traveling throughout your legs, bringing with it feelings of heaviness and warmth. Continue to breathe slowly and deeply and repeat, "My right leg and foot are heavy and warm." Shift your focus to your left leg and repeat, "My left leg and foot are heavy and warm." Shift your focus to both legs and repeat, "Both of my legs and feet are heavy and warm." "It would take a great deal of effort to lift my legs"

Wrap up. Continue to breathe deeply and slowly, visualizing the waves of warmth and relaxation washing over your body, and realize that you are totally and deeply relaxed. It is only in this state that you should repeat the statement, "I am calm and relaxed." Continue to breathe deeply and slowly, repeating the message to yourself. After a few breaths begin to get back in touch with where you are: the room and the time. You are safe, secure, and relaxed. Begin to count down from five:

> 5—Take a deep breath and visualize the room.
> 4—Take a deep breath and begin to stretch.
> 3—Take a deep breath and slowly open your eyes.
> 2—Take a deep breath. You are now mentally alert and ready to get back to whatever you were doing before this activity.
> 1—You are fully awake and ready to go.

To get the full benefits of autogenics you will need to practice on a regular basis. Slowly, you will find it easier to relax and fall into the autogenic state.

Biofeedback

Biofeedback is a technique that employs instruments that measure body functioning associated with stress (usually temperature, muscle tension, brain wave activity, and perspiration). If a stress response is present, that information is fed back to you through a signal such as a buzzer, light, or beeper (Fig. 8-6).

The physiological processes that are measured by the biofeedback equipment occur automatically as a result of involuntary, autonomic nervous system functioning. As you might recall from chapters 2 and 3, it was previously thought that people had no conscious control over these involuntary processes. As we have discussed, however, with practice we can slow down our breathing rates, increase our blood flow, influence our brain waves.

Biofeedback provides us with information about these various involuntary body processes that is used in two ways:

1. It makes you aware that these body functions have been activated (meaning you are stressed).
2. It helps you regulate these functions once you are aware they are operating.

As you are learning how to regulate the body processes associated with the stress response, biofeedback provides instant information about the

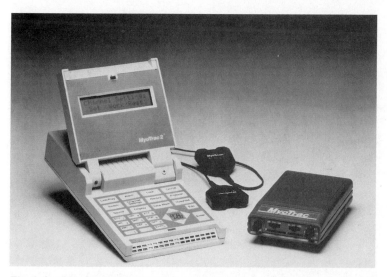

Fig. 8-6 All biofeedback equipment comes with some form of sensor, which is attached to your body to detect physiological changes, and a bell, buzzer, light, or meter to feed this information back to you.

success of your efforts. With the aid of biofeedback machines, you can train yourself to recognize stress and put your body into a relaxed state.

In time you can wean yourself off the machines, because you no longer need them to tell you either that you are under stress or that you are relaxing properly. The techniques that you would use to relax are those we have already discussed: deep breathing, muscle relaxation, visualization, and autogenics. The main difference with biofeedback is that you would employ those techniques while being hooked up to a biofeedback machine.

Biofeedback has been shown to be very effective in treating some stress-related disorders. It seems to be most effective in dealing with cardio-vascular disorders because of subjects' ability to increase circulation to the peripheries and to relax constricted blood vessels. Migraine headache, hyper-tension,[10] and Raynaud's syndrome, a disease characterized by reduced blood flow to the extremities,[4] have all been treated successfully with biofeedback (Fig. 8-7). Biofeedback is also used in the treatment of muscle-tension–related disorders, though there have been mixed results concerning the application of biofeedback in the treatment of tension headache.[10]

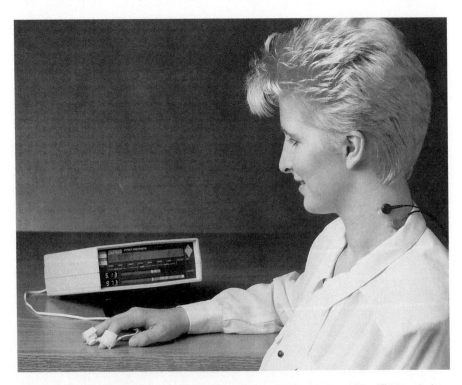

Fig. 8-7 This is what it looks like to be hooked up to a biofeedback machine. This particular type of machine senses temperature through a sensor that clips onto a finger.

Types of Biofeedback

There are three main types of biofeedback machines: thermal, electromyographical, and galvanic skin response. Each works differently according to the type of information it measures.

Thermal machines measure temperature at the extremities. During the stress response, temperature at the extremities drops as blood vessels servicing those areas constrict and reduce blood flow, concentrating blood in the vital organs.

Sensors are usually clipped to the fingers and are used to provide feedback as relaxation efforts warm the extremities by increasing their blood supply. A light, buzzer, or bell will signify that you are relaxed and that blood flow to the fingers has increased.

Electromyographic machines measure striate muscle tension. Both acute and chronic muscle tension associated with stress can be measured this way. Once muscle relaxation activities are begun, the machine provides feedback, again in the form of lights, bells, or buzzers, to let you know whether or not you have successfully relaxed your muscles.

Galvanic skin response machines work by sensing excess perspiration, which enhances the electrical conductivity of your skin. Increased sweating is a normal by-product of the stress response as your body prepares for fight or flight. The machine provides feedback concerning your success in reducing the stress-associated perspiration.

Biofeedback equipment ranges in price from under $100 for simple, palm-size, battery-operated galvanic skin response machines to several thousand dollars for more complex machinery that measures different functions. Each has its own limitations because conditions other than stress can influence temperature, skin conductivity, and muscle tension.

Remember, biofeedback is just a means of providing information concerning your body and your relaxation activities. Signals such as lights and buzzers tell us when our bodies have relaxed and help condition us concerning what relaxation feels like. You still must learn how to relax through breathing, muscle relaxation, and imagery. Biofeedback does not take the place of these techniques. However, it can provide positive reinforcement to people who have tried these techniques and others but are not sure they are doing them properly or have doubts about their effectiveness.

KEY
TO UNDERSTANDING

Remember that the biofeedback machine does not take the place of learning how to breathe and relax your muscles.

Summary

This chapter introduces us to the fourth line of defense against stress—relaxation. This level of defense works on the principle of reciprocal inhibition. In other words, the body cannot be both stressed and relaxed at the same time. Relaxation creates a physiological state that is incompatible with stress.

The various techniques discussed in this chapter are designed to put the body into a relaxed state. By doing so on a regular basis, you can begin to cancel out the effects of stress. Essentially what happens when you relax is that you shut down the stress response and allow its harmful by-products to dissipate. All of the autonomic responses, from increased breathing to blood pressure, either return to normal or drop below baseline levels, inducing a state of relaxation.

Deep breathing is the basis for all relaxation activities. By getting in touch with the rate and depth of your breathing, you can assess whether or not you are stressed. Becoming aware of your breathing is the first step in starting to control it. The chapter describes how to perform deep breathing correctly.

The next strategy described is meditation. Meditation is examined from its spiritual and physiological perspectives. The health benefits of meditation, from lowered respiration to changed brain waves, are examined. Benson's[1] relaxation response, a simplified way to meditate, is described in detail.

Imagery and visualization are relaxation techniques that revolve around the idea that visual images can induce either a stress or relaxation response. By visualizing warm, relaxing images, we can facilitate a relaxed state of being. Conversely, by conjuring up uncomfortable images, we induce a stress response.

Autogenics, a form of self-hypnosis, incorporates breathing and visualization to help us relax. Autogenic training uses images of warm, relaxed body parts to induce a tranquil state that is incompatible with stress.

The last technique introduced in this chapter is biofeedback. Biofeedback uses sophisticated instruments to monitor the autonomic processes set into motion as part of the stress response. These responses are fed back through lights and buzzers to help us monitor our efforts to relax. In time we can learn to do this without the aid of the equipment.

Study Questions

1. What are some of the physiological changes that occur during relaxation?
2. How does relaxation work in reducing stress?
3. Describe what the author refers to as a "passive mental state."
4. Why is deep breathing the foundation of all relaxation activities?
5. What are the four conditions required for performing Benson's relaxation response?
6. What is the quieting reflex?

7. What is visual imagery and how is it used to reduce stress?

8. Define autogenics and describe how it works to reduce stress.

9. What is biofeedback?

10. What is the ultimate goal of using biofeedback equipment?

References

1. Benson, H. (1975). *The relaxation response.* New York: Avon.

2. Charlesworth, E. & Nathan, R.G. (1984). *Stress management: a comprehensive guide to wellness.* New York: Ballantine.

3. Curtis, J. & Detert, R. (1985). *Learn to relax: a 14-day program,* LaCrosse, WI: Coulee Press.

4. Girdano, D.A., Everly, G.S., & Dusek, D.E. (1993). *Controlling stress and tension: a holistic approach.* Englewood Cliffs, NJ: Prentice Hall.

5. Syntonics Research. (1979). *Environments* (CD, disk 9). New York: Syntonics Research.

6. Holmes, D.S. (1984). Meditation and somatic arousal reduction: a review of the experimental evidence. *American Psychologist, 39, 1-10.*

7. Lehrer, P.M., et al. (1983). Progressive relaxation and meditation: a study of the psychophysiology and therapeutic differences between the two techniques. *Behavior Research and Theory, 21,* 651-652.

8. Schultz, J., & Luthe, W. (1959). *Autogenic training: a psychophysiological approach to psychotherapy.* New York: Grune & Stratton.

9. Segal, J. (1975). *The calming response.* Unpublished manuscript.

10. Stroebel, C. (1978). *The quieting response training: introduction.* New York: BMA.

11. Shapiro, D., & Surwit, R.S. (1979). In O. Pomerleau and J.P. Brady (Eds.), *Behavioral medicine: theory and practice.* Baltimore: William & Wilkins.

Name: _____ Date: _____

Relaxing Words, Sounds, and Images

Many of the passive relaxation strategies in this chapter revolve around the use of a relaxing word, sound, or image. This self survey is designed to help you clarify these relaxation aids. Try to come up with at least one entry for each of the three categories (words, sounds, and images). This will enhance your ability to perform the activities in this chapter.

Relaxing Words

Fill in a personally relaxing word for each category:

1. _____ human body (relax, slow, deep, etc.)
2. _____ interpersonal (love, sex, etc.)
3. _____ outdoors (sun, water, beach, etc.)
4. _____ vacation spot (Bahamas, Maui, etc.)
5. _____ other

Relaxing Images

Fill in a personally warming, relaxing, or meditative image for each category:

1. _____ human body (watching breathing, muscles stretching, etc.)
2. _____ interpersonal (making love, massage, etc.)
3. _____ outdoors (floating on a raft, etc.)
4. _____ vacation spot (beach, lake, etc.)
5. _____ inanimate object (candle flame, etc.)
6. _____ other

Relaxing Sounds

Fill in a relaxing, warming, or meditative sound for each category:

1. _____ human body (breathing, heart beat, etc.)
2. _____ exercise (breathing, foot falls during running, etc.)
3. _____ outdoors (rainstorm, wind, etc.)
4. _____ music (specific artist, type of music, etc.)
5. _____ object (metronome, air conditioner, etc.)
6. _____ other

9

Relax: Active Relaxation Strategies

CHAPTER OBJECTIVES

- Compare and contrast active and passive relaxation techniques.
- Explain how systematic muscle relaxation works.
- Demonstrate how to perform systematic muscle relaxation.
- Describe the similarities and differences between yoga and stretching.
- Describe how yoga and stretching reduce stress.
- Demonstrate how to perform a basic stretching routine.
- Describe how massage works to reduce stress.
- Demonstrate basic massage strokes.

Putting the body into a relaxed state on a regular basis is important. Relaxation has the ability to both cancel out the effects of stress and help prevent stressors from building up and triggering a stress response.

The types of techniques described in Chapter 8 all have one thing in common: they require a passive mental attitude. Additionally, techniques such as meditation, imagery, and autogenics are, for the most part, mental techniques. They really do not require active physical participation. Part of their appeal lies in their ability to help us acquire mental discipline. However, many people find the mental discipline required for these techniques restrictive and displeasing.

In this chapter more physical forms of relaxation are explored. There is an emphasis on techniques that reduce muscle tension and the buildup of stress by-products through more active physical participation. The level of activity we explore in this chapter is basic and increases in the next chapter.

Systematic Muscle Relaxation

As described earlier, acute and chronic muscle tension are common by-products of the stress response. In many cases we do not even realize that we are tense until our bodies send us warning signs in the form of pain, tightness, and reduced functioning. Practicing some form of muscle relaxation or stretching on a regular basis is key in the prevention of this tension.

KEY
TO UNDERSTANDING

Stretching and relaxation helps prevent muscle pain, tightness, and reduced functioning.

Systematic muscle relaxation is a technique developed by Edmund Jacobson,[7] a Chicago physician. His early work was with presurgical hospital patients. He noticed that patients awaiting surgery seemed stressed and had high levels of muscular tension, particularly in the neck and back. Jacobson felt that if he could help his patients relieve tension, it might reduce some of their suffering and help facilitate their recovery. When he made patients aware of their tension and asked them to relax, it did not work; they needed more help in relaxing their muscles.

Jacobson developed systematic muscle relaxation as a technique to help patients relax their muscles before surgery in order to enhance their response to treatment and care. Jacobson found that with practice, patients could learn to relax their skeletal muscles whenever they wanted to. The technique not only worked in reducing skeletal muscle tension, but it also had a calming effect on the mind and on the activity of internal organs. Once the perception of muscle tension was removed, the mind and the internal organs relaxed.

Jacobson also found that his technique could be used to prevent muscle tension from building up. Systematic muscle relaxation has been found to be effective in treating insomnia, nervous anxiety, depression, hypochondria, hypertension, colitis, and tension headaches.[12]

In its most basic use, systematic muscle relaxation helps people know what relaxed muscles and bodies feel like. By alternating the contraction and relaxation of muscles, students learn the difference between tension and relaxation. This can be used as a preventive approach to tension-related problems in the muscles by helping students become aware of their stress before it results in muscular disorders.

People with a history of low back pain, disk or other spinal problems, and any musculoskeletal disorders should speak to their physicians before engaging in these exercises. All exercises should be carried out as vigorously as possible to the point of feeling uncomfortable but short of pain.

Instructions for Systematic Muscle Relaxation

1. Find a quiet place away from others.
2. Minimize distractions by closing the door and turning off the radio, television, and phone.
3. Loosen any tight clothing and remove jewelry and shoes.
4. Lie on your back with your arms at your sides. Elbows flexed comfortably, with your hands gently resting on your stomach.
5. Let your legs assume a gentle flex, with your knees slightly bent and falling outward.
6. Your body should not need support to hold this position, but if it does, you may use a small pillow under the knees and/or the small of the back (Fig. 9-1).

Fig. 9-1 Starting position

Feet and calves

1. Point the toes of both feet back toward your face (similar to removing your foot from the gas pedal).
2. Hold for a few seconds, then gradually let your feet return to their normal resting position.
3. Repeat this activity once more.
4. Point the toes of both feet away from your face, pushing them down toward the floor.
5. Hold for a few seconds then gradually let your feet return to their normal resting position.
6. Repeat this activity once more (Fig. 9-2).

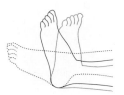

Fig. 9-2 Feet/calves

Spine

1. Straighten your legs, touching your feet together and push down on the floor with the bottoms of your legs and knees. (Be sure to take your pillow out if you have one under your knees.)
2. Hold for a few seconds and then gently let your knees pop up and your legs return to their normal resting position.
3. Repeat this activity once more.
4. Tense all of your stomach muscles (pull them in as if you were preparing to get punched in the stomach).
5. Hold them tightly for a few seconds and them let your stomach muscles return to their normal resting position.
6. Repeat this activity one more time.
7. Clench the muscles in your buttocks and anus tightly. If you are doing this correctly, your groin and genitals should push up.
8. Hold for a few seconds and then return to your normal resting position.
9. Repeat this activity once again.
10. Grasp your elbows with your hands and lift your arms over your head.
11. As you do this, tilt your head to the rear and arch your back as far as it will go (Fig. 9-3).
12. Hold for a few seconds and then gently let your head fall forward, let your spine straighten, and return your arms to their resting position on your abdomen.
13. Repeat this activity once more.

Fig. 9-3 Spine

Shoulders

1. Shrug your shoulders up toward your ears; try to touch your ears with your shoulder blades (Fig. 9-4).
2. Slowly let your shoulders return to their normal resting position.
3. Repeat this activity one more time.
4. Move your arms so your palms are pressing inward on the sides of your legs. Press as hard as you can against the sides of your legs.
5. Hold this for a few seconds and then let your arms return to their normal resting position.
6. Repeat this activity one more time.

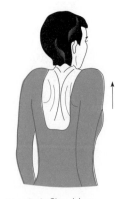

Fig. 9-4 Shoulders

Hands and arms

1. Clench both of your hands into tight fists (Fig. 9-5).
2. Hold for a few seconds and then slowly let your hands return to their normal resting position.

3. Repeat this activity one more time.

4. Clench both of your fists and curl your arms tightly so that your hands press up against your shoulders.

5. Hold for a few seconds then relax and let your arms return to their normal resting position.

Head and neck

1. Bend your head forward trying to touch your chest with your chin. Keep your shoulders flat against the floor while you are attempting this.

2. Hold this position for a few seconds and then gently let your head fall backward to its normal resting position.

3. Repeat this activity one more time.

4. Tilt your head backward trying to touch your nose to the wall behind you. Keep your shoulders on the floor.

5. Hold this for a few seconds and then gently let your chin fall forward, returning your head to its normal resting position.

6. Repeat this activity one more time.

7. Gently turn your head as far as it will go to the right side; try to touch your cheek to the floor (Fig. 9-6).

8. Hold this position for a few seconds and then gently return your head to its normal resting position.

9. Repeat this activity one more time.

10. Gently turn your head to the left side as far as it will go; try to touch your cheek to the floor (Fig. 9-6).

11. Hold this position for a few seconds and then gently return your head to its normal resting position.

Face

1. Scrunch up your face into the tightest, funniest expression you can make (Fig. 9-7).

2. Hold this for a few seconds and let your face return to its normal resting position.

3. Repeat this activity one more time.

4. Open your mouth and eyes as wide as they will go.

5. Hold this position for a few seconds and then return to your normal resting position.

6. Repeat this activity one more time.

With practice these activities will take less time to perform. Even though they seem simple, try to perform them exactly as directed to minimize any risk of injury and to maximize their effectiveness. A benefit of per-

Fig. 9-5 Hands and arms

Fig. 9-6 Head and neck

Fig. 9-7 Face

KEY
TO UNDERSTANDING

Increased awareness
of the functioning and
power of your mus-
cles is side benefit of
systematic muscle
relaxation.

forming these relaxation activities is that they promote muscle awareness and connect you to the inner power of these muscles and their intended motions.

Yoga and Stretching

It is not unusual that most of us start our day with a good stretch on awakening. It is a natural reaction to reduce the muscle tension associated with laying in one position for a prolonged period of time. You probably also find yourself stretching during the day when you have spent too long hunched over a desk, sitting too long at the computer terminal, or standing in one spot.

Common results of our modern sedentary lifestyle are chronically shortened muscles, tendons, and ligaments. As discussed in Chapter 4, the negative health effects of chronically shortened muscles include restricted range of motion, fatigue, and pain and spasms.

Most of us do not, as a regular part of our day, perform work that forces us to fully stretch our muscles. We perform a series of tasks that require an abbreviated range of motion. Hatha yoga and stretching exercises can help us reduce stress by reducing muscle tension and the consequent stress messages that tense muscles send to the brain.

Yoga and Static Stretching

The word *yoga* is derived from the Sanskrit (the ancient literary language of India) root word meaning to yoke or join. Yoga is an ancient Hindu ascetic philosophy that includes mental, physical, social, and spiritual components. Traditional yoga instruction involved a master teacher who passed his teachings on to his disciples through an integrated, eightfold process called asthanagayoga.[19] The eightfold process includes:

1. Yama—rules and restraints for productive living in society, such as being truthful.
2. Niyama—self-rules governing cleanliness and personal contentment.
3. Asaana—physical exercises called *postures*.
4. Pranayama—deep-breathing training.
5. Pratihara—freeing the mind from the senses.
6. Dharana—focused concentration on an object.
7. Dhyana—meditation.
8. Samadhi—cosmic meditation.

Yoga training, as initially intended, was a way of life and a way of being. As students progressed through the eight stages of training, they would liberate and control their life force believed to be located in the spinal cord and vital organs.

There are several different types of yoga, each one focusing on different aspects of the asthanagayoga. Bhakti yoga (the path of devotion), gyana yoga (the path of knowledge), and raja yoga (the path of wisdom, self-realization, and enlightenment) are examples of these.[19]

Hatha is a type of yoga that employs various stretching exercises called *postures.* They are designed to reduce muscle tension and facilitate a relaxed state of being that is conducive to meditation. However, one does not need to practice meditation to enjoy the benefits of tension reduction that can be attained through hatha yoga exercises.[11]

The type of stretching most similar to that used in hatha yoga is static stretching. Static stretching involves passively stretching a specific muscle by putting it into a maximally stretched state and holding it for an extended period of time. Recommendations for the length of holding time range from 6 to 60 seconds. Thirty seconds is most often recommended as the optimal time to build up to.[14]

Many people interested in stretching perform hatha yoga postures without realizing that they are doing so. Modern static stretching programs, designed to increase flexibility, draw many of their stretches from hatha yoga postures.[6] Our current interest in stretching has evolved in part out of the desire to achieve maximum flexibility for athletic purposes. *Flexibility* can best be defined as the ability of a joint to move through its full range of motion.[14] Flexibility has long been recognized as an essential component of fitness. Some athletic activities, such as gymnastics, ballet, and diving, require maximum flexibility. Athletes in other sports can also benefit from increased flexibility because it is related to a variety of other qualities, including stride length, balance, and reaction time.[14]

Interest in stretching spread from the athletic community to the general public during the fitness movement of the 1980s and 1990s. People realized that having more flexible joints that could move easily and smoothly through their full range of motion was essential to healthy living.

Yoga and stretching work by taking advantage of the elastic properties of muscles and connective tissue such as ligaments and the tissue that encapsulates joints. Through systematic stretching of muscles and tissue, it is possible to lengthen muscles and loosen the connective tissue. This increases the joint's range of motion. An additional advantage of stretching and yoga is the reduction of muscle tension. Through stretching, tension that has built up in immobile or braced muscles and joints is released.

Preparation for Yoga and Stretching

Yoga and stretching exercises are designed to be performed slowly and gently; therefore you should not rush. You are not trying to develop cardiovascular fitness. Never force yourself beyond the point of pain. The old maxim "no pain, no gain" does not hold true in the practice of yoga, static stretching, or any physical activity. Always stretch to the point of tension (just short of but never to the point of pain) and then hold that position. Initially, hold the stretch for a count of 10 seconds. In time you will find that you can stretch further and hold it longer. Do not rush this development. It took you a lifetime to get this tight. It will take a few months to loosen up. You may also find that because of your body type you are never able to stretch as far as others. This is normal. A key to success is to try to stretch to your personal limit.

Do not bounce when you stretch and hold. This is called *ballistic stretching*. Ballistic stretching employs rapid and forceful bouncing movements designed to push resistant muscle tissue beyond its normal stretching point. These quick, forceful movements have been shown to be effective in stretching, but they can also injure your muscles, tendons, and ligaments. If the forces generated by the jerks, bounces, and pulls are greater than the tissue's ability to extend, injury may result.[14] Ballistic stretching can also be counterproductive because, when you bounce, your muscles are forced to pull against themselves. The brain, sensing the bounces, sends a message to the muscles to contract rather than lengthen.[1]

When you are stretching and performing yoga, always breathe normally. Do not hold your breath and never lock your joints fully when extending your arms or legs. You should keep your knees and elbows slightly bent.

A Simple, Full-Body Hatha Yoga Routine

The following stretching exercises, called postures in yoga, are designed to stretch every part of your body. Take your time during the exercises. With practice you will be able to perform this routine in less than 30 minutes.

Sky Reach

This posture is designed to stretch your fingers, hands, arms, shoulders, chest, and back.

1. Stand with your feet shoulder-width apart, hands resting at your sides.
2. Slowly reach for the sky, trying to touch the clouds (or ceiling if you are inside).
3. As you reach, make sure you stretch your wrists, elbows, shoulders, and all of your fingers. Do not raise up on your toes.
4. When you reach maximum stretch, hold for a count of 10 seconds (Fig. 9-8).

Toe Touch

Although this exercise is designed to have you ultimately touch your toes, you will probably have to begin by aiming for your knees, then your shins,

KEY
TO UNDERSTANDING

Stretch to your personal limit.

Fig. 9-8 Sky reach

and in time, your feet. Do not cheat by bending your knees excessively. In time you will reach your toes. This posture will stretch your arms, hands, wrists, fingers, legs, neck, and back.

1. Stand with your feet shoulder-width apart.
2. Slowly, bend from the waist trying to touch your knees with your hands.
3. Let your head fall forward, nestling close to your thighs if possible. Try to keep your neck and head loose.
4. Bend your knees slightly.
5. When you reach your maximum stretch, hold for a count of 10 seconds.
6. Slowly return to the upright position.
7. Repeat this twice more, reaching for your shins and finally your toes (Fig. 9-9).

Fig. 9-9 Toe touch

Achilles Stretch

This posture is designed to stretch the achilles tendons and calf muscles.

1. Stand facing the wall, feet shoulder-width apart, arm's length away.
2. Keeping both heels on the ground, knees slightly bent, and feet flat, lean into the wall, touching it gently using your hands and arms to balance.
3. Keep leaning into the wall until you reach your maximum stretch. You will feel pressure in your calves and achilles tendons.
4. Hold for a count of 10 seconds.
5. Repeat twice more (Fig. 9-10).

Standing Side Trunk Bends

These bends are designed to stretch your hips, side abdominals, ribs, and shoulders.

Fig. 9-10 Achilles/calf stretch

1. Stand with your feet flat and shoulder-width apart, arms at your sides.
2. Slowly raise your arms overhead, palms facing forward.
3. Keeping your feet flat and your hips rigid, bend as far as you can to the right.
4. Stretch your arms out, keeping elbows slightly bent as you bend to the side.
5. Let your head follow gracefully, trying to keep your neck and head loose.
6. When you reach your maximum stretch, hold for a count of 10 seconds.

7. Slowly return to the starting position.
8. Repeat this posture, stretching this time to the left side.
9. Do three stretches to each side (Fig. 9-11).

Fig. 9-11 Side bends

Fig. 9-12 Back reach

Back Reach

This posture can be done either seated or standing and is designed to stretch the back, arms, and shoulders.

1. Either standing or sitting with your back straight, feet shoulder-width apart, clasp your hands together and extend your arms over your head.
2. Keeping your fingers intertwined, bend from the elbows and touch the base of your neck with your fists.
3. As you are doing this, push your arms and elbows back.
4. When you reach your maximum stretch, hold for a count of 10 seconds.
5. Repeat three times (Fig. 9-12).

Shoulder Roll

This posture is designed to stretch your shoulders, back, arms, and neck.

1. Stand straight with your feet flat and shoulder-width apart.
2. Clasp your hands together behind your back (Fig. 9-13).
3. Keeping your hands clasped and feet flat, lift your arms up toward your shoulders.
4. At the same time you are doing this, bend forward from the waist as far as possible.

Fig. 9-13 Shoulder roll

5. Keep your knees slightly bent when you are doing this and try to tuck your chin against your chest.
6. When you reach your maximum stretch, hold for a count of 10 seconds.
7. Repeat this exercise three times.

Forward Back Stretch

This posture is designed to stretch your back, neck, arms, and legs. Ultimately you will be trying to reach and hold your ankles. Do this in stages, however, aiming first for the knees then the shins, and finally the ankles.

1. Sit on the floor with your legs stretched out in front of you, feet together, hands at your sides.
2. Keeping the backs of your legs on the ground as much as possible and your knees slightly bent, slowly bend forward, sliding your palms along the sides of your legs until you reach your knees.
3. As you reach forward you can extend your elbows outward.
4. Try to keep your chin tucked in as close to your chest as possible for maximum stretch.
5. When you reach your maximum stretch, hold for a count of 10 seconds.
6. Repeat this activity three times (Fig. 9-14).

Fig. 9-14 Forward back stretch

Reverse Back Stretch

This posture is designed to stretch your spine in the opposite direction. It will also stretch your arms, chest, neck, and shoulders. Ultimately you will be fully extending your arms for maximum stretching of your spine. You will start however by rising to your elbows, eventually lifting them off the floor.

1. Lay on your stomach, feet together, hands to your side.
2. Bring your hands under your shoulders, palms flat on the ground, fingers pointing forward (similar to getting ready to do a push up).
3. Slowly push your torso off the floor, arching your back.
4. Keep your forearms and elbows on the floor as you arch and let your head stretch backward, chin trying to touch the ceiling.
5. Stretch until you feel mild discomfort and then hold this for a count of 10 seconds.
6. If you feel no pain, on the next repetition try to arch further by straightening your arms and letting your elbows come off the floor.
7. Repeat this posture three times (Fig. 9-15).

Fig. 9-15 Reverse back stretch

Hurdler's Stretch

This is a one-legged variation of the forward back stretch that puts additional emphasis on stretching the quadriceps (front of the thighs) and hamstrings (back of the legs), as well as the knees and groin (Fig. 9-16).

Fig. 9-16 Hurdler's stretch

1. Sit on the floor with your legs together.
2. Tuck one leg into your groin as illustrated in Fig. 9-16.
3. Keep the other leg extended, knee slightly bent.
4. Keeping the knee of the tucked leg as close to the ground as possible, tuck your chin and slowly bend your head forward toward your knee.
5. Stretch as close to your knee as possible then hold for a count of 10 seconds.
6. Do this three times and then switch to your other leg (Fig. 9-16).

Groin Stretch

As the title indicates, this posture is intended to stretch the muscles of the groin (Fig. 9-17).

Fig. 9-17 Groin stretch

1. Sit on the floor with your back straight, heels together, and knees bent pointing out to the side.
2. Keeping your head up, gently push down on your knees, forcing them closer to the floor.
3. Stretch until your feel discomfort in the groin and then hold for a count of 10 seconds.
4. Repeat this three times.

T'ai Chi Ch'uan

The purpose of this section of the chapter is not to teach you t'ai chi ch'uan; it takes years of study and practice to master this art. Rather, this section is designed to introduce the underlying concepts associated with t'ai chi ch'uan and to illustrate its value as a stress-management technique.

T'ai chi ch'uan is a form of self-defense that was developed in China and dates back several thousands of years. It is a unique blend of both physical movement and philosophical outlook. The physical movements of t'ai chi ch'uan (more than 100 exercises) are fluid, emphasizing the philosophical belief of flowing or harmonizing with one's opposition rather than fighting against it. T'ai chi ch'uan has adopted many of its philosophical underpinnings from Taoism which emphasizes the balance of opposing forces in life.

The blending of opposing forces referred to as yin and yang, characterizes the Taoist philosophy of life.[2] Yin can be described as a negative force and yang as a positive one. Crompton[4] uses an analogy of a battery and flashlight to describe how yin and yang can work together or against each other. When the flashlight is switched on, the electrical current flows from one pole of the battery to the other, resulting in the creation and harnessing of the energy. As with the flashlight, when we are in balance, our yin and yang are working in harmony; they serve as a source of energy and help light the way through the path of life. **Taoism** explores this essential duality of life and teaches how to flow with it rather than against it. This "going with the flow" is one of the characteristics that sets t'ai chi ch'uan apart from many other forms of self-defense.

Chi, is a Chinese word used to describe a life force, or subtle energy, that flows throughout the body. The Chinese believe that health involves the continual, unobstructed flow of chi; when our yin and yang are balanced, we are healthy and experience an unobstructed flow of chi. Disease and illness are not caused by pathogens per se but rather by a restriction or obstruction of the flow of chi. We are constantly surrounded by viruses, bacteria, and other disease-causing pathogens. What allows these and other invaders to enter and cause disease is a breakdown in the flow of life giving energy. **Acupuncture** and yoga are also practices that are believed to unblock constriction of the free flow of energy.[5]

taoism
a Chinese philosophy of life and religion founded by Lao Tzu that emphasizes the duality of life and opposing forces

acupuncture
the Chinese medical practice of puncturing the body with thin wire needles at precise points to free constricted or blocked energy centers

T'ai Chi Ch'uan and Stress Management

T'ai chi ch'uan, also referred to as *moving meditation,* teaches people to remain calm and centered against the forces of opposition. It emphasizes conserving energy, remaining balanced, and using rather than fighting the forces of opposition. It is not a violent exercise but an exercise in maintaining balance in life.[17]

In a sense, t'ai chi ch'uan teaches people how to maintain homeostasis in the face of stressors. The mental (staying calm, not giving into fear, harmonizing with the opposition) blends with the physical (keeping a low center of gravity, maintaining balance, using your opponents energy to conserve your own) in seeking to maintain equilibrium.

Learning t'ai chi ch'uan involves practicing and perfecting its many different exercises. The movements of t'ai chi ch'uan are graceful and continuous, and emphasize even, effortless, coordinated breathing. Seward[17] outlines six underlying concepts of t'ai chi ch'uan that illustrate some of its stress-reducing qualities:

1. Effortless, deep breathing—Breathing should be natural, and in time students learn to coordinate breathing with the specific exercises. Students get in touch with their breathing, making sure it comes from the abdomen rather than the chest.

2. Tension reduction—All exercises are performed gracefully. Students are taught to look for signs of tension that may inhibit the flow of energy.

3. A perpendicular stance—Students are taught to maintain their balance as they move from position to position, keeping their spinal column straight.

4. A low center of gravity—Keeping centered has a lot to do with maintaining a stable base, a lower center of gravity.

5. An even speed—Keep movements continuous and even flowing, conserving energy by avoiding sudden, jerky movements.

6. Mind/body integration—T'ai chi ch'uan is referred to as moving meditation because the student is instructed to concentrate on the body and visualize its movements. Students are instructed to get back to focusing on their movements when their minds stray.

These six underlying concepts illustrate how t'ai chi ch'uan blends strategies that we have already discussed (deep breathing, visualization, meditation, and muscle relaxation) with a philosophy of life that is flexible and emphasizes the need to adapt to change rather than to fight it.

Massage and Therapeutic Touch

The "laying on of hands," or massage, has long been recognized for its healing power. From biblical references to the work of Krieger,[10] who coined the term *therapeutic touch*, physical touching has a long history of effectiveness in reducing tension. The actual practice of massage was invented by the Chinese.[18]

While religious references to massage deal with healing through miracles and physical touch, Krieger[10] believes that each of us produces energy that can be transferred to another without the need of these devices. According to Krieger, people have an energy field that extends beyond the skin and creates an aura around each of us. We are most conscious of this energy field when it is invaded by others. For instance, when we are in a crowded elevator or forced to hold onto a strap in a packed subway, we feel as if our personal space is being invaded. Photographers using Kirlian, or heat-sensitive, filming techniques, have captured pictures of our personal energy auras on film.[8]

Although therapeutic touch does not involve actual touching and manipulating, Krieger[10] believes that trained practitioners can transfer their energy and its healing powers by passing their hands over their patients and merging the two energy fields. Wright[20] believes that our bodies and the environment are open systems that exchange energy. When we are ill or in pain, the flow between our bodies and the environment is disrupted. Therapeutic touch, Krieger believes, is a way to restore the natural harmony between our bodies and our environment. Therapeutic touch has been found to be effective in treating a wide range of physical and emotional health problems, ranging from anxiety disorders to physical pain.[16]

Whether or not you believe in the body's energy field and the power of therapeutic touch, you no doubt have experienced the simple pleasure and relaxation associated with a good back rub or full-body massage. The relaxation benefits of massage affect not only the person being massaged but also the masseur or masseuse. Giving a massage requires slowing down and becoming fully involved in the process. The person giving the massage must clear his or her head and focus on properly stroking and kneading the skin and muscles of the receiver. The feel of warm human flesh and the knowledge that you are pleasing someone else is also rewarding and relaxing for the masseur.

Massage has two major effects: it relieves muscle tension and stimulates circulation to the tissues and muscles.[18] This is why you feel warm and relaxed after a massage.

Massage is used in a variety of clinical and therapeutic settings. Hospitals, clinics, and other medical settings use it to help relax patients, increase circulation to injured parts of the body, and speed the healing process. Massage is especially effective in improving the circulation of bedridden patients who are unable to move freely. Lack of movement and being forced to lie in bed in the same position for extended periods put undue pressure on tissue and reduce circulation. Massage promotes circulation, which helps supply oxygen and other nutrients to all parts of the body while removing waste products.[9]

Massage is also used by athletes, trainers, and sports medicine specialists to prevent and treat **soft-tissue** injuries and speed the healing process. Massage is especially useful in the treatment of **sprains**, **strains**, and **contusions**, and works by stimulating blood flow to the injured area. This increased blood flow reduces swelling, promotes healing, and reduces the likelihood of **fibrosis**.[13]

Types of Massage

There are many different types of massage. Some of the more common are Swedish, shiatsu, and medical or sports massage.

Swedish massage

Swedish massage, or total body massage, is probably the form that most people are familiar with. Swedish massage is one of the most commonly

soft tissue
tissue other than bone

sprain
a traumatic injury to the tendons, muscles, or ligaments around a joint—characterized by pain, swelling, and discoloration of the skin

strain
minor muscular damage due to excessive physical effort

contusion
a bruise characterized by pain, swelling, and discoloration that does not break the skin

fibrosis
an abnormal condition where fibrous connective tissue spreads over smooth muscle tissue

used forms of massage and combines a variety of strokes that build in pressure. Swedish massage starts with light, flowing strokes called *effleurage*. These light, flowing strokes are followed by *petrissage*, a series of shorter, more pressurized squeezes and rolls. These are followed by deeper, penetrating kneading strokes (friction), chops (tapoment), and deep vibrating movements (vibration).

A person receiving a Swedish massage lies nude, face down on a massage table or bed, with a towel covering the buttocks. Massage oil is usually used to minimize friction. A Swedish massage progresses up and down the spine, working the neck, shoulders, buttocks, hamstrings, and calves. These are the areas most susceptible to the build-up of tension, associated aches and pains, strained muscles, fatigue, and insomnia.[3]

Shiatsu

Shiatsu, or acupressure massage, is similar to another healing technique — acupuncture. Both are based on the belief that stress, tension, and disease are due in part to a blocking of the body's vital energy. Acupuncture relieves the blockage of chi through stimulation of pressure points by inserting needles into them, while acupressure manipulates those pressure points through massage.

Acupressure involves applying pressure to the pressure points for a few seconds using the thumbs in a series of circular movements. The entire massage is shorter and simpler than Swedish massage. Unlike Swedish massage, which is best obtained in the nude, shiatsu does not require the removal of clothes.[3]

Medical/Sports Massage

Medical, or sports, massage is directed at healing muscle tissue that has been damaged by injury or overexertion. Sports masseurs and masseuses are eclectic in their approach, employing a variety of strokes, pulls, and touches during the application of pressure.

Sports massage is intended to help athletes recover from strenuous workouts by increasing the circulation of blood into specific muscles. This increased circulation helps carry nutrients to the tissue and facilitate the removal of waste products such as lactic acid. The accumulation of lactic acid within muscles is associated with fatigue and discomfort.[14]

Medical massage is also intended to increase circulation to the muscle tissue. In many cases bedridden patients, cannot walk or perform enough physical activity to stimulate their circulation, which can hinder their treatment and increase muscle tension and soreness. Massage can help counteract these physical conditions by reducing stress, relieving pain, and restoring a sense of emotional well-being.[15]

Preparation for Massage:
A Word About Sensuality and Sexuality

It is hard sometimes for us to separate our sensuality from our sexuality when it comes to massage. For many of us, the only time we touch others in such an intimate way is when we are being sexual. Massage is not an inherently sexual activity, however, it is sensual. Kneading, stroking, and manipulating another person's flesh requires that we be in tune with the sensation of touch. We must be acutely aware of pressure and motion when giving a massage. Also, many of the massage oils available are scented and bring into play our sense of smell. It may take time to both enjoy giving and getting a massage and viewing these as sensual delights that do not have to lead to sexual activity.

How to Give a Massage

Giving a massage is a natural behavior. Most of us massage others the way we like to be massaged. Instinctively, we believe that if it feels good to us,

STRESS IN OUR WORLD

Janet

Janet is an African-American returning student in her thirties, with two children. She had raised both of her sons while working part-time selling real estate on weekends. With both of the boys in high school and her husband doing well in his own business, Janet felt it was time to pursue her dream, earning her bachelor's degree in psychology. As a senior, she had finished all of her major courses and was taking all of the fun electives she could that were somewhat related to her field. She had one semester to go.

However, Janet was uneasy because in her stress management class the students were going to be giving each other warm-oil foot massages. The professor had explained that this was intended to be an exercise in stress relief. Janet understood this and really wanted to experience what a warm-oil foot massage was like, but she did not feel right about doing it. What would she do if she was paired up with an attractive young guy? What if she was paired up with another woman and found that she enjoyed the experience? Did that mean she was gay? Janet was filled with stress as the time got closer.

Put yourself in Janet's place. Would this affect you in a similar way? Are sensuality and sexuality that closely related? Could you separate the two? How could the stress of this activity be defused?

it will feel good to the person we are massaging. While this is true for the most part, some basic instructions in massage will help you refine your technique.

In general, it is easier to give a massage if you use some form of lubricating oil. Some people prefer powder as an agent to reduce friction and like the dry sensations powder offer, but most people prefer oil. Try both and decide for yourself.

If you use oil, make sure it is warm or at room temperature. Nothing gets a massage off to a worse start than having someone dump cold oil on your skin. If possible, let the oil sit at room temperature or warm the container under hot water in the sink before you start. Pour the oil into your hands and rub it around and then onto the body rather than squirting it directly onto the person's skin.

Make sure you have enough room to get completely around the person without having to lean on or jump over him or her. You should be able to position yourself over the person so you can apply firm pressure during some strokes. A massage table or high bed is ideal because it allows you to stand while giving a massage. You can also kneel next to the person receiving the massage. Additionally, a massage table has a well for the person's head to rest in, allowing him or her to lie comfortably with their face down, facilitating easy access to their neck, shoulders, and head. A professional table is not essential, however, when giving a massage. You can place a pillow under the person's head for support and have them rest their head gently to the side.

The most important thing about giving a massage is to take your time. The other person will instantly sense if you feel obligated to do this and are rushing through it. Giving a massage is an act of kindness and must be done slowly and lovingly, with no expectations for anything in return.

There are several types of strokes that can be used when giving a massage. A key element is to maintain contact with your partner, if possible, as you move from one stroke to the next. Try to have your strokes merge to form a sense of continuous motion with the muscles. Sometimes having a visual image of the muscular system can help.

Try to keep your strokes rhythmic and symmetrical. Do not worry if your strokes are not perfect; they will get better with practice. Try hard to keep your motion flowing. You will need to be use your whole hand to effectively master all of the strokes. Your fingers, palm, heel, and fist all come into play.

1. Kneading—In kneading, you grasp the flesh with all four fingers of both hands and rotate your thumbs in opposite directions. Kneading works beautifully with the muscles of the arms, legs, hands, feet, and shoulders.

KEY
TO UNDERSTANDING

Take your time when giving a massage.

2. Pressing—Pressing involves pushing against the body with the heel of the hand. For extra pressure you can use your other hand to apply pressure against the hand involved in the pressing. Pressing can be used in long strokes or circular motion and is very effective with thicker muscles such as those in the back.

3. Stroking—Stroking involves the fingertips and can be done by either pushing away from you in circles or drawing toward you. Stroking can also involve all five fingers gently drawing flesh toward you. Stroking is wonderful for the scalp, neck, and inner thighs but is also great for long continuous motion along the back, torso, arms, and legs.

4. Pulling—Pulling is very similar to stroking toward you, except it involves more pressure. In stroking your movements glide over the skin, but in pulling you actually grab hold and gently tug. You can pull with just your fingers or with your entire hand(s). Pulling is terrific for the head, hands, fingers, toes, feet, arms, and legs.

5. Lifting—In some cases, actually lifting a part of the body such as the head, torso, or leg, and supporting it in your hands is very relaxing. When you are lifting, your hands are cupped and used to cradle the part being elevated.

6. Pounding—Making a fist and gently pounding a body part can release the tension that has accumulated in it. Pounding obviously is not for everyone or every body part. However, it is very effective on the back.

You can give full-body or partial massages. Sometimes just a back massage or foot massage will do the trick. Other times, a full-body massage, complete with scented candles, is indicated.

When giving a full-body massage, you can start anywhere. Some people start with the feet and then work up to the head and finish at the hands. Other people give the massage in the reverse order or start at the abdomen because it is the center or our bodies and the place where blood pools when the body is stressed. Wherever you start, just remember to cover the entire body in a systematic way. Try not to jump around from feet to head to toes. Finish a part thoroughly and then move on to the next body part.

Feet

Begin the massage by having the person lie on his or her stomach. Apply the warm oil to your hands liberally and reapply as indicated.

1. Work on each foot separately.
2. Position yourself kneeling at the person's feet. Grasp the center of the foot with both hands and knead it.

3. Work down to the toes and pull on all five toes simultaneously.
4. Still holding the toes, switch to a circular pulling motion.
5. Work on each toe individually, gently pulling and kneading in a circular motion.
6. Press the arch of the foot from toes to heel.
7. Lift the foot and rotate it gently while holding onto the middle of it.
8. Finish off the foot by pressing the ball of the foot back and stroke the achilles tendon in the heel.
9. Repeat this on the other foot.

Legs

1. Straddle a leg while facing toward the person's head and work on the back of the leg using long pressing strokes. Press firmly all the way up to the back of the thigh and let your hands slide gently back along the outside of the leg on their way back. Try to maintain contact with the leg throughout this entire stroke.
2. After a few strokes grasp the leg on the return and gently lift and pull it as your hands return back. You may have to raise your body off the table, floor, or bed to make room for their leg.
3. Repeat this on the other leg.
4. Still straddling the leg, grasp the lower leg (calf) with both hands and knead deeply with the thumbs. The calf muscle is very dense, so you will be able to apply firm pressure.
5. Gently massage the back of the knee with mild circular kneading.
6. Repeat this on the other leg.

Buttocks

1. Work on the entire buttocks area at once.
2. Straddle the person's legs and firmly knead the buttocks with both hands.
3. After kneading the buttocks, grasp the person's hips and gently lift his or her hips off the floor, stretching this region.

Back

1. Either straddle the person's hips or lean over from the side and firmly massage the back using long presses from the small of the back to the neck.
2. Push hard using the heels of your hands as you press upward. Let your hands trail down the person's sides as they return to the small of the back.
3. After a few strokes, grasp the person's sides and gently pull and lift their back and hips as you return your hands to the starting position.

Head and Shoulders

1. Move up to the person's shoulders. Do not sit on the back as you do this. Lean over the person and grasp the meaty part of the shoulders on either side of the neck. This muscle, the trapezius, can be well developed in athletes and can be firmly kneaded.
2. Knead this muscle with the thumbs and entire hand. Use circular thumb motion.
3. Use the same motion on the rounded muscles (deltoids) at the end of the shoulders.
4. Return to the center of the back and, only with the thumbs, gently knead the base of the spine, from the shoulders to the base of the skull.
5. Using both hands, knead the entire neck. You should be able to grasp the neck gently as you use your thumbs and fingers simultaneously.
6. Using your fingers, massage the entire head with gentle circular pressing strokes. You may also use your entire hands to cradle and massage the head.

After asking the person to turn over, finish the massage by working on the arms, hands, torso, abdomen, and fronts of the legs.

Arms

1. Kneeling next to the person, grasp the arm closest to you and, starting at the wrist, knead toward to the underarm.
2. Let your hands slide down the sides of the person's arms on their way back to the starting position.
3. After a few strokes, grasp the arm and gently lift and pull on the way back.
4. Repeat the procedure on the other arm.

Hands

1. Grasp the person's hand in both of your hands. Firmly knead the backs and fronts of the hands using your thumbs and fingers.
2. Gently pull and rotate each finger.
3. Repeat the procedure on the other hand.

Front of the body

1. Either straddle the person's waist or lean over him or her. Using the heels of both hands simultaneously, press upward on his or her chest from the center outward. Be careful, especially with women, with the pressure exerted.
2. When you reach the shoulders, let your hands slide to the side for their return journey.

3. After a few strokes grasp the person's sides and lift as you pull your hands back to their starting place at the top of the stomach.

4. As an alternate to pulling or sliding down the sides, you can use long continuous finger strokes as you pull your hands back across the chest on their return journey.

5. The stomach/abdomen from the rib cage to the pubic area can be massaged using both hands simultaneously in a gentle circular stroking motion.

6. Kneel to the side of a leg and massage the front of it using a kneading stroke from the inner thigh down. Your hands should slide to the sides and maintain contact as you gently push them back to the top of the thigh.

7. After a few strokes, lift the leg and gently pull it toward you as you knead it with both hands.

8. As an alternate, you can use a pulling stroke to bring your hands down from the inner thigh to the ankle.

9. You may also spend some time kneading the inner thigh firmly with the thumbs, as this is an area where muscle tension seems to accumulate.

Many people feel relaxed and a little sleepy after a massage. Try to let him or her have some quiet time to savor the results. Hopefully, he or she will be appreciative enough to reciprocate.

See Assess Yourself 9-1 to record your personal experiences with the relaxation strategies described in this chapter.

Summary

We begin this chapter with a discussion of the differences between the types of relaxation techniques described in Chapter 8 and the ones discussed in this chapter. The previous chapter focuses on relaxation techniques that are more mental in their focus and required a high level of mental discipline. The relaxation techniques described in this chapter are more physical in nature and require more physical involvement.

In the first technique, systematic muscle relaxation, students alternate between contracting and relaxing specific muscles. They work on each muscle in a systematic fashion from their heads to their toes. This technique works not only in relaxing muscles and releasing muscle tension, but also teaches students what tension and relaxation feels like.

The chapter continues with a discussion of hatha yoga and static stretching, describing their effects on relieving muscle tension. Hatha yoga postures and static stretching stretch muscles to a point where the muscle is uncomfortable but not in pain, resulting in decreased muscle tension .

T'ai Chi Ch'uan, a Chinese form of self-defense, is also discussed. The underlying philosophy of t'ai chi ch'uan, which draws heavily from Taoism, emphasizes learning how to maintain balance in the face of opposition by going with the flow, not against it.

The chapter ends with a section on massage. Massage has two primary benefits—releasing muscle tension and stimulating increased circulation to the muscle, creating a sensation of warmth. Therapeutic touch, a type of healing massage based on the sharing of energy between the therapist and the patient is also discussed. The section ends with instructions for giving a full-body massage.

References

1. Anspaugh, D., Hamrick, M., & Rosato, F. (1994). *Wellness: concepts and Applications* (2nd ed.). St. Louis: Mosby.

2. Bynner, W. (1980). *The way of life: according to Lao Tzu.* New York: Perigee Books

3. Cohen-Suib, S. (1987). *The magic of touch.* New York: Harper & Row.

4. Crompton, P. (1987). *The t'ai chi workbook.* Boston: Shambhala.

5. Dunn, T. (1987 November/December). The practice and spirit of t'ai chi ch'uan. *Yoga Journal.*

6. Girdano, D.A., Everly, G.S., & Dusek, D.E. (1993). *Controlling stress and tension: a holistic approach.* Englewood Cliffs, NJ: Prentice Hall.

7. Jacobson, E. (1970). *You must relax.* New York: McGraw Hill.

8. Kirlian, S., & Kirlian, V. (1961). Photography and visual observation by means of high-frequency currents. *Journal of Scientific and Applied Photography, 6,* 145-148.

9. Kozier, B., Erb, G., & Olivieri, R. (1991). *Fundamentals of nursing: concepts, process, and practice* (4th ed.). Redwood City, CA: Addison Wesley.

10. Krieger, D. (1979). *The therapeutic touch: how to use your hands to help or heal.* Englewood Cliffs, NJ: Prentice Hall.

11. Luby, S.(1977). *Hatha yoga for total health.* Englewood Cliffs, NJ: Prentice Hall.

12. McGuinan, F.J. (1983). Progressive relaxation: origin, principles, and clinical applications. In P.M. Lehrer & R.L. Woolfolk (Eds.) *Principles & practice of stress management* (2nd ed.). 17-52. New York: The Guilford Press.

13. Mellion, M. (1994). *Sports medicine secrets.* St. Louis: Mosby.

14. Prentice, W. (1994). *Fitness for college and life* (4th ed.). St. Louis: Mosby.

15. Russel, J.K. (1994). Bodywork: the art of touch. *Nurse-Practitioner Forum, 5*(2), 85-90.

16. Sayre-Adams, J. (1994). Therapeutic touch in health visiting practice. *Health Visitation, 6*(9), 304-305.

17. Seward, B.L. (1994). *Managing stress: principles and strategies for well being.* Boston: Jones and Bartlett.

18. Tappan, F. (1980). *Healing massage techniques: a study of eastern and western methods.* Reston, VA: Reston.

19. Werner, K. (1980). *Yoga & Indian philosophy.* Delhi, India: Motilal Pubs.

20. Wright S.M. (1987). The use of therapeutic touch in the management of pain. *Nursing Clinics of North America, 22,* 705-713.

ASSESS YOURSELF 9-1

Active Relaxation Assessment

Try each of the active relaxation strategies described in Chapter 9 at least once in the next week. At the end of a week, rate each activity using the following instrument:

1. What I liked about the activity:

_____

_____

_____

_____

2. What I disliked about the activity:

_____

_____

_____

_____

3. Potential barriers to using this activity on a regular basis:

_____

_____

_____

_____

4. Types of stressors this activity might be effective against:

_____

_____

_____

_____

Release: Using Physical Activity

Watch a group of children at play. Observe the way they run and jump, roll and dive, stretch, and reach. There is a simple, almost primitive quality about their physical release. Thinking of their activity reminds us that we all have within us the ability to be physical and to return to a more primitive state.

For many, the benefits of physical release need no explanation. Physical activity, whether at work, at play, in sports, or in bed, seems like a natural outlet for stress and tension. These people know intuitively that they simply feel better after they have released tension through physical activity. Their minds are clear and their muscles have that tired but relaxed feeling. They feel content and at peace with themselves.

Unfortunately, many others somehow lose the ability to be physical. Somewhere along the way they disconnect from their physical selves. They become dualistic, separating their minds from their bodies and trying to think their way out of everything.

This chapter explores the relationship between exercise, fitness, sexual activity, and stress management. All of these activities form the basis of the third line of defense against stress—release, which uses active physical involvement to cope with stress. The first half of the chapter concentrates on exercise and fitness. The second half focuses on physical activity as it relates to stress management.

Fight or Flight Revisited

Chapter 3 discusses the physiology of the stress response. If you recall the phrase "fight or flight," it refers to the body's preparation either to confront or run away from potential threats to one's well-being. In the days of the cave person, you either fought or ran away from the saber-toothed tiger when you discovered that you both inhabited the same cave. The earliest humans were equipped with this incredible self-defense system that activated when they perceived a threat to their well-being.

We are still equipped with this ability to mobilize strength and energy to fight or flee, but we rarely have the opportunity to use this energy when confronted by the less life-threatening but just as real modern threats to our well-being. The irate boss, traffic jam, inconsiderate sales clerk, and excessively demanding professor all are capable of invoking the same intense stress response as the sabre-toothed tiger. Also unchanged is our ability to deal with these threats through physical release.

When we are under stress and our bodies have mobilized energy for the fight-or-flight response, we are prepared for action. We are in a state that calls for physical release. We have the energy, our muscles are tense and ready, and our mind is alert and willing. When we act, we use the byproducts of this response (blood sugars, hormones, muscle tension, and high blood pressure) constructively. If we do not act and dissipate this stress response, it begins to exact its toll. In time, as discussed in Chapter 4, the response will lead to a decreased quality of life, inefficient functioning, illness, and breakdown.

However, instead of fighting or fleeing, we can release our pent up energy by going for a run, swim, or bike ride. We can take a brisk walk or chop some firewood. We can dance or work out on exercise equipment. We can give a massage. We can constructively use up the byproducts of the stress response (Fig. 10-1).

Fitness and Stress

Fitness can best be described as the degree to which our bodies function efficiently. Your level of fitness at any given time can be charted on a continuum ranging from inefficient functioning to maximum efficiency.

How well our bodies perform the tasks required of them contributes not only to our overall health and longevity but also to our daily quality of

Fig. 10-1 Positive release. Exercise is a productive way to release stress.

life.[17] Having high levels of physical well-being means that not only are we able to meet the demands of a typical day but we have energy remaining to enjoy our lives—to get the most out of our being. In a way, being fit helps us cope with the demands of modern living.

Components of Fitness

Fitness has two sets of components: (1) health-related components and (2) motor-skill–related components. The health-related components of fitness include muscular strength, muscular endurance, cardiorespiratory endurance, flexibility, and body composition. The motor-skill–related components are speed, power, agility, neuromuscular coordination, balance, and reaction time.[17] We focus on the health-related components because they are more directly related to stress management and overall well-being.

Muscular Strength

Muscular strength is the ability of a muscle or muscle group to exert maximum force in an activity for one repetition. An example of this is a weight-training activity called the *dumbbell curl* (Fig. 10-2). In this activity a person holds a fully loaded dumbbell, sits on a preacher bench, and attempts to bring the dumbbell to the shoulder in a curl motion. The exercise almost exclusively isolates the biceps muscle in that arm. The muscular strength of that biceps is a function of how much weight it can curl.

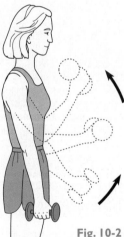

Fig. 10-2 Dumbbell curls. Performing a single dumbbell curl with maximum weight is a way to test muscular strength.

Muscular Endurance

Muscular endurance is the ability of a muscle or muscle group to sustain work (continuous repetitions) over time. Using the same dumbbell curl, we could measure the muscular endurance of that same biceps by reducing the weight and seeing how many times (or repetitions) a person could curl the dumbbell.

Cardiovascular Endurance

Cardiovascular endurance is the ability of the heart and lungs to pump blood, process oxygen, and sustain work over time. Long-distance runners, cross-country skiers, and other endurance athletes possess the best cardio-vascular fitness.

A stress test (Fig. 10-3) is a measure of cardiovascular endurance. While one is running on a treadmill, vital heart and lung functions, such as heart rate, blood pressure, lung volume, and rate of breathing, are measured to determine his or her level of performance.

Flexibility

Flexibility is the ability of a joint to run through its full range of motion. Common stretching activities, such as sitting, reaching, and toe touching, are ways to measure a person's flexibility.

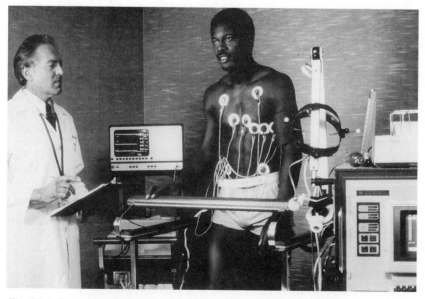

Fig. 10-3 Stress test. An exercise stress test is an excellent tool for measuring cardio-vascular endurance.

Body Composition

body composition

the ratio of fat to fat-free mass, such as muscle, bone, blood, organs, and other fluids exclusive of fat tissue

Body composition refers to the makeup of the body in terms of muscle, bone, fat, and other elements. Ideal body composition requires a certain percentage of lean vs. fat tissue.

Very few types of exercises or sports provide all five health-related components of fitness. One must pay attention to this when planning a fitness program. One must take care to incorporate activities that work on all five components if the desired effect is to achieve a truly high level of fitness. Assess Yourself 10-1 is designed to help you determine how well various kinds of activities incorporate the five components of fitness.

Principles of Fitness

specificity

the ability of an exercise to exert specific effects on targeted body parts or systems

Four principles affect fitness: specificity, reversibility, individual differences, and overload. Each is concerned with a particular facet of fitness.

Specificity refers to the fact that each type of exercise and individual activity has a specific effect on the body part it involves. For instance, dumbbell curls increase either the muscular endurance or the strength of the biceps muscle. They will not work the heart and lungs or contribute to agility. You can use your knowledge about the specificity of your physical activities to plan a well-rounded fitness program.

reversibility

the tendency of gains in endurance or strength to reverse after prolonged inactivity

Reversibility refers to the "use it or lose it" phenomenon in fitness. No fitness results are permanent. You begin to lose some of the benefits when you stop working out. Reversibility varies according to the component of fitness. In general, you will begin to experience some drop-off in fitness if you go more than 1 week without continuing to exercise.

individual differences

the need of each individual to begin and progress at different levels because of inherited, cultural, and historical differences

Individual differences are those genetic and behavioral factors that contribute to the speed and level of improvement in striving for fitness. Body type, body composition, growth and development, experience, and baseline level of fitness all are examples of individual differences that contribute to our progress (see the box on p. 331).

overload

systematically increasing the frequency, intensity, and/or time of exercise to force the body to physiologically adapt

Overload is the physiological adaptation of cells and tissue to increasing levels of demand. It involves systematically increasing one's exercise workload, forcing the body to adapt to this increased level of demand. One can employ overload by increasing the frequency, intensity, or time of exercise workouts.

Fitness, Exercise, and Energy Production

To become fit and continue to improve our level of fitness, we must exercise and employ overload. This requires the production and utilization of energy. Different types of exercise and activities use differing means of producing the energy necessary to perform work.

Factors that Affect Fitness

A wide variety of individual factors can influence our starting point and progress in any fitness program.

Age	Goals
Race	Hobbies
Gender	Self-image
Ethnicity	Peer group
Personality	Environment
Social class	Role model
General health	Responsibilities
Genetic predisposition	Knowledge about fitness

When we exercise, specific physiological processes occur. Our muscles contract and relax. We use energy in the form of glycogen stored in the skeletal muscles. Our lungs take part, causing oxygenation of the blood and removal of carbon dioxide. This richly oxygenated blood bathes all of the body's tissue, including the brain. Our heart and circulatory system must work harder to pump blood. Our sweat glands are activated, and our body temperature rises. In some cases, our liver churns out cholesterol and lipids, providing energy from stored fats. We burn these extra calories for the energy necessary to prolong this work.[14] Table 10-1 shows how many calories are burned through various types of exercise activities.

The cells in our bodies produce energy continually. Carbohydrates, proteins, or fats obtained through eating foods combine with oxygen, causing a chemical reaction within the cell that produces **adenosine triphosphate (ATP)**, a high-energy compound found in all living cells. ATP is the immediate source of cell energy and is produced in two ways—anaerobically and aerobically.

adenosine triphosphate (ATP)
a compound produced within the mitochondria of cells that is the energy storehouse in muscles

Anaerobic Energy Production

Energy needed to supply short-term, intensive bursts of activity is produced anaerobically. This type of activity is explosive, usually involves maximum effort, and lasts no longer than about 90 seconds. Sprinting (while running, swimming, or cycling) is an example of this type of activity. Anaerobic energy production can occur in the absence of oxygen. It relies on the rapid utilization of the ATP that is stored in the body's cells. When this stock of ATP is depleted, our bodies turn to stored glycogen as the energy source. Glycogen, stored in skeletal muscles, is broken down into glucose, which is

TABLE 10.1

Calories Expended During Exercise

Activity	Calories/min/lb*
Aerobic dance (vigorous)	0.062
Basketball (vigorous, full-court)	0.097
Bathing, dressing, undressing	0.021
Bed-making (and stripping)	0.031
Bicycling (13 mph)	0.071
Canoeing (flat water, 4 mph)	0.045
Chopping wood	0.049
Cleaning windows	0.024
Cross-country skiing (8 mph)	0.104
Gardening	0.062
Digging	
Hedging	
Raking	0.034
Weeding	0.038
Golf (twosome carrying clubs)	0.045
Handball (skilled, singles)	0.078
Horseback riding (trot)	0.052
Ironing	0.029
Jogging (5 mph)	0.060
Laundry (taking out and hanging)	0.027
Mopping floors	0.024
Peeling potatoes	0.019
Piano playing	0.018
Rowing (vigorous)	0.097
Running (8 mph)	0.104
Sawing wood (crosscut saw)	0.058
Shining shoes	0.017
Shoveling snow	0.052
Snowshoeing (2.5 mph)	0.060
Soccer (vigorous)	0.097
Swimming (55 yd/min)	0.088
Table tennis (skilled)	0.045
Tennis (beginner)	0.032
Walking (4.5 mph)	0.048
Writing while seated	0.013

*Multiply calories/min/lb by your body weight in pounds and then multiply that product by the number of minutes spent in the activity.
From Anspaugh, D., Hamrick, M., & Rosato, F. (1994). *Wellness: concepts and applications* (2nd ed.). St. Louis: Mosby.

metabolized within the cells to produce ATP. A small amount of glucose can be converted into ATP without the need for oxygen.[17] Anaerobic energy production results in the incomplete use of carbohydrates and creates **lactic acid** as a byproduct.

Aerobic Energy Production

Activities that extend beyond 4 minutes of continuous performance require energy derived by combining oxygen with nutrients. Aerobic literally means, "with oxygen." Running, cycling, and swimming laps are three examples of **aerobic exercise**.

Within our cells, components called *mitochondria* combine oxygen from respiration with the breakdown of carbohydrates, fats, or protein to produce ATP. This process generates considerably more ATP than anaerobic energy production and allows our bodies to sustain activities for long periods of time. During aerobic metabolism the cells utilize their carbohydrate, fat, or protein energy sources completely, producing ATP and releasing carbon dioxide and water as byproducts.[17]

Combined energy production

Activities that are 90 seconds to 4 minutes in duration produce energy through a combination of aerobic and anaerobic processes. Typically these activities involve intermittent bursts of motion that use up available ATP, requiring aerobic production of additional energy. Tennis, baseball, and touch football are examples of activities that incorporate intermittent bursts of high-intensity activity (Table 10-2).

lactic acid

a waste product, responsible for muscle soreness, produced by anaerobic energy production

aerobic exercise

exercise in which the amount of oxygen taken into the lungs is equal to or slightly more than that required to meet the body's energy demands; allows for ATP production with sufficient oxygen

TABLE 10.2

Energy Systems

Energy System	Length of Time	Type of Activity
Anaerobic	0-90 sec	Any type of sprint (running, swimming, cycling) Short duration, explosive activities
Combined systems	90 sec-4 min	Medium distance activities ($1/2$- to 1-mile run) Intermittent sports activities
Aerobic	>4 min	Long-distance events Long-duration intermittent activities

From Prentice, W. (1994). *Fitness for college and life*. St. Louis: Mosby.

Becoming Fit

Becoming fit requires a systematic approach and commitment to exercise, diet, and changing one's lifestyle. Assess Yourself 10-2 is designed to assist you as a first step in this process.

A carefully developed fitness plan incorporates a variety of exercises and activities to assess, develop, and maintain or improve your level of well-being across the five health-related components of fitness. Even a moderate amount of exercise, such as daily walking, can reduce your risk of heart disease and lower your serum cholesterol.[2]

Cardiovascular Fitness

Assessing Your Cardiovascular Fitness

Knowing how to begin a cardiovascular fitness program requires that you assess your baseline level of cardiac fitness. When you know your level of cardiovascular fitness, you can plan an exercise program that starts at the appropriate place. Assess Yourself 10-3 outlines the Cooper 12-minute walk/run test, which is a quick and simple way to assess your level of cardiovascular fitness and compare yourself with your peers.

Developing a Cardiovascular Fitness Program

Developing cardiovascular fitness involves using exercises that produce energy aerobically. As discussed previously, aerobic exercise involves continuous, rhythmic, and repetitive whole-body movements for extended periods of time at a pace that allows the body to fully utilize oxygen. Activities such as running, swimming, dancing, cross-country skiing, and cycling that last at least 20 minutes and force the heart and lungs to work at a certain level of demand (60% to 85% of maximum range) can produce an aerobic training effect.

The specific requirements for developing aerobic fitness are contained in the acronym *FIT*, which stands for *F*requency, *I*ntensity, and *T*ime.

cardiorespiratory
pertaining to the heart, lungs, and circulatory system

Frequency. A beginner trying to develop a moderate level of cardiovascular fitness needs to work out at least three times a week.

MHR (maximum heart rate)
the maximum number of heart beats/minute, obtained by subtracting one's age from 220 (220 - age)

Intensity. The intensity of the workout refers to the level of demand it places on the **cardiorespiratory** system. To achieve cardiovascular fitness, one must force the heart to work at a certain percentage of its maximum rate. Beginners and those with moderate levels of cardiovascular fitness should work out at 60% to 75% of their **maximum heart rate (MHR)** to achieve an aerobic training effect.[17] This percentage range is called an *aer-*

obic training zone. The formula in Assess Yourself 10-4 will help you calculate your aerobic training zone.

Heart rate often varies during a workout. Fig. 10-4 illustrates a typical heart rate during an aerobic training workout for beginners. As long as your rate stays within your aerobic training zone, you will achieve an aerobic training effect.

Time. Time refers to the duration of the workout. You must keep your heart rate in your training range for at least 20 minutes (30 minutes is preferred) to achieve an aerobic training effect.[17]

Run Your Way to Cardiovascular Fitness

Many activities can be used to develop cardiovascular fitness. One of the easiest and least-expensive activities is running (Fig. 10-5). The only piece of equipment you must to buy is a good pair of running shoes, which can cost less than $100. Fig. 10-6 illustrates some of the features available in quality running shoes.

You can run in old sweat clothes, shorts, a T-shirt, or whatever you feel comfortable wearing. Adjust your clothing to the weather. Remember, you will raise your body temperature as a result of the activity, so do not overdress.

Beginning Running. A beginning running program assumes you have not had any prior training or have not trained in the past 6 months. Even if you have trained in previous years, remember that your body needs time to adjust to this activity. Trying to do too much too soon will put too much stress and strain on your muscles, joints, and ligaments, causing pain and injury that will set back your training and become a stressor.

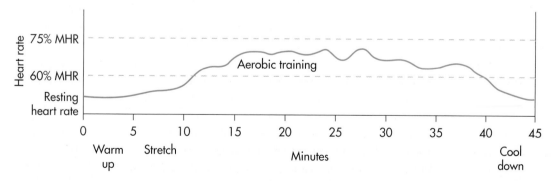

Fig. 10-4 A typical aerobic workout for a beginner. A typical aerobic workout lasts about 45 minutes and includes warm-up, stretching, and cool-down periods, as well as the training time. It is not unusual for one's heart rate to fluctuate within the training zone during the workout.

Fig. 10-5 Aerobic exercise. Running is an excellent form of aerobic exercise.

Beginning to run requires a progression from walking to jogging to eventual running. Walking means at least one foot maintains contact with the ground. Walking (regular walking, not race walking) generally is performed at a speed that requires more than 14 minutes per mile. While one is jogging or running, both feet are momentarily suspended off the ground between foot strikes. A combined walk/run usually results in a speed that requires 12 to 14 minutes per mile. Jogging is generally considered a slower form of running and occurs at speeds that require 9 to 12 minutes per mile. Anything faster than that is considered running.[11]

Running programs typically start with a combination of walking and jogging. As your fitness level improves, you walk less and jog more. Ultimately you stop walking altogether and begin jogging, moving up to a running pace as your strength and endurance increase.

Try to approach your training with an open mind. Remember, you are doing this to help combat stress. Do not make your training a source of

Running

Flexibility: ball of foot is flexible

Uppers: nylon or nylon mesh

Heel Flare: flared for greater stability

Cushioning: heel and sole well-padded

Soles: made of carbon-based material for greater durability

Tread: grip is enhanced by deep grooves

Fig. 10-6 Quality running shoes generally have at least these features.

stress. Look forward to your run. Enjoy each milestone in your training improvement. Do not rush—savor each minute you are out there running!

Jogging/Running Form. Although jogging and running are natural activities that anyone can perform, here are some guidelines to help you develop a smooth and efficient form:

1. Run tall and with a straight back. Try not to lean forward or back too much. Keep your head level. Focus on the area 10 to 15 feet ahead of you. Do not look at either your feet or the sky. Let your head float effortlessly on your neck, but do not allow it to bob.

2. Use your arms efficiently. Bend you elbows at about a 90-degree angle and let your arms swing naturally inward toward your chest. Try not to swing beyond the midline of the chest or trunk. Keep your hands relaxed, cupping them gently. Balling your fists creates tension. Let your relaxed hands swing back and forth with your arms. When your arms and hands tire or become tense, drop them and shake them out as you jog, returning them to their proper position when they are relaxed again.

3. Do not overstride. A shorter stride is more efficient than a longer one. Keep your feet under you. Your foot should land directly under your slightly bent knee, not out in front of the knee.

4. The slower you run, the flatter the landing. As you pick up speed, you move toward the front of the foot, eventually pushing off from the toes. If you are a beginner, you should try to land on the heels of the feet and roll forward as you push off again on your next stride. Try not to run on the balls of your feet or your toes for extended periods of time. This will cause cramping.

5. Breathe deeply and evenly as you run; do not hold your breath. Some joggers have no problem doing this, while others try to pace

their breathing with a specific number of leg strides. As your workout progresses, you probably will find it helpful to inhale and exhale through your mouth.

The running/jogging program outlined in Table 10-3 is designed for beginners or those who have not trained in 6 months. It starts with walking and progresses to a full running program within 10 weeks.

Maintain or Improve

After you have achieved a moderate level of cardiovascular fitness, you will need to modify your FIT guidelines to maintain or improve your fitness. You can employ the overload principle and force your body to adapt and become stronger by increasing the frequency, intensity, or time of your workouts. Do not attempt to increase all three at the same time unless you are a well-trained athlete.

Cooper's Aerobic Point System. Kenneth Cooper, director of the Aerobic Center in Dallas, Texas, and a pioneer in aerobic exercise, created a point system to help people develop and maintain their levels of cardiovascular fitness. To maintain adequate levels of cardiovascular fitness, you must acquire a certain number of points each week. Men are required to accumulate 32 points, and women need 27 points each week to maintain their cardiovascular fitness.[3] Points correspond to specific cardiovascular training activities.

Cooper developed a "chart pack," a series of activities with specific point values, to help men and women maintain their fitness levels. These charts incorporate frequency, intensity, time variables, and age to provide a simple way to plan and maintain adequate levels of cardiovascular fitness. Acquiring more points each week increases a person's level of aerobic fitness. The running chart (see Table 10-3) illustrates how far, how fast, and how often a person must run to maintain his or her current level of cardiovascular fitness.

Cooper[3] provides several charts covering a variety of cardiovascular fitness maintenance programs, such as walking, swimming, cycling, and stair climbing, for those interested in activities other than running.

Muscular Strength

One can develop muscular strength by performing exercises that produce energy through aerobic, anaerobic, or combined methods. Most strength activities, however, employ anaerobic energy production through resistance training. Resistance training can be performed through isometric, isotonic, or isokinetic exercise techniques.

TABLE 10.3

Cooper's[3] Jogging/Running 10-Week Program

Under 30 years of age

Week	Activity	Distance (miles)	Time Goal	Freq/Wk	Points/Wk
1	walk	2.0	32:00	3	13.5
2	walk	3.0	48:00	3	21.7
3	walk/jog	2.0	26:00	4	24.9
4	walk/jog	2.0	24:00	4	28.0
5	jog	2.0	22:00	4	31.6
*6	jog	2.0	20:00	4	36.0
7	jog	2.5	25:00	4	46.0
8	jog	2.5	23:00	4	49.5
9	jog	3.0	30:00	4	56.0
10	jog	3.0	27:00	4	61.3

*By the sixth week, a minimum aerobic fitness level has been reached (36 aerobic points per week), but it is suggested that a higher level of fitness be achieved. By the tenth week of the above program, a total of 61 points per week is being earned, consistent with the excellent category or aerobic fitness.

30-49 Years of Age

Week	Activity	Distance (miles)	Time Goal	Freq/Wk	Points/Wk
1	walk	2.0	34:00	3	12.2
2	walk	2.5	42:00	3	16.3
3	walk	3.0	50:00	3	20.4
4	walk/jog	2.0	25:00	4	26.4
5	walk/jog	2.0	24:00	4	28.0
6	jog	2.0	22:00	4	31.6
*7	jog	2.0	20:00	4	36.0
8	jog	2.5	26:00	4	43.7
9	jog	2.5	25:00	4	46.0
10	jog	3.0	31:00	4	53.7
11	jog	3.0	29:00	4	57.6
12	jog	3.0	27:00	4	61.3

*By the seventh week, a minimum aerobic fitness level has been reached (36 aerobic points per week), but it is suggested that a higher level of fitness be achieved. By the twelfth week of the above program, a total of 61 points per week is being earned, consistent with the excellent category or aerobic fitness.

Isometric Exercise

isometric exercise

a type of exercise that involves resisting an immovable object, causing muscle length to remain constant

An **isometric exercise** involves a muscle contraction against an immovable object, such as a door jamb. The contraction is held for 10 seconds and is repeated 5 to 10 times per day. During this contraction, the length of the muscle remains constant while tension produces maximum force against the immovable object. Another example is using a desk to develop arm strength. While sitting at the desk, you push up against it with your arms, exerting maximum force against the furniture.

Isometric exercises (Fig. 10-7) are simple, inexpensive, and can be used to develop considerable muscular strength. They were very popular in the 1960s and 1970s, but their popularity fell when investigators discovered that the strength they developed was specific to the angle in which they were performed. Because they do not involve a full range of motion, strength is concentrated at the angle in which the contraction is held and approximately 20 degrees more in either direction. To develop strength throughout the whole muscle, you must perform isometric contractions at several different points in the muscle's entire range of motion.[1]

Another problem with isometric exercises is that they raise blood pressure and put an increased workload on the heart throughout the contraction. This is partially attributed to holding one's breath during the contraction. One way to minimize this is to breathe throughout the exercise.

Despite their limitations, isometric exercises are still a valuable part of training for muscular strength because of their simplicity and low cost. They are particularly appropriate for athletes who need to increase strength at a particular point in a muscle's range of motion. An example is an Olympic weight-lifter who is stuck at a certain weight in a particular lift; he raises the bar to a certain point and cannot lift it any further. Performing an isometric exercise at that same angle can strengthen the lifter's muscles at that sticking point, so that he or she can improve the entire lift.[17]

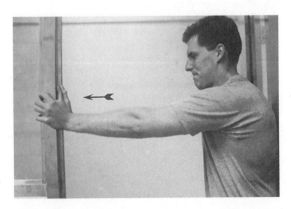

Fig. 10-7 Isometric exercises. Isometric exercises, like this one, involve applying resistance against a fixed object.

Isotonic Exercise

Isotonic exercise uses concentric and eccentric contractions to work a muscle as it changes in length. It is continuous and not static (unlike isometric exercise). Using a biceps curl as an example (Fig. 10-2), concentric contraction occurs as you lift the dumbbell and shorten the muscle. Eccentric contraction occurs as you lengthen the muscle, slowly straightening the arm against the resistance of the dumbbell without letting the weight fall.

Free Weight Training. Isotonic training can employ either free weights (Fig. 10-8) or machines that confine the resistance along a track. Free weights include bars, plates, and collars. The plates are of varied weight and are secured to the bar by collars. The bars can be short (as in dumbbells, which are designed to be used with one hand), long (as in barbells, designed to be used with two hands), or bent (as in a curling bar, designed to isolate specific muscles).

Free weights enable lifters to perform an almost endless array of exercises that can target every major muscle group and most individual muscles. Free weights also allow unrestricted movement and the ability to alter the range of motion of exercises. They also stimulate ancillary muscles that are not directly targeted in the exercise but that help support or stabilize the body as the motion is being performed. For instance, performing a standing arm curl with a barbell (an exercise that targets primarily the biceps muscles) also stimulates the muscles of the hips, legs, lower back, and shoulders as they hold the body in position to perform the arm exercise.

Variable-Resistance Exercise Equipment. Variable-resistance exercise machines are designed to provide safety, compactness, and specificity in targeting muscles. These machines contain weights confined to tracks that pre-

isotonic exercise
a type of exercise that involves concentric (shortening) and eccentric (lengthening) contractions

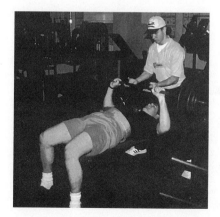

Fig. 10-8 Free weights. Free weights can provide an easy and inexpensive way to develop muscular strength and endurance.

vent them from falling onto the floor or the lifter. The machines configure the weights, bars, seats, and benches in such a way as to allow lifters to safely perform an array of exercises that work the entire body. Some machines also allow more than one lifter to work out simultaneously.

The machines are designed to offer maximum resistance along the entire range of motion of any given exercise. Various machines provide this resistance differently. Universal Gym equipment (Fig. 10-9) alters the lifter's leverage through positioning of the bars, weight tracks, and seating arrangements. Nautilus equipment (Fig. 10-10) uses cams (a type of toothed gear) shaped like a nautilus shell to provide equal resistance throughout the entire range of motion.

Isokinetic Exercise

isokinetic exercise

a type of exercise that involves muscle contractions at a constant speed

Isokinetic exercise involves exercising against resistance at a constant speed. Isokinetic exercise machines use special hydraulic, pneumatic, and pressure systems to regulate the speed and resistance of muscle activity. Most isokinetic machines are designed to resist both concentric and eccentric contractions at a preselected speed. This enables the safe application of maximum force to muscles through their full range of motion.

A major disadvantage of isokinetic training devices such as Cybex equipment (Fig. 10-11) for the average person is their excessive cost. Many of the machines are computerized and come with printers that record a person's training. These machines also are used as diagnostic and rehabilitative devices to help people recover from injuries. They enable people to safely select training levels that work injured muscles safely through their full range of motion under constant speed.[19]

Fig. 10-9 Universal weights. A universal weight machine provides safe, variable resistance training. Machines such as the universal allow individual lifters to exercise without the need for a spotter.

 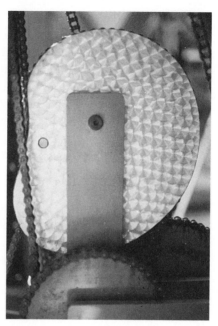

Fig. 10-10 Nautilus machines. Nautilus machines employ cams to equalize resistance through both concentric and eccentric contractions.

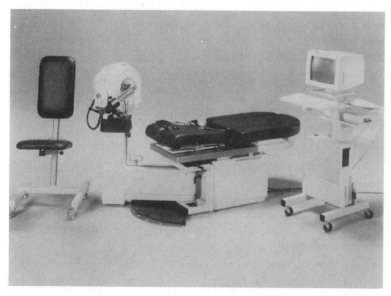

Fig. 10-11 Isokinetic equipment, such as the Cybex machines pictured here, are particularly important in rehabilitation, where one must carefully monitor exercise behavior

Frequency. Beginners should lift three times a week with at least 1 day of rest between exercise sessions. Beginner's weight-training programs typically consist of 8 to 10 exercises that target the body's major muscle groups (such as the chest, back, and shoulders).

Progressive-resistance training will produce delayed muscle soreness, especially in beginners. Eccentric contractions of muscles cause microscopic damage to muscle tissue fibers, which produces minor swelling and pressure on nerves.[1] During rest days the muscles repair themselves and begin to adapt to the increased demands placed on them as they grow and become stronger.

Intensity. Intensity in progressive resistance weight training is measured in repetitions, repetition maximum (RM), and sets. Repetitions are the number of times you repeat a specific exercise. RM is the maximum number of repetitions you can perform at a given weight. A set is a particular number of repetitions.

Beginners must set starting weights for each of the 8 to 10 exercises they will perform. One does this initially through trial and error. For any given exercise, the lifter should be able to perform six to eight repetitions RM in each of three sets, with a 60- to 90-second break between sets. If he or she cannot do at least six repetitions in each set, the initial weight is too high and the poundage should be dropped.

When the person is able to perform eight repetitions RM for three sets of an exercise, resistance should be increased by 10%. Increasing the weight resistance by 10% should enable the person to perform six repetitions RM at the new weight.[17] The person gains strength as the muscles are forced to adapt to the increasing level of demand.

Time. In strength training, specific time requirements are less critical than frequency and intensity guidelines. In general, however, a set of six to eight repetitions will take 15 to 30 seconds to perform. Rest between sets should be 60 to 90 seconds. Three sets of a specific exercise should take 5 to 6 minutes. A typical workout consisting of three sets of six to eight repetitions of 10 exercises could be completed in 1 hour. Add 5-minute warm-up and cool-down periods, and the workout could be completed in less than $1^1/_2$ hours.

Maintaining or Improving Muscular Strength

Several strategies can be employed to maintain or improve strength gains. To maintain a specific level of strength, one may choose to keep weights at a specific poundage for longer periods of time. Shifting to a workout that emphasizes muscular endurance is a way to maintain high levels of strength by changing the focus of the training.

Intermediate and advanced training to improve strength levels could involve increasing the frequency of training. This type of training often involves splitting routines and working out more frequently. For example, instead of working the entire body on Monday, Wednesday, and Friday, an advanced lifter might split the routine, working on half of the body for 3 days and the other half for an additional 3 days each week. This doubles the frequency of workouts from 3 to 6 days per week. Monday, Wednesday, and Friday might focus on the upper body. Instead of doing 5 upper-body exercises, the lifter might increase the number to 10. Tuesday, Thursday, and Saturday would be devoted to lower-body exercises, again with an increased number of exercises. Increasing the number of workouts usually increases their intensity, because lifters increase the level of demand on the half of the body being trained by employing a greater number of exercises.

Muscular Endurance

A certain amount of muscular endurance will develop as a byproduct of strength training. Generally, as muscles become stronger, they also are able to perform work for longer periods of time than untrained muscles. To further develop muscular endurance, one can employ the same weight training program used for developing muscular strength but change the intensity and time.

Frequency. The frequency of workouts in muscular endurance is the same as in strength development. Lifting three times a week with at least 1 day of rest between workouts is sufficient.

Intensity. To develop muscular endurance, use the same exercises recommended for strength development but with weights light enough to lift for 10 to 15 repetitions RM. When you are able to perform three sets of 15 repetitions RM, increase the weights.

Time. In general, the total workout time will not vary from that of a strength-training routine. Often, when one is working on muscular endurance training, time between sets will vary. One way to increase endurance is to cut back on rest between sets. The 60 to 90 seconds of rest between sets that accompany strength training can be reduced.

Circuit Training

circuit resistance training (CRT)

a type of muscular endurance training involving a circuit of exercise stations where the lifter performs many repetitions at a moderate weight

Circuit resistance training (CRT) is a way of working out that is designed to develop muscular strength, muscular endurance, cardiorespiratory endurance, and body composition simultaneously. Circuit training involves setting up a group of 8 to 15 exercise stations (a circuit), and progressing through the circuit with minimal rest, stopping to perform specific exercises at each station.

The weights selected (40% to 55% RM) at each station are substantially lower than those used for strength training. At each station you perform as many repetitions as possible for 15 to 30 seconds (time varies with specific exercises). The rest interval between stations is the same amount of time required to perform the exercise (15 to 30 seconds). The circuit is completed when you have finished all of the stations. You then repeat the circuit two to three times. One improves fitness through overload by: (1) increasing the intensity of the stations by adding weight or time or (2) decreasing the rest time between stations.[1] A sample circuit is illustrated in Table 10-4.

The only weakness of circuit training is that it does not allow for maximal strength development. More efficient development of muscular strength occurs with fewer repetitions and heavier weights.

TABLE 10.4

A Typical Circuit

The following is an example of a circuit. You should warm up before CRT and finish the workout with a cool down.

Station 1	Leg press or half-squat	15 to 30 sec
Station 2	Bench press	15 to 30 sec
Station 3	Back hyperextension	15 to 30 sec
Station 4	Biceps curl	15 to 30 sec
Station 5	Overhead press	15 to 30 sec
Station 6	Sit-up or abdominal crunches	15 to 30 sec
Station 7	Push-ups	15 to 30 sec
Station 8	Lateral raises	15 to 30 sec
Station 9	Hamstring curl	15 to 30 sec
Station 10	Pull-ups	15 to 30 sec

From Anspaugh, D., Hamrick, M., & Rosato, F. (1994). *Wellness: concepts and applications* (2nd ed.). St. Louis: Mosby.

Flexibility Training

Developing flexibility involves incorporating stretching into training activities. Stretching and yoga are explained in detail in Chapter 9. Chapter 9 also presents instructions for performing a full-body stretching routine that can be incorporated into any fitness program.

To develop optimal flexibility, one should perform stretching exercises twice during each workout: (1) at the beginning of the workout, after the body is warmed up, and (2) at the end of the workout as part of the cool-down process.

Body Composition

Maintaining ideal body composition requires more than just losing weight and keeping thin. The human body is composed of water, bone, lean tissue, such as muscles and organs, and fat tissue. The key to maintaining ideal body composition is keeping the percentage of fat tissue within a safe limit while maximizing bone integrity and the strength and endurance of lean muscle tissue.

There are two types of fat tissue—essential and nonessential. Among the many functions of essential fat tissue are the following: storing fat-soluble vitamins (A, D, E, and K), padding and protecting vital organs, playing a key role in hormone production, insulating nerves, and contributing to ovulation and menstruation. Because of the complex role of fat tissue in hormone regulation, ovulation, and menstruation, women require a higher percentage of essential fat tissue than men. A man's total body weight is 3% essential fat tissue, but a woman's body weight is 10% to 12% essential fat tissue.

All other fat tissue is considered nonessential, or storage fat. A certain amount of storage fat is necessary for insulation, reserve energy stores, and other functions. Excess body fat, however, is dangerous to one's health and is strongly associated with all forms of cardiovascular disease, cancer, and premature death. Adding essential body fat and storage fat percentages calculates the total body fat level. Table 10-5 illustrates the various levels of body fat.

Although three fat-related terms—*fat, overweight,* and *obese*—often are used interchangeably, they refer to three different issues. Of the three terms, *fat* is the least scientific. There are no acceptable scientific standards for determining whether someone is fat. It is totally subjective and is determined by prevailing cultural norms. What is considered curvaceous and attractive in one culture might be considered fat in another. The term *fat* has no useful application regarding ideal body composition and fitness.

TABLE 10.5

Body Fat Levels

Males	Females	Classification
<8%	<13%	Lean
8%-15%	13%-20%	Optimal
16%-20%	21%-25%	Slightly overfat
21%-24%	26%-31%	Fat
≥25%	≥32%	Obese

From Anspaugh, D., Hamrick, M., & Rosato, F. (1994). *Wellness: concepts and applications* (2nd ed.). St. Louis: Mosby.

Overweight refers to weighing more than is considered desirable for your specific age, gender, and frame size. Desirable weight is not determined subjectively; it is calculated according to actuarial tables that examine the relationship between body weight and the risk for premature disability and death.

Obesity is a condition in which a person's fat accumulation results in a body weight that exceeds the desirable weight by 25% in men and 32% in women. Obesity is associated with increased risk for premature disability and death resulting from cardiovascular disease and several other conditions.

Assessing Body Composition

Body composition is evaluated by measuring body weight and body fat. Overweight is usually assessed by comparing one's weight with a weight obtained from a standardized height and weight chart. The 1983 Metropolitan Life Insurance Height and Weight Table resulted from various studies that examined the relationships between body weight and premature illness, disability, and death (see Table 10-6). Although being overweight has a relationship to increased risk for premature disability and death, this type of assessment of body composition has problems.

One problem is that these charts use measures of gross weight instead of measures of percentage of body fat. Because lean muscle tissue is heavier than fat, well-trained athletes with more muscle packed on their frames than the average person will fall into the overweight categories. With modern training regimens, male and female athletes can be very heavily muscled yet have body fat percentages in the low or acceptable ranges.

Another problem is that the charts are subjective. People tend to deny that they are overweight and instead reevaluate their frame size. Small-framed people become big-boned or broad-shouldered and move up to the

TABLE 10.6

Metropolitan Life Height/Weight Tables

Does your weight fall within the range established by this table? Weight tables published in 1983 reflect the fact that today's adults are on the average somewhat heavier than in recent decades. Figures include 5 pounds of clothing for men, 3 pounds for women, and shoes with 1-inch heels for both.

	Men				Women		
Height	Small Frame	Medium Frame	Large Frame	Height	Small Frame	Medium Frame	Large Frame
5 ft 2 in	128-134	131-141	138-150	4 ft 10 in	102-111	109-121	118-131
5 ft 3 in	130-136	133-143	140-153	4 ft 11 in	103-113	111-123	120-134
5 ft 4 in	132-138	135-145	142-156	5 ft 0 in	104-115	113-126	122-137
5 ft 5 in	134-140	137-148	144-164	5 ft 1 in	106-118	115-129	125-140
5 ft 6 in	136-142	139-151	146-164	5 ft 2 in	108-121	118-132	128-143
5 ft 7 in	138-145	142-154	149-168	5 ft 3 in	111-124	121-135	131-147
5 ft 8 in	140-148	145-157	152-172	5 ft 4 in	114-127	124-138	134-151
5 ft 9 in	142-151	148-160	155-176	5 ft 5 in	117-130	127-141	137-155
5 ft 10 in	144-154	151-163	158-180	5 ft 6 in	120-133	130-144	140-159
5 ft 11 in	146-157	154-166	161-184	5 ft 7 in	123-136	133-147	143-163
6 ft 0 in	149-160	157-170	164-188	5 ft 8 in	126-139	136-150	146-167
6 ft 1 in	152-164	160-174	168-192	5 ft 9 in	129-142	139-153	149-170
6 ft 2 in	155-168	164-178	172-197	5 ft 10 in	132-145	142-156	152-173
6 ft 3 in	158-172	167-182	176-202	5 ft 11 in	135-148	145-159	155-176
6 ft 4 in	162-176	171-187	181-207	6 ft 0 in	138-151	148-162	158-179

From Payne, W. & Hahn, D. (1995). *Understanding your health* (4th ed.). St. Louis: Mosby.

next frame level in the charts, where their current body weight fits into the recommended weight guidelines.

The last major problem relates to underweight. Weighing less than the recommended body weight on a standardized height and weight chart does not necessarily mean that a person has ideal body composition. A person can be thin but have poor muscle tone, have unacceptable body fat levels, or be dangerously anorexic.

Another way to assess body composition by evaluating weight is to calculate body mass index. The most critical assessment of body mass is the amount of fat that accumulates around the abdominal cavity. Men and women with a "spare tire" are at a much greater risk for developing cardio-vascular disease than both those who maintain ideal body composition and those who are overweight but do not carry the extra weight around their middles. Assess Yourself 10-5 enables you to calculate your body mass.

The best way to assess body composition is to measure percentage of body fat. There are at least three different ways to assess body fat: electrical impedance, skin fold measures, and underwater weighing.

Electrical Impedance. Electrical impedance measures the resistance of small currents of electricity as they pass through the body. Fat tissue resists the current more than does lean tissue. This test uses sensors similar to those used during an ECG exam, measures electrical resistance, and prints the body fat percentage.

Skinfold Measures. Skinfold measures use special calipers to take pinches of skin at various body sites where fat accumulates (Fig. 10-12). These measures are entered into a formula that extrapolates from these measures to calculate overall body fat level.

Hydrostatic Weighing. Hydrostatic weighing involves measuring one's underwater weight and normal weight. The two weights then are compared and a formula is used that considers the fact that lean tissue is heavier and fat tissue is lighter than water. The comparison produces a very accurate percentage of overall body fat.

Developing Optimal Body Composition

A healthy approach to developing and maintaining ideal body composition is to create a program of sensible eating and exercise. The greatest contributing factor to the development of obesity is physical inactivity.

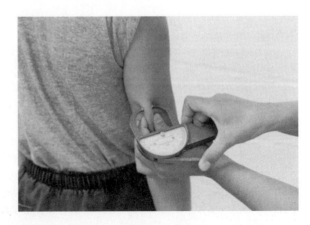

Fig. 10-12 Skinfold measures. By taking careful measures of skinfold thickness at critical points on the body, you can estimate your overall percentage of body fat.

The energy-balance equation (Fig. 10-13) is a theory that states if we burn fewer calories than we consume, the extra calories will accumulate as fat tissue and extra weight. If we burn more calories than we consume, we will lose fat tissue and body weight. If the number of calories burned matches the number consumed, we will maintain our body weight. Sensible eating and regular exercise help ensure that the calories we eat match those that we burn.

Not only does a program of regular exercise help burn calories, it helps elevate our basal metabolic rate, the amount of energy our bodies need to maintain basic functions such as breathing and circulating blood. About 50% to 70% of the total calories we need in a given day are used in maintaining our basal metabolic rate. Aerobic exercise can elevate our metabolic rate and keep it elevated for up to 8 hours.

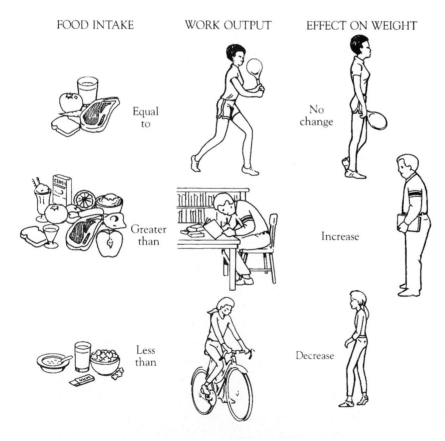

FOOD INTAKE   WORK OUTPUT   EFFECT ON WEIGHT

Equal to — No change

Greater than — Increase

Less than — Decrease

Fig. 10-13 The energy-balance equation. The energy-balance equation describes how weight loss, gain, or maintenance is related to calorie consumption and utilization.

Eating For Fitness

Eating for fitness means choosing foods that provide maximum energy and that contribute to maintaining ideal body composition and producing strong bones and a healthy heart. The best diet for improving one's fitness level also happens to be the one recommended for maintaining optimal health and preventing premature disability and death. Essentially, it is a diet high in complex carbohydrates and low in fat, with moderate protein intake.

Nutrients and Energy

Six nutrients are essential to our existence: carbohydrates, fats, protein, vitamins, minerals, and water. The first three (carbohydrates, fats, and protein) supply energy, while the last three (vitamins, minerals, and water) help our bodies utilize the energy.

Energy is measured in calories. A gram of carbohydrate or protein contains 4 calories of energy and a gram of fat contains 9 calories, more than twice the amount of the other nutrients. Although fat is dense with calories and a rich source of energy, consuming too much fat increases one's risk for obesity, heart disease, and cancer.

Fats. There are three types of fats, also known as lipids: (1) saturated, (2) monounsaturated, and (3) polyunsaturated fats. Saturation has to do with the number and alignment of hydrogen atoms within the fat molecule.

Saturated fats are animal products, such as meat and dairy foods, and normally are solid at room temperature. Monounsaturated and polyunsaturated fats are products from the plant kingdom, such as nuts and oils, and normally are liquid at room temperature. Some plant products, such as peanut butter, are hydrogenized (have extra hydrogen added during processing) to keep their natural oils from separating at room temperature.

Cholesterol is a fat-related substance in alcohol form that is produced by the liver and derived from the foods we eat. Most of the cholesterol (about 75%) in our bloodstream is produced by our livers despite what we eat. Cholesterol is a necessary body product; it helps produce bile acids, which assist in the digestion of fats. Cholesterol also helps protect nerve fibers and assists in vitamin D formation and in hormone production. Foods high in saturated fats (animal products) also are usually high in cholesterol. Foods high in monounsaturated and polyunsaturated fats, such as plant products, have little or no cholesterol. Polyunsaturated fats have been shown to reduce cholesterol levels by facilitating the removal of excess cholesterol from the bloodstream.

Cholesterol is carried through the bloodstream to cells and tissues by lipoproteins, a form of protein. There are three types of lipoproteins: (1) **high-density lipoproteins (HDLs)**, (2) low-density lipoproteins (LDLs),

high-density lipoproteins

"good cholesterol"; a type of protein that carries cholesterol to where it is needed by the body and brings the rest back to the liver to be excreted and (3) very-low-density lipoproteins (VLDLs). All lipoproteins carry cholesterol to the sites within the body where it is needed. However, only HDLs return the unused cholesterol to the liver, where it is broken down and eliminated; LDLs and VLDLs do not. LDLs and VLDLs return the excess into the body's circulation, where it accumulates on the walls of blood vessels, resulting in atherosclerosis.

Stress can elevate LDL cholesterol levels by triggering the liver to produce too much cholesterol. However, aerobic exercise increases HDL levels, helping to remove excess serum cholesterol.

Protein. Proteins are compounds comprising of chains of amino acids. There are more than 20 types of **amino acids**. Complete proteins contain nine essential amino acids; incomplete proteins do not contain all nine essential amino acids.

amino acids
organic chemical compounds that are the building blocks of proteins

Protein is a major component of almost every cell in the body. It builds muscle and other tissues, bones, and blood. Protein also is a major component of antibodies and enzymes. Protein assists in hormone production, carries iron, oxygen, and nutrients to cells, and serves as a source of energy.

Americans consume too much protein in general and get most of it from animal products, which are a major source of complete protein but also contain saturated fat and cholesterol. Plant sources of protein are incomplete but contain little fat and cholesterol. Plant products must be combined to get complete protein. This mixing of incomplete proteins to form complete ones is a major component of many ethnic diets, where combinations such as beans and rice, rice and vegetables, or corn or flour tortillas and beans often replace meat as the main source of dietary protein.

Carbohydrates. Carbohydrates come in two forms: simple sugars and complex carbohydrates. Simple sugars also are known as monosaccharides because they contain only one sugar molecule. Common simple sugars include sucrose (table sugar), fructose (fruit sugar), and galactose (milk sugar). Complex carbohydrates are formed by combining long simple sugar molecules.

Simple sugars often are described as empty calories because they provide energy but otherwise have little or no nutritional value. Table sugar is a good example. A packet of table sugar provides 16 calories of energy to fuel the body, but no additional water, vitamins, or minerals. Therefore simple sugars are inefficient energy sources; their energy is quick and does not last long. Foods high in simple sugars, such as candy, pastries, and soda, elevate blood sugar rapidly, but the energy they provide quickly peaks and dissipates, leaving you hungry in a short time. Because foods high in simple sugars also tend to be high in overall calories and provide only short bursts of energy, one can easily overindulge in these foods. Such overindulgence creates a pattern of high calorie and low nutrient intake, resulting in obesity and malnutrition.

Complex carbohydrates are very efficient energy sources. Foods high in complex carbohydrates also tend to be high in other nutrients and fiber. Fiber not only is essential for good digestive system health but also serves to slow the release of calories in complex carbohydrate foods. Whole-grain products, such as a bran muffin, are rich sources of energy and nutrients and also contain soluble and insoluble fiber.

Soluble fiber breaks down in the digestive system to form a gelatinous mass that slowly releases energy. Unlike the candy bar, high in fat and simple sugars, foods that contain complex carbohydrates leave you feeling satisfied long after you consume them. The insoluble fiber in the bran muffin binds together to form a bulky mass that passes through your digestive system, gathering up other wastes and facilitating their elimination as feces.

The slow, complete, and even release of energy is what makes complex carbohydrates the best source of energy for fueling fitness and other activities. The largest part of your energy supply, when you are eating for fitness, should come from foods high in complex carbohydrates.

Vitamins. Vitamins are organic compounds that serve as catalysts (or coenzymes) to help enzymes facilitate chemical reactions that utilize nutrients in foods. Vitamins have a host of functions in the body, ranging from cell repair to oxygen transport. To be used by the body, vitamins are dissolved (or are soluble) in either fat or water. The fat-soluble vitamins (A, D, E, and K) are dissolved, carried, and stored in fat. An excess of fat-soluble vitamins can be toxic. Water-soluble vitamins (the B vitamins and vitamin C) are dissolved and carried in water. Excess water-soluble vitamins that are not used by the body are excreted in urine as waste.

Minerals. Minerals are inorganic compounds that serve as the structural elements of body parts, such as teeth, bones, muscles, blood, and hormones. Minerals are needed for the regulation of various body processes, such as muscle contraction, cell permeability, and blood clotting.

Sodium, one of the major minerals, is responsible for water balance in cells and muscular contractions. As discussed in Chapter 3, excess sodium elevates blood pressure by causing an imbalance in water-volume regulation. Sodium is present as a naturally occurring nutrient in most foods and beverages; the most common form is table salt (sodium chloride), which contains about 2123 mg of sodium per teaspoon. Only a small amount of sodium is needed (1000 to 3300 mg, or about $1/8$ teaspoon) each day.

Calcium is a critical mineral for bone formation and maintenance, blood clotting, nerve transmission, muscle contraction, and fluid regulation.

Calcium shortages are associated with osteoporosis, a degenerative bone condition resulting in weak, hollow, brittle bones. Many adults get too little calcium because they do not consume enough milk and dairy products, dark, leafy vegetables, and fish, which are the best sources of calcium.

The Food Pyramid

One can eat for fitness best by following the dietary guidelines that accompany the food pyramid (Fig. 10-14), a dietary tool that simplifies food choice. The food pyramid breaks down the major food sources of all nutrients into six groups: (1) grains, (breads, cereals, rice, and pasta), (2) fruits, (3) vegetables, (4) meats, poultry, fish, dry beans, eggs, and nuts, (5) milk, yogurt, and cheese, and (6) fats, oils, and sweets. The pyramid explains how many servings from each group are necessary to supply your optimal level of nutrition. The food pyramid describes the portion size for each food group and how many portions of each group you need to consume per day.

Fats, Oils, & Sweets
USE SPARINGLY

KEY
◻ Fat (naturally occurring and added)   ◪ Sugars (added)
These symbols show fats, oils, and added sugars in foods.

Milk, Yogurt, & Cheese Group
2-3 SERVINGS

Meat, Poultry, Fish, Dry Beans, Eggs, & Nuts Group
2-3 SERVINGS

Vegetable Group
3-5 SERVINGS

Fruit Group
2-4 SERVINGS

Bread, Cereal, Rice, & Pasta Group
6-11 SERVINGS

Fig. 10-14 The food pyramid. The food pyramid provides a simple, easily understood way of ensuring proper nutrition. By consuming the recommended number of servings, you will meet all of your nutritional needs while consuming a high-carbohydrate, low-fat, moderate-protein diet.

If you plan your diet according to the recommendations of the food pyramid, you will consume the proper amount of nutrients and get the most of your calories from complex carbohydrates. Eating according to the food pyramid will provide optimal energy while helping to maintain ideal body composition. Assess Yourself 10-6 helps you determine whether you are eating according to the food pyramid.

Effects of Fitness on Stress

As illustrated in Fig. 10-15 there are many physiological and psychological benefits associated with being fit. Lifestyle changes, such as a healthful diet and regular exercise, not only benefit an individual's fitness level but are also essential for effective stress management.

Physiological Benefits

Tension Reduction

During all forms of physical activity, muscles are contracted and relaxed. The intensity of this is determined by the level of resistance and demand put on the muscles, but in general, they are forced to perform work. Exercise, then, is an appropriate use of our skeletal muscles and does not result in chronic muscle tension. Physical activity reduces the tension in our skeletal muscles that is associated with the stress response.

Physical activity is effective in reducing both acute and chronic muscle tension. When we are in a life-threatening situation and our bodies are primed to fight or flee, either fighting or running away reduces the intense muscle tension of this response. Likewise, action will reduce the tension associated with the low-level, chronic muscular contraction that can result from long-term, resistance stage stress.

Hormone Utilization

When the body is stressed, it secretes various hormones into circulation to mobilize energy to maintain homeostasis and cope with the stressor. These hormones, if not utilized, can create various problems, as documented in Chapter 4. Physical activity puts these hormones to use. Rather than allowing these hormones to wear down your immunity and place unusually high demands on your tissues, organs, and systems, you get rid of these chemicals during your physical activity.

Fat/Cholesterol Utilization

During the stress response, the liver works overtime, converting its stored glycogen to glucose for fuel. In addition, it produces extra cholesterol,

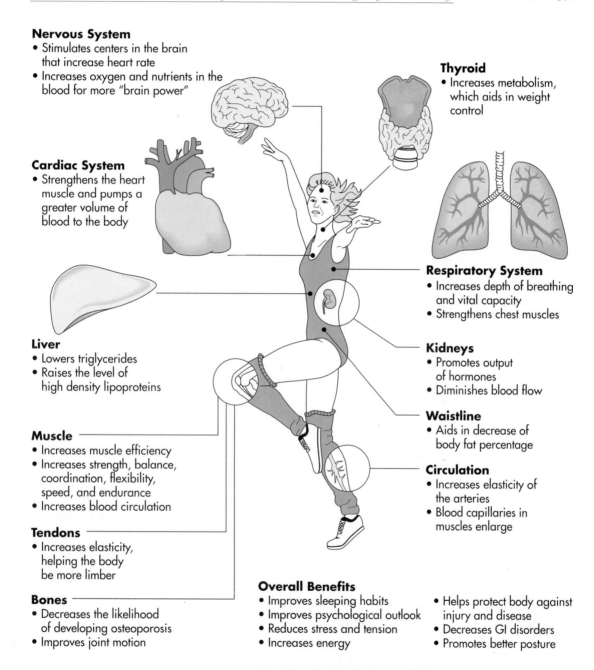

Nervous System
- Stimulates centers in the brain that increase heart rate
- Increases oxygen and nutrients in the blood for more "brain power"

Thyroid
- Increases metabolism, which aids in weight control

Cardiac System
- Strengthens the heart muscle and pumps a greater volume of blood to the body

Respiratory System
- Increases depth of breathing and vital capacity
- Strengthens chest muscles

Liver
- Lowers triglycerides
- Raises the level of high density lipoproteins

Kidneys
- Promotes output of hormones
- Diminishes blood flow

Waistline
- Aids in decrease of body fat percentage

Muscle
- Increases muscle efficiency
- Increases strength, balance, coordination, flexibility, speed, and endurance
- Increases blood circulation

Circulation
- Increases elasticity of the arteries
- Blood capillaries in muscles enlarge

Tendons
- Increases elasticity, helping the body be more limber

Bones
- Decreases the likelihood of developing osteoporosis
- Improves joint motion

Overall Benefits
- Improves sleeping habits
- Improves psychological outlook
- Reduces stress and tension
- Increases energy

- Helps protect body against injury and disease
- Decreases GI disorders
- Promotes better posture

Fig. 10-15 The benefits of exercise are plentiful. Exercise serves as a valuable way to release stress.

which normally is used to transport fats to the tissue where they are needed. Exercise helps remove the excess cholesterol produced by the liver during the stress response by triggering the production of extra high-density lipoproteins, which carry the cholesterol back to the liver, where it is broken down and secreted as **bile**.

bile
a bitter, yellow green fat emulsifier secreted by the liver

If the body's available calories and stored glycogen reserves cannot meet the demand of the activity being performed, storage fat is broken down into glucose, which provides the needed energy. If energy demands are acute, as in the stress response, the body will turn to the protein in muscle tissue to meet its needs for fuel. As discussed in Chapter 3, this process is called **gluconeogenesis**. Exercise serves a valuable function in protecting muscle tissue from this process and ensuring that calorie needs are met by storage fat rather than lean tissue: exercise keeps muscles toned while burning extra calories. This is a benefit for those trying to lose weight as well as manage their stress.

gluconeogenesis
the process of converting noncarbohydrate sources of energy into glucose

Enhanced Cardiorespiratory Function

The heart, lungs, and circulatory system take part in all forms of exercise by pumping oxygen-rich blood to tissue and removing carbon dioxide and other wastes. It is during aerobic exercise, however, that the greatest cardiorespiratory effects are realized. The net cardiorespiratory effects of exercise are increased energy, greater endurance, increased mental alertness and acuity, improved mood, and decreased risk of cardiovascular disease.

In general, when the heart and lungs work together effectively, they transfer oxygen and carbon dioxide more efficiently. Our heart pumps more efficiently, our blood vessels remain pliable and open, allowing maximum passage of blood, and our lungs have a greater depth and volume. The heart and lungs thus constantly supply the body with oxygen-rich blood. This affects our functioning at the cellular level and helps us get the most out of each organ and body system. This affects everything from the way our brains think and reason to the amount of energy we have to get us through the day. Our mood is improved, and we have a more positive outlook on life.

All of these physiological benefits of exercise help us cope with stress more effectively. We have more energy on reserve and we can think through things with a clearer brain that pays more attention to details.

Psychological Benefits

Release of Endorphins, Norepinephrine, Serotonin, and Dopamine

Almost everyone is familiar with the expression *runner's high*, the sense of euphoria long-distance runners experience as a result of the release of endorphins (see the box below). Although first discovered in long-distance runners, endorphins can be produced through other aerobic activities, such as dancing, if the duration of the activity is at least 20 to 30 minutes.[8]

Enhanced Self-Esteem and Self-Image

Sticking to a fitness program requires self-discipline, hard work, delayed gratification, and self-control. These are important qualities that habitual exercisers share and that improve self-esteem and self-image. Studies have shown that exercise can improve one's self-esteem, self-reliance, and self-efficacy.[12,13] In a sense, exercisers are more hardy. Hardiness, as discussed in Chapter 2, is related to reduced stress and a greater sense of being in control of life.

Runner's and Other's Highs

Have you ever felt that euphoric rush as you break through the wall on a long run or crest a glistening hill of snow on your cross-country skis? It is a combination of effortless motion (you feel as if your feet or skis are gliding over the surface of the ground, barely making contact), extra energy (your body is loose and energized; your lungs are exchanging air effortlessly), and blissful happiness. As you continue to run or ski, you are tempted to let out a yell, whooping it up just because you feel so alive and in tune with the moment. Such experiences are believed to result from the combination of endorphins and the neurotransmitters dopamine, serotonin, and norepinephrine.

Endorphins, as discussed in Chapter 7, are neuropeptides, amino-acid chains produced in the brain and spinal cord that act like opiates to block pain. These naturally occurring painkillers not only reduce pain, they also produce a feeling of well-being ranging from mildly better to ecstatic.[5] The pituitary gland produces extra amounts of endorphins during vigorous exercise.

Serotonin, dopamine, and norepinephrine are neurotransmitters related to mood that are produced in the brain and other regions of the central nervous system. All three are antidepressants that increase energy and elevate mood. Low levels of serotonin and dopamine have been related to depression. Serotonin, dopamine, and norepinephrine are released by the body as a byproduct of sustained exercise.[21]

These neurotransmitters act as keys to unlock the various regions of the brain capable of producing feelings of heightened well-being and euphoria. Naturally occurring chemicals, endorphins, act much like the legal (available by prescription) and illegal mood-enhancing drugs. The advantages are that you can produce endorphins by yourself, and they have no harmful side effects.

Increased Creativity and Ability to Focus

Exercise provides a break from reality. During exercise, one can dissociate from reality, take your mind off the task at hand, and take a "mini-vacation," as Mott[15] calls it. This break from reality also can provide an opportunity for creativity and a chance to explore options. Gondola[6] found that creative problem-solving abilities were improved by aerobic exercise. She found some improvement after just one exercise session.

Reduced Anxiety and Improved Outlook on Life

Ornstein and Sobel[16] report that exercise can also improve mood. They found that walking a mile or two, even at a mild to moderate pace, can substantially reduce an individual's anxiety level. Exercise can divert our attention away from our problems and to a more relaxing and positive focus.[17] Exercise also can serve as an outlet for relieving anger and anxiety in a positive, socially acceptable way.[19]

A key to using exercise as a stress-management technique is to incorporate all three types of energy-producing exercise (aerobic, anaerobic, and combined) and various sports and activities. This gives you a variety of options and provides a reasonable level of fitness. For instance, you may

KEY

TO UNDERSTANDING

An effective exercise program uses all three types of exercise and includes a variety of activities.

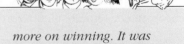

STRESS IN OUR WORLD

Ken and I

Ken is a fairly competitive guy. A frustrated high school athlete, Ken at 40 is still competing against everyone, all the time. He's so competitive, he would rather sacrifice a triple word space in a game of Scrabble than relinquish that tile to anyone.

I used to run with Ken. To me, running was a fun way to keep in shape. Being outside in all kinds of weather, listening to the sounds, and watching the horizon roll by as we ran along the path was terrific.

Then things changed. Running became a competition. We began to enter local middle-distance races. I thought we were both just in it for the t-shirts. Boy, was I mistaken. Ken became a maniac. Each run had to have a purpose. We either ran for time or distance, always trying to do "better" than the last time. I began to focus less on the scenery and more on winning. It was beginning to become work.

I stopped running with Ken after a while. Actually, I stopped running for a while, period. It was no longer fun. I feel bad about it now; it's as if I lost two friends, Ken and my running.

Has anything like this ever happened to you? Is something you truly enjoy beginning to turn into work or a source of stress? What did you do or can you do to prevent it from happening?

want to play golf for relaxation, even though you realize it offers very little if any cardiorespiratory exercise. Or you might take up running, not so much because it relaxes you, but because it is an efficient way to burn off those stress byproducts of your fast-paced lifestyle.

A final word of caution concerning exercise: Do not let it become a source of stress (see Stress in Our World box on p. 360). To get the benefits of stress reduction from your physical activity, you must maintain a mental attitude that keeps your activities in their proper perspective. If you really want to become a competitive athlete in a given sport, choose another type of physical activity to use as a stress-management technique.

KEY
TO UNDERSTANDING

When using exercise to reduce stress, make sure the activity does not become a source of stress.

Other Forms of Physical Release

Laughter

Chapter 6 discusses the importance of taking yourself lightly while you take your work seriously. It also discusses how laughter helps us put things into their proper perspective and maintain a rational frame of mind.

This chapter examines a byproduct of humor—laughter. What are the physiological effects of a good belly laugh? Is there something more to the stress-reducing effects of humor that go beyond the cognitive?

The answer is a resounding yes! It is physiologically impossible to be stressed when you are laughing. Laughter creates a physiological state that is incompatible with stress. Almost all of the body systems are involved: the skeletal and smooth muscles contract, your respiration increases in depth and rate, your heart rate and blood pressure elevate, your body temperature increases, and your central nervous system is activated.

The real benefit, as in orgasm, is that the levels of activity of these systems and physiological processes (breathing, blood pumping, and muscle contraction) initially are higher than they are when the body is at rest, but after a good laugh, fall below normal resting levels, resulting in the same sense of deep relaxation and contentment.[7]

At least five major muscle groups react rhythmically when you laugh: your abdomen, neck, shoulders, diaphragm, and face. When you are finished laughing, they all are more relaxed than when you started. Laughter is a good tonic for muscle tension.

Laughter also is a proven pain reliever, as described in Chapter 6. Laughter, like physical exercise, can trigger the release of endorphins. Hafen et al[7] ask, could there also be a "laugher's high" created by the release of these same endorphins? They think so.

As discussed in Chapter 6, Norman Cousins[4] used humor to help fight his life-threatening illness. He found that 10 minutes of laughter provided up to 2 hours of pain-free sleep. Not only has laughter been associated with a reduction in physical pain, it also has been shown to reduce psychological pain and suffering. Using "humor therapy," researchers in Sweden showed that humorous books, videotapes, and records can be used to reduce psychological pain in patients suffering from chronic degenerative diseases.[7]

Health Benefits of Laughter

Although the short-term benefit of laughter is mostly its ability to induce relaxation and reduce muscle tension and pain, humor may have a long-term benefit of increasing one's ability to ward off disease and prolong life. In studies at California's Loma Linda University, laughter has been found to enhance immune system functioning by increasing the concentration of lymphocytes, killer cell activity, and overall level of functioning.[18]

Laughter also halts the stress response, in particular, the production of excess hormones, which are related to decreased immune functioning. These immune-enhancing effects may suggest the use of humor and laughter in preventing disease.

Humor also seems to have a beneficial effect on recovery. Norman Cousins[4] has reported for 10 years on the effects of laughter and humor on several conditions, including his own serious illness. Simon[20] described the beneficial effects of humor and laughter in helping patients prepare for and cope with upcoming medical treatment. The box on p. 363 describes an activity designed to provide the beneficial effects of laughter.

Crying

Like a good laugh, a good cry also has stress-reducing power. Crying without tears is essentially a respiratory act. It involves a larger-than-normal inspiration of air followed by a large exhalation. Crying, like laughing, involves rhythmic contractions of major muscle groups and is followed by a more relaxed muscular state.[9]

Crying with tears adds another dimension. The fact that only humans shed emotional tears supports the power of crying in relieving emotional stress.[9] In addition, recent discoveries show that tears contain **enkephalins**, a form of natural opiates similar to the runner's endorphins. These enkephalins help the eye to flush irritants, but perhaps these natural opiates also are intended to help humans deaden the pain associated with stressful emotional trauma.

Anyone who has had a good cry can attest to its emotional healing power, but its power is more difficult to prove scientifically. The point is, do not suppress a good cry! It is nature's stress management for sadness, grief, and disappointment.

enkephalin

a type of painkilling neuropeptide

Emotional Exercise

1. Grin a little grin—get the zygomaticus major (your primary smiling muscle) working. Do not let the eyes, eyebrows, or cheeks get involved.
    - Grin, release
    - Grin, release

2. Squint a little squint—squint as if you forgot your glasses.
    - Squint, release
    - Squint, release
    Now try both;
    - Grin, squint, release
    - Grin squint, release

3. Raise the frontalis (forehead)—this wrinkles the forehead and bobs your eyebrows forward.
    - Raise, hold, relax
    - Raise, hold, relax
    Now try all three
    - Grin, squint, raise
    - Grin, squint, raise

4. Tighten the platysma (the set of muscles in the lower face and neck)—if you do it correctly, it will expose the bottom teeth.
    - Tighten, hold, relax
    - Tighten , hold, relax
    All together
    - Grin, squint, raise, tighten
    - Grin, squint, raise, tighten

5. Belly laugh—inhale deeply, from the belly up. Put your hand on your belly and feel it push out. As it pushes out, say "Ha," while exhaling sharply.
    - Inhale, exhale, saying "Ha"
    - Do this a dozen times quickly

6. Rock back and forth—as you do all the steps in sequence, rock back and forth.
    - Keep going for a few seconds

7. Contact—let the physical tension out by pounding on a table, your knee, a friend's back.
    - Grin, squint, raise, tighten, laugh, rock, pound

8. Tears—if they come, let them roll. Of course you can not force them, but do not fight them either.

Adapted from Metcalf, C.W. & Felible, R. (1992). *Lighten up: survival skills for people under pressure.* Redding, MA: Addison-Wesley.

STRESS IN OUR WORLD

Big Boys Don't Cry

I was watching Ted at the wrestling match the other day. His 7-year-old son Davey had just taken an incredible beating on the mat and wound up getting pinned in the third period. Davey had been tossed around by his more experienced opponent like a rag doll. He was slammed hard to the mat a couple of times, and his face was pushed into the mat ("eating mat," as it is called)

for most of the final period.

Davey, a tough little guy, had held up pretty well against this onslaught. Now, however, with his opponent's arm raised in victory, the flood gates burst open, and Davey broke down into tears. I watched as Ted approached his little son, unsure of what I should do. It seemed natural to me to want to put my arm around the little guy and comfort him, allowing the tears to wash away his sorrow. I stayed back, however,

and sadly watched as Ted handed Davey his sweatshirt and said, "Wipe those tears off, kiddo, big boys don't cry." They walked off the mat, Ted leading the way, Davey dragging behind, head bowed, fighting back the tears.

Do you know a Ted? What are your or your brother's experiences with the "big boys don't cry" mentality? Do men always have to be tough? Is this good training for the tough life we will have to lead?

Unfortunately, many of us do not allow ourselves the benefit of a good cry. Gender roles and cultural mores strongly influence our ability to let the tears flow. As discussed in detail in Chapter 14, the traditional American male role frowns on crying. Crying is tolerated in early childhood, but boys in this culture learn very early that "big boys don't cry."

Crying among all adults also seems to be influenced by culture. We all know the British stereotype of "keeping a stiff upper lip" or the Italian affinity for physical contact, kissing, and giving emotions, including crying, free reign. Adult crying has varying levels of acceptance among cultures that enable some people to express themselves more easily than others. Can you recall an instance where you felt like crying, were on the verge of tears, and held back because of an attitude related to your culture?

Summary

In this chapter we examine the roles of various forms of physical release. We discuss how all of us are born with the ability to use physical activity to release stress. We examine exercise, laughter, and crying as physical ways to release the tension and negative effects of stress.

We examine the physiological bases of these various release strategies and find that all have certain properties in common. All initially cause various body systems (cardiovascular, respiratory, and muscular systems) to increase their levels of activity. Immediately after the release activities, however, these body processes decrease to levels below those found before the activities. That is, after release activities, people become more relaxed, have lower blood pressure, and in general are more content and at peace.

Three different types of energy production are discussed: aerobic, anaerobic, and combined. Each type of exercise has stress-reducing properties and can be used as a coping strategy. The chapter examines the specific physiological and psychological benefits of exercise in stress management.

The chapter also discusses the specific physiological properties of laughter and how it reduces tension and stress. Laughter is incompatible with stress. A good laugh can provide relief from one's problems, as well as put the body into a relaxed state, canceling the effects of stress.

Finally, the chapter discusses crying, noting how it shares the stress-reducing properties of laughter. Crying, a uniquely human endeavor, produces tears that can wash away some of our stress.

Study Questions

1. Describe how release, the fourth level of defense against stress, works.
2. Define aerobic, anaerobic, and combined energy production.
3. What are the physiological stress-reducing properties of exercise?
4. What are the psychological stress-reducing properties of exercise?
5. Explain the acronym FIT.
6. How can one use FIT to improve his or her fitness?
7. What are the three principles of fitness?
8. Describe the physiological effects of laughter.
9. How are laughter and crying similar in their stress-reducing effects?

References

1. Anspaugh, D., Hamrick, M., & Rosato, F. (1994). *Wellness: concepts and applications* (2nd ed.). St. Louis: Mosby.

2. Blair, S. (1989). Physical fitness and all-cause mortality: a prospective study of men and women. *JAMA, 262*, 2395-2401.

3. Cooper, K. (1982). *The aerobics program for total well-being.* Toronto: Bantam.

4. Cousins, N. (1979). *Anatomy of an illness as perceived by the patient.* New York: Norton.

5. Flippin, R. (1989). Beyond endorphins: the latest research on runner's high. *American Health*, Oct, 78-83.

6. Gondola, J.C. (1990). In B.K. Williams & S. Knight, (Eds.), *Healthy for life.* Pacific Grove, CA: Brooks/Cole.

7. Hafen, B., et al. (1992). *The health effects of attitudes, emotions, and relationships.* Provo, UT: EMS Associates.

8. Hopson, J.L. (1988). A pleasurable chemistry. *PT* July/August, 29-33.

9. Marieb, E.M. (1992). *Human anatomy and physiology* (2nd ed.). Redwood City, CA: Benjamin Cummings.

10. Deleted in page proofs.

11. Mood, D., Musker, F., & Rink, J. (1995). *Sports and recreational activities* (11th ed.). St. Louis: Mosby.

12. Morgan, W.P. (1982). Psychological effects of exercise. *Behavioral Medicine Update*, 4, 25-30.

13. Morgan, W., & Goldstein, S. (Eds.). *Exercise and mental health.* New York: Hemisphere.

14. Montoye, H.J., et al. (1988). *Living fit.* Menlo Park, CA: Benjamin Cummings.

15. Mott, P. (1990). Mental gymnastics. *LAT*, (Oct 7), 18-19.

16. Ornstein, R., & Sobel, D. (1989). *Healthy pleasures.* Reading, MA: Addison-Wesley.

17. Prentice, W. (1994). *Fitness for college & life.* St. Louis: Mosby.

18. Robinson, R. (1989). He who laughs...lasts. *Vibrant Life*, (Sept 10), 5.

19. Sime, W.E. (1984). Psychological benefits of exercise. *Advances*, 1, 15-29.

20. Simon, J.M. (1988). Therapeutic humor: who's fooling who?. *Journal of Psychosocial Nursing and Mental Health Services*, 26, (4), 11.

21. Thibodeau, G. & Patton, K. (1993). *Anatomy and physiology* (2nd ed.). St. Louis: Mosby.

ASSESS YOURSELF 10-1

Fitness and Sports

Pick the activity that contributes the most to fitness

1. Softball
2. Tennis
3. Swimming
4. Aerobic dance
5. Football
6. Golf
7. Running
8. Bodybuilding
9. Walking
10. Stair-climbing machine

Discuss how your choice contributes to the five components of fitness (muscular strength, muscular endurance, flexibility, coordination, and cardiovascular endurance).

_____

_____

_____

_____

_____

_____

_____

_____

_____

_____

_____

_____

_____

Name: _____ Date: _____

Physical Activity Readiness Questionnaire (PAR-Q)*
A Self-Administered Questionnaire for Adults

PAR-Q and You

PAR-Q is designed to help you help yourself. Many health benefits are associated with regular exercise, and completing the PAR-Q is a sensible first step to take if you are planning to increase the amount of physical activity in your life.

For most people, physical activity should not pose any problem or hazard. PAR-Q has been designed to identify the small number of adults for whom physical activity might be inappropriate or those who should obtain medical advice concerning the type of activity most suitable for them.

Common sense is your best guide in answering these few questions. Please read them carefully and check YES or NO opposite the question if it applies to you.

Yes	No	
____	____	1. Has your doctor ever said you have heart trouble?
____	____	2. Do you frequently have pains in your heart and chest?
____	____	3. Do you often feel faint or have spells of severe dizziness?
____	____	4. Has a doctor ever said your blood pressure was too high?
____	____	5. Has your doctor ever told you that you have a bone or joint problem, such as arthritis, that has been aggravated by exercise or might be made worse by exercise?
____	____	6. Is there a good physical reason not mentioned here why you should not follow an activity program even if you wanted to?
____	____	7. Are you over age 65 and not accustomed to vigorous exercise?

If you answered "Yes" to one or more questions

If you have not recently done so, consult with your physician by telephone or in person *before* increasing your physical activity and/or taking a fitness test. Tell your physician what questions you answered "Yes" on PAR-Q.

If you answered "No" to all questions

If you answered PAR-Q accurately, you have reasonable assurance of your present suitability for:

■ A graduated exercise program—A gradual increase in proper exercise promotes good fitness development while minimizing or eliminating discomfort.

■ An exercise test—Simple tests of fitness (such as the Canadian Home Fitness Test) or more complex types may be undertaken if you so desire.

Postpone

If you have a temporary minor illness, such as a common cold.

Cont'd

Physical Activity Readiness Questionnaire (PAR-Q)*
A Self-Administered Questionnaire for Adults (cont'd)

If you had one or more "yes" answers on the previous page, follow the direction to consult with a physician. If you had all "no" answers on the PAR-Q, answer the additional questions below before beginning intensive training, particularly for sports.

Yes   **No**

___   ___   1. Do you plan to participate on an organized team that will play intense competitive sports (i.e., varsity team, professional team)?

___   ___   2. If you plan to participate in a collision sport (even on a less organized basis), such as football, boxing, rugby, or ice hockey, have you been knocked unconscious more than one time?

___   ___   3. Do you currently have pain from a previous muscle injury?

___   ___   4. Do you currently have symptoms from a previous back injury, or do you experience back pain as a result of involvement in physical activity?

___   ___   5. Do you have any other symptoms during physical activity that give you reason to be concerned about your health?

If your answer to any of these questions is "yes," then you should consult with your physician by telephone or in person to determine whether you have a potential problem with vigorous involvement in physical activity.

---

*Developed by the British Columbia Ministry of Health, conceptualized and critiqued by the Multidisciplinary Advisory Board on Exercise (MABE).
Reference: PAR-Q Validation Report, British Columbia Ministry of Health, May, 1978.
Produced by the British Columbia Ministry of Health and the Department of National Health & Welfare.

Name: _____ Date: _____

Cooper's 12-Minute Walking/Running Test

Purpose

To determine the level of cardiorespiratory endurance during a 12-minute running or walking activity.

Equipment

1. Measured running course, preferably a track
2. Stopwatch

Procedure

1. During a 12-minute period, the subject attempts to cover as much distance as possible by either running or walking.

Treatment of data

1. Distance covered should be rounded off to the nearest 1/8 mile.
2. Consult the table below. Locate the distance covered for either men or women under appropriate age classification and determine the level of fitness.

Sample worksheet for Cooper's 12-Minute Walking/Running Test	**Example**
1. Measure distance covered, and round off to nearest 1/8 mile _____.	1. 1.50
2. Locate this distance in appropriate "Age" column _____.	2. Age 20
3. Determine fitness level _____.	3. Good

12-Minute Walking/Running Test Distance (Miles) Covered in 12 Minutes

Fitness Category		Age (Years)					
		13-19	20-29	30-39	40-49	50-59	60 +
I. Very poor	(men)	<1.30*	<1.22	<1.18	<1.14	<1.03	<.87
	(women)	<1.0	<.96	<.94	<.88	<.84	<.78
II. Poor	(men)	1.30-1.37	1.22-1.31	1.18-1.30	1.14-1.24	1.03-1.16	.87-1.02
	(women)	1.00-1.18	.96-1.11	.95-1.05	.88-.98	.84-.93	.78-.86
III. Fair	(men)	1.38-1.56	1.32-1.49	1.31-1.45	1.25-1.39	1.17-1.30	1.03-1.20
	(women)	1.19-1.29	1.12-1.22	1.06-1.18	.99-1.11	.94-1.05	.87-.98
IV. Good	(men)	1.57-1.72	1.50-1.64	1.46-1.56	1.40-1.53	1.31-1.44	1.21-1.32
	(women)	1.30-1.43	1.23-1.34	1.19-1.29	1.12-1.24	1.06-1.18	.99-1.09
V. Excellent	(men)	1.73-1.86	1.65-1.76	1.57-1.69	1.54-1.65	1.45-1.58	1.33-1.55
	(women)	1.44-1.51	1.35-1.45	1.30-1.39	1.25-1.34	1.19-1.30	1.10-1.18
VI. Superior	(men)	>1.87	>1.77	>1.70	>1.66	>1.59	>1.56
	(women)	>1.52	>1.46	>1.40	>1.31	>1.31	>1.19

*<Means "less than"; > means "more than."

ASSESS YOURSELF 10-4

Beginner's Aerobic Training Zone

Steps involved in calculating your aerobic training zone:

1. Calculate your maximum heart rate (MHR):

   220 - your age = MHR (EQ)

2. Calculate your resting heart rate (RHR):

   Pulse rate upon waking in the morning

3. Identify your lower and upper training intensity (TI) levels:

   60% (lower level for beginners)

   75% (upper level for beginners)

4. Calculate your lower and upper target heart rates (THR):

   THR = (MHR - RHR) x (TI% + RHR)

   Lower THR = (MHR - RHR) x 60% + RHR

   Upper THR = (MHR - RHR) x 75% + RHR

   _____

   _____

   _____

5. As long as your heart rate during exercise falls between your lower and upper target heart rates, you are in your aerobic training zone.

   THR, target heart rate; MHR, maximum heart rate; RHR, resting heart rate; TI%, training intensity (% of maximum heart rate).

   _____

   _____

   _____

Example: 20-year-old student with a resting heart rate of 60 beats/minute.

1. 220 - 20 = 200 MHR = 200)

2. 60 = RHR

3. 60% lower limit; 75% upper limit

4. (200 - 60) x .60 + 60 = 84 + 60 = 144

   (200 - 60) x .75 + 60 = 105 + 60 = 165

5. Training zone = 144 to 165 beats/minute

Name: _____ Date: _____

Determining Your Body Mass Index (BMI)

Use the following two figures to determine your body mass index (BMI) and health risk. First determine your BMI using the calculations below. Then plot your number on the nomogram on p. 376.

To Determine Your BMI:

1. Divide your weight in pounds by 2.2 to convert it to kilograms.

    A = Weight (kg) = Your Weight (lb) ÷ 2.2

    _____

    _____

2. Multiply your height in inches by 2.54 and divide by 100 to convert height to meters.

    B = Height (m) = Your height (in) × 2.54 ÷ 100

    _____

    _____

3. Multiply B by B to get your height (in meters) squared.

    C = Height (m) × Height (m)

    _____

    _____

4. Divide A by C to determine BMI.

    BMI = Weight (kg) ÷ Height^2 (m)

    _____

    _____

Example: You weigh 176 pounds and you are 72 inches (6 feet) tall.

1. A = 176 ÷ 2.2 = 80

2. B = $\dfrac{72 \times 2.54}{100} = \dfrac{182.88}{100} = 1.83$

3. C = 1.83 × 1.83 = 3.35

4. BMI = $\dfrac{80}{3.35}$ = 23.88

Cont'd

Determining Your Body Mass Index (BMI) (cont'd)

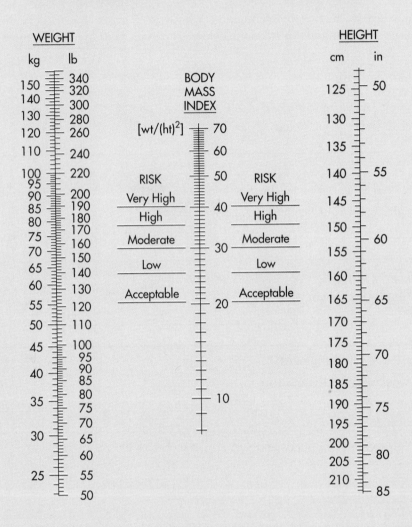

Nomogram for determining BMI. To use this nomogram, place a ruler or other straight edge between the body weight in kilograms or pounds (without clothes) located on the left hand column and the height in centimeters or in inches (without shoes) located on the right-hand column. The BMI is read from the middle of the scale and is in metric units.

ASSESS YOURSELF 10-6

How to Use the Daily Food Guide

What counts as one serving?

BREADS, CEREALS, RICE, AND PASTA
1 slice of bread
$1/2$ cup of cooked rice or pasta
$1/2$ cup of cooked cereal
1 ounce of ready-to-eat cereal

MILK, YOGURT, AND CHEESE
1 cup of milk or yogurt
$11/2$ to 2 ounces of cheese

VEGETABLES
$1/2$ cup chopped raw or
   cooked vegetables
1 cup of leafy raw vegetables

FRUITS
1 piece of fruit or melon wedges
$3/4$ cup of juice
$1/2$ cup of canned fruit
$1/4$ cup of dried fruit

MEAT, POULTRY, FISH, DRY BEANS, EGGS, AND NUTS
$21/2$ to 3 ounces of cooked lean
   meat, poultry, or fish
Count $1/2$ cup of cooked beans
   or 1 egg, or 2 tablespoons
   of peanut butter as 1 ounce of lean
   meat (about $1/3$ serving)

FATS, OILS, AND SWEETS
Limit calories from these, especially if you
need to lose weight

The amount you eat may be more than one
   serving. For example, a dinner portion of
   spaghetti would count as two or three
   servings of pasta.

A Closer Look at Fat and Added Sugars

The small tip of the pyramid shows fats, oils, and sweets. These are foods such as salad dressings, cream, butter, margarine, sugars, soft drinks, candies, and sweet desserts. Alcoholic beverages also are part of this group. These foods provide calories but few vitamins and minerals. Most people should go easy on foods from this group.

Some fats or sugar symbols are shown in the other food groups. That's to remind you that some foods in these groups also can be high in fat and added sugars, such as cheese or ice cream from the milk group, or french fries from the vegetable group. When choosing foods for a healthful diet, consider the fat and added sugars in your choices from all the food groups, not just fats, oils, and sweets from the pyramid tip.

Cont'd

How to Use the Daily Food Guide (cont'd)

How many servings do you need each day?

	Women and some older adults	Children, teenage girls, active women, and most men	Teenage boys and active men
Calorie level*	About 1600	About 2200	About 2800
Bread group	6	9	11
Vegetable group	3	4	5
Fruit group	2	3	4
Milk group	**2-3	**2-3	**2-3
Meat group	2, for a total of 5 ounces	2, for a total of 6 ounces	3, for a total of 7 ounces

*These are the calorie levels if you choose lowfat, lean foods from the five major food groups and use foods from the fats, oils, and sweets group sparingly.
**Women who are pregnant or breastfeeding, teenagers, and young adults to age 24 need three servings.

How many servings of each food group do you take in each day?

_____

_____

_____

_____

_____

_____

11

Reorganize: Coping by Putting It All Together

CHAPTER OBJECTIVES

■ List and describe the four levels of defense against stress.

■ Describe how the lines of defense mesh with the six dimensions of health and wellness to produce a synergistic effect.

■ Discuss how all stress transactions occur within the context of one's microenvironment and macroenvironment.

■ Compare a holistic approach to stress management to one that teaches only a variety of individual coping strategies.

■ Develop three strategies for improving social and spiritual functioning.

■ Develop three strategies for improving mental functioning.

- **Use a personal example to describe the four-phase process for improving emotional functioning described in the text.**
- **Develop a personal plan to integrate fitness into life year-round.**
- **Discuss the direction and movement toward wellness.**

This final chapter on coping discusses how to reorganize our lives and our stress-management strategies around the six dimensions of health and wellness, helping us become more holistic and at the same time more stress-resistant.

As you recall from Chapter 1, holistic health is the process of moving toward optimal functioning in the physical, intellectual, emotional, social, spiritual, emotional, and environmental domains. This book has explored the five dimensions of health and has discussed the importance of striving for optimal functioning in all five dimensions. It has also discussed the four *R*s of coping: rethink, reduce, relax, and release.

synergistic

tendency of two or more factors, when added together, to produce an effect greater than the sum of the parts

This chapter continues with these issues; however, it focuses on how to integrate them into a more unified whole rather than discussing them as separate stress-management strategies. By linking strategies from all six dimensions and four *R*s simultaneously, we can generate a **synergistic** effect against stress. That is, all of these strategies working together at the same time produce an effect greater than the sum of these strategies working independently.

The Importance of Holistic Health in Stress Management

KEY

TO UNDERSTANDING

The stress transaction does not occur in a vacuum. It is affected by your overall level of functioning.

A key to understanding the stress transaction, as discussed at several points in this book, is that stress does not occur within a vacuum. At any given moment, our ability to interpret potential stressors is influenced by our general level of wellness in all of the six dimensions of health. The reason something stresses us has as much to do with our general level of functioning as it does with the nature of the stressor itself. In addition, our belief in our ability to cope with potential stressors also is strongly influenced by our general level of wellness.

When we are functioning at maximum efficiency, we simply have more resources at our disposal to help us manage our stress. Our general level of health itself serves as a coping device. For instance, when we are functioning maximally, we possess excellent physical health and enjoy the energy it brings. Our muscles are strong and supple and can sustain longer periods of work. We are flexible. Our hearts and lungs process oxygen and remove waste efficiently, allowing our brains to think more clearly and process information better. This cardiovascular efficiency produced by physical fitness leads to high-level mental functioning because the brain can work better.

When we are functioning efficiently emotionally, we are in touch with and can control our emotions. We are less likely to react inappropriately or overreact to situations that might stress us if we were not functioning as well.

When we have high levels of social well-being, we have a support system or safety net to help us. Even if we do not need it, knowing that we have this support system puts our minds at ease. A strong social dimension ensures that we have various social resources to help us in times of need.

Spiritual well-being helps us resist stress by enabling us to have faith in the world and in the future. It gives us a sense of order, a feeling that things somehow will work out. People with a strong spiritual dimension possess an inner peace that helps them through the toughest of times.

When we are not whole, when we are functioning inefficiently, we have fewer resources, both within ourselves and elsewhere to help us manage our stress. The stress transaction then leads us to believe that we are unable to cope effectively. This belief probably is accurate because we do not have as broad a base of support as we need.

In a sense, we can plot our overall wellness level on a continuum of functioning. We range from high-level functioning to being dysfunctional, and from high-level wellness to low-level health or illness (see Stress in Our World box on p. 382).

Think Globally, Act Locally: The Macroenvironment and Microenvironment

So far we have talked about the six dimensions of health and wellness as if they exist in a vacuum. Nothing could be further from the truth! You always examine your life and stress within the context of your immediate environment (**microenvironment**) and the global community (**macroenvironment**). All of your experiences take place within this framework of reality. Although you constantly strive to be the best that you can be as an individual, this quest takes place within a neighborhood, a state, your country, and the world as a whole. This is why you never can ignore the quality of life within your environments.

**micro-
environment**
one's immediate environment, including their immediate family and friends, and living and work space

**macro-
environment**
the world at large

STRESS IN OUR WORLD

Elka

Elka was exhausted! Drenched with sweat, head pounding, muscles in her upper body burning with fatigue, she had glided over the finish line of her first marathon, her wheelchair coasting for the first time in several miles. She reveled in the ceremonial dousing from a garden hose and eagerly gulped down several cups of water.

As she coasted to a stop and was greeted by her friends and parents, she paused to reflect on how far she had come in the past years since her accident. An athlete and outdoor enthusiast, Elka had been injured in a skiing accident 4 years earlier. While skiing with friends, she hit a patch of ice, fell, skidded wildly off the trail and out of bounds, and hit a tree. She broke her back and was paralyzed from the waist down.

Elka was devastated! Her whole life and identity centered on sports and the outdoors. Wheelchairs and paralysis did not fit into her perception of health and fitness. A junior physical education major and varsity field hockey player, she had

plans to teach physical education and coach at the high school level. She spent most of her free time away from school swimming and riding her jet ski in the summer, snow skiing in the winter, and hiking and camping in the fall. She could not imagine a life without these pursuits that she loved so much.

For months after the accident, she refused to talk to anyone. She would not take part in her physical therapy program and rehabilitation activities, and she stopped talking to her athletic friends. Her rehabilitative process was very slow. She gained weight, became surly, and sank into chronic depression.

Not until she met Jane, a wheelchair marathoner and basketball player, did Elka begin to renew her interest in life. Jane had completed her rehabilitation at the same facility Elka was attending. She happened to be in town and came to give a lecture about wheelchair athletes. As Elka listened and watched Jane wheel around and have fun with the other clients, something began to stir within her. After her talk, Jane came over and introduced herself to Elka. The two had a lot in

common and, as they shared stories about their lives and their accidents, Elka began to see a glimmer of hope.

Within months of meeting Jane, Elka made a complete turnaround. She began to take her rehabilitation seriously, putting extra time and effort into her activities. She started to watch her diet and began to plan for her goal of competing in a road race.

As she savored her feelings about finishing her first marathon, Elka realized that many things about her had changed. For starters, she really did not feel sorry for herself any longer. Sure, she still wished that the ski accident never had happened and that she had the use of her legs. However, she did not really think of herself as unhealthy or unfit anymore. She worked hard and made the most of her abilities. Her weight was down, upper-body strength and cardiorespiratory endurance were better than ever, and she had the same zest for life that she had before the accident.

Elka thought she was in excellent health. What do you think? Can someone be physically challenged and still possess excellent physical health?

Health educators and environmentalists have a phrase to illustrate this concept: "Think globally, act locally." That is, pay attention to events in the world around you and do what you can to improve your world but put most of your energies into your immediate community, where the daily quality of life directly affects you and your family.

For example, Roger was trying to live a more holistic life. He worked out aerobically three to four times a week, watched his diet, and kept his weight within reasonable limits. He did not smoke and always used his seat belt. He tried to think rationally and logically and used his mind to minimize stressors in his life. He was in touch with his emotions and sought opportunities to express and explore his spirituality. He was moving toward optimal functioning in his life.

However, Roger's previously peaceful, environmentally clean little town began to change. Developers sought permission from his town's zoning board to develop 5000 acres of farmland. They wanted to build 10,000 cluster housing units, two industrial parks, and a trash transfer station. The developers claimed this would spur growth in this mostly rural town. These changes began coming when a national and worldwide recession had claimed countless jobs and resulted in high unemployment locally and nationally.

Roger realized that the quality of life he enjoyed and that contributed to his well-being was threatened by the proposed changes. Roger could have chosen to ignore the events and restricted his activities to his personal pursuit of wellness or he could have chosen to think globally and act locally.

Roger chose the latter and began to meet with his neighbors. They agreed that this particular type of development was threatening their lifestyle. They attended the next planning board meeting en masse, and in a show of solidarity, they expressed their concerns to the town council and the developers.

As the months passed, Roger and his group began to appreciate the importance of planned growth for the community, and the politicians and the developers began to understand the need to scale down their plans and include recreational and environmental facilities that improve rather than destroy the quality of life in the town. In time, both sides compromised and reached an agreement.

Over the months, as Roger has led the struggle against runaway development in his town, he has become more sophisticated about how global events trickle down to his community. Roger has begun to pay attention to events in this country and in the world. He has begun to see how the policies of a nation affect not only the livelihood of government and big business but also his town. For instance, his group's fight against excess growth had legal support from federal and state statutes intended to protect wetlands. This caused Roger to think about the importance of these types of regulations for other communities throughout the world, which led him to join an international organization dedicated to preserving the environment throughout the world. He even worked up enough nerve to attend a chapter meeting in a nearby town.

For the first time, Roger has begun writing to his elected representatives, telling them how he feels about important issues here and abroad. Roger indeed has expanded his horizons and has taken a stand on the things that matter to him.

Roger has found that all of this work and involvement has given him some personal dividends that have enriched his life. He no longer feels powerless. He feels that, although he may not change the world, he at least is an active participant in it. This has given him a sense of power and control over his destiny. He also feels closer to his community and his neighbors. Their common struggle has brought them closer together and given them a common bond that they previously lacked. He even began talking to the elderly gentleman down the street whom he had thought was aloof and uncaring. They discovered that they share a passion for the outdoors, which led them to spend time together on hikes in the nearby woods (Fig. 11-1). Now, when Roger takes his daily runs, he feels much more connected and serene.

Roger has learned something many of us never learn—that we do not live in a vacuum, that we cannot divorce ourselves from the events going on around us, no matter how much might want to at times. We all are in this together.

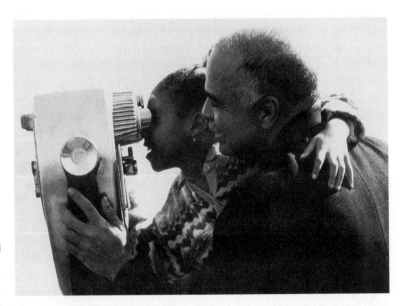

Fig. 11-1 Opportunities for learning abound when we expand our friendships to include older people who have a wealth of life experience to share with us.

Strengthening the Social and Spiritual Dimensions

Chapters 6 and 7 discuss several strategies for rethinking and reducing stressors that affect our spiritual and social dimensions. Values clarification, goal setting, lightening up, and slowing the pace are examples of these. As stand-alone activities, they are excellent methods for coping with stress. We can use social and spiritual strategies as one-shot attempts to cope with specific stressors (Assess Yourself 11-1).

However, we also can strengthen our spiritual and social dimensions in general by becoming involved in a host of activities even when we are not feeling stressed. We do this in an attempt to shore up these dimensions of our health for preventive purposes. In a sense, this provides a protective effect, giving us faith and inner strength that help us resist stress in general.

To fully develop our social and spiritual dimensions, we must commit to serving some good greater than our own needs. For some of us, this means serving others. Whether it is volunteering to lead your church youth group, managing your local little league team, being a friend to a person with AIDS, or becoming a volunteer firefighter, the commitment and action in serving others is what is important. Commitment and action together are the keys to success.

KEY
TO UNDERSTANDING
Commitment and action are keys to successful change.

By thinking globally but acting locally, Roger enriched his social and spiritual dimensions. Instead of seeking artificial social and spiritual issues, Roger became involved in issues that were real for him. He experienced real social and spiritual change because his involvement was based on issues that mattered to him. A key to becoming actively involved in serving others is to focus on something that has meaning to you.

KEY
TO UNDERSTANDING
Your chances of success are greater if you volunteer for work that you enjoy.

Roger's sense of control began changing from feeling controlled by others to having greater control over his life. He began experiencing the "commitment and control" that Kobassa[3] identified as part of the hardy personality. Roger never intended for this to happen. In fact, he was very reluctant to commit the time needed by such a project. When he finally did, it was not an intentional attempt to enrich his social and spiritual life, his goal was to solve a problem. In time, however, he came to enjoy the effort and began to view it as a challenge. Roger put more effort into his community because it mattered to him.

Another benefit to all of Roger's labor was his development of a sense of connectedness to something greater than himself. This connection began simply. He became connected to his group and committee out of necessity to accomplish the task. His connection grew, however, into something greater than that. Roger took a few months to put his finger on it, but he finally realized that he was becoming connected to his life. He began to develop a passion for living. It was strange, but he was beginning to become energized by all of this. He began to feel that something in his life truly mattered. He felt that it was not him against the world—it was him of and with the world. He began to feel at one with his neighbors, his community, his earth, the creatures that inhabit the earth, and the future of all this.

Roger had discovered his spirituality, although he did not label it as such. This is the kind of secular sense of spirituality that grows out of connectedness to others and to a greater good, which further strengthens our connections to the world around us.

Roger learned that his spirituality increased as a result of his social action. In other cases the reverse is true; our need for others and a desire for social connectedness is increased by more solitary explorations of our spirituality.

Finding Your Own Walden Pond

In 1854, Henry David Thoreau[5] wrote about his need to seek a place away from the crowds, in a more natural environment, where he could explore the meaning of his life and the trappings of the civilized world. He was not renouncing society, merely stepping back from society to better look at his life.

Similarly, in our fast-paced culture, we must get off the fast track to find the spiritual element in our lives. By doing this, we can return to our daily responsibilities and commitments renewed and refreshed. Although vacations are meant to do this, unfortunately they have become a source of stress for many. We often cram so much into our vacations visiting places that provide more, rather than less, stimulation, that we need a vacation to recuperate from our vacation.

Thoreau's pilgrimages to Walden Pond were his attempts to find a more natural place to slow down, be among the elements of nature, and sort through the trials and tribulations of his life in civilized society.

Colin Fletcher[2], in *The Complete Walker*, talks about his need to escape from the travails of everyday life by going hiking and backpacking for a few days or weeks at a time. He describes how this recharges his life. His time with no telephone, television, radio, or newspaper allows him to pause and think, without interference from media noise. His trips also renew his sense of awe of the natural world. In addition, he now appreciates coming home to clean sheets and a hot bath, simple things that we take for granted.

Different cultures and religions have a variety of ways to build time and special places for contemplation into the fabric of daily life. The Japanese have gardens, replete with miniature bonsai trees. These gardens offer a sanctuary from the hurried pace of industrialized Japanese society. Moslems set aside time every day to turn toward their holy city, Mecca, and pray to Allah. Buddhist monks isolate themselves in desolate monasteries high in the mountains where, removed from the trappings of civilization,

STRESS IN OUR WORLD

Finding Your Walden

"I suppose you could say that going out in this older world is rather like going to church. I know that it is in my case, anyway. For me, praying is no good: my god is not interested in what happens to me personally. By walking out alone into the wilderness I can elude the pressures of the pounding modern world, and in the sanctity of silence and solitude—the solitude seems to be a very important part of it—I can after a while begin to see and to hear and to think and in the end to feel with a new and exciting accuracy. And that, it seems to me, is just the kind of vision you should be hoping to find when you go to church."

In this passage from The Complete Walker, Colin Fletcher[2] talks about the sense of spirituality he encounters when he ventures into the wilderness, or the older world, as he describes it. He likens it to the serenity and clarity one experiences, or should experience, after attending church. The wilderness is his church, and walking in it is his worship and perhaps his salvation. Does this work for you? What kinds of natural experiences put you in touch with your spirituality?

they can contemplate the meaning of their existence. Catholic priests and nuns also have their monasteries, where they spend long hours in quiet contemplation of the spiritual world, far removed from the hustle and bustle of everyday life. Native Americans seek the sanctuary of special places: hilltops, meadows, or other places in the wilderness where they retreat into their quest for inner peace. Wherever we find our Walden Pond, we must make the time to visit it often. We must build time into our schedules to disconnect from our busy lives, so we may reconnect with something greater than ourselves.

Strengthening the Intellectual Dimension

The fact that you attend a college is a step toward improving your intellectual dimension. Mental functioning is the ability to think and process information clearly and accurately. This book emphasizes the importance of rational thinking in the stress transaction. Our ability to see and hear through all of the noise, mixed messages, and misinformation in our society affects not only our stress levels but also our overall quality of life.

Being able to distinguish fact from fiction depends on our knowledge and the way we use it. This book discusses several cognitive strategies for stress management. Among them are Ellis and Harper's[1] ABCDE technique for rational thinking and improving creativity, a model for problem solving, and the DESC model. Regularly practicing these strategies will increase one's ability to think clearly and logically and to act rather than react to potential stressors. This will give you a more rational perspective on potential stressors.

More important than practicing these strategies, however, is the need to commit to thinking clearly and using reason and logic to guide you. This must be a conscious commitment that extends beyond yourself. This means that you expect the same from your family, friends, and significant others and that you gently try to get others to use their reason and logic. Not only do you change, but you become an agent of change for a more reasoned, intelligent life.

A big component of this intelligent life is a commitment to continually expand your knowledge. Knowledge gives you power and control in your life. A key to reducing stress is knowing as much as you can about a potential stressor. This can help defuse the stressor by reducing the fear it may cause you as fear often is a product of ignorance.

Because you are in college and have come this far, you probably have made a good start in your quest for an intelligent life (Fig. 11-2). This does more than just give you more information than the average person; it gives you a broader perspective and an appreciation of events in the world

KEY
TO UNDERSTANDING

Knowing as much as you can about a potential stressor can reduce the stress associated with it.

Fig. 11-2 Although graduation day may be the culmination of our formal academic training, it is only the beginning of lifelong learning.

around you. This perspective can improve your ability to cope because it makes you more sophisticated in your understanding of potentially stressful situations.

One of the virtues of a broad academic background is that it helps one develop a multicultural perspective on life. By exposing yourself to different cultures and histories, you begin to appreciate different people and beliefs. Research has shown that hatred for people because of their race (racism) or their sexual orientation (homophobia/heterosexism) is caused in part by ignorance and fear of people who are different.

Remember, the stress response begins in your brain with your perception of events. Having objective knowledge about different people can help reduce your fear, mistrust, and hatred and can become another tool in your repertoire of coping devices (see the Stress in Our World box below).

Being a lifelong learner is another tool. Your brain works best when it is stimulated. Learning and thinking are processes that can continue far beyond your college years. The discipline and skills you develop now can be the foundation for a lifelong commitment to thinking and learning. Being a student of life, always seeking the facts and the truth, always listening to

STRESS IN OUR WORLD

On Homophobia

Tom hated homosexuals. The thought of men loving other men in either a romantic or sexual sense really disgusted him. In fact, it disgusted him so much that he felt fearful and angry enough to consider physically hurting any man who might "come onto" him. Tom was homophobic. Of course, he did not describe himself this way and did not know what the term meant until the subject came up in his personal health class.

Tom always had assumed that homosexuals at some point in their lives consciously decided to be gay. He was amazed to learn that for both gay and straight people, the process of psychosexual development and the formation of sexual orientation were similar. This was not a planned, conscious decision. It just happened.

Tom also learned that most of his beliefs about all homosexuals being promiscuous, HIV positive, and child molesters were myths.

As Tom's myths were replaced by facts, his fears

began to decrease. He was amazed to learn that a classmate of his was gay and that the classmate's sexual orientation never had been an issue in their relationship. Tom's stress about homosexuality began to be replaced by acceptance. He still was glad he was a heterosexual, but he did not feel that everyone had to be.

Have you had similar experiences about sexual orientation or other differences in other people? How has your knowledge about diversity helped you reduce your stress?

both sides, and always seeing the grays and not just the black and white of issues keeps our intellectual dimension healthy.

People who stop being active learners, who become passive recipients of "news," are less able to accurately assess a potentially stressful situation because they are less able to identify the real harm or threat. They can be manipulated more easily by the media and by those who choose to twist the facts, stretch the truth, and try to scare people. Assess Yourself 11-2 gives tips for becoming a lifelong learner.

The Emotional Dimension

While the mental dimension addresses the cognitive aspects of our minds, the emotional domain involves our feelings and how we deal with them. Chapter 2 discusses the relationship of psychological factors to stress, listing facets of the stress-prone as well as the stress-resistant personality. Two emotions in particular, anger and hostility, are related to a variety of negative health outcomes. Loneliness also is a contributor to stress and illness. Positive emotions, such as happiness, commitment, challenge, and a sense of humor are related to improved health status.

This book presents several strategies for understanding and dealing with our emotions. Morita psychotherapy, for example, is a strategy that recognizes and channels negative emotions into positive behaviors. Recognizing and changing destructive, negative self-talk also helps us reduce destructive emotions. Finally, lightening up and looking at the bright side is a straight-forward way to deal with emotional stress.

KEY
TO UNDERSTANDING

Moving toward mental wellness requires regularly assessing your happiness and staying in touch with your feelings and how you are managing them.

These individual strategies are great and with practice will help you reduce and cope with stressors. What is equally important, however, is a commitment to staying emotionally healthy and moving toward being emotionally well. A key to this is regularly assessing your happiness, staying in touch with your feelings, and examining how well you are managing your feelings rather than being controlled by them.

Emotional health means being proactive for your emotional well-being—seeking the company of those who nurture your feelings rather than hurt them. It means building time into your life to play, laugh, and have fun (Fig. 11-3). It means seeking the help of friends and professionals when you need it, without feeling shame, guilt, or denial.

Commitment to your emotional well-being requires paying attention to the major decisions that affect your emotional well-being. This means examining how your choices in your work, friends, spouse, living environment, and lifestyle affect your emotional health. For instance, you may decide to forgo a promotion if it requires moving to a place you do not like. Or you may decide to cut back on activities that require you to spend an inordinate

Fig. 11-3 True friends understand and support you. They are there when you need them and they boost, not destroy, your self-esteem.

amount of time doing things that you do not enjoy or bring you down (e.g., working, yard care, commuting, worrying about money).

Being proactive about your emotional health may require you to change your plans. Sometimes this can pose problems for others who have certain expectations for you. It may mean taking 5 years instead of 4 to finish college, or waiting an extra year to get married or buy that new car.

As you begin to pay attention to and better control the factors that affect your emotional well-being, individual coping strategies have more effect because you need to draw on them less frequently and for fewer major issues. You are moving toward optimal functioning in the emotional dimension (Assess Yourself 11-3).

The Physical Dimension

Many people fail in their attempts to become fit because they fail to develop a four-season plan. They start in the summer with a program of swimming, and when fall rolls around and the pool closes, they have no back-up plan. They become very inactive during the fall and winter months, fall grossly out of shape, and then must start over in the spring.

This is a destructive cycle for several reasons. First, it stops the momentum toward optimal functioning. Instead of progressing to greater heights of fitness, they always are playing catch-up. Second, it wreaks havoc on weight control, because the body must readjust to reduced calorie expenditure (and possibly greater calorie consumption) during the winter months.

From a psychological perspective, moving indoors and being less physically active may contribute to seasonal affective disorder (SAD) if a person is predisposed to this disorder. As Chapter 5 discusses, SAD sufferers are victims of winter depression. The short, gray days of winter that begin in October and end in March can make them feel depressed, sluggish, and uninterested in life. Deprived of both physical activity and sunshine, the person sinks lower into inactivity and depression.

There is no reason for people to cease physical exercise or outdoor activities in winter. There are a variety of indoor pursuits that provide exercise to compensate for the lack of outdoor opportunities. Health clubs, YMCAs and YWCAs, and local recreational programs abound.

You may be able to pursue your activities all year long if you live in a temperate climate or you can adjust to changes in weather or temperature. Try not to let your activity level lapse while you switch from your summer activities to your winter ones. The more time you take off, the more difficulty you will have getting back on track.

If you want to continue your outdoor pursuits in winter, consider the new, space-age materials, such as Polarfleece and Gore-Tex, that are light and waterproof and provide the right amount of warmth by holding heat in and allowing perspiration to exit. An alternate to wearing these newer materials is dressing in lightweight layers of cotton and wool. This is an excellent and inexpensive way to stay warm and save money.

A key to keeping active all year is to have at least one indoor activity and one outdoor activity that you enjoy for each season (see Stress in Our World box on p. 393). For instance, in the summer you might jog outdoors and do aerobic dance indoors. In the winter you could cross-country ski or snowshoe outdoors and play racquetball indoors. By having both indoor and outdoor activities, you will be less likely to go without exercise for too long.

KEY
TO UNDERSTANDING

Have at least one indoor and one outdoor physical activity for each season.

Moving Toward Optimal Functioning

KEY
TO UNDERSTANDING

The process of moving toward wellness is as important as the end result.

As you can see, the way to start controlling your stress is to improve your level of functioning across all of the dimensions of health. To do this you must understand that the process of moving toward optimal functioning is as important as the results you achieve. As Fig. 11-4 shows, your direction is the key. We strive to gain more control and responsibility for our health while developing the support systems we need to help us in our journey.

STRESS IN OUR WORLD

Let's Get Physical

Many people make physical activity the core of their leisure and recreational pursuits. They play sports, work out, or go for hikes or walks in the woods as much for the sheer pleasure of the activities as for their benefits in stress management or health. These people view physical activity as a core value and would not think of letting a week go by without planning some physical activity, even in the depths of winter. They plan for fitness when thinking of their weekends, vacations, and spare time. Their time with family and friends may well center on physical activity. Instead of sitting around watching football on television all day Sunday, they organize a coed game of touch football first, while the sun is shining, and then come indoors to enjoy hot drinks and to catch the late afternoon game. They do not eschew the intellectual delights of life; they just balance their sedentary passions with a penchant for physical pursuits.

What do you think about this idea? Can you come up with eight physical activities (two per season) for a four-season fitness program? How do physical activities fit into your recreational plans?

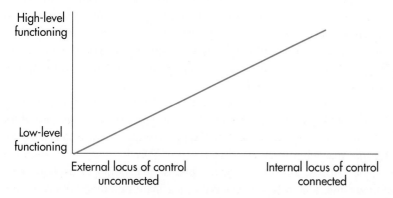

Fig. 11-4 Movement in wellness is away from illness and toward optimal functioning. It also involves moving away from an external locus of control and toward connections to support systems and a spiritual life.

This model also helps us appreciate the role of time. When it takes years to reach our current level of health and stress, it may also take years to reorganize our lives so we can improve wellness. Enjoy the time you spend doing this. Do not try to rush it.

As we improve our level of functioning, we develop more reserve energy and personal resources to help us stay well and cope with stress. As our lives become more whole, we become more well-rounded and develop a more preventive outlook toward health. We begin to choose daily activities and long-range goals more carefully, always considering our health and stress management.

At times, we act in ways that may slow our progress, but we generally move in the right direction. We also forgive ourselves and realize that to be human is to give into temptation sometimes and eat or drink too much, or overextend ourselves for a time. We realize that we are not perfect beings, and we allow ourselves these imperfections without excess guilt, shame, or anger. We lighten up and readjust.

Wellness and Coping

By adopting this long-range focus, we prevent some stress because we now view life differently and plan accordingly. We consider the six dimensions of wellness and the four *R*s when planning our lives and making decisions.

For example, we would not plan a vacation without including some kind of physical exercise or recreation. We know that to be healthy and to cope with demands we need exercise.

We would not seriously consider a job change that would demand so much of our time that we would have to give up the hours that we now allot to exercise or community activities. We protect our time and are careful about who we share it with and how we spend it. We know that a commitment to wellness and stress management requires us to spend time on preventive and restorative activities.

We think twice before forming relationships with people whose values conflict seriously with ours. We realize that our support system is crucial to our ability to cope, and we avoid becoming too intimate with people who do not support or who mock our efforts.

In other words, as we approach wellness, we begin to examine our commitments, the demands they placed on our lives, and their effects on the six dimensions of health. Our values change. Health and stress management become core values. They are priorities as we consider choices in our lives. We have changed; we are moving toward wellness.

Contracting for Change

We already have discussed the importance of goal setting. It is time to set some health-related goals using a behavior change contract (Assess Yourself 11-4). A behavior change contract establishes and formalizes your commitment to change and rewards you for your success. When you commit to something and sign your name to it, you are giving your word that you will honor this contract.

Start small. Try to set manageable goals that you have a good chance to achieve. As you reach your goals, remember that this process should not itself create stress. Remember the stress curve from Chapter 7. More is not necessarily better. If you set manageable goals, you will feel the exhilaration that accompanies challenge. If you set unmanageable goals, you will feel the anxiety associated with threat. Use your awareness of these feelings to plan and to change plans when necessary.

Take your time! You took your whole life to get where you are. You will take a while to improve. Enjoy the journey!

Summary

This chapter explains how holistic stress management combines a commitment to wellness with the four lines of defense, rethink, reduce, relax, and release. These defenses complement each other and create a synergistic effect. The benefits that result from improving one's general wellness can improve the specific coping skills of the four *R*s.

Moving toward optimal functioning, the pursuit of wellness, also can empower us with more energy, greater social resources, better overall intellectual abilities, and the faith in the future to carry on. These generic life skills provide extra resources in the fight against stress. Those who are in better shape mentally, physically, socially, spiritually, and environmentally have more strength and greater resources in coping with stress.

Those with a greater level of wellness also have an improved perspective on life and on potential stressors. Little things that used to be sources of stress are now amusing interludes to be enjoyed or simply handled. Their life force has new value. It is not to be wasted on trivial stressors.

Committing to a stress-management plan such as this requires reshaping one's entire life. Thus this level of coping is called *reorganize*. This means reorganizing one's life to center on health and stress management. These issues must become core values. They guide and shape one's choices, perceptions, and experiences.

Student Study Questions

1. Describe the four levels of defense against stress and explain how they differ.
2. What is synergy? Describe how the four levels of defense work with high-level wellness to achieve a synergistic effect.
3. What are the effects of one's microenvironment and macroenvironment on stress transactions?
4. Describe three strategies for improving social and spiritual functioning.

5. What role does college play in improving mental functioning and reducing stress?

6. Describe three ways to integrate fitness into your year-round activities.

7. "The process of moving toward optimal functioning is more important than the outcome." Explain this quote.

Reference List

1. Ellis, A., & Harper, R. (1979). *A new guide to rational living.* Englewood Cliffs, NJ: Prentice Hall.

2. Fletcher, C. (1972). *The complete walker.* New York: Knopf.

3. Kobassa, S. (1979). Stressful life events, personality & health: an inquiry into hardiness. *Journal of Personality and Social Psychology, 37*(1), 1-11.

4. Payne, W., & Hahn, D. (1995). *Understanding your health.* St. Louis: Mosby.

5. Thoreau, H.D. (1854). *Walden.* Boston: Houghton.

Name: _____ Date: _____

Social and Spiritual Health Begins at Home

Although you should have a perspective on the world and the global things that stress you, you probably will have the greatest ability to affect stressful events that are closest to you. The following five tips can help you in this process.

1. Identify issues and situations in your community that either create stress or reduce the quality of your life.

   _____

   _____

   _____

   _____

2. Involve your family if you can. Can you work as a family on any of the issues identified in #1?

   _____

   _____

   _____

   _____

3. Identify community resources that you and your family can use in your work and that can link you with other people.

   _____

   _____

   _____

   _____

4. Call or meet with the director of social services, recreation, or health and welfare of your town or city. This person is responsible for coordinating all social services in your area.

5. Volunteer for the kind of activities that you enjoy. Do not let your volunteer activities become a source of stress.

Name: _____ Date: _____

10 Tips for Becoming a Lifelong Learner

1. Realize that your education is never finished.

2. Believe that you can teach an old dog new tricks. What is something you want to learn about?

   _____

   _____

3. Keep an open mind; you may learn something.

4. Seek the wisdom of senior citizens. Write down the names of some senior citizens you could talk to.

   _____

   _____

5. Travel; learn by absorbing the ideas of different cultures. List five places you would like to visit.

   _____

   _____

6. Expose yourself to opinions that are different from your own.

7. Read something daily! Name five books you are interested in reading.

   _____

   _____

8. Listen to talk radio.

9. Take continuing education courses just for fun. What kind of continuing education classes would you like to take?

   _____

   _____

10. Become active in groups and attend their meetings. Name two organizations in which you would like to participate.

    _____

There are countless others, but these are relatively painless and easily achievable. Keep your mind active. Exercise it by exposing it to new ideas and ways of viewing the world. This will keep you forever young.

ASSESS YOURSELF 11-3

Staying Emotionally Well: A Four-Phase Process

1. Constructing—Write a description of yourself; your values, goals, good qualities, and weaknesses.

   _____

   _____

   _____

2. Accepting—After you have completed the first step, acknowledge that this is who you really are. Accept this reality.

   _____

   _____

   _____

3. Undertaking—Decide what you want to improve. Examine who you are and decide which aspects of your self or your life you want to improve. Develop a plan, similar to the behavioral contract on p. 403 of this chapter, to help you implement these changes.

   _____

   _____

   _____

4. Reframing—Construct, based on the results of your undertakings, a new picture of yourself, complete with the new emotions that accompany it.

   _____

   _____

   _____

Use this model periodically as an assessment tool to help you keep in touch with your perception of yourself and the direction of your life.

Adapted from Payne, W. & Hahn, D. (1992). *Understanding your health*. St. Louis: Mosby.

Behavior Change Contract

There are many types of behavior change contracts. They all attempt to help you structure your plans for changing your behavior. The key is to start with a manageable goal that you have a good chance of achieving. Following are the steps in creating a behavior change contract:

1. Desired goal

_____

2. Intermediary objectives

_____

3. Potential barriers
   - Predisposing factors (knowledge, attitudes, and values)

   _____

   - Enabling factors (financial and other resources)

   _____

   - Reinforcing factors (support system)

   _____

4. Strategies for overcoming barriers

_____

5. Timeline for goal and objectives

_____

6. Reward

_____

7. Signature

_____

8. Witness

Each of these steps is conducted as follows:

1. Start with a manageable goal, one you are likely to accomplish.

2. Break this goal into smaller segments. List each segment in the sequence it occurs.

3. Identify potential barriers to success. Predisposing factors are your knowledge, attitudes, and values about your goal that may impede your progress. Enabling factors are those resources, from financial to geographical, that help you to reach your goal. Reinforcing factors support your change, motivating you to maintain your change.

4. If you have identified any of these barriers, you must develop a plan to overcome them.

5. Give yourself a reasonable amount of time to reach your objectives and ultimate goal.

6. Reward yourself for success. Put aside some money or make plans to do something special when you reach your goal. This will nudge you along toward success.

7. Sign the document to make a commitment.

8. Have a friend or loved one witness your commitment. This reinforces your sense of commitment.

Sample contract

1. Goal: To run three times a week to reduce stress.

2. Intermediate objectives:

    a. Read a book on how to begin a running program

    b. Buy running shoes.

    c. Learn how to stretch

    d. Walk 1 mile, 3x/week, at a 12-minute/mile pace.

    e. Walk 2 miles, 3x/week, at a 12-minute/mile pace.

    f. Begin to run 1 mile, 3x/week, at a 9-minute/mile pace.

3. Barriers:
Predisposing:

    a. Knowledge—don't know anything about running.

    b. Attitudes—none.

    c. Values—none.

Enabling: have the necessary resources, a high-school track across the street from my house.

Reinforcing: family is very unathletic but dad wants to lose some weight.

4. Overcoming barriers:

    a. Knowledge—borrow the necessary books from the library.

    b. Lack of family support—have dad run with me.

5. Timeline:

    1 month—Read material, develop plan for stretching, begin walking program.

    2 months—walking program going strong, ready to start running.

    3 months—running 1 mile, 3x/week, 9 minute/mile pace.

III

Stress: A Developmental Perspective

This, the third and final part of the text, examines stress through a developmental perspective rather than addressing specific stressors in separate chapters as most textbooks do. Each chapter in Part 3 will use Erikson's[9] eight stages of development (see the table on p. 407) as a rough guide to the tasks normally associated with psychosocial development. In a sense, one might consider Erickson's tasks to be potential stressors, because mastery of them involves trial and error, over a variety of situations and experiences.

As we mature as individuals, we bring with us all of the skills and competencies established by working through the tasks associated with previous stages of life. A key to understanding the significance of these tasks as far as stress is concerned is realizing that mastery of or failure to master these tasks feeds into our perceived ability to cope with future tasks. The potential stressors of future stages are therefore appraised in light of the strength of our perceived past coping resources.

We could illustrate this by examining how two different 9-year-old little leaguers of similar physical maturation and pitching ability respond to the pressures associated with having to pitch in the final inning of a game in which the score is tied. Successful mastery of the tasks associated with previous developmental stages come into play when each little leaguer appraises the situation.

The first player, Joel, feels intense stress. He feels that he cannot get the job done. He is worried about his pitching ability, the crowd, and what his teammates think about him. Joel has little self-confidence in general. His self-esteem is lacking, and for the most part he has not experienced much success in other facets of his life. He has lead a sheltered life with few opportunities to test his abilities.

The second pitcher, Will, views this as the ultimate challenge. He wants to be here, in a position to win the game. He is supremely confident in his ability to do his job, get the ball over the plate, and let his teammates make the outs. He does not feel that the win or loss is entirely up to him. Will has high levels of self-esteem and self-confidence. He has succeeded at many other things in the past, ranging from other sports to Cub Scouts and academics. He has been given ample opportunities by his parents to test his abilities under a variety of situations.

Later in life, unless each boy changes and grows, experiencing new things that help them master tasks still unresolved from earlier stages, their perceived ability to cope with potential stressors will be handicapped. Joel, for instance, may be stressed more easily than Will simply because his lack of self-esteem negatively affects his perceived ability to cope with potential stressors.

In addition to one's overall level of stress, our ability to cope also is developmental in nature. As we experience success with various coping strategies, we begin to have faith that they can help us deal with potential stressors. We begin to trust our own ability to handle things, and our over-all perceived ability to cope is enhanced. We feel confident in our ability to cope regardless of the type of potential stressor and the factors that surround it. Children's coping is more problem-specific, but as they grow, they adopt a more generic emotion-focused basis of coping that builds on their earlier problem-focused approach.[1]

This final part of the book examines the key tasks associated with normal development and the potential for stress that is associated with them. It also examines common experiences that we go through in mastering the developmental tasks.

Each chapter in this part ends with an illustration of how the four *R*s of coping—rethink, reduce, relax, and release—could be used in managing stressors associated with the specific developmental stage.

TABLE 12.1

Erikson's States of Development

Age	State of Development	Task/Area of Resolution	Concepts/Basic Attitudes
Birth–18 months	Infancy	Trust versus mistrust	Ability to trust others and a sense of one's own trustworthiness; a sense of hope **or** Withdrawal and estrangement
18 months–3 years	Early childhood	Autonomy versus shame and doubt	Self-control without loss of self-esteem; ability to cooperate and to express oneself **or** Compulsive self-restraint or compliance; defiance, willfulness
3–5 years	Late childhood	Initiative versus guilt	Realistic sense of purpose; some ability to evaluate one's own behavior **or** Self-denial and self-restriction
6–12 years	School age	Industry versus inferiority	Realization of competence, perseverance **or** Feeling that one will never be "any good," withdrawal from school and peers
12–20 years	Adolescence	Identity versus role diffusion	Coherent sense of self; plans to actualize one's abilities **or** Feelings of confusion, indecisiveness, possibly antisocial behavior
18–25 years	Young adulthood	Intimacy versus isolation	Capacity for love as mutual devotion; commitment to work and relationships **or** Impersonal relationships, prejudice
25–65 years	Adulthood	Generativity versus stagnation	Creativity, productivity, concern for others **or** Self-indulgence, impoverishment of self
65 years to death	Old age	Integrity versus despair	Acceptance of the worth and uniqueness of one's life **or** Sense of loss, contempt for others

From Erikson, E.H. (1963). *Childhood and Society*. (2nd ed.). New York: WW Norton.

Childhood Stress

CHAPTER OBJECTIVES

- Understand the developmental nature of personality and stress.

- Describe how coping with stress also is a developmental process.

- Describe Erikson's major developmental tasks for the first four stages of life (childhood, early childhood, late childhood, school age).

- Understand how the developmental tasks could be perceived as either stressors or challenges.

- Understand how the four *R*s of coping could be employed to reduce childhood stress.

Infancy: Birth to 18 Months

The major task of infancy according to Erikson[9] is the development of a sense of trust. That trust wins out over mistrust is central to the continued healthy psychological development in all of us.

Infancy is a time of total dependence. Infants rely entirely on caregivers (Fig. 12-1), whether they are mothers, fathers, other family members, or legal guardians, to provide for all of their survival needs. One can easily see that our ability to trust in the world as a safe place and in ourselves as deserving, worthwhile beings, is entirely dependent on others.

Infants have basic needs that must be met. They must be fed when they are hungry, changed when they are wet or soiled, and hugged when they need nurturance. To develop as healthy humans, they must have these needs met in a timely, caring fashion. If they are met consistently and with positive nurturing emotions, they begin to believe that the world is safe. They also begin to believe that others are worthy of their trust.

However, if these basic needs are not met consistently and correctly, infants do not fully develop this sense of trust in themselves and others. If a healthy sense of trust is not fully established by the end of the infant stage, then it will not be brought to the next level of growth, when it is time to move on to other developmental tasks. The infant will become emotionally disadvantaged—handicapped by the lack of development of the foundation of our personality: a sense of trust (see Stress in Our World box on p. 411).

Fig. 12-1 Children need nurturing from parents or a caregiver to develop a sense of trust in the world and themselves.

STRESS IN OUR WORLD

Nina

Nina is a "crack baby." Her mother, Jacqueline, was a prostitute addicted to crack. Jacqueline did not even know she was pregnant until nearly the end of her first trimester. She would have had an abortion except that by being pregnant she qualified for a special assistance program that entitled her to a better apartment and other benefits. Shortly after Nina's birth, Jacqueline left town and left no forwarding address.

Nina lived in a hospital intensive-care ward for the first 6 months of her life. Because of her low birth weight and crack addiction, she had to live in a special incubator-like crib, connected to various life-monitoring devices. One of 20 addicted, abandoned babies in the hospital, Nina received little extra attention. The nurses, physicians, hospital staff, and volunteers were wonderful— caring, attentive, and nurturing. Their time was limited, however, and most of Nina's waking hours were spent alone in her crib.

Nina was placed in a foster home after 6 months in intensive care. Her initial foster parents returned her after 6 months because she was unresponsive to their care; she never smiled, and she spent many hours crying in her crib.

Nina was adopted at 13 months by a loving woman and her husband who had three other children just like her. They understood the special needs of a child like Nina and were prepared for the extra effort that went into caring for a baby like her. After 3 months, Nina was beginning to respond to her new parents. They were even able to get a smile out of her, something she had never done in 16 months.

How could a start like Nina's influence someone's sense of trust in themselves and the world?

Early Childhood: 18 to 36 Months

In early childhood our major task is the development of a sense of autonomy. In this stage, children begin to develop self-control and self-esteem. They learn how to express themselves and begin to cooperate with others. Empowered by their newfound mobility, they walk about, exploring their environment and mastering simple tasks that give them some degree of control and freedom.

Children need freedom within limits to explore their world and begin to act independently (Fig. 12-2). However, with this mobility and freedom, they are at risk for varying types of danger ranging from assorted bumps and bruises to poisoning, abduction, and sexual abuse. Although scary, a key to understanding the early childhood stage is that, without being given a certain amount of freedom to take chances and explore their world, children run the risk of not developing the self-esteem and self-control that will be critical in progressing through childhood and life.

KEY
TO UNDERSTANDING

To develop self-esteem and self-control requires mobility and freedom to suffer from life's bumps and bruises.

Fig. 12-2 Children are naturally inquisitive. Left alone in a protected environment, they will explore endlessly.

For most children and their parents, the early childhood years are pure delight. Many landmark events take place during this period that allow the child to master the key developmental tasks of this stage.

Toilet training is an example of an event where mastery is essential for completion of the developmental tasks of this stage and for building a solid foundation of stress-coping skills. The toilet training process is empowering for children. Along with mastery of bowel control, children gain a measure of self-control, self-esteem, and independence. The wearing of "big boy pants" is how one friend's son refers to his newfound freedom from diapers.

If toilet training is not rushed and handled skillfully by parents or caregivers, children develop a sense of pride in accomplishing something very important to them. However, if toilet training is rushed, or if children are punished or criticized too harshly for the inevitable mistakes and soiled underpants, they can pass through this stage without developing those all-important feelings of self-control and self-esteem.[18]

Learning to walk is another major developmental task that usually occurs during the early childhood stage. Children who are helped but are not overly protected from the bumps and falls that are a normal part of learning to walk develop a sense of control over their environment. They learn about the literal "bumps and bruises" that are a normal part of achieving anything meaningful in life. Children that are overly protected and shielded from even the most minor stumble have a harder time becoming autonomous.

When children can walk around independently, they need to be able to explore their environment (see Stress in Our World box below). They need to have both hazard-free environments and the freedom to explore them autonomously to develop a sense of self-control and self-esteem. Children whose exploratory play is restricted or unsafe face a retarded development of autonomy. They may even become fearful of being alone or taking a risk at later points in their lives.

The skills that are essential for the development of autonomy are critical for coping with stress. If someone grows up without fully developing a sense of autonomy, this will affect his or her perceived ability to cope with potential stressors and the stress appraisal process in general.

STRESS IN OUR WORLD

Rob

Rob is like most 2 year olds; he tries to get into everything. He explores his world through his senses, examining even a simple blade of grass with the utmost curiosity. He looks it over carefully, smelling it as he rubs it between his fingers, crushing it. He listens to the sounds the grass makes as he rips it out of the ground and ultimately tastes a sample, chewing it thoughtfully. He is also beginning to do things for himself, like picking out his favorite socks and trying to put them on himself. This takes forever, and he usually winds up with two different colored socks, half on his feet, one inside out.

Rob would like to explore and do a lot more things by himself, but his grandmother is a bit overprotective. She is responsible for Rob from 7:00 AM until dinner time because both his mom and dad work full-time. Rob's dad often is not home until after 7:30 PM and does not get a lot of time to see his son. Rob's mom is a bit frazzled after getting home from work, carpooling his older brother around, making dinner, and cleaning up.

Both Rob's mom and grandmother are fearful people. They want to protect Rob from most of life's hard knocks. Whenever Rob does get a chance to play outside, his mom or grandmother is right behind him, watching out that he does not bump into anything or fall down. They will not let him on the jungle gym at the playground because they believe it is too advanced for him.

Rob would like to help his mom cook but she is afraid he might hurt himself. He tried to help her make brownies one day, but he tipped over the bowl of batter trying to get a finger-full and it fell on his toe, injuring it slightly.

Rob is trying to gain some mastery over his environment but is finding it slow going with the restrictions being placed on his autonomy.

Late Childhood: 3 to 5 Years

In this stage of development, children continue to gain freedom and begin to be exposed to a variety of people and experiences as they further explore their environment. The major task for this stage is the development of initiative. Children's actions become more purposeful as they evaluate their competencies and initiate behaviors that are consistent with this. Their likes and dislikes are more firmly established, and their behavior reinforces this.

Children at this age struggle with an overwhelming preoccupation with self as they are increasingly exposed to other youngsters in a variety of play and social situations. They are put in situations with other youngsters that force them to share, take turns, and accommodate others. This socialization is a vital and necessary developmental step that prepares children for the kinds of social interactions necessary for future success in school. This is also a potentially stressful time as children need to satisfy their own **egocentric** needs while learning to live in an increasingly social world.

Caregivers also can be stretched to their limits as they try to provide opportunities for children to grow. Children need the freedom and space to initiate and take responsibility for their behavior, but they also must have some limits imposed on their freedom. Children who are given unlimited freedom may be stressed simply because they do not have the cognitive or moral development to act rationally and logically when given too many choices. They are either unable to decide or make choices that are based on unrealistic perceptions or expectations. However, children who are not allowed to make independent decisions and initiate actions will never develop the ability to act purposefully and learn to trust their abilities. They also will never experience the pain of failure, which can be a great learning tool. Children need to learn that some choices are bad choices and that all of our desires are not always achievable.

Children learn to tolerate frustration by being put into situations that require them to decide, act, and sometimes experience defeat or failure. If these failures are handled properly, caregivers can turn them into valuable learning experiences that promote initiative and self-confidence through a realistic perception of abilities (see Stress in Our World box on p. 415).

egocentric
feeling as if you and your needs are central focus of everything and everyone

School Age: 6 to 12 Years

The main developmental task of the childhood stress stage is the development of **industry**; children develop their perseverance and sense of competence and they learn about the necessity of working hard and sticking to the things they initiate.

industry
a sense of industriousness or productivity

STRESS IN OUR WORLD

Kuanray

Kuanray is a fairly well-adjusted 5 year old. He has his days but for the most part he is a happy, well-rounded boy. Kuanray's parents have been careful in structuring his world so that he has gotten an equal blend of freedom and protection from life's little bumps. They have been careful about setting up rigid rules and punishments for Kuanray, saving those for the things that really matter, like his personal safety or courtesy and behavior toward others. For the most part, Kuanray is allowed to pick his own clothes and decide who he would like to play with or what TV shows

he wants to watch. He cannot do things like cross the street or go to the schoolyard by himself.

Kuanray's parents have tried to expose him to athletics and sports so he can develop a sense of mastery of his physical world. He got a bicycle with training wheels for his birthday this year, and by the end of the summer Kuanray was able to ride without training wheels. Kuanray is proud of this accomplishment and has the autonomy to ride his bicycle around the parking lot of his parents' condominium during the day and early evening.

Kuanray's social skills have been improving. His parents have been taking him

to the playground every day so he can play in the sand and climb on the equipment. They try to sit in the background and let Kuanray get used to playing with the other children, at times sharing his sand toys with the others. There have been some difficulties for Kuanray as he learned that not all of the other kids share or treat his toys with respect. He has even gotten into some arguments and near fights as he has defended his rights to either play by himself or with his own toys.

It has not been easy but Kuanray has learned a lot of valuable lessons by being allowed to suffer some frustrations and setbacks.

Beginning school greatly affects children's lives (Fig. 12-3). Their day changes dramatically. For those whose lives were relatively unstructured up until this point, the school day can represent a radical departure. For others with preschool or organized recreation experience that introduced them to structure at an earlier age, the school day is not such a new and unusual experience.

School also puts children in a situation where their main caregivers and disciplinarians are no longer their parents or someone else with whom they are familiar. Some children have never been separated from their primary caregiver before this point and have a difficult time getting used to school. Other children who have either been in preschool or day care may not find the adjustment that difficult. In fact, children who have interacted

Fig. 12-3 An elementary school classroom should be a place of cooperation and working together toward goals.

with other children and adults may look forward to the new experience of kindergarten and elementary school.

Besides the generic differences between school and home or child-care facilities, school introduces children into a formalized world of learning with strict rules, regulations, and work expectations. This is a time when formal competition begins. Children begin to compete for grades, athletic prowess, social connectedness, and attention. It is a competition that, in our society, never ends. How students cope with this is contingent on their success in working through the previous developmental stages and the strategies they learned in the past.

Besides the competition, students begin to be categorized. For many, this categorization has already begun in preschool. In many communities, readiness for kindergarten is assessed by preschool teachers and formal entrance tests. Rarely is this labeling overt, but students learn (often from older siblings) what the A, B, or C group stands for or what reading level 1, 2, or 3 means. Although they are intended to help students progress at their own pace and work in an appropriate class level, labels sometimes follow students through a school system providing for easy future categorization.

Schools provide an unlimited opportunity for the development of industry and competence. They provide a rich milieu of academic, social, athletic, and recreational experiences in which students grow. Children can test their limits: they can experience a variety of things that challenge them and push them on to higher levels. In a safe, protected environment, children can grow not just as students but into competent, whole persons.

School as a Stressor

Schools, as we have hinted, can also be potentially stressful. Eliss[5] identified the following sources of school stress: overemphasis on academic acceleration, competition, evaluation, and test-based accountability. Eliss cautions that the phrase *overemphasize* is important. Although academic acceleration is important and beneficial for some students, not all students are able to deal with being pushed academically. Emphasizing competition and test-based evaluation over self-improvement can add extra stress to the school experience.

Helms and Gable[13] found that interactions with both teachers and peers are also often sources of stress for children. Communicating with, and being acknowledged and accepted by teachers and peers is especially stressful for students with low academic self-concept. Perceiving oneself as being not smart or below average could be a source of stress, especially in overly competitive school settings. Other researchers, Murphy and Della-Cortes,[19] also found that pressure to conform and live up to the expectations of others at school is a significant source of stress for children.

Children who are unprepared for school can suffer their first bitter taste of failure. If they have not successfully worked their way through the previous developmental issues, the effects can be devastating and long-lasting. Some of these students fall behind early and never catch up. Many just give up on school, feeling they cannot succeed. See the box on p. 418 for an overview of the Head Start program.

Many children find the social aspects of school very stressful. They are not ready to share anything, let alone the spotlight, with others. Some children may be seen as different and thus become the target of taunts and abuse. In time, most find their niche and a good friend or two who will help them through.

Coping With Childhood Stressors: The Four *R*s

Helping children learn to cope with stress is not always easy. Even under the best circumstances, children can have a short attention span, can be irrational, and can test your patience. Parents, caregivers, and friends must approach children with compassion, kindness, tolerance, and above

Head Start

The Head Start program was one of the many social programs initiated by President Lyndon Johnson in the 1960s. The program was part of a broader package of measures proposed as an investment against criminal activity and welfare dependency. Its original purpose was to give disadvantaged children a head start in school, helping to ensure their success and keep them from getting behind, dropping out, and falling into a cycle of poverty, welfare, and crime. The original Head Start program was intended to be an 8-week summer educational experience that included provisions for a healthy breakfast and lunch, as well as opportunities for academic and social enrichment.[11]

Head Start attracted much media attention in 1993 when President Clinton announced that he was in favor of vastly increasing the scope and funding of the program.[10] President Clinton expanded the program to reach 721,268 disadvantaged preschoolers, increasing its budget to $2.8 billion. The time-frame was also extended from 8 weeks in the summer to 5 days a week for a full year. The scope of services was expanded to include medical and social services to participants and their families.

Critics of the program claim that evaluations of Head Start have questioned its effectiveness in meeting its educational, medical, and social goals. Studies have shown that gains made by participants in reading and math were lost later in their educational careers.[15] A study by the United States Department of Health and Human Services (USDHHS) showed that the actual success rates for various health goals for participants were much lower than claimed: 43% of the participants were immunized, social services were extended to 23% of participant families, and 54% of the children received medical services. All three percentages were well below stated goals for the program.

After 30 years of operation, Head Start has also failed to affect the problems of high drop-out rates, crime, and juvenile delinquency that it was originally intended to improve. Many critics contend that the money and resources could be better spent elsewhere. Some believe that the money should be spent on a voucher system that would allow disadvantaged children to attend the schools of their choice.[14] Others believe that the short-term benefits demonstrated by Head Start may be provided more effectively through various private and community initiatives or through comprehensive child-development centers, family service centers, and day-care service providers.[3]

Supporters believe that total involvement and investment in the program will help achieve its goals. They argue that that with increased funding the program can be improved by hiring better teachers, lengthening the school day, and extending the program to 2 years.[3,16]

In 1993, USDHHS Secretary Donna Shalala's Advisory Committee on Head Start Quality called for refocusing and reenergizing the Head Start program to upgrade the quality of existing services.[22]

all, a sense of humor. If one thing does not work, try something else. If you try something and it seems like the wrong time to bring it up, don't. Come back at a later time and try again. Do not become a source of stress or get stressed yourself while trying to help children learn how to cope with their stress.

The best way for parents and caregivers to teach children to cope with stress using the four *R*s is to use a combination approach that includes: 1) being a role model, 2) talking to children about stress and the five *R*s coping strategies, and 3) helping them try some of the activities for themselves.

Being a role model involves commitment to understanding and action. Reading this and other books will provide caregivers with the basic information and tools they need to put the four *R*s into practice in their own homes. Adults with poor stress-management skills will not be good role models for their children. Parents and caregivers can get additional help from professionals associated with local colleges, community mental health and social work agencies, local health departments, and religious organizations.

Beyond knowing what to do, parents and caregivers must act. They must begin to use the four *R*s themselves. This will create a home atmosphere and a lifestyle for their families that is stress-resistant. Children growing up in this kind of environment learn by observation and role modeling of appropriate stress-management activities.

The next component of teaching children to cope with stress using the four *R*s is to talk to them at appropriate times. Talking to them in advance of potentially stressful situations helps them learn about anticipatory stress. It can help prevent stress from occurring. Talking to them when they are stressed helps them cope with current stressors and can also reduce the likelihood of the same problem occurring in the future.

Most parents and caregivers know their child's limits and can anticipate conditions and situations that will become stressful if they are allowed to occur. Adults need to discuss these situations clearly and simply with their children before they are allowed to occur.

For instance, imagine 9-year-old Denise coming home from school one day with a flyer announcing the school's after-school recreation programs. She tells her mother that she wants to sign up for three different activities that her friends are taking part in: girl's basketball, chorus, and cheerleading. Even though she could do all three (they meet at different times, are affordable, and transportation and child-care arrangements could be arranged), her mother knows that this would stretch both of them to their limits and would be too stressful. This is the time when Denise's mom needs to sit down with her and discuss why signing up for all three is not a good idea. Issues such as time management, overextending oneself, and so on could be discussed.

Talking to children about coping with stressors that could not be prevented is also important. Children, like adults, can learn from their mistakes. When children and adults make bad decisions that result in stress, they can sit down and discuss how to cope with the problem and prevent it from happening again.

For example, imagine that Denise was allowed to sign up for all three activities and it did result in her and her mom being stressed. Her mother could use the opportunity to talk to Denise about what is going on, how she is feeling, and how to use the four *R*s to cope with her stress. Her mother could help Denise pick one or two coping strategies that would work for her. Finally, the two could discuss how they could use this information to reduce the chances of this type of stress occurring again.

The third component in teaching children about four *R*s is helping them try some of the strategies (see the box below). Children learn by doing, especially when parents help facilitate conditions for learning. Rather than do it for them, parents and caregivers need to set things up, obtain materials, give simple, clear instructions, and let children do the activity themselves.

Using the example of Denise again, imagine that she and her mom decided that one way Denise could cope with her stress was to listen to relaxation tapes of soothing music or natural sounds. Denise's mom could acquire the tape (purchase or borrow from the library), read the instructions, and set up the ideal environment for listening (quiet room, minimal distractions). All Denise would have to do is agree to listen. If she liked the activity and it seemed to help, her mom could teach her how to set things up for herself in the future.

Helping Children Cope With Stress Using the Four *R*s

Rethink—Help children examine the way they view potential stressors and their lives. Sometimes changing their illogical or irrational thoughts about things can defuse stress.

Reduce—Help children cut back on the sheer volume of stressors in their lives. Help them manage their time and level of commitment.

Relax—Help children learn to relax. Provide opportunities for quiet, relaxing activities.

Release—Help children release the byproducts of stress and tension. Teach them safe, healthy outlets for stress and tension.

Putting it all together—Work with children in building healthy, holistic lifestyles. Be a role model for high-level functioning in the intellectual, emotional, physical, spiritual, social, and environmental domains.

Rethink

The first line of defense, logical thinking, or reasoning, is a skill that begins to develop at around ages 11 to 12 years, during what developmental psychologist Jean Piaget[20] described as the formal operational period of development. Before this age, children are very self-centered and have a difficult time subjugating their own wants, even in the face of good, objective information to the contrary.

Even though this is true, parents can set the stage for helping children think logically by being role models. Setting an example by using rational thinking and behavior is very important, even if children at this time are not developmentally ready to apply this in their own lives. Parents can share their decision-making processes with their children, helping them understand the thoughts and emotions that underlie these decisions. In some cases, common family issues (not major problems) that affect the whole family can be addressed together. Choosing the family car, deciding where to go on vacation, and deciding about moves, job changes, and a host of other issues that affect the whole family can be discussed as a group with an emphasis on how the way we think about these things affects whether or not they are sources of stress for us.

Using a formal model like Ellis and Harper's[4] ABCDE (see Chapter 6) technique can be helpful in sorting through issues as a group and modeling rational thinking. Having periodic family meetings is a good way to set aside time to examine family issues in a logical, thoughtful way.

Family meetings can also serve as an emotional safety valve where members can vent their frustrations in an acceptable way. Sometimes referred to as "bitch ins," these meetings can give family members a chance to let off steam and prevent emotions from building up and becoming overwhelming. From this experience, children can learn that it is okay to have these emotions and that there are acceptable ways to deal with them. They also can learn that the positive expression of emotions can be helpful in their relationships.

Reduce

Children need help managing their time and commitments. The challenge is to give them increasingly more autonomy and decision-making ability while protecting them from making too many bad decisions that will hurt them.

Children have very little conception of time, their physical limits, and how far they can stretch themselves. If allowed total autonomy, they will stay up late every night, try to attend every function, sign up for all the clubs and teams, and generally point themselves in too many directions. Parents and caregivers must set limits to help children grow by experiencing a variety of things without exhausting themselves (Fig. 12-4).

Initially, parents need to use their time management skills to assess their children's schedules and pare down the sheer number of their children's commitments when necessary. As children move from early childhood through the school years, they can be taught time-management skills themselves. Parents can give children options by limiting the number of different activities their children can be involved in while letting their children make the decisions without excess parental pressure regarding which things they will get involved in.

Decision-making skills are important. Parents can teach kids to put the pros and cons of various decisions down on paper and use a formal decision-making model to help them. Parents can also help children make decisions that are consistent with their values by assisting children in values clarification.

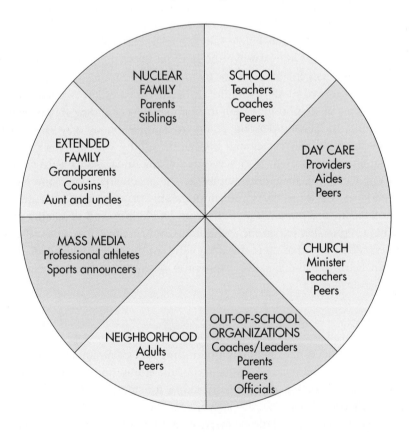

Fig. 12-4 Kids too can sometimes feel as if they are being pulled in too many different directions at the same time.

Parents can teach their children to be assertive and be able to say no when they truly do not want to do or to commit to something. Parents can actually role-play with their children to help them become assertive and thus reduce stress by not overcommitting themselves in the first place.

Parents and caregivers can also reduce the amount of stressors in their children's lives by not rushing them. In his classic work more than 20 years ago, psychologist David Elkind[6] coined the term the *hurried child* to describe children who are rushed through their childhood. These children were pushed too hard too fast and not allowed to "be children."

They are pushed into competitive academic, athletic, and social situations before they are developmentally ready for them. Elkind[6] warns that children need a lot of unstructured time for free, noncompetitive play. Often, in an attempt to help their children get a head start on the competition, parents push them too much, rush them into experiences too soon, and generally hurry them along through their childhood. In many cases, children are pushed because of their parent's own narcissistic desires to make their children into geniuses.[8]

Elkind[7] warns that children are not merely adults in small bodies, capable of understanding and handling the pressures and responsibilities that adults can. He argues that children do need to be protected from some of the pressures and decisions adults face. Exposing children to all of the facts concerning the tough issues that adults face, like money problems, divorce, and other relationship issues, is not always the best way to handle these problems. Exposing children to these things does not toughen them up and prepare them for the hard road that life often presents. Children are not developmentally ready for this exposure. They often blame themselves and worry over problems that they have no responsibility for or control over. In a sense, this shielding and protecting is a reduce strategy because it cuts back on the volume of potential stressors children face.

Relax

Children, like adults, need time to relax and play. They need to slow down and be allowed to be children, to be able to relax, and to have less structure in their activities. Children need both passive and active forms of relaxation. They need to develop a variety of ways to relax that work for them. A key to understanding this is to realize that as adults, we cannot assume that what works for us will work for them.

Passive relaxation can be interwoven into family practices, ranging from quiet time without television or video games to activities like walking in the woods or cultivating a garden. Children can also be introduced to

KEY
TO UNDERSTANDING

Hurried children are
ones who are not
allowed to be children.

KEY
TO UNDERSTANDING

Adults cannot assume
that what works for
them in reducing
stress will work for
their children.

deep breathing and visualization activities. An activity like the calming response[21] is quick and easy for children to learn.

Children like music. Adults can help them choose some soothing music to listen to when they are tense. We need to help them understand the differences between soothing, calming sounds and melodies and the pounding, hard driving rock and roll that may be enjoyable to listen to but not soothing in a stress-management sense. Care must be taken in not putting down their tastes in music while introducing them to relaxing sounds.

We can also teach them, from an early age, the virtues of active, physical forms of relaxation. The healing touch of physical contact is something that can be introduced at birth and continue through a child's life. Children crave physical comforting through hugging, stroking, rocking, and sometimes just holding hands. Children also love back rubs and massage. Incorporating this touching into one's daily contact with children can be very stress reducing and serve as a model for coping that can carry over into adulthood.

Stretching is something that is very natural for children. Teaching them a few basic stretches and how to incorporate these into their relaxation habits is very easy. Have them start each day with a couple of minutes of stretching.

Release

In spite of the effectiveness of passive relaxation techniques, most children prefer more vigorous ways to get rid of tension and stress. They need time to run and play and stretch and climb, and caregivers need to provide daily outlets for these things. Children can really test their competence, autonomy, self-confidence, and self-esteem through vigorous physical activities.

Children enjoy motion. Whether it is riding a bicycle, skateboard, or roller blades, or swinging on a rope or a swing, children like to be in motion. They get a chance to rid their bodies of any pent-up anger, frustration, or muscular tension of the day. They also scream and yell with delight, purging tension and emotions along the way if we let them. As caregivers, we need to encourage these physical pursuits while providing supervision and safety (Fig. 12-5).

Unintentional childhood injuries are a major source of discomfort, disability, and death in the United States. Children need to be protected against falls, a risk that is highest in ages birth to 5 years, and then declines throughout childhood.[24] The nature of falls changes from the early years (birth to 5) when they are associated with falling off household things (beds, changing tables) over things (furniture, rugs), down things (stairs) and out of things (windows) to falling off recreational equipment and products (playground equipment, trees, bicycles, or roller skates) in the school age years (6 to 12).[24]

Fig. 12-5 Caregivers must be sure that play areas are safe, clean, and well protected. Play area groundcover must be sufficiently soft to cushion the impact of jumps and falls off equipment.

Children can be protected against fall-related injuries by ensuring that during early childhood safety restraints are used, such as rails on beds and changing tables, gates to cordon off unsafe areas, and bars on upper level windows, decks, and porches to block exits. Fall-related injuries in older children can be reduced by providing adequate cushioning in all play areas (mats for tumbling, sand or mulch for playgrounds) and requiring that protective gear be used (helmets, knee and elbow pads) when bicycling and roller-skating.[24]

We also can teach children how to cycle and skate safely. We can insist that children take precautions and use safety equipment, and we can teach them how to do safety checks on their equipment. Once empowered, we must learn how to leave them alone and experience life, scraping a few knees and taking some knocks along the way.

It is important that children have multiple opportunities and types of situations for experiencing physical release. Many children only experience this joy when involved in formal activities like a gymnastics class or Little League. Experiencing the joy of physical release is something that can be done informally, inexpensively, and by oneself at almost any time. Children need to know that this is something they can control.

Another form of release is self-pleasuring. Self-pleasuring types of touch, including fondling and masturbation, are a normal part of childhood development. They serve many functions ranging from stress reduction to learning about one's body to understanding one's sexual response.[18] Although sensual in nature, this form of pleasuring does not have the same sexual connotations for children as it does for adults.[18]

There is no scientific evidence that masturbation poses any physical or psychological harm. Religious arguments against masturbation have no scientific basis but need to be respected on sacred importance. Overreaction to masturbation and fondling can send negative sexual messages to a child and set the stage for shame, guilt, and secrecy, all of which can negatively affect sexual pleasure in adulthood.[2]

Caregivers can set guidelines about self-pleasuring concerning such issues as privacy and hygiene. It is important for children to realize that, although self-pleasuring is normal and acceptable, they need to respect the rights of others who may not be comfortable with their public displays of such behavior.

Putting It All Together

As we have seen, childhood is a potentially stressful time. Children need to have high levels of wellness to ensure that they have a solid foundation on which to build their ability to cope with life's stressors.

Physical Wellness

High levels of physical wellness are essential. Childrens' bodies need to function well to provide the energy needed to cope with daily stressors. They also need strong immune systems to help them resist the myriad infectious agents they will be exposed to in school and to bounce back quickly from illness. (See the box on p. 427.)

Parents and caregivers need to be sure that their children have received their immunizations for the preventable childhood diseases, such as polio, measles, mumps, and so on. Most school districts require that all children have their recommended immunizations before attending school. School districts usually have set policies concerning how to deal with children who do not comply. Local or state health departments are required to provide immunization services for all childhood diseases. Children may attend federally funded public health clinics to obtain these immunizations free of charge or at a very low cost.

Children also need to have their hearing and vision checked at least once a year. Routine hearing and vision screening tests can help identify those students who may need corrective glasses or hearing aids. Impaired vision or hearing is a major contributing factor to underachievement in the classroom. Children who cannot hear well or see the chalkboard or screen are at a disadvantage in the classroom. Most schools have programs of free vision and hearing screening or have referrals available directing students to free or low-cost providers for such services.

Proper nutrition, which involves eating well from the five food groups, is essential. Parents and caregivers can pressure schools to provide adequate meals and healthful policies on snacks and other food items available from the cafeteria.

Although most states have some provision for physical education, many schools are lax in ensuring that students receive ample opportunity to develop fitness. Schools that emphasize competitive athletics over lifetime fitness education could be pressured to adopt curricular changes that promote fitness in addition to sports.

Children with AIDS

Of all the sad stories associated with the AIDS epidemic, the saddest concern children. By the end of 1993, more than 5000 cases of AIDS had been reported in children under the age of 13.[24] Many of these children are able to lead normal lives. They can attend school, go out and play with their friends, and try to maintain their normal activities while they wage a life-and-death battle to try to fight the AIDS virus.

These children are practically incapable of transmitting the virus to anyone else. In fact, they are much more likely to become infected with germs their classmates and playmates spread around casually by coughing and sneezing. For the AIDS victim, these and other common environmental germs can be deadly.

Despite this, there are those who persecute these children, creating tremendous stress for them and generally making their lives miserable. These are the parents of other children, school board members, teachers, and principals who bar the door and deny access to children with AIDS. They mistrust public health authorities who try to downplay the likelihood of nonsexual disease transmission. They want certainty and to be told that their children are 100% safe. Fueled by misinformation and fear, they want absolute answers to a disease that is still shrouded by many unanswered questions.

In communities across the country, these otherwise rational, good-thinking people are acting like zealots, afraid that this disease is going to claim their children. They are denying a whole generation of children with HIV/AIDS the right to live out their remaining days with some degree of decency and normalcy.

How would you feel if your child had a classmate with AIDS?

Caregivers must take responsibility in participating in family fitness activities. Families need to exercise at least three times a week for a minimum of 30 minutes to help children incorporate fitness into their lifestyles. Parents can use fitness activities (walking, bicycling, swimming, running, and hiking) as opportunities for modeling behavior and for helping their children develop healthy coping styles.

Emotional Wellness

Emotional well-being for children is also critical. Parents need to understand the developmental tasks that children face during these childhood years and provide support for them as they work through these issues. Parents need to read and learn about what the normal developmental tasks of each stage are so they can provide their children with opportunities for experiential learning.

Parents also need to know where to get help when problems arise and should feel comfortable asking for help if they cannot handle a problem by themselves. They need to know what community resources exist to help them with their children and how to get access to them. Most towns, either through their health departments, hospitals, mental health agencies, school continuing education programming, or local colleges, offer parenting courses or programs. Most community health programs are provided free or at a very minimal cost. In most cases, grants or scholarships are available for parents and caregivers who cannot afford to pay for courses.

Caregivers also need to be good role models for stress management. Coping with emotional distress in positive ways without relying on alcohol or drugs or excessive emotional outbursts is a key to the development of these skills in children. The Yeager Group[23] developed a list of ways parents can help their children cope with stress (see the box on p. 429).

Parents who lack this ability need to get professional help to ensure that this style of inappropriate coping is not passed on to their children. Local health departments, community mental health centers, public hospitals, and colleges and universities are excellent sources of help. Most of these providers offer mental health services on a sliding scale based on one's ability to pay.

Children need to be taught to recognize their emotions and to learn that it is normal and acceptable to feel sad, hurt, angry, or any of a range of emotions. Children also need to know that it is okay to share these emotions and ask for help in dealing with them; there are people who care about them and can help.

Intellectual Wellness

Intellectual well-being is an area that most parents assume is being handled by the schools. However, many school teachers do not have the knowledge or time to help individual students improve their learning skills.

KEY
TO UNDERSTANDING

Coping with emotions in a positive way is a key to developing such skills in your children.

KEY
TO UNDERSTANDING

Children need to know that it is okay to have negative emotions and to share them with others and ask for help.

Things Parents Can Do To Teach Their Children About Stress

- Give your children permission to relax.

- Remember that children are not short adults, so learning these skills should not be a "graded project."

- Share with your child the value of using relaxation to be creative. This will flow easier if you believe it and practice it yourself.

- Allow for "solo" time for your child during the day.

- Occasionally monitor your child's daily schedule.

- Parental guilt is a needless worry.

- Try not to judge your family to another's (e.g., The Cleavers).

- Validate the feelings of fears and exultations of your child.

- Use age-appropriate metaphors in teaching skills to younger children.

- Pace your child's breathing in assisting in the calming after a crisis.

- Be a good role-model.

Modified from Yaeger, et al. (1990). *Managing parental stress in the eighties.*

Parents can help children improve their study skills by assisting them in organizing their work, setting aside adequate study time, breaking assignments down into manageable parts, learning how to outline, and so on.

Introducing students to technology also can help. Working with students in performing computerized information searches and using word processing and educational CD ROM programs are some examples of technological skills that can improve cognitive abilities.

Social Wellness

Social well-being is a very important part of children's coping with stress. Children need friends and playmates and to have free time for unstructured play. Because school imposes such a high degree of structure on children, caregivers have to be careful that children do not become overburdened with highly structured play activities outside of school.

This period in a child's life has great potential for the development of strong social networks if caregivers take the time and care necessary for helping children make friends and get involved in social activities. Children have a variety of settings ranging from formal and informal play groups to organizations such as scouts, boys' and girls' clubs, and Little League in which to become involved and to cultivate social networks.

Parents and caregivers serve as role models for their children's socialization skills. Parents who themselves have strong social networks can assist their children in making friends and getting involved in group activities. Children can also benefit from the warmth and support of an extended family if aunts, uncles, cousins, and grandparents are nearby. Once our primary social network, the extended family is but a memory for many Americans because of our mobility and frequent job changes.

Children, like adults, pay a price for inclusion in social groups and networks. A key to understanding this is Lazarus and Folkman's[17] findings that the benefits we derive from social networks are offset by the stress they can create. Socialization takes time and energy. Inclusion in groups often requires that we subjugate a little of our individuality and control. We must decide whether the benefits we derive from inclusion in certain social relationships offsets and exceeds the costs we have to pay.

Each child, like every adult, has a limit to the extent of social networking they can handle. Children need to understand that it is acceptable to not get involved if they do not want to. They also need to hear that it is

STRESS IN OUR WORLD

Greg

Greg is a nice kid: he has very highly developed social skills, he is polite in front of adults, has excellent manners, and is very verbal. Unfortunately, he is also a nervous wreck at times. His life is so scheduled that he needs his own appointment book to keep track of his commitments. Besides attending the local public school's fourth grade, Greg is enrolled in his Temple's Hebrew classes on Tuesday night. He is on the local club soccer team. They practice on Fridays and have games on Sundays, but sometimes they schedule extra practices or have make-up games on other nights. He also plays Little League baseball, with games on varying evenings and on Saturdays. Sometimes Little League practices are scheduled on Tuesday or Friday night. When this happens, Greg finds himself scurrying from one place to the other, gulping a burger down in between. He is also in Cub Scouts. They meet on Wednesday evenings at 7:00 PM. If he has a game on Wednesdays, he will sometimes leave early or rush right out immediately following the game.

He drives his Little League coach nuts. During team meetings and games, Greg is constantly fidgeting. He seems unfocused and unable to sit still and pay attention to instructions. It seems like he wants to do two things at once. As a pitcher, the coach constantly has to remind him to slow down, get control, and pitch. Greg rushes through everything.

Do you know someone like Greg?

fine if they want to be alone and not play or not get involved with others all the time. Finally, they need to understand that sometimes this is not always crystal clear, and they may not know why they want or do not want to be involved with some people and some activities. They need to be able to trust their intuition and be supported in this.

Spiritual Wellness

Children are very spiritual beings. They are curious about life and death, religion and God, nature and the universe. Although they may not be able to understand all of the subtleties of life, death, and the universe, they are open to ideas and experiences. Feeling connected to something beyond themselves is something that can be nourished and encouraged. Unfortunately, children can also become quite dogmatic and overzealous about spiritual issues because they are so malleable.

Children can benefit from activities that nourish their spirituality. Whether it is inclusion in formal religious activities or involvement with animal husbandry and protection, environmental protection, feeding or housing the hungry and homeless, or any of a variety of activities that reach out beyond themselves, these types of activities are enriching and renewing (Fig. 12-6). They also serve as possible avenues of social networking.

Summary

This chapter explores the childhood years from birth through 12 years of age, examining these years using Erikson's model to explain the tasks normally associated with growth and development. These tasks range from the development of trust to the feelings of competence and industry.

Fig. 12-6 Getting involved in environmental projects can provide a sense of connectedness to something greater than oneself.

Erikson's tasks in themselves can be perceived as either stressors or challenges, depending on how children perceive them. The developmental tasks are presented in this chapter as not only building blocks for healthy psychosocial development, but also for coping with stress. If children successfully work through the stages and master the developmental tasks, they develop a sense of competence. This competence feeds into their perceived ability to cope with life's stresses. As you recall, our belief in our ability to cope with situations factors into our perception of them as either stressors or challenges. If children do not master the tasks associated with their particular stage of development, they will have a harder time coping with life's stresses because their repertoire of psychosocial skills and strengths will be limited or incomplete. They may be unable to use certain coping strategies because they lack adequate development of certain personality constructs, such as self-esteem.

The chapter ends by applying the four *R*s of coping to the stressors associated with this stage, demonstrating how specific coping strategies rethink, reduce, relax, and release can be used to manage childhood stress. It also describes how a high level of wellness in general is protective against some of the stressors of this stage.

Student Study Questions

1. List and describe Erikson's eight stages of development.
2. Describe the major developmental task for each of Erickson's stages.
3. Explain how these tasks could be perceived as either stressors or challenges.
4. Describe the developmental nature of coping with stress.
5. How does failure to master a developmental task relate to stress?
6. Describe how the first *R*, reorganize relates to coping with childhood stress.
7. Describe three reduce strategies for coping with childhood stress.
8. Explain two rethink strategies that could be used in coping with childhood stress.
9. Describe three relax strategies that could be used in coping with childhood stress.
10. Describe how rethink can be employed with irrational children.
11. Describe the role of safety is using the release strategy with children.

References

1. Compas, B., Banez, G.A., Makcarne, V., & Worsham, N. (1991). Perceived control and coping with stress: a developmental perspective, *Journal of Social Issues, 47*(4), pp 23-35.

2. Crooks, R., & Baur, C. (1993). *Our sexuality*. Redwood City, CA: Benjamin Cummings/Addison Wesley.

3. Edelman, M.W., & Hood, J. (1993). Should the Head Start program be expanded? *CQ Researcher, 3*, p 305.

4. Ellis, A., & Harper, R. (1975). *A guide to rational living*. North Hollywood: Melvin Powers.

5. Eliss, M. (1988). Schools as a source of stress to children: an analysis of causal and administrative influences. *Journal of School Psychology, 27* (1), 383-407.

6. Elkind, D. (1981). *The hurried child*. Reading, MA: Addison Wesley.

7. Elkind, D. (1987). The child yesterday, today, and tomorrow. *Young Children, 4*, 6-11.

8. Elkind, D. (1991). Instrumental narcissism and parents. *Bulletin of the Meminger Clinic, 55* (3), 299-307.

9. Erikson, E. (1978). *Childhood and society* (2nd ed.). New York: WW Norton.

10. Friedman, D. (1993). A reputation that outruns reality. *US News & World Report, 114*, pp 63-65.

11. Glazer, S. (1993). Head Start. *CQ Researcher, 3*, pp 291-299.

12. Hales, D. (1993). *An invitation to health*. Redwood City, CA: Benjamin Cummings/Addison Wesley.

13. Helms, B.J., & Gable, R.K. (1990). Assessing and dealing with school-related stress in grades 3-12 students. Paper presented at Annual Meeting of the American Educational Research Association, Boston, April 1990.

14. Hood, J. (1993). Caveat emptor: the Head Start scam. *USA Today, 121*, pp 74-79.

15. Kantrowitz, B. (1992). A Head Start does not last. *Newsweek, 119*, pp 44-46.

16. Kramer, M. (1993). Getting smart about Head Start. *Time, 141*, p 43.

17. Lazarus, R., & Folkman, S. (1985). *Stress appraisal and coping*. New York: Springer.

18. Masters, V., Johnson, W., & Kolodny, R.(1992). *Human sexuality* (4th ed.). New York: Harper Collins.

19. Murphy, L., & Della-Cortes, S. (1990). School related stress and the special child. *Special Parent/Special Child, 6* (1), pp 15-20.

20. Piaget, J. (1950). *The psychology of intelligence*. London: Rutledge & Kegan Paul.

21. Segal, J. (1986). *Calming response*. (Cassette Tape). Philadelphia.

22. Shalala, D.E. (1993). Shalala calls for refocusing, re-energizing the Head Start program. *Children Today, 22*, pp 4-6.

23. Yaeger Group. (1990). *Managing parental stress in the eighties*. Boston: Yaeger Group.

24. USDHHS, (1993). *Position Papers from the Third National Injury Control Conference*. Washington, DC: US Government Printing Office.

ASSESS YOURSELF 12-1

Unfinished Sentences

Completing unfinished sentences is a helpful way to assess the effect of something that occurred in the past and continues to exert an influence on the way you feel today. Unfinished sentences provide some structure for helping you think about the past. They also allow you to begin to control some of the emotions associated with the events captured in the sentences.

Instructions:

Finish each of the sentences using the blank lines provided. Use additional paper if necessary. Restrict your memories to your childhood years (0-12).

1. The three major stressors of my childhood were _____
   _____

2. One particularly stressful event for me was _____
   _____

3. I still feel guilty about _____
   _____

4. I am still angry about _____
   _____

5. I am still confused about _____
   _____

6. The pace of my childhood life was _____
   _____

7. As a child, I coped with stress by _____
   _____

8. My parent(s)/guardian coped with stress by _____
   _____

9. My parent(s)/guardian told me the following about coping with stress: _____
   _____

Unfinished Sentences (cont'd)

10. As far as stress is concerned, my brothers and sisters _____

    _____

11. The person who coped with stress most effectively was _____

    _____

12. The greatest strength I had as a kid for dealing with stress was _____

    _____

13. The most positive coping experience I remember was _____

    _____

Adolescent Stress

CHAPTER OBJECTIVES

- Describe Erikson's major developmental task of adolescence.
- Describe the influence of puberty on adolescent stress.
- Differentiate between reproductive readiness and psychosocial readiness.
- Describe the influence of school on adolescent stress.
- Describe how to cope with adolescent stress using the four Rs model.

Adolescence Defined

adolescence

a psychosocial term used to define the early teen to middle teenage years

KEY
TO UNDERSTANDING

Adolescents need to keep focused on goals while trying out new things and taking chances.

The major task associated with **adolescence** is the development of self-identity.[13] Finding out who we are and accepting this while at the same time feeling pulled in a hundred different directions can be very stressful for the average adolescent. It can also be a time of great excitement and joy as we literally move from childhood to adulthood. During adolescence, our bodies and our minds change and grow. We outgrow not only our old clothes but often our old ideas and sometimes our old friends as we struggle to come to grips with who we are and where we are going.

Usually we only hear about the problems and the failures of adolescents. We hear about teenage drug and alcohol use, AIDS, teen pregnancy, satanic cults, and defiant behavior. Movies are made that glorify adolescent rebelliousness and juvenile delinquency.

As Michael Carrera,[5] a respected adolescent sexuality expert, notes, most teenagers go through this time without major problems and emerge into young adulthood strong, competent, and whole. They try new things and expose themselves to new experiences to foster this discovery (Fig. 13-1). The key is keeping focused on goals and dreams while trying new things and taking chances.

Fig. 13-1 Exciting sports like rock climbing can help build self-esteem and confidence through mastery of a very demanding task.

Finding out who we are, and taking action to further this new-found self is complicated by others trying to pull us in several different directions. Family and friends, media images, and societal traditions all put pressure on us to conform to sets of rules and roles that may not be the right ones for us. Confusion and tension can arise as we work through our own feelings and desires and the pressures from others.

On top of all of this, our bodies are changing from children to adults. Puberty is a time of profound physiological change as our bodies mature. We become reproductively ready with fully adult genitalia, reproductive systems, and hormones coursing through our bloodstreams, sending messages to our brains that we have arrived sexually. For most of us, psychosocial readiness for sexual activity with another person takes a while to catch up to reproductive readiness. We become caught in a state of confusion as our bodies send our minds messages about sex that we may not be ready to handle.

This chapter examines some of the types of experiences that confront adolescents and discuss how, for some, these are perceived as stressors, while for others, they are challenges.

Puberty

One of the overwhelming influences on the adolescent stage of development is puberty. While adolescence is a psychosocial term denoting a period of years, **puberty** is the biological term used to describe myriad physiological events that characterize this stage of life (Fig. 13-2).

By the end of puberty our bodies reach a stage of reproductive readiness as mentioned previously. **Reproductive readiness** is a physiological state that has two major components: mature reproductive anatomy and hormonally influenced sexual desire.

At this time, our sex organs are fully developed and capable of being used for procreation as well as recreation. Not only are such anatomical parts as penises and vaginas fully mature and capable of responding to sexual desire, ovaries and testes are fully able to produce viable ova and sperm, respectively. In nature's eyes, we are able and ready to propagate the species.

We are given a boost by nature in that our gonads (testes and ovaries), which have long been silent, now begin to produce hormones that stimulate sexual desire. Androgens, primarily testosterone, stimulate sexual receptor centers in our brains that trigger feelings of sexual desire. All of the cold showers in the world will not quell this sexual desire and interest because to a certain extent it is being fueled by hormones that are circulating in our bloodstreams.

We are ready in a purely physiological sense to do what nature intended us to do: mate with others of our species. In our culture, however, many if not most adolescents are not ready in a psychosocial sense to carry out

puberty
a biological term used to describe a variety of bodily changes associated with physical maturation from childhood to adulthood

reproductive readiness
the state of complete adult physiological maturation

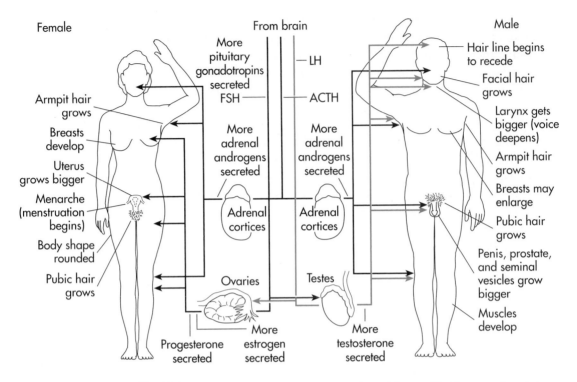

Fig. 13-2 Puberty is a time of many changes when adolescents' bodies move from being childlike to fully adult.

these sexual urges with others. This is a key to understanding adolescent sexuality. This creates a disparity between being ready for intercourse in a physiological sense but not being ready in terms of social skills and emotional readiness.

There are many factors that contribute to this disparity between physiological and psychosocial readiness. First and foremost is the fact that most parents view adolescent intercourse with disfavor. Masters, Johnson, and Kolodny[26] assert that most American parents, regardless of their own sexual lifestyles, tend to be less permissive about their children's premarital sexual activity.

American culture in general views adolescent sexual intercourse as a problem that will only lead to negative outcomes (unintended pregnancy, sexually transmitted disease including AIDS, sexual abuse, and others). Other cultures however view this matter entirely differently and celebrate this time in a young person's sexual life. Indeed, in some Pacific island cultures, adolescent sexual behavior is encouraged.

Another reason contributing to the lack of psychosocial readiness during adolescence is what Martinson[25] refers to as retarded sexual development. He claims that American youth are not retarded in terms of sexual behavior, citing statistics concerning the average age of first intercourse, but rather in terms of their knowledge, attitudes, and values. Martinson feels this is due to having grown up in a culture that fosters sexual naiveté and guilt. These findings cut across all racial and ethnic groups. American society is very homogeneous in terms of how it views adolescent sexuality. The negative effects of such experience, he claims, inhibits children's quest for knowledge and positive affirmation of a normal part of their development.[25]

Martinson[25] argues further that it is this combination of retarded sexual development and the early onset of teenage intercourse that is the root of this country's high adolescent pregnancy rate. In a multinational study of teenage pregnancy and sexuality, American youth scored the lowest of five similar industrialized nations (Canada, Sweden, France, England, and the Netherlands) on tests of knowledge and attitudes concerning sexuality and conception.[9] Lack of basic information concerning sexual anatomy and physiology, contraception, and pregnancy were cited among other findings as indicators of what international experts would consider arrested sexual development.

Many cultural factors contribute to this slowed sexual development among American youth. Foremost among them is our conservative sexual history. American culture evolved from our devoutly religious, puritanical forefathers and mothers who escaped persecution for their views in Europe by coming to this country. American patriarchal culture has always placed a great emphasis on the family and historically has viewed sex as something that occurs only within the context of a marriage with the primary function being procreation.[26]

There is a strong legacy of this sexual conservation both institutionalized formally in law and enforced informally through cultural taboos and parenting styles. The United States is still a country where sex education is not universally taught in school and even when it is, it is more a course in reproductive anatomy than anything else.[15] In most states the practice of noncoital sexual acts is illegal.[26]

Besides having a moral tradition that prohibits adolescent sexual education and experimentation, the United States, like many industrialized societies, prolongs adolescent and young adult dependency. To succeed, adolescents in most cases need to further their education. For most of them, this means remaining indebted to their parents and pursuing additional training and education while either living at home or remaining financially obligated to their parents. In a sense, what this does is delay the transition from childhood to adulthood and with it, adult privileges such as sexual experimentation. In other cultures, adolescents are encouraged to begin to separate from their parents, and in many cultures this separation is institutionalized in a formal rite of passage (see the box on p. 442).

Rites of Passage[26]

Marriage rituals usually contain sexual motifs, as do adolescent rituals or initiation rites that remove individuals from the status of child and place them in the status category closer to adulthood. For girls, these ceremonies often occur near the time of the first menstruation and sometimes signify that they are ready to begin sexual activity or to be married. For boys, there is rarely any physical marker for these rites, but in many societies the penis is physically altered during initiation.

Schlegel and Barry (1979, 1980) examined the distribution of adolescent ceremonies in a sample of 192 societies. They found that 80 societies had no adolescent initiation ceremonies; 17 had ceremonies for boys only, 39 had rites for girls only, and 46 had ceremonies for both genders. Larger societies with intensive agriculture and more complex forms of social organization tend not to have ceremonies for either gender. The fact that American culture lacks a formal initiation rite for boys and girls thus agrees with the finds of Schlegel and Barry. Schlegel and Barry (1980) see initiation ceremonies as ritualized communication about gender status and suggest that such rituals occur in societies where gender plays an important role in the organization of social life.

Most food-collecting societies have a division of labor based on gender: men hunt and women gather. Thirty-four of the 45 food-collecting societies in the Schlegel and Barry sample perform initiation ceremonies for at least one gender. Two have rites for boys only, 20 have rites for girls only, and 12 perform rituals for both genders. The content of the rituals in the 32 societies that have rites for girls indicates that most of these societies ceremonially emphasize a girl's first menstrual flow. Schlegel and Barry suggest two reasons for this concern. First, many of these societies believe that if a man or his weapons come into contact with menstrual blood his ability to hunt will be destroyed. The initiation ceremony notifies the new woman that she must observe menstrual taboos to avoid risking the band's meat supply. Another possibility is that these rather small groups ritually celebrate evidence that a woman is capable of bearing children, which ensures the continued existence of the group.

From Masters, W.H., Johnson, V.E., & Kolodny, R.C. (1992). *Human sexuality* (4th ed.). New York: Harper Collins.

Differences in Sexual Development

The preceding section is not presented as an indictment of American sexual mores. America is not a Polynesia island where the tribe will look after adolescents who marry and bear children when they are in their teens. Unlike Polynesia, American society expects that at some point, married couples will be self-sufficient. This requires having a job, living apart from one's family, and caring for oneself. Although parents and family sometimes help, the prospect of teenage marriage and parenthood (see Stress in Our World box on p. 443) is fraught with problems and, consequently, most teen marriages in the United States fail.[26]

STRESS IN OUR WORLD

Nelson and Sandra

Nelson and Sandra are two 17-year-old high school seniors who decided to get married and have their baby, Rebecca. Sandra's parents let them live rent free in the apartment over their garage until Sandra and Nelson finish high school.

Although they are getting help from Sandra's parents (in addition to providing the apartment, Sandra's mom watches Rebecca on the evenings when Sandra attends night school), they have been having a hard time adjusting to the demands of marriage and parenting and have discussed separation.

Both are in their last year of high school. Nelson is attending during the day full time while Sandra watches Rebecca. Sandra attends night school while either Nelson or Sandra's mom provides childcare. Both Nelson and Sandra work 15 to 20 hours a week on weekends and whenever they can fit the hours in during the week.

During a typical day Nelson and Sandra get up about 6:00 AM (Rebecca is an early riser and wakes up at about 5:30, amusing herself in her crib until her parents get up). Nelson showers and gets ready for school (he has to leave at 7:00) while Sandra feeds, washes, and changes Rebecca. Sandra takes Rebecca for a ride at 7:30 as she drives her mom and dad to their jobs. Sandra then takes the family car and goes to the supermarket, library, pediatrician, or wherever else she needs to go that morning. Around mid-morning, she puts Rebecca down for a nap and tries to do her homework from the previous evening. After she does her homework, she cleans her apartment and her mom's house and tries to catch up on the laundry.

Sometimes, when Rebecca will not take her nap, is sick, or just needs more attention, Sandra gets very tense because all of her work gets backed up and she worries if she can get it all done. On other days she feels so tired that she just lies down with Rebecca and rests, even though she knows this will put her behind in her work. On days when Rebecca has been up all night with a cold or some other problem or has woken up several times during the evening, Sandra is exhausted and stumbles through her day like a zombie.

When Nelson is done with school, he stops home for 30 minutes to change into his work clothes (he pumps gas and is a mechanic-in-training at a local gas station), grab a quick bite, and bicycles over to work. He works until 7:00 PM when Sandra has to leave for night school. He bathes Rebecca, reads her a story or plays with her for a while, and puts her to bed. Nelson then sits down, has dinner, and begins his homework, working until Sandra gets home from night school.

After a long day Sandra and Nelson try to relax—watch a little television or rent a movie—but they often find themselves falling asleep in front of the TV only to be woken up by Rebecca in the middle of the night when the routine starts anew.

Of the estimated 11 million unmarried, adolescent women who are having intercourse, about 1 million become pregnant each year. Of these 1 million pregnancies, about 50% result in live births, 40% are aborted, and the remaining 10% end in stillbirth or spontaneous abortion.[27]

Teenage mothers are more likely to have pregnancy-related problems than women who delay childbearing until they are in their twenties. Adolescents are more likely to experience toxemia, hemorrhaging, and miscarriages than women who delay pregnancy. Additionally, teens are more likely to have low birthweight babies, and the infant mortality rate among teen mothers is 200% higher than that of older women.[27]

Most of the negative health outcomes associated with teenage pregnancy used to be believed to be caused by biological immaturity—women having children before their bodies were physiologically ready for them. However, recent evidence has disproved this myth. Teenagers, given adequate prenatal care and proper nutrition, have as good as or better pregnancy outcomes than older women.[32]

Unfortunately obtaining adequate prenatal health care is the exception rather than the norm for most teenage women who get pregnant. Many are not under the care of a physician, midwife, or other health-care provider for all three trimesters. Because of this, routine testing and screening is delayed or is not done. When routine trimester examinations are not performed, close monitoring of the size, weight, positioning, and vital signs of the fetus is impossible. Additionally, these visits provide an opportunity for the health-care provider to assess the health of the pregnant teen and talk about such critical issues as nutrition, substance use, plans for delaying future pregnancies, and adequately caring for the child if the pregnancy is to be carried to full term.

Approximately 95% of unmarried teenage mothers keep their babies (see Stress in Our World box on p. 445).[31] These mothers face a harder future than their peers who delay bearing children until they are older and married. Although it is illegal to keep pregnant teens out of public school, most (approximately 80%) drop out and do not return.[35] Because of the twin burdens of the lack of a high school degree and the need for childcare, these teens earn less, have a lower level of schooling, work in blue collar professions, and in general have a lower standard of living than their peers who delay marriage and childbirth.[26]

Other teenage women who become pregnant decide that they are not ready to become mothers and decide to use foster care or give their babies up for adoption. Foster care is designed to provide temporary help for mothers or parents who feel they cannot take care of their child now but will be able to do it in the near future. Under foster care, mothers still have legal rights to their children, have formal visitation privileges, and are

STRESS IN OUR WORLD

Tamika

Tamika is 17. She and her 2-year-old baby, Ayesha, her two brothers, her mother, and her grandmother live in a large public housing project and receive welfare assistance. She is a high school drop out who has tried to go back to school to get her high school equivalency degree but has not been able to attend class consistently.

Tamika got pregnant at age 14. Although she had not planned it, she did not take any precautions to prevent it.

"I hadn't planned to get pregnant but deep-down inside, I really wanted a baby," recalls Tamika. "I had been messing around with Bobby (Ayesha's father) for about a year, not using any birth control, and kind of expected something to happen. All my friends were doing the same thing and some were already pregnant. Trisha already had a baby at 14 and we all kinda envied her. I wanted one for myself, something I could call my own, that no one could take away from me."

Tamika paused to pick up Aeysha, who had started to cry. "It was hard at first," she continued. "My mother got all mad and stuff, and threatened to throw me out of the house if I didn't get an abortion. I told her I didn't want to get an abortion, that I wanted to have my baby. I even did leave for a while, moved in with my aunt, but after a couple of weeks my mom let me move back home. I think she was mad because the same thing happened to her when she was 18 and she was always talking to me about not making the same mistakes as she did and how hard life had been for her as a teenage mother, and all that stuff."

Tamika put Aeysha back in her crib and continued talking about the past couple of years. "I wasn't like the other girls who get pregnant and try to hide it. I told my mom I wanted to treat my baby right. I knew all about the kind of things that could hurt my baby and went to the clinic when I found out I was pregnant. I had a real hard time being pregnant. I got sick almost every day the first couple of months and couldn't eat anything but cereal and milk shakes. It got better about half-way through and I could eat mostly anything. I stopped going to school after 7 months because I was getting tired all the time, and anyway school was boring. The other kids were okay about me being pregnant and all, but I just didn't really care about it anymore. All I could think about was my baby.

"After I had Aeysha, things got real tough. There was hardly any room for anybody to move around with Aeysha's crib in the middle of the living room. My brothers were always getting mad about Aeysha waking them up, and I would yell at them about coming in late and waking her up. I was always tired. My grandma helped a lot. She always seemed to be there to talk to my mom or brothers when everybody got on me or when I needed someone to watch Aeysha. I don't think I could have made it through the first year without her. My mom's been okay but she's got enough to do, working two jobs and trying to keep my brothers in school."

When asked about what her life is like now and what she wants to do, Tamika

cont'd

STRESS IN OUR WORLD (CONT'D)

Tamika (cont'd)

looked out the window and sighed, "Sometimes, I think I'll go crazy, cooped up in this little three-room apartment with nowhere to go and nothing to do but watch my baby. I miss running the streets with my friends and Bobby doesn't come around much anymore. I've been seeing this other boy, Harold,

for about a year. I thought I was pregnant again last year but it turned out I was just late with my period. After that I got on the pill 'cause I don't want another baby yet. I love Aeysha and am glad I have her, but I know now how tough it is to do anything with a baby to take care of.

"Sometimes I can't see any way out of here. I'm

thinking of getting into this program they have for kids with babies. You can get your high school degree and learn something like how to use a word processor. They watch your baby while you're there and even help you find a job when you graduate. Someday, I'd like a place of my own to raise my kid in."

actively involved with their children. Women who give their children up for adoption permanently give over their rights as parents to another person or family.

Both foster care and adoption offer viable options for teenage mothers who are unable to cope with the demands of being a parent. Although each offers an option for coping with an unintended pregnancy, deciding on which course of action to take, carrying the pregnancy to term, and following through with giving the baby up can be extremely stressful.

Many pregnant teens choose to terminate their pregnancies rather than carry them to full term. The majority of American women who have abortions are young. More than 400,000 abortions are performed on women between the ages of 11 and 19 years. This accounts for almost 30% of all abortions performed in America.[26]

About 90% of all abortions are performed at or before 12 weeks of gestation. Early abortion (first trimester) is a relatively safe medical procedure. There are minor risks associated with perforation of the uterus, hemorrhaging, or partial removal of the uterine contents. Studies show that early abortions have little effect on subsequent fertility.[8] Despite the overall healthy prognosis of abortion, being pregnant, deciding what to do about it, and having an abortion are potentially very stressful (see Stress in Our World box on p. 447).

STRESS IN OUR WORLD

Carol Ann

Carol Ann is a 29-year-old mother of one. A successful small business owner, Carol Ann has been married to John for about 5 years.

"I grew up in a small town and was raised to think that abortion was killing. I remember seeing those films about little babies being tossed out in the garbage after their mothers had abortions and all the posters and billboards with pictures of fully-developed fetuses and the headings, 'Abortion is murder.' I couldn't imagine anyone ever having an abortion. But then I got pregnant and began to look at things differently.

"I was away at college. I was a 19-year-old sophomore and had been having sex with my boyfriend, Michael, for about 6 months. We were using my diaphragm for birth control and to tell you the truth, I don't ever remember having any problems with it. I used it faithfully, every time we had sex.

"I couldn't believe I was pregnant. I was frantic. I must have had five pregnancy tests until I finally accepted the fact. I couldn't have this baby! I cried for 2 days and Michael was very supportive. Sometimes we cried together as we tried to figure out what to do. I knew in my heart that I wasn't ready to be a mother. I still had 3 years of school left, plus graduate school. I had no job, no time, and psychologically I just couldn't handle it.

"I went to a local abortion clinic. The people were great. They gave me all of the information I needed, took tests, and assured me that because I was only 3 weeks' pregnant, the procedure they would use was safe and relatively simple. I scheduled an appointment and went home to think about it.

"It wasn't an easy decision but I felt I had no acceptable choice. I didn't think I could handle being pregnant, having a baby, and then giving it up for adoption or foster care. I didn't want to tell my parents. I wasn't sure how they'd react and I didn't want to jeopardize my being away at school. They were paying for everything and I wasn't sure if they'd force me to drop out.

"I guess the hardest thing for me was rationalizing what I considered the taking of a human life. I'm not a pacifist and I do believe in capital punishment so I guess I don't feel that human life is sacred under all conditions. This was different though because I wasn't talking about soldiers or prisoners, I was talking about a life that I carried within me. I always believed that life began at conception. I vividly recall from biology how quickly embryos turn into fetuses and how the various body parts and systems grow. I really felt that I was carrying a life within me and that regardless of the stage of my pregnancy, or viability of life outside of the womb, aborting this fetus was taking a life.

"I felt sad for a few weeks after my abortion. I wished I hadn't gotten pregnant and didn't have to make the decision, but sometimes life doesn't always work out the way you plan. I got over it gradually, finished out the school year, and graduated on time 2 years later. Now, 10 years later as the mother of a 2-year-old girl, I know I never could have been the mom I am now. Although it was a tough decision, it was the right one for me at the time.

There are other negative health consequences associated with adolescent intercourse. Adolescents have higher STD rates of syphilis, gonorrhea, and pelvic inflammatory disease (PID) than do all other age groups. Adolescents also engage in sexual behavior that puts them at high risk for contracting HIV/AIDS.[22] Although the number of AIDS cases in the 13- to 19-year-old age bracket is small (872 through June 1992), many more young people are thought to be infected with HIV. Additionally, since one in five of all reported AIDS cases is between 20 and 29 years old (44,495 cases through June 1992), and the incubation period for AIDS can last several years, many, if not most of these people acquired AIDS as teenagers.[6]

Puberty, Sex, and Stress

It is easy to see why emerging sexuality can be a major source of stress for adolescents. You can see why many people try to protect adolescents from this stress by trying to avoid the subject all together. Maybe, they believe, if we do not talk about it, it will disappear. Many people try to rechannel adolescent sexual energy into other pursuits. They feel that maybe if teens can be kept busy enough with schoolwork, sports, cultural pursuits, and so on it will take their minds off of sex.

Unfortunately, as you have seen, this is not the case. There are strong biological and, some would argue, evolutionary forces at work, driving adolescent sexual interest. To deny that it exists, or to rechannel it without first acknowledging it and explaining its power to young people, is unethical and doomed to fail.

A key to understanding this is to realize that it is one thing for a society to honestly admit to young people that sex is a powerful force in their young lives and that as a culture America would prefer adolescents to redirect that sexual energy into other pursuits. It is another to deny its existence, hoping it will go away, or to trivialize sexual urges.

The mixed messages that adolescents receive about sex can be a real source of stress. On the one hand, their bodies are telling them, "yes, yes, yes," but adult society is telling them, "no, no, no." Media (music stars, television, movies, and so on) that target adolescents are telling them that it is okay and a normal part of teenage rebelliousness to give into, even glorify, their sexual urges, yet parents want them to wait and to fear the power of sex.

This is a hard dilemma to work through. For American adolescents, many of whom lack the most rudimentary sexual knowledge, working through these conflicting sexual messages and urges can be overwhelmingly stressful (see Stress in Our World boxes on pp. 449 and 450).

KEY
TO UNDERSTANDING

In handling adolescent sexuality, honestly admit its power and explain why it is important to channel it appropriately.

STRESS IN OUR WORLD

Growing Up Straight: Rich

Rich's adolescence was a fairly typical experience for a straight, lower-middle-class young man growing up in urban America. Rich's parents were high school graduates who worked in factories as piece-work tailors. Although both were very loving and attentive parents, neither was skilled at communicating openly with Rich about the issues he would face as an adolescent. Indeed, neither really even knew about the key developmental aspects of puberty and adolescence, let alone felt comfortable talking to Rich about these issues. Consequently, Rich's adolescence was a kind of hit-or-miss, trial-and-error experience for which he was totally unprepared.

Rich remembers experiencing such things as wet dreams, his first "true" love, masturbation, his first ejaculation, and how puzzled he was trying to figure out how male and female genitalia came together during sexual intercourse.

Rich desperately wanted to talk to his mom or dad about some of the things he was going through but remembers feeling as if these issues were off limits. He remembers agonizing about his first ejaculation, feeling as if perhaps he had injured himself or something had gone wrong because all of a sudden there was this liquid coming out of the end of his penis. Rich had to be content with asking his friends or older brother about some of these things. He knew, based on the responses he received, that some of the answers were not the right ones.

Rich also remembers reading the "girlie" magazines his father hid in the closet, hoping to get some answers from them. He somehow knew that these also were not what he was looking for.

The only comforting thing about Rich's adolescence was that he did not go through it alone. Mike, his closest friend, had almost the exact experience. He also felt normal because he was "just one of the guys." They were all going through the same things and shared a common attraction to girls and other "manly" pursuits like football, basketball, and fixing cars.

It took Rich several years to get over much of the guilt and shame he had about his sexual feelings and behavior during adolescence. He spent the better part of his twenties looking for the answers to unresolved questions and issues from his adolescence.

School and Stress

The primary task of adolescence is coming to terms with ourselves—finding out who we really are and what we really care about. It is a time of struggling with being an individual, while at the same time wanting to fit in and be what society wants us to be.

STRESS IN OUR WORLD

Growing Up Gay: Paul

Paul, like Rich, had a very tumultuous adolescence. The only son of immigrant parents, Paul had very little preparation for what he would experience during puberty and adolescence. As adults, Paul and Rich met and discussed the similarities they had going through this troubling time. Paul also had a tremendous amount of curiosity and guilt about his sexual desires. A Roman Catholic, Paul recited the Hail Mary after each time he masturbated. He had a tremendous amount of confusion about his and his church's feelings about this practice but felt he had no

one with whom to discuss it. He remembers trying to talk to a priest about it once during confession, but instead of being helped he was told to ignore his sexual feelings and pray when he had the urge to masturbate.

Paul had one major difference from Rich. Paul was gay. Going through adolescence as a gay young man was doubly troubling for Paul. Paul just never felt any sexual desire toward females. Inside, however, Paul was very troubled because he really felt attracted to some of the boys in his class. Paul agonized all through his adolescence as he tried to figure out who or what he really was. He tried dating girls but

found it unsatisfactory. Paul kind of suspected he was gay but did not want to admit it and felt that he had no one he could confide in and explore this facet of himself.

Paul coped with this by suppressing most of his sexual feelings. He would deny that they existed and spend most of his time immersed in studying. It was not until he entered college as a pre-med student that he finally gave in to his urges to explore this part of himself. Later, when he was in medical school and involved in a steady relationship with another male student, Paul was able to work through some of the pain and confusion of his adolescence.

KEY
TO UNDERSTANDING

School is a powerful potential stressor because it is where academic, athletic, and social pressure to succeed all come to a head.

The arena in which this task is played out to a great extent is school. As adolescents move through middle school, high school, and into college, the classroom, school yard, and playing fields can exert a great deal of pressure.

Developing a sense of self and self-esteem occurs in part by succeeding in our interests, pursuits, and friendships. Feeling competent is a big part of developing self-esteem. An adolescent's competence is severely tested in school. A key to understanding the influence of school as a potential stressor is to view it as the place where academic, social, and athletic pressures to succeed come to a head.

Prior success in elementary school makes the transition to middle and high school easier because it represents a continuation of prior patterns of success. Despite past success, however, the adolescent school experience is vastly different.

The physical environment of most middle and high schools is a major change from elementary school. Physically, everything is larger. Buildings, hallways, and even the chairs and desks are larger and thus intimidating. The mix of students is different. Typically, students from several elementary schools funnel into a middle school. Likewise, a community may have more than one middle school channeling students to a high school. Some high schools are regional, serving students from different communities. Essentially, these differences make middle and high schools mixing pots, where there are a lot of new, unfamiliar faces and places to get used to. Instead of the familiar, intimate elementary school serving kids from the neighborhood that they have been around since they began school, adolescents are in unfamiliar territory with unfamiliar faces.

Couple this with the dramatic physiological changes occurring in adolescent bodies as a result of puberty and on top of this add the social, academic, and athletic pressures that are part of school, and you get a sense of how much potential stress adolescents face (Fig. 13-3).

Social Pressures

Adolescence is a time of developing a personal style. Most adolescents go through several styles as they explore new and different interests, friends, and experiences, adding to those parts of their personalities that have evolved up to this point.

Fig. 13-3 School: the idyllic haven for adolescents or the epicenter of their stress?

Peers and the media compete with parents in exerting a tremendous amount of pressure on adolescents as they attempt to develop their own unique personal styles. Pop culture idols and media that pander to them start the trends that set broad standards for dress, language, and other lifestyle choices. Friends put on additional pressure to conform to their expectations concerning these standards for dress, language, and behavior. Adolescents are caught in the middle as they try to be true to themselves and follow their own instincts while being bombarded by their family, peers, and the media.

Adolescents who possess high self-esteem because it was nurtured and developed throughout their childhood have an easier time of sorting through the conflicting messages of adolescence. They may relish this task and view it as a challenge. Their decision-making skills, self-confidence, and trust enable them to hold true to their values, despite the pressure from others.

One of the strengths these adolescents possess is a greater sense of control over their lives. Compas et al[7] found that a sense of control is related to an increased ability to cope with stress and that it affects how adolescents cope. Adolescents with a sense of control are still bombarded with the new ideas, experiences, situations, and temptations. However, they are more in control of their emotions, better able to sort through potential stressors, make better choices, and feel better about their decisions than adolescents that do not have a strong foundation of self-esteem.

These adolescents are struggling with issues that are part of normal acculturation into mainstream society. They are not rebelling against society per se but rather are struggling with the conflicting messages, urges, restrictions, and pressures that are part of their transition from childhood to adulthood in American society (see Stress in Our World box on p. 453).

Adolescents who do not have high levels of self-esteem because of deficiencies in their childhood development will struggle more with peer, media, and parental pressure. Unsure of themselves and their abilities and fearful of failure or rejection, they will struggle with decisions and make inappropriate choices and decisions.

Many of them may feel disenfranchised, with no vested interest in the future. Unlike their more confident peers, who are working through the process of becoming a part of mainstream American culture and who look forward to the future, disenfranchised youth have no such vision. They will latch onto peers and even go as far as joining gangs to gain the approval and self-esteem they so dearly crave (see the box on p. 454). A key to understanding the lore of youth gangs is to understand that they are filling a void in the lives of adolescents with low self-esteem and self-control.

KEY
TO UNDERSTANDING

Gangs fill a void that is missing in the lives of their members.

Planning for the Future

The last aspect of adolescence that contributes to the development of self-identity is planning for the future. Our hopes, dreams, and plans for the future reflect who we really are. They spring out of our self-knowledge, attitudes, values, beliefs, and likes and dislikes.

STRESS IN OUR WORLD

Alex: Rebel Without a Cause

Alex had a stormy adolescence. He probably met or exceeded every stereotype about the pitfalls of adolescence that has ever been written. He was arrested several times, was a multiple drug abuser, acquired gonorrhea as an junior in high school, and fought regularly with anyone who looked at him the wrong way. On the other hand, Alex had a lot of potential. He was intelligent, a talented musician, was accepted to college on a musical scholarship, and was liked by most of his teachers and fellow classmates.

Most of Alex's problems stemmed from the friends he had and a tremendous lack of self-esteem. Alex was physically small. As a junior, he was only 5 feet 6 inches tall and weighed about 120 lbs. When he tried out for the high school football team he

was literally laughed off the field by the coach who told him to try out for the marching band. This left a lasting impression and soon thereafter Alex's best friends were ex-football players who were thrown off the team for a variety of reasons.

It seemed like Alex's adolescence was one big fight. He fought in defense of his own manhood whenever it was questioned. He fought in defense of his friends character whenever that was threatened. His friends all drank and did drugs, and in order to fit in Alex joined in. He found that drinking and drugs made him feel big and powerful and he liked feeling that way. Nothing in his life had ever made him feel that important or powerful. In fact, he felt so big and so tough, that he used every opportunity to prove it.

When he was sober, Alex knew that his life was headed in the wrong direction. He

knew that his friends were trouble but he also protected them. After all, these people, more than anyone else, accepted him for what he was. These were kids from broken homes, abusive situations, the cast-offs that no one else wanted. Alex found refuge in his band of castaways.

Fortunately Alex survived his adolescence. He took advantage of his college scholarship and found that in college people respected him for his mind and his talent. In time he even stopped fighting. He got involved in political action, representing the plight of the have-nots in society.

Alex still has a drinking problem and has never learned how to cope with life without alcohol or drugs, but he no longer feels the need to defend his manhood at the drop of a hat. He often wonders how his life would have turned out if things had been different during his adolescence.

Street Gangs

Belonging to gangs is nothing new for boys and men. Gangs are just one example of the grouping together in which men have always been involved. Sports teams, clubs, fraternities and social groups provide a way for men to turn loneliness and bitterness into social interaction, claims Logsdon.[24] Their rituals and codes provide an identity and sense of connectedness to their members.

Street gangs also provide these rewards but add to them a mix of crime, violence, and murder that has turned the streets of some American towns and cities into free-fire zones. Like all clubs, street gangs have their initiation rites. While members of a fraternity may have to prove themselves by surviving hazing, the price of admission into a street gang is often murder. The "code of the streets" governs the lives of gang members. This code is based on gaining respect by demonstrating toughness through violent behavior.[3] The senseless, brutal execution of innocent people has often been used as a test of demonstrating toughness and as a means of gaining respect and admission into gang.

Social and demographic trends point to an increase in violent crimes and murder by youth in the 1990s and in the first decade of the twenty-first century.[16] The Children's Defense Fund reports that a grim future of poverty, violence, and neglect lies ahead for many U.S. children if the government does not take action to stop this trend.[10] Eisenman[11] reports that most juvenile offenders come from dysfunctional families and have been the victims of physical, psychological, or sexual abuse. Many of these troubled youth find that membership in gangs gives them the protection and unconditional love they never received elsewhere.

Gangs are no longer the sole province of males. Young female gang members, so-called "gangsta girls," are becoming more common. These girls join gangs for the same reasons that boys do. In many instances the girls gain entry into the gangs through their relationships with friends and family members who are gang members.[1]

Gangs are often divided along racial or ethnic lines. Although African-American and Latino gangs, such as Los Angeles' Crips and Bloods, have gotten national attention, other ethnic gangs are on the increase. An increasing number of Vietnamese and other Southeast Asian

cont'd

Although formulating plans for the future is a normal part of adolescent development that can prove to be challenging, it can also be a major source of stress. As this chapter shows, knowing who we are and understanding what we believe in and value is not always easy. This is especially true when we are bombarded with others' opinions about who we should be and what we should do with our lives. It seems as though everyone has an opinion about what we should do with our future.

Street Gangs (cont'd)

youth are becoming runaways and joining gangs. These Americanized youth feel alienated from their parents and are rejecting their culture and tradition and seeking their fortunes on the street in illegal activities.[20] Other Asian youth gangs are on the rise. In locations as diverse as Minneapolis/St. Paul, Minnesota and Queens, New York, Asian youth gangs, such as New York's Green Dragons, prey on Asian-American businessmen, frequently venturing out of the cities to victimize suburbanites.[30] The predominantly white, middle-class Spur Posse of Lakeland California shocked the nation with its members' casual attitudes toward molesting and raping young girls.

Gangs are also no longer confined to large cities such as Los Angeles and New York. Small cities such as Topeka, Kansas (population 120,000) have experienced increases in gang-related activities. One reason cited is the exporting, by gang families, of their children and relatives to their relatives in smaller cities and towns across America.[17]

While street gangs have been part of the tapestry of urban America for several decades, it is only within the past 10 years that the level of violence and murder associated with gangs in general, and youthful members in particular has increased so dramatically. Every 100 hours, more youths die on the streets of America than were killed in Operation Desert Storm.[36] The amount of teenagers arrested for murders jumped 85% from 1987 to 1991. Many of the victims of teenage violence and murder are teenagers themselves.[23]

While sociologists and psychologists point to the family, poverty, and feelings of hopelessness and alienation as reasons for gang membership, the easy availability of semiautomatic weapons and the glamorization of violence by the media have contributed to the increases in actual violent murders.[16,19] Automatic weapons, the killing tools of choice among gang members, are readily available on the street. These weapons of destruction have been glamorized in popular songs, movies, and evening-news coverage of gang murders. "Gangsta Rap" fills the airwaves of radio programming, and music-video television stations broadcast endless hours of violent images daily. Miller[28] says marketers, who capitalize on violence in their "tough guy" marketing approaches must be more responsible for their role in contributing to the glamour associated with gang images.

Parents and caregivers, often acting in what they feel are our best interests try to steer us in one direction. "Go to college," they tell us. "You can't get a good job without a college degree." Others might say, "Get a job and earn some money," or "Join the service and grow up a little."

Friends try to pressure us to follow their lead. "Come on", they tell us. "Go to this college. It's the hot school this year," even though we know we have no desire to go there. Or they might say, "School is for chumps. You can make more money in a week dealing drugs than you would in your first year out of college." Others, with no plans for the future, encourage us to "kick back, get high, and let things work out for themselves."

The media tells us which jobs are hot and which are not. The evening news goes on and on about how job prospects for this year's crop of college graduates is the worst in a decade. Or the field that really interests you is predicted to have a decline in the anticipated number of job vacancies over the next decade.

Adding to this confusing adolescent search for self and decision-making is a sense of time-urgency. Adolescents feel that not only do plans have to be formulated, but decisions have to be made now or opportunities may be lost. Parents, friends, guidance counselors, and a host of others push adolescents to make critical decisions that affect their futures.

In some cases the need for expediency is real. Certain courses must be taken in school as prerequisites for more advanced studies. Application deadlines must be adhered to for college admission, scholarships, enrollment into the armed forces, and so on. Some choices do preclude missed opportunities elsewhere. Pursuing certain tracks in high school, such as college prep or business and secretarial, may make it difficult to take certain courses or pursue other interests in the future. There can also be conflict between the desire to participate in extracurricular activities and the desire or need to work. Deciding to play fall sports for instance may limit the ability to work during the summer and earn enough money to buy a car or other items. In other cases it can work the other way; deciding to, or having to work part-time while attending school may rule out the possibility of getting involved in extracurricular activities.

In other cases, however, decisions do not have to be made right away. Some issues, like going to college, choosing the right career, or deciding what you want to be can be delayed or postponed until a later date. Most adolescents are unsure of what they really want to do in terms of school, work, or a career.

In some cases postponing decisions about going to college or other forms of schooling is actually the best answer. Many adolescents opt for joining the armed forces and taking a couple of years to decide about their career plans. In many cases the armed forces can prepare them for civilian jobs by providing valuable training and experience. Other adolescents may decide to seek employment right out of high school, preferring to work as they sort through what they ultimately want to do with their lives.

All of these decisions about the future are potentially stressful if the adolescent feels unable to cope with them.

Coping With Adolescent Stress Using The Four *R*s

Rethink

Thinking clearly and rationally is essential for adolescents to reduce stress. Using a decision-making model and writing down pros and cons can be very helpful in deciding on everything from which college to attend to whether or not to do drugs or have sex with somebody. Formalizing decision-making about issues and peer pressure helps adolescents focus rationally on the issues, thereby reducing their emotional involvement.

Ellis'[12] ABCDE model of rational thinking can help adolescents assess whether or not the stress they feel about sexual matters is real and based on accurate data or unreal and based on illogical beliefs that can be rethought (see the box below). If you remember from Chapter 6, this model helps us examine the irrational and illogical beliefs that we have regarding potential stressors and substitute more rational thinking in their place.

Rethinking also entails having concerned caregivers provide accurate information about adolescent concerns about sexuality, career choices, and a myriad of other topics. Caregivers need to either know the facts, know where to get them, or know where to refer their children for accurate, objective information. Having accurate information is invaluable in weighing advantages and disadvantages or the risks and benefits of decisions.

Evaluating decisions objectively and rationally is important. Equally important, however, is to assess these same decisions from a personal values position. A key to understanding this is to realize that often, something may seem right or okay from a purely informational point of view but is not acceptable in terms of a values assessment. Adolescents need to be able to assess their personal values and be supported in holding to these values.

KEY
TO UNDERSTANDING

Some things may appear correct from an informational standpoint but do not feel right in terms of personal values.

Ellis and Harper's ABCDE Model

Activating Event—the actual potential stressor itself (person, place, situation, etc.)

Beliefs—the irrational or illogical beliefs one has about the activating event

Consequences—the physical, social, emotional, and behavioral consequences of one's beliefs

Dispute—the process of substituting more rational and logical beliefs for one's illogical beliefs

Evaluate—the process of determining the effects of the consequences and dispute

Caregivers also need to do this and to clearly communicate their personal stand and values concerning particular issues, despite their rational assessment of the information. Caregivers also need to be role models for standing for their values. For example, parents who preach honesty yet cheat on their taxes contribute to the mixed messages that adolescents receive.

Reduce

Adolescents also need to know that they have a right to say no. Assertiveness training can be extremely helpful in assisting adolescents reduce the amount of stress in their lives by saying no to people, offers, situations, and commitments that will either put them into stressful predicaments or overtax their ability to cope. The DESC model (see Chapter 7) for verbal assertiveness can be very helpful. Learning about time management by keeping a time log can show adolescents how they use their time and how to more effectively manage their time. Writing commitments down on a wall calendar and getting used to waking up to their own alarms are simple ways to learn to manage time more effectively.

Having a family appointment calendar sets a good example for time management. Parents can show their children their work calendars and appointment books as examples of how they manage their time. Parents can also explain how they have to put off or not take part in certain activities because of lack of adequate time. Caregivers still may have to curtail some activities because adolescents may overbook themselves if allowed to do so.

Relax

Adolescents need lots of personal time and space. Being able to kick back, listen to some music, or watch TV without interruption is something that they need. For many teenagers this is difficult. Parents and caregivers may not understand their teenagers' need to be alone and have privacy. There may not be sufficient room in the house for personal alone space. They may have to share their room with a brother, sister, or other family member.

Adolescents need help in expanding their relaxation and privacy options. They are at an age where music is very important. Giving them a relaxation tape that utilizes soothing music or natural sounds is an excellent way for them to get used to passive relaxation (Fig. 13-4). They can learn and practice visualization fairly easily. The calming response (see Chapter 8) is a simple, quick passive relaxation strategy that is perfectly suited to adolescents.

Fig. 13-4 Music and natural sounds can be very healing and have a natural appeal for adolescents

Release

Having cathartic physical outlets that purge their tension is particularly important to adolescents because in most cases they have not yet learned how to understand and control their emotions like adults. Their emotions have a tendency to run wild and can lead to secondary stress quite easily if not purged.

Fortunately for most adolescents, play and sport are things they enjoy and are still involved in. Vigorous physical activity is an excellent way to rid their bodies of stress. Dancing, for example, is an outlet that combines their love of music with physical tension release. Encouraging dance and other noncompetitive forms of release is helpful. Weight lifting, hitting a punching bag, jumping rope, and so on are forms of play that encourage physical release while diminishing competition, which can be stressful.

Putting it All Together

As with the other stages of childhood development, having high levels of wellness can be a great help in coping with stress. Adolescence is a very exhausting time of life for the average teenager. With everything that is going on in their lives and with the sheer physical demands of puberty, high levels of wellness are essential and a key to protecting against the many stresses of adolescence.

KEY
TO UNDERSTANDING
High levels of wellness are protective against the many stressors of adolescence.

Physical Wellness

Physical wellness is very important. Not only do the behaviors and habits developed by physical wellness affect the day-to-day energy levels and quality of life of adolescents, they also set the foundation for good health or illness in adulthood.

Many adolescents use this time in their lives to participate in intramural and varsity athletics. While this is an excellent way to stay in shape, there are some cautions against relying on organized sports to achieve high levels of fitness. One of the major concerns of using organized sports to achieve fitness (and stress management) goals is that they are seasonal. Athletes need to have off-season fitness options for the majority of the year when they are not participating with their team. Athletes also need to be cautious about the trade-offs involved in participation in organized sports. The competition and pressures involved in performing at a high level can be a major source of stress. Sometimes adolescents are pressured into participating by parents, peers, and coaches even when they would rather not.

Parents, older siblings, and caregivers can be good role models for adolescents in adopting a four-season fitness plan. If these significant people are engaged in a year-round program of physical activity that includes both indoor and outdoor pursuits, it will help set an example for their children to adopt lifelong wellness choices. A year-round fitness program will also help adolescents maintain a desirable body weight and contribute to their having a positive body image. Feeling good about one's body is essential to self-esteem and healthy sexual development.

Teenagers are always running from one activity to another and frequently eat a lot of their meals on the run. They need to learn how to differentiate between fast food and junk food. Junk food is food that is devoid of the essential nutrients necessary for growth. Fast food is anything that is ready in a short time. Adolescents can be taught how to eat well, regardless of whether their meals are from a drive-through fast food restaurant or a convenience store.

Social Wellness

Social wellness is very important as adolescents begin to be motivated more by their friends and peers than by parents. Adolescents need to understand that their choices of friends and the social settings they frequent will strongly influence their exposure to either health-enhancing behavior or risky behavior. It is important that dialogue between parents and adolescents be open, direct, and honest, with extra attempts made at clearing up miscommunications. Adolescents can accept limitations on their social lives if they understand the reasons for parental decisions and can be involved in negotiating rules and regulations.

There is a good chance that social patterns set in late childhood will continue to exert a strong influence. That is, if an adolescent's friends up to now typically were health conscious and did not take excessive risks, these same type of people will be sought out for new friends or will continue to be part of

KEY
TO UNDERSTANDING

Sports can be a source of stress, and adolescents need other physical outlets to cope.

KEY
TO UNDERSTANDING

Junk food is different from fast food.

the adolescent's social network. This is a time, however, when changing schools (new middle schools and high school) will expose adolescents to a wider circle of potential friends, some of whom may engage in risky health behavior.

Because peer pressure is difficult to resist, caregivers should assist adolescents in developing a supportive versus destructive circle of friends. Limits need to be set and with clear reasons given for denying adolescents access to certain places, people, and things.

Intellectual Wellness

Once again, using RET (see Chapter 6) and formal decision-making models can help adolescents use their brains when evaluating situations and making decisions. Success in school can also help reduce stress by building self-esteem. Pride in tackling difficult academic work can go a long way in developing competence, self-esteem, and confidence, attributes that help adolescents increase their perceived ability to cope. The more they feel that they can cope, the less stress they will have, and the more they will perceive potential stressors as challenges.

Helping adolescents find something they are good at is a key to this. Adolescents need support and reinforcement for a job well done, whether it is completing a school assignment, holding down a part-time job, or changing the oil in the car (Fig. 13-5).

Emotional Wellness

Emotional wellness is critical during adolescence. With the myriad changes going on both physiologically and psychosocially during this time, life for adolescents and their caregivers can be an emotional roller-coaster.

Fig. 13-5 Teenagers need to feel that they can do something right. Reward them for a job well done, whether it is changing the oil or getting an *A* on a test.

The same hormones that influence sexual desire also contribute to rapidly shifting emotional states. Adolescents need to know that these things are normal and that they will survive them. They need to feel that there is someone with whom they can discuss anything that is on their minds, no matter how bizarre they think it is (Fig. 13-6). They need to believe that they are not alone with their problems.

Adolescents also need to know that it is normal to get depressed at times. Short-term depression (less than 2 months) that is related to a loss or disappointment is common during adolescence. **Chronic depression,** however, is a serious condition that significantly reduces the quality of a person's life. Chronic depression can make you feel constantly fatigued, cause you to overeat or undereat, can give you feelings of hopelessness and low self-esteem, and generally make you disinterested in life.[2]

Chronic depression is also a risk factor for suicide. Suicide is the second leading cause of death among people aged 15 to 24 years in the United States.[34] The reasons are many and varied, but basically young people take their lives because they feel that there is no other way out. There are several risk factors for suicide that contribute to this sense of hopelessness (see the box on p. 463).

Sometimes adolescents considering suicide have suffered a loss that has deeply hurt them (divorce, death of loved one). In other cases they feel they simply cannot keep pace with the pressures in their life or they have failed and let someone down. In any case a key to understanding suicide is

chronic depression

depression that lasts most of the day, more days than not, and persists for more than 2 months (1 month in children and adolescents)

Fig. 13-6 Adolescents need to feel that there is someone who will listen to them. Talking things out can help relieve stress.

Suicide Risk Factors[18]

Researchers have looked for explanations for suicide by studying everything from phases of the moon to birth order in the family, yet they have found no conclusive answers. They have, however, identified certain characteristics that affect the likelihood of suicide:

Age. In the past, the risk of suicide has increased with age, peaking among people in their late seventies. But in the last thirty years, the rate of suicide among adolescents and young adults has tripled. However, college students commit suicide at about half the rate of nonstudents their age, and suicide rates at highly competitive schools are not significantly different from those at less rigorous ones.

Sex. Men commit suicide more frequently than women, but women attempt suicide four to eight times as often as men. Men and women also choose different methods: men tend to use knives and guns; women turn to poison and drugs.

Race. The suicide rate is generally higher for whites but it is rising among young blacks in ghettos. Native Americans have a suicide rate five times higher than that of the general population.

Marital status. Suicide rates are lowest among the married and highest among the separated, divorced, or widowed. In general, people who live alone are at higher risk.

Employment. The unemployed are at higher risk than those working in or out of the home. Professionals (particularly male physicians) also have high suicide rates.

Physical health. People who commit suicide are more likely to be ill or to believe that they are. More than 80% see a doctor about a medical complaint within 6 months before suicide.

Mental illness. Depression, schizophrenia, and other psychiatric disorders are correlated with a high risk of suicide. One symptom in particular—hopelessness—is more highly correlated with suicide than depression itself.

Heavy drinking. This self-destructive behavior greatly increases suicide risk.

Previous suicide attempts. Individuals who have tried to kill themselves are more than twice as likely to try again.

Loss. Divorce, death of a loved one, or the end of other important relationships increases the risk.

Life stresses. Those who commit suicide tend to have experienced a high frequency of major life events—job changes, births, financial reversals, divorces, menopause, retirement—in the previous 6 months.

Interpersonal conflict. Long-standing, intense conflict with family members or other important people adds to the danger of suicide.

Suicide's Warning Signs[18]

Usually a person considering suicide says or does something that should serve as a warning signal; 75% of suicide victims give verbal or behavioral clues to what they are planning. The most obvious clue is a previous attempt. Others are dramatic changes for no apparent reason in familiar routines of eating, drinking, or sexual activity. Among young people, the most frequent indications are the following:

■ Increased moodiness, seeming down or sad

■ Feelings of worthlessness or discouragement

■ A withdrawal from friends, family, and normal activities

■ Changes in eating and sleeping habits

■ Specific suicide threats

■ School compositions revealing a preoccupation with death

■ Persistent boredom

■ A decline in the quality of schoolwork

■ Violent, hostile, or rebellious behavior

■ Running away

■ Breaking off of friendships

■ Increased drug and alcohol use

■ A failed love relationship

■ An unusual neglect of personal appearance

■ Difficulty in concentrating

■ A radical personality change

■ Complaints about physical symptoms, such as headache or fatigue

A teenager planning suicide also may give verbal hints with statements such as "It's no use" or "Nothing matters anymore." The suicidal teenager may give away favorite possessions, clean his or her room, or otherwise tie up loose ends. The person may suddenly become cheerful after a depression.

realizing that it is a permanent solution to a temporary problem that in most cases can be worked out. Adolescents need to know that feeling sad and depressed is a normal part of adolescence but if it persists for more than 2 months they need to get help. They need to know that even if they cannot approach their parents or caregivers, there is someone out there who can help. All adolescents need to know the warning signs of suicide so that they can either help themselves or their friends.

Adolescents also need to know how to help a friend who they think is contemplating suicide. The box below describes guidelines for helping a friend who you think is contemplating suicide.

Spiritual Wellness

Spiritual well-being can help sustain adolescents in these potentially troubling times by giving them faith in the future. Sometimes an adolescent's problems seem overwhelming. They wonder if they will ever be able to overcome them. They ask themselves if it is worth it to go on. Being con-

KEY
TO UNDERSTANDING

Adolescents need to develop confidence and build self-esteem by finding something they are good at.

How to Help Someone Contemplating Suicide[18]

If someone you know has talked about suicide, behaved unpredictably, or suddenly emerged from a severe depression into a calm, settled state of mind, do not rule out the possibility that he or she may attempt suicide.

- Encourage your friend to talk. Ask concerned questions. Listen attentively. Show that you take the person's feelings seriously and truly care.

- Do not offer trite reassurances or list reasons to go on living.

- Do not analyze the person's motives or try to shock or challenge him or her.

- Suggest solutions or alternatives to problems. Make plans.

- Encourage positive action, such as getting away for a while to gain a better perspective on a problem.

- Do not be afraid to ask whether your friend has considered suicide. The opportunity to talk about thoughts of suicide may be an enormous relief, and—contrary to a long-standing myth—will not fix the idea of suicide more firmly in a person's mind.

- Do not think that people who talk about killing themselves never carry out their threat. Most individuals who commit suicide give definite indications of their intent to die.

nected to something other than themselves, either through a formal religious affiliation or working as a volunteer in an organization dedicated to helping the environment or the poor, can give adolescents a mission or purpose.

It also connects them to others, particularly other youth, who are involved, have faith in their future, and are committed to making things better. In a sense, you become part of a group of caring individuals from whom you can gain support. Often, religious and other secular organizations committed to the public's good offer social and recreational opportunities to heighten the fellowship of their members. Caring for oneself comes with caring for others.

Summary

This chapter provides a brief overview of the tasks and stressors associated with adolescence. It begins with a short description of Erikson's major developmental task for adolescence—the development of a coherent sense of self.

Finding out who they are can be a major source of stress for adolescents who feel caught between trusting their own instincts and the demands of parents and the pressure from peers and media images.

Three major factors—puberty, school, and planning for the future—are presented as issues that influence the development of a coherent sense of self. All three greatly affect an adolescent's search for self.

The chapter describes the difference between puberty and adolescence. Specific physiological changes associated with puberty are discussed in detail. In particular, the emergence of reproductive readiness, the point of full maturation of the male and female reproductive systems, is discussed, with emphasis on its role as a potential stressor. A discussion of the differences between physiological and psychosocial readiness is presented with a description of how these two states of readiness rarely coincide with American youth and how this can be a source of stress.

Some of the stressful consequences of premature sexual intercourse are discussed. Among them are teenage pregnancy, abortion, and sexually transmitted disease.

School is presented as an arena in which the quest for self-discovery is played out. Various school-related issues are discussed. The chapter concludes with an application of the four Rs of coping with the developmental stressors of this period and how the dimensions of wellness affect adolescent stress.

Student Study Questions

1. Describe Erickson's major developmental task for adolescence.
2. Define adolescence and puberty. Explain the differences.
3. How can one be reproductively ready but not psychosocially ready?
4. List and describe three potential adolescent stressors associated with school.
5. Describe two coping strategies adolescents can use to reduce, rethink, relax, and release.
6. How can the dimensions of wellness be used to cope with stress in the absence of more specific strategies?

References

1. Abner, A. (1994). Gangsta girls: gang membership among young black girls is rising. *Essence*, July, pp 64-70.
2. American Psychiatric Association (1987). *Diagnostic and statistical manual* (3rd ed.). Washington DC: American Psychiatric Association.
3. Anderson, E. (1994). The code of the streets. *The Atlantic, 273*, pp 80-91.
4. Deleted in page proofs.
5. Carrera, M. (1981). *Sex: the facts, the acts, & your feelings.* New York: Crown.
6. Centers for Disease Control. (1992). *HIV/AIDS prevention fact book 1992.* Washington DC: U.S. Government Printing Office.
7. Compas, B., Banez, G.A., Makcarne, V., & Worsham, N. (1991). Perceived control and coping with stress: a developmental perspective. *Journal of Social Issues, 47* (4), pp 23-35.
8. Crooks, R. & Baur, C. (1993). *Our sexuality.* Redwood City, CA: Benjamin Cummings/Addison Wesley.
9. Dryfoos, J. (1985). What the United States can learn about prevention of teenage pregnancy from other countries. *SIECUS Report, 14* (2), pp 1-7.
10. Edwards, R.T. (1994). Crimes against youth. *National Catholic Reporter, 30,* p 5.
11. Eisenman, R. (1994). The young desperados. *USA Today, 122,* pp 27-29.
12. Ellis, A. & Harper, R. (1979). *A new guide to rational living.* Englewood Cliffs, NJ: Prentice Hall.
13. Erickson, E. (1978). *Childhood and society* (2nd ed.). New York: WW Norton.
14. Fields, S. (1993). Rape as sport: the culture is at the root. *Insight on the News, 9,* pp 19-21.
15. Forrest, J.D. & Silverman, J. (1989). What public school teachers teach about preventing pregnancy, AIDS, and sexually transmitted diseases. *Family Planning Perspectives, 21,* p 65-72.
16. Fox, A., & Pierce, G. (1994). American killers are getting younger. *USA Today, 122,* pp 24-27.

17. Furhmans, V. (1992). Youth gangs hit the small time. *Governing*, pp 28-30.
18. Hales, D. (1993). *An invitation to health*. Redwood City, CA: Benjamin Cummings/Addison Wesley.
19. Harrington-Leuker, D. (1992). Blown away by school violence. *Education Digest, 58*, pp 50-54.
20. Ingrassia, M. (1994). America's new waves of runaways. *Newsweek*, April 4, pp 64-66.
21. Insel/Roth
22. Jemmott, J.B., Jemmott, L., & Fong, G.T. (1992). Reductions in HIV risk-associated sexual behaviors among black male adolescents: effects of an AIDS prevention intervention. *American Journal of Public Health, 82* (3), 372-377.
23. Kantrowitz, B. & Leslie, C. (1993). Wild in the streets. *Newsweek 122,* Aug 2, pp 40-47.
24. Logsdon, G. (1992). Those old gangs of mine. *Men's Health, 7*, pp 24-26.
25. Martinson, F.M. (1982). Against sexual retardation. *SIECUS Report, 10* (3), p.3.
26. Masters, W.H., Johnson, V.E., & Kolodny, R.C. (1992). *Human sexuality* (4th ed.). New York: Harper Collins.
27. McGrew, M. & Shore, W. (1991). The problem of teenage pregnancy. *The Journal of Family Practice, 32*, 17-25.
28. Miller, A. (1991). Do gangs deserve a rap? Marketing using youth gang image. *Newsweek, 118*, Oct. 21, p. 55.
29. Payne, W. & Hahn, D. (1995). *Understanding your health*. St. Louis: Mosby.
30. Robson, B. (1992). Lost boys. *MPLS-St. Paul Magazine, 20*, pp 90-101.
31. Steven-Simon, C. & White, M. (1991). Adolescent pregnancy. *Pediatric Annals, 20*, 322-331.
32. Trussel (1988)
33. United States Department of Health & Human Services. (1992). Preventing risk behaviors among students. *HIV/AIDS Prevention Newsletter, 3* (3), pp 1-2.
34. United States Department of Health & Human Services. (1991). Attempted suicide among high school students: United States, 1990. *MMWR, 40* (37), 35-37.
35. White, S. & DeBlassie, R. (1992). Adolescent sexual behavior. *Adolescence, 27*, 183-191.
36. Witkin, G. (1991). Kids who kill: disputes once settled with fists are now settled with guns. *US News & World Report, 110*, April 8, pp 27-33.

Name: _____ Date: _____

Unfinished Sentences

The following sentence stems were designed to help you remember significant issues related to your stress as an adolescent. Completing them can help you understand your present stress level and coping style.

Instructions:

Finish each of the sentences using the blank lines provided. Use additional paper if necessary. Restrict your memories to your adolescent years (early to mid-teens).

1. The most stressful thing about adolescence is _____

_____

2. The three major stressors of my adolescence were _____

_____

3 A particularly stressful event for me was _____

_____

4. I still feel guilty about _____

_____

5. I am still angry about _____

_____

6. I am still confused about _____

_____

7. The pace of my adolescence was _____

_____

8. As an adolescent, I coped with stress by _____

_____

9. My parent(s)/guardian told me the following about stress and coping_____

_____

Unfinished Sentences (cont'd)

10. My parent(s)/guardian told me the following about stress and coping _____
_____

11. As far as stress is concerned, my brothers and sisters _____
_____

12. As far as stress is concerned, my friends_____
_____

13. The person who coped with stress most effectively was _____
_____

14. The greatest strength I had as an adolescent for coping with stress was _____
_____

15. The most positive coping experience I remember was _____
_____

16. A coping strategy that has evolved from my adolescence is _____
_____

CHAPTER 14

Young Adulthood Stress: College and Other Challenges

CHAPTER OBJECTIVES

- Describe Erikson's major developmental task of young adulthood.
- Discuss the importance of friendship.
- Define intimacy and describe how it develops.
- Describe four barriers to intimacy.
- Define love according to Sternberg.
- Compare and contrast friendship, intimacy, and love.
- Describe how to cope with intimacy-related stress.
- Describe some of the stresses associated with academic and other work.
- Explain how to cope with work-related stress using the four *Rs*.

The primary task we face as young adults, according to Erikson,[8] is to develop intimacy. We begin to move away from our adolescent focus on ourselves and are ready to begin exploring mutually satisfying relationships. This stage emphasizes commitment, in both our intimate relationships and our work.

This is an exciting time of life, when we meet new friends, explore intimate, loving relationships, and test the waters of career possibilities. For many college students, this is the first time they live apart from their parents and is a time of unparalleled freedom. Students who have mastered the developmental tasks of childhood and adolescence enter this period of their lives ready and eager to sample all that life has to offer.

This also can be a time of great stress. The same tasks that are perceived as challenges by some are viewed as stressors by others. Not everyone is equally prepared for the freedom, the work, and the tasks of young adulthood. Many have yet to work through some of the key developmental tasks of earlier periods in their lives and are unable to handle the pressures of young adulthood. Many lack work and study skills. Others have limited resources for managing pressures. All of these factors and many others affect our perceived ability to cope with the normal developmental tasks of this period. If we feel unable to cope or are unsure of our ability to cope, these daily challenges will be perceived as stressors.

This chapter examines some of the key stressors that normally accompany this developmental period. Most of these stressors are associated with interpersonal intimacy, academic, and work issues.

Friendship and Intimate Relationships
Forming Friendships

The major developmental task of young adulthood is forming committed, intimate, loving relationships. In most cases, our friendships form the basis of our intimate relationships. Intimacy grows out of friendships as people become more trusting and comfortable with each other.

Pals, buddies, chums, comrades, sisters, brothers, amigos, and amigas are some names we give to our friends. Joel Block,[1] in his book *Friendship,* contends that humans are "wired" with a basic desire for contact with others. Our friendships, Block believes, make us whole. Friends enrich our existence and bond with us to form a conspiracy against the world; we like one another, understand each other, share interests, and have similar lifestyles or problems in life.[1]

What draws friends together? Many friendships grow from shared interests and experiences. These similarities provide the initial attraction. If the initial attraction is strong enough, it provides the basis for the friends to spend further time together. As the friendship progresses, the friends share more time and experiences, reinforcing their commonality, deepening their bonds, and enriching their lives.

Friendship is a unique bond. Although it is fraught with entanglements similar to those that characterize romantic relationships, such as competition, jealousy, and betrayal, it offers what Block[1] calls *psychological space*. Friendships are more open-ended than relationships with family, mates, or lovers. Unlike these more intimate relationships, we and our friends live separate lives that allow time away from entanglements. Consequently, the relationship has a greater tolerance for growth and change. In many cases, when we do not see our friends for days, weeks, or months, we pick up where we left off, renewed and eager to share where we have been or what we have done. In a sense, true friendships are timeless.

With our friends, we are most truly ourselves. "A friend is one who knows you as you are, understands where you've been, accepts who you've become, and still invites you to grow."[11] Sometimes our true friendships are so unforced and seem so natural that we take them for granted. We assume they will always be there, and we start to neglect our friends. The box below offers some excellent tips for maintaining friendships.

Maintaining Friendships

Like all relationships, friendships require attention and work to survive. Here are some behaviors that can keep you close to those you care about most:

- Be willing to open up. The more you share, the deeper the bond between you and your friend will become.

- Be sensitive to your friend's feelings. Keep in mind that, like you, your friend has unique needs, desires, and dreams.

- Express appreciation. Be generous with your compliments. Let your friends know you recognize their kindnesses.

- See friends clearly. Admitting their faults need not reduce your respect for them.

- Know that friends will disappoint you from time to time. They, too, are only human.

- Talk about your friendship. Evaluate the relationship periodically. If you have any gripes or frustrations, air them.

Forming Intimate Relationships

Intimacy is an often-misunderstood phenomenon. Many people equate intimacy with sexual activity and love, yet these are three separate entities. One can be intimate and sexual with another person but not love him or her. One also can be intimate with but not sexually involved with another person. Finally, one can be sexual with another person but neither love nor be intimate with him. As you can see, this can be very confusing and sometimes very stressful.

Most people agree that the best possible combination of all three would be to be sexual with someone toward whom you feel both intimate and loving. Blumstein and Schwartz[3] found this to be true in a survey of more than 10,000 adults (Fig. 14-1). Most young adults learn this through trial and error as they pass through this stage of their development. People usually maintain multiple types of relationships simultaneously; they are intimate with some people, friends with others, and sexual and loving toward others. If they have worked through the other stages of development competently, they are ready to sample the range of these deeper, committed, intimate relationships (Fig. 14-2).

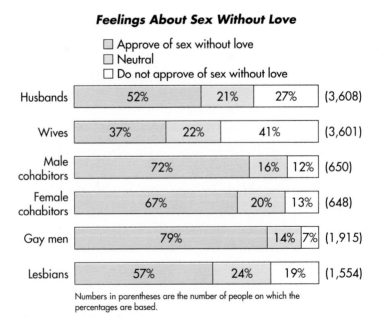

Feelings About Sex Without Love

☐ Approve of sex without love
☐ Neutral
☐ Do not approve of sex without love

Husbands	52%	21%	27%	(3,608)
Wives	37%	22%	41%	(3,601)
Male cohabitors	72%	16%	12%	(650)
Female cohabitors	67%	20%	13%	(648)
Gay men	79%	14%	7%	(1,915)
Lesbians	57%	24%	19%	(1,554)

Numbers in parentheses are the number of people on which the percentages are based.

Fig. 14-1 American adults' attitudes towards the propriety of sex without love are shown in this survey.

Fig. 14-2 Intimate relationships can be a source of great comfort and enjoyment.

Intimacy

We live in a culture of instant intimacy. Our lives are fast paced and mobile, with drive-in services, call waiting, cellular telephones, faxed lunch menus, express check-out counters, and computerized dating services. People relocate every 7 years on average, leaving old friends and making new ones. Television soap operas play out several entire romantic encounters in one 30-minute segment. People expect that their own intimate relationships will develop as quickly. A key to understanding intimacy, however, is realizing that an intimate relationship takes time to develop.

The word *intimacy* comes from the Latin word for within. Intimacy is the process of gradually sharing one's innermost feelings with another. Intimacy involves risk; sharing feelings requires making oneself vulnerable, which requires trust and takes time. For intimacy to grow, people must share and then step back to assess how the other person handles the situation.

We share not only thoughts and feelings with intimate friends but also our experiences. Intimacy often springs from the shared experiences of friendship. We develop a camaraderie between ourselves and another person when we share difficult, challenging, or enjoyable times. A special bond develops between us.

In time, if the other person treats our intimate revelations with caring, confidentiality, and respect, and if in turn reveals his or her own innermost feelings, intimacy will grow between us. If not, and the other person violates our trust or does not respect our feelings, our desire for intimacy wanes. In some cases, this can make us leery about wanting to develop new

KEY
TO UNDERSTANDING

Intimacy takes time to develop.

intimate relationships. (The Assess Yourself box on p. 505 provides a tool for measuring a person's capacity for intimacy.)

Another key to understanding intimacy is that it does not necessarily include sexual relations. Many of us have intimate relationships with people to whom we are not sexually attracted. This can be confusing, as we try to sort through the feelings we have for the person. Are we looking for a sexual relationship or is it intimacy we desire? Should we have sex with someone with whom we are not intimate, or should intimacy grow out of sexuality? We may think we should have sexual feelings for someone with whom we share our deepest feelings, yet we may not be ready for that special kind of commitment.

Intimate relationships can form between members of the same or opposite gender. Traditionally, women have enjoyed same-gender intimate relationships more frequently than men. Women typically share intimate information with female confidants much more so than men (Fig. 14-3). Most men perceive intimate sharing of any feelings with another man as unmanly or feminine and therefore to be avoided. Men are socialized to keep their feelings to themselves,[19] much to the detriment of their mental and emotional well-being.

Intimacy knows no racial or ethnic boundaries. If allowed to develop, intimate relationships and love can flourish between people of different races and cultures (Fig. 14-4). Indeed, the racial and cultural differences often attract us to each other in the first place (see Stress in Our World box on p. 477).

KEY
TO UNDERSTANDING

Intimacy does not
necessarily involve sex.

Fig. 14-3 Females in our culture have been raised to be intimate with their friends. It is sometimes hard for males to become intimate with their male friends.

STRESS IN OUR WORLD

Robert and Monica

Robert and Monica have been lovers for about a year. Both are juniors attending a large, urban, Midwestern university. They started dating as freshmen and last year stopped dating other people. Robert is white, Protestant, and from a middle-class farming family in Wisconsin. Monica is black, Baptist, and from a middle-class business family in Baltimore.

"I'll have to admit," Rob says, "that when I first saw Monica, it was her blackness that attracted me. Growing up on a farm in Wisconsin, I'd never really met any black girls in school. Unlike me, Monica is dark, and I found myself staring at her in freshman English class.

"He was aroused all right," says Monica. "I could tell from across the lecture hall that Rob was having a hard time concealing his interest in me. My friend Clarissa was the first to notice, elbowing me to look at that 'crazy white boy over there staring at us.' Boy was he hot! With those beautiful blue eyes, white skin, and bulging farm-boy muscles popping out from all over, I felt my knees getting a little weak as I found myself staring back."

"I remember that first lecture," Rob interjects, cutting Monica off with a smile and a gentle touch of her knee. "All through the class I fantasized about Monica. As a matter of fact, I missed most of the notes because I was paying more attention to her than the professor." Rob laughs, and continues, "It worked out all right though, because I went up to her after class and asked her for her notes. We started talking and made plans to see each other later on that evening. That was our first date and the start of our 3-year relationship."

"It was weird," Monica continues. "The last thing I needed or wanted was a white guy messing up my life. My mom and dad, although not racist, wanted me to meet someone of 'my own kind' and warned me about all of these lily-white farm boys who had never seen any black women before. I really wasn't interested in meeting a white guy, and explaining things to my parents, but I must admit, when I saw Rob staring at me, I also kind of lost track of what the professor was lecturing about. Later on in our relationship Rob and I had a good laugh when we each confided about what was going on in our minds during class that day and how we ever passed freshman English."

"It's funny," says Rob. "Although the thing that first attracted me to Monica was the differences between us, as our intimacy and love grew, I found her more similar to me than different. The color thing that everyone still makes such a big deal about kind of vanished in my mind. What's really funny is that I tend to like the things that most people associate with black people and African-American culture. I love rap music; she hates it and can listen to classical for hours. I like cities; she prefers the quiet and solitude of the mountains. I'm liberal, she's conservative politically and questions the value of federal entitlement programs."

Do you know a Robert and Monica?

Barriers to Intimacy

Sometimes we are reluctant to become intimate with others. We are unable to let down our guards and share our innermost feelings. In the box on p. 479 Masters, Johnson, and Kolodny[13] identify six specific barriers to intimacy. Any or all of these can be a source of stress that we could address.

Date Rape. In recent years, date rape has become a serious issue young adults must face as they begin to explore intimate relationships with one another. Date rape is forced sexual intercourse by a dating partner. Studies from a number of college campuses show that as many as 20% of all college women report having experienced date rape. The reports of other forms of sexual violation, including being touched and kissed against their will, are even higher.[15] Although some men report similar experiences, the occurrence of female-to-male date rape is very limited.

Date rape can be very traumatic because the sexual assault violated a special kind of relationship. In most cases the perpetrator was someone with whom the victim had a degree of trust. Date-rape victims feel particularly violated because the rapist was someone they knew and trusted. Because of this, victims often experience post-traumatic stress disorder (PTSD).[15] As described in Chapter 5, PTSD sufferers experience anxiety, sleeplessness, eating disorders, depression, and hyperactive neural functioning. Date-rape victims also have considerable anxiety about future dating and establishing trust within intimate relationships. The box on p. 481 provides some date-rape precautions.

Fig. 14-4 Attraction and intimacy are not bound by race or color. Often what first attracts lovers is the uniqueness of their differences.

Barriers to Intimacy

Some people seem to be able to forge close relationships easily, while others have a difficult time getting past the social acquaintance stage. The fortunate few who can comfortably develop closeness and rapport with others in a seemingly effortless way are a distinct minority. Most of us have to work at developing intimacy, and most of us, at one time or another, find that our intimacy overtures are ignored or rejected. Here is a list of common reasons for difficulty initiating or maintaining intimate relations.

1. *Shyness.* People whose shyness causes them to avoid social interactions or to isolate themselves in social settings are unwittingly restricting their opportunities for intimacy. Paradoxically, shy people often long for intimacy and companionship in their lives, but they seem unwilling or unable to take the risks necessary to overcome their shyness.

2. *Aggressiveness.* People who behave aggressively often scare others away or cause them to adopt a defensive posture. The typical concern seems to be "I'll be overpowered by this person," and few people look for relationships in which they will be dominated by somone else. Toning down aggressive language and behavior can improve a person's chances for intimacy.

3. *Self-centeredness.* Being preoccupied with one's self commonly turns others off. We all know people who insist on being center-stage all the time, who ignore the needs of others (not out of malice but because of lack of awareness), who monopolize conversations, and who are generally unwilling to do what a partner wants unless it coincides with their own needs. These people frequently initiate intimacy by telling others a great deal about themselves, but they tend to have a more difficult time maintaining long-term relationships.

4. *Selfishness.* Going beyond self-centeredness, selfishness is apt to be far more damaging to the development of genuine intimacy. Selfish people are often manipulative and try to gain a tactical advantage over others to get their own way. The selfish person does not care much about what is best for the relationship or best for the other person; instead, he or she seeks to exert control for personal gain.

5. *Lack of empathy.* The person who is unwilling or unable to accept and understand another's views, thoughts, or feelings has a difficult time in intimate relationships. Often, these people seem to have difficulty listening: either they block out what their partner says, or they fail to internalize the message and look at the situation from the partner's point of view. Empathetic people do not just sympathize with the feelings and needs of others, they try to respond to these feelings and needs as well.

6. *Conflicting or unrealistic expectations.* Many people are so idealistic about intimacy that they expect the impossible, creating a situation that frequently leads to disappointment, frustration, or possibly to giving up. In other intimate relationships the partners' goals may be so different that the relationship fails. For instance, if one person is looking primarily for companionship and entertainment in a friendship while the other is looking for a deeply philosophical, intellectual relationship, they are not likely to find a pleasing intimacy together.

cont'd

Barriers to Intimacy (cont'd)

Needless to say, this is not a complete list of all possible barriers to intimacy. There are other conditions, such as depression, drug abuse, or severe physical illness, that may make intimacy extremely difficult even when the other ingredients seem to be in place. It is also important to realize that intimacy is often extraordinarily resilient, making its own way in the face of unforeseen obstacles. Perhaps this is one reason why so many of us are concerned with finding and keeping intimacy in our lives.

From Masters, W., Johnson, V., & Kolodny, R. (1992). *Human sexuality.* New York: Harper Collins.

Love

KEY
TO UNDERSTANDING

Respect is central to mature love.

What is love? There are many kinds of love, such as the love parents have for their child, the love of God, or the love you may have for your pet. Erich Fromm[9] in his classic work, *The Art of Loving,* defines mature love between two adults as a union under the condition of preserving one's integrity and one's individuality, in which lovers become one yet remain two. A key to understanding Fromm's conceptualization of mature love is realizing the role of respect in loving relationships. Fromm[9] believed that self-respect and respect for one's lover are essential ingredients for love. Although Fromm refers to this type of love as mature love and refers to "adult" lovers, adolescents and young adults are capable of forming love relationships built on the same respect.

More recently, Sternberg[17] developed a triangular theory of love to characterize the relationship between two adults. According to Sternberg, there are three facets to adult love, or what Fromm would characterize as mature love: passion, intimacy, and decision or commitment. Passion involves romance, physical attraction, and sexual desire. Intimacy is the desire for bonding, sharing, warmth, and emotional closeness. Decision or commitment is the conscious decision to love another person and remain committed to him or her despite the inevitable problems that will arise in any relationship. Decision or commitment might be viewed as the rational or cognitive aspect of love while passion and intimacy could be viewed as the motivational and emotional components respectively.

friendship

characterized by intimacy but is without passion and commitment

companionate love

involves intimacy and commitment but lacks passion

When all three components of love occur in equal proportions, the partners have consummate love, according to Sternberg.[17] Ideally, both partners have consummate love at the same time. More typically, however, one or both of the lovers lack one or more of the three components (Fig. 14-5).

Friendship is a state characterized by intimacy alone. There is no passion nor any decision or commitment. **Companionate love**, which often is

---

Date Rape Precautions[15]

The following are some ways for both men and women to avoid a date rape situation:

Men	Women
Know your sexual desires and limits. Communicate them clearly. Be aware of social pressures. It is okay not to "score."	*Know your sexual desires and limits.* Believe in your right to set those limits. If you are not sure, stop and talk about it.
Being turned down when you ask for sex is not a rejection of you personally. Women who say no to sex are not rejecting the person; they are expressing their desire not to participate in a single act. Your desires may be beyond control, but your actions *are* within your control.	*Communicate your limits clearly.* If someone starts to offend you, tell them so firmly and immediately. Polite approaches may be misunderstood or ignored. Say no when you mean no.
Accept the woman's decision. No means no. Do not read other meanings into the answer. Do not continue after you are told no!	*Be assertive.* Often men interpret passivity as permission. Be direct and firm with someone who is sexually pressuring you.
Do not assume that just because a woman dresses in a "sexy" manner and flirts that she wants to have sexual intercourse.	*Be aware that your nonverbal actions send a message.* If you dress in a "sexy" manner and flirt, some men may assume you want to have sex. This does not make your dress or behavior wrong, but it is important to be aware of a possible misunderstanding.
Do not assume that previous permission for sexual contact applies to the current situation.	*Pay attention to what is happening around you.* Watch the nonverbal clues. Do not put yourself into vulnerable situations.
	Trust your intuitions. If you feel you are being pressured into unwanted sex, you probably are.
Avoid excessive use of alcohol and drugs. Alcohol and drugs interfere with clear thinking and effective communication.	*Avoid excessive use of alcohol and drugs.* Alcohol and drugs interfere with clear thinking and effective communication.

characteristic of couples who have been together for many years, has everything but passion. In **empty love**, the partners are committed to each other, but the fires of passion and the deep personal warmth of intimacy have long been extinguished.

empty love

involves commitment without passion and intimacy

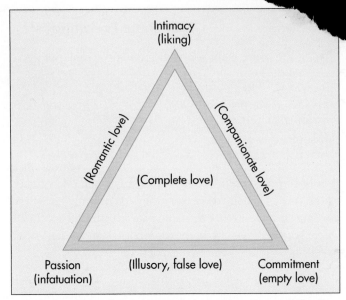

Sternberg's theory allows us to depict a couple's compatability–how well their feelings match. The closer the match, the more satisfying the partner's relationship.

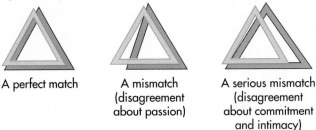

Fig. 14-5 Sternberg's triangular theory of love.

infatuation

characterized by passion without intimacy and commitment

romantic love

involves passion and intimacy but no commitment

fatuous love

passionate and committed but not intimate

Infatuation is immature love; it is shallow in that there is neither an intimate bind nor a long-term commitment between the partners. **Romantic love** is characterized by passion and intimacy. It is intense and overwhelming but not longstanding and committed. Similar is **fatuous love**, in which partners are passionate and have a commitment. The rapidity and intensity of this commitment, however, is usually short term and based on an unrealistic perception of the nature of the partner.

Sternberg[17] believes that passion and intimacy develop early and intensely in relationships and level off as the relationship matures. Decision and commitment, however, take more time to develop but intensify as the relationship matures and endures. A key to understanding Sternberg's[17] model is realizing that although equality of all three components character-izes consummate love, each can occur in varying degrees for each partner at any stage of the relationship.

Sternberg[17] developed a scale to help one determine the nature and type of your loving relationship (see the Assess Yourself box on p. 511).

Consummate love involves loving another individual for who he or she really is, not for whom we want that person to be. Sternberg[17] believes that consummate love grows out of self-love. In other words, before one can love another, one first must love oneself. Self-love grows out of a healthy sense of self-esteem and self-control, issues that arise during childhood (see Chapters 12 and 13). Consummate love involves sacrifice, caring, and shar-ing, qualities that result only from working through developmental tasks related to the self.

Intimacy and Love as a Source of Stress

Someone who never developed a strong sense of self-esteem and competence during childhood and adolescence will have a hard time mak-ing the sacrifices necessary to develop consummate love. Until one satisfies the tasks of the earlier developmental years, that person will remain needy and unable to fully give to another person in a mature loving relationship. Developing consummate love often requires some soul-searching as we determine whether we are ready for an intense, intimate relationship with another person (see Stress in Our World box on p. 484).

Coping With Intimacy-Related Stress: The Four *R*s

Rethink

Thinking rationally is difficult when one is romantically involved with someone, yet this often is exactly what is necessary to cope effectively. Using Ellis and Harper's[7] ABCDE model, described in Chapters 6 and 13, can help organize your thoughts so that you can better determine whether you are thinking clearly about your relationships.

Use values-clarification activities to determine whether your intimate friends and lovers enhance or weaken your values. Intimate relationships often are a source of stress because our significant others force us to con-front our long-held values. In some cases this helps us reaffirm or change values.

Sometimes putting your thoughts down on paper can help you look objectively at the data and make a decision. Using a formal decision-mak-

STRESS IN OUR WORLD

Ken

Ken is a college freshman in a large, urban, Midwestern university. He is living away from home for the first time and is slowly adjusting to his new roommate, classmates, and sexual freedom. He misses his home, a small suburb of Boston. His roommate Jeff grew up on a farm in Iowa and also is away from home for the first time. They are very different, and Ken is adjusting to the demands of developing an intimate friendship with this new person. Ken also has begun dating a very attractive young woman from one of his classes who is approaching him sexually. Ken is a virgin with very traditional beliefs about premarital sexual intercourse. Despite these stressors, however, Ken is coping with college life successfully because he is trying to apply the four Rs of coping and is trying to maintain a high level of wellness.

Ken has been paying attention to his health in general because he is a baseball player and wants to stay in shape year-round. He eats a balanced diet from the dor-

mitory meal plan and has lots of healthy snacks (e.g., fruit, granola bars, and juice packs) in his dormitory room. He runs every afternoon and gets plenty of rest. He is in good physical condition.

Ken also is trying to maintain his social support system while away at school. He keeps in touch with his friends and family at home. He writes to his best friend, who also is away from home, and calls him once a week to touch base. Ken went home on Thanksgiving break to visit his family and friends. He also has begun to develop a support system at school. He has made friends with other members of the baseball team and is exercising with them three times a week.

Ken takes time to enjoy the natural beauty of his new home. He frequently visits the park in his new city and has visited the zoo a few times. He has attended the non-denominational religious service at the school chapel and feels connected spiritually. He also has used this time to think about his values concerning sex.

Ken was depressed for the first few weeks of the school

year. He missed home and was not sure he had made the right decision to live away from home. Rather than ignore these feelings, Ken made an appointment with one of the counselors at the counseling center. After a few visits to the counselor, Ken felt better about being away from home, and his depression lifted. Just knowing the counselors were there to help made Ken feel less alone and more in control of his life.

Ken also has been paying attention to his studies. He makes sure his homework does not accumulate. He took a study skills course at the student center for academic support, and this helped him study more effectively.

In addition to Ken's efforts to improve his overall wellness, he has adopted a few specific techniques for coping effectively with the stress he feels over forming new relationships. He has used time management (reduce) effectively to help him control his schedule. This has enabled him to fit everything he likes into his busy schedule. He relies on Ellis and Harper's ABCDE techniques (rethink) to examine

STRESS IN OUR WORLD (CONT'D)

Ken (cont'd)

his illogical thoughts about his new friendships. He has realized, for instance, that he is normal in his fear and misgivings about sharing his deepest feelings with his roommate as their relationship becomes more intimate. He also has realized that the stress he feels about his long-held sexual values is normal, and he can use some techniques to cope with this stress.

A few times a week Ken takes advantage of the college's large collection of musical recordings. He goes to the library and listens to his favorite recordings in one of the school's private audio cubicles. He finds that this helps him slow down (relax). He also has found a side benefit to his off-season exercise program. The running and weight lifting are an invaluable outlet for his stress-related tension and energy (release).

Ken also has allowed himself to release his sexual tensions through intimate yet nonintercourse outlets.

Ken has suffered some setbacks in his intimate relationships. He has had some arguments with his roommate. Ken and his roommate are very different, and occasionally Ken loses his temper over his roommate's sloppiness. After Ken cools off, however, they talk and keep communicating. Ken's girlfriend often is impatient with his sexuality. She is not a virgin and does not understand his desire to remain a virgin. He is not sure where all of this is leading, but he is keeping an open mind and enjoying the process, viewing his relationships more as a challenge than a source of stress.

ing model will enable you to list the pros and cons involved in making a decision regarding intimate or loving relationships. One side often will outweigh the other. When listing pros and cons, weighting is important. You may have only one or two pros or cons, but if they are very important and represent your core values, they carry enough weight to sway your decision.

Reduce

Intimacy is nurtured over time. One must devote time to a relationship to develop intimacy. This means using the various *reduce* strategies explored in Chapter 7, which may require you to use your time better.

This also may require you to use the three *As* of coping (abolish, avoid, and alter) to more effectively manage the stressors in your life. By eliminating excess stressors and managing your commitments more effec-

KEY
TO UNDERSTANDING

When one weighs the pros and cons of a decision, the weighting of the variables is important. Often each variable has a different value.

tively, you should gain the additional time needed for your new intimate relationships.

Communicating effectively will also help reduce the stress of your intimate relationships. Miscommunication is a source of stress in new relationships. Getting to know another person and ensuring that that person knows who you are requires open, clear, and continuous communication. Be precise and specific about your thoughts and feelings. Listen actively and seek clarification of unclear statements. Chapter 7 reviews communication theory and methods to communicate effectively.

Masters, Johnson, and Kolodny[13] identify three main causes for lack of clarity in intimate communication:

1. *Not saying what you mean.* People often cannot find the right words to express how they truly feel, particularly in intimate conversation. In many cases, people may not be fully in touch with their feelings. At other times, people may avoid saying how they really feel or what they really mean out of fear of hurting the other person's feelings or to avoid risking rejection.

2. *Sending mixed messages.* Mixed messages carry contradictory information. Messages can be mixed by body language or a tone of voice that does not fit the spoken. When someone says "nothing is wrong" but has a rigid body posture or avoids eye contact, the message is mixed. Saying "I don't really care" through tight, gritted teeth leaves the receiver of the message doubting its validity. Mixed messages also can result when the ending of a sentence is inconsistent with its beginning. "I really like you, but I think we are seeing a little bit too much of each other," might be construed as a mixed message.

3. *Not being specific.* Statements that are vague or general leave a person frustrated and wondering what the sender really means. "We're really not cut out for each other," "You're no fun anymore," and "We could use more time apart" all are vague messages that need further clarification.

Do not allow miscommunication to sabotage your intimacy. If you are unsure about something your partner said or implied, take responsibility for clearing this up. Do not assume that your partner is even aware of the issue. A key to understanding this is realizing that the partner may not even know the implications of what they said. Do not let unresolved miscommunications grow into underlying sources of mistrust, confusion, anger, or resentment. Masters, Johnson, and Kolodny[13] offer seven suggestions for improving clarity in communications (see the box on p. 487).

KEY
TO UNDERSTANDING

People often are unaware that the interpretation of their words is a source of stress.

Clearing Up Miscommunication

One can improve communications in several ways. Here are some general suggestions to consider:

1. Think through what you want to say and how you will say it, particularly if it is an important or emotionally charged message.

2. Let your partner know your priorities; try not to crowd in so many requests and instructions that it is difficult to grasp your key points.

3. Be concise. Long-winded discussions are more likely to confuse than clarify. On the other hand, being concise does not mean being simplistic or superficial. Do not leave out important information about your feelings or desires in an effort be brief.

4. Do not talk *at* your partner. Give him or her a chance to respond and interact.

5. Try not to begin communications by criticizing or blaming your partner. Starting on a negative note puts your partner on the defensive and makes objective listening difficult.

6. Do not be afraid to put what you need to say in a letter if you are having trouble saying it face to face. Writing it down shows that you care enough to take the time to say it carefully.

7. Ask for feedback from your partner to be sure your partner has understood and to get his or her reactions.

Modified from Masters, W., Johnson, V., & Kolodny, R. (1992). *Human sexuality*. New York: Harper Collins.

Relax

Relaxation techniques will help you cope with stressors by putting your body into a state that is incompatible with stress. This will stop the stress response and recharge you. This will slow your body and cancel the harmful effects of the stress response.

You may choose passive relaxation techniques, such as imagery, meditation, and visualization, discussed in Chapter 7. You may prefer the more active relaxation strategies from Chapter 8, such as systematic muscle relaxation, yoga, or t'ai chi ch'uan. These activities not only will relax your muscles but will slow your mind as well, giving you a break from the rumble of thoughts about your relationships.

Release

Vigorous physical activity is an excellent method for purging the tension and stress of a relationship. Other outlets such as sports or exercise are excellent ways to constructively use up the energy that the body mobilizes in response to relationship-related stress.

Putting it All Together

As mentioned in Chapters 1 and 5, being well in a holistic sense means functioning well across the five dimensions of health: physical, mental, emotional, spiritual, social, and environmental. Wellness is your core defense against potential stressors.

The greater your physical wellness, the more energy you will have at your disposal to meet the demands of the stress response. Your mental functioning will help you process information, weigh facts, and make better decisions. A greater emotional well-being will enable you to recognize and control your intimacy-related emotions without questioning your sanity. Having a strong social network will give you a greater array of social resources for advice and help. Your spiritual wellness will serve as an anchor to steady you when you feel adrift. Your environmental wellness keeps your perspective of the world around you in check to help you avoid excess stressors.

Academic Coursework and Stress

The second major developmental task of early adulthood is a commitment to work. For most college students, this work is their school work. However, many students also are employed at least part-time and have some commitment to a paying job in addition to their school work.

College-level academic work can be very demanding. For some students, this represents a great change from their work in high school. In most cases, college classes require much more reading and writing. Each class might require students to read hundreds of pages of text in a week, write at least one major research paper and take three examinations in a semester, and always be prepared to discuss the current topic in class.

In addition, many colleges emphasize communication skills and require students to present their work to their classmates and participate in classroom discussions. Debates, group discussions, and role playing are common parts of classes.

The workload can be difficult to manage even under the best of circumstances, when students are full-time, live on campus, and do not have to work. When students must commute, work part-time or full-time, and raise families, they have difficulty finding the time to prepare for their classes.

Commuter students and evening students also may have difficulty fitting in and developing the kind of support systems available to full-time, residential students. Commuters and part-time evening students often do not have the luxury of spending their free time on campus, making friends, joining clubs, and participating in extracurricular activities. They also frequently have more difficulty accessing some of the college's resources, ranging from career counseling to equipment that may not be available in the evening. Because of this, commuters and part-time evening students sometimes feel estranged from their schools. Many colleges are acknowledging the special needs of these and other nontraditional students and are developing special services to meet them. This includes extending the hours of key college personnel such as advisors, registrars, and counselors into the evening. Many colleges have special commuter or evening-student organizations, complete with full privileges to vote in the school's elections.

Not only are college classes much more demanding than high school classes, but college students also are much more independent. Students are expected to track assignments and test dates by reading their class syllabus. Attendance usually is not as closely watched as in high school, and students must be self-motivated to attend class. Absent students are held accountable for all information presented in class.

To survive, students must be focused, self-motivated, and able to work autonomously. Some students perceive the rigors of academia as a challenge. They are focused and motivated to do well. They perceive coursework as a test of their abilities and respond favorably to its demands. They relish their freedom and autonomy.

For others, coursework is extremely stressful. Rather than perceiving it as a challenge, they perceive it as a stressor. Some may feel overwhelmed by the sheer volume of work. Others feel inadequate, and unable to cope with the intellectual demands of college. They lack the study skills required to wade through hundreds of pages of text and to compose research papers. Still others cannot handle the autonomy. With no one nagging them to get up and go to class or study, they fall behind in their classes. They lack the self-discipline necessary to do their work. They prefer to party rather than delay any gratification. The temptations are many and varied. Many students use alcohol and other drugs to cope with college stressors. Binging on alcohol and other drugs becomes part of the social fabric of their college experience.

Wechsler et al.[20] studied the binge-drinking behavior of more than 17,000 students on 140 4-year college campuses across the United States. The researchers defined binge drinking as having four or five drinks in a row within the past 2 weeks. Students were asked a series of questions to determine whether they binged on alcohol, how frequently, and with what consequences. (The box on p. 491 can help assess a person's alcohol use.)

This study confirmed the results of several smaller studies of college drinking.[12,16] About one out of six (16%) of all the respondents was a non-drinker (15% of the men; 16% of the women). About two out of five (41%) were drinkers but did not binge. Almost half (44%) of all the students were binge drinkers. About one in five (19%) was a frequent binge drinker (17% of the women and 23% of the men). These students had three or more binge drinking occasions in the past 2 weeks.

The consequences of binge drinking are many and varied. The researchers found that binge drinkers were more likely than nonbinge drinkers and abstainers to engage in unplanned sexual activity, not use protection when having sex, get hurt or injured, damage property, argue with friends, miss classes, fall behind in school work, and do something they later regretted. Frequent binge drinkers were 10 times more likely than other binge drinkers to have unplanned and unprotected sex, get into trouble with campus police, and be injured or damage property.

Binge drinkers also negatively affect nondrinkers and other students who encounter bingers. Colleges with the highest percentages of bingers also had the highest rates of secondary binge effects. Nonbingers at these institutions reported such problems as having their sleep or studying interrupted (68%), having to take care of a drunk student (54%), being insulted or humiliated (34%), experiencing an unwanted sexual advance (26%), having a serious argument (20%), being pushed, hit, or assaulted (13%), or being a victim of date rape (2%)

When asked to evaluate the seriousness of their binging and its repercussions, less than 1% of the binge drinkers identified themselves as problem drinkers.

Although Wechsler[20] did not attempt to determine why students binged, they did find that prior drinking behavior in high school influenced binging in college. Most of the students reported the same drinking patterns for high school and college. About half (47%) did not binge in either high school or college. About 22% binged in both high school and college. An additional 22% binged in college but not high school, and the remaining students (approximately 10%) were bingers in high school but not in college.

These findings suggest that interventions for curtailing alcohol binging may need to be targeted to precollege populations as well as college freshmen because many of the latter learned their behavior as high school students. Wechsler et al.,[21] in a previous study of 611 college freshmen and sophomores, found that students who were heavy drinkers in high school were much more likely to become bingers in college. College programs

How Do You Drink?

Answer the following questions about your alcohol use. Total your yes and no responses in the box at the end of each column.

	Yes	No
1. Do you drink more often than you did a year ago?	_____	_____
2. Do you drink more heavily than you did a year ago?	_____	_____
3. Do you drink to get drunk?	_____	_____
4. Do you drink to cope with stress?	_____	_____
5. Do you go drinking to meet people?	_____	_____
6. Do you drink to feel accepted by others?	_____	_____
7. In the past 2 weeks, have you had five drinks in a row at one sitting?	_____	_____
8. Have you had five or more drinks at one sitting more than three times in the past month?	_____	_____

9. After one or more episodes of drinking this year have you:

	Yes	No
■ Had a hangover?	_____	_____
■ Missed class?	_____	_____
■ Done something you regretted?	_____	_____
■ Forgotten where you were?	_____	_____
■ Argued with friends?	_____	_____
■ Gotten into trouble with campus police?	_____	_____
■ Gotten injured or hurt?	_____	_____
■ Gotten into a fight?	_____	_____
■ Had unplanned sex?	_____	_____
■ Not used protection during sex?	_____	_____
Totals	_____	_____

Scoring

Total your yes answers. If you had two or more yes answers, you may be exhibiting a pattern of unacceptable alcohol use and should consider exploring this with someone at your college's counseling center.

should focus on early identification and intervention among college freshmen who were heavy high school drinkers.

Wechsler et al.[20] noted that despite the overall decline in drinking in America the studies on college campuses fail to show a corresponding decrease. Drinking among college students often centers on the social nature of alcohol consumption. Gleason[10] found that college women perceive drinking as a way to be around others and seek acceptance from peers. Montgomery et al.[14] found that alcohol was consumed more for social than for personal reasons. Men and women reported using alcohol more for the purpose of meeting members of the opposite sex than for personal reasons, although alcohol did make them feel better about themselves.

Although the previous studies examined the motivation for alcohol use in general, Wechsler et al.[20] reported that drinking behavior that elsewhere would be characterized as alcohol abuse often is socially acceptable and even desirable behavior on certain college campuses. These "party schools" foster reputations that binge drinking is part of their college life. Conversely, institutions that do not have alcohol outlets within 1 mile of campus and colleges that prohibit alcohol use by anyone (even those older than 21 years) have lower rates of alcohol binging.

Others who have studied alcohol use among college students have found that interpersonal stress often is related to binging. Bradstock et al.,[4] in a study of 12,467 college women, found interpersonal stress to be significantly related to binge drinking. They also found high-risk behaviors (e.g., smoking, binge drinking, lack of seat-belt use) to be synergistically related to alcohol misuse. That is, women who binged on alcohol also were more likely to engage in multiple risk behaviors simultaneously (see Stress in Our World box on p. 493). Carver and Scheier[5] found that students used alcohol as a way to cope with the threat associated with course grades. They also found that using alcohol to cope did not always reduce stress. In many instances, drinking increased the feelings of threat.

As a result of these and other factors, most college students have difficulty maintaining the same high grade point averages they had in high school. Many who do not plan to continue their education beyond a bachelor's degree have difficulty staying motivated and studying hard for each class to maintain the highest possible grade point average. This is very unlike their high school days, when each grade was important and could determine whether they were accepted by the college of their choice or not accepted anywhere.

Some students cut corners in one class to concentrate on another. Others try to determine what will earn a good grade and focus on mastering those assignments and tasks rather than learning the subject matter. Still others lower their sights and accept lower grades to cope with college's increased academic demands.

STRESS IN OUR WORLD

Robin: A Party Animal

Robin is in big trouble. She is a second-semester sophomore at a large southern school and is on academic probation. Robin is a "party animal." She barely passed her freshman year by dropping two classes and earning the lowest possible grade point average.

As a freshman, Robin went wild. The daughter of very conservative parents,

Robin led a very regulated life before college. She had curfews, could date only certain guys, and was not allowed much independence. Now at school and living away from home for the first time, she broke all the rules. She stayed out late, cut class, dated anyone who interested her, got drunk frequently, and generally acted as if there were no tomorrow. When she did attend class, she often was hung over.

This year she is pledging a sorority and is spending even less time on her studies. Her sorority sisters have warned her about flunking out, but Robin dismissed them as "alarmists." Now on academic probation, Robin must begin to change her lifestyle if she is to remain in college.

Do you know a Robin? How do you feel about students who go wild? Is Robin's behavior typical? Ethical?

Most students, however, try to get the highest possible grade and find grades a significant source of stress. In analyzing several years' worth of students' self-reported stress logs, the author found that grades are consistently among the top five student stressors.[2] This applies to both the students who try to achieve the highest possible grade point average and those who are willing to sacrifice a high grade in one class to concentrate on another.

Paying for College

College students face many types of work-related stressors. College was much different 20 or more years ago. Freshmen were young, came directly from high school, and were full-time day students. Average tuition was much lower, and most students worked only during the summer to help defray costs incurred during the academic year.

The government helped reduce college costs and easily obtainable, low-interest loans to almost everyone. Students who could not afford tuition almost always could borrow what they needed or work part-time to pay their way.

Changing demographic and economic trends have reduced the number of traditional freshmen. The post-baby boom generation of college-age students is smaller than in recent decades. Colleges have been forced to compete for a smaller pool of applicants. Many colleges have changed their marketing strategies to target older returning students, second-degree students, and part-time evening and weekend students to maintain adequate numbers of students. Most nontraditional students do not work part-time just to earn pocket money for miscellaneous expenses. They and many traditional younger students work full-time and raise families as well as pay tuition and fees and buy books.

College tuition, room and board, and fees have soared. In 1977, 4 years of tuition, room, and board at a typical private liberal arts institution cost less than $20,000. In 1991 the same education cost slightly more than $50,000.[18] Conservative estimates for college costs per year are $12,635 for private colleges and $4,733 for public colleges. Average college tuition is expected to increase at about 6% to 7% annually through the 1990s.[18] Enrollment at any prestigious private colleges is falling dramatically because of a combination of fewer applicants and higher college costs.

While college costs have continued to escalate, government support for higher education has steadily decreased since 1980. The national student loan program that helped many students of the 1960s and 1970s has gone bankrupt. Qualifications for government student loans have become so restrictive that only the poorest students now qualify. The middle class, which makes up the bulk of student enrollment, essentially finds itself frozen out of loan programs. Private lenders also have raised their income requirements, eliminating most middle-class students. Other restrictions on loans, such as stricter family income and assets reporting, have made loans much harder to obtain for subsequent generations of students. Problems in the banking community, such as the high default rate on college loans and the savings and loan scandal, have made lenders leery about loaning money.

Even students who can borrow are concerned about their ability to repay their college debts after they graduate. With college costs escalating and the job market of the 1990s bleaker than in many decades, students are much less inclined to finance their entire education. Many students are choosing public colleges and 2-year institutions to further their education because costs at these institutions are much lower than at private schools.[18]

Work and Stress

As a result of this change in work and college over the past 20 years, work-related stress has taken on a new meaning. Students not only are stressed about future work and career decisions, they also are under a tremendous amount of pressure to perform their current jobs and simply survive economically.

For many, college hardly represents idyllic strolls across campus with hours of free time to discuss Plato and the meaning of life. Rather, it is a mad dash across campus to get to their cars and race to their jobs so they can pay their tuition.

Many fear that if they lose their jobs, they will have to drop out of school. Many would like to spend more time on campus, participate in activities, or simply study, but cannot because they must work and return home to care for children, spouses, or aging parents.

Job Versus Career

After college many students also find themselves having to take a pay cut to take an entry-level job in the career for which they have been preparing. These students, who have worked their way through college, find themselves earning more money from their current job than they could from a new job in their chosen discipline. Many of these students also face the prospect of working without benefits (e.g., health insurance) until these benefits take effect in their new job, in many cases only after several months.

Facing this kind of scenario, many students choose to keep their current jobs rather than start in their chosen discipline (see Stress in Our World box on p. 496). They are afraid to lose their salary and benefits, even though they probably would eventually surpass these levels in their new careers. A key to understanding this dilemma is realizing that occasionally one must take a step backward to move forward.

KEY
TO UNDERSTANDING

Sometimes we must step backward to move forward in life.

Coping With Academic and Work Stress: The Four *R*s

Rethink

Rethinking your views about school and work begins with values clarification. You must determine what is truly important to you. Use the values-clarification activities described in Chapter 6, to determine the role of money, job, career, grades, and academic success in your life.

For some students, earning *C*s and *D*s is acceptable. Having a good time at college is most important for them. For others, anything less than an *A* is unacceptable. They are not in college for the social diversions. They want to learn as much as possible. They would feel extremely guilty if their grades slipped because they partied rather than studied. Most students fall somewhere between these two extremes. They want to do well academically but also take advantage of the social opportunities of college life.

STRESS IN OUR WORLD

Laura

Laura just graduated with a degree in physical education. She student-taught in a nearby elementary school, and the school offered her a job teaching physical education. This was exactly the kind of position Laura has always wanted. She loves working with children.

Laura currently works for a caterer. When she told her boss about the teaching offer, he asked Laura to stay and work for his catering service full-time. He said he would give her a raise that would make her salary about 40% higher than the entry-level teaching salary she was offered. Laura decided to stay with her current job as a caterer rather than put her new degree to work.

Laura is making good money. As a freshman 4 years ago, she worked for minimum wage during the school year. She mostly prepared food for the catering service. She was a good worker and received two raises during her first year. Her job provided the money she needed for tuition, fees, books, and other expenses. She viewed her job as a means to getting her degree.

As a sophomore, Laura was promoted to head chef and was put in charge of food preparation. She performed well and received another raise. Although she liked the job and the money, she still viewed it as something to do until she graduated. She mostly worked weekends, and the job did not interfere with her schoolwork.

In her junior year, Laura was allowed to try the sales end of the business, and she did very well. Her commissions were a nice incentive to work harder. She made much more money than she ever thought possible for a part-time job, but this job still was not the goal of her education.

By her senior year, Laura no longer prepared food. She worked in sales and marketing and spent her hours meeting with prospective clients and promoting her caterer. The money was good, and she had a very flexible job. The job even allowed her to do her student teaching.

Laura agonized over her decision. She really wanted to teach but is attracted by the higher salary of the catering position. She is not challenged by her current job but feels comfortable there and is used to her current standard of living.

What should Laura do? Do you know anyone like Laura? Do you expect to take a pay cut to work in your discipline?

Some students are committed to graduating in 4 years and view their course load as fixed and unchangeable. They would not consider stretching the college experience over more than 4 years.

Clarify how you view your current job and the importance of your future career. Consider such issues as the type of job you need, salary requirements, and working conditions (see Assess Yourself 14-3). Your thoughts about these and other related issues influence how you divide your time among course work, socializing, and working at a job. Depending on the area you value most, you may decide to reduce the demands in one of these areas. Coping skills, such as Ellis and Harper's[7] ABCDE described in Chapters 6 and 13, will help you determine whether you are thinking rationally and logically about school and work. Making sound decisions based on a logical rethinking of your priorities will help reduce your stress.

Get accurate information on which to base your decisions. College career service officers are dedicated to helping you find the information about work that you need.

Reduce

After entering college, you may find you no longer can meet the demands on your time. A full load of academic course work can be very time-intensive. Just keeping up with the reading can be an incredible burden. If you find that you cannot keep current with your studies, something must change (see Stress in Our World box on p. 499).

Working through college can be a major source of stress. One example is schedule-related problems. Working enough hours to maintain one's lifestyle can be very difficult. To reduce this stress, develop a budget for each week, month, semester, or academic year, and stick to it (see Assess Yourself box on p. 515).

One can apply reduce strategies to academic stress in two ways. You can either reduce your lifestyle demands (personal activities that cut into study time) or reduce your course work demands (academic activities that cut into your personal time). You cannot have both.

Most traditional students choose to reduce lifestyle activities that cut into their study time. They employ time-management techniques, such as the three *A*s (abolish, avoid, and alter), to rank the demands on their time and ultimately reduce the less important activities.

Other students choose to reduce their academic demands so they can maintain their lifestyle. These students take fewer credits per semester and stay in school longer. This is becoming increasingly common as more students must work to pay for school. They learn that they cannot perform effectively if they try to maintain a full academic course load and work enough hours to pay their bills. By taking fewer classes each semester, these students can spend less time on their schoolwork. There is no one correct route for everyone; the choice depends on the individual.

Communicating effectively can help reduce work and school stress. Students' stress about work and classes often is intensified by the expectations and demands of significant others. Parents usually want the best for their children, but they often place great pressure on students. Many parents push students in directions contrary to what their children need and want.

Using the communication skills discussed in Chapter 7 will help you communicate effectively and prevent misunderstandings and miscommunications from contributing to work-related stress. The DESC model of assertive communication discussed in Chapter 7 is especially effective in helping you tell others how you feel.

Relax

Completing academic course work can be physically draining. Sitting in a wooden library chair for hours or poring over a computer terminal as you search journal articles can be very tiring. Studying for exams until late hours and hunching over a typewriter or word processor can create great muscular tension.

Taking breaks from your work and relaxing helps manage academic stress. Make a habit of taking frequent relaxation breaks when studying or writing. Get up, stretch, go for a walk around your room or floor, or better yet, go outside. Take a 5-minute break about every 45 minutes.

Quick and simple relaxation strategies, such as visual imagery, diaphragmatic breathing, and the calming response, discussed in Chapter 8, or yoga, stretching, and t'ai chi ch'uan, described in Chapter 9, can be performed for a few minutes and provide a respite from the demands of studying.

Take 20 minutes after you finish studying to fully relax before continuing with your day. Also try to build relaxation time into your work schedule. If you have morning and afternoon coffee breaks, use them wisely. Take time to do some stretching, deep breathing, and visualization. Get up from your desk and take a walk around your floor. Use your lunch hour to take a walk, exercise, or relax rather than eat a heavy meal. Get away from your telephone and desk. Try to break the habit of eating at your desk.

Release

You may find that you need more than gentle relaxation activities to help you cope with the demands of work and school. Exercise vigorously before and after study sessions of several hours. As a preparation for studying, vigorous physical activity will help loosen tense muscles and circulate oxygen-rich blood throughout your brain. When you have finished studying, exercise will help rid your body of accumulated tension.

Exercise helps clear your mind after several hours of focusing on a specific topic, whether it is work or study. Exercise also relaxes you and helps you sleep well, replenishing the energy you expended throughout the day.

STRESS IN OUR WORLD

Donna

Donna is a 22-year-old college junior. A commuter, she attends school full-time but takes only 12 credit hours. She works 20 hours per week and has found that this combination of work hours and credit hours suits her. She had great difficulty her first 2 years of college. She was taking 18 credit hours and working 25 hours a week. She never exercised, her diet was a disaster (she lived on coffee and fast food), she had low self-esteem, and her social life was a wasteland. She was exhausted, stressed, and doing poorly in all of her classes. She never seemed to have any time for study or for her friends. She was very unhappy and considered dropping out of school.

After much introspection and some help from the college counseling center, she made some changes in her life. First, she decided that something had to be eliminated. She needed to work to meet a car payment, tuition, and other expenses. She lived with her family, but they could not afford to help her financially beyond providing her room and board. She eliminated 5 hours (one evening) from her job schedule. However, freeing this one evening did not seem to make much difference. She still carried 18 credits and felt overwhelmed.

Not until she accepted the fact that she was carrying too many credit hours and cut back to 12 did Donna begin to enjoy school. Her grades began to improve because she could devote more time to studying. She even had enough time to go to the college's center for academic support and take a study-skills course. She found that she could use that extra evening to go to the school library and use their computer center.

Studying at the computer center gave her access to word processing, laser printers, and on-line data searches. She not only had more time to study but she was using her time more effectively.

In her second year, Donna took a health course and learned about wellness. She began to pay attention to her diet and realized that she could eat well on the run by choosing her fast foods more carefully. She even began exercising four times a week with an aerobics tape. She began to pay attention to her friends again and joined a commuter support group on campus. She felt connected both at home and on campus.

Now in her third year, Donna has accepted the fact that it will take her at least 5 years to graduate. However, this is not a problem anymore. She is focused, in control of her life, and enjoying every day.

Take advantage of any exercise or recreational programs your place of employment offers during lunchtime. If not, try to start a lunchtime aerobics program. Learn whether your place of business has showers or locker rooms. At the least, you can walk at lunchtime (stair walking can be very intensive).

Your college is an excellent source of recreational programs and exercise facilities. Most colleges have intramural athletic programs or open gymnasium hours for students who do not compete in varsity athletics. These programs offer an opportunity to play a friendly game of basketball, volleyball, or many other sports without the need to commit to an organized team.

Most colleges also offer classes in aerobic exercise, weight training, and swimming and have nonclass open hours at the pool, weight room, and workout rooms. Some colleges even offer squash and racquetball rooms and tennis courts to students and faculty.

Putting it All Together

Coping with the demands of undergraduate coursework requires a tremendous amount of physical energy. Attending class, reading assignments, writing reports and papers, and studying for tests all require energy. More than simply staying awake and performing these tasks, our brains need energy to work at peak efficiency. We need good food to fuel our bodies, sufficient rest to regenerate it, and enough exercise to keep it fit.

Physical Wellness

The greater one's physical well-being, the more efficiently one can perform the tasks of college-level academic work. We simply have more staying power. Our minds process information more efficiently, and we can work harder and longer.

Your physical well-being also directly affects your ability to cope with work-related stressors because it affects the amount of energy you can devote to work over time. High levels of fitness will give you greater energy, strength, endurance, and flexibility. All of these facets of fitness can help you meet the demands of work and keep you energized, thinking clearly and performing efficiently. If your job is physically demanding, from waitressing to operating heavy equipment, being fit will help ensure that you still have energy at the end of your day so that you can attend to your studies, relationships, or community.

Emotional Wellness

High levels of emotional well-being enable you to focus on the rigors of college work. It is much more difficult to focus on studies if you are on an emotional rollercoaster every day. College students must be able to draw on their self-esteem, courage, and positive emotions in times of intense pressure.

Your emotional well-being also will affect how well you handle your thoughts and feelings about your work and co-workers. An inability to understand and cope with the emotions evoked on the job may affect your school work or interfere with your ability to focus on your studies when you leave the job.

Employers often offer employee assistance benefits, which usually include mental health services. **Employee assistance professionals** can help you cope with the demands of the job. Colleges also usually provide help with emotional problems through their counseling centers. These facilities provide help to day and evening students, and in many cases, their families. They can help students understand and cope with the emotional challenges of juggling the demands of school, work, and family.

Intellectual Wellness

High-level mental functioning is essential to college success. Utilizing specific study skills that you have mastered up until this point is essential. Most colleges run study skills courses through their office of academic support if you have never mastered these skills. These courses will teach you skills, such as reading more effectively, outlining, writing papers, and improving your memory.

Become familiar with the college's library. Learn how and where to find the information that you will need to succeed. The library staff is committed to helping you find the information you need.

Learn how to use technology to improve your performance. Mastering a simple word-processing computer program will save you countless hours in rewriting papers and other assignments. Learn how to perform computer information searches to save time. Learn the locations and operation of your college's fax machines. These machines can move information at the speed of a telephone call when you need information quickly.

Work to improve your creativity. Expand your methods of solving problems. Take chances and try new approaches. Sharpening your mental skills will help you cope with the rigors of work as well as school. Take advantage of seminars and continuing education programs offered at work or school to help you refine your professional skills.

Use your mental skills to evaluate careers and jobs. Take advantage of your college's career services office. Professionals at this office can help you evaluate career trends and potential employers and can identify regions of the country that have a need for your skills. Career service offices also offer aptitude and interest testing for students unsure of their desires or aptitudes for specific careers.

Social Wellness

Having a strong social support system both on campus and at home can provide valuable resources in coping with coursework-related stress. Maintain old social networks and develop new ones. Join a study group, or form one with your friends. Such a group will help keep you motivated to study and will give you a forum in which to test your new ideas. Make at least

employee assistance professional (EAP) a human resource specialist responsible for a broad range of employee services ranging from retirement planning to mental health

one friend in each class. Get the person's home and school telephone numbers and arrange with him or her to exchange notes whenever either of you is absent. Include your professors in your social networks. Visit your professors during their office hours to show them you care about their classes. Ask them to clarify your unresolved class issues before they turn into problems.

Make sure your parents, brothers, and sisters understand the rigors of your class assignments. Try to arrange your schedule at home to give you the time and space your studies require. Tell your family what you need from them to complete your coursework. Perhaps your family can give you financial, emotional, or intellectual help in coping with your studies. Use your family for such tasks as proofreading, quizzing you, or testing your debating skills. Simply having friends and family nearby for play is a valuable resource for temporarily putting aside your worries.

Spiritual Wellness

Pay attention to your spirituality; connect to something beyond yourself. This connection will enable you to put your schoolwork in a broader perspective. It will enable you to compare the demands of academia with the concerns of others and your entire community.

Developing your spiritual side can help maintain or restore your faith in the future when you begin to question your motives and doubt whether the sacrifices are worthwhile.

Summary

This chapter examines the stress associated with Erikson's major developmental tasks of young adulthood, forming intimate relationships and committing oneself to work. It discusses how these issues are merely potential stressors until we perceive them differently. Some of us are more prepared than others to handle the demands and the confusion associated with developing relationships and focusing on a job and career.

The chapter examines intimacy and how it often is confused with love and sexual relations, while in fact these three are related yet different. Stress often arises from the strong emotions evoked by trying to understand these confusing relationships. Intimate relationships often are stressful because they force us to confront our long-held beliefs and values about life.

For many students, living independently for the first time creates the opportunity to explore intimate relationships. Dealing with roommates, making new friends, and developing romantic relationships all create potentially challenging or stressful situations. The chapter examines this transition, including the factors that influence how we interpret these opportunities to develop intimacy.

The chapter discusses coping with relationship-related stress, combining the four *R*s in a holistic, lifestyle-oriented approach.

The second major developmental task of young adulthood is committing to one's work. The two major sources of work for young college students are academic coursework and part-time or full-time employment.

The chapter compares the the academic rigors of college with those of high school. These differences can be perceived as either challenges or stressors. Issues such as the nature of college classes, autonomy, time requirements of academic work and outside demands on students' time are factors that influence the perception of academic work as stressful. Specific coping strategies, combining the four *R*s into a wellness model of coping are effective in dealing with the stresses of college.

Finally, the chapter examines work-related stress, exploring current and future work-related issues and analyzing some of the factors that contribute to the perception of work as a stressor or challenge. The role of employment for college students has changed in the past 20 years. Many students must work to pay for their education. The part-time jobs of some students become lucrative options, often rivaling entry-level salaries for their profession.

For all working students, balancing the requirements of work and school may be perceived as stressful. Again, a framework for coping with work-related stressors incorporates a variety of techniques from all of the four *R*s.

Student Study Questions

1. Describe Erikson's major developmental task of young adulthood.
2. Why does intimacy take time to develop?
3. Describe four barriers to intimacy.
4. How does Sternberg define consummate love?
5. Describe two other types of love that lack components of consummate love.
6. Explain how communication skills are a *reduce* coping strategy for intimacy-related stress.
7. Describe the changing role of employment in paying college expenses.
8. Explain how values clarification can be used as a *rethink* strategy for coping with academic and other work-related stress.
9. Describe three relaxation skills that can be used easily on the job.
10. Describe how to incorporate two release strategies into a typical school or work day.

References

1. Block, J.D. (1980). *Friendship: how to give it, how to get it.* New York: MacMillan.
2. Blonna, R. (1994). Unpublished manuscript.

3. Blumstein, P. & Schwartz, P. (1983). *American couples.* William Morrow.

4. Bradstock, K., Forman, M., Binkin, N., & Gentry, E. (1988). Alcohol use and health behavior lifestyles among U.S. women: the behavioral risk factor surveys. *Addictive Behaviors, 13* (1), 61-71.

5. Carver, C.S. & Scheier, M.F. (1994). Situational coping and coping dispositions in stressful transactions. *Journal of Personal and Social Psychology, 66* (1), 184-195.

6. Crooks, R. & Baur, C. (1993). *Our sexuality.* Redwood City, CA: Benjamin Cummings/Addison-Wesley

7. Ellis, A. & Harper, R. (1975). *A guide to rational living.* North Hollywood, CA: Melvin Powers.

8. Erikson, E. (1978). *Childhood & society,* (2nd ed.). WW Norton.

9. Fromm, E. (1956). *The art of loving.* New York: Harper & Row.

10. Gleason, N.A. (1994). College women and alcohol: a relational perspective. *Journal of American College Health, 42* (6), 279-289.

11. Hales, D. (1991). *Your health.* Redwood City, CA: Addison Wesley/Benjamin Cummings.

12. Johnston et al. (1991). Drug use among American high school seniors, college students, and young adults, 1975-1990. Publication ADM 91-1835 (Vol. 2). Washington DC: US Government Printing Office.

13. Masters, W., Johnson, V., & Kolodny, R. (1992). *Human sexuality.* New York: Harper Collins.

14. Montgomery, R., Benedicto, J., & Haemmerlie, F. (1993). Personal vs. social motivations of undergraduates for using alcohol. *Psychological Reports, 73* (3), 960-962.

15. Payne & Hahn (1992). *Understanding your health.* St. Louis: Mosby.

16. Presley et al. (1993). Alcohol and drugs on American campuses: use, consequences and perceptions of the campus environment. (Vol. 1). Carbondale, IL: The Core Institute.

17. Sternberg, R.J. (1988). *The triangle of love: intimacy, passions, commitment.* New York: Basic Books.

18. Stoffel, J. (1991). College economics 101. *Fidelity Focus,* Summer.

19. Thompson, C. (1993). The male role stereotype. In Cyrus, V. *Experiencing race, class, and gender in the United States* (pp 146-148). Mountain View, CA: Mayfield.

20. Wechsler, H., Davenport, A., Dowdell, G., Moeykens, B., & Castillo, S. (1994). Health and behavioral consequences of binge drinking in College. *JAMA, 272* (21), 1672-1677.

21. Wechsler, H., Isaac, N., Grodstein, F., & Sellers, D. (1994). Continuation and initiation of alcohol use from the first to the second year of college. *Journal of Studies of Alcohol, 55* (1), 41-45.

Name: _____ Date: _____

IQ Test[11]

This exercise is designed to measure your capacity for intimacy—how well you have fared in and what you have learned from your interpersonal relationships from infancy through adulthood. In a general way, it helps measure your sense of security and self-acceptance, which gives you the courage to risk the embarrassment of proffering love or friendship or respect and getting no response. This exercise can provide insight and can alert you to weaknesses that may be reducing your performance in everything from meeting and interacting with potential mates to ordering food in a restaurant.

Directions

Read each question carefully. If your response is yes or mostly yes, place a plus (+) on the line preceding the question. If your response is no or mostly no, place a minus (-) on the line. If you honestly cannot decide, place a zero (0) on the line, but try to enter as few zeros as possible. Even if a particular question does not apply to you, try to imagine yourself in the situation described and answer accordingly.

Compare any significance in the number or the frequency of plus or minus answers. Simply be honest when answering the questions.

_____ 1. Do you have more than your share of colds?

_____ 2. Do you believe that emotions have very little to do with physical ills?

_____ 3. Do you often have indigestion?

_____ 4. Do you frequently worry about your health?

__+__ 5. Would a nutritionist be appalled by your diet?

__+__ 6. Do you usually watch sports rather than participate in them?

_____ 7. Do you often feel depressed or in a bad mood?

__+__ 8. Are you irritable when things go wrong?

_____ 9. Were you happier in the past than you are right now?

_____ 10. Do you believe it possible that a person's character can be read, or one's future foretold by means of astrology, tarot cards, or the like?

_____ 11. Do you worry about the future?

__+__ 12. Do you try to hold in your anger as long as possible and then sometimes explode in a rage?

_____ 13. Do your loved ones often make you feel jealous?

__+__ 14. If your intimate partner were unfaithful one time, would you be unable to forgive and forget?

Cont'd

IQ Test (cont'd)

_____ 15. Do you have difficulty making important decisions?

_____ 16. Would you abandon a goal rather than take risks to reach it?

_____ 17. When you go on vacation, do you take some work along?

_____ 18. Do you usually wear clothes that are dark or neutral in color?

_____ 19. Do you usually do what you feel like doing, regardless of social pressures or criticism?

_____ 20. Does a beautiful speaking voice turn you on?

_____ 21. Do you always take an interest in where you are and what is happening around you?

_____ 22. Do you find most odors interesting rather than offensive?

_____ 23. Do you enjoy trying new and different foods?

_____ 24. Do you like to touch and be touched?

_____ 25. Are you easily amused?

_____ 26. Do you often do things spontaneously or impulsively?

_____ 27. Can you sit still through a long committee meeting or lecture without twiddling your thumbs or wiggling in your chair?

_____ 28. Can you usually fall asleep and stay asleep without the use of sleeping pills or tranquilizers?

_____ 29. Are you a moderate drinker rather than either a heavy drinker or teetotaler?

_____ 30. Do you smoke not at all or very little?

_____ 31. Can you put yourself in another person's place and experience their emotions?

_____ 32. Are you seriously concerned about social problems even when they do not affect you personally?

_____ 33. Do you think most people can be trusted?

_____ 34. Can you talk to a celebrity or a stranger as easily as you talk to your neighbors?

_____ 35. Do you get along well with salesclerks, waiters, service-station attendants, and cab drivers?

_____ 36. In mixed company, can you discuss sex easily and without feeling uncomfortable?

_____ 37. Can you express appreciation for a gift or a favor without feeling uneasy?

_____ 38. When you feel affection for someone, can you express it physically as well as verbally?

ASSESS YOURSELF 14-1 (cont'd)

IQ Test (cont'd)

_____ 39. Do you sometimes feel that you have extrasensory perception?

_____ 40. Do you like yourself?

_____ 41. Do you like others of your own gender?

_____ 42. Do you enjoy an evening alone?

_____ 43. Do you vary your schedule to avoid doing the same things at the same times each day?

_____ 44. Is love more important to you than money or status?

_____ 45. Do you place a higher premium on kindness than on truthfulness?

_____ 46. Do you think it is possible to be too rational?

_____ 47. Have you attended, or would you attend, a sensitivity encounter group session?

_____ 48. Do you discourage friends from visiting unannounced?

_____ 49. Would you feel it a sign of weakness to seek help for a sexual problem?

_____ 50. Are you upset when a homosexual seems attracted to you?

_____ 51. Do you have difficulty communicating with someone of the opposite sex?

_____ 52. Do you believe that men who write poetry are less masculine than men who drive trucks?

_____ 53. Do most women prefer men with well-developed muscles to men with well-developed emotions?

_____ 54. Are you generally indifferent to the kind of place in which you live?

_____ 55. Do you consider it a waste of money to buy flowers for yourself or others?

_____ 56. When you see an art object you like, do you pass it up if the cost would mean cutting back on your food budget?

_____ 57. Do you think it pretentious and extravagant to have an elegant dinner when alone or with members of your immediate family?

_____ 58. Are you often bored?

_____ 59. Do Sundays depress you?

_____ 60. Do you frequently feel nervous?

_____ 61. Do you dislike the work you do to earn a living?

_____ 62. Do you think a carefree hippie lifestyle would have no delights for you?

_____ 63. Do you watch television selectively rather than simply to kill time?

Cont'd

IQ Test (cont'd)

_____ 64. Have you read any good books recently?

_____ 65. Do you often daydream?

_____ 66. Do you like to cuddle with pets?

_____ 67. Do you like many different forms and styles of art?

_____ 68. Do you enjoy watching an attractive person of the opposite sex?

_____ 69. Can you describe how your date or mate looked the last time you went out together?

_____ 70. Do you find it easy to talk to new acquaintances?

_____ 71. Do you communicate with others through touch as well as through words?

_____ 72. Do you enjoy pleasing members of your family?

_____ 73. Do you avoid joining clubs and organizations?

_____ 74. Do you worry more about how you present yourself to prospective dates than about how you treat them?

_____ 75. Are you afraid that if people knew you too well the would not like you?

_____ 76. Do you fall in love at first sight?

_____ 77. Do you always fall in love with someone who reminds you of your parent of the opposite sex?

_____ 78. Do you think love is all you currently need to be happy?

_____ 79. Do you feel a sense of rejection if a person you love tries to preserve his or her independence?

_____ 80. Can you accept your loved one's anger and still believe in his or her love?

_____ 81. Can you express your innermost thoughts and feelings to the person you love?

_____ 82. Do you talk over disagreements with your partner rather than silently worry about them?

_____ 83. Can you easily accept the fact that your partner has loved others before you and not worry about how you compare with them?

_____ 84. Can you accept a partner's disinterest in sex without feeling rejected?

_____ 85. Can you accept occasional sessions of unsatisfactory sex without blaming yourself or your partner?

_____ 86. Should unmarried adolescents be denied contraceptives?

_____ 87. Do you believe that even for adults in private there are some sexual acts that should remain illegal?

ASSESS YOURSELF 14-1 (cont'd)

IQ Test (cont'd)

_____ 88. Do you think that hippie communes and Israeli kibbutzim have nothing useful to teach the average American?

_____ 89. Should a couple put up with an unhappy marriage for the sake of their children?

_____ 90. Do you think that mate swappers necessarily have unhappy marriages?

_____ 91. Should older men and women be content not to have sex?

_____ 92, Do you believe that pornography contributes to sex crimes?

_____ 93. Is sexual abstinence beneficial to a person's health, strength, wisdom, or character?

_____ 94. Can a truly loving wife or husband sometimes be sexually unresponsive?

_____ 95. Can intercourse during a woman's menstrual period be as appealing as at any other time?

_____ 96. Should a woman concentrate on her own sexual pleasure during intercourse rather than pretend enjoyment to increase her partner's pleasure?

_____ 97. Can a man's effort to bring his partner to orgasm reduce his own pleasure?

_____ 98. Should fun and sensual pleasure be the principal goals in sexual relations?

_____ 99. Is pressure to perform well a common cause of sexual incapacity?

_____ 100. Is sexual intercourse an uninhibited romp rather than a demonstration of sexual ability?

Explanation of Scoring

Questions 1-18, count your minuses: _____ 11

Questions 19-47, count your pluses: _____ 17

Questions 48-62, count your minuses: _____ 12

Questions 63-72, count your pluses: _____ 5

Questions 73-79, count your minuses: _____ 2

Questions 80-85, count your pluses: _____ 5

Questions 86-93, count your minuses: _____ 7

Questions 94-100, count your pluses: _____ 6

Total: _____ 63

Cont'd

IQ Test (cont'd)

To obtain your correct score, subtract half the total number of zero answers from this total.

If your corrected score is under 30, you have a shell like a tortoise and tend to withdraw your head at the first sign of psychological danger. Probably life handed you some bad blows when you were too young to fight back, so you have erected strong defenses against the kind of intimacy that chould leave you vulnerable.

If you scored between 30 and 60, you are about average, which shows that you have potential. You have erected some strong defenses, but you have matured enough and have had enough good experiences that you are willing to take a few chances with other human beings, confident that you will survive regardless.

Any score over 60 means you possess the self-confidence and sense of security not only to run the risks of intimacy but also to enjoy it. This could be a little discomforting to another person who does not have your capacity or potential for close interpersonal relationships, but you are definitely ahead in the game, and you can make the right person extremely happy just by being yourself. If your score approaches 100, either you are an intimate superstar or you are worried too much about giving the right answers.

If convenient, do this exercise with someone with whom you feel intimate. Afterward, compare and discuss your answers. The results may indicate how compatible you are, socially or sexually.

Capacity for intimacy is one aspect of interpersonal relationships in which opposites do not necessarily attract. A person of high intimacy capacity can intimidate someone of low capacity who fears to respond, but those of similar capacities will tend to make no excessive demands on each other and, for that reason, will find themselves capable of an increasingly intimate and mutually fulfilling relationship.

From Hales, D. (1991). *Your health*. Redwood City, CA: Addison Wesley/Benjamin Cummings.

ASSESS YOURSELF 14-2

Sternberg's Love Scale

The blanks represent the person with whom you are in a relationship. Rate each statement on a 1-to-9 scale, where 1 equals "not at all," 5 equals "moderately," and 9 equals "extremely." Use intermediate points on the scale to indicate intermediate feelings.

1. I am actively supportive of _____ 's well-being.
2. I have a warm relationship with _____.
3. I am able to count on _____ in times of need.
4. _____ is able to count on me in times of need.
5. I am willing to share myself and my possessions with _____.
6. I receive considerable emotional support from _____.
7. I give considerable emotional support to _____.
8. I communicate well with _____.
9. I value _____ greatly in my life.
10. I feel close to _____.
11. I have a comfortable relationship with _____.
12. I feel that I really understand _____.
13. I feel that _____ really understands me.
14. I feel that I can really trust _____.
15. I share deeply personal information about myself with _____.
16. Just seeing _____ excites me.
17. I find myself thinking about _____ frequently during the day.
18. My relationship with _____ is very romantic.
19. I find _____ to be very personally attractive.
20. I idealize _____.
21. I cannot imagine another person making me as happy as _____ does.
22. I would rather be with _____ than anyone else.
23. There is nothing more important to me than my relationship with _____.
24. I especially like physical contact with _____.
25. There is something almost "magical" about my relationship with _____.
26. I adore _____.

Cont'd

Sternberg's Love Scale (cont'd)

27. I cannot imagine life without _____.

28. My relationship with _____ is passionate.

29. When I see romantic movies and read romantic books I think of _____.

30. I fantasize about _____.

31. I know that I care about _____.

32. I am committed to maintaining my relationship with _____.

33 Because of my relationship to _____, I would not let other people come between us.

34. I have confidence in the stability of my relationship with _____.

35. I could not let anything get in the way of my commitment to _____.

36. I expect my love for _____ to last for the rest of my life.

37. I will always feel a strong responsibility for _____.

38. I view my commitment to _____ as a solid one.

39. I cannot imagine ending my relationship with _____.

40. I am certain of my love for _____.

41. I view my relationship with _____ as permanent.

42. I view my relationship with _____ as a good decision.

43. I feel a sense of reponsibility toward _____.

44. I plan to continue my relationship with _____.

45. Even when _____ is hard to deal with, I remain commited to our relationship.

Average _____

Items 1 to 15 are for measuring the intimacy component; 16 to 30, for the passion component; and 31 to 45 for the decision/commitment component. To obtain your score, add your rating for each of the component subscales in the space below and divide the total by 15. This will give you an average rating for each item. (As generally administered, the scale items appear in random order, rather than clustered by component as they are here.)

From Masters, W., Johnson, V., & Kolodny, R. (1992). *Human sexuality.* New York: Harper Collins.

Name: _____ Date: _____

Values Clarification

Rate from one to five the following statements about school, work, and career.

1	2	3	4	5
strongly agree	agree	uncertain	disagree	strongly disagree

1. I must finish school in 4 years or less.
2. I would feel guilty about taking fewer credit hours per semester.
3. I could accept getting a lower grade in one class to concentrate on my other classes.
4. I feel guilty about taking difficult courses on the pass/fail system.
5. I must put the same amount of effort into all of my classes.
6. Grades are not as important as enjoying school and life.
7. Grades really do not matter to me.
8. I like to space my classes so I do not feel rushed.
9. I do not like to waste time between classes.
10. I will not sacrifice my lifestyle just for school.
11. I cannot reduce my work hours at all.
12. I will take fewer classes rather than reduce my work hours.
13. Schoolwork is not as important as my job.
14. Working so that I can buy things and have extra spending money is more important than taking a full load of courses.
15. Students are supposed to be stressed.
16. Money is the most important factor in my career choice.
17. I could not take a pay cut to work in my profession.
18. I would never recoup my loss if I took a pay cut to work in my profession.
19. Doing something I like is more important than my salary.
20. I could do without certain luxuries for a while to break into the job of my choice.

Examine each of your responses in light of the information in this chapter about the role of school, work, and career. Is your current lifestyle or academic style consistent with your values?

Name: _____ Date: _____

Developing a Budget

When one develops a budget, the top priority is to be honest. Be truthful about your earnings, expenses, and ability to save. The best-looking budget will work only if it is followed. The following is a sample budget.

Expenses		Income	
School	$3500	College savings	$7500
■ Tuition/fees		Summer Job (net)	2000
■ Books		Part-time job (net)	2700
Room and board or	5000	(during school year,	
■ Rent (month)	300	15 hr/week at $5/hr	
■ Utilities (month)	50	net for 36 weeks)	
■ Telephone (month)	15		
■ Food (month)	190		
Clothing	125		
Travel/auto			
■ Car payments (month)	50		
■ Insurance	67		
■ Gas/oil	75		
■ Repairs	15		
Savings	320		
Miscellaneous	400		
Totals	$11,900		$11,900

The proposed budget is for a typical college student sharing an off-campus apartment with two roommates. Room and board costs would be similar to those for dormitory students.

In this budget the student is drawing $7500 a year from an existing college savings plan. This budget also assumes that the student works during the summer and clears (after taxes) $2000. The student also works 15 hours a week during the school year and nets $5 an hour.

This is a fairly tight budget, even though the income is high. It does not allow for credit card debt or extensive travel, such as a trip at spring break.

Cont'd

Developing a Budget (cont'd)

This budget breaks down expenses (including anticipated car maintenance expenses) into monthly amounts and compares these with available income. This budget could be tightened considerably if the student would forgo a car entirely (savings of $3680) or forgo a new car ($1800 yearly car payment).

This budget would not apply to all students. It does illustrate that students must set their budgets according to their income, and ensure that they plan for predictable expenses, and have some money in reserve for emergencies. Credit cards should be used only in emergencies, debit cards (payment deducted immediately from checking account or due by the end of the month) are preferable so balances do not grow.

How does your budget compare to this student's?

Expenses

School _____
- Tuition/fees
- Books

Room and board or _____
- Rent (month) _____
- Utilities (month) _____
- Telephone (month) _____
- Food (month) _____

Clothing _____

Travel/auto
- Car payments (month) _____
- Insurance _____
- Gas/oil _____
- Repairs _____

Savings _____

Miscellaneous _____

Totals _____

Income

College savings _____

Summer Job (net) _____

Part-time job (net) _____

(during school year, 15 hr/week at $5/hr net for 36 weeks)

Totals _____

Stress in Adulthood

CHAPTER OBJECTIVES

- Know the major tasks associated with Erikson's adult stage of development.
- Know the two major sources of stress associated with this stage.
- Be able to describe the six major sources of job stress.
- Understand the relationship between job stress and negative health outcomes.
- Understand how to reduce the major sources of job stress by employing the four *Rs* of coping.
- Be able to discuss some of the stressors associated with singlehood, cohabitation, marriage, and divorce.
- Be able to describe the four major sources of stresses associated with cohabitation and marriage.
- Describe how to cope with relationship stress using the four *Rs* of coping.

This chapter examines Erikson's next-to-last stage of development, adulthood. The major task associated with adulthood is what Erikson calls *generativity versus stagnation*. During this stage we strive to be productive, creative, and nurturing versus self-indulgent and impoverished. This is a time of building and solidifying relationships and becoming gainfully employed and productive in our work. It is a time when many people choose to enter into committed relationships and raise families.

It is also a time when we are most likely to make our mark and leave our legacy as individuals. It is a time for taking care of our personal and family needs and then giving something back so that others may share in our success. For some people, this means being a good parent, for others it means getting involved in politics and shaping public issues, still others serve their community as volunteers, helping in everything from youth sports to environmental protection.

For those who have mastered the earlier developmental tasks, this is a time of wanting to give back, to help out, and to ensure the continuity of life and happiness. It is a time of hard work and then enjoyment of the fruits of one's labors. For others, it is a continuation of the self-indulgence and self-centeredness of their unfulfilled lives. It is a time of total freedom to focus on the self with no limits and no moral obligations to anyone or anything else.

This chapter focuses on two of the main sources of stress and challenge in our adult years—work and relationships. Regardless of one's race, gender, socioeconomic status, and ethnicity, adulthood is a time of seeking permanence, productivity, and commitment in our work and our relationships. Much of the youthful trial and error is past us as we seek stability in these areas of our lives.

Work Stress

KEY
TO UNDERSTANDING

Work, even in the best of times, creates a multitude of potential stressors.

A key to understanding work as a potential stressor is to realize that even in the best of times work creates a multitude of potentially stressful situations and scenarios. Finding a job that is satisfying and productive, performing well in the job, growing with it, establishing friendships and collegiality, earning the rewards and perks that are part of the job, and then retiring from it, are difficult tasks. Work can be hard, competitive, inflexible, demanding, confusing, ironic, and demeaning. However, it also can be challenging, rewarding, enabling, satisfying, heroic, and even noble.

In tough economic times, when the global economy and marketplace are changing the way America and companies do business and view work and workers, a job can be extremely stressful. Not only do we have to cope with the normal demands of working, but we must worry about the permanence of things that our parents took for granted, such as companies standing by their employees in tough times, rising salaries, increased benefits over time, a guaranteed job for life if one performs well, dependable retirement benefits, and a solvent social security system to supplement one's retirement.

As Chapter 6 discusses, Americans use work more than any other variable to define who they are. Americans live to work. Ask any American who he or she is and you are likely to hear a dissertation about his or her work. Americans define themselves by their vocation. They are teachers, doctors, mechanics, computer programmers, housewives, and firefighters. Conversely, people from other cultures work to live; they view work as a means to an end, not merely an end in itself.

Costs of Worker Stress

Americans pay a tremendous price for their obsession with work. The health-care costs associated with occupational stress are staggering. Job stress costs American industry more than $150 billion a year in lost productivity, accidents, and medical claims.[25] Job stress causes underproductivity, absenteeism, illness, injury, excessive employee turnover, theft, sabotage, and substance abuse. These losses are estimated to total about $1700 per employee per year for a medium-size manufacturing firm.[25]

The fastest-growing category of workmen's compensation claims is related to job stress. Occupational-stress–related claims accounted for 15% of all workmen's compensation claims in 1989, up from 5% in 1980.[36] This increase is related to the changing face of the American economy. LeVan et al.[36] attributes the rise to the following factors: increase in mergers, plant closures, relocation, growth of the highly stressful service industry, and more claims being filed by employees who historically were healthy and had no record of filing claims previously. More than half of all claims were filed by workers aged 30 to 39 years, a relatively young group for workmen's compensation.

In California the law asks the courts to rule in favor of employees in cases where there is any doubt about the validity of the claims. Rather than pay the huge legal bills associated with fighting suspected bogus claims in court, most employers are opting to settle with claimants at an average cost of $5000 to $15,000 per case.[44]

Many workers turn to alcohol and drugs to deaden their pain and help them cope. Unfortunately, this creates a vicious circle that further contributes to mental distress and illness, sapping workers of their energy, vitality, and a competitive edge. This reduces productivity, which threatens their companies' ability to compete in the marketplace, leading to more stressful layoffs, shutdowns, and reorganizations.[25]

KEY
TO UNDERSTANDING

The increase in stress-related worker's compensation claims has paralleled the rise in plant closings and relocations, downsizing of businesses, and growth of the service industry.

Burnout

In addition to the actual dollars spent, Americans pay another price—one that has more to do with our emotional well-being and spirit. Many workers simply burn out, losing their zest for their work life (Fig. 15-1). To burn out by definition is to fail, to wear out, or become exhausted because of excessive demands on energy, strength, or resources. Cherniss[11] identifies the eight signs of worker **burnout** in the box on p. 521.

One of the principal causes of burnout is overload. Overload is simply having too much work to do and not enough time to do it. This is particularly common among "helping" professionals, workers whose primary responsibility is to help others. Overload or perceived overload was reported as a primary cause of burnout among teachers,[7] social workers,[11] social work supervisors,[17] school psychologists,[30] and nurses.[52]

Other sources of burnout are inadequate orientation, leading to unrealistic expectations concerning the job,[11,43] lack of adequate resources,[30] ambiguity,[11,17] and lack of professional autonomy.[35] The accompanying box on p. 521 lists some ways to avoid burnout.

Fig. 15-1 Trying to accomplish too many tasks at once can cause burnout, a state of total exhaustion.

Signs of Burnout

Working with human service professionals, Cherniss[11] identified the following symptoms of burnout:

1. Loss of concern for the client

2. A tendency to treat client's concerns in a detached fashion

3. Increasing discouragement, pessimism, and fatalism about one's work

4. A decline in motivation, effort, and involvement in work

5. Apathy, negativism, irritation, and anger with clients and peers

6. Preoccupation with one's own comfort and welfare

7. Tendency to rationalize failure by blaming clients and "the system"

8. Resistance to change, growing rigidity, and loss of creativity

From Cherniss, C. (1980). *Stress and burnout in human service professionals.*

Preventing Burnout

■ Develop healthy lifestyle habits, which will increase your resistance to stress and your ability to cope.

■ Reach out and build a network of supportive friends, family members, neighbors, and co-workers.

■ Learn to recognize situations that you cannot change so that you do not waste energy trying to change them.

■ Draw a line between your personal life and your professional responsibilities. Do not let problems with one affect the other.

■ Practice at least one stress-management technique (exercise, meditation, relaxation, or the like) regularly.

■ Be nice to yourself. For example, reward yourself with a new tape or compact disc if you feel good about your performance on a test or on the job. Accept others' compliments.

■ Develop positive addictions, such as exercise, instead of negative addictions, such as smoking or drinking. Remember, however, that even a good behavior like exercise, carried to extremes, can hurt rather than help.

From Hales, D. (1991). *Your health.* Redwood City, CA: Benjamin/Cummings.

Sources of Job Stress

One can assess the sources of job stress in many different ways. We will use a model that puts the individual in the center of everything, emphasizing the importance of one's cognitive appraisal of potential stressors and perceived ability to cope as the key factors in job stress (Fig. 15-2).

Under this model, the individual's overall level of wellness is critically related to the individual's ability to appraise potential job stressors and use a repertoire of strategies for coping with these demands. Many potential sources of stress converge on the individual and test his or her ability to cope.

Potential job-related stressors in this model come from the economy, the job itself, the organization, the physical environment, management's style, and nonmanagement interpersonal relationships. They become stressors only if appraised as such. Some people will appraise these issues as challenges.

The Individual Worker

As this book emphasizes throughout, one's individual level of wellness greatly affects one's stress levels. This applies especially to work stress. One's overall level of well-being affects everything from the worker's ener-

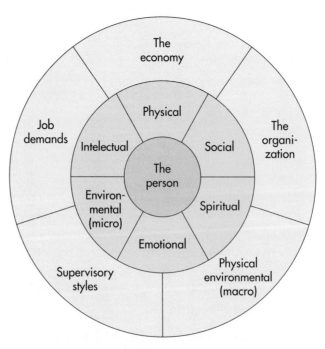

Fig. 15-2 Sources of stress for an individual.

gy and stamina to keep up with the demands of the job, to the worker's intellectual ability to keep pace with the demands of rapid technological advances, to see things differently and creatively, or to learn new ways of doing the job. Level of well-being also affects one's perceived ability to cope with work stress. The individual filters the remaining sources of job stress through this level of wellness and perceived ability to cope, and thus these sources may or may not represent stressors to the individual.[34]

The Economy

As is mentioned in Chapter 4, economic insecurity, which Catalano[9] defines as either the rate of unemployment in an area (ecologic view) or the loss of a job and the inability to pay bills (individual view), was related to both psychological distress and physical illness.

Belle[3] et al. in Chapter 4 describe the relationships between poverty and unemployment from their perspective of their effects on the individual. As a more global issue, the economy in general creates problems for business that force massive changes in the way companies, shops, and stores do business. This trickle-down effect changes worker's job expectations, which can be stressful (see Stress in Our World box on p. 524).

Zemke[53] found that job stress is more prevalent in industries that are under severe cost-cutting and recessionary pressures. Whether they are downsizing, reorganizing, or engaging in some other new procedure to reduce the size of the work force, the effects are potentially stressful for employees. Often, those most vulnerable to these cutbacks are employees who have given the best years of their lives to the company. Instead of enjoying the twilight of their careers and eagerly planning for retirement, these employees are anxious and fear that they may not survive in the company long enough to collect a pension.

A key to understanding economy-related stress is that downsizing and cutbacks also are stressful for workers who retain their jobs. Even when workers retain their jobs, economy-based stressors have an effect. A study by Northwestern National Life Insurance Company found that 46% of American workers experience stress and burnout partially because of the recession. Four out of 10 feel high job stress, 50% point to stress as the major factor in their loss of productivity, and 36% want to quit.[37]

The workers retained after downsizing harbor resentment. With fewer employees remaining, those who were retained often are required to work overtime to finish the job. The same Northwestern Life study found that while 45% of those interviewed (1299) work extra hours, 34% thought that overtime work was not enough to get their jobs done.[37] Further, these same employees felt pressured by their employers to produce more to cope with the demands of the recession.[47] This combination

KEY
TO UNDERSTANDING

The effects of layoffs and downsizing are stressful even for those employees who are retained.

STRESS IN OUR WORLD

José

José is 58 years old. A high school graduate with a year of college, José has been in the building supply business for more than 20 years. He manages a large building supply store in the Northeast. His company operates 12 of these stores in the tristate area; they supply local contractors and other smaller building supply outlets. José's company is owned by a much larger corporation that is involved in many other facets of the building trade, ranging from construction to logging. Much of their business is international. José's company is the smallest and least profitable of all the ventures. Small companies like José's have lost most of their business to large national home-supply stores. Consumers, eager to save, have flocked to these stores because they offer rock-bottom prices. These stores buy in much larger quantities than José's business can, and they move huge quantities of merchandise daily.

José was given his pink slip this morning. Although he saw the writing on the wall for more than a year, he still cannot believe it. His store dropped from 10 full-time employees to 3 in the past year, with much of the work picked up by part-timers and the remaining full-time staff. José's boss said he was sorry to have to do this but the parent company was selling their division, and the new owners want to clean house in all 12 locations and bring in "their own people." José will receive 6 months severance pay and a lump sum for his retirement, but all benefits will cease in 1 month.

José is in a state of shock. He has a son finishing his third year of college at an expensive private school. His daughter will graduate from high school next year, and her plans are uncertain. José's wife, a high school graduate, has a part-time job as a secretary, but the job does not pay well, and the benefits will not carry the family. They have managed to save a small amount for their son's final year of college.

José is concerned that he may have difficulty finding a job at his age. At 58, he feels too old to adapt to a new occupation, but he realizes that the building supply business has changed and probably will never return to what it was. He is not yet ready to retire. He believes he is too young to retire and has not accumulated as much in his retirement plan as he would like. Besides, he may have to tap his retirement funds if he is unable to find work. He is considering all of his options.

José has had some health problems over the past few years. A high-strung guy, José suffers from high blood pressure and ulcers, and the last thing he needs in his life right now is more worries.

of events creates a pressure to do more with less in a very insecure economy, a very stressful scenario for most people, especially managers and supervisors at the end of their careers who were looking forward to winding down their work lives.

The Organization

Organizational structure, regardless of the size of the business, can be a source of stress. Potential stressors resulting from organizational structure include power struggles, advancement opportunities, and organizational policies and processes.[25]

Power struggles occur when employees or groups of employees form political alliances and compete for positions, choice assignments, or overtime. Power struggles also can result from managerial styles that pit workers against management. Power struggles between peers are stressful enough; power struggles that pit older, higher-paid workers against newer, lower-paid employees in a cost-conscious job market are particularly frightening (see Stress in Our World box on p. 526).

Discrimination based on race, gender, age, or sexual orientation is an abuse of power. Discrimination is one group or individual blocking participation from another group or individual. Title 7 of the 1964 Civil Rights Act makes such discrimination illegal in the United States. **Affirmative Action** legislation originally was intended to ensure that all groups have equal access to employment and promotion. The guidelines were designed to assist employers in developing policies concerning the hiring and promotion of minorities. These Affirmative Action policies can be a source of stress to nonminority candidates for employment and promotion if workers perceive these policies as a way of merely filling quotas rather than an attempt to increase diversity by hiring equally qualified minority applicants.

Sexual harassment is probably the most blatant misuse of power on the job. Sexual harassment can be defined as "any unwarranted attention of a sexual nature from someone from the workplace that creates discomfort and/or interferes with the job."[14]

Sexual harassment on the job can come in many forms. A common form involves a male boss, supervisor, or manager who uses his power to make sexual demands on a female subordinate. If she refuses, his threats may range from loss of her job, to a denial of promotion or a transfer, to a demotion to a lesser job.

Sexual harassment can be a devastating source of stress. Many victims simply cannot afford to lose their jobs or be forced into lower paying positions. Quitting a job and applying for unemployment benefits may not be possible because harassment sometimes is perceived as an inadequate reason for leaving a job. Even if unemployment benefits are allowed, they often do not meet expenses.[14]

Victims also may suffer a variety of physical and mental health effects. Crooks and Baur[14] report that in two separate studies 75% to 85% of victims of sexual harassment suffered some negative effects, which included feeling angry, humiliated, ashamed, embarrassed, cheap, nervous, irritable, and

Affirmative Action
federal legislation enacted to force employers to pursue vigorous enforcement of the specific requirements of Title 7 of the 1964 Civil Rights Act

sexual harassment
any unwarranted attention of a sexual nature from someone in the workplace that creates discomfort and/or interferes with the job.

STRESS IN OUR WORLD

William

William is 48 years old. He holds an MBA in finance and works as a middle manager for a multinational bank on Wall Street in New York City. William is bright, articulate, and funny. He also is good at what he does but realizes that somewhere along the way and for some reason, advancement has passed him by. He has seen many bright-eyed, 26-year-old whiz kids pass him by on their way to an assistant vice president's position and a private office with a view. For the past 5 years, William seems to have been one more project away from consideration for promotion. He has made so many lateral moves within his job level that he feels like a halfback on a broken-field run.

William has long since resolved that he probably will not get that office with a view. After he accepted that fact, he was fairly content for a couple of years. He did his job, stayed late when necessary, and took advantage of the excellent perks of his job. With full health benefits (including optical and dental), a good

salary, a retirement plan, and profit sharing, William thought he could do a lot worse. He basically liked what he was doing, although the grind and expense of commuting 2 hours each way from central New Jersey got to him at times. William had committed to staying until he was 55, taking an early retirement, and getting into something enjoyable, such as teaching high school or junior college.

William was called into the boss's office today and told that his operation was closing up shop in New York. His division's work would to be transferred to the Brussels, Belgium office, where the costs were much lower and the proximity to the European banking community much greater. The Brussels office might have a spot for him, but the job probably would be a demotion, perhaps another lateral move. If he accepted, he would have to be ready to move in a month. If he declined, they would keep him on in New York for 6 months in a temporary position while he conducted a job search. The company had no other position for him.

At termination, he would receive 6 months' severance pay and his retirement benefits in a lump sum. As an ex-employee, he could continue to purchase his health benefits, but the company would stop paying for them.

William was stuck. He would not go to Brussels, even if he could. He really could not go because his son was enrolled in a special school and was doing well. His son was scheduled to graduate next year, and William could not bear to move him. Besides, his daughter would start high school and his youngest son would begin grammar school next year. His wife and the kids really loved where they lived and had no desire to move across the ocean to start a new life.

Speaking of starting a new life, William was not sure he was ready to do this either. Although he was less than fulfilled with his job, he worked for a very prestigious company on Wall Street known internationally for banking. He realized he probably was earning too much to be considered for a job in central New Jersey. A smaller bank might be afraid

STRESS IN OUR WORLD (CONT'D)

William (cont'd)

to take a chance on him, figuring he would become
bored or restless. They might
think that at 48 he would be
too old and set in his ways.
He might have a harder time,
however, finding work in
New York. Banks there would

think that "there must be
some reason" this guy was
never promoted to assistant
vice president. Retirement
was out. William thought he
had too many productive
work years left in him to
retire, even if he could afford
to retire. With three kids to
put through college and a

wife who did some child care
out of the house but had no
benefits, William could not
afford to retire. He tried to
stay calm and focus on his
options. This was hard, however, as the date of his job's
elimination crept closer.

unmotivated. Many also felt guilty, helpless, and alienated from co-workers.
Such feelings can result in a tremendous loss of productivity for both the
employee and the employer.

Ageism is another form of discrimination. Ageism is common in the era
of downsizing, as businesses attempt to purge older employees, who generally are paid more and have more substantial benefits. Even Fortune 500
companies, which were perceived as unshakable in most conditions and
protective of workers, have fired those they label as "surplus employees."[24]

Another major organizational stressor is lack of opportunity for
advancement. Becoming stuck in a dead-end job can be a major source of
stress. Turnage et al.,[49] in a study of 68 managerial, 171 professional, and 68
clerical workers, found lack of opportunity for advancement as one of the
highest-rated job stressors.

Organizational policies also are a major source of stress. In general,
ambiguous organizational policies are major contributors to employee stress.
Areas of ambiguity include time frames, work objectives and goals, lines of
responsibility, procedures and protocols, worker's and management's
expectations about the job, and job performance. The relationship between
ambiguous organizational policies and stress was found in both American
and foreign studies of workers.[8,17,23,45]

Time urgency comes in many forms: sales deadlines, production quotas, pay for piecework, seasonal work limitations, time estimates for specific
jobs, and more. The negative effects of time urgency on cardiovascular function were documented 20 years ago by Friedman and Rosenman.[20] Other
researchers have documented the relationship between time urgency and
stress in work settings ranging from dressmaking to accounting.[6,13,29,43,49]

Rotating shifts are another type of time stressor. Giordano et al.[23] describe the changes the human body must make to adapt to changes in the work day. For example, the body needs several weeks to fully adjust to a switch from day shift to night shift. Typically, however, police officers, fire-fighters, and airline crews change shifts more often than that, producing symptoms similar to jetlag: headache, gastrointestinal problems, loss of appetite, alteration of sleep patterns (e.g., insomnia, nightmares), and blurred vision. Jamal and Baba[32] report shift-work stress as a problem for nurses who work rotating schedules.

Company travel policies can be particularly stressful for both employees and their families. Frequent travel disrupts not only **body cycles** and **biorhythms** of the employee but also family schedules, patterns, and routines. Szwergold[48] notes that chronic travelers are constantly torn between their professional duties and obligations to family members.

Forced relocation is another potential stressor. Many business men and women are forced to relocate and continuously live in fear of their next relocation (see Stress in Our World box on p. 529). In many businesses and industries, promotion requires relocation. Employment with the federal government and armed forces is contingent on signing a work agreement that allows forced relocation. Military relocation often involves moving to another country, where the stress of adapting to an entirely new culture is added to the usual stress of moves within the United States.

Transfers can be very stressful to families, as children are forced to change schools, make new friends, and start all over. Spouses must adjust and find new employment, make new friends, and establish new relationships with doctors and dentists.[42] Having to do this every couple of years can make families unwilling to fully unpack after each move unless the organization finds ways to smooth the process.[19]

Organizational Processes

Besides the written organizational policies, an organization's informal method of conducting its business and implementing policy can be a source of stress.

Inadequate orientation can be a major source of stress for new and experienced employees. By failing to properly orient new employees to the organization, employers set the stage for much of the ambiguity-related stress discussed in this chapter.[12] Inadequate orientation also can lead to unrealistic expectations that, if unmet, can be a source of stress and burnout.[43]

Gaining access to resources and acting on policies in the workplace can also be a source of stress. These stressors result from an employee's attempts to understand the bureaucratic procedures established in most

body cycles

cyclical time frames governing basic physiological processes such as hunger, thirst, and sleep

biorhythms

naturally recurring cycle of biological activities governed by the nervous and hormonal systems

STRESS IN OUR WORLD

The Smiths

The Smiths have moved six times in the past 10 years as Craig Smith has pursued his dream of becoming a regional sales manager for his company, a large pharmaceutical firm located in New Jersey. He, his wife, Mary, and their three children, Sharon (14 years old), Craig Jr. (12), and Robbie (7), started in New Jersey 10 years ago and moved to Buffalo, Indianapolis, San Diego, Houston, and Chicago.

The moves were necessary, as the company put it, for Craig to learn new skills, understand the nuances of different territories and regions, and gain experi-ence at various sales levels within the company. Craig has applied for what he hopes is his last transfer, back to New Jersey, to become a regional sales vice president based in corporate headquarters.

Craig hopes this is his final move because moving and uprooting his family so often is stressing his family to its limits. Mary even gave him an ultimatum: only one last move, or she will consider a divorce. Sharon and Craig, Jr. would like to go through their high school years at one school and, for once, hang onto their friends for more than a year. Robbie is the only one who does not seem to mind too much.

Craig has had enough, too. The sagging housing market over the past few years has given his family a beating on their home sales. They will face a higher cost of living in New Jersey. At this level, however, the company pays all relocation costs, and his raise will put Craig at a very comfortable salary. Furthermore, he will not have to transfer again, because this is the highest sales level within the company. At 40, Craig is tired of fighting his way up the corporate ladder. He would like to coach his son's Little League team and watch his other kids grow up.

large organizations. Bureaucracies have four components: specialization of labor; formal rules governing all aspects of behavior; objective, emotion-less management intended to treat everyone the same; and a formal hier-archy of positions and lines of communication within and across these positions.[23]

This rigidity can be a source of stress. Girdano et al.[23] summarizes the seven major criticisms of bureaucracies: frustration of professional and per-sonal development, encouragement of mediocrity on the job, reinforcement of complex rules (red tape), discouragement of communication caused in part by excessive paperwork (more red tape), impersonality in supervisory practices, arbitrary rules that are virtually impossible to rescind, and stifling of creativity.

Supervisory Styles

Role conflicts, caused by the way jobs are assigned and performed, were cited in several studies as a source of stress.[8,22,23,45] In these instances, workers thought that what they were asked to do conflicted with their stated job functions. Stress is created by the way supervisors and managers require that the jobs are performed, not the jobs or policies themselves.

Ginsburg[22] identifies specific supervisory behaviors that contribute to a management style that creates job stress for workers. This style includes the following behaviors, which are a reflection of the way a manager deals with workers: letting subordinates unfairly take the blame for problems, delegating too much or too little authority, displaying emotions that are inappropriate for their position, and being distrustful.

Communication styles also were cited as a source of stress. Er[16] reports that supervisors create unnecessary stress by confusing aggressiveness with assertiveness in their dealings with employees. Supervisors often must be assertive in enforcing organizational policies and goals. Supervisors must use assertiveness correctly and not confuse it with aggressive behavior, which creates unnecessary stress in employees.

Job Demands and Stress

Some occupations are more stressful than others simply by virtue of their demands or their settings. The following types of job demands can be stressful: excessive time urgency, critical decision-making responsibility, excessive complexity and/or difficulty, repetitiveness/simplicity/boredom, and risk to personal safety.

As already discussed, some jobs heap excessive time demands on workers. All jobs require that tasks be completed on time. Excessive time demands, however, are those based on unrealistic expectations of the worker's abilities.

Some jobs require that workers take full responsibility for critical, in some cases life-and-death, decisions. Emergency medical workers arriving at the scene of an accident must quickly survey the scene and decide which victims require immediate care and who can wait. They must decide which procedures to institute immediately. Failure to act correctly could result in death. Police officers must decide instantly whether to draw their weapons and fire or hold off and risk being shot.

Some jobs are exceedingly precise and complex. Girdano et al.[23] found that the higher the complexity of the job, the greater the stress. They found that the following factors are related to the complexity of a job: increase in the amount of information that must be used, increase in the sophistication of skills, increase in the number of alternative ways of performing the job, and the introduction of contingency plans.

KEY
TO UNDERSTANDING

Role conflict can be associated with the way others interpret our jobs, not in the work itself.

In many cases, jobs follow procedures and protocols but have several options along the way. For instance, nurses often make decisions about patient management depending on the results of complicated diagnostic procedures.

Other jobs can be stressful because they are repetitive, boring, and monotonous or offer little challenge and opportunity to make decisions. This kind of work is best illustrated by the assembly line worker, who is responsible for performing countless repetitive tasks throughout the day. Whether it is bolting, welding, or soldering one specific part as it moves along a conveyer belt, or sewing a specific part of a garment before it is passed along to the next seamstress, this type of work can be mastered in a short time and soon results in boredom.

Girdano et al.[23] describes a condition called *assembly line hysteria* characterized by nausea, muscle weakness, severe headaches, and blurred vision. It was found to be caused by four conditions characteristic of assembly-line work: boredom with the job, repetitive tasks on the job, lack of ability to communicate and converse with other workers, and low job satisfaction. In other cases, work becomes a stressor when people feel underutilized and unchallenged. In these cases, skills and abilities go unused, and frustration builds.

Other jobs are stressful simply because they are dangerous. Soldiering is a good example. Being on guard or in battle puts the body under continual stress. The work of police officers and firefighters at times is life threatening.

Physical Environment

An occupational stressor similar to job demands is the physical environment, the place where one's work is pursued and the **ergonomics** of the equipment used. Most physical environmental stressors seem to be found in blue-collar occupations ranging from manufacturing to mining. Some of these are noise, poor temperature control, overcrowding, poor arrangement and design of work space, and poor lighting. The stressors can be life threatening, as in the case of toxic chemicals, pollution, and dangerous people (e.g., encountered by prison guards and police officers).[25]

Recent studies have examined the role ergonomics plays in occupational stress, particularly in white-collar occupations that require repetitive motions. With the increasing use of computers in the workplace has been a corresponding rise in illness resulting from repetitive motion in computer operation. The repeated arm and hand motions involved in using a keyboard can result in muscle and tendon strain and inflammation. Symptoms include pain, swelling, numbness, and weakness in the hands and arms.

ergonomics
an applied science concerned with the characteristics of people that must be considered in the design and arrangement of the environment so that the two will interact more efficiently and safely

**carpal tunnel
syndrome**

an inflammation of
the carpal tunnel of
the wrist leading to
painful swelling, ten-
derness, and loss of
strength in the hand,
wrist, and arm

**cumulative
trauma disorder**

injuries associated
with similar and
repetitive motions

Sewing machine operators experience similar effects as a result of sewing on machines all day long. **Carpal tunnel syndrome** is a disorder that results from the cumulative trauma of these repetitive tasks. **Cumulative trauma disorder** resulting from computer, sewing, and other industry-related stress now accounts for almost 50% of all occupational disorders.[26]

Relationship Stress

The second major task of our adult years is to continue, to deepen, and possibly to end, the relationships that began in young adulthood. For most Americans this means a commitment to marriage and a family. For many, the commitment to another is not marriage but cohabitation. For others this period is marked by divorce or the death of a spouse. The remainder of this chapter examines adult relationships and the stress they produce.

Singlehood

A significant percentage of Americans choose to remain single for life. The decision to remain single for life usually is made by men and women aged 25 to 30.[46] Reasons for remaining single include delaying marriage, changes in sexual standards, increased financial independence for women, changing economic times, and changing conceptions of marriage. Postponing marriage sometimes results in an inadvertent slide into permanent singlehood.[10]

Regardless of the reasons, those who choose to remain single for life report that they are happy. Contrary to popular belief, most singles are not lonely, and they develop alternative social patterns based on friendships and nonmarital love relationships. The satisfaction singles derive from these relationships and from their careers is more than adequate for their happiness.[10]

Stress Associated with Being Single

In many cases the stress associated with being single is derived more from the attitudes and reactions of others than from the single person's own perceptions. Cavanaugh[10] reports that the two most stressful issues for single people are how they should handle dating and other's expectations that they should marry.

Some of the potentially stressful dating issues are dealing with role expectations, handling sexual involvement, dating without becoming too serious too fast, and initiating close friendships without coming on too strongly.[10]

A key to understanding singles stress is realizing that America is a "couples-oriented" society that puts a premium on adults interacting social-

KEY
TO UNDERSTANDING

America is a couples-
oriented culture that
puts an inordinate
amount of pressure on
single people to marry.

ly as a heterosexual couple. Most Americans assume that everyone will get married someday. This puts an inordinate amount of pressure on single people, especially when friends and associates always are trying to "fix them up." Singles often find themselves having to defend their position. Singles also tend to lose old friendships as their friends marry and raise families.

Gay single people find themselves in a double bind. Everyone tries to fix them up with members of the opposite sex so they can find someone and settle down. When gay singles finally do find someone, they usually cannot share their relationship with their straight friends.

Cohabitation

Cohabitation is defined as two members of the opposite gender who live together but who are not married (see the box below). Unmarried couples who live together are not much different from married couples. They share, argue, and make decisions about money, sex, and household labor.

The reasons for living together but not marrying are many and varied, but generally there are three forms of cohabitation: casual or temporary involvement, preparation or testing for marriage, and substitution for marriage.[38]

cohabitation
living arrangement of two members of the opposite gender sharing a home

---

Cohabitation Facts

- About 3 million Americans currently are cohabiting.
- The age breakdown is as follows:
  38% of the women and 25% of the men are under 25;
  36% of the women and 41% of the men are 25 to 34;
  20% of the women and 28% of the men are 35 to 64;
  6% of both sexes are 65 or older.
- Most cohabiting couples either break up or get married within 2 years; two out of five break up within 1 year.
- 25% of college undergraduates have had at least one cohabitation relationship.
- Couples who have cohabited tend to have more disagreements and less marital satisfaction in the early years after marriage than couples who have not cohabited.
- Cohabitation does not seem to help people choose their mates more effectively than noncohabitants do; 36% of married couples who cohabited before marriage separate or divorce within 10 years, compared with 27% who did not live together before marriage.

From Masters, W.H., Johnson, V.E., & Kolodny, R.C. (1992). Human sexuality (4th ed.). New York: Harper Collins.

Stress Associated With Cohabitation

The stresses associated with cohabitation are similar to those experienced by married individuals and generally result from four issues: unrealistic expectations, communication problems, money, and sex. These are examined in detail after the section on marriage.

Cohabitors also may experience a unique type of stress resulting from others' perceptions and expectations of their relationship. Parental disapproval is a common problem among cohabitors. Parents often expect those living together to be taking the first step toward marriage, an assumption that is not always valid.

Another type of stress is lack of legal recognition of the bond. Cohabitors often have difficulties with property ownership and rights of survivorship after the death of one of the couple. Unless the couple has a current will, the survivor has no clearly established legal property rights. Gay couples experience similar stressors.

Marriage

Unquestionably, the vast majority of Americans want to marry, although they are postponing it longer than in the past (Fig. 15-3). The median age at first marriage has been rising for Americans for the past 3 decades. Although an integral part of most cultures, marriage takes many forms and assumes

Fig. 15-3 For most Americans, marriage is something they believe in.

many purposes throughout the world. In America, most people make the following assumptions about marriage: a legal bond, permanence, heterosexuality, sexual exclusivity, emotional exclusivity, and monogamy.[14]

Most Americans also expect more from marriage than do those in many other cultures. This is because, historically, marriages were intended to provide a stable economic unit in which to raise children. Today, most Americans expect marriage to fulfill their social, emotional, financial, and sexual needs.[14]

When they do marry, many people find that many of these expectations are unrealistic. This can lead to frustration, disillusionment, separation, and divorce. They also find that marriage is hard work. Even under the best of circumstances and with a good match in a partner, successful marriage requires continual assessment, communication, commitment, willingness to change, and hard work.

The Developmental Course of Marriage

Berry and Williams[4] propose a developmental model of marriage that spans adulthood (Fig. 15-4).

In the early, honeymoon phase, marriage is at its most intense. The partners spend considerable time together, talking, sharing interests and leisure, establishing their roles within the relationship, and arguing and making up. As the honeymoon phase winds down, the couple settles into a rou-

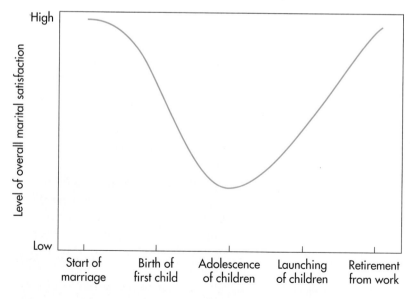

Fig. 15-4 The Berry and Williams scale shows marital satisfaction across adulthood. However, not all couples show a significant decline in satisfaction.

tine. The intensity of the honeymoon phase diminishes and, along with it, marital satisfaction. The birth of children reduces the amount of time the spouses have for the relationship.

Marital happiness reaches rock bottom during the mid-life phase of the relationship (see the box on p. 537), which also coincides with adolescence in the couple's children. Myriad problems ranging from financial considerations, to coping with teenagers, to changing roles for husband and wife contribute to this phase (see Stress in Our World box on p. 538).

Happiness begins to rebound as the adult children leave home. This frees time and money. The partners find that they have the time, money, and privacy to reestablish the practices in their relationship that give them pleasure, as well as to investigate new ideas together.

Marital happiness continues to rise in the later adult years and into retirement. Depending on several factors ranging from health to retirement income, the couple can continue to enjoy their freedom, and in some cases, relationships with their children and grandchildren.

Stress Associated with Marriage

As we have seen, marriage has many potential sources of stress, ranging from loss of initial sexual passion to economic stability in retirement. Hales[27] poses an interesting way of grouping common stressors associated with intimate relationships, including marriage and cohabitation. There are four main sources of relationship stress: unrealistic expectations, communication problems, money, and sex. This chapter examines these and two others, care of children and care of elderly parents.

Unrealistic Expectations. Many relationships are doomed from the start because they are based on a set of unrealistic expectations that never can be fulfilled. As discussed in Chapter 14, many unrealistic expectations in relationships are due to an immature or romantic perception of relationships. Romantic love, unlike consummate love, is based on unrealistic perceptions of never-ending bliss, sexual passion, happiness, absence of conflict, and beauty. The harsh reality is that bliss turns to boredom and aggravation, passion turns to comfort, happiness gives way to periods of sadness, arguments sometimes are necessary to work out problems, and your spouse is not very beautiful at 6:00 AM before he shaves or she fixes her hair.

Unrealistic expectations are not limited to the spouse or the relationship, however. As illustrated in Chapter 2, people who tend to be illogical and view the world irrationally are under more stress than those who are more rational and objective. If a person's dominant personality construct is irrational or illogical, the person is more apt to subscribe to a set of illogical beliefs about life in general.[15] They might, as Walen et al.[51] asserts, view

Midlife Crisis or Middle-Age Myth?

You have heard the story before. A happy, successful 45-year-old businessman quits his job, leaves his wife and kids, and runs off to Tahiti with his 25-year-old secretary. Or, perhaps it is the 40-year-old mother of two facing the "empty nest" who jumps into her convertible BMW with her 20-year-old tennis instructor and heads west into the sunset in a torrid blaze of passionate sex.

These and other "midlife crises" that have been popularized by the print and film media make interesting stories and pose a romantic solution to many of the difficult issues that appear during middle age. In real life, however, relatively few people experience such catastrophic, radical changes. New information fueled by long-term research on aging is showing that middle age is the very best time of life. It is a developmental stage unlike most others, because it is not tied particularly to changes in the body, such as early childhood, adolescence, and old age. Midlife is characterized more by psychological adaptations and is very reality based.

By midlife, many of the stressful questions that faced us as young adults are answered, such as: Will anyone ever love me? Will this marriage workout? Will I ever find a job? What kind of lifestyle can I afford to lead?

By midlife, most people have found love. If they are married, they are more likely to stay married (the overwhelming majority of divorces occur within the first 6 to 8 years of marriage). They have settled into a job and have a pretty good idea of where they are headed (most professionals who are going to "make it" have made it by this time). They have a good sense of their earning capacity and therefore can gauge the kind of lifestyle they can expect.

Although the myth of midlife is that this period is characterized by unrest, discomfort, dissatisfaction, and upheaval, the reality is that it is a comfortable, satisfying time. It is a time to enjoy the rewards of 10 to 20 years of scuffling. It is a time to push a little easier at work, to get off a little early to watch your kid's Little League game. It is a time to focus on vacations and social gatherings, to take a class to learn how to paint, or improve your backhand. It is a time to lighten up a little.

Midlife is a period of gradual adjustment, not tumultuous change. It gradually unfolds and is based on several adjustments to reality. For most people it is based in reality, not fantasy. Those most likely to experience a true crisis (about 5%) are people who generally have experienced similar crises in all developmental stages of their lives. Their lives are based on unrealistic (therefore unrealized) notions and expectations. One of the major criticisms of earlier studies of midlife is that they were based on small numbers of case studies of atypical populations (mostly affluent, professional, and white). In the recent cross-sectional studies of more representative samples of Americans, researchers found that the average person's midlife adjustment is based on reality. People gradually adjust their expectations to fit the reality of their lives. By the time they settle into midlife, they have learned to make the best of what they have and are not constantly longing for things that are beyond their reach.

From Gallagher, W. (1993) *The Atlantic, 271*(5), 51-63; Harris, P., & Lyon, D. (1990). *Reader's Digest, 136*(818), 108; Forrest, D. (1992). *Canadian Business, 65*(9), 96-100.

STRESS IN OUR WORLD

Lynn

Lynn is 40 years old. She has been married for 15 years and has four children, ages 13, 11, 10, and 7. Lynn married immediately after junior college and never worked full-time in her field of preparation, accounting. She has done some part-time bookkeeping and child care in her home over the years, but for the most part she has been a full-time mother and housewife.

Lynn is excellent at what she does. She has managed to raise four children, keep her house clean and efficient, and work in several school, church, and community organizations. She has served as a class mom, den mother, Sunday school teacher, and school board member. Lynn, although a little frazzled at times, has managed to care for her family well.

Lynn is ready for a change, however. Money has been tight lately. Her husband decided a few years earlier to go back to school in the evening to earn his mas-

ter's degree so he could keep pace in his chosen profession. Tuition has greatly eroded their meager savings. The kids all have needed braces, and the youngest needed a cardiac specialist to repair a congenital heart defect.

Lynn went back to work 6 months ago. Her youngest child is in all-day kindergarten, and her husband now works flexible hours so he can pick up the kids from the after-school program. Lynn tried to work as a bookkeeper but found she did not like it anymore. She always wanted to get into retail, so she landed a sales job at one of the more fashionable women's stores at the new mall nearby.

Lynn has done exceptionally well in retail. In 6 months she was promoted to assistant manager of her section (women's evening wear), and she loves it. She thrives on the interpersonal contact, the fashion, getting dressed up, and attending sales meetings. She has decided to return to school to get her

bachelor's degree in retail management. Her company offers a distributive education program through a local state college, in which she can go to class and earn credit for her retail sales work. She enrolled in the program, and in 3 years she will have enough credits to graduate, and with a little luck, earn a position as a sales manager with her company.

It has not been easy. Juggling the demands of motherhood, housework, school, and work has been trying. Her husband has been very supportive and has learned to cook. The kids are helping wherever they can, and everyone tries to respect mommy's "quiet time" when she is studying. Lynn's house is not as clean as it once was, her husband's shirt collars could use a little more ironing (he is learning), and the kids' lunches occasionally get mixed up, but it is working. Lynn has successfully passed into a phase of her life that will help her continue to grow.

Lessons from Happy Marriages[27]

Many long-running relationships not only survive but also thrive through the years. What is the secret? Here are some of the characteristics that researchers have found in happy couples:

- They are best friends. They share secrets, work, and play; they hang out together; and they laugh a lot.

- They listen to, and confide in, each other. They discuss and debate everything—and they reveal their innermost feelings and fears to each other.

- They are tuned in to each other's feelings. Unlike the stereotype of silent, cold men, the husbands in good marriages are just as expressive as the women.

- They can deal with negative emotions and keep them from getting out of control.

- They know how to handle conflict. Happy couples focus on an issue; deal only with the current problem; and criticize the spouse's action, not the spouse.

- They are less than brutally honest. Although they express their feelings clearly, they know that hurtful words can leave sores.

- They trust each other. In a good marriage, partners can show their weakest side and know they will still be loved.

- They are committed to making the marriage work. Even in the roughest times, they choose to stick it out with each other.

- They share interests and values, and their common interests create a bond that keeps their relationship strong.

- They are flexible enough to change and tolerate change. In fact, their marriages endure and improve—not despite the changes and challenges but because of them.

From Hales, D. (1991). *Your health*. Redwood City, CA: Benjamin/Cummings.

the world through a set of unrealistic expectations and therefore be predisposed to stress of all kinds, including relationship stress.

Communication Problems. Communication problems can sabotage any relationship. They usually result from the inability to talk about problems or misunderstandings in the relationship. Sometimes they are rooted in a lack of assertiveness, where one or both partners are unable to stand up for themselves. Communication problems also can arise when partners are unable to express positive and constructive thoughts and feelings. Many people are raised in an environment where communication focuses on problems and the expression of negative emotions. However, relationships can wither from a lack of expression of caring, tenderness, compassion, and recognition of worth. Communication problems grow from three issues: lack of skill, lack of desire to communicate effectively, or a combination of both.

The easiest communication problem to remedy is the skill-based problem. If one or both partners do not know how to communicate clearly and effectively or do not know how to fight fairly, they can learn how, assuming that they have the desire. If either partner does not have the desire to solve the problem, all of the skill in the world is meaningless. Loss of desire to talk and solve problems is a warning sign of a deteriorating relationship.

In the last case, one or both partners may want to communicate but may feel a particular problem is too difficult to discuss. In some cases, partners may want to communicate more effectively but lack the energy and commitment that is necessary to solve their problems.

Money Problems. Money, or what money means to each partner, is a major source of stress in long-term relationships. If each partner's perception of money is different, this can be a chronic source of stress in the relationship. For instance, if one partner views money as relatively unimportant and only a means to obtaining goods necessary for survival and the other perceives money as a ticket to a better life, higher status, possessions, luxury, this couple is in trouble because their core values about money are complete opposites.

Money problems also can result from different conceptions of credit. One person may view credit as a fundamental economic necessity and carry outstanding balances on credit cards, personal loans, and home-equity lines of credit. The other may be uncomfortable with even a mortgage or car loan and prefer to delay all purchases until they can be made in cash (see Stress in Our World box on p. 541). The problem is confounded by the easy availability of credit and the aggressive marketing of everything from credit cards to home-equity loans. The declining real estate market of the late 1980s and early 1990s drove many homeowners into bankruptcy or reduced their wealth drastically as the value of their homes fell below the loans against their property.

Gender roles also enter this issue, as couples decide issues such as whether one or both partners will work, whose job is more important, and whether one person will leave his or her job if the couple has children. If one partner has traditional expectations about gender roles concerning money and the other does not, this can be a major source of stress.

Sexual Stress. Sexual problems can spring from the first two problems in long-term relationships, unrealistic expectations and poor communication. Unrealistic expectations about sex within the marriage can lead to dissatis-

STRESS IN OUR WORLD

Tom and Susan

Tom and Susan have an interesting way of handling family finances. They met in graduate business school when they were in their late twenties and pursuing their MBAs. Both had lived alone for a few years and had several years of work experience under their belts. They each had their own savings and checking accounts and retirement funds.

When they discussed marriage, they were concerned about maintaining financial independence and protecting their individual savings, income, and spending patterns. Susan was a saver. She had well over $20,000 in savings before she met Tom and wanted to preserve this money. She was disciplined and always paid cash, even for her automobiles.

Tom was a spender. He believed in the virtues of credit and never saw a catalog he did not like. Saving was something you did when you turned 50 and began to think about retirement. For as long as he could remember, he had carried outstanding balances on his credit accounts, but eventually he repaid them.

Being so different about money but so alike in several other ways, Tom and Susan decided that after they were married they would have three separate accounts: his, hers, and ours. The "ours" account would be used for all joint bills (rent, food, joint vacations, and child rearing, if it came up). Tom wanted it to cover other expenses, such as car purchases and retirement savings, but Susan, knowing that he was a spender and that she would wind up contributing

more, refused to accept this. Each would contribute the same amount to the joint account despite their individual salaries. If one made more than the other, he or she could use it as he or she wished.

Tom and Susan have done all right, despite some stress. She is still a saver and still has more than $20,000 in her bank account. He is still a spender and has a $15,000 car loan and credit card debts exceeding $3000. Susan considered helping him with some payments but decided that he never would learn if she bailed him out of his spending problems.

Some of their friends think they are a little eccentric and that their marriage seems more like a business than a loving partnership, but it seems to work for them. What do you think?

faction. If a partner is unable or unwilling to communicate about sexual concerns, the concerns invariably worsen and become a source of stress within the relationship.

Sexual incompatibility is a major source of stress and a factor in the dissolution of relationships. Research shows that many couples who cohabit in preparation for marriage do so to gauge sexual compatibility before marrying.[38]

Sexual activity changes after people leave the single life and either cohabit or marry. It no longer is as frantic or isolated from the rest of their lives as it was when the partner lived separately. Although sexual pleasure is not sacrificed, sex becomes more integrated into the ebb and flow of the couple's life. It is balanced with other needs and responsibilities, which is an important developmental task in this stage of the relationship.[38] Those who cannot adjust to this change become sexually dissatisfied and may turn to extramarital sex, counseling, or divorce.

The frequency of sexual intercourse declines as relationships age (Table 15-1). Sexual activity peaks within the first year of marriage and then begins to diminish. The average frequency for marital coitus is two to three times a week for couples in their twenties and thirties, a frequency that gradually declines with increasing age.[14]

The frequency of sexual relations is highly correlated with marital satisfaction. Blumstein and Schwartz[5] found that 9 out of 10 married couples who were having sex three or more times a week reported satisfaction with their relationships (Fig. 15-5). On the other hand, only 50% of those couples having sex one to four times a month were satisfied with their relationships.

Physiologically, sex does not necessarily improve or worsen as couples age, it just changes. Most men and women experience little change during their thirties and early forties. Women begin to experience noticeable changes in sexual response at menopause. About 25% of women experience menopause before age 45, 50% from 45 to 50, and the remaining 25% after the age of 50.[33]

Menopause brings the following changes in sexual response:

1. Women require more time to respond physiologically to sexual stimuli.
2. Vaginal lubrication takes more time and generally is less effective in reducing vaginal irritation.
3. The vagina is less elastic and has reduced expansibility.
4. The clitoris is reduced in size but not responsiveness.

TABLE 15.1

Frequency of Marital Intercourse

	Number of Couples Surveyed	Mean Frequency of Intercourse per Month
First year	12	14.8
Second year	10	12.2
Third year	19	11.9
Fourth year	7	9.0
Fifth year	18	9.7
Sixth year	8	6.3

From Masters, W.H., Johnson, V.E., & Kolodny, R.C. (1992). *Human sexuality* (4th ed.). New York: Harper Collins.

Fig. 15-5 Married couples who have fun and are spontaneous can keep sex in their relationship.

5. The intensity of orgasmic contractions diminishes slightly.
6. The ability to have multiple orgasms does not change.[38]

Changes in sexual physiology are less noticeable among most men in their forties and fifties. Although sperm production slows after 40, it continues into the eighties and nineties. Similarly, although male sexual hormone levels decline gradually after age 55, most men notice no loss in sexual desire. About 5% of men over 60 experience a syndrome called the *climacteric*, which produces symptoms similar to those of menopause.[38]

The following physiological changes have been observed in men over 55:

1. Men require more time to become aroused and erect and may require manual stimulation of the penis.
2. Erections tend to be less firm.
3. The amount of semen ejaculated is reduced.
4. Men feel less need to ejaculate.
5. The intensity of orgasmic contractions also is slightly reduced in men.
6. Men need more time to get another erection.[38]

These physiological changes, which all result from a physiological slowing and a slight reduction in the intensity of sexual response, are more than offset by increased comfort about sexuality, an absence of fear of pregnancy, familiarity with one's partner, and an increased time allowed for the sex act.

Care of children. Children can be a major source of sexual stress for adults. Whether the partners are married or cohabiting, straight or gay, children change the couple's patterns of interaction. Berry and Williams[4] show in their analysis of marital happiness and adult developmental phases that satisfaction within the marriage reaches its lowest point around the time the couple's children reach adolescence. Even though this seems to indicate that adolescents are responsible for the greatest stress associated with children, parenting poses formidable stressors at all stages of child development. Although there is no comparable analysis of the effects of children on the developmental phases of gay or unmarried heterosexual parents, we can assume that these parents would experience similar effects.

Parenthood contributes to adult stress in several different ways. Parenting requires a tremendous amount of time at every stage of child development. The specific demands change, but the time requirement remains. Newborns require constant supervision. Even when the parents sleep, they sleep only lightly, ready to react to their children's cries for help in the night. Young children need help with everything from washing and dressing to cutting the food on their plates. Older children need their parents' help with everything from homework to transportation. Parents of adolescents spend countless hours driving their children all over town, while parents of older teens wait until all hours of the night for the safe return of their teenager and the family car.

Children reduce the amount of time partners have for shared activities by up to half.[10] The demands they impose on their parents cut into the time that parents have for themselves and their spouse. This can disrupt everything from a couple's sexual relationship to their hobbies.

Besides the stress of the time demands of children, the unpredictability of children's needs (time and otherwise) creates stress. From feeding babies early in the morning, to driving car pools, to waiting for one's adolescent to return home from a date, parents must bear unpredictable demands on their time, temperament, and sexual desire. Assess Yourself 15-1 helps couples examine their feelings about parenthood.

Care of Elderly Parents. The last stress associated with marriage (and adulthood in general) is care of aging parents. Daughters are more than three times as likely as sons to be the primary caretaker of elderly parents.[10] In many cases, care involves deciding whether or not to take the aging parent in to live with the middle-aged child and his or her family. This is a particularly hard choice, because after living apart for many years, often both the child and the parent prefer to remain alone.

Cavanaugh cites two main sources of stress in caring for aging parents: adult children often have difficulty coping with their parents' deteriorating state of mental functioning, and many adult children find the caring role confining. In many cases the adult children must care for a parent after years of raising their own children. If caring for a parent severely restricts their new freedom, middle-age children can become very resentful. This can be even more stressful for single children used to years of total freedom and mobility.

Divorce

Not all marriages progress completely through Berry and Williams[4] phases. More than half of all first marriages end in divorce (Table 15-2).[14] Although raw divorce statistics are misleading, the divorce rate has been rising during the past 20 years, reaching a high of 5.3 divorces per 1000 residents in 1981.[14]

Most people marry with the hope that the relationship will last forever. Therefore divorce often represents a loss of this hope. This often accompanies a loss of economic status (particularly for low- and middle-income women), lifestyle, and security of familiarity, friends, and sometimes children.[14]

TABLE 15.2

Marriage and Divorce Rates and Ratios

Number and Ratio of Divorces to Marriages, 1950, 1977, and 1991

	1950	Ratio	1977	Ratio	1991	Ratio
Number of divorces	385,000	1:4	1,091,000	1:2	1,179,000	1:2
Number of marriages	1,667,000		2,176,000		2,446,000	

From: U.S. Bureau of the Census, 1978 and 1985; and National Center for Health Statistics, 1982, 1985, 1989, and 1992.

Number of Marriages and Divorces per 1000 U.S. Residents, 1970-1991

	1970	1971	1972	1973	1974	1975	1976	1977	1978	1979	1980
Marriages	10.6	10.6	10.9	10.8	10.5	10.0	9.9	9.9	10.3	10.4	10.6
Divorces	3.5	3.7	4.0	4.3	4.6	4.8	5.0	5.0	5.1	5.3	5.2

	1981	1982	1983	1984	1985	1986	1987	1988	1989	1990	1991
Marriages	10.6	10.6	10.5	10.5	10.2	10.0	9.9	9.7	9.7	9.8	9.7
Divorces	5.3	5.0	5.0	4.9	5.0	4.8	4.8	4.8	4.7	4.7	4.7

From Crooks, R., & Baur, K. (1993). *Our sexuality* (4th ed.). Redwood City, CA: Benjamin/Cummings.

The grief associated
with divorce is similar
to the grief associated
with the death of a
loved one.

A key to understanding the psychological effects of divorce is to compare divorce with the grieving process of those who have experienced the death of a loved one. They experience initial shock followed by disorganization. Volatile emotions and guilt usually follow. Loneliness also often accompanies divorce. Finally, after several months to a year, these feelings are replaced by a sense of relief and acceptance.[14] This grieving process leads to a healing of wounds that allows the divorced person to move on with his or her life and begin again. If the divorced person has not recovered from the divorce and begun to accept what has happened after several months to a year, counseling and psychotherapy may be needed.[14]

Approximately three out of four divorced people remarry, most within 3 years of their divorce. Most remarried people report that their second marriage is better than their first, but this marriage is even more likely than first marriages to end in divorce.[14] The reasons are not known for certain but some possibilities are less willingness to stay in a second marriage when it turns sour, closer scrutiny of a second marriage, financial problems (e.g., alimony, child support) and reduced trauma of divorce after already experiencing it.

Stress Associated With Divorce

Coping with divorce entails a stressful grieving process. However, the intensity and duration of this stress varies, and in most cases the stress of divorce is less than the stress of remaining in the marriage. This is especially true in childless marriages in which both spouses return to work and continue the kind of lifestyle that preceded the marriage.

Child care, child support, and alimony can be formidable stressors in divorces involving children. Even under the most amicable of arrangements, single-parent families usually have more stress than traditional families with two parents. Children still usually remain in the custody of mothers after the divorce, with fathers responsible for child support and, in most cases, alimony. This usually places additional financial strain on both former spouses.

Two households now must be maintained, sometimes still on one income, especially if there very young children are involved. Women, especially low- and middle-income women, usually have a reduced standard of living after divorce, while men seem to fare better. In traditional relationships, the father's job provided most of the family's income, and newly divorced mothers are either just entering the workforce or returning to lower-paying jobs while trying to maintain the same standard of living for themselves and their children. Under optimal circumstances, the father pays a fair and equitable amount of child support and alimony to minimize the stress associated with this adjustment and to allow the woman to meet the family's needs.

In less-than-optimal situations, fathers fail to pay child support and alimony, creating stress for the former wife and children, who wonder where they will find the money to meet expenses. Long and frequent litigation can create additional stress.

Besides financial stress, divorce involving children creates a new kind of stress in relationships between children and the absent spouse. Visitation, decision-making about child-rearing issues, and issues concerning the parents' new partners are just a few of the many potential stressors.

In many cases, remarriage merges families of one spouse with those of the other to form a new "blended" family. Adjusting to step-parents and half-siblings can stress children. Blended families pose a unique challenge, as they combine all of the usual components of family life and child-rearing with the merging of two families, each with its own history, lifestyle, habits, and patterns of interaction. Each family needs time to adapt to the new living situation. Parents and children must decide how to merge their patterns and expectations of family life with new standards for their new family. Much of the success of this process depends on the interpersonal skills and resources each family brings to the new relationship and their desire to work out issues as they create a new unit.

Coping With Work and Relationship Stress: The Four *R*s

Rethink

Changing irrational beliefs about work and relationships can reduce occupational and relational stress. Zingle and Anderson[54] show how teachers' irrational beliefs about work contribute to their stress. Many irrational beliefs about work are related to unrealistic or ambiguous expectations, roles, and goals. One can clear up unrealistic expectations by communicating effectively with supervisors and workers and by studying organizational policies and goals.

One can use Ellis' ADCDE model, described in Chapter 6 and throughout this text, to examine illogical beliefs. A formal decision-making model also can help one to think more clearly about job-related stressors. Such a tool can be particularly helpful in mapping out retirement strategies, including income and benefits.

Just as we rethink the meaning of work as we mature, we must rethink the meaning of our changing relationships. Talking with our spouse and significant other, reading, and taking courses will help us think through situations in a logical, rational way. This objective information and insight can help us assess potential relationship stressors, reducing their intensity or eliminating many of them. For instance, learning that passion normally fades somewhat in any long-term love relationship may help you assess this occurrence in your life.

Reduce

Although certain types of occupational stress, such as recessions, cannot be reduced at the worksite level, most occupational stress can be reduced. Much occupational stress can be reduced through changes in organizational policies and procedures and the physical environment. Although emergencies inevitably will arise and major events will occur in the life of any organization, much of the daily organizational stress is within the control of management. The box on p. 549 highlights strategies for reducing occupational stress.

Reducing relationship stress begins with minimizing unrealistic expectations, communication problems, sexual incompatibility, and money problems.

Relationships built on unrealistic expectations are doomed to failure. Both partners must examine their expectations periodically to learn whether they are close. The relationship contract (Assess Yourself 15-2) is a good tool for this purpose.

Partners must also work on their communication problems to reduce relationship stress. The strategies discussed in Chapter 7 can be employed. Hales[26] devised a set of guidelines for "fighting fairly" that can be used to communicate about relationship problems (see the box on p. 551).

Setting aside a certain amount of family meeting time each week also is a good way of ensuring that stressful issues do not remain submerged for too long. Children can use these meetings to deal with stressors that cut across generational lines, and grandparents can participate if desired.

One way to reduce stress associated with sex within a relationship is to assess the sexual compatibility of the partners before they marry. Some couples cite this as a reason for cohabitation before marriage. Initial sexual happiness in a relationship is a good predictor of future sexual happiness. Couples who are dissatisfied with their sex lives initially in their relationship and hope that their sex lives will improve over time learn that this generally does not happen. If sexual problems, ranging from inhibited sexual desire to painful intercourse to impotence, do not improve, sex therapy may be necessary.

Even though initial satisfaction is a good predictor of sexual happiness in marriage, many changes occur in the course of a relationship that affect sexual activity, including the following: health problems, routines, intellectual growth, childbirth, job pressures, in-law problems, and physiological changes associated with aging. These and countless other issues can lead to

Reducing Occupational Stress

Reducing Ambiguity and Unrealistic Expectations
Employers can:
- Give new employees a thorough orientation that covers such issues as:
  - realistic salary, benefits, and advancement potential
  - organizational chart
  - lines of communication
- Develop and post written policies and procedures
- Encourage open communication, including:
  - assertiveness and communication training
  - rewards for employees who use these skills

Employees can:
- Take responsibility for clearing up ambiguity and unrealistic expectations
- Take advantage of opportunities to ask questions and communicate
- Use *I* language when communicating needs

Reducing Time Urgency
Employers can:
- Use teams consisting of management and workers to establish time estimates for various jobs
- Review time estimates regularly
- Provide time-management training for all employees
- Foster an environment that encourages employees to report unrealistic time estimates

Employees can:
- Take responsibility for reporting unreasonable time estimates or time urgency
- Take advantage of time-management training programs

Reducing Boring/Repetitive Tasks
Employers can:
- Cross-train workers in a variety of tasks
- Use team approaches to projects that allow individual team members to perform a variety of tasks
- Rotate repetitive tasks
- Ensure that workers take breaks when appropriate

Cont'd

Reducing Occupational Stress (cont'd)

Reducing Boring/Repetitive Tasks (cont'd)

Employees can:

- Take advantage of team approaches if available
- Use breaktime and lunch hour to release stress and tension

Reducing Travel and Relocation Stress

Employers can:

- Minimize travel through greater use of video teleconferencing, conference telephone calls, and other technological methods
- Condense travel periods (fewer trips but longer duration)
- Limit weekend travel
- Limit forced relocation of employees
- Minimize making promotion contingent on relocation

Employees can:

- Minimize family disruption and inconvenience associated with travel by spending more time before and after trips attending to family needs

Reducing Worksite Stress

Employers can:

- Fully comply with public occupational health standards
- Be proactive in ensuring employee health, including:
  - soliciting employee suggestions for improving work conditions
  - encouraging employee reporting of stressful/hazardous conditions

Employees Can:

- Fully comply with public health standards and practices, including:
  - wearing protective equipment etc.
  - taking responsibility for reporting stressful/hazardous conditions

Reducing Retirement Stress

Employers can:

- Implement retirement training programs on issues such as:
  - financial planning, benefits, leisure and fitness programs, and aging
- Reward participation in retirement savings plans, including:
  - offering matching funds
- Establish volunteer programs for retired employees to "mentor" new employees
- Give retirees opportunities to use company services and programs

Reducing Occupational Stress (cont'd)

Reducing Retirement Stress (cont'd)

Employees can:

- Take responsibility for learning about retirement and related services and programs (both at work and in public sector)

- Take advantage of services and programs

- Begin to plan for retirement in their forties and fifties (if not earlier)

From Barling, J., & Kryl, I.P. (1990). *Work and Stress, 4*(4), 319-329; Leiter, M. (1991). *Canadian Psychology, 32*(4), 547-558; Matsui, T., & Onglatco, M.L. (1992). *Journal of Vocational Behavior, 41*(1), 79-88; Szwergold, J. (1991). *HR Focus, 68*(11), 5.

Fighting Fairly

- Start your sentences with "I," not "you." Instead of attacking with a statement such as, "You're jealous and immature," say "I feel hurt when you quiz me about my old relationships."

- Make sure you are arguing about the right issue. Are you angry simply because your partner is never on time or because you do not seem to be the top priority?

- Do not embarrass each other by fighting in front of others.

- Even if you are alone, do not attack each other so viciously that one of you is backed into a corner.

- Avoid generalizations such as, "You always interrupt me."

- Be fair. Whenever there is a cheap shot, one of you should stop the fighting by crying, "Foul!"

- Focus on the issue at hand.

- Think before you open your mouth. Taking a few deep breaths will give you a chance to weigh your words.

- Learn to listen. Rather than thinking about what you will say next, tune in to your partner's words, gestures, or expression.

- If you cannot come to terms on a particular issue, agree to disagree or to keep talking about your differences in the future.

From Hales, D. (1991). *Your health*. Redwood City, CA: Benjamin/Cummings.

sexual stress in a relationship. Consequently, one cannot foresee and prevent all potential problems through an initial assessment of sexual compatibility. Couples must be willing to assess their sexual happiness continually and communicate their needs and desires to their partners. In this way the partners deal with problems and concerns before they get worse.

The best way to reduce money problems is to ensure that you and your partner are compatible in your perception of money and its place in the relationship. Assessing your relationship together is a good way to gauge this.

Setting up and following a budget is another way to reduce money problems. This will ensure that each partner has an equal say in how money is earned and spent. Chapter 14 provides guidelines for dealing with money issues.

Setting up three different savings and checking accounts (mine, yours, and ours) and deciding how bills will be paid from these accounts also is a helpful way for couples to deal with money. The specific amounts contributed by each partner are less important than the fact that the couple agrees to the idea in concept. Each couple will adjust the specifics differently, but as long as partners agree on the mechanism, stress will be reduced.

Relax

All of the relaxation techniques discussed in this text can be applied to work and relationship stress. There are many opportunities to build relaxation techniques and breaks into the work day, as discussed in Chapter 14. Take advantage of breaks and lunch time by practicing deep breathing, meditation, stretching, walking, imagery, and other relaxation techniques.

One technique for coping with relationship stress that also can help bring couples together in a sensual way is massage. Massage is excellent for both reducing stress and communicating caring to your partner. One of the simplest things you can do to relax your partner is to give him or her a massage. Sometimes a simple back rub or hand and foot massage can be very relaxing.

Release

The more technical your job, the more you need to escape technology, both during your work breaks and after hours, and participate in physical and nontechnical activities to release your tensions.[1] As discussed thoroughly in Chapter 14, more organizations are realizing the benefits of exercise as a way for their employees to relieve occupational stress. If your company offers fitness facilities, take advantage of them.

Many employers do not have on-site fitness facilities but offer incentives to employees to join private clubs. Some employers offer reduced rates at participating health clubs or discounted memberships in recreation programs.

Take advantage of these activities and save money. Better yet, take advantage of the reduced rates and sign up your significant other and family members.

Regardless of our age, we need release of tension through active, physical means. Couples can make these activities both a method of stress management and a relationship builder. If the partners have used physical activities throughout their lives as a method of stress relief, they can continue, assuming that they remain in good health. If the partners have intentionally cultivated sports or recreational interests that can be continued for life (e.g., tennis, golf, swimming, walking, and hiking), they will find the freedom of retirement a blessing because they can enjoy these pursuits whenever they want.

For couples, sexual release through intercourse can play an important part in stress management throughout adulthood, despite the increased time needed for sexual responses. If adults understand and can accept these physiological changes, they often can derive more pleasure from sexual activity as they age.

Putting it All Together

As we enter adulthood and advance into old age, the cumulative effects of our lifestyle begin either to pay dividends or to exact a toll. If we have maintained a healthy lifestyle and practiced behaviors that are consistent with high-level wellness, we find that we still have a zest for life and the energy to cope with the demands of work, family, and life in general.

Physical Wellness

Maintaining physical well-being throughout our most productive adult years becomes more difficult as demands on our time and resources increase. Finding the time to exercise and maintain a high level of fitness becomes more difficult as we settle into relationships, raise families, and commit time to work and community.

If, over the course of our adult lives, we have developed a lifestyle based on fitness and good nutrition, we find that we are fit and trim, do not suffer from the many debilitating conditions that plague many other older Americans, and can enjoy the fruits of our labor. We have more energy to devote to our relationships. We can share time and recreational pursuits with our partners and families, carrying this activity level into retirement and old age. Retirement and old age are filled with activities such as playing golf and tennis, swimming, and enjoying free time together. Our sexual response is also better than our peers because of our good physical health (Fig. 15-6).

Even if injured or chronically ill, our bodies will respond to exercise and changes in eating habits. We can lose weight through dieting and exer-

Fig. 15-6 Exercise can promote fitness as well as strengthen relationships as we age.

cise. We can increase strength, endurance, and flexibility at any time in our lives. Further, we can approach this challenge as a couple, joining forces and offering mutual support.

Social Wellness

Opportunities to expand our social resources abound during our adult years. We meet new people through work, our neighborhood, our children's activities, community functions, church, and groups that interest us, ranging from political to leisure groups.

If we have paid attention to maintaining old friendships and cultivating new ones, we will find that our social networks are strong and broad. If we have reached out to strengthen ties in young and middle adulthood, we will find these friendships easier to continue in older adulthood and retirement. If we have put down roots and established some sense of community and permanence in our early adult years, we find that as we age, we feel a part of our community. We have a rich network of friends and associates we constantly encounter while shopping, recreating, or participating in community activities. This gives us a circle of other couples with whom to interact. In addition, these friends can help us work through the relationship problems we will face. Often, just talking with friends who are in the same situation can be a method of coping.

If we have not paid attention to developing and maintaining our social networks, we still can begin to develop them. We can take advantage of formal and informal activities in our towns through recreation commissions, adult education programs, churches, and other organizations. We can take classes together, join organizations, and rekindle common interests while meeting like-minded others.

Spiritual Wellness

In a sense, our social wellness merges into our spiritual wellness as we contemplate the meaning of our lives and relationships and our purpose in living. If we have stayed busy raising a family, participating in civic and religious activities, and giving back to the world, we arrive at middle-to-older adulthood with a sense of fulfillment. We see the continuity of life and the interconnections among family, community, and the world. We see friends and neighbors reaching out to help each other, and we feel connected. We see our children growing and our parents aging, and we sense the circularity of life.

If, on the other hand, we have neglected this aspect of our lives and have lived a selfish, self-centered existence, we may feel isolated and resentful as we contemplate our mortality and see our vitality begin to fade. We may feel alone, especially in times of need. The omnipotence we once felt is replaced by a vulnerability that we never imagined we could feel.

We can strengthen our spirituality by joining groups from formal religious institutions to conservation and environmental organizations. Our maturity may be a bonus by providing a broader and deeper framework for understanding our spiritual dimension than when we were younger. Sensing our own mortality, we finally may be able to appreciate the sense of interconnectedness that characterizes spiritual development.

Intellectual Wellness

If we have paid attention to our intellectual well-being, we have stayed current. We have continued to learn about ourselves and our significant other. We have read books on psychology, aging, even the latest surveys of marital satisfaction reported in magazines. We have done this not only to understand what makes us and our partners tick but also to keep our minds active and our brains working. We have taken on new challenges, read interesting books, attended adult education courses, and traveled. We have allowed ourselves to play with technology. We have welcomed the computer age and tried to stay current with the flow of information. We also have realized that being open to new ways of seeing and doing things has kept us vibrant. We have listened to they young and learned from them, not content to be satisfied with the wisdom of our age.

If we did not try to stay mentally sharp by being a lifelong learner, we might have difficulty starting now; but it is never too late to grow and change. We can learn new information and ways of viewing our world. We can learn new skills and improve our abilities to think clearly and rationally. With more life experience, we sometimes can grasp concepts and make connections more easily than when we are young.

Emotional Wellness

If we have paid attention to our emotional well-being throughout young adulthood, we realize that one normally has occasionally confusing or painful feelings about our partners, our children, our aging bodies, or any other issues. We realize that we weathered other emotional storms and we also can handle these emotions. If we cannot, we know people who will listen, people who can help. Having asked for help in the past, we have no problems seeking help now. We can face our partners and our own aging and mortality with clarity, dignity, and strength.

If we have not worked to understand and strengthen our emotional well-being throughout our lives, doing this now is a greater challenge because we face issues that may have been festering below the surface for years. On the other hand, we may have the maturity and insight finally to be able to come to grips with issues that have eluded us for years. We may only now be ready to face some of the painful emotions that have plagued us for years. Sometimes the death of a parent or loved one frees us to examine our feelings toward them and ourselves.

Summary

This chapter takes us through Erikson's next-to-last stage of development, adulthood. We review the major tasks associated with this stage—generativity and integrity. Both are manifested primarily through the work we do and the relationships we develop. We continue the relationships and work established in young adulthood.

Some of us make our mark and leave a legacy that makes us proud. We are productive in our work, moving through our chosen careers with honor, integrity, and commitment. We build a history of accomplishment and growth. Others are not so successful. For myriad reasons and obstacles, they never reach the zenith of their careers. They become stuck, fixed, overlooked, passed over by others on the fast track to a top career. For many, work means reporting in, doing the job, putting in the hours, and counting the days until retirement, when they can enjoy life.

Along the way, we encounter many stressors associated with work. These stressors result from the following five facets of work stress: the individual, the economy or marketplace, job demands, organizational issues, and the physical environment. Further, these stressors evolve as we move through different stages in our work lives on our way to eventual retirement. Things that stressed us as we worked up the ladder sometimes do not seem as important as we reach the twilight of our careers.

We also assess our generativity and integrity by the success of our relationships. Our successes and failures as lovers, spouses, parents, and caregivers are the raw data we use to gauge the productivity of our relationships.

For some of us, our legacy is one of loving partner, devoted parent, or caring child. We move through the stages of our relationships, eagerly anticipating the changes and tasks that await us. We acknowledge the changing nature of our roles as lovers, spouses, parents, and caregivers to our parents, realizing that with each new role come fresh challenges and experiences that make us uniquely human. We seek to understand these challenges and do our best at meeting them. We leave a legacy of one who cared and tried.

Others move through life and their relationships with a self-centeredness that obscures all thought for caring, sharing, and nurturing. Adulthood and old age are viewed as opportunities for greater self-indulgence. For many, this is a period of taking and not giving. The challenges of relationships are resented and seen as infringements on the self. These people leave a legacy of self-centeredness that may have been very productive materially but very empty spiritually.

This chapter applies the four *R*s of coping to work and relationship stressors. Although many of the generic coping strategies presented throughout the book apply to these stressors, others, such as using rational information about the effects of aging on sexuality, are specific to the stressors of adulthood and old age.

Student Study Questions

1. Describe the major tasks associated with Erikson's adulthood.
2. Explain the two major sources of stress in adulthood.
3. Describe at least three major costs associated with job stress in America.
4. Define burnout and describe how it is related to overload.
5. Describe the six major sources of job stress covered in this chapter.
6. Describe three ways to reduce job stress mentioned in this chapter.
7. Describe how *rethink* strategies can be employed to cope with job stress.

8. Describe two stresses associated with each of the following: singlehood and divorce.

9. Describe the four major sources of stress associated with cohabitation and marriage.

10. Explain how *reduce* strategies can be used to cope with the four sources of stress associated with cohabitation and marriage.

11. Describe how *rethink* strategies can be used to cope with the four sources of stress associated with cohabitation and marriage.

12. Describe some of the normal changes associated with sexuality in adulthood.

References

1. Baldwin, B. (1990). Managing the stress of technology. T*he CPA Journal, 60* (10), 94-97.

2. Barling, J., & Kryl, I.P. (1990). Moderators of the relationship between daily work stressors and mood. *Work and Stress, 4* (4), 319-329.

3. Belle, D. (1992). Poverty and women's mental health. *American Psychologist, 45* (3), 385-388.

4. Berry, R.E., & Williams, (1987). Assessing the relationship between quality of life and marital and income satisfaction: a path analytic approach. *Journal of Marriage and the Family, 49,* 107-116.

5. Blumstein, P., & Schwartz, P. (1983). *American couples.* New York: Morrow.

6. Brisson, C., Vezina, M., & Vinet, A. (1992). Health problems of women employed in jobs involving psychological and ergonomic stressors: the case of garment workers in Quebec. *Women and Health, 18* (3), 49-65.

7. Burke, R.J., & Greenglass, E.R. (1989). Psychological burnout among men and women in teaching: an examination of the Cherniss model. *Human Relations, 42* (3), 26-39.

8. Buttner, E.H. (1992). Entrepreneurial stress: is it hazardous to your health? *Journal of Managerial Issues, 4* (2), 223-240.

9. Catalano, R. (1991). The health effects of economic insecurity. *The American Journal of Public Health, 81* (9), 1148-1152.

10. Cavanaugh, J.C. (1993). *Adult development and aging.* Belmont, CA: Wadsworth.

11. Cherniss, C. (1980). Stress and burnout in human service professionals.

12. Cherniss, C. (1992). Long-term consequences of burnout: an exploratory study. *Journal of Organizational Behavior, 13* (1) 1-11.

13. Collins, K., & Killough, L.N. (1992). An empirical examination of the stress in public accounting. *Accounting, Organizations, and Society, 17* (6), 535-548.

14. Crooks, R., & Baur, K. (1993). *Our sexuality* (4th ed.). Redwood City, CA: Benjamin/Cummings.

15. Ellis, A., & Harper, R. (1975). *A guide to rational living.* Englewood Cliffs, NJ: Prentice Hall.

16. Er, M.C. (1989). Assertive behavior and stress. *SAM Advanced Management Journal, 54* (4), 4-5.

17. Erera, I.P. (1991). Supervisors can burn out too. *Clinical Supervisor, 9* (2) 131-148.

18. Forrest, D. (1992). Now for something completely different: success and midlife crisis. *Canadian Business, 65* (9), 96-100.

19. Forster, N.S. (1990). Employee job mobility and relocation. *Personnel Review, 19* (6), 18-25.

20. Friedman, M., & Rosenman, R. (1974). *Type A behavior and your heart.* New York: Knopf.

21. Gallagher, W. (1993). Midlife myths. *The Atlantic, 271* (5), 51-63.

22. Ginsburg, S.G. (1990). Reducing the stress you cause others. *Supervisory Management, 35* (11), 5.

23. Girdano, D.A., Everly, G.S., & Dusek, D.E. (1990). Englewood Cliffs, NJ: Prentice Hall.

24. Grant, L. (1993). White collar wasteland. *US News and World Report, 114* (25), 42-52.

25. Hafen, B.Q., Frandsen, K.J., Karren, K.J., & Hooker, K.R. (1992). *The health effects of attitudes, emotions, and relationships.* Provo, UT: EMS Associates.

26. Hales, D. (1992). *An invitation to health* (5th ed.). Redwood City, CA: Benjamin/Cummings.

27. Hales, D. (1991). *Your health.* Redwood City, CA: Benjamin/Cummings.

28. Harris, P., & Lyon, D. (1990). Midlife crisis: a myth? *Reader's Digest, 136* (818), 108.

29. Homer, C.J., Sherman, J., & Siegal, E. (1990). Work-related psychosocial stress and risk of pre-term low-birthweight delivery. *The American Journal of Public Health, 80* (2), 173-175.

30. Huebner, E.S. (1992). Burnout among school psychologists: an exploratory investigation into its nature, extent, and correlates. *School Psychology Quarterly, 7* (2), 129-136.

31. Inkeles, & Todis. (1972). *Art of sensual massage.* San Francisco: Straight Arrow Books.

32. Jamal, M., & Baba, V.V. (1992). Shiftwork and department-type related to job stress, work attitudes, and behavioral intentions: a study of nurses. *Journal of Organizational Behavior, 13* (5), 449-464.

33. Kart, S.S. (1994). *The realities of aging.* Boston: Allyn & Bacon.

34. Lazarus, R.S. (1991). Psychological stress in the workplace. *Journal of Social Behavior and Personality, 6* (7), 1-13.

35. Leiter, M. (1991). The dream denied: professional burnout and the constraints of human service organizations. *Canadian Psychology, 32* (4), 547-558.

36. LeVan, H., Katz, M., & Hochwarter, W. (1990). Employee stress swamps workers comp. *Personnel, 67* (5), 61-65.

37. Managers Magazine. (1992). Recession fuels worker stress, cuts productivity. *Managers Magazine, 67* (3), 3.

38. Masters, W.H., Johnson, V.E., & Kolodny, R.C. (1992). *Human sexuality* (4th ed.). New York: Harper Collins.

39. Matsui, T., & Onglatco, M.L. (1992). Career self-efficacy as a moderator of the relation between occupational stress and strain. *Journal of Vocational Behavior, 41* (1), 79-88.

40. Morrison, E., & Price, M.U. (1974). *Values in sexuality: a new approach to sex education.* New York: Hart.

41. Mullen, Gold & Bellcastro. (1990). *Connections for health.* Dubuque, IA: WC Brown.

42. Munton, A.G. (1990). Job relocation, stress and the family. *Journal of Organizational Behavior, 11* (5), 40-46.

43. Nelson, D.L., & Sutton, C.D. (1991). The relationship between newcomer expectations of job stressors and adjustment to the new job. *Work and Stress, 5* (3), 241-251.

44. Nichols, D. (1993). Stress claims costing California owners plenty. *Restaurant Business Magazine, 92* (2), 15-17.

45. Peiro, J.M., Gonzalez-Roma, V., & Ramos, J. (1992). The influence of work-team climate on role stress, tension, satisfaction and leadership perceptions. *European Review of Applied Psychology, 42* (1), 49-58.

46. Phillis, D.E., & Stein, P.J. (1983). Sink or swing? The lifestyles of single adults. In E.R. Allegeir and N.B. McCormick (Eds.), *Changing boundaries: gender roles and sexual behavior.* Palo Alto, CA: Mayfield.

47. Small Business Reports. (1992). Less stress is best. *Small Business Reports, 17* (10), 30.

48. Szwergold, J. (1991). Surviving the stress of business travel. *HR Focus, 68* (11), 5.

49. Turnage, J.J., & Spielberger, C.D. (1991). Job stress in managers, professionals, and clerical workers. *Work and Stress, 5* (3), 165-176.

50. US Department of Health and Human Services. (1991). *Sexually transmitted disease clinical practice guidelines,* Washington, DC: US Government Printing Office.

51. Walen, S., Di Guisseppi, R., & Dryden, W. (1980). *A practitioner's guide to rational emotive therapy.* New York: Institute for Rational Emotive Therapy.

52. Wilson, H.S., & Kneisl, C.R. (1992). *Psychiatric nursing.* Redwood City, CA: Addison Wesley.

53. Zemke, R. (1991). Workplace stress revisited. *Training, 28* (11), 35-40.

54. Zingle, H., & Anderson, S. (1990). Irrational beliefs and teacher stress. *Canadian Journal of Education, 15* (4), 445-449.

ASSESS YOURSELF 15-1

Am I Parent Material?

For some people the answer to "Do I want to be a parent?" is obvious and unquestioned, but for others it is not. If we are uncertain, we can seek advice from others and try to learn from other people's experiences, but ultimately the decision is our own. Here is a sample of questions you might ask yourself in exploring your feelings about parenthood.

Does Having and Raising a Child Fit the Lifestyle I Want?

1. What do I want out of life for myself? What do I think is important?
2. Could I handle a child and a job at the same time? Would I have the energy for both?
3. Would I be ready to give up the freedom to do what I want to do when I want to do it?
4. Would I be willing to cut back my social life and spend more time at home? Would I miss my free time and privacy?
5. Can I afford to support a child? Do I know how much it takes to raise a child?
6. Do I want to raise a child in the neighborhood where I live now? Would I be willing to move?
7. How would a child interfere with my growth and development?
8. Would a child change my educational plans? Do I have the energy to go to school and raise a child at the same time?
9. Am I willing to give a great part of my life—at least 18 years—to being responsible for a child? And spend a large portion of my life being concerned about my child's well-being?

What Is In It For Me?

1. Do I like doing things with children? Do I enjoy activities that children do?
2. Would I want a child to be like me?
3. Would I try to pass on to my child my ideas and values? What if my child's ideas and values turn out to be different from my own?
4. Would I want my child to achieve things that I wish I had but did not?
5. Would I expect my child to keep me from being lonely in my old age? Do I do that for my parents? Do my parents do that for my grandparents?
6. Do I want a boy or girl child? What if I do not get what I want?
7. Would having a child show others how mature I am?
8. Will I prove I am a man or woman by having a child?
9. Do I expect my child to make my life happy?

Cont'd

Am I Parent Material? (cont'd)

Raising a Child—What Is There To Know?

1. Do I like children? When I am around children for a while, what do I think or feel about having one around all of the time?

2. Do I enjoy teaching others?

3. Is it easy for me to tell other people what I want or need or what I expect of them?

4. Do I want to give a child the love he or she needs? Is loving easy for me?

5. Am I patient enough to deal with the noise and the confusion and the 24-hour-a-day responsibility? What kind of time and space do I need for myself?

6. What do I do when I get angry or upset? Would I take things out on a child if I lost my temper?

7. What does discipline mean to me? What does freedom, setting limits, or giving space mean? What is being too strict or not strict enough? Would I want a perfect child?

8. How do I get along with my parents? What will I do to avoid the mistakes my parents made?

9. How would I take care of my child's health and safety? How do I take care of my own?

10. What if I have a child and find out I made a wrong decision?

Have My Partner and I Really Talked about Becoming Parents?

1. Does my partner want to have a child? Have we talked about our reasons?

2. Could we give a child a good home? Is our relationship a happy and strong one?

3. Are we both ready to give our time and energy to raising a child?

4. Could we share our love with a child without jealousy?

5. What would happen if we separated after having a child or if one of us should die?

6. Do my partner and I understand each other's feelings about religion, work, family, child raising, and future goals? Do we feel pretty much the same way? Will children fit into these feelings, hopes, and plans?

7. Suppose one of us wants a child and the other does not? Who decides?

8. Which of the questions listed here do we need to really discuss before making a decision?

From: Mullen, Gold, and Bellcastro. *Connecting for health.*

ASSESS YOURSELF 15-2

Relationship Contract[41]

If you could plan the perfect relationship, what would it be? Answer the following questions with your partner to compare your ideas of the perfect relationship.

Name:
Should the wife take on the husband's last name, the husband take on the wife's name, both take a hyphenated name, both take a new name, or both keep their own names?

If there are children, what will their surname be?

Birth Control:
What kind?

Whose responsibility?

Household Duties:
Who does what?

Leisure Time:
Should evenings and weekends be spent together?

Who decides what to do?

Should vacations be spent together?

   With Children?

   Separate?

Living Arrangements:
Where will you live?

What kind of privacy to you want?

Shared bedroom?

Do you want to live with others?

What will you and your partner do if you want to live in different places because of jobs or for any other reason?

Money:
Will both partners be wage earners?

If so, will you pool your income?

Each keep own salary?

Share equally the cost of living expenses and keep the remainder for yourselves?

Cont'd

Relationship Contract (cont'd)

Sexual Rights:

Commitment to monogamy?

Who initiates sex?

Is either partner free not to respond?

Children:

How many?

When?

Adopt?

Who will take primary responsibility for raising the children?

Will one partner have to quit a job?

Other Relationships:

Are you and your partner free to make relationships with other people?

With those of the same sex?

With those of the opposite sex?

What is to be the extent of these relationships?

Do you include each other in these relationships?

From: Morrison, E., & Price, M.U. (1974). *Values in sexuality: a new approach to sex education*. New York: Hart.

Stress in Old Age

CHAPTER OBJECTIVES

- Know the major tasks associated with Erikson's old-age stage of development.

- Describe four normal physical and mental changes associated with aging.

- Compare some of the chronic diseases in elderly men and women.

- Analyze the effects of socioeconomic status on retirement.

- Describe the influence of social support on retirement and aging.

- Describe the changing nature of relationships among elderly couples.

- Compare long-term heterosexual and homosexual relationships.

- Explain how living environments sometimes change as people age.

- Describe the pros and cons of various living environments for the elderly.

- Define death anxiety and describe how various groups react to it.

- Describe how to use the four *R*s to cope with stressors associated with old age.

KEY
TO UNDERSTANDING

The elderly need to relive the past to assess the meaning of their lives.

In Erikson's[14] final stage, old age, the major developmental task is maintaining integrity in the face of despair. The last stage begins in older adulthood with a growing awareness of the nearness of death. It is a time for facing mortality and accepting the worth and uniqueness of our lives.

Maintaining integrity in the face of despair requires us to evaluate our lives and accomplishments. In a sense, we are verifying our existence and seeking its meaning. We do this by looking back at where we have been, what we have accomplished, and whom we have touched. The process of verifying and finding meaning in our lives often involves reminiscing with family, friends, and others. This reliving of the past helps give it meaning and aids in the resolution of this stage's developmental task. A key to understanding the aged is to recognize their need to relive past events. Successful resolution of this task gives us wisdom and the strength to look to the future without despair. Students can get a feeling for this task by performing the activity in Assess Yourself 16-1.

Those who look back on their lives and feel meaningless will anticipate old age with despair. They will question the meaning of their lives and wonder how their lives might have been. Those who have met the challenges of the earlier stages of life and who have successfully completed the developmental tasks that precede old age do not nervously anticipate this final stage. Rather, they have a sense of inner peace and look back on their lives with a sense of accomplishment and contribution.

Many also will look to the future. Confident in the integrity of their lives, they look for continued opportunities to be productive. The context is different from their early adulthood, when their productivity was directed at careers and other responsibilities. Now, free of these responsibilities, they take on new roles, such as grandparents or community volunteers.

There are many potential challenges or stressors during this stage, as bodies age, health status changes, careers wind down, relationships and living environments change, and we contemplate our ultimate death. As we have learned, our perceived ability to cope with the realities of aging affects how we view these events. In this chapter, we will examine some of the changes associated with aging and the potential stress associated with them.

Health Changes Associated with Aging

Many theories seek to explain how and why the body ages. These theories can be grouped into two categories: damage theories and programmed theories. Damage theories assert that the body ages because of damage that affects normal functioning. Whether the damage is due to the effects of free radicals (damage inflicted on cells by highly unstable molecules formed from incomplete cellular oxidation) or accumulation of harmful waste products within the cells (such as amyloid, a protein-related waste associated with altered cell oxidation), these theories assert that physical aging is due to some type of cellular damage.[41]

Programmed theories assert that aging is the result of a programmed limitation of life. Programmed theories suggest that cells have a programmed life span determined by the number of times they can regenerate. In a sense, this represents an "aging clock" that slows after a specific number of cellular replications. Other programmed theorists believe that humans have a "death gene" that causes gradual changes in important biological functions, eventually resulting in death.[41]

Physiological Changes

Regardless of which theory is correct, specific physiological changes are associated with the aging process. The box on p. 568 summarizes the major physiological changes associated with aging.

Although these changes are commonly associated with aging, their onset and effects are affected by one's overall level of health and well-being.

Changes Associated with Aging

- Decrease in number of brain cells
- Decrease in cerebral blood flow
- Diminished immune response
- Decline in acuity of special senses
- Decreased connective tissue elasticity
- Thinning and wrinkling of the skin
- Decreased vital capacity of the lungs
- Decreased cardiac output
- Loss of muscle mass
- Decreased stomach acid output
- Decreased kidney filtration rate
- Enlarged prostate
- Decreased bone density
- Joint degeneration

KEY
TO UNDERSTANDING

The normal physiological changes associated with aging need not detract from the elderly's quality of life.

A key to understanding this relationship is to realize that the normal changes associated with aging generally do not significantly reduce one's quality of life.

As long as people feel well, have enough energy, and do not suffer from restricted mobility, they can continue to enjoy the physical activities they always have enjoyed. Their level of performance may decline, and they may need more time to warm up and recover, but they still can participate.

Sexual response changes but does not end. Older adults take longer to become sexually aroused, and the strength of their orgasms decreases slightly, but aging does not decrease sexual pleasure or desire. Sexual desire in old age tends to mirror that of young and middle adulthood.

The effects of aging on intellectual abilities is very difficult to study because of the confounding effects of physical disease on mental functioning. Although the cerebral cortex and other parts of the brain shrink in size, these changes do not necessarily reduce functioning. Reaction time and work speed may fall slightly, but vocabulary, understanding, and verbal abilities remain about the same. Lifelong patterns of learning and interest in new ideas seem to affect the individual's mental functioning in old age as much as the size of the cortex.

Chronic Disease

The incidence of chronic disease increases with age. Table 16-1 illustrates the 12 most common chronic diseases and the differences in morbidity for 45- and 65-year-old men and women.

Health generally deteriorates with age through an accumulation of chronic diseases and disabilities. **Comorbidity** grows as the effects of one condition affect another (e.g., atherosclerosis affects high blood pressure).

Tables 16-2 and 16-3 rank the 12 most common chronic diseases of men and women aged 65 to 74 and 75-plus. Although the normal aging process need not affect one's quality of life, affliction with one or more of these chronic conditions can limit daily activities. Table 16-4 lists the ten most common chronic health problems limiting activity for men and women aged 65 to 74. These chronic conditions can reduce energy level, movement, range of motion, balance, coordination, breathing ability, and endurance, and can increase the risk of a life-threatening condition, such as a heart attack. Thus the development of chronic diseases can reduce the quality of life and contribute to stress.

Although the tables overwhelmingly support the idea that the likelihood of chronic limiting conditions increases significantly with age, the increases are not uniform for all people. A key to understanding this variability is realizing that the development of chronic disease is affected by one's overall level of well-being and lifestyle. Those who have modified their risks for these condi-

comorbidity
state of having two or more chronic diseases at the same time

KEY
TO UNDERSTANDING

The development of chronic disease is affected by lifestyle and overall level of well-being.

TABLE 16.1

Chronic Health Problems in Men and Women Aged 45 to 64

Rank	Men (45 to 64 years of age)	Women (45 to 64 years of age)
1	High blood pressure	Arthritis
2	Arthritis	High blood pressure
3	Hearing impairment	Chronic sinusitis
4	Chronic sinusitis	Hearing impairment
5	Coronary artery disease	Hay fever without asthma
6	Orthopedic impairment—lower back	Orthopedic impairment—lower back
7	Hay fever without asthma	Varicose veins
8	Hemorrhoids	Hemorrhoids
9	Orthopedic impairment—lower extremity	Chronic bronchitis
10	Visual impairment	Migraine headache
11	Diabetes	Diabetes
12	Ringing in ear	Bursitis

From Payne, W., & Hahn, D. (1992). *Understanding your health.* St. Louis: Mosby.

TABLE 16.2

Chronic Health Problems in Men and Women Aged 65 to 75

Rank	Men (65 to 74 years of age)	Women (65 to 74 years of age)
1	Arthritis	Arthritis
2	High blood pressure	High blood pressure
3	Hearing impairment	Hearing impairment
4	Coronary artery disease	Chronic sinusitis
5	Chronic sinusitis	Cataracts
6	Ringing in ear	Coronary artery disease
7	Diabetes	Diabetes
8	Visual impairment	Varicose veins
9	Other heart diseases	Orthopedic impairment—lower back
10	Atherosclerosis	Ringing in ear
11	Orthopedic impairment—lower back	Hemorrhoids
12	Hemorrhoids	Heart rhythm disorders

From Payne, W., & Hahn, D. (1992). *Understanding your health.* St. Louis: Mosby.

TABLE 16.3

Chronic Health Problems in Men and Women Aged 75-plus

Rank	Men (75+ years of age)	Women (75+ years of age)
1	Hearing impairment	Arthritis
2	Arthritis	High blood pressure
3	High blood pressure	Hearing impairment
4	Cataracts	Cataracts
5	Coronary artery disease	Chronic sinusitis
6	Visual impairment	Visual impairment
7	Chronic sinusitis	Coronary artery disease
8	Atherosclerosis	Frequent constipation
9	Other hearing diseases	Atherosclerosis
10	Cerebrovascular disease	Varicose veins
11	Diabetes	Heart rhythm disorders
12	Ringing in ear	Other heart diseases

From Payne, W., & Hahn, D. (1992). *Understanding your health.* St. Louis: Mosby.

TABLE 16.4

Chronic Health Problems Causing Limited Activity in Men and Women Aged 65-plus

Rank	Men (65+ years of age)	Women (65+ years of age)
1	Diseases of the heart	Arthritis
2	Arthritis	Diseases of the heart
3	High blood pressure	High blood pressure
4	Emphysema	Diabetes
5	Arteriosclerosis	Orthopedic impairment—lower back
6	Visual impairment	Visual impairment
7	Diabetes	Arteriosclerosis
8	Orthopedic impairment—lower extremity	Orthopedic impairment—lower extremity
9	Cerebrovascular disease	Other musculoskeletal disorders
10	Paralysis	Cerebrovascular disease
11	Other musculoskeletal disorders	Paralysis
12	Orthopedic impairment—lower back	Cancer

From Payne, W., & Hahn, D. (1992). *Understanding your health.* St. Louis: Mosby.

tions over the course of their lives by eating well, exercising, not smoking, and controlling their weight have a lower incidence of chronic disease in old age.

Changing Health Status as a Source of Stress

Poor health is cited as a reason for early (forced) retirement and for perceiving retirement as stressful.[7] Failing health can be a source of stress in itself, because it can quash retirees' plans for travel, entertainment, and relaxation. Poor health also can contribute to stress by draining income for health-care costs. Logue[32] found that minorities and less-educated whites suffer disproportionately from long-term disability. In addition, lower socioeconomic status is related to a higher level of long-term disability and a decreased quality of life in old age and retirement (see Stress in Our World box on p. 572). Minorities and less-educated whites also are disproportionately represented at the lower end of the socioeconomic scale[32]

Some retirees also must face the issue of caring for their own sick parents. As life expectancy continues to increase, some retirees in their fifties and sixties face the need to care for their parents, who now are living into their eighties and nineties. This can put additional physical, psychological, and financial strain on retirees who are in the midst of coping with their own changing health status.

STRESS IN OUR WORLD

Louise

Louise is 58 years old. She is a first-generation Italian American who worked as a seamstress in a dress factory. Louise recently was forced to retire after she discovered she had carpal tunnel syndrome.

About 2 years ago, Louise started complaining of pain in her hands and wrists. Her doctor told her it was arthritis and that he could not do much about it. He gave Louise some medication for pain and told her to take aspirin for the pain after she finished her prescription medication. Louise did this and, despite the pain, continued to work.

After 6 months, the pain became unbearable. Louise was experiencing shooting pain in her wrists and forearms and was unable to lift heavy loads. She continued to work but became less productive as she needed to rest her arms frequently. Because she

worked on a piecework basis, and her pieces were moved to the next seamstress for completion, when Louise's work slowed, her co-workers became angry and complained to the floor supervisor. Louise's boss told her she had to produce more or he would have to let her go.

By this time Louise was ready for a second opinion. She visited a new doctor on the recommendation of a co-worker. This new doctor correctly diagnosed carpal tunnel syndrome and prescribed complete rest, a supportive brace, and antiinflammatory medication. The doctor also recommended surgery, but Louise refused, fearing "being cut" needlessly. Louise explained her condition to her boss and he promptly fired her. Louise began receiving unemployment benefits and tried to find another sewing job. No one would hire her because of her condition.

When Louise's unemployment benefits expired, she applied for long-term disability benefits. The application required an exhaustive series of medical examinations, and her employer hotly contested because Louise had refused the surgery. After a long battle that involved three separate medical evaluations, Louise was approved for long-term disability benefits until she became eligible for retirement. Because she was forced to stop working before she had worked the required number of years, Louise did not qualify for her full pension from her union. Consequently, her retirement income was substantially lower than it would have been if she had stayed for a few more years. The combination of suffering from a chronic disease and receiving a limited retirement income has been a major source of stress for Louise.

Retirement Stress

Old age usually is accompanied by a change in work status. The young and midadult periods were characterized by a career-building phase in which most people strove to achieve a high level of productivity. In the later years of middle adulthood, the individual strives to maintain the standards set in the younger years. Most workers begin to reduce their effort, reappraise the role of work in their lives, and plan for their retirement. In old age, most workers retire.

Retirement is very difficult to define. Most people view retirement as complete withdrawal from the work force. This definition is inadequate, however, because many people continue to work part-time, sometimes out of a need for income and often because of a need to feel productive and maintain their identity and status. Retirement is a complex process leading to withdrawal from a full-time occupation.[7] This process begins with thinking about retirement. Retirement brings tremendous change in everything from one's self-perception to daily schedule and interactions with other people.

Changes in Status

As discussed in chapter 15, Americans use work, more than any other activity, to define who they are. Americans live to work. Consequently, when they retire, they must redefine who they are because they no longer are full-time workers.

When people retire, their status changes. Even though many continue to work part-time, in a sense, they are perceived by others as moving from the ranks of the working to the nonworking, from the employed to the unemployed. With this change in work status comes the potential for changes in the way retirees view themselves. Regardless of the type of work performed, when people spend 10, 20, 30, or more years getting up, going to an office or factory, and working 8 or more hours, this routine influences how they perceive themselves. In a way, people develop an identity as workers who perform a specific job, fulfill a task, or meet a need.

Changes in Perception

Our job or career influences our self-worth and identity. The more we define ourselves by our work (rather than by a more holistic view that includes other roles, such as parent, community member, or spouse), the greater the chance that we will perceive any change in our employment as a stressor. A key to understanding why many people fight retirement is that they are not prepared or willing to renounce their identity as workers. They still view themselves as workers and are not ready to abandon this identity. Parnes and Sommers[40] found that having a higher level of education, being married to a working wife, and having good physical and psychological health are more common in men in their seventies and eighties who continue to work and shun retirement.

KEY
TO UNDERSTANDING

Many people fight retirement because they are not prepared or are unwilling to renounce their identities as workers.

Attitudes toward retirement differ according to the nature of the work one has performed. People with rewarding jobs typically are not happy to see them end. These jobs have been a source of gratification, pleasure and, in many cases, financial reward. Those who have viewed work as a lifetime of drudgery often eagerly anticipate the day they can quit. Blue-collar workers tend to desire retirement, while professionals and self-employed people may not.[7]

Changes in Finances

Retirement often reduces income. A feeling of financial security is a major factor in both early retirement and enjoyment of being retired.[7] Financial security can temper the loss of worker status because retirees can see and enjoy the fruits of their labor. Financial security allows retirees to maintain the lifestyles to which they are accustomed, or in many cases, improve the quality of their lives.

Lack of financial security often works in exactly the opposite way. Retirees who are not financially secure may view their working lives as a failure or wonder where they went wrong. Their identities and self-worth may be tarnished if they feel that they did not fulfill their earning potential or were not rewarded fairly for their worth as workers. Lack of financial security also may influence a retiree's perceived ability to cope with retirement and the loss of full-time income.

Financial insecurity can be a major stressor as the cost of living continues to escalate. Retirees on fixed incomes may find that increased costs in basic necessities such as housing, food, and medical coverage outpace their savings and retirement income (see Stress in Our World box on p. 575). Financial insecurity also can reduce a retirees' ability to enjoy the activities they associate with retirement, such as travel and recreation. As discussed previously in this chapter, minority retirees are more likely than their white counterparts to have less income in retirement and therefore are more susceptible to escalating living expenses and health crises.

Changes In Daily Activities

One's daily schedule can change dramatically with retirement, depending on one's preretirement work and schedule. Those retiring from a job with traditional, fixed work hours, will face the prospect of a day that begins and ends when they want it to end. They no longer must set an alarm clock, fight rush hour traffic, report to work by a specific time, and then fight traffic again at the end of the work day. These retirees need time to adjust to their new freedom after years of following a work schedule. Those retiring

STRESS IN OUR WORLD

Ralph and Florence

Ralph and Florence both are recently retired from their jobs in the clothing industry. Ralph is 65 and will receive maximum retirement benefits. Florence is 59 and will receive disability benefits and limited retirement benefits because she does not have 25 years of continuous service and has not reached the age of 65. Ironically, Florence has worked in the industry longer than Ralph because she started at age 14, but she had several breaks in service resulting from illnesses and the birth of her two children.

Ralph was a presser, operating a machine that pressed men's suits and jackets. Florence was a seamstress, putting pockets and linings into ladies garments. Ralph retired in moderate health. He is about 50 pounds overweight, has hypertension and glaucoma, and has led a very sedentary life for the past 40 years. Florence stopped working because she developed carpal tunnel syndrome as a result of the vibrations and pressure of operating a heavy sewing machine. In addition, Florence is overweight, smokes, has hypertension, and suffers from arthritis. Like her husband, she has led a very sedentary life for the past 40 years.

Ralph and Florence have no personal retirement savings plan. Both are entitled to pensions from their respective unions. Ralph will receive $350 per month, and Florence, $200 per month. In addition, they will receive social security benefits of about $1000 per month. They recently sold their home because they needed the money to survive and because their inner-city neighborhood had become too unsafe. Just a few months ago, a neighbor had been beaten and robbed while walking home one block from the bus stop.

Ralph and Florence moved into an apartment in another town about 25 miles away where they will be closer to Florence's sister, nieces, and nephews. Their housing expenses have tripled because their new rent is much higher than their old mortgage payments on the house. Florence misses her house. It was much bigger than the apartment and had a dining room and a yard. Her new apartment is small, dark, and too small for her formal dining room set. She feels that a part of her has died with the move.

Since their retirement, Florence and Ralph spend most of their time at home together in front of the television, although they have joined the local senior citizens' group and see their families regularly. They worry about whether they will outlive their retirement benefits or how they would survive the effects of a catastrophic illness.

from more flexible jobs, who owned their own businesses, set their own schedules, worked off hours, or worked out of their home or from their car, will find less change in their daily schedule.

Regardless of their preretirement work schedule, all retirees have much more free time. Many factors, such as disposable income, health status, hobbies, recreational pursuits, and interest in community service, affect how this time is spent.

KEY TO UNDERSTANDING

People usually spend their retirement years pursuing the same activities and interests that characterized their preretirement lives.

A key to understanding how retirees will spend their time is to examine the lifestyle they led before retirement. This pattern usually will predict how they will spend their time during retirement. People with various interests outside of work, such as hobbies, sports, and community service, can pursue these activities during retirement (Fig. 16-1). Their retirement years probably will be as full as, or fuller than, the years they spent working full-time. People whose lives center on work or who have few outside interests will face much more difficulty adjusting to retirement.

In addition to one's daily schedule, one's interactions with other people change in retirement. Work is the primary source of social interaction for many people. The work day provides opportunities for interactions with co-

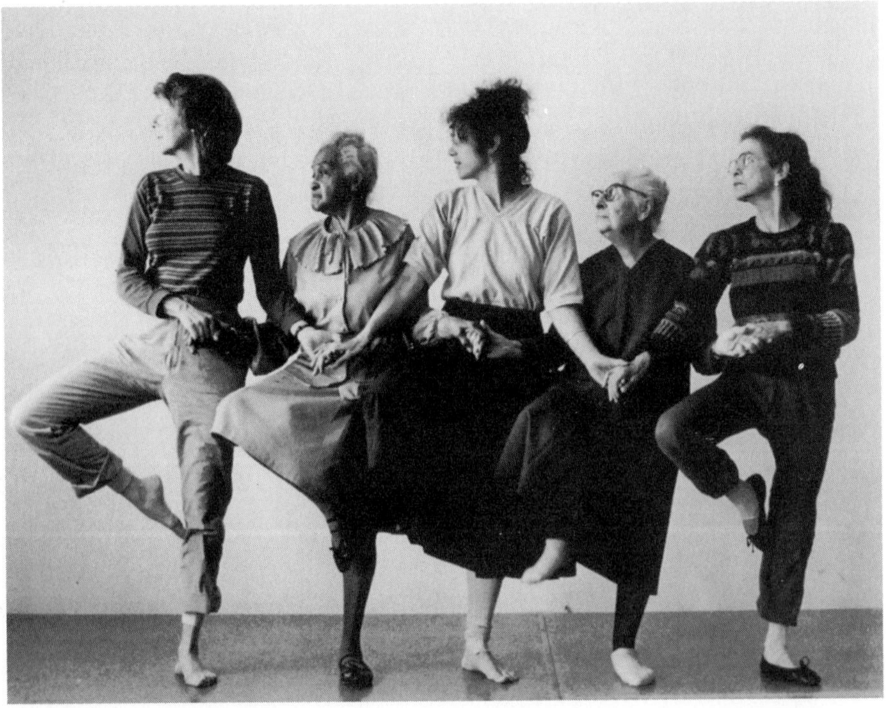

Fig. 16-1 Retirement provides us with many opportunities to pursue old interests and explore new ones.

workers, colleagues, and the public. Many people find the social aspects of work as rewarding as the work itself. Retirement ends this interaction. In some cases, this interaction is replaced by increased interaction with family and friends, pursuing hobbies, recreational activities, or community service. In other cases, particularly for widowed or divorced retirees, retirement brings endless hours of solitude in a quiet house.

Changing Relationships Associated with Aging

Old age often is affected by changes in relationships and family life, as the commitment to relationships that began in young adulthood continues, deepens, or ends. For many, this is a period marked by divorce or the death of a spouse or lover. The box below presents an oft-cited theory of the stages of the family life cycle.[12]

Duvall's stage eight, the postparental years, generally coincides with late adulthood and old age. Many events blend during this time, such as menopause and other physiological changes of aging, retirement, older children leaving home, and the emergence of grandchildren. Although often characterized negatively as a time of loss and failed health, this stage also is a dynamic period in which new freedom, psychological and social stability, and wisdom can be a springboard to increased happiness for couples.

Most older couples today have grown old together. The average couple can expect to live together at least 15 years after the last child leaves.

Duvall's Family Life Cycle

Stage 1.   Establishment (newly married, childless)

Stage 2.   New parents (infant to 3 years)

Stage 3.   Preschool family (oldest child 3 to 6 years, possibly younger siblings)

Stage 4.   School-age family (oldest child 6 to 12 years, possibly younger siblings)

Stage 5.   Family with adolescent (oldest child 13 to 19 years, possibly younger siblings)

Stage 6.   Family with young adult (oldest child 20, until first child leaves home)

Stage 7.   Family as launching center (from departure of first child to departure of last child)

Stage 8.   Postparental family (after all children have left home)

From Duvall, E.M. (1977). *Family development.* (5th ed.). Philadelphia: Lippincott.

This is different from the turn of the century, when half of all marriages were affected by the death of one of the spouses before the last child left the house.[23]

There are mixed findings concerning marital satisfaction and happiness in the older years. In general, most of those who remain married report high levels of marital satisfaction in their older years, but divorce among older people has doubled since 1960 and is predicted to increase among those over 65 in the future.[23]

Marriage

Chapter 15 discusses Berry and Williams'[4] developmental theory of marriage. They found that, as married couples reached middle adulthood, the happiness that had reached an all-time low in their early forties began to rebound with the departure of adult children. As children leave home, free time and money also increases. The partners find they have the time, money, and privacy to reestablish the activities in their relationship that give them pleasure, as well as to investigate new activities together.

Marital happiness continues to rise in the later adult years and into retirement. Depending on several factors, ranging from health to retirement income, the partners continue to enjoy their freedom and, in some cases, relationships with their children and their grandchildren.[7]

We all know couples who have celebrated their fiftieth, or golden, wedding anniversary. We marvel at their longevity and wonder about the secret to their success. Researchers have studied this question, but the findings are inconsistent. Part of this inconsistency results from varying definitions of happiness. Older couples differ from younger ones in their standards for happiness. Older couples share a history that includes memories of the great depression, world wars, more traditional roles in marriage, and marital satisfaction.

In a long-term study of 17 happily married couples, Weishaus and Field[45] found that the most significant factor in marital satisfaction was their ability to adapt to change. These couples had the ability to adapt to changing circumstances that normally might be interpreted as stressful and potentially damaging to the relationship. A serious illness, for example, might be viewed as an opportunity for increased caring and closeness rather than anger and alienation.

Divorce

Marital happiness ebbs and flows over a couple's lifetime. Marriages are shaped over this time by each partner's level of dependence on the other. When dependence is mutual and equal, relationships are strong and close. When dependence is unequal and one partner's needs are much greater than the other's, the marriage has a greater risk of stress and conflict.[7] When dependence is not equal and mutual, normal developmental issues, such as a return to school, retirement, or relocation are perceived as threatening and become a source of resentment, discontent, and stress.

Other issues that reduce marital happiness in old age are health problems,[15] a need to care for sick parents and children,[1] and financial problems.[7] In many cases, marital dissatisfaction in older adulthood is not related to age but rather resurfaces after years of being subordinate to issues of child-rearing. With the children grown and out of the house, old tensions and discontent resurface and produce stress.

Divorce is particularly distressing to older adults because of the long investment of time in another's life. In general the longer the marriage, the greater the trauma. In many cases, an elderly person's identity is closely tied to being another person's husband or wife. Loss of this status often results in a loss of economic status, lifestyle, friends (who often choose sides), and self-concept.[7]

Divorce carries a much greater stigma for the elderly than for the young. Kart[23] reports that, because of this stigma, many elderly underreport their status as divorced when completing forms or applying for services. Divorce among the elderly, particularly for women, also may produce a much greater loss than for younger adults because of retirement, the empty nest, and relocation of family. Although younger divorced people still have a job, young children, and friends and family to visit, the elderly often face a loss of these important connections.[5]

Widowhood

Widowhood can occur at any time during a marriage but is much more likely later in life. Widowhood is more common for women; more than half of all women over 65 are widows, but just 15% of men at that age are widowers. This difference is due primarily to two factors: men have shorter life expectancies than women, and women tend to marry men older than themselves. Consequently, most American married women can expect to live 10 to 12 years as a widow if they choose not to remarry.[7]

Widowhood can be stressful in several ways besides the stress of an ended partnership. Widowed people do not have well-defined social roles in our society. Widowed people therefore often are left alone by family and friends, who do not know how to respond to them. Widowed people also may feel awkward as single people trying to fit into a coupled world.[7]

Men generally are older when they become widowed. Many people believe that men are more stressed by the death of their wives than women

Widowhood Behavior Patterns

Not all women find widowhood equally stressful or stressful at all. Lopata,[33] in studying more than 300 widows in Chicago, found six different behavior patterns that women used after the deaths of their husbands:

1. "Liberated wives" were able to grieve the loss of their spouse and move on to live full, productive lives.

2. "Merry widows" went on to live lives of fun, dating, and various forms of entertainment.

3. "Working widows" continued their careers or took a new job.

4. "Widows' widows" continued to live alone, were independent, and enjoyed the company of primarily other widows.

5. "Traditional widows" moved in with their children and took an active role in the lives of their grandchildren.

6. "Grieving widows" were unable to work through their loss and willingly isolated themselves from others.

are by the death of their husbands. Cavanaugh[7] speculates that this may result from several factors: the way men are raised, the fact that a wife is usually a man's only close confidant, the difficulty most men have in living alone because of their inability to cook or clean, and the tendency of men to be more socially isolated than women.

Loss and Bereavement Stress

Researchers long have noticed an association between human loss, bereavement, and illness. For more than 2000 years, physicians and philosophers have recognized that the strong emotions that follow loss are the precursors to physical and mental illness.[17] **Bereavement** is a form of depression with anxiety and is a common reaction to the loss of a loved one. Loss of a loved one is significantly related to increased stress and illness.

bereavement

a form of depression with anxiety that is a common reaction to the loss of a loved one

In studies of patients with a variety of diseases ranging from cancer to respiratory and cardiovascular disease, a common thread was the earlier loss of a loved one. This loss led to feelings of helplessness, hopelessness, and emptiness in one's life.[17]

Cohen and Syme[8] studied 4500 adults over age 45 who lost a spouse to premature death. Their study became known as the "broken heart" study because they found that nearly 40% of the surviving spouses died of heart problems during the first 6 months after the death of their spouses. The death rate steadily dropped after this time and returned to that of the control group after 5 years. Other studies have confirmed these findings and have reported that one of the factors that return the risk of death to a normal rate is remarriage of the surviving spouse.[17]

Studies have implicated human loss in the survivor's decline of immune function, resulting in an enhanced susceptibility to illness. A variety of studies have found the following changes in the immune status of subjects who recently lost a spouse or family member: significant drops in T-cell and B-cell activity, reduced activation of lymphocytes, significantly reduced killer cell activity, and higher levels of corticosteroids, which dampen antibody response.[17]

Grief is the nearly universal pattern of physical and emotional responses to bereavement separation and loss. **Grief** is a natural process, essential to healing from the pain of loss. Kubler-Ross[27] identified six stages of grief:

grief
the nearly universal pattern of physical and emotional responses to bereavement

1. Denial—disbelieving that the loss has occurred.
2. Anger—strong displeasure over the loss, which could be expressed at anyone or anything.
3. Bargaining—trying to bargain with God or oneself to reverse the loss.
4. Depression—intense sorrow over the loss.
5. Acceptance—accepting the inevitable.
6. Hope—faith in the future.

One must successfully work through each of the stages of grief to heal after a loss (Fig. 16-2). The grieving process cannot be rushed. On average, the grieving process lasts 18 to 24 months, but it can last for years.[17] A key to understanding grief is realizing that people vary in the amount of time they need to fully recover from the loss of a loved one. Trying to rush the grieving process can leave the individual stages uncompleted.

KEY
TO UNDERSTANDING

People vary in the amount of time they need to grieve over the loss of loved ones.

In a study of grief and loss among those in nontraditional relationships (extramarital affairs, cohabitation, and homosexual relationships), Doka[11] found that the normal stages of grief are compounded by the nontraditional nature of the relationships. In homosexual and other relationships, conflicting needs compound the process of healing from grief. A need to declare and demonstrate one's sorrow and affection for the loved one is tempered by a need to maintain secrecy and a fear of disclosure of the relationship. The need for social support and to grieve with other mourners is countered by a sense of social isolation.

Among homosexual couples who are not keeping their relationship a secret, these compounding factors are minimized. Quam and Whitford[42] found that being active in the gay community helps gay couples develop social support networks that enable them cope more effectively with a variety of issues associated with grief.

Fig. 16-2 Grief evokes feelings of profound loss.

Loss of possessions

The loss that leads to disease is not always the loss of a person or a relationship. Depression and disease may follow the loss of a career, self-respect, economic security, or a treasured possession.[37] Possessions, especially for the elderly and especially the home, often are viewed as extensions of oneself or as a personal record of memories, accomplishments, and experiences. Loss of possessions can result in a loss or destruction of identity. This can be observed in the elderly, who, because of illness or death of a spouse, lose their home and their wealth and are forced to move in with children or into a nursing home.

Easing the Grieving Process[41]

Realizing that there is no single guaranteed formula for helping the bereaved, friends and caregivers can help by performing some or all of the following:

- Make few demands on the bereaved; allow him or her to grieve.

- Help with the household tasks.

- Recognize that the bereaved person may vent anguish and anger and that some if it may be directed at you.

- Recognize that the bereaved person has painful and difficult tasks to complete; mourning cannot be rushed or avoided.

- Do not be afraid to talk about the deceased person; this lets the bereaved know that you care for the deceased.

- Express your own genuine feelings of sadness but avoid pity. Speak from the heart.

- Reassure the bereaved person that the intensity of his or her emotion is very natural.

- Advise the bereaved to get additional help if you suspect continuing major emotional or physical distress.

- Keep in regular contact with the bereaved; let him or her know that you continue to care.

From Payne, W., & Hahn, D. (1992). *Understanding your health*. St. Louis: Mosby.

Long-Term Gay and Lesbian Relationships

The large majority of research about relationships focuses on married heterosexuals; comparatively little has been written about long-term gay and lesbian relationships. In a prospective study of 65 gay and 47 lesbian long-term relationships, Kurdak[29] found that the duration of the relationship was a predictor of satisfaction. Gay and lesbian subjects in relationships lasting longer than 8 years reported greater satisfaction than those of shorter duration. Kurdak also found that lesbian couples reported higher levels of relationship satisfaction than gays. Lippman[31] found that as homosexuals age, those in close, committed relationships are the happiest. Variables related to happiness in relationships, such as commitment, companionship, intimacy, and fulfillment of needs, were the same for homosexual and heterosexual couples.

The stereotypical picture of old age for gay men and women is that of unhappiness, loneliness, and aloneness. In reality, it is the opposite. As a rule, homosexual men and women may be better prepared for the challenges of old age than many traditional heterosexual couples. Traditional heterosexual marriages are much more likely, because of stereotypical male and female gender roles, to be built on dependency. Husbands rely on wives for certain activities (e.g., cooking, cleaning, and child-care), and wives depend on husbands for other needs (e.g., wages, long-term financial security, and heavy household work). Gay and lesbian relationships are, out of necessity, more egalitarian. Each partner has been socialized to be self-reliant because gay male and female relationship roles have no social norms. The absence of gender role stereotypes forces homosexual men and women to communicate more effectively and be more flexible and creative in meeting relationship needs.[28] Masters, Johnson, and Kolodny[34] found gay men and women are also more willing to communicate, experiment, and attend to detail in their sexual behavior.

In one of the most extensive, long-term prospective studies of male homosexuals to date, McWhirter and Mattison[35] followed 156 gay couples for more than 20 years. The subjects were gay couples who had been together approximately 9 years before enrolling in the study. McWhirter and Mattison found that gay relationships, like their heterosexual counterparts, go through a series of stages. Stage one, the *blending stage*, occurs in the first year of the relationship. As with heterosexual couples, this year is characterized by the highest levels of sexual activity, strong love and passion, and a blending of personal interests. Stage two, the *nesting stage*, occurs during years 2 to 3, and emphasizes building the relationship and starting a home together. Ambivalence, problems, and doubts about the relationship are most common at this stage. Stage three, the *maintaining stage*, is characterized by a decline in passion and frequency of sexual activity and an emphasis on conflict resolution and reassertion of some of the individuality subverted during the initial stages of the relationship. Stage four, the *building stage,* occurs during years 6 through 10 and is marked by increased personal productivity and independence but also increased collaboration, trust, and dependability between partners. Stage five, from years 11 to 20, is labeled the *releasing stage*. This stage is characterized by the merging of money and other assets and a tendency to take each other for granted. Sexual activity decreases noticeably in this stage. The final stage, *renewing,* extends beyond 20 years and is marked by personal security and a restored sense of partnership based on remembering shared experiences and good times.

Homosexual men and women may be better prepared for dealing with losses such as the death of their partner and retirement because of better planning throughout their relationship. Many homosexuals have planned for their own financial support and have consciously developed supportive social networks.[25] They also may be better prepared to cope with hardship, having lived a life of adversity as a member of a stigmatized group.[10] This combination of attitude, social and financial resources, and self-reliance may help gay men and women cope with the demands of aging. Berger[3] found that older homosexual men matched or exceeded the general population in measures of life satisfaction.

Changes in Living Environment Associated with Aging

People do not live in only a house, they live in an environment that includes friends, family, community resources, and history. A common part of aging for many elderly people is a change in living environment. A change in living environment can be a major source of stress or a challenge, depending on how one perceives the change and the resources and background one brings to the situation (see Stress in Our World box below).

STRESS IN OUR WORLD

Tony and Elaine

Tony is 66, and Elaine is 60, although each could pass for at least 15 years younger. Tony and Elaine have been married for more than 30 years, have two grown children with families, and are retiring from professional careers. Tony, an engineer by training, has been a successful developer for more than a decade, having built a string of shopping centers along the East Coast. He has been actively involved in a self-directed retirement savings plan for more than 25 years and will retire with more than $1 million in the account. Elaine, an elementary school teacher for more than 25 years, will retire with a pension of more than $40,000 a year and partial health benefits.

Tony and Elaine are fit, slim, and very physically active. They play tennis, dance, and jog regularly. They took up sailing at age 40 and have successfully navigated through most of the waterways of North America.

Tony and Elaine's passion for sailing is so great that they plan to sell their home and buy a small condominium in Maine and a large sailboat, on which they will live for half of the year. They plan to spend their winters on their boat in Florida and the Caribbean. In the summer, they will sail up the East Coast, stopping to visit their children and grandchildren in North Carolina and New Jersey.

They have no desire to live in a retirement community, their current house, or anywhere permanently. They believe they have saved enough money to live in this style for at least 20 years and are not worried about relocating.

Age-Integrated, Single-Family, Owner-Occupied Homes

Most Americans, including the elderly, live in single-family, owner-occupied homes (see Stress in Our World box below). Of about 20 million households headed by the elderly, about 76% are owner-occupied and 24% are rental units.[23] Owners who are 75 years and older are more likely to rent and live alone than those under that age. Elderly men are more likely than women to own their own home.[23] Homes owned by the elderly tend to be

STRESS IN OUR WORLD

Yvanna

Yvanna is 70 years old and retired for 5 years from her job as a factory worker in the meat-packing industry. A small, trim woman with bright blue eyes and a quick smile, she raised six children in the same small, brick row house, in a major Midwestern city where she has lived for the past 40 years. All of her children have moved away from home except for her youngest son, who serves in the navy and lives at home between his tours of duty. Yvanna is in good health but occasionally is bothered by arthritis in her hands and fingers.

Stephen, Yvanna's husband of 50 years, recently died of lung cancer. She misses him terribly and feels alone in their empty house. Many of her neighbors have moved away or died, and the neighborhood is changing as new residents renovate the aging structures. Last week, Mrs. Olson, an elderly woman across the street and Yvanna's favorite neighbor, broke her hip on the ice in front of the house and moved into a nursing home.

Money is not a concern because Yvanna has no mortgage, and she has a pension and survivor's benefits from her husband's job.

Marie, Yvanna's oldest daughter, has offered to let Yvanna live with her family. Marie lives in North Carolina in a large, suburban home, with a guest room and plenty of space. Her three children would love to have their nanny live with them, and the idea is fine with Marie's husband George. George travels extensively and would not mind having his mother-in-law around to keep his wife company.

Yvanna is feeling very confused. She would really like to see more of her daughter and grandchildren but is not sure she wants to give up her freedom. She likes her house and the neighborhood. It is home to her. She knows the area, its residents, and she has a lot of friends and acquaintances around the city. She likes being able to get by without a car, walking to the market and other stores. She feels safe here and likes the urban environment. She really has no desire to relocate anywhere, least of all to a suburban area where she would be lost without a car and totally dependent on her daughter to get around. She thinks she will get over her husband's death easier if she stays where she is but the uncertainty is causing her a lot of stress.

older (43% built before 1950) than those owned by younger people. Contrary to popular media images of the elderly flocking to the retirement communities of the South and Southwest, most elderly remain in the same house in which they have lived in for most of their lives. Most elderly homeowners over 65 years of age have lived in their houses for more than 30 years.[23] Most elderly live in age-integrated communities, where people of all ages live together; only about 6% of the elderly live in age-segregated communities.

Age-Segregated Housing

Age-segregated housing for the elderly appears in several types: retirement communities based on single family homes, apartment complexes for the elderly, congregate communities, nursing homes, and continuing-care retirement communities. Each poses unique opportunities, challenges, and stresses to the elderly.

Single Family–Home Retirement Communities

In this type of community, residents purchase their own detached, single-family home. These houses typically are smaller than standard houses, have only one level, and feature appliances and fixtures that are adapted to the needs of the elderly. These houses usually offer low-maintenance features, such as vinyl siding and self-cleaning appliances. Lawn care, trash pickup, and snow removal usually are provided through a monthly maintenance fee. The community has planned recreational activities and amenities, typically including a clubhouse (for parties, games, and other activities), a pool, tennis courts, and shuffleboard. These communities are designed to reduce the stress associated with home ownership and maximize the possibilities for social interaction and recreation.

Limited studies show that these communities tend to have overwhelmingly white, financially secure, educated, healthy, married, adult residents. Residents report high life satisfaction, social participation, and a desire to stay in the community.[7] Jacobs[19,20] found conflicting results. In a study of a retirement community southeast of Los Angeles, Jacobs found that participation in social activities was limited (500 out of 6000 participated regularly), and there also was a strong undercurrent of racism against African Americans, Hispanics, and Native Americans. Further studies are needed to clarify these issues.

Apartment Complexes for the Elderly

Most of these age-segregated housing complexes feature rent-controlled apartments, common meeting areas, and planned activities, although the nature and extent of organized activities vary considerably. Studies differ about the desirability of such a living environment. Carp,[6] Lawton and Cohen,[30] and Messer[36] found that the elderly living in age-segregated apartment complexes had better psychological and social well-being, better health, lower disease and death rates, better social participation, and lower rates of institutionalization than those remaining in their own homes. Jacobs[20] found, however, that many residents were apathetic, passive, isolated, and fearful. The complex had an undercurrent of racism against African Americans and resentment against the frail elderly. Kart[23] concluded that making a successful community requires more than just putting together a collection of like-aged people. Experience, needs, and attitudes must be considered to ensure the development of a real community.

Congregate Communities

Congregate housing represents an intermediate step between independent living arrangements (single-family homes and apartment complexes) and institutionalized settings (nursing homes and some continuing-care retirement communities). Congregate care is a type of communal housing arrangement that combines the privacy of self-contained apartments with the security and socialization of common facilities. Features include a central office with trained staff, medical clinic, cleaning staff, and dining hall. Studies in England, where congregate housing has flourished for more than 2 decades, show that this type of living arrangement allows residents to avoid becoming institutionalized in nursing homes while it meets needs that could not be met if residents lived in private homes.[7]

Nursing Homes

A nursing home is any facility that houses elderly residents who require 24-hour supervision and medical care. Nursing homes are regulated by state and federal governmental standards and may be nonprofit or for-profit institutions. Nursing homes are equipped to handle the special physical, emotional, social, and spiritual needs of elderly people who no longer can take care of themselves (Fig. 16-3). The facilities vary according to one's ability to pay. Not all facilities accept residents who must rely on government subsidies to pay for their care.

Approximately 5% of the adult population over 65 years of age resides in a nursing home. The typical nursing home resident is very old, female, widowed or divorced, financially disadvantaged, and without children. Nursing home care is extremely expensive (average cost is $25,000 a year), and only a small portion of the cost is covered by private medical insurance and Medicare (2% and 1% respectively). Average nursing home residents typically must deplete their life savings to pay for care. Government subsidies for nursing home care take over the payments when the elderly no longer can pay.[7]

Fig. 16-3 Nursing homes play a vital role in the lives of elderly people who need constant supervision and medical care.

Studies of the elderly residing in nursing homes show that they are more maladjusted, depressed, and unhappy; have a lower range of interests and activities; and die sooner than noninstitutionalized aged people.[23] Although these results seem to indict nursing homes for these problems, three factors contribute to these unfavorable outcomes: the stress of relocation and a change in living environment, preadmission effects, and the total institution.

Relocation. As we discuss in Chapter 15, relocation can be stressful at any age but is particularly stressful for the aged. Researchers generally agree that moving an elderly person from a familiar home setting to an unfamiliar institutional setting can be very distressing, even if the move is voluntary. The stress is compounded when the move is forced.[23]

Preadmission Effects. The negative effects of institutionalization on the elderly may be related to preadmission effects in some cases. One theory is that the negative emotional states, impaired cognitive functioning, and diminished affective responses associated with institutionalization actually are set into motion as an anticipatory, adaptive response. In a sense the individual assumes this negative state of functioning even before entering the institution as a way of adapting to anticipated changes. The other theory states that negative effects of institutionalization are related to selection bias and are not caused by the nursing home. The differences in functioning between people living in institutions and those in the community are due to general differences in the population as a whole. The negative outcomes associated with institutionalization occur within a segment of the population as a whole.

Total Institution. The last factor contributing to the overall negative outcomes associated with nursing home life is the total institution. Several aspects of nursing home life can contribute to the aforementioned negative outcomes. Admissions procedures can be depersonalizing. In some cases, individuals are stripped of personal possessions, are issued institutional clothing, and in a sense, lose their individuality. Institutional barriers prevent residents from behaving and playing roles as they did outside the nursing home. It is hard to be someone's mother, father, grandmother, or lover while behind an institution's walls. A lack of privacy and freedom often inhibits accustomed behavior. Because institutionalization is designed to meet all of one's needs, cooperation between staff and residents is vital.

Thinking About Death

We all must die. As cold and cruel as these four words sound, they are one of the few truisms of life. The meaning of death varies for people. For some, it is a source of great anxiety. Others are more accepting of death. Some of the variables that seem to contribute to fear of death are pain, body malfunction, humiliation, rejection, nonbeing, punishment, interruption of goals, and negative effect on survivors.[7] In a sense, these variables represent threats to our well-being and to continuing life as we know it and enjoy it.

The preceding factors are related to one's anxiety about death; other variables affect our perception of these factors. Considerable research has studied the demographic and personality variables associated with death anxiety. Death anxiety has been shown to vary by gender, race and ethnicity, religiosity, and age.

Studies differ about the influence of gender on death anxiety. Some research indicates that women score higher than men on measures of death anxiety, but other studies do not support this conclusion.[7] In studies that found differences between the way men and women perceive death, researchers found that the women tended to view death more emotionally while the men considered death in more cognitive terms. Although this seems to indicate that, because women view death more emotionally, they would have more difficulty accepting it, Kalish[21] found that the opposite is true. Although women become more emotionally aroused by the prospect of their own death, they also demonstrate higher levels of acceptance of their demise than men.

Conclusions about racial differences in death anxiety also are mixed. Bengston, Cuellar, and Rage[2] found no significant differences in death anxiety among African Americans, Mexican Americans, and whites. Myers, Wass, and Murphey,[38] however, found that elderly African Americans had a higher death anxiety than white subjects. Bengston, Cuellar, and Rage[2] also found that, although three groups showed no differences in death anxiety, African Americans are most likely to expect to live a longer life.

Some of the differences in death anxiety between blacks and whites can be attributed to the influence of religion, religiosity, social support, and kinship ties.[26] African Americans were found to have more extensive kinship ties with nuclear and extended families and greater levels of social support than whites. As discussed in Chapter 4, a high level of social support is related to physical and mental health and improved outcomes in the treatment of illnesses.

Social support and kinship networks are so strong within the African-American community that they have been recognized by gerontologists, social service providers, and government officials as major resources available to the black elderly. However, Gratton and Wilson[16] warn that the strength of the African-American community in meeting the needs of its elderly should not be used as an excuse to cut funding for programs that target this population.

Church has long been a source of strength in African-American communities. Religiosity and church involvement is an underlying thread that binds black families to the African-American community and is a source of strength in troubled times. In many African-American communities, life centers on church activities. The church is a rallying point for everything from political activism to social support. Even in urban America, church is a greater focal point for African Americans than for whites.

This relationship to the church is especially important in aging because much research has documented the relationship between religiosity and reduced death anxiety. Religiosity can have several dimensions, such as belief in an afterlife, prayer, church attendance, and participation in fellowship activities. Church attendance and participation are related to lower death anxiety, while belief in an afterlife is not.[21]

One of the essential characteristics of religion and church attendance is that it provides a forum for the practice of faith and spirituality. As discussed in Chapter 4, one's social and spiritual activities are significantly related to reduced stress and increased health. Faith and spirituality also are related to death anxiety. Faith and spirituality help one to understand the meaning of one's life and the inevitability of death. Faith and spirituality also assist people in understanding, coping with, and recovering from crises and loss. Reed,[43] in a study of 300 terminally ill patients, found spirituality and faith positively related to low death fear, positive death perspectives, and better emotional adjustment.

Little is known about the relationship between the more secular definitions of spirituality, discussed in Chapter 4, and death anxiety.

Age is another demographic variable related to the way we view death. Nagy,[39] in a classic study, examined the perceptions of death in postwar Hungarian children. Nagy found that children under age 5 viewed death as a temporary state. Children from Nagy's study believed that dead people, like the television cartoon characters who recover after being run over by a truck or exploded by a bomb, are only temporarily departed. Between 5 and 9 years old, children viewed death as irreversible but not necessarily inevitable for the individual child. Death existed but was remote; it affected other people. By 9 or 10, children began to view death as inevitable and final, part of the life cycle of all living organisms. Critics have argued that Nagy's findings cannot be generalized to modern children in other cultures. Kastenbaum[24] argues that children are more sophisticated in their perception of death and actually characterize death in scientific terms. He cites one 7 year old who characterizes death as being like "when the computer is down." In reality, this child might have the same view of death as Nagy's postwar Hungarian children but use a more modern metaphor. Despite the criticism that Nagy's findings cannot be generalized across all cultures and eras, the study does provide a context for viewing death. Death perception does change over the life cycle.

Even though the elderly think about death more than any other age group, they generally fear death less and accept it more.[7] Kalish[22] gave several explanations for this—they have completed the most important tasks in their lives and therefore do not worry that they have not had the time to accomplish everything; they have suffered from more chronic diseases; they realize they are unlikely to improve and therefore view death as relief; they already have lost many of their friends and loved ones; and they already have spent much time thinking about death.

Coping With Stress Related to Aging: The Four *R*s

Rethink

As in all the stages of life, one begins coping with stress in old age by taking a more rational and logical look at the people, places, and objects that are a source of stress. The realities of aging force us to reexamine our beliefs about ourselves and our lives. Accepting the changes of our aging bodies, reduced work responsibilities or retirement, relationships, and living environments requires us to objectively appraise these situations. The changes associated with aging often reduce or eliminate functioning once taken for granted. Cavanaugh[7] believes that a fundamental developmental task of old age is accepting the nature and extent of the changes and losses.

The first step in accepting change and loss in old age is confirming their existence. Payne and Hahn[41] propose a three-part process for confirming change or loss in functioning. One way to verify a decline in functioning is by *testing* for its presence. The elderly can test their level of functioning by trying to take part in activities that they previously could perform. Failure to perform at the usual level can confirm the nature and extent of the loss. *Observing others* is another way of confirming functional, structural, or emotional loss. Observing the loss in others sometimes can confirm the loss in ourselves much more easily than seeing it in ourselves. The last way to confirm our losses is to *consult experts*. Physicians and gerontologists can confirm the type and extent of decline.

The reality of our changing lives sometimes becomes clouded by our emotions. Attempts at verifying loss and decline can be difficult when they arouse strong emotions, such as anger, fear, or denial. Ellis and Harper's[13] ABCDE model provides a framework for logically examining the changes associated with aging. Whether one views the changes of aging as challenges or stressors depends on one's ability to consider these changes rationally. The ABCDE model can help do this.

Reduce

Old age, more than any other time, gives one the opportunity to slow the pace of life. Freed from the responsibilities of reporting to a full-time job every day and raising young children, one has the perfect opportunity to gain control of one's life. As previously discussed, one of the major tasks of this stage of life is reflecting on one's life and accomplishments.

The elderly are blessed with the wisdom of a lifetime to assist them in reducing stress. Strategies introduced in Chapter 7, such as the triple *A*s of coping (abolish, avoid, and alter) and time management, are easier to employ because we understand more fully what is truly important to us and our priorities are much clearer than in our youth. We have less pressure from others to continually push, and our attempts at such activities as downscaling (see Chapter 7) are more likely to be supported by significant others in our lives.

One of the keys to understanding *reduce* strategies at this stage of our lives is to realize that some stimulation and demand is crucial for getting the most out of our lives. As discussed in Chapter 7, insufficient demand and

KEY
TO UNDERSTANDING

People need a certain amount of stimulation and demand to be fully alive.

stimulation can be as harmful as excess stimulation, and the elderly must avoid reducing their activities too much or they risk stagnation and stress from understimulation. Knowing one's own abilities will guide one in accepting new challenges and staying active while avoiding excess stress (see Stress in Our World box below).

Relax

The need for rest and relaxation increases as we age. All of the relaxation techniques discussed in this text can be applied to coping with stress in old age. The passive relaxation strategies of Chapter 8 apply especially to this stage of life because they are gentle and facilitate contemplation. Deep breathing, imagery, and meditation can help one reflect on the meaning of one's life, an essential task at this stage.

More active forms of relaxation, such as yoga and stretching, are perfect activities for the elderly as long as one takes care not to force movements or progress too rapidly. Stretching and yoga will help keep muscles and joints limber and relaxed while providing an antidote to stress (Fig. 16-4).

STRESS IN OUR WORLD

Marie: Active at 80

Marie is simply too busy to think about getting old. Marie is 80 and still going strong. Married to Bill for 55 years, Marie is vibrant, healthy, and always on the run. Her three daughters all are married adults in their forties and fifties and have blessed Marie and Bill with seven grandchildren. Marie and Bill own a small house which is easy to maintain and debt-free.

Since retiring more than 10 years ago, Marie has turned her attention to community activities in her church and local senior citizens' group. She has held various leadership positions in these organizations and is always involved in some project. An avid knitter, seamstress, quilter, and craftsperson, Marie still draws great pleasure from making a quilt or sweater, or craft for one of her daughters or grandchildren. Marie likes to sew while watching television and amazes her visitors as her deft hands whirl about.

Although osteoporosis and vision problems have caused Marie some trouble, she enjoys her life and does not view these health problems as major impediments to her happiness. Marie is very active in church activities, and her faith has carried her through her bouts with these conditions. Marie is very happy with her life and is too busy to worry about her own death.

Fig. 16-4 Stretching is an excellent way for older people to relieve tension.

Massage is one relaxation strategy that brings couples together in a sensual way. Massage is excellent for both reducing stress and communicating caring to one's partner. It is simple to provide and is relaxing for one's partner.

Release

Even in old age, the release of tension through active, physical means is important. Exercise habits developed throughout life can be continued if one's health is good. The pace, intensity, and duration of exercise may diminish slightly, but this reduction need not inhibit participation in activities that are enjoyable and that reduce stress.

People of all ages can become more active and physical even if they were not physically active in their earlier years. However, they must undergo a complete physical examination by their physician, and they must follow a graduated program of exercise that slowly builds strength and endurance. Water activities such as swimming and aquatic exercise are especially beneficial because they put less strain on bones and joints (Fig. 16-5).

If couples have used physical release throughout their lives as a way to deal with stress, this habit simply continues, assuming they remain in

Fig. 16-5 Exercising in a pool is a way to get a good workout that is gentle on the body's joints.

good health. If couples have intentionally cultivated sports and recreational interests that have lifelong potential (e.g., tennis, golf, swimming, walking, and hiking), they will find the greater free time of retirement a blessing because they can enjoy these pursuits whenever they want (Fig. 16-6).

Orgasm can continue to serve as a potent stress reducer until death. As discussed, sexual response changes in measurable ways as we age. If older adults understand and can accept these physiological changes, they often can derive more pleasure from sexual activity as they age.

Putting it All Together

Physical Wellness

As we advance into old age, the cumulative effects of our lifestyle begin to either pay dividends or exact a toll. If we have maintained a healthy lifestyle and have practiced behaviors that are consistent with high-level wellness, we find that we still have a zest for life and the energy to live each day to its fullest. We exercise as we have exercised for years. We watch our diets, paying particular attention to avoiding excess fat, salt, and sugar. We get enough rest and relaxation.

Fig. 16-6 Some older people may be better conditioned than young adults.

We find that we are fit and trim, do not suffer from the many debilitating conditions that plague many other older Americans, and can enjoy the fruits of our labor. We have more energy to devote to our relationships. We can share time and recreational pursuits with our partners. Our sexual response is better than that of our peers because of our good physical health.

If we have lived an unhealthful life, our habits now will begin to catch up to us. Those extra pounds we have been carrying and those bad habits, such as smoking and drinking excessively, will rob us of the energy we need to cope with life and recuperate from the wear and tear of living.

In addition, we are at greater risk of the lifestyle diseases, such as cardiovascular disease and cancer, which can drastically change our relationships with our partners by making us more dependent and less involved. We probably already have seen the writing on the wall, as we have been prescribed medication for hypertension and have been warned about our high cholesterol and poor results on our most recent stress test.

Social Wellness

If we have maintained old friendships and cultivated new ones, we will find that our social network is strong and wide. If we have reached out

Fig. 16-7 Although sexual physiology changes somewhat as we age, intimacy, sensuality, and pleasure can continue until we die.

and strengthened ties in young and middle adulthood, we will find this trend easy to continue in older adulthood.

If we have put down roots and established some sense of community and permanency in our early adult years, we find that as we age, we feel a part of our community. We have a rich network of friends and associates whom we constantly encounter while shopping, recreating, or participating in community activities. This network gives us a sense of belonging to a community and a safety net in case we suffer a setback.

If we have not paid attention to developing and maintaining our social network, we may find this task even harder because we have missed many opportunities to form new friendships and solidify old ones. We also may find that we now need these social networks the most to help us with such stressors as illness, retirement, and widowhood.

Fortunately, opportunities abound for senior citizens to make new friends and develop support groups. Most communities offer an essential service by organizing senior citizen groups. These groups usually operate out of an office on aging at the local, county, or state level. The services can range from simply facilities for regular meetings to social gatherings, trips, and low-cost meals. Most churches also provide services for the elderly. The box on p. 599 provides a list of resources for senior citizens.

Spiritual Wellness

In a sense, our social wellness merges into our spiritual well-being as we contemplate the meaning of our lives and relationships and our contri-

Resources for Seniors

The following national organizations can help senior citizens find information and obtain services. Similar organizations can be found at the state and local levels.

U.S. Commissioner
Administration on Aging
Department of Health and
Human Services
Kohen Building
330 Independence Avenue,
S.W.
Washington, DC 20201
(202) 619-0724

Alzheimer's Disease and
Related Diseases
Association (ARDA)
70 E. Lake St., Suite 600
Chicago, IL 60601
(800) 572-6037
In Illinois (800) 572-6037

American Association of
Homes for the Aging
901 E St., N.W., Suite 500
Washington, DC 20049
(202) 296-5960

American Association of
Retired Persons
Washington, DC 20049
(202) 872-4700

American Health Care
Association
1201 L St., N.W.
Washington, DC 20005
(202) 842-4444

American Society on Aging
833 Market St., Suite 512
San Francisco, CA 94103
(415) 543-2617

Children of Aging Parents
2761 Trenton Rd.
Levittown, PA 19056
(215) 345-5104

Foundation for Hospice
and Home Care
519 C St., N.E.
Washington, DC 20002
(202) 547-6586

Gray Panthers
1424 16th St., N.W., Suite 602
Washington, DC 20036
(202) 387-3111

National Association for
Home Care
519 C St., N.E.
Washington, DC 20002
(202) 547-7424

National Council of
Senior Citizens
1331 F St., N.W.
Washington, DC 20004-1171
(202) 347-8800

National Council on the
Aging, Inc.
409 3rd St., S.W., 2nd Floor
Washington, DC 20024
(202) 479-1200

National Hospice
Organization
1901 N. Moore St., Suite 901
Arlington, VA 22209
(703) 243-5900

National Rehabilitation
Information Center
(NARIC)
8455 Colesville Rd., Suite 935
Silver Spring, MD 20910
(800) 34-NARIC;
In Washington, DC area:
(301) 588-9284

National Senior Citizens
Law Center
1815 H St., N.W., Suite 700
Washington, DC 20006
(202) 887-5280

The Older Women's League
(OWL)
730 11th St., N.W., Suite 300
Washington, DC 20001
(202) 783-6686

From Payne, W., & Hahn, D. (1992). *Understanding your health*. St. Louis: Mosby.

bution to the world. If we have stayed busy, raising a family, participating in civic and religious activities, and giving something back to the world, we look back on our lives with a sense of fulfillment. We see the meaning of our lives and our effect on a family, community, and the world. We see our children and grandchildren growing and our own aging, and we sense the circularity of life.

As discussed previously in this chapter, elderly people whose spirituality is manifested in religion and who actively participate in church-related activities gain an important benefit. Old age also gives the elderly the opportunity to reexamine religious and spiritual beliefs as they reassess the meaning of their lives and attempt to come to grips with their own mortality.

If, on the other hand, we have neglected this aspect of our lives and have lived a selfish, self-centered existence, we may feel isolated and resentful as we contemplate our mortality and see our vitality fade. We may feel alone, especially in times of need. The omnipotence we once felt is replaced by a vulnerability and despair that we never imagined could exist. Having never taken steps to reach out and connect with something greater than ourselves, we find it hard to do so now. We begin to resent our spouse, as we see his or her body and youthful looks age.

Intellectual Wellness

If we have paid attention to our intellectual well-being, we have been life-long learners. We have continued the learning habits we cultivated over a lifetime. We still read, keeping our minds active and our brains working. We still relish a challenge, take an occasional course, and travel. We embrace technology and are open to new ways of seeing and doing things. We listen to our young and give them the wisdom of our age.

If we never paid attention to keeping mentally sharp by being a lifelong learner, we may have difficulty starting now. We may find that we resent change and do not want to grow. We want to remain comfortable, and we resent anyone or anything that forces us to see things with a fresh perspective.

Emotional Wellness

If we have paid attention to our emotions and tried to understand them over the years, we realize that the fears and concerns of old age are not unlike those of all the other stages of our life. We realize that we weathered other storms and we also can handle these emotions. If we cannot, we have people who will listen and can help. Having asked for help in the past, we have no problem seeking help now. We can face our partner's and our own aging and mortality with clarity, dignity, and strength. We are not afraid to admit that we may need professional help in sorting through our feelings about our own aging.

If we have not tried to understand and strengthen our emotional well-being throughout our lives, we find that the pressures of an aging body, retirement, widowhood, and other issues overwhelm us. Never having asked for help in the past, we do not know how or where to begin. We feel scared, alone, and helpless.

Summary

This chapter examines Erikson's final stage of development, old age. We review the major task of this stage: maintaining integrity in the face of despair.

In old age, we look back on our life to assess its meaning. Some of us leave a legacy that makes us proud. We were productive in our work, moving through our chosen careers with honor, integrity, and commitment. We retire, leaving a history of accomplishment. Others are not so successful. For myriad reasons and obstacles, they never reach the zenith of their professions. They become stuck, fixed, overlooked, or passed over by others on the fast track to a top career. For many, work means reporting in, doing the job, putting in the hours, and counting the days until retirement, when they can enjoy life.

We also measure our generativity and integrity by the success of our relationships. Our successes and failures as lovers, spouses, parents, and caregivers illustrate the productivity of our relationships.

Some of us leave a history as a loving partner, devoted parent, or caring child. We move through the stages of our relationships, eagerly anticipating the changes and tasks that await us. We acknowledge the changing nature of our roles as lovers, spouses, parents, and caregivers to our parents, realizing that with each new role comes fresh challenges and experiences that make us uniquely human. We seek to understand these challenges and do our best to meet them. We leave a legacy of one who cared and tried.

Others move through life and their relationships with a self-centeredness that obscures all thought for caring, sharing, and nurturing. Adulthood and old age are viewed as opportunities for greater self-indulgence. For many, this is a period of taking but not giving. The challenges of relationships are resented and seen as infringements on the self. These people leave a legacy of self-centeredness that may have been very productive materially but is very empty spiritually.

This chapter examines six common potential stressors of old age—aging bodies, changing health status, retirement, changing relationships, changing living environments, and fear of death. Each is examined as either a challenge based on the realities of aging, or as a stressor arising from illogical thoughts and feelings.

Finally, we describe specific applications of the four *R*s of coping to the stressors associated with old age. Although many of the generic coping strategies presented throughout this book apply to these stressors, others, such as considering rational information about the physiological effects of aging, are specific to the stressors of old age.

Study Questions

1. What is the primary task associated with Erikson's old-age stage of development?
2. Describe five major sources of stress for the elderly.
3. What are some of the major physiological changes associated with aging?
4. Describe the effects of aging on cognitive functioning.
5. Describe the effects of aging on sexual response.
6. How does lifestyle affect the development of two chronic diseases associated with aging?
7. What are two of the main benefits associated with work that a retiree loses?
8. How does aging affect long-term heterosexual and homosexual relationships?
9. Describe how living arrangements might change as people age.
10. What is death anxiety?
11. How might culture affect death anxiety?

References

1. Barusch, C. (1988). Problems and coping strategies of elderly spouse care-givers. *The Gerontologist, 27,* 667-685.
2. Bengston, V.L., Cuellar, J.B., & Raga, P.K. (1977). Stratum contrasts and similarities in attitudes toward death. *Journal of Gerontology, 30,* 688-695.
3. Berger, R. (1982). *Gay and gray.* Urbana, IL: University of Illinois Press.
4. Berry, R.E., & Williams, W. (1987). Assessing the relationship between quality of life and marital and income satisfaction: a path analytic approach. *Journal of Marriage and the Family, 49,* 107-116.
5. Cain, B. (1982). Plight of the gray divorcee. *New York Times Magazine,* Dec 19, 89-94.
6. Carp, F.M. (1976). Housing and living environments of older people. In R.H. Binstock & E. Shanas (Eds.), *Handbook of aging and the social services* (pp. 244-271). New York: Van Nostrand.
7. Cavanaugh, J.C. (1993). *Adult development and aging.* Belmont, CA: Wadsworth.
8. Cohen, S. & Syme, S.L. (1985). *Social support and health.* Orlando, FL: Academic Press.

9. Crooks, R. & Baur, K. (1993). *Our sexuality* (4th ed.). Redwood City, CA: Benjamin/Cummings.

10. Dawson, K. (1982). Serving the older gay community. *SIECUS Report, 11,* 5-6.

11. Doka, K.J. (1987). Silent sorrow: grief and loss of significant others. *Death Studies, 11* (8), 455-469.

12. Duvall, E.M. (1977). *Family development* (5th ed.). Philadelphia: Lippincott.

13. Ellis A. & Harper R. (1975). *A guide to rational living.* Englewood Cliffs, NJ: Prentice Hall.

14. Erickson, E. (1986). *Childhood and society.* New York: WW Norton.

15. Gilford, R. (1984). Contrasts in marital satisfaction throughout old age: an exchange theory analysis. *Journal of Gerontology, 39,* 325-333.

16. Gratton, B. & Wilson, V. (1989). Family support systems and the minority elderly: a cautionary analysis. *Journal of Gerontological Social Work, 13,* (1-2), 91-93.

17. Hafen, B.Q., et al. (1992). *The health effects of attitudes, emotions, and relationships.* Provo, UT: EMS Associates.

18. Hales, D. (1992). *An invitation to health* (5th ed.). Redwood City, CA: Benjamin/Commungs.

19. Jacobs, J. (1974). *Fun city: an ethnographic study of a retirement community.* New York: Holt, Reinhardt, and Winston.

20. Jacobs, J. (1975). *Older persons and retirement communities.* Springfield, MA: Charles C Thomas.

21. Kalish, R.A. (1985). The social context of death and dying. In R.H. Binstock and E. Shanas (Eds.), *Handbook of aging and the social sciences* (2nd ed.). (pp. 149-170). New York: Van Nostrand.

22. Kalish, R.A. (1987). Death and dying. In P. Silverman (Ed.), *The elderly as modern pioneers* (pp. 320-334). Bloomington, IN: Indiana University Press.

23. Kart, C. (1994). *The realities of aging: an introduction to gerontology.* Boston: Allyn & Bacon.

24. Kastenbaum, R. (1991). *Death, society, and human experience.* Columbus, OH: Charles E. Merrill.

25. Kelly, J. & Rice, S. (1986). The aged. In H. Gochros, J. Gochros & J. Fischer, (Eds.). *Helping the sexually oppressed.* Englewood Cliffs, NJ: Prentice Hall.

26. Krause, N. & Wray, L. (1991). Psychosocial correlates of health and illness among minority elders. *Generations, 15,* (4) 25-30.

27. Kubler-Ross, E. (1969). *On death and dying.* New York: MacMillan Publishing.

28. Kurdak, L. (1993). The allocation of household labor in gay, lesbian, and heterosexual married couples. *Journal of Social Issues, 49,* (3) 127-139.

29. Kurdak, L. (1989). Relationship quality of gay and lesbian cohabiting couples. *Journal of Homosexuality, 15,* (3-4) 93-118.

30. Lawton, M.P. & Cohen, J. (1974). The generality of housing impact on the well-being of older people. *Journal of Gerontology, 29,* 194-204.

31. Lipman, A. (1986). Homosexual relationships. *Generations, 10,* (4) 51-54.

32. Logue B. (1990). Race differences in long-term disability: middle aged and older American Indians, blacks, and whites in Oklahoma. *Social Sciences Journal, 27,* (3) 253-272.

33. Lopata, H.Z. (1973). *Widowhood in an American city.* Cambridge, MA: Schenkman.

34. Masters, W.H., Johnson, V.E., & Kolodny, R.C. (1992). *Human sexuality* (4th ed.). New York: Harper Collins.

35. McWhirter, D., & Mattison, A. (1984). *The male couple.* Englewood Cliffs, NJ: Prentice Hall.

36. Messer, M. (1967). The possibility of an age-concentrated environment becoming a normative system. *Gerontologist, 7,* 247-251.

37. Murrell, S.A., Himmelfarb, S., & Phifer, J.E. (1988). Effects of bereavement/loss and pre-event status on subsequent physical health in older adults. *International Journal of Aging/Human Development, 13,* (2) 89-107.

38. Myers, J.E., Wass, H., & Murphey, M. (1980). Ethnic differences in death anxiety among the elderly. *Death Education, 4,* 237-244.

39. Nagy, M. (1959). The child's theories concerning death. In H. Feifel (Ed.), *The meaning of death.* New York: McGraw Hill.

40. Parnes, H.S. & Sommers, D.G. (1994). Shunning retirement: work experience of men in their seventies and early eighties. *Journal of Gerontology, 49,* (3) 117-124.

41. Payne, W. & Hahn, D. (1992). *Understanding your health.* St Louis: Mosby.

42. Quam, J.K. & Whitford, G.S. (1992). Adaptation and age-related expectations of elder gay and lesbian adults. *Gerontologist, 32,* (3) 367-374.

43. Reed, P.G. (1987). Spirituality and well-being in terminally ill hospitalized adults. *Research in Nursing and Health, 10,* 335-344.

44. Simon, S.D., Howe, L.W., & Kirschenbaum, H. (1972). *Values clarification: a handbook of practical strategies.* New York: A & W Visual Library.

45. Weishaus, S., & Field, D. (1988). A half century of marriage: continuity or change? *Journal of Marriage and the Family, 50,* 763-774.

ASSESS YOURSELF 16-1

My Epitaph[44]

Purpose

Sometimes contemplating death helps one gain perspective on live. What is life all about? What difference would it make if you were not alive? This strategy has us look at the meaning of our lives in a simple but challenging way.

Procedure

The teacher says, "Have any of you ever been to old graveyards and read some of the inscriptions on the tombstones? For example:

"Here lies Mary Smith. She had more love to give than was ever wanted.

"Sara Miller, A Woman of Valor.

"Ezra Jones lived as he died. Out of debt, out of sight, and out of sorts.

"What would you want engraved on your own tombstone? What would be an accurate description of you and your life in a few short words?

_____

_____

_____

_____

_____

_____

Note:

Extend to any student the right to pass in this exercise. Death can be frightening, and some students are superstitious enough to believe that if you talk about your own death, it will happen. Be sensitive to this.

Sometimes students may be given time to consult *Bartlett's Quotations* or old yearbooks to choose appropriate statements for their epitaphs.

The teacher can help by having an epitaph of his own ready to read. The teacher must be willing to put his own values on the line if he expects the students to learn to do so. In keeping with this notion, the authors of this book would like to share their epitaphs:

From Simon, S.D., Howe, L.W., & Kirschenbaum, H. (1972). *Values clarification: a handbook of practical strategies.* New York: A & W Visual Library.

EPILOGUE

People are always asking me, "What can I do to cope with stress?" Everyone always wants to know the one technique that will end all of their stress forever. By now, you probably realize that there is no one technique. In a sense, techniques are bandages applied after the harm has already occurred.

After all of these years of thinking, writing, and teaching about stress, I am convinced that stress management is not about stress dots, learning how to meditate, or thinking about warming scenes and positive thoughts (although these techniques and many others are useful in reducing stress). The real secret to coping with stress in a changing world is contained in two words: *challenge* and *lifestyle*.

Challenge is significant because stress management begins with our perception—an attitude that we develop about our lives and the world we live in. Coping with stress in a changing world is based on a perception of life founded on the belief that each day brings change and the challenges that are inherent in change. When we embrace change we feel challenged. Being challenged makes us confident, strong, optimistic, and energized. We realize that we are never "home free" and must continue to adapt to change. This perception of change and the challenges it brings evolves each day, enriching our lives and helping us grow.

I am convinced that growth and lifelong learning are a big part of stress management. When we stop growing, we stop learning. When we stop growing, we entrench and try to defend what we know rather than seek to understand what we do not know. We become leery of change because it makes us uncomfortable. Instead we should embrace it and allow it to invigorate us.

Lifestyle is a key element in coping with stress because our perception of the world around us is intimately linked to a style of living that is always moving forward toward optimal functioning. Although we have seen how high levels of well being across the six dimensions of health can assist us in coping with stress, this is not the only reason we strive for optimal functioning. The journey, the quest for optimal functioning, is equally as important.

Striving for optimal functioning involves living a life that is disciplined yet joyful, hard-working yet playful and full of healthy pleasures. Setting goals that challenge us each day and across all six dimensions of well-being keeps us invigorated and focused. We do not dread change; we embrace it and assess how we can use it to help us meet our goals.

Our lives have different focus. Rather than living day-to-day, we have a long-range focus that puts each day into a broader perspective. By adopting this long-range focus, we prevent a certain amount of stress from ever occurring because we take into account the six dimensions of wellness and the four *R*s when planning our lives and making decisions. In other words, as we strive for optimal functioning, we begin to examine our commitments and the demands placed on our lives in the context of their relationship to all six dimensions of health and their effects on these domains.

As mentioned in Chapter 11, in a sense what happens is that our values change. Health and stress-management become core values. They become things that are no longer an afterthought. They earn priority status as we consider the options and choices that our lives present. Our values and perception change and our lifestyles begin to reflect the changes as we move toward wellness.

As I look back over the book and think about some things that help me cope with stress and live each day to the fullest, I come up with the "magic 11" (I tried to limit it to 10 but could not):

1. *Embrace change.* Substitute positive self-talk about change for negative, fearful messages. Change is good—it will help you grow. The only constant in life is change!

2. *Have some fun every day.* Life is hard. Allow yourself the luxury of some fun. Make time to have some fun each day by building it into your schedule. Take charge of your life and begin to drop activities and people that weigh you down and kill your fun.

3. *Lighten up.* As Metcalf said, "Learn how to take yourself lightly and your work seriously." You are not the center of the universe. The sun would still shine tomorrow if you no longer existed. We are all expendable.

4. *Stop and think before you act.* Sometimes counting to 10 before you act does help when you feel as if you are going to explode from stress. Your mother or father probably told you this several years ago. It is still good advice. Rational thinking begins with learning to control your emotions.

5. *Simplify your life.* I have found that having a few high quality things (including relationships) is more satisfying than trying to have it all. More is not always better. Sometimes more is less (less time, less quality, less energy, less fun).

6. *Be kind to others.* Your expressions of kindness will help you as much as they help others. It is hard to be angry and hostile when you are being kind.

7. *Forgive.* It is so easy to screw up in life. I know too many people who are still angry about something that their parents or others did to them years ago. They blame them for their unhappiness today. Take responsibility for your unhappiness and learn how to forgive.

8. *Slow down.* Very few things in life are worth the rush. Rushing to get somewhere usually only gets you there a little quicker and a lot more frazzled. Rushing to get everything you want out of life now usually reduces the quality of experiences rather than enhancing them. You can realize all of your hopes and dreams if you spread them out over your lifetime. There is no need to rush.

9. *Hug more.* It is hard to be stressed when you are hugging another living thing (e.g., a loved one, pet). Physical expressions of caring are important in keeping you connected to others.

10. *Get physical.* Getting some exercise every day will help you release tension and other stress by-products as well as increase your overall health.

11. *Take a chance on love.* I cannot think of anything that has helped me cope with stress more than the love of my wife, my children, my parents, and my friends. Their caring and my commitment to them has been a source of strength and inspiration through my most troubled times. Do not give up on love, even if your initial attempts have failed.

Coping with stress in a changing world requires your active participation in your life. You control your destiny. You chart your course through your life's journey. I wish you well on your journey. Enjoy the trip!

INDEX